Historic Documents
of 2013

Historic Documents
of 2013

Heather Kerrigan, Editor

Los Angeles | London | New Delhi
Singapore | Washington DC

Los Angeles | London | New Delhi
Singapore | Washington DC

FOR INFORMATION:

CQ Press

SAGE Publications, Inc.

2455 Teller Road

Thousand Oaks, California 91320

E-mail: order@sagepub.com

SAGE Publications Ltd.

1 Oliver's Yard

55 City Road

London, EC1Y 1SP

United Kingdom

SAGE Publications India Pvt. Ltd.

B 1/I 1 Mohan Cooperative Industrial Area

Mathura Road, New Delhi 110 044

India

SAGE Publications Asia-Pacific Pte. Ltd.

3 Church Street

#10–04 Samsung Hub

Singapore 049483

Cover image: © Getty Images.

"Award Ceremony Speech." December 10, 2013. © The Nobel Foundation 2013. Used with permission.

"Climate Change 2013: The Physical Science Basis." Summary for Policymakers. September 27, 2013. IPCC, 2013: Summary for Policymakers. In: Climate Change 2013: The Physical Science Basis. Contribution of Working Group I to the Fifth Assessment Report of the Intergovernmental Panel on Climate Change [Stocker, T. F., D. Qin, G.-K. Plattner, M. Tignor, S. K. Allen, J. Boschung, A. Nauels, Y. Xia, V. Bex and P. M. Midgley (eds.)]. Cambridge University Press, Cambridge, United Kingdom and New York, NY, USA. Used with permission.

"Eulogy by President Jacob Zuma at the State Funeral of the late former President of the Republic and former Commander in Chief of the Armed Forces, His Excellency Nelson Rolihiahla Mandela, Qunu, Eastern Cape." December 15, 2013. © GCIS2014: ALL RIGHTS RESERVED. Used with permission.

"IARC: Outdoor air pollution a leading environmental cause of cancer deaths." October 17, 2013. From IARC. Outdoor air pollution a leading environmental cause of cancer deaths, Press release n°221, 17 October 2013. Available from http://www.iarc.fr/en/media-centre/iarcnews/pdf/pr221_E.pdf, accessed on 11 April 2014. Used with permission.

"KCNA Report on Successful 3rd Underground Nuclear Test." February 12, 2013. Korea News Service.

"PM Statement on Algeria Hostage Crisis" January 21, 2013, and "Same sex marriage: Prime Minister's statement" July 18, 2013. Open Government License. http://www.nationalarchives.gov.uk/doc/open-government-licence/version/2.

"Statement by the Prime Minister of Canada on the Death of Venezuelan President Hugo Chavez Frías." March 5, 2013. Source: Prime Minister of Canada. © Her Majesty the Queen in Right of Canada, 2014. Used with permission.

"Statement from the IOC President on terrorist attacks in Russia" December 30, 2013. Used with permission from the International Olympic Committee.

Printed in the United States of America.

A catalog record of this book is available from the Library of Congress.

ISBN 978-1-4833-4787-5 (cloth)

This book is printed on acid-free paper.

Assistant Editor: Laura Notton

Managing Editor: Heather Kerrigan

Contributors: Brian Beary, Anastazia S Clouting, Hilary Ewing, Linda Fecteau, Melissa Feinberg, Sarah Gall, Heather Kerrigan

Editorial Assistant: Jordan Enobakhare

Production Editor: David C. Felts

Copy Editor: Deanna Noga

Typesetter: C&M Digitals (P) Ltd.

Proofreader: Kristin Bergstad

Indexer: Joan Shapiro

Cover Designer: Michael Dubowe

Marketing Manager: Carmel Schrire

SFI® Certified Sourcing
www.sfiprogram.org
SFI-00453

14 15 16 17 18 10 9 8 7 6 5 4 3 2 1

Contents

JANUARY

FEBRUARY

MARCH

APRIL

MAY

JUNE

JULY

AUGUST

SEPTEMBER

OCTOBER

NOVEMBER

of Foreign Affairs regarding the terrorist attacks in Volgograd; and a December
30, 2013 statement from IOC President Thomas Bach regarding security for the
Games.

DECEMBER

Thematic Table of Contents

GOVERNMENT AND POLITICS

HEALTH AND SOCIAL SERVICES

INTERNATIONAL AFFAIRS
AFRICA

INTERNATIONAL AFFAIRS
ASIA

INTERNATIONAL AFFAIRS
EUROPE

INTERNATIONAL AFFAIRS
LATIN AMERICA AND THE CARIBBEAN

INTERNATIONAL AFFAIRS
MIDDLE EAST

INTERNATIONAL AFFAIRS
RUSSIA AND THE FORMER SOVIET REPUBLICS

INTERNATIONAL AFFAIRS
GLOBAL ISSUES

NATIONAL SECURITY AND TERRORISM

RIGHTS, RESPONSIBILITIES, AND JUSTICE

List of Document Sources

CONGRESS

EXECUTIVE DEPARTMENTS, AGENCIES, FEDERAL OFFICES, AND COMMISSIONS

INTERNATIONAL GOVERNMENTAL ORGANIZATIONS

JUDICIARY

NONGOVERNMENTAL ORGANIZATIONS

NON-U.S. GOVERNMENTS

INTERNATIONAL NONGOVERNMENTAL ORGANIZATIONS

U.S. STATE AND LOCAL GOVERNMENTS

WHITE HOUSE AND THE PRESIDENT

Preface

The implementation of expansive health care coverage in the United States amidst a federal government shutdown, landmark Supreme Court rulings on same-sex marriage and DNA collection, new members welcomed to the European Union and eurozone, milestones in space exploration, major scientific reports on pollution and climate change, the resignation of Pope Benedict and the election of his successor, scandals involving the National Security Agency (NSA) surveillance program and U.S. document leaks, increasing tensions in the Middle East as the civil war in Syria marches on, and terrorist bombings in Russia and the United States are just a few of the topics of national and international significance chosen for discussion in *Historic Documents of 2013*. This edition marks the forty-first volume of a CQ Press project that began with *Historic Documents of 1972*. This series allows students, librarians, journalists, scholars, and others to research and understand the most important domestic and foreign issues and events of the year through primary source documents. To aid research, many of the lengthy documents written for specialized audiences have been excerpted to highlight the most important sections. The official statements, news conferences, speeches, special studies, and court decisions presented here should be of lasting public and academic interest.

Historic Documents of 2013 opens with an "Overview of 2013," a sweeping narrative of the key events and issues of the year that provides context for the documents that follow. The balance of the book is organized chronologically, with each entry comprising an introduction and one or more related documents on a specific event, issue, or topic. Often an event is not limited to a particular day. Consequently, readers will find that some events include multiple documents that may span several months. Their placement in the book corresponds to the date of the first document included for that event. The event introductions provide context and an account of further developments during the year. A thematic table of contents (page xix) and a list of documents organized by source (page xv) follow the standard table of contents and assist readers in locating events and documents.

As events, issues, and consequences become more complex and far-reaching, these introductions and documents yield important information and deepen understanding about the world's increasing interconnectedness. As memories of current events fade, these selections will continue to further understanding of the events and issues that have shaped the lives of people around the world.

How to Use This Book

Each of the seventy entries in this edition consists of two parts: a comprehensive introduction followed by one or more primary source documents. The entries are arranged in chronological order by month. Entries with multiple documents are placed according to the date of the first document. There are several ways to find events and documents of interest:

By date: If the approximate date of an event or document is known, browse through the titles for that month in the table of contents. Alternatively, browse the table of contents that appears at the beginning of each month's articles.

By theme: To find a particular topic or subject area, browse the thematic table of contents.

By document type or source: To find a particular type of document or document source, such as the White House or Congress, review the list of document sources.

By index: The index allows researchers to locate references to specific events or documents as well as entries on the same or related subjects.

An online edition of this volume, as well as an archive going back to 1972, is available and offers advanced search and browse functionality.

Each entry begins with an introduction. This feature provides historical and intellectual contexts for the documents that follow. Documents are reproduced with the original spelling, capitalization, and punctuation of the original or official copy. Ellipsis points indicate textual omissions (unless they were present in the documents themselves indicating pauses in speech), and brackets are used for editorial insertions within documents for text clarification. The excerpting of Supreme Court opinions has been done somewhat differently from other documents. In-text references and citations to laws and other cases have been removed when not part of a sentence to improve the readability of opinions. In those documents, readers will find ellipses used only when sections of narrative text have been removed.

Full citations appear at the end of each document. If a document is not available on the Internet, this too is noted. For further reading on a particular topic consult the "Other Historic Documents of Interest" section at the end of each entry. These sections provide cross-references for related entries in this edition of *Historic Documents* as well as in previous editions. References to entries from past volumes include the year and page number for easy retrieval.

Overview of 2013

In the United States, 2013 was characterized by political brinksmanship that culminated in the shutdown of the federal government in October. The shutdown was predicated on disagreement over the Affordable Care Act (ACA), President Barack Obama's landmark health care legislation that passed in 2010. And the failure to pass a federal budget was just one on a long list of issues on which Democrats and Republicans in Congress could not reach a consensus. Other highly charged debates revolved around the debt ceiling, immigration, and gun control. The U.S. economy continued to improve throughout 2013 with unemployment reaching a low of 6.7 percent in December. However, despite positive gains, the lower and middle classes still struggled to regain footing following the 2007–2009 recession.

Internationally, the year was dominated by continuing turmoil in the Middle East, most specifically in Syria where the ongoing civil war entered its third year. The conflict spilled over into neighboring nations, reigniting ethnic and political tensions. The international community failed to mount a strong response, even after it was confirmed that Syria's president had used chemical weapons against civilians. The Turkish government faced an uprising of its own that, while unsuccessful, brought international attention to the prime minister's failure to protect the rights of citizens. In Egypt, the newly elected president was ousted by the nation's military and the constitution was temporarily suspended while new amendments were drafted and new elections held. In Europe, the European Union (EU) welcomed its newest member, Croatia, while the eurozone welcomed Latvia. At the same time, the EU worked to stop a crisis in Cyprus's banking sector. The EU also opened free trade negotiations with the United States, but a planned trade pact with Ukraine was dismantled under pressure from Russia.

DOMESTIC ISSUES

In January 2013, President Obama delivered his second inaugural address before a crowd of one million. Although omitting specific policy proposals, which he saved for his February State of the Union speech, the president outlined the broad liberal agenda that he had planned for the next four years. Fixing both income inequality and social inequality were at the top of the president's list. Concerning the latter, the president called for equal benefits for same-sex couples, and by the end of the year, seventeen states and the District of Columbia had laws on the books permitting same-sex marriage within their borders.

Throughout his campaign and into his second term, President Obama repeatedly reiterated the importance of fixing America's wealth inequality. A significant part of bridging the gap between the wealthiest and poorest Americans was continuing to replace the millions of jobs lost during the 2007–2009 recession. Throughout 2013, the unemployment rate continued to decline, but the public and private sectors were still not keeping pace with job creation prior to the recession. By December, the unemployment rate fell to 6.7 percent but the workforce participation rate hovered near 63 percent, meaning that a growing number of people were continuing to leave the job market, likely frustrated by their inability to find work. According to economists, if the workforce participation rate was taken into account, the unemployment rate would be above 10 percent.

With the unemployment rate continuing to decline, it was unsurprising that the official 2012 poverty rate released by the U.S. Census Bureau in September did not record a significant change over 2011. According to the Census Bureau, 46.5 million Americans lived below the poverty line in 2012. This statistic combined with other economic data proved that the most impoverished Americans, and even those in the middle class, were still struggling to get back to where they were before 2007.

While the economic outlook was bright for most of the country, some areas continued to struggle. In July, the city of Detroit, Michigan, filed for Chapter 9 bankruptcy protection with a debt estimated at between $18 billion and $20 billion. The filing came after emergency financial measures put in place by the state failed to produce the necessary reforms to shore up the city's finances. The bankruptcy filing was approved on December 3, and the city set to work restructuring its finances. Perhaps the biggest roadblock to accomplishing this will be the city employee unions that have filed suit in federal court to block the city from reducing pension payouts as a means to save money.

White House Under Fire

In the first year of its second term, the Obama administration came under fire for apparent civil liberty violations. Over the period of a few weeks in June, confidential government documents were published by Britain's *The Guardian* newspaper detailing top-secret National Security Agency (NSA) surveillance programs. These surveillance programs collected information on electronic communications in bulk without individual warrants. According to the newspaper, much of what was being collected came from millions of Verizon customers in the United States under an order from the U.S. Foreign Intelligence Surveillance (FISA) Court. The order directed Verizon to provide law enforcement agencies with phone numbers, call details, and location data on calls within the United States as well as those between someone in the United States and someone in another country, although the calls were not recorded, and the content of the calls was not provided. Moreover, those under surveillance were not necessarily suspected of conducting any illegal activity. As the case began to unravel, allegations were raised that the United States had targeted some world leaders, including German Chancellor Angela Merkel.

On June 9, *The Guardian* released the identity of the source of the top-secret documents. Edward Snowden was a former Central Intelligence Agency (CIA) employee, who at the time of the leaks was on leave from a position as an NSA contractor. Snowden, who fled to Hong Kong before the leaks became public, contended that he released the documents to keep the public informed about what the government was doing in secret. The United States called on Hong Kong to extradite Snowden, but by the time Hong Kong responded, Snowden had applied for asylum in more than twenty countries and had already flown to Russia. Snowden lived in the international terminal in Moscow's airport because he did not have valid travel documents to enter Russia legally. In August, Snowden was granted temporary asylum in Russia. As of the end of 2013, Snowden had not been granted permanent asylum in any nation and was still living in an undisclosed location in Russia.

For its part, the White House continued to stand by the program, arguing that it was approved by Congress, recorded only calls of non-U.S. persons, and was a key component of thwarting terrorist activity aimed at the United States. In response to the ongoing crisis, President Obama commissioned a report seeking recommendations on conducting surveillance activities moving forward. The report with forty-six recommendations was released on December 18, and recognized the necessity of limited surveillance programs but expressed concern that the current NSA surveillance programs were neither effective nor valuable. Two different legal challenges decided in federal court on the NSA program reached separate conclusions—one upheld the constitutionality of the program while the other considered it entirely illegal.

Shortly before the NSA leaks came to light, the White House battled with the Associated Press (AP) over the secret collection of reporter phone records. In response to a May 2012 article published by the AP on a covert CIA operation that thwarted an attempt to plant a bomb on a plane bound for the United States, the Department of Justice subpoenaed the records of more than twenty AP phone lines. The Department argued that it was trying to determine who had leaked information about the operation to the AP and this was its only means of doing so. The AP contended that the Justice Department had violated First Amendment principles to the detriment of media outlets everywhere. The case revived the debate on Capitol Hill about whether to reintroduce a media shield law for consideration that would protect journalists from such action.

The Obama administration also drew sharp criticism from the right when an Internal Revenue Service (IRS) targeting program was brought to light. In 2012, conservative groups raised questions about why their applications for 501(c)(4) tax-exempt status were being held up in the approval process, and why they were being asked to provide information, such as donor names, which was outside the realm of traditional status reviews. An audit by the Inspector General found that for eighteen months in 2011 and 2012 the IRS used a "Be On The Lookout" (BOLO) list to target certain groups applying for tax-exempt status for additional scrutiny. The directive specifically raised a red flag on applications containing the words "tea party," "Patriots," and "9/12 Project." Although use of the list was discontinued later in 2012, conservative members of Congress demanded that those responsible be held accountable. Both Steve Miller, the interim head of the IRS, and Lois Lerner, head of the division in charge of tax-exempt status reviews, left their positions.

Congressional Inaction

The dominant issue in American public life in 2013 was Congressional inaction in a number of high-profile areas, most notably immigration, gun control, the debt ceiling, and the federal budget. Less than two months into his second term, on March 1 President Obama signed an executive order setting in motion a series of budget cuts known as the sequester. The $85 billion across-the-board federal spending reductions were born out of Congressional inability in 2011 to reach an agreement on how to offset the increase in the debt ceiling as well as the subsequent 2012 failure to agree on how to replace the across-the-board cuts with something more targeted. Both parties floated a number of proposals to stop or defer the cuts, which impacted defense and domestic spending equally. Republicans wanted deeper cuts to nondefense programs and changes to entitlement programs such as Medicaid. Democrats wanted to replace the sequester while subsequently increasing federal spending. At the end of March, the president signed a bill that made changes to the sequester by adding funding for military pay, Food and Drug Administration (FDA) inspections, and research grants. The bill also reduced military furlough days. By the end of 2013, the sequester was still in place. Between 2014 and 2021, annual spending cuts of $109 billion will be made, and it is up to Congress to determine how federal budgets will be impacted.

On two issues—immigration and gun control—members of Congress faced increasing pressure from the public and the White House to act. In his inaugural address, the president expressed his hope that one day the country would "find a better way to welcome the striving, hopeful immigrants who still see America as a land of opportunity." The Senate took a major step toward this end in June when it passed a bill that would create a thirteen-year path to citizenship for those illegal immigrants in the United States who met certain qualifications, while also enhancing border security and opening new opportunities for skilled laborers to come to the United States legally. The bipartisan legislation took into account the president's 2012 and 2013 executive orders that temporarily decriminalized the status of undocumented or illegal immigrants who were brought to the United States at a young age. The House failed to take up the bill, instead deciding to develop its own legislation. In June, four different bills moved out of committee for consideration by the full House, but by the end of the year the House had failed to vote on any measure.

In the wake of a number of mass shootings in 2012, the gun control debate reached a fever pitch. In January, Republicans and Democrats in both houses released a variety of bills, some which sought to renew the assault weapons ban that expired in 2004, while others attempted to expand gun rights. As the debate wore on, an additional thirty mass shootings took place in the United States in 2013, including one at the Washington, D.C., Navy Yard that resulted in twelve deaths. Although Congress did not pass any gun legislation in 2013, President Obama used his executive authority to take matters into his own hands. In January, the president released twenty-three executive actions including new incentives for states to share background check information. On August 29, the president released two additional gun-based executive orders. One order closed a background check loophole while the second required the military to deny most private requests for importing surplus U.S. military firearms from overseas.

The greatest illustration to date of Congress' inability to reach a consensus came on October 1 when the federal government shut down for sixteen days because the two houses could not agree on a budget to keep the country running. In late September, the Republican-led House passed a budget that would fund the government through December 15, but would entirely defund the ACA. Senate debate on the bill was lackluster because it was clear such a bill would not pass with a Democratic majority, but it culminated in a twenty-one hour filibuster during which Sen. Ted Cruz, R-Texas, gave a marathon speech against the president's signature law. The bill was amended by the Senate to remove the ACA provision and sent back to the House, but the House refused to pass it in its current form. The budget moved back and forth, but a compromise bill did not pass both houses before the September 30 expiration of the continuing resolution that had kept the government funded since March.

The October 1 shutdown impacted all federal government services considered nonessential, including national parks, airport inspections, and federal housing loans; essential services, such as Social Security checks and military pay, were kept intact. Additionally, some 800,000 federal employees were furloughed. Over the course of sixteen days, Republicans and Democrats tried to reach an agreement to reopen the federal government. It was not until near midnight on October 16 when the two parties formulated a bill that would fund the federal government until January 15, 2014. The Continuing Appropriations Act of 2014 was immediately signed by the president and made only minor adjustments to the ACA. According to Standard & Poor's, the shutdown cost the country approximately $24 billion and would impact fourth-quarter economic growth.

The compromise bill that reopened the federal government addressed another pressing issue—the debt ceiling, the Congressional limit on how much the federal government can borrow to pay its debts that have already been incurred, such as Social Security. If Congress failed to increase the nation's borrowing limit, the federal government would default on its debts and would eventually need to begin picking and choosing which payments to make. This would harm Americans as well as deal a significant blow to investor confidence and the financial image of the United States abroad. During debate on the issue, Republicans asked for concessions that would help offset the cost, including food stamp reductions, tax reform, a retirement age increase, and the privatization of Medicare and Social Security. Democrats refused to negotiate, arguing that they had already agreed to budget cuts under the sequester. Ultimately, Republicans relented and passed a clean bill that was contained in the October 16 agreement on the federal budget. The agreement raised the debt ceiling through February 2014 without budget cuts.

The shutdown coincided with the opening of the federal health exchanges through which Americans could purchase health insurance coverage required under the ACA individual mandate. The online system, HealthCare.gov, which was one of many methods by which Americans could sign up for care, was instantly criticized for its inability to handle the volume of users. The site drew eight million users in its first week and was slowly repaired to keep up with traffic. The District of Columbia and the eighteen states that chose to open their own health care exchanges for their citizens experienced greater success, with Kentucky touted as a national model.

SUPREME COURT DECISIONS

In 2013, the Supreme Court ruled on a number of high profile civil liberty cases. Perhaps the two most highly anticipated rulings were on the issue of same-sex marriage. On June 26, the Supreme Court released its rulings in both *Hollingsworth v. Perry* and *United States v. Windsor*. In the former, a divided court ruled 5–4 that the private group bringing a case in support of California's Proposition 8, which outlawed same-sex marriage in the state, had no standing in federal court. The decision meant that the lower court ruling, which invalidated Proposition 8 and made same-sex marriage legal in California, would be upheld. *United States v. Windsor* dealt with the federal Defense of Marriage Act (DOMA), which, for the purpose of federal benefits, defines marriage as between one man and one woman. In its 5–4 decision, the Court ruled that DOMA was a violation of the Equal Protection Clause of the U.S. Constitution. The ruling meant that same-sex couples who married and resided in a state in which their marriage was legally recognized would receive all the federal benefits received by their heterosexual counterparts.

In its 2012–2013 term, the Court also ruled on the Voting Rights Act (VRA) in the case of *Shelby County v. Holder*. The VRA, a landmark piece of legislation signed in 1965, was intended to stop racial discrimination at the polls by placing specific enforcement provisions on those states with a history of disenfranchising minority voters. In its 5–4 ruling, the Court kept most of the VRA intact but removed the list of states, counties, and municipalities that must seek preclearance from the Department of Justice before enacting new voting policies. While the ruling did not end the preclearance requirement, by negating the list of those to which it applied, the requirement lost most of its enforcement capabilities. Shortly after the ruling, states that had been subject to the preclearance requirement passed new election laws, including new identification requirements that, as a whole, tended to disproportionately affect minorities.

Another decision that dealt with race, this time in the college admissions process, was decided on June 24, 2013. In the case of *Fisher v. University of Texas*, the Court failed to rule on whether the University of Texas' use of race in the admissions process was unconstitutional. Instead, in its 7–1 decision, the Court established a new, rigorous level of scrutiny that should be applied to affirmative action cases. The Court found that a school could use an affirmative action policy to establish a diverse student body so long as a compelling state interest in using such a method could be established. The case at hand was sent back to the lower courts for review against the new standard.

Today, all fifty states require DNA testing for anyone convicted of a felony. However, the laws are varied on when DNA testing can be required for those arrested for, but not convicted of, a serious crime. On June 3, the Supreme Court ruled 5–4 in the case of *Maryland v. King* that the use of DNA testing constitutes a legitimate police booking activity akin to fingerprinting and is therefore not a violation of the Constitution's prohibition against unreasonable search and seizure.

On June 13, the Court released its ruling in the case of *Association for Molecular Pathology v. Myriad Genetics* in which the Court was tasked with determining whether human genes can be patented. The case was of notable significance to those with a family history of certain types of cancer, such as breast cancer, who can complete a screening to determine whether they have the gene mutation that can lead to the disease. Myriad held a patent on the human BRCA genes that are used in determining the mutation and, prior to the case, was the only company offering the BRCA screening at a cost upwards of $3,000, thus limiting the number of people who could afford the test. In its ruling, the Court determined that a naturally occurring human gene could not be patented, although synthetic genes could be patented as long as they could not be created in nature. Immediately following the ruling, a number of companies began offering their own BRCA cancer screenings at lower prices.

Foreign Affairs

Internationally, the major focus of 2013 was the ongoing civil war and humanitarian crisis in Syria that was quickly raising tensions across the Middle East. In September, the United Nations released a report confirming that President Bashar al-Assad used chemical weapons against civilians in an attempt to end the rebel incursion. The Syrian president fiercely denied such allegations. UN Secretary General Ban Ki-moon pressured member nations to work together to force Assad to end the civil war, but by year-end there was little consensus on how to do so. Russia and China, two permanent members of the Security Council with veto power, thwarted attempts to sanction Syria or take any other action against the Middle Eastern nation. President Obama raised the prospect of United States unilateral action, potentially through targeted missile strikes, to stop Assad from further use of his chemical weapons stockpiles. In October, the United States and Russia reached an agreement with Syria that would begin dismantling and removing all the nation's chemical weapons. The task was to be completed by the Organisation for the Prohibition of Chemical Weapons (OPCW), and a February 2014 deadline was set. In December, OPCW announced that despite its ongoing efforts it would likely not meet the deadline.

The three-year civil war in Syria spilled over into neighboring countries, causing tensions to rise in Lebanon, Israel, Jordan, Iraq, and Turkey. Refugees flooded into these nations, with Turkey and Lebanon bearing the brunt of the humanitarian crisis. Both nations were ill-equipped to handle the influx of refugees whose numbers soared into the millions. Refugees from Syria have cost Turkey upwards of $750 million. The ongoing conflict also reignited regional power struggles, pitting nations who supported Assad, such as Iran, against their neighbors, such as Saudi Arabia, who supported the rebels. The creation of rebel camps along the Turkish and Lebanese borders also sparked ethnic tensions— Assad draws most of his support from the Alawite, Christian, Druze, and Sunni sects, groups that operate in direct conflict with the Shiites in neighboring nations.

Elsewhere in the Middle East, the Egyptian and Turkish governments faced rebellion of their own. Throughout early 2013, Egyptian citizens took to the streets to protest the government of Mohamed Morsi, who was elected to replace Hosni Mubarak after the latter was deposed during the 2011 Arab Spring uprisings. Egyptian citizens claimed that Morsi imposed strict Islamic law on their country and pushed through a constitution that did not reflect the will of the majority but consolidated his executive power. Morsi refused to step down from his position, instead reaching out to opposition groups in an effort to form a consensus government. On July 3, the Egyptian military arrested the president, suspended the constitution, and called for new elections to be held and a new constitution drafted. The United States was highly critical of the move and the way in which the military went about drafting and approving the new constitutional amendments. When new presidential elections are held in 2014, it is likely that the Egyptian army chief will win, which sparked concern in the international community that he would further consolidate his power and continue limiting the rights of Egyptians.

In Turkey, protests against the government of Prime Minister Recep Tayyp Erdoğan took shape in May 2013 when Erdoğan announced the destruction of a park in Istanbul. What started as a demonstration by fifty environmentally conscious Turks quickly turned into a nationwide movement against the power of the prime minister. The millions of protesters who turned out across the country in 2013 demanded that the prime minister step down, arguing that since first coming to office in 2003 he had stripped Turkish citizens of their basic rights and imposed Islamic values on their traditionally secular country. Erdoğan remained defiant, and by the close of 2013 still held on to his seat. In total, approximately 5,000 protests took place in Turkey in 2013. Less than one dozen people were killed, about 8,000 were injured, and an estimated 3,000 more were arrested.

In Europe, the year started with an EU-International Monetary Fund (IMF) bailout for the Mediterranean island of Cyprus in an effort to prevent a financial meltdown that had the potential to significantly harm the eurozone. In the agreement, Cyprus made a number of difficult economic reforms, including raising taxes and lowering public spending. The wealthy Russians who sought out Cyprus as a cheap place to shelter their money were forced to take a significant financial hit in the deal. Despite the EU's ongoing financial struggles, it welcomed Latvia in July to become the newest eurozone member. At the same time, it also approved the application of Croatia to become the 28th EU member, the first new country to join since the economic crisis began in 2008. Observers questioned whether the inclusion of Croatia was a financially sound decision because the country has significantly high debt and unemployment levels.

As the United States and the European Union opened negotiations on what could be the world's largest free trade agreement, the EU's planned trade pact with Ukraine was crumbling under pressure from Russia. The pact signing was expected during a

November EU summit, but, following threats from Russia that it would set up trade barriers against Ukraine if the agreement was signed, Ukrainian president Viktor Yanukovych canceled the plan. The decision sent shockwaves through Ukraine, where many of its pro-Western citizens thought the agreement would be a first step toward EU membership. Protests in the capital of Kiev sprang up against Yanukovych, and by the end of the year, anti-Russia radicals joined the pro-Europe demonstrators and the movement grew increasingly violent.

The nuclear ambitious nations of Iran and North Korea made headlines again in 2013. In February, North Korea conducted its third underground nuclear test under direction from its new leader, Kim Jong Un. North Korea stated that the test was meant to prepare the nation to protect itself against any U.S. incursion into its affairs. While the yield of the blast was small, it was still stronger than the country's last two tests. North Korea now claims that it has developed a bomb small enough to be attached to a missile. This claim, along with allegations that North Korea could fire a long-range missile at the United States, was widely disputed by international experts. In response to the nuclear test, the United Nations Security Council called an emergency meeting, and, despite some pushback from China, passed a third set of sanctions against North Korea in March. Although China, one of North Korea's few allies, was generally opposed to such action, the nation determined that sanctions might be the best way to encourage the country to restart denuclearization discussions.

In June, the Iranian people elected a new president, Hassan Rouhani. Mahmoud Ahmadinejad, the former president who had a tense relationship with the West, was prohibited from running again due to term limits. Rouhani was largely viewed as a more moderate leader than his predecessor, and his past attempts at cooperation with other nations raised hopes that the relationship between Iran and the West could be improved. One long-running point of contention with the West is Iran's nuclear activities. The Iranian government claims that the program is intended for peaceful, electricity generation, but its secretive methods for conducting such activities raised suspicion in the international community that there was a more sinister desire behind the program. While Ahmadinejad had been unwilling to negotiate with Western nations to limit the country's nuclear activities, Rouhani was instrumental in restarting talks with the United States, United Kingdom, Russia, China, France, and Germany. And in November, the group reached a landmark interim agreement that would see Iran halting most of its nuclear activities in return for access to billions of dollars in funds that had been frozen under financial sanctions.

—Heather Kerrigan

January

President Obama Delivers Second Inaugural Address

JANUARY 21, 2013

Although he had officially been sworn into office one day earlier, President Barack Obama addressed a crowd of approximately one million to deliver his inaugural address on January 21, 2013. The address was themed "Faith in America's Future," and Obama described his ambitions for a second term. The eighteen-minute speech contained few specific proposals but laid out a broad liberal agenda, which drew ire from the right. In a clear message to a Congress that had been gridlocked on many issues the previous year, the president called on Democrats and Republicans to work together at this key moment in history to move the nation forward. "Being true to our founding documents does not require us to agree on every contour of life; it does not mean we will all define liberty in exactly the same way, or follow the same precise path to happiness," the president said. But, he added, "We cannot mistake absolutism for principle, or substitute spectacle for politics, or treat name-calling as reasoned debate. We must act, knowing that our work will be imperfect." He concluded, "My fellow Americans, we are made for this moment and we will seize it, so long as we seize it together."

DECIDEDLY LIBERAL TONE

Obama used his inaugural address to describe, in nonspecific terms, his goals for the next four years. At the top of that list included fixing both income inequality and social inequality. The president called for significant action on civil rights and human rights, noting that "what makes us exceptional, what makes us America, is our allegiance to an idea articulated in a declaration made more than two centuries ago: We hold these truths to be self-evident, that all men are created equal." The president spoke at length about the importance of providing women with equal pay for equal work and ensuring that sexual minorities receive the same benefits as heterosexual individuals. Our work will not be complete, the president said, "until our wives, our mothers, and daughters can earn a living equal to their efforts." In a ringing endorsement of same-sex marriage rights, he added, "Our journey is not complete until our gay brothers and sisters are treated like anyone else under the law—for if we are truly created equal, then surely the love we commit to one another must be equal as well." The topic of equality drew an evocative response from the audience gathered to hear the speech.

The president also reiterated the importance of fixing America's wealth inequality. "We are true to our creed when a little girl born into the bleakest poverty knows that she has the same chance to succeed as anybody else, because she is an American, she is free, and she is equal, not just in the eyes of God but also in our own," Obama said. Without making specific policy proposals, the president described some of the methods that would put America on this path, including reducing health care costs and the deficit, but doing so in a way in which the nation would not be forced to choose between caring for future generations and taking care of the neediest Americans. Speaking directly to Republicans in Congress who have criticized the president for supporting only limited entitlement reform, Obama noted that "the commitments we make to each other—through Medicare and Medicaid and Social Security—these things do not sap our initiative; they strengthen us. They do not make us a nation of takers; they free us to take the risks that make this country great."

Obama described his desire to work toward reaching agreements on other domestic issues including climate change and immigration. Tying the importance of embracing clean, renewable energy to America's continued economic growth, the president said, "We cannot cede to other nations the technology that will power new jobs and new industries, we must claim its promise. That's how we will maintain our economic vitality. . . . That is how we will preserve our planet." On immigration, the president expressed his hope that the United States would one day be a place that would embrace bright, young immigrants rather than deporting them. "Our journey is not complete until we find a better way to welcome the striving, hopeful immigrants who still see America as a land of opportunity," Obama said.

Foreign affairs received very little attention despite the ongoing civil war in Syria, American presence in Afghanistan, and the nuclear ambitions of North Korea and Iran, with the president noting only that he intended to continue to make America "the anchor of strong alliances in every corner of the globe." He did not mention any country by name, but instead spoke in vague terms about America's position in global politics.

Analysts said Obama's speech reflected his position as a second-term president who would not face reelection. David Gergen, the director of the Center for Public Leadership at Harvard University's Kennedy School of Government, said the speech was "the strongest embrace of 20th-century liberalism since Lyndon Johnson and the Great Society." Republican congressional leadership offered a tempered response to the speech, noting both hope for a fresh start with the president and a desire to overcome differences to pass legislation to serve the American people. "Republicans are eager to work with the president on achieving this common goal and we firmly believe that divided government provides the perfect opportunity to do so. Together, there is much we can achieve," said Senate Minority Leader Mitch McConnell, R-Ky.

Other Republicans were far less positive, noting that if the president intended to press an agenda like that in his speech, it would do nothing but cause a deeper rift in Washington. "This is not the approach of a leader attempting to find solutions to problems but rather the tactics of a partisan trying to pick political fights. His vision for the next four years is clear: defend a broken system, ignore the fiscal crisis, and drive future generations further into debt," said Sen. Mike Lee, R-Utah.

ADDRESS SETS STAGE FOR FRAUGHT POLITICAL YEAR

Although Sen. McConnell expressed a desire to forge bipartisan agreements, he made clear the key difference facing Republicans and Democrats in 2013. The president's agenda as defined in his inaugural address, said McConnell, is "certainly not designed to deal with the transcendent issue of our era, which is deficit and debt. Until we fix that problem, we can't fix America and we cannot leave behind for our kids the kind of America our parents left behind for us." Obama himself spent little time discussing the deficit in his inaugural address—he mentioned it only once while noting "we reject the belief that America must choose between caring for the generation that built this country and investing in the generation that will build its future." But the president had already defined his position on the issue in his first term, arguing that the best way to solve the nation's debt and deficit crisis was to increase tax revenue. Republicans had long rejected such a solution, calling instead for entitlement reforms.

The political gamesmanship surrounding these disagreements was set in motion from the beginning of the year as Congress and the White House debated the best way to lessen the impact of the automatic spending cuts known as the sequester. Republicans painted Obama's refusal to accept deep entitlement reforms without tax increases as a desire to create a bigger government. The debate over government's reach was reprised later in the year as Congress decided whether to raise the debt ceiling to allow the government to maintain its borrowing authority. The sequester cuts, coupled with the impending debt ceiling deadline, created few significant compromises on long-term debt and deficit solutions.

A Cabinet Lacking Diversity

At the close of 2012, a number of cabinet members announced their intent to leave the administration at the end of the president's first term. This included Secretary of State Hillary Clinton, whom many speculated was leaving to prepare herself for a presidential run in 2016, Treasury Secretary Timothy Geithner, Defense Secretary Leon Panetta, and Environmental Protection Agency chief Lisa Jackson. Hilda Solis, the Secretary of Labor, announced her intent to depart after President Obama was sworn in for a second term, as did Transportation Secretary Ray LaHood. Seven cabinet secretaries were asked to remain in their positions: Attorney General Eric Holder, Secretary of Agriculture Tom Vilsack, Secretary of Education Arne Duncan, Health and Human Services Secretary Kathleen Sebelius, Secretary of Homeland Security Janet Napolitano, Housing and Urban Development Director Shaun Donovan, and Veterans Affairs Secretary Eric Shinseki.

Given the continuing economic recovery, as well as the state of foreign affairs, the two highest profile appointments Obama needed to make were that of Treasury Secretary and Secretary of State. For the former, Obama chose his Chief of Staff Jack Lew, who had served in his administration as budget director. Lew had a long history in Washington, including directing the Office of Management and Budget, and holding a high-level policy position at the State Department. Prior to working in the public sector, Lew worked at Citi Global Wealth Management and Citi Alternative Investments.

To replace Clinton, the president first nominated his U.N. Ambassador Susan Rice. Rice, however, faced significant backlash related to the response to the attack on the U.S. consulate in Benghazi, Libya, that left the ambassador and three other Americans dead. In the end, she withdrew her name from consideration. Obama later went on to successfully nominate her to the position of National Security Advisor in mid-2013. When Rice withdrew her nomination, Obama turned to Sen. John Kerry, D-Mass., the unsuccessful 2004 Democratic presidential nominee. Kerry spent twenty-eight years in the Senate and had a solid foreign affairs background having served his full tenure on the Committee on Foreign Relations, the last four years of which he spent as chairman.

Obama's nomination of Lew and Kerry, coupled with his decision to nominate Chuck Hagel for the position of Secretary of Defense, raised the eyebrows of many who saw the cabinet as lacking in gender and ethnic diversity, specifically in the most powerful positions. Including both cabinet-level and cabinet-rank officials (like the EPA administrator and UN ambassador), the new cabinet had seventeen Caucasian, three African American, one Hispanic, and one Asian American member. Eight of the cabinet members were female.

Few of Obama's cabinet selections faced strong opposition in the Senate, except for Hagel. The former Nebraska senator was an outspoken critic of the Patriot Act and former President George W. Bush's handling of the Iraq War, and his comments on other sensitive issues, such as American military intervention in nations like Iran, were key points of contention for many Republicans in the Senate. Sen. Ted Cruz, R-Texas, even questioned whether Hagel, who refused the senator's call to release five years of financial information rather than the requisite two, had received income from rogue nations like North Korea. A group of Republican senators, led by John Cornyn of Texas, complained that Hagel had failed in making a case for his nomination during his confirmation hearings, which they considered an automatic disqualification from the position of Defense Secretary. "There is simply no way to sugarcoat it. Senator Hagel's performance before the Senate Armed Services Committee was remarkably inept, and we should not be installing a defense secretary who is obviously not qualified for the job and who holds dangerously misguided views on some of the most important issues facing national security policy for our country," Cornyn said. To the latter point, some Republicans were concerned that Hagel would jeopardize the already tenuous relationship between Israel and the United States based on past comments he made about the Jewish community. Fifteen Republican senators sent a letter to President Obama urging him to withdraw Hagel's nomination, but the president stood by his decision. Despite an attempt to stall the nomination process, Hagel was ultimately confirmed 58 to 41 on February 26.

—Heather Kerrigan

Following is the text of the inaugural address delivered by President Barack Obama on January 21, 2013.

DOCUMENT *President Obama's Inaugural Address*

January 21, 2013

Thank you. Thank you so much.

Vice President Biden, Mr. Chief Justice, Members of the United States Congress, distinguished guests, and fellow citizens:

Each time we gather to inaugurate a President we bear witness to the enduring strength of our Constitution. We affirm the promise of our democracy. We recall that what binds this Nation together is not the colors of our skin or the tenets of our faith or the origins of our names. What makes us exceptional—what makes us American—is our allegiance to an idea articulated in a declaration made more than two centuries ago:

We hold these truths to be self-evident, that all men are created equal; that they are endowed by their Creator with certain unalienable rights; that among these are life, liberty, and the pursuit of happiness.

Today we continue a never-ending journey to bridge the meaning of those words with the realities of our time. For history tells us that while these truths may be self-evident, they've never been self-executing; that while freedom is a gift from God, it must be secured by His people here on Earth. The patriots of 1776 did not fight to replace the tyranny of a king with the privileges of a few or the rule of a mob. They gave to us a republic, a government of and by and for the people, entrusting each generation to keep safe our founding creed.

And for more than 200 years, we have.

Through blood drawn by lash and blood drawn by sword, we learned that no union founded on the principles of liberty and equality could survive half-slave and half-free. We made ourselves anew, and vowed to move forward together.

Together, we determined that a modern economy requires railroads and highways to speed travel and commerce, schools and colleges to train our workers.

Together, we discovered that a free market only thrives when there are rules to ensure competition and fair play.

Together, we resolved that a great nation must care for the vulnerable and protect its people from life's worst hazards and misfortune.

Through it all, we have never relinquished our skepticism of central authority nor have we succumbed to the fiction that all society's ills can be cured through government alone. Our celebration of initiative and enterprise, our insistence on hard work and personal responsibility, these are constants in our character.

But we have always understood that when times change, so must we; that fidelity to our founding principles requires new responses to new challenges; that preserving our individual freedoms ultimately requires collective action. For the American people can no more meet the demands of today's world by acting alone than American soldiers could have met the forces of fascism or communism with muskets and militias. No single person can train all the math and science teachers we'll need to equip our children for the future, or build the roads and networks and research labs that will bring new jobs and businesses to our shores. Now more than ever, we must do these things together, as one nation and one people.

This generation of Americans has been tested by crises that steeled our resolve and proved our resilience. A decade of war is now ending. An economic recovery has begun. America's possibilities are limitless, for we possess all the qualities that this world without boundaries demands: youth and drive; diversity and openness; an endless capacity for risk and a gift for reinvention. My fellow Americans, we are made for this moment and we will seize it—so long as we seize it together.

For we, the people, understand that our country cannot succeed when a shrinking few do very well and a growing many barely make it. We believe that America's prosperity must rest upon the broad shoulders of a rising middle class. We know that America thrives when every person can find independence and pride in their work; when the wages of honest labor liberate families from the brink of hardship. We are true to our creed when a little girl born into the bleakest poverty knows that she has the same chance to succeed as anybody else, because she is an American; she is free and she is equal, not just in the eyes of God, but also in our own.

We understand that outworn programs are inadequate to the needs of our time. So we must harness new ideas and technology to remake our government, revamp our Tax Code, reform our schools, and empower our citizens with the skills they need to work harder, learn more, reach higher. But while the means will change, our purpose endures: a nation that rewards the effort and determination of every single American. That is what this moment requires. That is what will give real meaning to our creed.

We, the people, still believe that every citizen deserves a basic measure of security and dignity. We must make the hard choices to reduce the cost of health care and the size of our deficit. But we reject the belief that America must choose between caring for the generation that built this country and investing in the generation that will build its future. For we remember the lessons of our past, when twilight years were spent in poverty and parents of a child with a disability had nowhere to turn.

We do not believe that in this country freedom is reserved for the lucky, or happiness for the few. We recognize that no matter how responsibly we live our lives, any one of us at any time may face a job loss or a sudden illness or a home swept away in a terrible storm. The commitments we make to each other through Medicare and Medicaid and Social Security, these things do not sap our initiative, they strengthen us. They do not make us a nation of takers; they free us to take the risks that make this country great.

We, the people, still believe that our obligations as Americans are not just to ourselves, but to all posterity. We will respond to the threat of climate change, knowing that the failure to do so would betray our children and future generations. Some may still deny the overwhelming judgment of science, but none can avoid the devastating impact of raging fires and crippling drought and more powerful storms.

The path towards sustainable energy sources will be long and sometimes difficult. But America cannot resist this transition, we must lead it. We cannot cede to other nations the technology that will power new jobs and new industries, we must claim its promise. That's how we will maintain our economic vitality and our national treasure—our forests and waterways, our crop lands and snow-capped peaks. That is how we will preserve our planet, commanded to our care by God. That's what will lend meaning to the creed our fathers once declared.

We, the people, still believe that enduring security and lasting peace do not require perpetual war. Our brave men and women in uniform, tempered by the flames of battle, are unmatched in skill and courage. Our citizens, seared by the memory of those we have lost, know too well the price that is paid for liberty. The knowledge of their sacrifice will keep us forever vigilant against those who would do us harm. But we are also heirs to those who won the peace and not just the war; who turned sworn enemies into the surest of friends—and we must carry those lessons into this time as well.

We will defend our people and uphold our values through strength of arms and rule of law. We will show the courage to try and resolve our differences with other nations peacefully—not because we are naive about the dangers we face, but because engagement can more durably lift suspicion and fear.

America will remain the anchor of strong alliances in every corner of the globe. And we will renew those institutions that extend our capacity to manage crisis abroad, for no one has a greater stake in a peaceful world than its most powerful nation. We will support democracy from Asia to Africa, from the Americas to the Middle East, because our interests and our conscience compel us to act on behalf of those who long for freedom. And we must be a source of hope to the poor, the sick, the marginalized, the victims of prejudice—not out of mere charity, but because peace in our time requires the constant advance of those principles that our common creed describes: tolerance and opportunity, human dignity and justice.

We, the people, declare today that the most evident of truths—that all of us are created equal—is the star that guides us still; just as it guided our forebears through Seneca Falls and Selma and Stonewall; just as it guided all those men and women, sung and unsung, who left footprints along this great Mall, to hear a preacher say that we cannot walk alone; to hear a King proclaim that our individual freedom is inextricably bound to the freedom of every soul on Earth.

It is now our generation's task to carry on what those pioneers began. For our journey is not complete until our wives, our mothers and daughters can earn a living equal to their efforts. Our journey is not complete until our gay brothers and sisters are treated like anyone else under the law—for if we are truly created equal, then surely the love we commit to one another must be equal as well. Our journey is not complete until no citizen is forced to wait for hours to exercise the right to vote. Our journey is not complete until we find a better way to welcome the striving, hopeful immigrants who still see America as a land of opportunity—until bright young students and engineers are enlisted in our workforce rather than expelled from our country. Our journey is not complete until all our children, from the streets of Detroit to the hills of Appalachia, to the quiet lanes of Newtown, know that they are cared for and cherished and always safe from harm.

That is our generation's task—to make these words, these rights, these values of life and liberty and the pursuit of happiness real for every American. Being true to our founding documents does not require us to agree on every contour of life. It does not mean we all define liberty in exactly the same way or follow the same precise path to happiness. Progress does not compel us to settle centuries-long debates about the role of government for all time, but it does require us to act in our time.

For now decisions are upon us and we cannot afford delay. We cannot mistake absolutism for principle or substitute spectacle for politics or treat name-calling as reasoned debate. We must act, knowing that our work will be imperfect. We must act, we must act knowing that today's victories will be only partial and that it will be up to those who stand here in 4 years and 40 years and 400 years hence to advance the timeless spirit once conferred to us in a spare Philadelphia hall.

My fellow Americans, the oath I have sworn before you today, like the one recited by others who serve in this Capitol, was an oath to God and country, not party or faction. And we must faithfully execute that pledge during the duration of our service. But the words I spoke today are not so different from the oath that is taken each time a soldier signs up for duty or an immigrant realizes her dream. My oath is not so different from the pledge we all make to the flag that waves above and that fills our hearts with pride.

They are the words of citizens and they represent our greatest hope. You and I, as citizens, have the power to set this country's course. You and I, as citizens, have the obligation to shape the debates of our time—not only with the votes we cast, but with the voices we lift in defense of our most ancient values and enduring ideals.

Let us, each of us, now embrace with solemn duty and awesome joy what is our lasting birthright. With common effort and common purpose, with passion and dedication, let us answer the call of history and carry into an uncertain future that precious light of freedom.

Thank you. God bless you, and may He forever bless these United States of America.

SOURCE: Executive Office of the President. "Inaugural Address." January 21, 2013. *Compilation of Presidential Documents* 2013, no. 00032 (January 21, 2013). http://www.gpo.gov/fdsys/pkg/DCPD-201300032/pdf/DCPD-201300032.pdf.

Other Historic Documents of Interest

Prime Minister Cameron Remarks on Algerian Hostage Crisis

JANUARY 21, 2013

Before dawn on January 16, 2013, gunshots rang out at an Algerian gas plant, signaling the beginning of a four-day hostage crisis that eventually left sixty-nine dead. The terrorist group responsible for the attack, Signed-in-Blood Battalion, claimed they were motivated by France's recent intervention in Mali against Islamic extremists operating there. The terrorists targeted foreigners at the plant, many of whom made daring escapes with the aid of their Algerian counterparts. The intervention of the Algerian government to free the hostages drew swift criticism from other nations which believed a more precise solution would have led to a lower death toll. The Algerian government defended its action, especially in light of the recent deterioration of security in the region.

TIMELINE OF EVENTS

The terrorists reportedly entered Algeria mainly through Libya, thirty-one miles from the site of the In Amenas gas plant, which is jointly owned by the Algerian state-owned gas company, Sonatrach, British Petroleum (BP), and Statoil, a Norwegian company. The facility accounts for approximately 10 percent of natural gas production in Algeria and houses around 800 employees, 130 of whom are foreign. The attack began before dawn, when thirty-two gunmen attacked two buses carrying plant employees from their barracks. The armed escort was effective in repelling the attack, and only two workers were killed. A short time later, the gunmen forced their way into the plant and set up explosives in their path to try to prevent hostages from escaping. A plant guard tripped a plant-wide alarm to alert workers of a crisis. This gave some employees the opportunity to hide and shut down operations. The guard was subsequently killed. The gunmen split up, with some going to the employee living quarters while others tried to access the plant operations facilities. Those gunmen who went to the barracks told all Algerians that they were free to leave—the terrorists wanted foreign workers only. Algerian workers tried to hide their foreign counterparts as gunmen went door-to-door, searching the employee living quarters. Many who tried to run were shot. Those who refused to leave their quarters were beaten and dragged out. The foreign hostages who were captured had their hands bound, mouths taped, and bombs strapped to them.

During the siege, the terrorists issued their demands, first and foremost that French forces leave Northern Mali, where they were targeting Islamic extremists. In return, the terrorists said they would release the hostages. They also requested the release of two suspected terrorists being held by the United States and the release of hundreds of Islamic prisoners being held in Algeria. The Algerian government refused to negotiate with the terrorists or meet their demands, instead launching their own offensive to end the standoff.

On the first day of the attack, the Algerian military, which is in charge of security for the plant, surrounded the site. On January 17, the military entered the gas plant and met stiff resistance from the hostage takers. Using helicopters and heavy weapons, they were able to free a number of the hostages as the terrorists attempted to transport them out of the country. During this initial assault, thirty hostages and eleven terrorists were killed, according to Algerian security officials. The final assault to retake the plant came on January 19, after the Algerian government received word that the terrorists were planning to blow up the plant. As Algerian troops cleared out the remaining hostages, eleven of the terrorists were killed, along with seven hostages. Only one Algerian at the plant (the security guard) was killed. The remaining thirty-eight hostages killed included workers from Japan, the Philippines, Norway, the United Kingdom, the United States, Malaysia, Romania, Colombia, and France.

Following the four-day standoff, the Algerian government announced that twenty-nine of the hostage takers had been killed, while the remaining three were captured alive.

RESPONSIBLE PARTY

Shortly after the incident began, Mokhtar Belmokhtar, the leader of the al Qaeda-linked Signed-in-Blood Battalion (or Masked Men Brigade) took responsibility for the attack. Belmokhtar previously served as a commander of al Qaeda in the Islamic Maghreb (AQIM) but left the group in late 2012. Belmokhtar, known as Mr. Marlboro because his cigarette smuggling operation funds his jihad activities, is responsible for a number of earlier kidnappings and murders. The Signed-in-Blood Battalion operates out of Northern Mali, where there is currently a large presence of Islamic extremists.

According to the Algerian government, those responsible for the In Amenas attack traveled to Algeria from Northern Mali and Libya. Those in the group came from several countries including Tunisia, Algeria, Canada, Niger, Egypt, Mali, and Mauritania. The terrorists claimed that they were motivated by France's January incursion into Northern Mali; however, some international crisis experts noted that the attack appeared too well planned for the terrorists to have come up with an attack strategy so quickly. At various points throughout the siege, the hostage takers also stated that they were responding to the imprisonment of Islamists by Algeria and the Algerian decision to shut its border with Mali to refugees. It is believed that those planning the attack had informants in the In Amenas plant.

CRITICISM OF ALGERIAN RESPONSE

Immediately following the Algerian military operation to retake the gas plant, those nations with hostages at the facility criticized the tough response, questioning whether the government had considered all options to avoid the bloody battle that ensued. The United States, which did not issue an official criticism, said it had offered surveillance assistance to the Algerian government, which it hoped would be used to gain a better understanding of the situation inside the plant in order to avoid casualties. Both current and retired military officials said a U.S.-planned response using this method would have been carried out with greater precision.

Other nations, like France, supported the Algerian response, noting that the crisis was so unexpected and rapidly unfolding that Algeria may have felt it had no other option. "It's easy to say that this or that should have been done. The Algerian authorities took a decision and the toll is very high but I am a bit bothered . . . when the impression is given that the Algerians are open to question. They had to deal with terrorists," said French Foreign Minister Laurent Fabius. Algerian Prime Minister Abdelmalek Sellal said quick action was called for because "when the security of the country is at stake, there is no possible discussion." The prime minister said it was the aim of the terrorists to "take the foreign workers directly to northern Mali so they could have hostages, to negotiate with foreign countries."

The Algerian government did not give advance notice of its response plans to the other nations with hostages inside the plant. British Prime Minister David Cameron expressed disappointment that he had not been notified but said that the blame for those killed "lies squarely with the terrorists." U.S. President Barack Obama issued a similar response: "The blame for this tragedy rests with the terrorists who carried it out, and the United States condemns their actions in the strongest possible terms."

Co-owner of the gas plant, Statoil, commissioned a report into the attack and response by the Syrian government (to date, BP has not investigated the attack). The findings were released in September 2013, and were highly critical of the Algerian military unit charged with protecting the plant. "Neither Statoil nor the joint venture could have prevented the attack," the report stated, "but there is reason to question the extent of their reliance on Algerian military protection." The report went on to indicate that the military should have intervened prior to the attack when the gunmen crossed the border, or in the outer or inner military zones at the plant.

NORTH AFRICA TERRORIST THREAT

Following the crisis in Algeria, Prime Minister Cameron expressed his concern that the extremist threat in Northern Africa is quickly growing and spreading to various countries. He called on the international community to come together to develop a long-term solution to rooting out the terrorists. "What we face is an extremist, Islamist, al Qaeda-linked terrorist group. Just as we had to deal with that in Pakistan and in Afghanistan so the world needs to come together to deal with this threat in North Africa," Cameron said.

In Northern Mali alone, a number of terrorist organizations are operating, including AQIM, the Signed-in-Blood Battalion, Mujao, and Ansar Dine. Ansar Dine, in particular, took control of a large swath of the area following an attempted coup in January 2012, and has imposed Islamic law on the residents. In Somalia, known terrorist organization al-Shabaab is linked with al Qaeda in the Arabian Peninsula and is also reportedly training the Boko Haram Islamic extremist group that operates out of Nigeria. Al-Shabaab was responsible for a terrorist attack on a mall in Nairobi, Kenya, in September 2013, which left more than sixty people dead. Together, these groups have imposed a bloody reign of terror across the region. International counterterrorism experts note that one of the most troubling facts about these groups is that they attract foreign fighters from all over the world, including Western nations. A majority of these terrorist organizations operate by taking hostages and demanding ransoms. If possible, they aim for Westerners because the terrorists believe Western governments are willing to pay higher sums in return for their countrymen.

—Heather Kerrigan

Following is a statement by British Prime Minister David Cameron on January 21, 2013, in response to the Algerian hostage crisis.

Prime Minister Cameron on the Algerian Hostage Crisis

DOCUMENT

January 21, 2013

With permission, Mr Speaker, I would like to update the House on the despicable terrorist attack in Algeria and the tragic events of the last few days.

It is with great sadness that I have to confirm that we now know three British nationals have been killed and that a further three are believed to be dead, as is a Colombian national who was resident in Britain.

I am sure the whole House will join with me in sending our deepest condolences to the families and friends of all of those who have lost loved ones.

Mr Speaker, first let me update the House on developments over the weekend and the steps we have taken to get survivors home.

And then let me begin to set out how we will work with our allies to overcome the terrorist scourge in this region.

UPDATE

The Algerian Prime Minister told me on Saturday afternoon that the Algerian military had completed their offensive and that the terrorist incident was over.

Since then Algerian forces have undertaken a further operation to clear the site of potential explosives and booby traps.

This is still being completed and it will allow our Embassy-led team to access the site.

It is important to put on record the scale of what happened.

There is still some uncertainty around the precise facts, but we believe that in total there were some 800 employees working at the In Amenas site at the time of the attack, about 135 of whom were foreign nationals, over 40 were taken hostage.

At least 12 were killed with at least a further 20 unaccounted for and feared dead.

The Algerian Prime Minister has said recently today 37 foreign hostages were killed.

The number of terrorists was over 30. Most were killed during the incident but a small number are in Algerian custody.

Our immediate priorities have been the safety of the British nationals involved, the evacuation of the wounded and freed hostages, and the repatriation of those who have been tragically killed.

Working closely with BP—and side by side with our US, Japanese and Norwegian partners—a swift international evacuation effort has been completed.

The last British flights out on Saturday night, brought not only the remaining freed Britons but also Germans, Americans, New Zealanders, Croats, Romanians and Portuguese.

As of yesterday all 22 British nationals caught up in the attack, who either escaped or were freed, had been safely returned to Britain, to be debriefed by the police and of course reunited with their families.

Now, our most vital work is bringing home those who died.

An international team of British, American and Norwegian experts, is in close cooperation with the Algerian Ministry of Justice, undertaking the task of formally identifying their bodies.

We want this process to happen as swiftly as possible, but it will involve some intensive forensic and policing work—and so may take some time.

Mr Speaker, throughout the last five days, the British Ambassador to Algeria and staff from across government and beyond have been working around the clock to support British citizens and their families—and I am sure the House would like to join me in thanking them for their efforts.

We should also recognise all that the Algerians have done to confront this dreadful attack.

I am sure the House will understand the challenges that Algeria faced in dealing with over 30 terrorists bent on killing innocent people in a large and extremely remote and dangerous industrial complex.

This would have been a most demanding task for security forces anywhere in the world and we should acknowledge the resolve shown by the Algerians in undertaking it.

Above all the responsibility for these deaths lies squarely with the terrorists.

TERRORIST THREAT

Mr Speaker, many questions remain about this whole incident.

But one thing is clear.

This attack underlines the threat that terrorist groups pose to the countries and the peoples of that region—and to our citizens, our companies and our interests too.

Four years ago the principal threat from Islamist extremism came from the Afghanistan and Pakistan region.

A huge amount has been done to address and reduce the scale of that threat.

Whereas at one point three quarters of the most serious terrorist plots against the UK had links to that region today this has reduced to less than half.

But at the same time Al Qaeda franchises have grown in Yemen, Somalia and parts of North Africa.

The changing nature of the threat we face was highlighted in our National Security Strategy in 2010 and it did shape the decisions that we made.

While of course there were difficult decisions to make, we increased our investment in Special Forces, Cyber Security, key intelligence capabilities, while also increasing our investment in fragile and broken states.

In North Africa, as in Somalia, terrorist activity has been fueled by hostage ransoms and wider criminality.

To date, the threat it poses has been to these North African states themselves and, of course, as I've said, to Western interests in those states.

But as it escalates it is also becoming a magnet for jihadists from other countries who share this poisonous ideology.

Indeed there are already reports of non-Algerian nationals involved in this attack.

Mr Speaker, more than ever this evolving threat demands an international response.

It must be one that is tough, intelligent, patient and based on strong international partnerships.

First, we should be clear that this murderous violence requires a strong security response.

We must be realistic and hard headed about the threats that we face.

Our role is to support the Governments of the region in their resolve to combat this menace, as many are doing at a high cost.

So we will work closely with the Algerian government to learn the lessons of this attack, and to deepen our security cooperation.

And we will contribute British intelligence and counter-terrorism assets to an international effort to find and dismantle the network that planned and ordered the brutal assault at In Amenas.

We must work right across the region.

In Nigeria, we will continue our close security partnership with the Government as it confronts Islamist-inspired terrorism.

In Libya, we will continue to support the new Government on the urgent priority of building new and effective security forces.

And In Mali, we will work with the Malians themselves, with their neighbours and with our international allies to prevent a new terrorist haven developing on Europe's doorstep.

Mr Speaker, we support the French intervention that took place at the request of the Malian Government and we are working to ensure that an African-led military force can—with the appropriate training and support—help to ensure Mali's long-term stability.

That support will include the EU Training Mission that was agreed by EU Foreign Ministers in Brussels last week.

Second, our tough security response must be matched by an intelligent political response.

Al Qaeda franchises thrive where there are weak political institutions, political instability and the failure to address long-standing political grievances.

So we must need a political approach that addresses these issues.

EFFECTIVE AND ACCOUNTABLE GOVERNMENT

We must support effective and accountable government back people in their search for a job and a voice and work with the UN and our international partners to solve long-standing political conflicts and grievances.

Third, we must be patient and resolute.

Together with our partners in the region, we are in the midst of a generational struggle against an ideology which is an extreme distortion of the Islamic faith, and which holds that mass murder and terror are not only acceptable but necessary.

We must tackle this poisonous thinking at home and abroad and resist the ideologues' attempt to divide the world into a clash of civilisations.

The underlying conflicts and grievances that are exploited by terrorists are in many cases long-standing and deep.

And, of course, the building blocks of democracy: the rule of law and the independence of the judiciary, the rights of minorities, free media and association, and a proper place in society for the army. These are a big part of the solution but they all take a long time to put in place.

But this patient, intelligent but tough approach is the best way to defeat terrorism and to ensure our own security.

We must pursue it with an iron resolve.

And I will use our chairmanship of the G8 this year to make sure this issue of terrorism and how we respond to it is right at the top of the agenda where it belongs.

In sum, we must frustrate the terrorists with our security, we must beat them militarily, we must address the poisonous narrative they feed on, we must close down the ungoverned space in which they thrive and we must deal with the grievances they use to garner support.

This is the work that our generation faces and we must demonstrate the same resolve and sense of purpose as previous generations have with the challenges they faced in this House and in this country.

And I commend this statement to the House.

SOURCE: Government of the United Kingdom. "PM Statement on Algeria Hostage Crisis." January 21, 2013. https://www.gov.uk/government/speeches/pm-statement-on-algeria-hostage-crisis. License for reuse: http://www.nationalarchives.gov.uk/doc/open-government-licence/version/2.

OTHER HISTORIC DOCUMENTS OF INTEREST

FROM THIS VOLUME

■ African Union Condemns Mall Shooting, p. 448

FROM PREVIOUS *HISTORIC DOCUMENTS*

■ United Nations Approves Intervention in Mali, *2012,* p. 627

February

PM Netanyahu Charged With Forming New Israeli Government

FEBRUARY 2, MARCH 16, AND JULY 28, 2013

Although a parliamentary election was not due to be held until October 2013, in October 2012, Israeli Prime Minister Benjamin Netanyahu called an early election after his governing coalition failed to approve budgetary measures that would reduce the deficit. The election was held in January 2013, and although the prime minister's right-wing Likud party lost some seats to more moderate newcomers, it still walked away with the biggest victory. As Likud's leader, Netanyahu formed a governing coalition and was chosen prime minister for a second consecutive, and third overall, term. One of the biggest challenges facing Netanyahu's government was reaching some form of peace agreement with Palestine, and as such, the two nations resumed talks in July, with the United States acting as mediator.

ISRAELI LEGISLATIVE ELECTION CAMPAIGN AND RESULTS

In the 2013 election, thirty-two parties vied for seats in the Israeli parliament. A new centrist party entered the field, called Yesh Atid (There is a Future), led by former television star Yair Lapid, and campaigned on socioeconomic issues such as fixing the housing shortage, improving the education system, and ending the military draft exception for Jewish seminary students. The latter is considered a key method to encourage religious men to join the workforce rather than devoting their lives to religious study.

Netanyahu and his Likud party shied away from discussion of Palestinian peace talks during the election, instead emphasizing curbing Iranian nuclear power. The prime minister placed considerable focus on the increase in Islamist governments following the 2011 Arab Spring uprisings, noting that it was time to think more about national security, to which he saw Iran as a serious credible threat. Netanyahu told the United Nations in 2012 that by mid-2013, the Iranians would be in the late stages of building capacity to develop a nuclear weapon. Iran, however, calls Israel the biggest threat to Middle East security, because it is believed to have the only nuclear weapons in the region. Polling of voters showed little interest in the Iran issue, with a greater focus placed on domestic priorities, such as slow to nonexistent economic growth.

From the outset of the campaign season, Netanyahu's right-wing Likud party, and its close partner, the Yisrael Beiteinu group, expected to be handed an easy victory. But as the election drew closer, it became clear that the prime minister's coalition would lose some votes to opponents of the two-state solution for Israel and Palestine. In the end, those on the right, along with their Orthodox supporters, took half of the 120 parliamentary seats. Of those seats, Netanyahu's coalition, Likud-Beiteinu, won 31 seats. This was a stark contrast to the last election, which gave the coalition 42 seats. Despite being a newcomer to the Israeli political scene, Yesh Atid took 19 seats. The Israeli Labor party claimed 15 seats; Jewish Home, an ultra-nationalist group, took 12; the Shas, an ultra-Orthodox group, took 11; United Torah Judaism, a coalition of two ultra-Orthodox parties, won 7; Hatnua, a center-left party, took 6; as did Meretz, a left-wing party. The United Arab List-Ta'al and Hadash each took 4 seats, while Balad won 3. Kadima, one of the biggest winners in the 2009 election, only won 2 seats. Following the 2009 election, under its former leader, Tzipi Livni, Kadima was given the opportunity to form a governing coalition but was unable to do so. Livni now leads the Hatnua party.

By weakening Likud-Beiteinu's power in parliament, Yesh Atid was given a key seat at the negotiating table as the new government was formed. Addressing his campaign workers after the election, Lapid said, "I call on the leaders of the political establishment to work with me together, to the best they can, to form as broad a government as possible that will contain in it the moderate forces from the left and right, the right and left, so that we will truly be able to bring about real change."

Minority party leaders called the election results a referendum on Netanyahu's leadership, but there was no credible opponent to challenge the prime minister's seat. Netanyahu was, however, forced to admit that he would have to work toward a broader consensus with his government, noting the strong showing of Yesh Atid against his right-wing religious block. "I believe the election results are an opportunity to make changes that the citizens of Israel are hoping for and that will serve all of Israel's citizens. I intend on leading these changes, and to this end we must form as wide a coalition as possible," Netanyahu said.

New Governing Coalition

Israel's electoral system is based on proportional representation so that no one party can win an absolute majority in parliament. This forces the largest political forces in the country to work with smaller, less powerful parties to govern effectively. As the leader of the party with the greatest number of seats in parliament, Netanyahu was given the first right to form a coalition government. In the past, Netanyahu worked only with his closest allies, but the results of the 2013 election forced him to look to those formerly viewed as enemies or his party risked loss of influence. Noting the biggest challenges facing Israel as security and the economy, Netanyahu remarked, "I call upon those who said they would not sit in the government to reconsider and to come and find common ground. I call upon all sections of society and all the parties, including those who didn't recommend me, to join a responsible national unity government which will be as wide as possible, a government which will ensure the security, the unity and the future of the State of Israel."

Netanyahu was given until March 16 to form a governing coalition, which he did with an eleventh-hour deal. "I formed a government," Netanyahu announced, adding, "We face a decisive year in the fields of security and economy, in efforts to promote peace and in Israelis' desire to effect change. There is cooperation in this government and I believe we will bring change to all Israeli citizens in all areas." The final agreement had been held up for weeks because of internal disputes regarding who would hold which cabinet positions. The coalition, which included Yesh Atid, Jewish Home, and the Hatnua party, was united on domestic issues but heavily divided on how to handle the issue of Palestine. Ultra-Orthodox parties were notably absent from Netanyahu's coalition, reflecting the electorate's move toward the center. The Labor party refused to join the coalition, noting their own strict adherence to the development of a two-state solution and Netanyahu's economic policies that they claim hurt Israel's most vulnerable. The new coalition held 68 of parliament's 120 seats.

LACKLUSTER PEACE TALKS RESUME

Prior to the election, Western diplomats warned Netanyahu's government that international support was waning in light of continued Israeli development in East Jerusalem and the West Bank. These areas are considered crucial to Palestinians if a two-state solution is to come to fruition. Few in the international community saw the election as indicative of a change in the tense relationship between Israel and the West, specifically the United States. Following the election, the United States maintained its support for a two-state solution with Palestine, and encouraged Netanyahu's government to work toward such an agreement.

In July, U.S.-led peace talks between Israel and Palestine began, the first since the 2010 breakdown of similar negotiations. Heading into the meetings, there was little hope that the new round of talks would produce any significant outcomes. Israel-Palestine peace talks have become increasingly less meaningful than they were two decades ago, and both sides seem to recognize this. During negotiations in the 1990s, Israel released 4,000 Palestinian prisoners as part of an agreement to resume peace talks. In 2013, slightly more than 100 would be released over a nine-month period.

The impetus for the 2013 talks was mainly driven by a U.S. desire to reach a conclusion rather than a want on either side of the conflict. Israel sent two representatives—Minister of Justice Livni and prime ministerial aide Isaac Molcho—as did Palestine, which was represented by Saeb Erekat, a senior negotiator, and Muhammed Shtayyeh, a senior Fatah official. U.S. Middle East Peace envoy Martin Indyk and his deputy were named as mediators on the U.S. side. The talks were formally launched on July 29 and 30. Both sides agreed to put all issues pertaining to a peaceful resolution on the table, including a two-state solution, border security, settlements, Jerusalem, final borders, and refugees. The United States said no timeframe would be set for the negotiations but that it hoped an agreement could be reached in nine months. All parties involved agreed not to release details of the meetings. Such secrecy was considered vital to not only keep the talks progressing but also to allow negotiators to consider potential new solutions.

The negotiations were rife with disagreement, as Palestine maintained its desire to have East Jerusalem become its capital, while Israel demanded that Jerusalem be left intact and kept the capital of Israel. It was also indicated that Israel wanted to maintain some of its developments in the West Bank. Leaders in Palestine and Israel faced internal disagreement over the talks as well. The Jewish Home party does not support the two-state solution, and even members of Netanyahu's Likud party disagree with the establishment of a Palestinian state. In Palestine, Hamas, which controls the Gaza Strip, and some other factions, condemned any negotiations with Israel.

As with earlier peace talks, it did not take long before negotiations stalled. On November 13, the Palestinian delegation resigned amid what they considered a lack of progress. This froze the peace talks until a new delegation could be brought in, which Abbas suggested would happen in little time. It was largely speculated, however, that the breakdown occurred after it was announced that the Israeli building minister commissioned plans for more than 20,000 new Jewish settler homes in the West Bank and East Jerusalem. Under international law, such developments are considered illegal. Netanyahu, a long-time supporter of settlement building, immediately called for the halting of such projects and claimed he had no knowledge of them. For their part, U.S. negotiators tried to downplay the situation and remained hopeful the talks would soon resume.

—Heather Kerrigan

Following are two press releases from the Israel Ministry of Foreign Affairs—the first, dated February 2, 2013, details the president's calling on Prime Minister Benjamin Netanyahu to form a new coalition government following the legislative election; and the second, dated March 16, 2013, announces Netanyahu's successful creation of a coalition government—and one press release from the U.S. Department of State on July 28, 2013, announcing the resumption of Israel-Palestine peace talks.

Israeli President Peres Calls for Formation of New Government

February 2, 2013

President Shimon Peres, this evening (Saturday, 2 February 2013), announced, at an official ceremony, that Member of Knesset and current Prime Minister, Benjamin Netanyahu, will be tasked with forming the next government. Earlier President Peres signed a letter to Benjamin Netanyahu in which he tasks him with the responsibility of forming the government, as demanded by Basic Law: The Government.

President Peres said, "I was handed the official results of the elections to the 19th Knesset by the Central Elections Committee Chairman Judge Elyakim Rubinstein, on Wednesday late afternoon.

"Basic Law: The Government empowers me with the responsibility to task one of the Members of Knesset with the responsibility to form the government, within seven days from receipt of the official results. The country needs the new government at the earliest possible opportunity. And so, immediately after receiving the results I began a round of consultation meetings with representatives of the parties elected to the 19th Knesset, as demanded by the law.

"The discussions with the representatives of the parties were conducted with full transparency, with professionalism and dignity. I wish to thank all the party representatives who made themselves heard clearly and responsibly.

"Representatives of 82 members of the 19th Knesset recommended to me that I should task the current Prime Minister, Benjamin Netanyahu, with forming the government. I considered the matter and decided to task Benjamin Netanyahu with the formation of the government, after I received his agreement, as stipulated by law.

"The representatives of the different parties raised important issues with me during our discussions and asked that they be considered when the government is formed. Included amongst them: the national deficit, social justice, the fight against discrimination, equitable sharing of the national burden, conscription to the IDF, restarting diplomatic negotiations to achieve peace and ways to deal with the security threats facing Israel. I will pass these issues on to the Prime Minister.

"I hope that the work will be concluded quickly. The State of Israel needs diplomatic and economic stability so that the government can make the necessary decisions which are on the agenda. The challenges are many, serious and urgent. The people expect a worthy government to be formed quickly so that it can roll up its sleeves and get to work. With the responsibility given to me by the Basic Law of The Government, I am pleased to task the formation of the government upon Member of Knesset Benjamin Netanyahu. I do that with the utmost respect and I wish him luck with this commendable duty."

Prime Minister Netanyahu said, "Thank you, President Peres.

"Dear citizens of Israel, I wish you all a good week. I thank you for the trust you have placed in me. It is an honor and a major responsibility to receive the mandate from you, for what is now third time, to lead our country.

"We have many internal issues to deal with. But firstly, in the Middle East, we must ensure our security. The primary mission of the next government is to stop Iran from becoming armed with nuclear weapons. We will also have to deal with other lethal weapons which are building up in our area and with threats against our cities and our citizens.

"We must continue to strengthen the Israeli economy. The next government which I will form will be committed to peace. I call upon Abu Mazen to return to the negotiating table.

"I am committed to dramatically increase the equitable sharing of the national burden. I am sure we can do this in a responsible manner, which will bring about a fundamental change without tearing apart. Tasks of this nature demand a national unity government, as wide and stable as possible. The reality in which we live has no place for boycotts.

"And so, I call upon those who said they would not sit in the government to reconsider and to come and find common ground. I call upon all sections of society and all the parties, including those who didn't recommend me, to join a responsible national unity government which will be as wide as possible, a government which will ensure the security, the unity and the future of the State of Israel."

SOURCE: Israel Ministry of Foreign Affairs. Press Room. "President Peres Charges Benjamin Netanyahu With Forming Next Government." February 2, 2013. http://mfa.gov.il/MFA/PressRoom/2013/Pages/President_Peres_charges_Netanyahu_forming_government_2-Feb-2013.aspx.

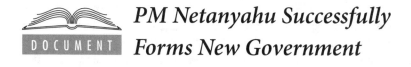

PM Netanyahu Successfully Forms New Government

March 16, 2013

Following the signing of coalition agreements with Yesh Atid and Habayit Hayehudi, Prime Minister Benjamin Netanyahu met with President Shimon Peres on Saturday evening, March 16, to inform him that he has succeeded in the task of forming a government. The new government is scheduled to be sworn in on Monday at the Knesset.

PM Netanyahu: "As you know, I formed a government. We face a decisive year in the fields of security and economy, in efforts to promote peace and in Israelis' desire to effect change. There is cooperation in this government and I believe we will bring change to all Israeli citizens in all areas. That is my mission."

President Peres: "The task of forming a government is complex and requires great efforts and resourcefulness. There were difficulties in the creation of this government and I congratulate Prime Minister Netanyahu that succeeded in forming the government in time. There are problems pending but they are also full of opportunities in the fields of security, welfare and in making peace in progressing the peace process. The country needs it and the people need it. The time has come. Good luck and my blessings to Prime Minister Netanyahu and the new government."

The White House issued the following statement: "President Obama congratulates the Israeli people, Prime Minister Netanyahu, and the new members of the Prime Minister's governing coalition on the successful formation of Israel's new government. President Obama looks forward to working closely with the prime minister and the new government to address the many challenges we face and advance our shared interest in peace and security. The United States places a high value on its deep and enduring bonds with Israel and the Israeli people. The President looks forward to further strengthening those bonds when he travels to Israel next week to meet with Israeli officials and to speak directly with the Israeli people."

SOURCE: Israel Ministry of Foreign Affairs. Press Room. "Netanyahu to Peres: I Have Formed a Government." March 16, 2013. http://mfa.gov.il/MFA/PressRoom/2013/Pages/Netanyahu-to-Peres-government-16-Mar-2013.aspx.

State Department Announces Resumption of Peace Talks

July 28, 2013

Today, Secretary Kerry spoke with Palestinian Authority President Mahmoud Abbas and Israeli Prime Minister Netanyahu and personally extended an invitation to send senior negotiating teams to Washington to formally resume direct final status negotiations. Initial meetings are planned for the evening of Monday July 29 and Tuesday July 30, 2013.

The Israelis will be represented by Justice Minister Tzipi Livni and Yitzhak Molcho, and the Palestinians will be represented by Chief Negotiator Saeb Erekat and Mohammad Shtayyeh. As Secretary Kerry announced on July 19 in Amman, Jordan, the Israelis and Palestinians had reached agreement on the basis for resuming direct final status negotiations. The meetings in Washington will mark the beginning of these talks. They will serve as an opportunity to develop a procedural workplan for how the parties can proceed with the negotiations in the coming months.

In his invitation, the Secretary again commended the courage shown by Prime Minister Netanyahu and President Abbas. The Secretary said, "Both leaders have demonstrated a willingness to make difficult decisions that have been instrumental in getting to this point. We are grateful for their leadership."

The United States and the parties are looking forward to beginning these substantive discussions and in moving forward toward a final status agreement.

SOURCE: U.S. Department of State. Bureau of Public Affairs. "Resumption of Israeli-Palestinian Direct Final Status Negotiations." July 28, 2013. http://www.state.gov/r/pa/prs/ps/2013/07/212503.htm.

OTHER HISTORIC DOCUMENTS OF INTEREST

FROM THIS VOLUME

FROM PREVIOUS *HISTORIC DOCUMENTS*

Vatican Announces Resignation of Pope Benedict; Conclave Chooses New Pope

FEBRUARY 11 AND MARCH 13, 2013

On February 11, 2013, Pope Benedict XVI stunned the world by announcing his resignation of the papacy during a routine meeting of the College of Cardinals. Vatican observers described Benedict's declaration as one of the most dramatic moments in the papacy's history, as no other pontiff had resigned his post since Pope Gregory XII stepped down in 1415 to end the Great Western Schism. A month after Pope Benedict's announcement, the College of Cardinals held a conclave to elect a new pope and selected Argentine Cardinal Jorge Mario Bergoglio as the Roman Catholic Church's new leader.

POPE BENEDICT XVI

Cardinal Joseph Aloisius Ratzinger was elected as the 265th pope on April 19, 2005, following the death of Pope John Paul II. He was very conservative in his theology, taking firm, traditional Catholic stands on social issues such as abortion, birth control, and divorce, and was a strong advocate for creating a purer Catholic Church that emphasized fundamental Christian values. Benedict also renewed the church's relationship with artists and encouraged church leaders to incorporate art into liturgy, opened a new Latin academy at the Vatican to help promote use of the language, and reintroduced traditional papal garments, earning him the name "the pope of aesthetics."

Benedict became pope during the height of the child molestation scandal involving Catholic priests, and issues of child abuse dominated his papacy. As pope, he acknowledged "the shame which we have all felt" over the reports of abuse, and that priests had "disfigured their ministry" and brought "profound shame and regret" on the church. In 2010, he announced new rules aimed at stopping the abuse, which allowed the church to prosecute suspected molesters for twenty years after incidents occurred (the previous limit was ten years); made it a church crime to download pornography; and enabled the pope to remove a priest from the church without a formal Vatican trial.

Yet those who suffered abuse as children claimed the pope's actions were insufficient. "In our view, we were let down in terms of promises of inquiries, reform and most importantly of all the Vatican continuing not to acknowledge that any priest or religious bodies found guilty of child abuse would face the civil authorities and be tried for their crimes in the courts," said John Kelly, a cofounder of the support group Survivors of Child Abuse. The Survivors Network of those Abused by Priests also pressed the International Criminal Court to prosecute Benedict in the child abuse scandal.

Benedict faced an internal, but very public, scandal in 2012. A Vatican butler stole and leaked official correspondence, which was later published in a book portraying the

Vatican as a place of intrigue and corruption. The incident prompted a lengthy internal investigation of the Vatican's finances and governing bodies.

THE POPE RESIGNS

At the time of his resignation, Benedict was eighty-five and beginning to show signs of age and fatigue. He told the College of Cardinals that his physical and mental states were key considerations in his decision to resign. "In today's world, subject to so many rapid changes and shaken by questions of deep relevance for the life of faith, in order to govern the barque of Saint Peter and proclaim the Gospel, both strength of mind and body are necessary, strength which in the last few months, has deteriorated in me to the extent that I have had to recognize my incapacity to adequately fulfill the ministry entrusted to me," Benedict said. He added that he wished to continue serving "the Holy Church of God in the future through a life dedicated to prayer" and noted the need to hold a conclave to elect a new pope.

Vatican spokesperson Rev. Federico Lombardi acknowledged that "the pope took us by surprise," but noted Pope Benedict had been weighing his decision for several months. Italian Prime Minister Mario Monti captured the shock many felt on hearing the news, characterizing the resignation as "immense and unexpected." Others applauded Benedict for his decision, including Irish Prime Minister Enda Kenny. "It reflects his profound sense of duty to the Church, and also his deep appreciation of the unique pressures of spiritual leadership in the modern world," Kenny said.

Benedict's resignation took effect on February 28 at 8:00 p.m., at which time he retired to his summer home in Castel Gandolfo before taking residence in a monastery in Vatican City.

A PAPAL ELECTION

Following a papal vacancy, the College of Cardinals assumes governance responsibilities of the Catholic Church and holds a series of meetings to discuss the current needs and challenges of the church and prepare for a conclave, or papal election. Only cardinals under the age of eighty are able to vote, and the number of electors is limited to 120. Cardinals vote by secret ballot, and they must vote for one of the other eligible cardinals. A cardinal must receive two-thirds of the vote to become pope. After each round of voting, the ballots are burned in the chapel's stove. If there is no decisive vote, the ballots are mixed with a chemical that produces black smoke, signaling to those outside that the voting must continue. Once a cardinal receives enough votes to become pope, the final ballots are burned with chemicals that produce white smoke.

The conclave following Benedict's resignation began on March 12, and included 115 cardinals from forty-eight countries. Participating cardinals gathered in the Sistine Chapel where they took an oath of secrecy before the chapel doors were sealed. There was no clear front-runner for the papacy among the cardinals when the conclave began, though Vatican observers speculated that they would elect someone from the developing world, in recognition of the significant and growing Catholic population in those countries. Others surmised that whoever was selected would follow a conservative path similar to that of Benedict, as he had appointed more than sixty-five of the cardinals participating in the conclave.

On March 13, following the fifth round of voting, white smoke could be seen coming from the Sistine Chapel's chimney at 7:06 p.m. local time. The cardinals had elected Bergoglio as the 266th pope. Bergoglio was a seventy-six-year-old who had served as the archbishop of Buenos Aires since 1998. He was also a pope of many firsts: he was the first pope in history to come from the Western Hemisphere, the first non-European to be elected in nearly 1,300 years, the first member of the Jesuit order to be elected, and the first pontiff to choose Francis as his papal name.

At 8:12 p.m., French Cardinal Jean-Louis Tauran, the senior cardinal in the order of deacons, announced to the crowd gathered in St. Peter's Square that a new pope had been selected. Pope Francis emerged roughly ten minutes later on the balcony of St. Peter's Basilica to offer the traditional blessings of Rome and the world, and to ask the crowd to pray for Benedict. In a break with tradition, Francis asked the crowd to pray for him as well.

POPE FRANCIS

As a young man, Francis had trained to become a chemist, but he joined the priesthood instead at age thirty-two. He was known as a humble man who lived simply. He chose a simple apartment in Buenos Aires over the traditional archbishop's palace, rode the bus, and cooked his own meals. He was also a staunch defender of the poor, stating in 2007 that "we live in the most unequal part of the world, which has grown the most yet reduced misery the least. The unjust distribution of goods persists, creating a situation of social sin that cries out to Heaven and limits the possibilities of a fuller life for so many of our brothers."

Many said his choice of Francis as his papal name further reflected these qualities, because his namesake, St. Francis of Assisi, had also devoted himself to the poor and acts of mercy. "Cardinal Bergoglio had a special place in his heart and his ministry for the poor, for the disenfranchised, for those living on the fringes and facing injustice," said Thomas Rosica, the Vatican's deputy spokesperson. "Francis of Assisi is . . . someone who turned his back on the wealth of his family and the lifestyle that he had, and bonded with lepers and the poor."

As a cardinal, Francis frequently spoke about Argentina's economic, social, and political problems in public. He provided counsel on these issues to Buenos Aires officials and was highly involved in mediating many social and political conflicts. He formed new parishes, streamlined the church's local administrative offices, and initiated several new programs aimed at providing spiritual guidance, including a commission for divorcees. He was an outspoken critic of same-sex marriages and had encouraged Catholics to protest Argentina's legalization of gay marriage in 2010, claiming it could "seriously injure the family." He also opposed same-sex adoption and had been critical of Argentina's attempt to legalize abortion under certain circumstances.

Some controversy surrounded Francis' actions during Argentina's period of military dictatorship from 1976 to 1983. Thousands of the military regime's political opponents were either killed or forcibly disappeared during this time, including a couple of young priests who were detained by the regime. Some said Francis did not do enough to help protect the two priests and other church workers from the regime, but others defended him, arguing that he'd worked behind the scenes to secure the priests' release.

Francis was officially inaugurated as pope on March 19, and delivered his first homily to tens of thousands of people gathered in St. Peter's Square. The homily focused on the need to care for the poor and the sick, as well as nature, stressing the importance of "protecting people, showing loving concern for each and every person, especially children, the elderly, those in need, who are often the last we think about."

Francis continued to break with a number of church traditions early in his papacy. He celebrated the Mass of the Lord's Supper, one of the major events marking the Holy Week before Easter, at the Casal del Marmo youth detention center, where he washed the feet of twelve juvenile delinquents, including two women. This service is traditionally held at the Basilica of St. John Lateran, the official seat of the bishop of Rome, and involves washing the feet of twelve priests to symbolize Jesus' washing of the apostles' feet. Catholic traditionalists criticized Francis' action, saying the rite should be limited to men, but Vatican spokesperson Rev. Lombardi responded that the pope's decision was "absolutely licit" for a rite that is not a sacrament.

In July, Francis made headlines when, on a plane back from Brazil, he said to reporters, "If someone is gay and he searches for the Lord and has good will, who am I to judge?" His remarks took a more compassionate tone than his predecessors, including Benedict, who had described homosexuality as "a strong tendency ordered toward an intrinsic moral evil." Vatican experts noted that Francis did not suggest in his remarks that priests or anyone else should act on their homosexual tendencies, but said his comments and even his use of the word "gay" were revolutionary.

In a September interview with Rev. Antonio Spadaro for *La Civiltà Cattolica*, an Italian Jesuit journal, Francis said the church was "obsessed" with abortion, gay marriage, and contraception, and that he had specifically chosen not to speak about those issues since becoming pope. He was critical of the church for what he described as prioritizing dogma and moral doctrines over loving all and helping the poor. While the remarks, again, did not change church doctrine, they did stir hope among some more liberal Catholics that those policies may someday change.

Francis has also been outspoken on a number of current issues, including the use of chemical weapons and military action in Syria, and the flaws of capitalism, and has emphasized the importance of strengthening relationships between the Catholic Church and other religions.

—Linda Fecteau

Following are two press releases from the Vatican. The first, dated February 11, 2013, announces Pope Benedict's resignation; and the second, dated March 13, 2013, details the election of a new pope.

DOCUMENT   *Pope Benedict Announces Resignation*

February 11, 2013

The Holy Father, at the end of today's consistory for causes for canonization, announced his resignation from ministry as Bishop of Rome to the College of Cardinals. Following is the Holy Father's complete declaration, which he read in Latin:

"I have convoked you to this Consistory, not only for the three canonizations, but also to communicate to you a decision of great importance for the life of the Church. After having repeatedly examined my conscience before God, I have come to the certainty that my strengths, due to an advanced age, are no longer suited to an adequate exercise of the Petrine ministry. I am well aware that this ministry, due to its essential spiritual nature, must be carried out not only with words and deeds, but no less with prayer and suffering. However, in today's world, subject to so many rapid changes and shaken by questions of deep relevance for the life of faith, in order to govern the barque of Saint Peter and proclaim the Gospel, both strength of mind and body are necessary, strength which in the last few months, has deteriorated in me to the extent that I have had to recognize my incapacity to adequately fulfil the ministry entrusted to me. For this reason, and well aware of the seriousness of this act, with full freedom I declare that I renounce the ministry of Bishop of Rome, Successor of Saint Peter, entrusted to me by the Cardinals on 19 April 2005, in such a way, that as from 28 February 2013, at 20:00 hours, the See of Rome, the See of Saint Peter, will be vacant and a Conclave to elect the new Supreme Pontiff will have to be convoked by those whose competence it is."

"Dear Brothers, I thank you most sincerely for all the love and work with which you have supported me in my ministry and I ask pardon for all my defects. And now, let us entrust the Holy Church to the care of Our Supreme Pastor, Our Lord Jesus Christ, and implore his holy Mother Mary, so that she may assist the Cardinal Fathers with her maternal solicitude, in electing a new Supreme Pontiff. With regard to myself, I wish to also devotedly serve the Holy Church of God in the future through a life dedicated to prayer."

SOURCE: Vatican Information Service. "Pope Renounces Papal Throne." February 11, 2013. http://www.vis.va/vissolr/index.php?vi=en&dl=26c5547c-7ea3-3625-2e10-51191b83d912&dl_t=text/xml&dl_a=y&ul=1&ev=1.

DOCUMENT *Cardinals Elect New Pope*

March 13, 2013

Cardinal Jorge Mario Bergoglio, S.J., has been elected as Supreme Pontiff, the 265th successor of Peter, and has chosen the name Francis. He is the first Latin American Pope, the first Jesuit Pope, and the first "Francis" in the pontificate.

At 8:12pm—54 minutes after the appearance of the white "fumata" at 7:06pm—the Cardinal proto-deacon Jean-Louis Tauran made the solemn announcement to the people from the external Loggia of the Hall of Blessings of the Vatican Basilica.

Following are the words pronounced by Cardinal Tauran:

> Annuntio vobis gaudium magnum;
>
> habemus Papam;
>
> Eminentissium ac Reverendissium Dominum,
>
> Dominum Georgium Marium

Sanctae Romanae Ecclesiae Cardinalem Bergoglio

Qui sibi nomen imposuit Franciscum.

[I announce to you with great joy;

We have a Pope;

The most eminent and most reverend Lord

Lord Jorge Mario

Cardinal of Holy Roman Church Bergoglio

Who has taken the name Francis.]

Conclave Notes

The conclave that led to the election of Pope Francis began on Tuesday, 12 March 2013 in the Sistine Chapel of the Vatican Apostolic Palace, with the "Extra omnes" pronounced at 5:33pm by Msgr. Guido Marini, master of the Liturgical Celebrations of the Supreme Pontiff, following the taking of the oath by the 115 cardinal electors.

The first black "fumata" took place at 7:42pm the same day.

On Wednesday, 13 March, there was black smoke at 11:40am.

On Wednesday, 13 March, there was white smoke at 7:06pm.

First "Urbi et Orbi" Blessing of the New Holy Father Francis

Before the new Pope appeared at the balcony, an honour guard of Swiss Guards in full military regalia and bearing the pontifical standard marched into the square and took their places under the Loggia followed by a representation of the various Italian armed forces that, since 1929, have paid homage to the Pope on important occasions as a sign of the reconciliation between the Holy See and the Italian State. The Holy See marching band accompanied the wait. As soon as they heard the name of the new pontiff, the crowd began to chant together: "Francesco, Francesco."

At 8:24pm, the Holy Father Francis, preceded by the Cross, appeared at the Loggia of the brightly lit Vatican Basilica. Before imparting the "Urbi et Orbi" ("to the city and the world) apostolic blessing, he greeted the enormous crowd that had been gathering all afternoon in cold and rainy St. Peter's Square saying:

"Dear brothers and sisters,

Good evening. You know that the duty of the Conclave was to give Rome a bishop. It seems that my brother cardinals picked him from almost the ends of the earth. But here we are! I thank you for the warm welcome. The diocesan community of Rome has its bishop. Thank you! First and foremost I would like to say a prayer for our Bishop Emeritus Benedict XVI. Let us pray together for him, that the Lord bless him and the Virgin keep him."

After leading the Our Father, Hail Mary, and Gloria, Pope Francis again addressed the crowd saying:

"And now let us begin this journey, bishop and people, this journey of the Church of Rome, which is the one that leads all the churches in charity. A journey of fraternity, of trust between us. Let us always pray for one another. Let us pray for the world so that this might be a great brotherhood. I hope that this journey of the Church that we begin today, and in which my Cardinal Vicar here present will assist me, will be fruitful for the evangelization of this beautiful city."

"Now I would like to impart the blessing, but first, first I ask a favour of you. Before the bishop blesses the people, I ask that you pray to the Lord that He bless me: the prayer of the people asking a blessing for their bishop. Let us pray in silence, this your prayer for me."

"Now I will impart the blessing to you and all the world, to all men and women of good will."

After imparting the apostolic blessing Pope Francis added: "Brothers and sisters, I take my leave. Thank you for your warm welcome. Pray for me and we will meet again soon. Tomorrow I'm going to pray to the Virgin that she will safeguard all of Rome. Good night and rest well."

Source: Vatican Information Service. "Cardinal Jorge Mario Bergoglio Elected Pope, Takes Francis as Name." March 13, 2013. http://www.vis.va/vissolr/index.php?vi=en&dl=736682ec-4e95-bc32-3e4f-5141aabca832&dl_t=text/xml&dl_a=y&ul=1&ev=1.

Other Historic Documents of Interest

From previous Historic Documents

- Vatican Prohibition on Gay Seminarians, *2005,* p. 863
- Cardinal Ratzinger's Homily for Pope John Paul II, *2005,* p. 290
- National Review Board on Sexual Abuse in the Catholic Church, *2004,* p. 82
- Catholic Bishops on Sexual Abuse by Priests, *2002,* p. 867
- Joseph Cardinal Bernardin on Sexual Abuse by Priests, *1992,* p. 507

State of the Union Address and Republican Response

FEBRUARY 12, 2013

Just three weeks after delivering his inaugural address, President Barack Obama stood before a joint session of Congress on February 12, 2013, to give the first State of the Union of his second term. The president's address was less idealistic and more of a task list when compared to the speech he delivered during his inauguration. Topping Obama's second term "to-do" list were domestic priorities like reinvigorating the economy, creating a world-class education system, and growing the middle class. The latter was a key tenet of Obama's speech, and was included in his 2011 address and his 2012 campaign speeches. While the country could be confident that the worst of the economic recession had passed, Obama said that the nation must "reignite the true engine of America's economic growth: a rising, thriving middle class."

A Thriving Middle Class

Obama's address made it clear that the economy would be his number one focus for the year. "Every day, we should ask ourselves three questions as a nation: How do we attract more jobs to our shores? How do we equip our people with the skills to get those jobs? And how do we make sure that hard work leads to a decent living?" Obama asked. To that end, the president said the economy could not continue on its upward trajectory without a thriving middle class: "Our economy is adding jobs, but too many people still can't find full-time employment. Corporate profits have rocketed to all-time highs, but for more than a decade, wages and incomes have barely budged."

To make the middle-class dreams of thousands of Americans come true, Obama urged Congress to invest in infrastructure and manufacturing to stop jobs from going overseas. And he asked them to raise the minimum wage from $7.25 to $9 per hour. President Obama also linked economic vitality to improvements in the American education system and renewed his calls for universal preschool and finding a way to lower college tuition to make higher education accessible to all Americans. To solve this growing higher education challenge, the president proposed tying some federal grants in part to tuition to encourage colleges and universities to keep tuition increases to a minimum.

One of the preeminent issues facing economic growth in the near term was the $85 million in automatic spending cuts, known as the sequester, set to take effect on March 1. On January 1, 2013, Congress voted to delay implementation of the cuts from January 2 to March 1, but at the time of the president's speech had failed to reach a compromise on how to replace, or at least lessen the impact of, the sequester. Obama said the cuts "would jeopardize our military readiness. They'd devastate priorities like education, energy, and medical research. They would certainly slow our recovery and cost us hundreds of thousands of jobs." Democrats wanted to see new tax revenue replace the sequester, while Republicans called for extensive entitlement reform, an idea the president called "even worse" than the sequester itself.

Maintaining the integrity of entitlement programs like Medicare, Medicaid, and Social Security were paramount to reinvigorating the middle class, the president said. He backed Democrats in Congress, calling for a revised tax code that closed loopholes and forced the wealthiest Americans to pay their fair share. "Why would we choose to make deeper cuts to education and Medicare just to protect special interest tax breaks?" the president asked. "Why is it that deficit reduction is a big emergency justifying cuts in Social Security benefits, but not closing some loopholes? How does that promote growth?" President Obama added that he would be willing to negotiate for some entitlement reform that would not seek deep benefit cuts, saying "I realize that tax reform and entitlement reform will not be easy. The politics will be hard for both sides. None of us will get a hundred percent of what we want. But the alternative will cost us jobs, hurt our economy, [and] visit hardship on millions of hard-working Americans."

Domestic Issues

President Obama won a solid majority of Hispanic votes in the 2012 presidential election, and intended to deliver on a key promise he made on the campaign trail: immigration reform. Republicans had a significant stake in the issue as well because they would need the support of the growing Hispanic population in future elections. In his State of the Union address, Obama urged Congress to work to draft bipartisan immigration legislation that would include background checks, English language requirements, and taxes and penalties for those currently in the country illegally while still providing them a path to legal status. "Our economy is stronger when we harness the talents and ingenuity of striving, hopeful immigrants," the president said, adding that he would sign a comprehensive immigration reform bill as soon as it came to his desk.

In the most emotional portion of his speech, Obama took on the issue of gun control. In the audience were more than two dozen Americans who had been touched by gun violence, including the parents of Hadiya Pendleton, a fifteen-year-old who was shot in Chicago just weeks after performing at Obama's inauguration. "They deserve a vote," Obama said of the victims and their families. Noting tragic events of the past few years, the president continued, "Gabby Giffords deserves a vote. The families of Newtown deserve a vote. The families of Aurora deserve a vote. The families of Oak Creek and Tucson and Blacksburg, and the countless other communities ripped open by gun violence, they deserve a simple vote." He asked legislators to work together to pass a gun law that included background checks at gun sales, a ban on some semi-automatic weapons, a limit on the size of magazines, and new policies to prevent guns from being sold to criminals. He noted that a majority of Americans support some form of gun control legislation and made clear that he did not intend to infringe on Second Amendment rights.

The president also addressed energy issues, linking them to climate change and devastating natural events like 2012's Hurricane Sandy. "We can choose to believe that Superstorm Sandy and the most severe drought in decades and the worst wildfires some States have ever seen were all just a freak coincidence. Or we can choose to believe in the overwhelming judgment of science and act before it's too late," Obama said, pushing Congress to pass legislation that would address climate change and transition the United States to cleaner, more sustainable energy methods such as solar and wind power. If

Congress failed to act, the president said he would tell his "Cabinet to come up with executive actions we can take, now and in the future, to reduce pollution, prepare our communities for the consequences of climate change, and speed the transition to more sustainable sources of energy." In a nod to Republicans, the president did add that he would also work to speed up approval of oil and gas drilling permits.

President Calls for Bipartisan Effort

Although the president took a decidedly liberal tone in his inaugural address, when it came to the State of the Union, Obama used a bipartisan approach. The American people "expect us to put the nation's interest before party. They do expect us to forge reasonable compromise where we can. For they know that America moves forward only when we do so together and that the responsibility of improving this union remains the task of us all," Obama said. In what had become a hallmark of the Obama administration, the president scolded Congress for its political gamesmanship that jeopardized the economy, weakened America's position on the world stage, and threatened the public's trust in its elected leaders. "Let's set party interests aside and work to pass a budget that replaces reckless cuts with smart savings and wise investments in our future. And let's do it without the brinksmanship that stresses consumers and scares off investors. The greatest nation on Earth cannot keep conducting its business by drifting from one manufactured crisis to the next," Obama said. If Congress refused to forge a new path and take action on the challenges facing the country, Obama said he was prepared to use his executive power to take action himself.

Despite Obama's call for bipartisanship, few believed it would come to fruition. According to a CNN/ORC poll taken after the speech, 53 percent said they did not think the speech would lead to more cooperation in Congress.

Foreign Affairs

As in his past State of the Union addresses, Obama spent little time, only 15 percent of his one-hour speech, focusing on international affairs. The countries of note mentioned included Afghanistan, North Korea, and Iran. On Afghanistan, Obama announced that 34,000 troops would be withdrawn within the next year. That would leave less than 30,000 troops in Afghanistan, where the United States is expected to end its mission in 2014. And because al Qaeda had been weakened, the president noted that the United States would now place more focus on counterterrorism efforts and training Afghani troops.

Despite questions surrounding the potential involvement of the United States in the ongoing civil war in Syria, the president made it clear that it was not his intent to become entrenched in another ground operation. "We don't need to send tens of thousands of our sons and daughters abroad or occupy nations," Obama said. Instead, the president proposed providing aid to Middle Eastern nations that would not only support the U.S. mission to root out global terrorism, but would also promote democracy abroad. "In the Middle East," he said, "we will stand with citizens as they demand their universal rights and support stable transitions to democracy."

Given North Korea's nuclear test the day of the president's speech, and Iran's continued uranium enrichment program, Obama highlighted the importance of working with the United States' international partners to reduce nuclear weapon stockpiles. He also warned the new leader of North Korea, Kim Jong Un, that continued defiance of international sanctions would only lead to further isolation and eventual retaliation.

Obama spoke briefly about his desire to finalize a free trade agreement with the European Union, which has the potential to create the world's largest free trade zone. Obama said such a comprehensive partnership "supports millions of good-paying American jobs." However, the president will likely continue to face stiff opposition from some in his own party who argue, with the backing of labor unions, that such free trade pacts send jobs overseas and only stand to hurt America's manufacturing base.

REPUBLICAN RESPONSE

The Republicans chose Florida Senator Marco Rubio to give the official response to the State of the Union address. Like the president, Rubio also focused on the importance of helping the middle class, but argued that the proposals made by President Obama would do more harm than good. "Mr. President, I don't oppose your plans because I want to protect the rich. I oppose your plans because I want to protect my neighbors," Rubio said. He was highly critical of Obama's desire to increase tax revenue while cutting spending, staying close to the Republican opinion that the best way to reduce the deficit is to reform entitlement programs rather than raising taxes. "The idea that more taxes and more government spending is the way to help hardworking middle class taxpayers, that's an old idea that has failed every time it's been tried," Rubio said. "More government isn't going to help you get ahead. It's going to hold you back." The proposals the president made, Rubio said, "will cost [middle class families] their raises. It will cost them their benefits. It may even cost some of them their jobs."

Responding to Democratic criticism that Republicans are simply seeking to serve the wealthiest Americans, Rubio agreed with some of Obama's tax proposals, such as lowering the corporate tax rate. However, he criticized the president for not also demanding enough from entitlement reform, arguing that without radical change, programs like Medicare will soon be bankrupt. "I would never support any changes to Medicare that would hurt seniors like my mother," Rubio said. "But anyone who is in favor of leaving Medicare exactly the way it is right now, is in favor of bankrupting it."

On social issues, Rubio touched briefly on gun control, stating that while it was clear a method was needed to deal with gun violence in America, Democrats could not undermine constitutional gun ownership rights as a means to do so. Rubio, the son of Cuban immigrants, also advocated for "a responsible, permanent solution to the problem of those who are here illegally" but noted the importance of also securing the borders and enforcing current immigration law.

Like the president, Rubio appealed to Republicans and Democrats to work together to solve America's most pressing challenges. "Each time our nation has faced great challenges, what has kept us together was our shared hope for a better life," Rubio said. "Now, let that hope bring us together again. To solve the challenges of our time and write the next chapter in the amazing story of the greatest nation man has ever known."

—Heather Kerrigan

Following is the complete text of the State of the Union Address delivered by President Barack Obama on February 12, 2013, and the Republican response, delivered by Sen. Marco Rubio, R-Fla., also on February 12, 2013.

DOCUMENT *State of the Union Address*

February 12, 2013

Please, everybody, have a seat. Mr. Speaker, Mr. Vice President, Members of Congress, fellow Americans: Fifty-one years ago, John F. Kennedy declared to this Chamber that "the Constitution makes us not rivals for power, but partners for progress." "It is my task," he said, "to report the state of the Union; to improve it is the task of us all."

Tonight, thanks to the grit and determination of the American people, there is much progress to report. After a decade of grinding war, our brave men and women in uniform are coming home. After years of grueling recession, our businesses have created over 6 million new jobs. We buy more American cars than we have in 5 years and less foreign oil than we have in 20. Our housing market is healing, our stock market is rebounding, and consumers, patients, and homeowners enjoy stronger protections than ever before.

So together, we have cleared away the rubble of crisis, and we can say with renewed confidence that the state of our Union is stronger.

But we gather here knowing that there are millions of Americans whose hard work and dedication have not yet been rewarded. Our economy is adding jobs, but too many people still can't find full-time employment. Corporate profits have skyrocketed to all time highs, but for more than a decade, wages and incomes have barely budged.

It is our generation's task, then, to reignite the true engine of America's economic growth: a rising, thriving middle class.

It is our unfinished task to restore the basic bargain that built this country: the idea that if you work hard and meet your responsibilities, you can get ahead, no matter where you come from, no matter what you look like or who you love.

It is our unfinished task to make sure that this Government works on behalf of the many, and not just the few; that it encourages free enterprise, rewards individual initiative, and opens the doors of opportunity to every child across this great Nation.

The American people don't expect government to solve every problem. They don't expect those of us in this Chamber to agree on every issue. But they do expect us to put the Nation's interests before party. They do expect us to forge reasonable compromise where we can. For they know that America moves forward only when we do so together and that the responsibility of improving this Union remains the task of us all.

Now, our work must begin by making some basic decisions about our budget, decisions that will have a huge impact on the strength of our recovery.

Over the last few years, both parties have worked together to reduce the deficit by more than $2.5 trillion, mostly through spending cuts, but also by raising tax rates on the wealthiest 1 percent of Americans. As a result, we are more than halfway towards the goal of $4 trillion in deficit reduction that economists say we need to stabilize our finances.

Now we need to finish the job. And the question is, how?

In 2011, Congress passed a law saying that if both parties couldn't agree on a plan to reach our deficit goal, about a trillion dollars' worth of budget cuts would automatically go into effect this year. These sudden, harsh, arbitrary cuts would jeopardize our military readiness. They'd devastate priorities like education and energy and medical research. They would certainly slow our recovery and cost us hundreds of thousands of jobs. And that's why Democrats, Republicans, business leaders, and economists have already said that these cuts—known here in Washington as the sequester—are a really bad idea.

Now, some in Congress have proposed preventing only the defense cuts by making even bigger cuts to things like education and job training, Medicare, and Social Security benefits. That idea is even worse.

Yes, the biggest driver of our long-term debt is the rising cost of health care for an aging population. And those of us who care deeply about programs like Medicare must embrace the need for modest reforms; otherwise, our retirement programs will crowd out the investments we need for our children and jeopardize the promise of a secure retirement for future generations.

But we can't ask senior citizens and working families to shoulder the entire burden of deficit reduction while asking nothing more from the wealthiest and the most powerful. We won't grow the middle class simply by shifting the cost of health care or college onto families that are already struggling or by forcing communities to lay off more teachers and more cops and more firefighters. Most Americans—Democrats, Republicans, and Independents—understand that we can't just cut our way to prosperity. They know that broad-based economic growth requires a balanced approach to deficit reduction, with spending cuts and revenue and with everybody doing their fair share. And that's the approach I offer tonight.

On Medicare, I'm prepared to enact reforms that will achieve the same amount of health care savings by the beginning of the next decade as the reforms proposed by the bipartisan Simpson-Bowles Commission.

Already, the Affordable Care Act is helping to slow the growth of health care costs. And the reforms I'm proposing go even further. We'll reduce taxpayer subsidies to prescription drug companies and ask more from the wealthiest seniors. We'll bring down costs by changing the way our Government pays for Medicare, because our medical bills shouldn't be based on the number of tests ordered or days spent in the hospital; they should be based on the quality of care that our seniors receive. And I am open to additional reforms from both parties, so long as they don't violate the guarantee of a secure retirement. Our Government shouldn't make promises we cannot keep, but we must keep the promises we've already made.

To hit the rest of our deficit reduction target, we should do what leaders in both parties have already suggested and save hundreds of billions of dollars by getting rid of tax loopholes and deductions for the well-off and the well-connected. After all, why would we choose to make deeper cuts to education and Medicare just to protect special interest tax breaks? How is that fair? Why is it that deficit reduction is a big emergency justifying making cuts in Social Security benefits, but not closing some loopholes? How does that promote growth?

Now is our best chance for bipartisan, comprehensive tax reform that encourages job creation and helps bring down the deficit. We can get this done. The American people deserve a Tax Code that helps small businesses spend less time filling out complicated forms and more time expanding and hiring; a Tax Code that ensures billionaires with high-powered accountants can't work the system and pay a lower rate than their hardworking secretaries; a Tax Code that lowers incentives to move jobs overseas and lowers tax rates for businesses and manufacturers that are creating jobs right here in the United States of America. That's what tax reform can deliver. That's what we can do together.

I realize that tax reform and entitlement reform will not be easy. The politics will be hard for both sides. None of us will get a hundred percent of what we want. But the alternative will cost us jobs, hurt our economy, visit hardship on millions of hard-working Americans. So let's set party interests aside and work to pass a budget that replaces reckless cuts with smart savings and wise investments in our future. And let's do it without the brinksmanship that stresses consumers and scares off investors. The greatest nation on Earth cannot keep conducting its business by drifting from one manufactured crisis to the next. We can't do it.

Let's agree right here, right now to keep the people's Government open and pay our bills on time and always uphold the full faith and credit of the United States of America. The American people have worked too hard, for too long, rebuilding from one crisis to see their elected officials cause another.

Now, most of us agree that a plan to reduce the deficit must be part of our agenda. But let's be clear: Deficit reduction alone is not an economic plan. A growing economy that creates good, middle class jobs, that must be the north star that guides our efforts. Every day, we should ask ourselves three questions as a nation: How do we attract more jobs to our shores? How do we equip our people with the skills they need to get those jobs? And how do we make sure that hard work leads to a decent living?

Now, a year and a half ago, I put forward an American Jobs Act that independent economists said would create more than 1 million new jobs. And I thank the last Congress for passing some of that agenda. I urge this Congress to pass the rest. But tonight I'll lay out additional proposals that are fully paid for and fully consistent with the budget framework both parties agreed to just 18 months ago. Let me repeat: Nothing I'm proposing tonight should increase our deficit by a single dime. It is not a bigger Government we need, but a smarter Government that sets priorities and invests in broad-based growth. That's what we should be looking for.

Our first priority is making America a magnet for new jobs and manufacturing. After shedding jobs for more than 10 years, our manufacturers have added about 500,000 jobs over the past 3. Caterpillar is bringing jobs back from Japan. Ford is bringing jobs back from Mexico. And this year, Apple will start making Macs in America again.

There are things we can do right now to accelerate this trend. Last year, we created our first manufacturing innovation institute in Youngstown, Ohio. A once-shuttered warehouse is now a state-of-the-art lab where new workers are mastering the 3-D printing that has the potential to revolutionize the way we make almost everything. There's no reason this can't happen in other towns.

So tonight I'm announcing the launch of three more of these manufacturing hubs, where businesses will partner with the Department of Defense and Energy to turn regions left behind by globalization into global centers of high-tech jobs. And I ask this Congress to help create a network of 15 of these hubs and guarantee that the next revolution in manufacturing is made right here in America. We can get that done.

Now, if we want to make the best products, we also have to invest in the best ideas. Every dollar we invested to map the human genome returned $140 to our economy— every dollar. Today, our scientists are mapping the human brain to unlock the answers to Alzheimer's. They're developing drugs to regenerate damaged organs, devising new materials to make batteries 10 times more powerful. Now is not the time to gut these job-creating investments in science and innovation, now is the time to reach a level of research and development not seen since the height of the space race. We need to make those investments.

Today, no area holds more promise than our investments in American energy. After years of talking about it, we're finally poised to control our own energy future. We produce more oil at home than we have in 15 years. We have doubled the distance our cars will go on a gallon of gas and the amount of renewable energy we generate from sources like wind and solar, with tens of thousands of good American jobs to show for it. We produce more natural gas than ever before, and nearly everyone's energy bill is lower because of it. And over the last 4 years, our emissions of the dangerous carbon pollution that threatens our planet have actually fallen.

But for the sake of our children and our future, we must do more to combat climate change. Now, it's true that no single event makes a trend. But the fact is, the 12 hottest years on record have all come in the last 15. Heat waves, droughts, wildfires, floods—all are now more frequent and more intense. We can choose to believe that Superstorm Sandy and the most severe drought in decades and the worst wildfires some States have ever seen were all just a freak coincidence. Or we can choose to believe in the overwhelming judgment of science and act before it's too late.

Now, the good news is we can make meaningful progress on this issue while driving strong economic growth. I urge this Congress to get together, pursue a bipartisan, market-based solution to climate change, like the one John McCain and Joe Lieberman worked on together a few years ago. But if Congress won't act soon to protect future generations, I will. I will direct my Cabinet to come up with executive actions we can take, now and in the future, to reduce pollution, prepare our communities for the consequences of climate change, and speed the transition to more sustainable sources of energy.

And 4 years ago, other countries dominated the clean energy market and the jobs that came with it. And we've begun to change that. Last year, wind energy added nearly half of all new power capacity in America. So let's generate even more. Solar energy gets cheaper by the year; let's drive down costs even further. As long as countries like China keep going all in on clean energy, so must we.

Now, in the meantime, the natural gas boom has led to cleaner power and greater energy independence. We need to encourage that. And that's why my administration will keep cutting redtape and speeding up new oil and gas permits. That's got to be part of an all-of-the-above plan. But I also want to work with this Congress to encourage the research and technology that helps natural gas burn even cleaner and protects our air and our water.

In fact, much of our new-found energy is drawn from lands and waters that we, the public, own together. So tonight I propose we use some of our oil and gas revenues to fund an energy security trust that will drive new research and technology to shift our cars and trucks off oil for good. If a nonpartisan coalition of CEOs and retired generals and admirals can get behind this idea, then so can we. Let's take their advice and free our families and businesses from the painful spikes in gas prices we've put up with for far too long.

I'm also issuing a new goal for America: Let's cut in half the energy wasted by our homes and businesses over the next 20 years. We'll work with the States to do it. Those States with the best ideas to create jobs and lower energy bills by constructing more efficient buildings will receive Federal support to help make that happen.

America's energy sector is just one part of an aging infrastructure badly in need of repair. Ask any CEO where they'd rather locate and hire, a country with deteriorating roads and bridges or one with high-speed rail and Internet, high-tech schools, self-healing power grids. The CEO of Siemens America—a company that brought hundreds of new jobs to North Carolina—said that if we upgrade our infrastructure, they'll bring even more jobs. And that's the attitude of a lot of companies all around the world. And

I know you want these job-creating projects in your district. I've seen all those ribbon-cuttings.

So tonight I propose a Fix-It-First program to put people to work as soon as possible on our most urgent repairs, like the nearly 70,000 structurally deficient bridges across the country. And to make sure taxpayers don't shoulder the whole burden, I'm also proposing a partnership to rebuild America that attracts private capital to upgrade what our businesses need most: modern ports to move our goods, modern pipelines to withstand a storm, modern schools worthy of our children. Let's prove there's no better place to do business than here in the United States of America, and let's start right away. We can get this done.

And part of our rebuilding effort must also involve our housing sector. The good news is, our housing market is finally healing from the collapse of 2007. Home prices are rising at the fastest pace in 6 years. Home purchases are up nearly 50 percent, and construction is expanding again.

But even with mortgage rates near a 50-year low, too many families with solid credit who want to buy a home are being rejected. Too many families who never missed a payment and want to refinance are being told no. That's holding our entire economy back. We need to fix it.

Right now there's a bill in this Congress that would give every responsible homeowner in America the chance to save $3,000 a year by refinancing at today's rates. Democrats and Republicans have supported it before, so what are we waiting for? Take a vote and send me that bill. Why are—why would we be against that? Why would that be a partisan issue, helping folks refinance? Right now overlapping regulations keep responsible young families from buying their first home. What's holding us back? Let's streamline the process and help our economy grow.

These initiatives in manufacturing, energy, infrastructure, housing, all these things will help entrepreneurs and small-business owners expand and create new jobs. But none of it will matter unless we also equip our citizens with the skills and training to fill those jobs.

And that has to start at the earliest possible age. Study after study shows that the sooner a child begins learning, the better he or she does down the road. But today, fewer than 3 in 10 4-year-olds are enrolled in a high-quality preschool program. Most middle class parents can't afford a few hundred bucks a week for a private preschool. And for poor kids who need help the most, this lack of access to preschool education can shadow them for the rest of their lives. So tonight I propose working with States to make high-quality preschool available to every single child in America. That's something we should be able to do.

Every dollar we invest in high-quality early childhood education can save more than 7 dollars later on: by boosting graduation rates, reducing teen pregnancy, even reducing violent crime. In States that make it a priority to educate our youngest children, like Georgia or Oklahoma, studies show students grow up more likely to read and do math at grade level, graduate high school, hold a job, form more stable families of their own. We know this works. So let's do what works and make sure none of our children start the race of life already behind. Let's give our kids that chance.

Let's also make sure that a high school diploma puts our kids on a path to a good job. Right now countries like Germany focus on graduating their high school students with the equivalent of a technical degree from one of our community colleges. So those German kids, they're ready for a job when they graduate high school. They've been trained for the jobs that are there. Now at schools like P-TECH in Brooklyn, a collaboration between New York Public Schools and City University of New York and IBM, students will graduate with a high school diploma and an associate's degree in computers or engineering. We need to give every American student opportunities like this.

And 4 years ago, we started Race to the Top, a competition that convinced almost every State to develop smarter curricula and higher standards, all for about 1 percent of what we spend on education each year. Tonight I'm announcing a new challenge to redesign America's high schools so they better equip graduates for the demands of a high-tech economy. And we'll reward schools that develop new partnerships with colleges and employers and create classes that focus on science, technology, engineering, and math: the skills today's employers are looking for to fill the jobs that are there right now and will be there in the future.

Now, even with better high schools, most young people will need some higher education. It's a simple fact: The more education you've got, the more likely you are to have a good job and work your way into the middle class. But today, skyrocketing costs price too many young people out of a higher education or saddle them with unsustainable debt.

Through tax credits, grants, and better loans, we've made college more affordable for millions of students and families over the last few years. But taxpayers can't keep on subsidizing higher and higher and higher costs for higher education. Colleges must do their part to keep costs down, and it's our job to make sure that they do.

So tonight I ask Congress to change the Higher Education Act so that affordability and value are included in determining which colleges receive certain types of Federal aid. And tomorrow my administration will release a new college scorecard that parents and students can use to compare schools based on a simple criterion: where you can get the most bang for your educational buck.

Now, to grow our middle class, our citizens have to have access to the education and training that today's jobs require. But we also have to make sure that America remains a place where everyone who's willing to work—everybody who's willing to work hard—has the chance to get ahead.

Our economy is stronger when we harness the talents and ingenuity of striving, hopeful immigrants. And right now leaders from the business, labor, law enforcement, faith communities, they all agree that the time has come to pass comprehensive immigration reform. Now is the time to do it. Now is the time to get it done. [*Applause*] Now is the time to get it done.

Real reform means stronger border security, and we can build on the progress my administration has already made: putting more boots on the southern border than at any time in our history and reducing illegal crossings to their lowest levels in 40 years.

Real reform means establishing a responsible pathway to earned citizenship, a path that includes passing a background check, paying taxes and a meaningful penalty, learning English, and going to the back of the line behind the folks trying to come here legally.

And real reform means fixing the legal immigration system to cut waiting periods and attract the highly skilled entrepreneurs and engineers that will help create jobs and grow our economy.

In other words, we know what needs to be done. And as we speak, bipartisan groups in both Chambers are working diligently to draft a bill, and I applaud their efforts. So let's get this done. Send me a comprehensive immigration reform bill in the next few months, and I will sign it right away. And America will be better for it. Let's get it done. Let's get it done.

But we can't stop there. We know our economy is stronger when our wives, our mothers, our daughters can live their lives free from discrimination in the workplace and free from the fear of domestic violence. Today the Senate passed the "Violence Against Women's Act" that Joe Biden originally wrote almost 20 years ago. And I now urge the House to do the same. Good job, Joe. And I ask this Congress to declare that women should earn a living equal to their efforts, and finally pass the "Paycheck Fairness Act" this year.

We know our economy is stronger when we reward an honest day's work with honest wages. But today, a full-time worker making the minimum wage earns $14,500 a year. Even with the tax relief we put in place, a family with two kids that earns the minimum wage still lives below the poverty line. That's wrong. That's why, since the last time this Congress raised the minimum wage, 19 States have chosen to bump theirs even higher.

Tonight let's declare that in the wealthiest nation on Earth, no one who works full-time should have to live in poverty and raise the Federal minimum wage to $9 an hour. We should be able to get that done.

This single step would raise the incomes of millions of working families. It could mean the difference between groceries or the food bank, rent or eviction, scraping by or finally getting ahead. For businesses across the country, it would mean customers with more money in their pockets. And a whole lot of folks out there would probably need less help from government. In fact, working folks shouldn't have to wait year after year for the minimum wage to go up while CEO pay has never been higher. So here's an idea that Governor Romney and I actually agreed on last year: Let's tie the minimum wage to the cost of living so that it finally becomes a wage you can live on.

Tonight let's also recognize that there are communities in this country where no matter how hard you work, it is virtually impossible to get ahead: factory towns decimated from years of plants packing up; inescapable pockets of poverty, urban and rural, where young adults are still fighting for their first job. America is not a place where the chance of birth or circumstance should decide our destiny. And that's why we need to build new ladders of opportunity into the middle class for all who are willing to climb them.

Let's offer incentives to companies that hire Americans who've got what it takes to fill that job opening, but have been out of work so long that no one will give them a chance anymore. Let's put people back to work rebuilding vacant homes in rundown neighborhoods. And this year, my administration will begin to partner with 20 of the hardest hit towns in America to get these communities back on their feet. Now, we'll work with local leaders to target resources at public safety and education and housing.

We'll give new tax credits to businesses that hire and invest. And we'll work to strengthen families by removing the financial deterrents to marriage for low-income couples and do more to encourage fatherhood, because what makes you a man isn't the ability to conceive a child, it's having the courage to raise one. And we want to encourage that. We want to help that.

Stronger families. Stronger communities. A stronger America. It is this kind of prosperity—broad, shared, built on a thriving middle class—that has always been the source of our progress at home. It's also the foundation of our power and influence throughout the world.

Tonight we stand united in saluting the troops and civilians who sacrifice every day to protect us. Because of them, we can say with confidence that America will complete its mission in Afghanistan and achieve our objective of defeating the core of Al Qaida.

Already, we have brought home 33,000 of our brave service men and women. This spring, our forces will move into a support role, while Afghan security forces take the lead. Tonight I can announce that over the next year, another 34,000 American troops will come home from Afghanistan. This drawdown will continue, and by the end of next year, our war in Afghanistan will be over.

Beyond 2014, America's commitment to a unified and sovereign Afghanistan will endure, but the nature of our commitment will change. We're negotiating an agreement with the Afghan Government that focuses on two missions: training and equipping Afghan forces so that the country does not again slip into chaos and counterterrorism efforts that allow us to pursue the remnants of Al Qaida and their affiliates.

Today, the organization that attacked us on 9/11 is a shadow of its former self. It's true, different Al Qaida affiliates and extremist groups have emerged, from the Arabian Peninsula to Africa. The threat these groups pose is evolving. But to meet this threat, we don't need to send tens of thousands of our sons and daughters abroad or occupy other nations. Instead, we'll need to help countries like Yemen and Libya and Somalia provide for their own security and help allies who take the fight to terrorists, as we have in Mali. And where necessary, through a range of capabilities, we will continue to take direct action against those terrorists who pose the gravest threat to Americans.

Now, as we do, we must enlist our values in the fight. That's why my administration has worked tirelessly to forge a durable legal and policy framework to guide our counterterrorism efforts. Throughout, we have kept Congress fully informed of our efforts. I recognize that in our democracy, no one should just take my word for it that we're doing things the right way. So, in the months ahead, I will continue to engage Congress to ensure not only that our targeting, detention, and prosecution of terrorists remains consistent with our laws and system of checks and balances, but that our efforts are even more transparent to the American people and to the world.

Of course, our challenges don't end with Al Qaida. America will continue to lead the effort to prevent the spread of the world's most dangerous weapons. The regime in North Korea must know they will only achieve security and prosperity by meeting their international obligations. Provocations of the sort we saw last night will only further isolate them, as we stand by our allies, strengthen our own missile defense, and lead the world in taking firm action in response to these threats.

Likewise, the leaders of Iran must recognize that now is the time for a diplomatic solution, because a coalition stands united in demanding that they meet their obligations, and we will do what is necessary to prevent them from getting a nuclear weapon.

At the same time, we'll engage Russia to seek further reductions in our nuclear arsenals and continue leading the global effort to secure nuclear materials that could fall into the wrong hands, because our ability to influence others depends on our willingness to lead and meet our obligations.

America must also face the rapidly growing threat from cyber attacks. Now, we know hackers steal people's identities and infiltrate private e-mails. We know foreign countries and companies swipe our corporate secrets. Now our enemies are also seeking the ability to sabotage our power grid, our financial institutions, our air traffic control systems. We cannot look back years from now and wonder why we did nothing in the face of real threats to our security and our economy.

And that's why, earlier today, I signed a new Executive order that will strengthen our cyber defenses by increasing information sharing and developing standards to protect our national security, our jobs, and our privacy.

But now Congress must act as well, by passing legislation to give our Government a greater capacity to secure our networks and deter attacks. This is something we should be able to get done on a bipartisan basis.

Now, even as we protect our people, we should remember that today's world presents not just dangers, not just threats, it presents opportunities. To boost American exports, support American jobs and level the playing field in the growing markets of Asia, we intend to complete negotiations on a Trans-Pacific Partnership. And tonight I'm announcing that we will launch talks on a comprehensive transatlantic trade and investment partnership with the European Union, because trade that is fair and free across the Atlantic supports millions of good-paying American jobs.

We also know that progress in the most impoverished parts of our world enriches us all, not only because it creates new markets, more stable order in certain regions of the world, but also because it's the right thing to do. In many places, people live on little more than a dollar a day. So the United States will join with our allies to eradicate such extreme poverty in the next two decades by connecting more people to the global economy, by empowering women, by giving our young and brightest minds new opportunities to serve and helping communities to feed and power and educate themselves, by saving the world's children from preventable deaths, and by realizing the promise of an AIDS-free generation, which is within our reach.

You see, America must remain a beacon to all who seek freedom during this period of historic change. I saw the power of hope last year in Rangoon, in Burma, when Aung San Suu Kyi welcomed an American President into the home where she had been imprisoned for years; when thousands of Burmese lined the streets, waving American flags, including a man who said: "There is justice and law in the United States. I want our country to be like that."

In defense of freedom, we'll remain the anchor of strong alliances from the Americas to Africa, from Europe to Asia. In the Middle East, we will stand with citizens as they demand their universal rights and support stable transitions to democracy.

We know the process will be messy, and we cannot presume to dictate the course of change in countries like Egypt, but we can and will insist on respect for the fundamental rights of all people. We'll keep the pressure on a Syrian regime that has murdered its own people and support opposition leaders that respect the rights of every Syrian. And we will stand steadfast with Israel in pursuit of security and a lasting peace.

These are the messages I'll deliver when I travel to the Middle East next month. And all this work depends on the courage and sacrifice of those who serve in dangerous places at great personal risk: our diplomats, our intelligence officers, and the men and women of the United States Armed Forces. As long as I'm Commander in Chief, we will do whatever we must to protect those who serve their country abroad, and we will maintain the best military the world has ever known.

We'll invest in new capabilities, even as we reduce waste and wartime spending. We will ensure equal treatment for all servicemembers and equal benefits for their families, gay and straight. We will draw upon the courage and skills of our sisters and daughters and moms, because women have proven under fire that they are ready for combat.

We will keep faith with our veterans, investing in world-class care—including mental health care—for our wounded warriors, supporting our military families, giving our veterans the benefits and education and job opportunities that they have earned. And I want to thank my wife Michelle and Dr. Jill Biden for their continued dedication to serving our military families as well as they have served us. Thank you, honey. Thank you, Jill.

Defending our freedom, though, is not just the job of our military alone. We must all do our part to make sure our God-given rights are protected here at home. That includes one of the most fundamental rights of a democracy: the right to vote. Now, when any American, no matter where they live or what their party, are denied that right because they can't afford to wait for 5 or 6 or 7 hours just to cast their ballot, we are betraying our ideals.

So tonight I'm announcing a nonpartisan commission to improve the voting experience in America. And it definitely needs improvement. I'm asking two long-time experts in the field—who, by the way, recently served as the top attorneys for my campaign and for Governor Romney's campaign—to lead it. We can fix this, and we will. The American people demand it, and so does our democracy.

Of course, what I've said tonight matters little if we don't come together to protect our most precious resource: our children. It has been 2 months since Newtown. I know this is not the first time this country has debated how to reduce gun violence. But this time is different. Overwhelming majorities of Americans—Americans who believe in the Second Amendment—have come together around commonsense reform, like background checks that will make it harder for criminals to get their hands on a gun. Senators of both parties are working together on tough new laws to prevent anyone from buying guns for resale to criminals. Police chiefs are asking our help to get weapons of war and massive ammunition magazines off our streets, because these police chiefs, they're tired of seeing their guys and gals being outgunned.

Each of these proposals deserves a vote in Congress. Now, if you want to vote no, that's your choice. But these proposals deserve a vote. Because in the 2 months since Newtown, more than a thousand birthdays, graduations, anniversaries have been stolen from our lives by a bullet from a gun—more than a thousand.

One of those we lost was a young girl named Hadiya Pendleton. She was 15 years old. She loved Fig Newtons and lip gloss. She was a majorette. She was so good to her friends, they all thought they were her best friend. Just 3 weeks ago, she was here, in Washington, with her classmates, performing for her country at my Inauguration. And a week later, she was shot and killed in a Chicago park after school, just a mile away from my house.

Hadiya's parents, Nate and Cleo, are in this Chamber tonight, along with more than two dozen Americans whose lives have been torn apart by gun violence. They deserve a vote. They deserve a vote. They deserve a vote. Gabby Giffords deserves a vote. The families of Newtown deserve a vote. The families of Aurora deserve a vote. The families of Oak Creek and Tucson and Blacksburg, and the countless other communities ripped open by gun violence, they deserve a simple vote. They deserve a simple vote.

Our actions will not prevent every senseless act of violence in this country. In fact, no laws, no initiatives, no administrative acts will perfectly solve all the challenges I've outlined tonight. But we were never sent here to be perfect. We were sent here to make what difference we can, to secure this Nation, expand opportunity, uphold our ideals through the hard, often frustrating, but absolutely necessary work of self-government.

We were sent here to look out for our fellow Americans the same way they look out for one another, every single day, usually without fanfare, all across this country. We should follow their example.

We should follow the example of a New York City nurse named Menchu Sanchez. When Hurricane Sandy plunged her hospital into darkness, she wasn't thinking about how her own home was faring. Her mind was on the 20 precious newborns in her care and the rescue plan she devised that kept them all safe.

We should follow the example of a North Miami woman named Desiline Victor. When Desiline arrived at her polling place, she was told the wait to vote might be 6 hours. And as time ticked by, her concern was not with her tired body or aching feet, but whether folks like her would get to have their say. And hour after hour, a throng of people stayed in line to support her, because Desiline is 102 years old. And they erupted in cheers when she finally put on a sticker that read, "I voted." There's Desiline.

We should follow the example of a police officer named Brian Murphy. When a gunman opened fire on a Sikh temple in Wisconsin and Brian was the first to arrive—and he did not consider his own safety. He fought back until help arrived and ordered his fellow officers to protect the safety of the Americans worshiping inside, even as he lay bleeding from 12 bullet wounds. And when asked how he did that, Brian said, "That's just the way we're made."

That's just the way we're made. We may do different jobs and wear different uniforms and hold different views than the person beside us. But as Americans, we all share the same proud title: We are citizens. It's a word that doesn't just describe our nationality or legal status. It describes the way we're made. It describes what we believe. It captures the enduring idea that this country only works when we accept certain obligations to one another and to future generations; that our rights are wrapped up in the rights of others; and that well into our third century as a nation, it remains the task of us all, as citizens of these United States, to be the authors of the next great chapter of our American story.

Thank you. God bless you, and God bless these United States of America.

SOURCE: Executive Office of the President. "Address Before a Joint Session of Congress on the State of the Union." February 12, 2013. *Compilation of Presidential Documents* 2013, no. 00090 (February 12, 2013). http://www.gpo.gov/fdsys/pkg/DCPD-201300090/pdf/DCPD-201300090.pdf.

DOCUMENT

Sen. Rubio Delivers Republican Response

February 12, 2013

[As prepared for delivery.]

Good evening. I'm Marco Rubio. I'm blessed to represent Florida in the United States Senate. Let me begin by congratulating President Obama on the start of his second term. Tonight, I have the honor of responding to his State of the Union address on behalf of my fellow Republicans. And I am especially honored to be addressing our brave men and women serving in the armed forces and in diplomatic posts around the world. You may be thousands of miles away, but you are always in our prayers.

The State of the Union address is always a reminder of how unique America is. For much of human history, most people were trapped in stagnant societies, where a tiny minority always stayed on top, and no one else even had a chance.

But America is exceptional because we believe that every life, at every stage, is precious, and that everyone everywhere has a God-given right to go as far as their talents and hard work will take them.

Like most Americans, for me this ideal is personal. My parents immigrated here in pursuit of the opportunity to improve their life and give their children the chance at an even better one. They made it to the middle class, my dad working as a bartender and my mother as a cashier and a maid. I didn't inherit any money from them. But I inherited something far better—the real opportunity to accomplish my dreams.

This opportunity—to make it to the middle class or beyond no matter where you start out in life—it isn't bestowed on us from Washington. It comes from a vibrant free economy where people can risk their own money to open a business. And when they succeed, they hire more people, who in turn invest or spend the money they make, helping others start a business and create jobs.

Presidents in both parties—from John F. Kennedy to Ronald Reagan—have known that our free enterprise economy is the source of our middle class prosperity.

But President Obama? He believes it's the cause of our problems. That the economic downturn happened because our government didn't tax enough, spend enough and control enough. And, therefore, as you heard tonight, his solution to virtually every problem we face is for Washington to tax more, borrow more and spend more.

This idea—that our problems were caused by a government that was too small—it's just not true. In fact, a major cause of our recent downturn was a housing crisis created by reckless government policies.

And the idea that more taxes and more government spending is the best way to help hardworking middle class taxpayers—that's an old idea that's failed every time it's been tried.

More government isn't going to help you get ahead. It's going to hold you back.

More government isn't going to create more opportunities. It's going to limit them.

And more government isn't going to inspire new ideas, new businesses and new private sector jobs. It's going to create uncertainty.

Because more government breeds complicated rules and laws that a small business can't afford to follow.

Because more government raises taxes on employers who then pass the costs on to their employees through fewer hours, lower pay and even layoffs.

And because many government programs that claim to help the middle class, often end up hurting them instead.

For example, Obamacare was supposed to help middle class Americans afford health insurance. But now, some people are losing the health insurance they were happy with. And because Obamacare created expensive requirements for companies with more than 50 employees, now many of these businesses aren't hiring. Not only that; they're being forced to lay people off and switch from full-time employees to part-time workers.

Now does this mean there's no role for government? Of course not. It plays a crucial part in keeping us safe, enforcing rules, and providing some security against the risks of modern life. But government's role is wisely limited by the Constitution. And it can't play its essential role when it ignores those limits.

There are valid reasons to be concerned about the President's plan to grow our government. But any time anyone opposes the President's agenda, he and his allies usually respond by falsely attacking their motives.

When we point out that no matter how many job-killing laws we pass, our government can't control the weather—he accuses us of wanting dirty water and dirty air.

When we suggest we strengthen our safety net programs by giving states more flexibility to manage them—he accuses us of wanting to leave the elderly and disabled to fend for themselves.

And tonight, he even criticized us for refusing to raise taxes to delay military cuts—cuts that were his idea in the first place.

But his favorite attack of all is that those who don't agree with him—they only care about rich people.

Mr. President, I still live in the same working class neighborhood I grew up in. My neighbors aren't millionaires. They're retirees who depend on Social Security and Medicare. They're workers who have to get up early tomorrow morning and go to work to pay the bills. They're immigrants, who came here because they were stuck in poverty in countries where the government dominated the economy.

The tax increases and the deficit spending you propose will hurt middle class families. It will cost them their raises. It will cost them their benefits. It may even cost some of them their jobs.

And it will hurt seniors because it does nothing to save Medicare and Social Security.

So Mr. President, I don't oppose your plans because I want to protect the rich. I oppose your plans because I want to protect my neighbors.

Hard-working middle class Americans who don't need us to come up with a plan to grow the government. They want a plan to grow the middle class.

Economic growth is the best way to help the middle class. Unfortunately, our economy actually shrank during the last three months of 2012.

But if we can get the economy to grow at just 4 percent a year, it would create millions of middle class jobs. And it could reduce our deficits by almost $4 trillion dollars over the next decade.

Tax increases can't do this. Raising taxes won't create private sector jobs. And there's no realistic tax increase that could lower our deficits by almost $4 trillion. That's why I hope the President will abandon his obsession with raising taxes and instead work with us to achieve real growth in our economy.

One of the best ways to encourage growth is through our energy industry. Of course solar and wind energy should be a part of our energy portfolio. But God also blessed America with abundant coal, oil and natural gas. Instead of wasting more taxpayer money on so-called "clean energy" companies like Solyndra, let's open up more federal lands for safe and responsible exploration. And let's reform our energy regulations so that they're reasonable and based on common sense. If we can grow our energy industry, it will make us energy independent, it will create middle class jobs and it will help bring manufacturing back from places like China.

Simplifying our tax code will also help the middle class, because it will make it easier for small businesses to hire and grow.

And we agree with the President that we should lower our corporate tax rate, which is one of the highest in the world, so that companies will start bringing their money and their jobs back here from overseas.

We can also help our economy grow if we have a legal immigration system that allows us to attract and assimilate the world's best and brightest. We need a responsible, permanent solution to the problem of those who are here illegally. But first, we must follow through on the broken promises of the past to secure our borders and enforce our laws.

Helping the middle class grow will also require an education system that gives people the skills today's jobs entail and the knowledge that tomorrow's world will require.

We need to incentivize local school districts to offer more advanced placement courses and more vocational and career training.

We need to give all parents, especially the parents of children with special needs, the opportunity to send their children to the school of their choice.

And because tuition costs have grown so fast, we need to change the way we pay for higher education.

I believe in federal financial aid. I couldn't have gone to college without it. But it's not just about spending more money on these programs; it's also about strengthening and modernizing them.

A 21st century workforce should not be forced to accept 20th century education solutions. Today's students aren't only 18 year olds. They're returning veterans. They're single parents who decide to get the education they need to earn a decent wage. And they're workers who have lost jobs that are never coming back and need to be retrained.

We need student aid that does not discriminate against programs that non-traditional students rely on—like online courses, or degree programs that give you credit for work experience.

When I finished school, I owed over 100,000 dollars in student loans, a debt I paid off just a few months ago. Today, many graduates face massive student debt. We must give students more information on the costs and benefits of the student loans they're taking out.

All these measures are key to helping the economy grow. But we won't be able to sustain a vibrant middle class unless we solve our debt problem.

Every dollar our government borrows is money that isn't being invested to create jobs. And the uncertainty created by the debt is one reason why many businesses aren't hiring.

The President loves to blame the debt on President Bush. But President Obama created more debt in four years than his predecessor did in eight.

The real cause of our debt is that our government has been spending 1 trillion dollars more than it takes in every year. That's why we need a balanced budget amendment.

The biggest obstacles to balancing the budget are programs where spending is already locked in. One of these programs, Medicare, is especially important to me. It provided my father the care he needed to battle cancer and ultimately die with dignity. And it pays for the care my mother receives now.

I would never support any changes to Medicare that would hurt seniors like my mother. But anyone who is in favor of leaving Medicare exactly the way it is right now, is in favor of bankrupting it.

Republicans have offered a detailed and credible plan that helps save Medicare without hurting today's retirees. Instead of playing politics with Medicare, when is the President going to offer his plan to save it? Tonight would have been a good time for him to do it.

Of course, we face other challenges as well. We were all heart broken by the recent tragedy in Connecticut. We must effectively deal with the rise of violence in our country. But unconstitutionally undermining the 2nd Amendment rights of law-abiding Americans is not the way to do it.

On foreign policy, America continues to be indispensable to the goal of global liberty, prosperity and safeguarding human rights. The world is a better place when America is the strongest nation on earth. But we can't remain powerful if we don't have an economy that can afford it.

In the short time I've been here in Washington, nothing has frustrated me more than false choices like the ones the President laid out tonight.

The choice isn't just between big government or big business. What we need is an accountable, efficient and effective government that allows small and new businesses to create middle class jobs.

We don't have to raise taxes to avoid the President's devastating cuts to our military. Republicans have passed a plan that replaces these cuts with responsible spending reforms.

In order to balance our budget, the choice doesn't have to be either higher taxes or dramatic benefit cuts for those in need. Instead we should grow our economy so that we create new taxpayers, not new taxes, and so our government can afford to help those who truly cannot help themselves.

And the truth is every problem can't be solved by government. Many are caused by the moral breakdown in our society. And the answers to those challenges lie primarily in our families and our faiths, not our politicians.

Despite our differences, I know that both Republicans and Democrats love America. I pray we can come together to solve our problems, because the choices before us could not be more important.

If we can get our economy healthy again, our children will be the most prosperous Americans ever.

And if we do not, we will forever be known as the generation responsible for America's decline.

At a time when one showdown after another ends in short-term deals that do little or nothing about our real problems, some are starting to believe that our government leaders just can't or won't make the right choices anymore.

But our strength has never come from the White House or the Capitol. It's always come from our people. A people united by the American idea that, if you have a dream and you are willing to work hard, nothing should be impossible.

Americans have always celebrated and been inspired by those who succeed. But it's the dreams of those who are still trying to make it that sets our nation apart.

Tonight, all across this land, parents will hold their newborn children in their arms for the first time. For many of these parents, life has not gone the way they had planned.

Maybe they were born into circumstances they've found difficult to escape. Maybe they've made some mistakes along the way. Maybe they're young mothers, all alone, the father of their child long gone.

But tonight, when they look into the eyes of their child for the first time, their lives will change forever. Because in those eyes, they will see what my parents saw in me, and what your parents saw in you. They will see all the hopes and dreams they once had for themselves.

This dream—of a better life for their children—it's the hope of parents everywhere. Politicians here and throughout the world have long promised that more government can make those dreams come true.

But we Americans have always known better. From our earliest days, we embraced economic liberty instead. And because we did, America remains one of the few places on earth where dreams like these even have a chance.

Each time our nation has faced great challenges, what has kept us together was our shared hope for a better life.

Now, let that hope bring us together again. To solve the challenges of our time and write the next chapter in the amazing story of the greatest nation man has ever known.

Thank you for listening. May God bless all of you. May God bless our President. And may God continue to bless the United States of America.

SOURCE: Office of the Speaker of the House John Boehner. "FULL TEXT: Sen. Marco Rubio Delivers the Republican Address to the Nation." February 12, 2013. http://www.speaker.gov/press-release/full-text-sen-marco-rubio-delivers-republican-address-nation.

OTHER HISTORIC DOCUMENTS OF INTEREST

North Korea Conducts
Third Nuclear Test

FEBRUARY 12 AND MARCH 7, 2013

In yet another show of defiance to the international community, on February 12, 2013, North Korea conducted its third underground nuclear test. This was the first such test under North Korea's new leader, Kim Jong Un, who assumed power after the death of his father in December 2011. North Korea gave the United States advance warning of the test, but made it clear that it was acting in an effort to prepare itself to protect against any U.S. incursion into its affairs pertaining to what it considered a hostile response to its 2012 "satellite" launch. "If the United States continues to come out with hostility and complicates the situation, we will be forced to take stronger, second and third responses in consecutive steps," the nation announced through its state-run media service.

TESTING HISTORY

On February 12, 2013, North Korea conducted a successful underground nuclear explosion, in defiance of international sanctions. "The test was conducted in a safe and perfect way on a high level with the use of a smaller and light A-bomb unlike the previous ones, yet with great explosive power," state-run Korean Central News Agency (KCNA) reported. The news agency went on to add that the successful test would help ensure peace on the Korean peninsula. It remains unclear whether the explosion involved uranium or plutonium, and because underground tests are difficult to verify, it is also unknown how miniaturized the device actually was. North Korea has made clear its intent to build a nuclear weapon small enough to fit on a warhead, but the international community is as yet unsure of whether it has actually done so.

The nation's last two nuclear explosions were conducted in October 2006 and May 2009. Both were claimed by North Korea to have been successful; however, the international community largely believes both attempts failed to produce the results North Korea had intended. The 2006 explosion involved plutonium and was quickly followed by UN sanctions. According to North Korea's KCNA, the second nuclear test was "part of measures to enhance the Republic's self-defensive nuclear deterrent in all directions." As with the first test, the United Nations increased economic sanctions against North Korea, and the United States followed suit.

In an effort to counter North Korea's nuclear ambition, there has been a significant amount of effort put toward negotiating with the nation to encourage it to end its nuclear program. The negotiations with the most promise, a series of Six-Party Talks between North Korea, the United States, China, South Korea, Japan, and Russia, stalled in 2008 when North Korea accused the other nations of failing to meet their side of the agreement after North Korea closed its Yongbyon nuclear facility. The Six-Party Talks have yet to be resumed, and North Korea has since reopened its facility. Year after year, the United States and its partners have encouraged North Korea to return to the talks, but due to North Korea's refusal, the United States has been forced to negotiate in one-off meetings. Shortly before Kim assumed power in 2011, U.S. and North Korean officials met in Beijing to offer food assistance if North Korea would stop enriching uranium. These talks, while they did not result in an immediate deal, were considered a breakthrough and a possible turning point. Once Kim was in office, he agreed to halt nuclear activity at Yongbyon and to end all long-range missile launches. However, in April 2012, North Korea announced that it would be launching a rocket with a satellite attached. While North Korea maintained that the purpose of the launch was for peaceful, meteorological means, it was widely believed that the launch was intended to test a long-range ballistic missile. The April 13, 2012, launch was a failure, but a second attempt on December 12, 2012 put a "working satellite" into orbit. The launch drew strong condemnation from the international community, but interested parties were unable to act through the United Nations because China and Russia, two permanent members of the Security Council, refused to take action, arguing that it was not their place to deal with the internal policies and politics of another nation.

The United Nations did expand sanctions against North Korea in January 2013, to which North Korea responded by announcing that it would resume its nuclear testing and rocket launches. All its efforts, North Korea announced, were aimed at "the U.S., the sworn enemy of the Korean people."

GAINING STRENGTH

Prior to North Korea's announcement on state-run television that the test had been successful, U.S. Geological Survey equipment detected the explosion, which had an initial magnitude of 4.9 and was later revised upward to 5.1. A variety of international organizations estimated the yield of the explosion at anywhere between 6 to 40 kilotons, but the most reliable estimates place it somewhere between 6 and 9. By comparison, the atomic bombs dropped by the United States on Nagasaki in 1945 yielded an explosion of approximately 20 kilotons.

Despite its somewhat small yield, it is still considered stronger than North Korea's last two tests. North Korea now claims that it has developed a bomb small enough that can be attached to a missile; however, this claim is widely disputed by international experts. The South Korean Defense Ministry released a report in September 2013 detailing its opinion that North Korea could "weaponize" its nuclear technology. The Defense Ministry said there was a high probability that North Korea could attach a ballistic missile to a nuclear warhead; however, it did not indicate the range that such a missile might be able to reach. But even a short-range missile could have dire effects in South Korea.

INTERNATIONAL RESPONSE AND FURTHER PROVOCATION

With North Korea's aggressions clearly aimed at the United States, the Western nation worked to resume denuclearization talks and called on its international partners to act to stop North Korea's aggression. "The danger posed by North Korea's threatening activities warrants further swift and credible action by the international community," said President Barack Obama. "The United States will also continue to take steps necessary to defend ourselves and our allies." Although he did not say it at the time, this would certainly include defending South Korea if North Korea chose to fire on its neighbor. An unnamed North Korean spokesperson deemed this rhetoric "hostile" and added, "Action for action is the basic principle for resolving the nuclear issue on the Korean Peninsula, and we will never move first unilaterally." One month after its nuclear test, North Korea threatened to fire on U.S. military bases in the Pacific over what it considered to be an attempt to remove Kim from power. Such threats never came to fruition.

In nearby South Korea, where a new president had recently taken office, the government stepped up its military presence and put the country on high alert for a possible missile strike. In March, North Korea declared an end to the 1953 armistice that ended the Korean War, a move that came as South Korea and the United States were conducting annual joint military training exercises, which North Korea called "a clear declaration of war against our republic." Additional steps were taken to punish South Korea for its participation in the drills, including cutting off a Red Cross hotline, temporarily closing a joint work facility on the border, and temporarily stopping reunifications for families split by the Korean War. By the end of April, North Korea had ratcheted down its threats, and both sides began looking at ways to reopen the work center and restart reunifications. Before an agreement was reached, in May, North Korea fired a series of short-range missiles off the east coast of the Korean Peninsula. While such testing was conducted in violation of UN sanctions, in an effort to maintain status quo, South Korea refrained from any meaningful response.

The most stunning response to the February nuclear test came from one of North Korea's only allies, China. Immediately following the test, North Korea's ambassador was summoned to Beijing to allow the country to make a formal protest against North Korea's actions. According to Chinese Foreign Minister Yang Jiechi, China, which was in the midst of a leadership transition, was "strongly dissatisfied and resolutely opposed" to the explosion and urged North Korea to "stop any rhetoric or acts that could worsen situations and return to the right course of dialogue and consultation as soon as possible." While China protested the explosion, international analysts said the response proved that the influence Beijing had over the reclusive state was beginning to crumble. "China's inability to dissuade North Korea from carrying through with this third nuclear test reveals Beijing's limited influence over Pyongyang's actions in unusually stark terms," said Suzanne DiMaggio, an analyst for the Asia Society, an organization focused on educating Americans about Asia.

In response to the February nuclear test, the United Nations called an emergency meeting of the Security Council. Members, however, understood that their options were limited because despite China's opposition to the test, it feared an increase in economic sanctions could further ignite tensions in the region and send a flood of North Korean refugees into China. As such, the test was simply "strongly condemned" by the Security Council, although it did promise to immediately begin reviewing additional measures to stop North Korea's continued aggression. In March, the Security Council passed a third set of sanctions against North Korea (the first two came in 2006 and 2009), drafted by the United States and China. Although China resisted earlier action against North Korea, it determined that sanctions might be the best method to encourage the country to come back to denuclearization talks and focus on a diplomatic solution to the problem. The sanctions restricted overseas travel and some luxury purchases by senior leaders, and blocked certain types of cash transfers in the hopes of stopping North Korea from gaining additional weapons technology. The unanimously approved sanctions were decried by North Korea, but the nation's Foreign Ministry said the country would retain the right to "a preemptive nuclear attack to destroy the strongholds of the aggressors."

POSSIBLE FURTHER TESTS PLANNED

Only three days after their third nuclear test, officials in North Korea informed China that they planned to conduct two more nuclear tests in 2013, although they did not specify the timing. Throughout the spring of 2013, South Korean officials kept a close watch on the Punggye-ri tunnels where North Korea conducted its February nuclear test. South Korea suspected that a new tunnel was being built, and in October, the U.S.-Korea Institute at the Johns Hopkins School of Advanced International Studies concluded, after a review of recent satellite images, that two new tunnel entrances had been dug. This, the report said, could be an indication that the nation is planning to ramp up nuclear tests, or it could mean simply that they are connecting other underground tunnels.

The expansion of the underground tunnels, coupled with an announcement from North Korea's Foreign Ministry that it intended to continue expanding its nuclear program, ended hopes for any new negotiations in 2013. The United States made clear that it would not reenter negotiations until North Korea began working toward denuclearization. North Korea vehemently refused, and it is believed that the country has both ramped up uranium enrichment activities and restarted the nuclear reactors at Yongbyon. Satellite imagery suggests that the size of the facility may have doubled as well.

Despite North Korea's threats, a fourth nuclear test did not take place in 2013. It is difficult for parties on any side of the North Korea problem to determine what the country is doing or when it may act. Its secretive nature makes its actions unpredictable. International experts believe the delay in a fourth test has to do with North Korea's relationship with China. So while it is possible that North Korea may delay a future nuclear test in an effort to smooth over relations with Beijing, it is also possible that the country will ramp up its nuclear program to put more pressure on the United States to negotiate for food aid and other economic supplements.

—Heather Kerrigan

Following is a statement from the Korean Central News Agency on February 12, 2013, announcing a successful underground nuclear test; and a press release from the United Nations on March 7, 2013, condemning the nuclear test.

DOCUMENT *North Korea Announces Nuclear Test*

February 12, 2013

The Korean Central News Agency released the following report on Tuesday:

The scientific field for national defence of the DPRK succeeded in the third underground nuclear test at the site for underground nuclear test in the northern part of the DPRK on Tuesday.

The test was carried out as part of practical measures of counteraction to defend the country's security and sovereignty in the face of the ferocious hostile act of the U.S. which wantonly violated the DPRK's legitimate right to launch satellite for peaceful purposes.

The test was conducted in a safe and perfect way on a high level with the use of a smaller and light A-bomb unlike the previous ones, yet with great explosive power. It was confirmed that the test did not give any adverse effect to the surrounding ecological environment.

The specific features of the function and explosive power of the A-bomb and all other measurements fully tallied with the values of the design, physically demonstrating the good performance of the DPRK's nuclear deterrence that has become diversified.

The nuclear test will greatly encourage the army and people of the DPRK in their efforts to build a thriving nation with the same spirit and mettle as displayed in conquering space, and offer an important occasion in ensuring peace and stability in the Korean Peninsula and the region.

Source: Korean Central News Agency (KCNA). "KCNA Report on Successful 3rd Underground Nuclear Test." February 12, 2013. http://www.kcna.co.jp/item/2013/201302/news12/20130212-18ee.html.

DOCUMENT

UN Security Council Responds to Nuclear Test

March 7, 2013

The Security Council today passed unanimously a resolution strengthening and expanding the scope of United Nations sanctions against the Democratic People's Republic of Korea by targeting the illicit activities of diplomatic personnel, transfers of bulk cash, and the country's banking relationships, in response to that country's third nuclear test on 12 February.

Acting under the Charter's Chapter VII, through resolution 2094 (2013), the Council strongly condemned the test and maintained the sanctions it first imposed on the Democratic People's Republic of Korea in 2006 under resolution 1718, deciding that some of those, along with additional restrictions, would apply to the individuals and entities listed in two annexes of today's text.

In that connection, a travel ban and asset freeze were imposed on the Chief and Deputy Chief of a mining trading company it deemed "the primary arms dealer and main exporter of goods and equipment related to ballistic missiles and conventional weapons," as well as on an official of a company designated by the Sanctions Committee to be the main financial entity for sales of conventional arms, ballistic missiles and goods related to assembly and manufacture.

The Council also froze the assets of a national-level organization responsible for the research and development of advanced weapons systems, and a conglomerate, designated by the Sanctions Committee in 2009, to be specializing in acquisition for the country's defence industries and support to related sales. Further, it added to the list of prohibited equipment and technologies, and included a list of luxury goods that cannot be imported.

States are directed under the resolution to enhance their vigilance over the diplomatic personnel of the Democratic People's Republic of Korea, in a provision aimed at halting any activities that could contribute to the country's weapons programme, or which would violate any prohibited activities.

More specifically, States are directed to prevent the provision of financial services or the transfer of any financial or other assets or resources, including "bulk cash," which might be used to evade the sanctions. They are also called on to prohibit in their territories the opening of new branches or offices of "DPRK" banks and to prohibit such banks from establishing new joint ventures.

Moreover, in the effort to prevent the direct or indirect supply, sale or transfer to or from the Democratic People's Republic or Korea or its nationals of any banned items, States are authorized to inspect all cargo within or transiting through their territory that has originated in the Democratic People's Republic of Korea or that is destined for that country. They are to deny permission to any aircraft to take off from, land in or overfly their territory, if they have reasonable grounds to believe the aircraft contains prohibited items.

States were also asked to supply any information on non-compliance and to report to the Council within 90 days, and thereafter, at the Committee's request, on measures they have taken to implement the text. The Sanctions Committee is directed to respond to violations and is authorized to add to the list. The expert panel, under the Committee's auspices, was extended until 7 April 2014.

The Council promised to keep the situation under continuous review and stated it was "prepared to strengthen, modify, suspend or lift the measures as may be needed in light of the DPRK's compliance," or to "take further significant measures in the event of a further DPRK launch or nuclear test."

The meeting began at 10:11 a.m. and ended at 10:14 a.m.

RESOLUTION

The full text of Security Council resolution 2094 (2013) reads as follows:

"The Security Council,

"*Recalling* its previous relevant resolutions, including resolution 825 (1993), resolution 1540 (2004), resolution 1695 (2006), resolution 1718 (2006), resolution 1874 (2009), resolution 1887 (2009) and resolution 2087 (2013), as well as the statements of its President of 6 October 2006 (S/PRST/2006/41), 13 April 2009 (S/PRST/2009/7) and 16 April 2012 (S/PRST/2012/13),

"*Reaffirming* that proliferation of nuclear, chemical and biological weapons, as well as their means of delivery, constitutes a threat to international peace and security,

"*Underlining* once again the importance that the DPRK respond to other security and humanitarian concerns of the international community,

"*Expressing* the gravest concern at the nuclear test conducted by the Democratic People's Republic of Korea ("the DPRK") on 12 February 2013 (local time) in violation of resolutions 1718 (2006), 1874 (2009) and resolution 2087 (2013), and at the challenge such a test constitutes to the Treaty on Non-Proliferation of Nuclear Weapons ("the NPT") and to international efforts aimed at strengthening the global regime of non-proliferation of nuclear weapons, and the danger it poses to peace and stability in the region and beyond,

"*Concerned* that the DPRK is abusing the privileges and immunities accorded under the Vienna Convention on Diplomatic and Consular Relations,

"*Welcoming* the Financial Action Task Force's (FATF) new Recommendation 7 on targeted financial sanctions related to proliferation, and *urging* Member States to apply

FATF's Interpretative Note to Recommendation 7 and related guidance papers for effective implementation of targeted financial sanctions related to proliferation,

"*Expressing* its gravest concern that the DPRK's ongoing nuclear and ballistic missilerelated activities have further generated increased tension in the region and beyond, and *determining* that there continues to exist a clear threat to international peace and security,

"*Acting* under Chapter VII of the Charter of the United Nations, and taking measures under its Article 41,

"1.   *Condemns* in the strongest terms the nuclear test conducted by the DPRK on 12 February 2013 (local time) in violation and flagrant disregard of the Council's relevant resolutions;

"2.   *Decides* that the DPRK shall not conduct any further launches that use ballistic missile technology, nuclear tests or any other provocation;

"3.   *Demands* that the DPRK immediately retract its announcement of withdrawal from the NPT;

"4.   *Demands further* that the DPRK return at an early date to the NPT and International Atomic Energy Agency (IAEA) safeguards, bearing in mind the rights and obligations of States parties to the NPT, and underlines the need for all States parties to the NPT to continue to comply with their Treaty obligations;

"5.   *Condemns* all the DPRK's ongoing nuclear activities, including its uranium enrichment, *notes* that all such activities are in violation of resolutions 1718 (2006), 1874 (2009) and 2087 (2013), *reaffirms* its decision that the DPRK shall abandon all nuclear weapons and existing nuclear programmes, in a complete, verifiable and irreversible manner and immediately cease all related activities and shall act strictly in accordance with the obligations applicable to parties under the NPT and the terms and conditions of the IAEA Safeguards Agreement (IAEA INFCIRC/403);

"6.   *Reaffirms* its decision that the DPRK shall abandon all other existing weapons of mass destruction and ballistic missile programmes in a complete, verifiable and irreversible manner;

"7.   *Reaffirms* that the measures imposed in paragraph 8 (c) of resolution 1718 (2006) apply to items prohibited by paragraphs 8 (a) (i), 8 (a) (ii) of resolution 1718 (2006) and paragraphs 9 and 10 of resolution 1874 (2009), *decides* that the measures imposed in paragraph 8 (c) of resolution 1718 (2006) also apply to paragraphs 20 and 22 of this resolution, and *notes* that these measures apply also to brokering or other intermediary services, including when arranging for the provision, maintenance or use of prohibited items in other States or the supply, sale or transfer to or exports from other States;

"8.   *Decides further* that measures specified in paragraph 8 (d) of resolution 1718 (2006) shall apply also to the individuals and entities listed in annexes I and II of this resolution and to any individuals or entities acting on their behalf or at their direction, and to entities owned or controlled by them, including through illicit means, and *decides further* that the measures specified in paragraph 8 (d) of resolution 1718 (2006) shall apply to any individuals or entities acting on the behalf or at the direction of the individuals and entities that have already been designated, to entities owned or controlled by them, including through illicit means;

"9. *Decides* that the measures specified in paragraph 8 (e) of resolution 1718 (2006) shall also apply to the individuals listed in annex I of this resolution and to individuals acting on their behalf or at their direction;

"10. *Decides* that the measures specified in paragraph 8 (e) of resolution 1718 (2006) and the exemptions set forth in paragraph 10 of resolution 1718 (2006) shall also apply to any individual whom a State determines is working on behalf or at the direction of a designated individual or entity or individuals assisting the evasion of sanctions or violating the provisions of resolutions 1718 (2006), 1874 (2009), 2087 (2013), and this resolution, and further *decides* that, if such an individual is a DPRK national, then States shall expel the individual from their territories for the purpose of repatriation to the DPRK consistent with applicable national and international law, unless the presence of an individual is required for fulfilment of a judicial process or exclusively for medical, safety or other humanitarian purposes, provided that nothing in this paragraph shall impede the transit of representatives of the Government of the DPRK to the United Nations Headquarters to conduct United Nations business;

"11. *Decides* that Member States shall, in addition to implementing their obligations pursuant to paragraphs 8 (d) and (e) of resolution 1718 (2006), prevent the provision of financial services or the transfer to, through, or from their territory, or to or by their nationals or entities organized under their laws (including branches abroad), or persons or financial institutions in their territory, of any financial or other assets or resources, including bulk cash, that could contribute to the DPRK's nuclear or ballistic missile programmes, or other activities prohibited by resolutions 1718 (2006), 1874 (2009), 2087 (2013), or this resolution, or to the evasion of measures imposed by resolutions 1718 (2006), 1874 (2009), 2087 (2013), or this resolution, including by freezing any financial or other assets or resources on their territories or that hereafter come within their territories, or that are subject to their jurisdiction or that hereafter become subject to their jurisdiction, that are associated with such programmes or activities and applying enhanced monitoring to prevent all such transactions in accordance with their national authorities and legislation;

"12. *Calls upon* States to take appropriate measures to prohibit in their territories the opening of new branches, subsidiaries, or representative offices of DPRK banks, and also *calls upon* States to prohibit DPRK banks from establishing new joint ventures and from taking an ownership interest in or establishing or maintaining correspondent relationships with banks in their jurisdiction to prevent the provision of financial services if they have information that provides reasonable grounds to believe that these activities could contribute to the DPRK's nuclear or ballistic missile programmes, or other activities prohibited by resolutions 1718 (2006), 1874 (2009), 2087 (2013), and this resolution, or to the evasion of measures imposed by resolutions 1718 (2006), 1874 (2009), 2087 (2013), or this resolution;

"13. *Calls upon* States to take appropriate measures to prohibit financial institutions within their territories or under their jurisdiction from opening representative offices or subsidiaries or banking accounts in the DPRK if they have information that provides reasonable grounds to believe that such financial services could contribute to the DPRK's nuclear or ballistic missile programmes, and other activities prohibited by resolutions 1718 (2006), 1874 (2009), 2087 (2013), and this resolution;

"14. *Expresses* concern that transfers to the DPRK of bulk cash may be used to evade the measures imposed in resolutions 1718 (2006), 1874 (2009), 2087 (2013), and this resolution, and *clarifies* that all States shall apply the measures set forth in paragraph 11 of this resolution to the transfers of cash, including through cash couriers, transiting to and from the DPRK so as to ensure such transfers of bulk cash do not contribute to the DPRK's nuclear or ballistic missile programmes, or other activities prohibited by resolutions 1718 (2006), 1874 (2009), 2087 (2013), or this resolution, or to the evasion of measures imposed by resolutions 1718 (2006), 1874 (2009), 2087 (2013), or this resolution;

"15. *Decides* that all Member States shall not provide public financial support for trade with the DPRK (including the granting of export credits, guarantees or insurance to their nationals or entities involved in such trade) where such financial support could contribute to the DPRK's nuclear or ballistic missile programmes, or other activities prohibited by resolutions 1718 (2006), 1874 (2009), 2087 (2013), or this resolution, or to the evasion of measures imposed by resolutions 1718 (2006), 1874 (2009), 2087 (2013), or this resolution;

"16. *Decides* that all States shall inspect all cargo within or transiting through their territory that has originated in the DPRK, or that is destined for the DPRK, or has been brokered or facilitated by the DPRK or its nationals, or by individuals or entities acting on their behalf, if the State concerned has credible information that provides reasonable grounds to believe the cargo contains items the supply, sale, transfer, or export of which is prohibited by resolutions 1718 (2006), 1874 (2009), 2087 (2013), or this resolution, for the purpose of ensuring strict implementation of those provisions;

"17. *Decides* that, if any vessel has refused to allow an inspection after such an inspection has been authorized by the vessel's flag State, or if any DPRK-flagged vessel has refused to be inspected pursuant to paragraph 12 of resolution 1874 (2009), all States shall deny such a vessel entry to their ports, unless entry is required for the purpose of an inspection, in the case of emergency or in the case of return to its port of origination, and *decides* further that any State that has been refused by a vessel to allow an inspection shall promptly report the incident to the Committee;

"18. *Calls upon* States to deny permission to any aircraft to take off from, land in or overfly their territory, if they have information that provides reasonable grounds to believe that the aircraft contains items the supply, sale, transfer or export of which is prohibited by resolutions 1718 (2006), 1874 (2009), 2087 (2013), or this resolution, except in the case of an emergency landing;

"19. *Requests* all States to communicate to the Committee any information available on transfers of DPRK aircraft or vessels to other companies that may have been undertaken in order to evade the sanctions or in violating the provisions of resolution 1718 (2006), 1874 (2009), 2087 (2013), or this resolution, including renaming or re-registering of aircraft, vessels or ships, and *requests* the Committee to make that information widely available;

"20. *Decides* that the measures imposed in paragraphs 8 (a) and 8 (b) of resolution 1718 (2006) shall also apply to the items, materials, equipment, goods and technology listed in annex III of this resolution;

"21. *Directs* the Committee to review and update the items contained in the lists specified in paragraph 5 (b) of resolution 2087 (2013) no later than 12 months from the adoption of this resolution and on an annual basis thereafter, and *decides* that, if the Committee has not acted to update this information by then, the Security Council will complete action to update within an additional 30 days;

"22. *Calls upon* and allows all States to prevent the direct or indirect supply, sale or transfer to or from the DPRK or its nationals, through their territories or by their nationals, or using their flag vessels or aircraft, and whether or not originating in their territories of any item if the State determines that such item could contribute to the DPRK's nuclear or ballistic missile programmes, activities prohibited by resolutions 1718 (2006), 1874 (2009), 2087 (2013), or this resolution, or to the evasion of measures imposed by resolutions 1718 (2006), 1874 (2009), 2087 (2013), or this resolution, and *directs* the Committee to issue an Implementation Assistance Notice regarding the proper implementation of this provision;

"23. *Reaffirms* the measures imposed in paragraph 8 (a) (iii) of resolution 1718 (2006) regarding luxury goods, and *clarifies* that the term "luxury goods" includes, but is not limited to, the items specified in annex IV of this resolution;

"24. *Calls upon* States to exercise enhanced vigilance over DPRK diplomatic personnel so as to prevent such individuals from contributing to the DPRK's nuclear or ballistic missile programmes, or other activities prohibited by resolutions 1718 (2006), 1874 (2009), 2087 (2013), and this resolution, or to the evasion of measures imposed by resolutions 1718 (2006), 1874 (2009), 2087 (2013), or this resolution;

"25. *Calls upon* all States to report to the Security Council within 90 days of the adoption of this resolution, and thereafter upon request by the Committee, on concrete measures they have taken in order to implement effectively the provisions of this resolution, and *requests* the Panel of Experts established pursuant to resolution 1874 (2009), in cooperation with other UN sanctions monitoring groups, to continue its efforts to assist States in preparing and submitting such reports in a timely manner;

"26. *Calls upon* all States to supply information at their disposal regarding non-compliance with the measures imposed in resolutions 1718 (2006), 1874 (2009), 2087 (2013), or this resolution;

"27. *Directs* the Committee to respond effectively to violations of the measures decided in resolutions 1718 (2006), 1874 (2009), 2087 (2013), and this resolution, *directs* the Committee to designate additional individuals and entities to be subject to the measures imposed in resolutions 1718 (2006), 1874 (2009), 2087 (2013), and this resolution, and *decides* that the Committee may designate any individuals for measures under paragraphs 8 (d) and 8 (e) of resolution 1718 (2006) and entities for measures under paragraph 8 (d) of resolution 1718 (2006) that have contributed to the DPRK's nuclear or ballistic missile programmes, or other activities prohibited by resolutions 1718 (2006), 1874 (2009), 2087 (2013), or this resolution, or to the evasion of measures imposed by resolutions 1718 (2006), 1874 (2009), 2087 (2013), or this resolution;

"28. *Decides* that the mandate of the Committee, as set out in paragraph 12 of resolution 1718 (2006), shall apply with respect to the measures imposed in resolution 1874 (2009) and this resolution;

"29. *Recalls* the creation, pursuant to paragraph 26 of resolution 1874 (2009), of a Panel of Experts, under the direction of the Committee, to carry out the tasks provided for by that paragraph, *decides* to extend until 7 April 2014 the Panel's mandate, as renewed by resolution 2050 (2012), *decides further* that this mandate shall apply with respect to the measures imposed in this resolution, *expresses its intent* to review the mandate and take appropriate action regarding further extension no later than twelve months from the adoption of this resolution, *requests* the Secretary-General to create a group of up to eight experts and to take the necessary administrative measures to this effect, and *requests* the Committee, in consultation with the Panel, to adjust the Panel's schedule of reporting;

"30. *Emphasizes* the importance of all States, including the DPRK, taking the necessary measures to ensure that no claim shall lie at the instance of the DPRK, or of any person or entity in the DPRK, or of persons or entities designated for measures set forth in resolutions 1718 (2006), 1874 (2009), 2087 (2013), or this resolution, or any person claiming through or for the benefit of any such person or entity, in connection with any contract or other transaction where its performance was prevented by reason of the measures imposed by this resolution or previous resolutions;

"31. *Underlines* that measures imposed by resolutions 1718 (2006), 1874 (2009), 2087 (2013) and this resolution are not intended to have adverse humanitarian consequences for the civilian population of the DPRK;

"32. *Emphasizes* that all Member States should comply with the provisions of paragraphs 8 (a) (iii) and 8 (d) of resolution 1718 (2006) without prejudice to the activities of diplomatic missions in the DPRK pursuant to the Vienna Convention on Diplomatic Relations;

"33. *Expresses* its commitment to a peaceful, diplomatic and political solution to the situation and welcomes efforts by Council members as well as other States to facilitate a peaceful and comprehensive solution through dialogue and to refrain from any actions that might aggravate tensions;

"34. *Reaffirms* its support to the Six-Party Talks, *calls for* their resumption, *urges* all the participants to intensify their efforts on the full and expeditious implementation of the 19 September 2005 Joint Statement issued by China, the DPRK, Japan, the Republic of Korea, the Russian Federation and the United States, with a view to achieving the verifiable denuclearization of the Korean Peninsula in a peaceful manner and to maintaining peace and stability on the Korean Peninsula and in north-east Asia;

"35. *Reiterates* the importance of maintaining peace and stability on the Korean Peninsula and in north-east Asia at large;

"36. *Affirms* that it shall keep the DPRK's actions under continuous review and is prepared to strengthen, modify, suspend or lift the measures as may be needed in light of the DPRK's compliance, and, in this regard, *expresses its determination* to take further significant measures in the event of a further DPRK launch or nuclear test;

"37. *Decides* to remain seized of the matter."

ANNEX I

Travel ban/asset freeze

1. YO'N CHO'NG NAM
   (a) *Description:* Chief Representative for the Korea Mining Development Trading Corporation (KOMID). The KOMID was designated by the Committee in April 2009 and is the DPRK's primary arms dealer and main exporter of goods and equipment related to ballistic missiles and conventional weapons.

2. KO CH'O'L-CHAE
   (a) *Description:* Deputy Chief Representative for the Korea Mining Development Trading Corporation (KOMID). The KOMID was designated by the Committee in April 2009 and is the DPRK's primary arms dealer and main exporter of goods and equipment related to ballistic missiles and conventional weapons.

3. MUN CHO'NG-CH'O'L
   (a) *Description:* Mun Cho'ng-Ch'o'l is a TCB official. In this capacity he has facilitated transactions for TCB. Tanchon was designated by the Committee in April 2009 and is the main DPRK financial entity for sales of conventional arms, ballistic missiles, and goods related to the assembly and manufacture of such weapons.

ANNEX II

Asset freeze

1. SECOND ACADEMY OF NATURAL SCIENCES
   (a) *Description:* The Second Academy of Natural Sciences is a national-level organization responsible for research and development of the DPRK's advanced weapons systems, including missiles and probably nuclear weapons. The Second Academy of Natural Sciences uses a number of subordinate organizations to obtain technology, equipment, and information from overseas, including Tangun Trading Corporation, for use in the DPRK's missile and probably nuclear weapons programmes. Tangun Trading Corporation was designated by the Committee in July 2009 and is primarily responsible for the procurement of commodities and technologies to support DPRK's defence research and development programmes, including, but not limited to, weapons of mass destruction and delivery system programmes and procurement, including materials that are controlled or prohibited under relevant multilateral control regimes.
   (b) *AKA:* 2ND ACADEMY OF NATURAL SCIENCES; CHE 2 CHAYON KWA-HAKWON; ACADEMY OF NATURAL SCIENCES; CHAYON KWAHAK-WON; NATIONAL DEFENSE ACADEMY; KUKPANG KWAHAK-WON; SECOND ACADEMY OF NATURAL SCIENCES RESEARCH INSTITUTE; SANSRI
   (c) *Location:* Pyongyang, DPRK

2. KOREA COMPLEX EQUIPMENT IMPORT CORPORATION
   (a) *Description:* Korea Ryonbong General Corporation is the parent company of Korea Complex Equipment Import Corporation. Korea Ryonbong General Corporation was designated by the Committee in April 2009 and is a defence conglomerate specializing in acquisition for DPRK defence industries and support to that country's military-related sales.
   (b) *Location:* Rakwon-dong, Pothonggang District, Pyongyang, DPRK

ANNEX III

Items, materials, equipment, goods and technology

Nuclear items

1. Perfluorinated Lubricants

   They can be used for lubricating vacuum pump and compressor bearings. They have a low vapour pressure, are resistant to uranium hexafluoride (UF6), the gaseous uranium compound used in the gas centrifuge process, and are used for pumping fluorine.

2. UF6 Corrosion Resistant Bellow-sealed Valves

   They can be used in uranium enrichment facilities (such as gas centrifuge and gaseous diffusion plants), in facilities that produce uranium hexafluoride (UF6), the gaseous uranium compound used in the gas centrifuge process, in fuel fabrication facilities and in facilities handling tritium.

Missile items

1. Special corrosion resistant steels—limited to steels resistant to Inhibited Red Fuming Nitric Acid (IRFNA) or nitric acid, such as nitrogen stabilized duplex stainless steel (N-DSS).

2. Ultra high-temperature ceramic composite materials in solid form (i.e. blocks, cylinders, tubes or ingots) in any of the following form factors:
   (a) Cylinders having a diameter of 120 mm or greater and a length of 50 mm or greater;
   (b) Tubes having an inner diameter of 65 mm or greater and a wall thickness of 25 mm or greater and a length of 50 mm or greater; or
   (c) Blocks having a size of 120 mm x 120 mm x 50 mm or greater.

3. Pyrotechnically Actuated Valves.

4. Measurement and control equipment usable for wind tunnels (balance, thermal stream measurement, flow control).

5. Sodium Perchlorate.

Chemical weapons list

1. Vacuum pumps with a manufacturer's specified maximum flow-rate greater than 1 m3/h (under standard temperature and pressure conditions), casings (pump bodies), preformed casing-liners, impellers, rotors, and jet pump nozzles designed for such pumps, in which all surfaces that come into direct contact with the chemicals being processed are made from controlled materials.

ANNEX IV

Luxury goods

1. Jewelry:
   (a) Jewelry with pearls;
   (b) Gems;
   (c) Precious and semi-precious stones (including diamonds, sapphires, rubies, and emeralds);
   (d) Jewelry of precious metal or of metal clad with precious metal.

2. Transportation items, as follows:
   (a) Yachts;
   (b) Luxury automobiles (and motor vehicles): automobiles and other motor vehicles to transport people (other than public transport), including station wagons;
   (c) Racing cars.

SOURCE: United Nations Security Council. Department of Public Information. "Security Council Strengthens Sanctions on Democratic People's Republic of Korea, in Response to 12 February Nuclear Test." March 7, 2013. http://www.un.org/News/Press/docs/2013/sc10934.doc.htm.

OTHER HISTORIC DOCUMENTS OF INTEREST

FROM PREVIOUS *HISTORIC DOCUMENTS*

Lebanese Prime Minister on Impact of Syrian Civil War

FEBRUARY 18, 2013

With the Syrian civil war entering its third year, the impact was being felt far beyond the nation itself. Live fire was reported on all sides of Syria's border with Lebanon, Israel, Jordan, Iraq, and Turkey. Refugees flooded into surrounding countries, with Turkey and Lebanon bearing the brunt of the humanitarian crisis. Syria's conflict reignited regional power struggles, such as those between Saudi Arabia and Iran, as the latter backed the regime of Bashar al-Assad, while the former funneled weapons to the rebels. Tensions increased among the region's ethnic groups as well—Assad's government draws a majority of its support from Alawites, Christians, Druze, and some portions of the Sunni sect, which caused conflict with Shiites in neighboring nations.

LEBANON

In Lebanon, the tenuous political balance has been threatened by the Syrian conflict. Syria has exuded a significant amount of influence over Lebanese politics in the past, and had troops stationed in the country until 2005. Hezbollah, a Shiite militia, is one of the two most powerful political organizations in the country and strongly supports the Assad regime. A majority of Lebanese citizens, however, back the rebel cause. Violence spiked in October 2012 following the assassination of Wissam al-Hassan, a Lebanese intelligence chief. His death was blamed on Hezbollah, whom Lebanese officials accused of acting on behalf of Syria.

Although violence did not escalate through 2013, the situation remained dire driven primarily by the influx of refugees fleeing Syria. Lebanon already had a poorly funded and run social welfare structure, which did little for its own citizens let alone refugees. According to the United Nations, more than 900,000 refugees have entered Lebanon since the beginning of the Syrian conflict. The Lebanese government estimates that number to be closer to one million.

The spillover of refugees and the creation of rebel camps on the Lebanon border reignited the tension between members of the Sunni and Shiite communities. This has played out not only neighbor-to-neighbor, but also on a grander scale between elected officials. Towns where a majority of the population was loyal to Hezbollah faced rocket attacks. Lebanon's biggest political powers—Hezbollah and the Future Movement—are at greater odds with each other. Hezbollah has faced a significant amount of criticism both within Lebanon and around the world for its strong support for Assad. The Future Movement, although viewing its counterpart as politically vulnerable, has not yet been able to capitalize on that and has actually seen its clout diminish as Shiite communities heed Hezbollah's call for jihad against those who oppose Assad.

In response to the ongoing conflict, Lebanese Prime Minister Najib Mikati instituted a policy of disassociation, meaning that while Lebanon would take part in regional dialogue to bring the Syrian conflict to a peaceful resolution, it might not take part in any decisions that are made or action that is called for, instead preferring to distance itself from the conflict. "Because of the political, historical, and geographic connection between Lebanon and Syria, and the deep polarization of the Lebanese between those who support the Syrian uprising and those who support the Syrian regime, we adopted a dis-association policy that aims to safeguard Lebanon from the overspill of the Syrian crisis," the prime minister said.

TURKEY

Along Turkey's 566-mile border with Syria, those who support the Assad regime began to clash with rebels who often stage operations on Turkish soil. In June 2012, a fighter jet conducting a routine mission was shot down by Assad's forces after veering momentarily into Syrian airspace before returning to international airspace. Fearing additional missile or chemical weapons strikes, Turkey called on the North Atlantic Treaty Organization (NATO) to hold an emergency session to determine whether member states could act to prevent further Syrian aggression. NATO members decided not to take action, so Turkey instead strengthened its own military presence along the border.

To date, Turkey has been one of the biggest recipients of refugees from Syria, at a cost of upwards of $750 million. The United Nations estimates that by the start of 2014 at least 500,000 had flowed across the border, with thousands more thought to have entered the country without registering. Smaller border towns that have welcomed both refugees and opposition forces have benefited economically from the increase in those frequenting local businesses. However, a growing number of refugees have begun looking for work inside Turkey, and they are willing to work for far less than Turkish citizens, a situation that is slowly reaching a breaking point. To prevent an anticipated outbreak of violence, Turkey called on the United Nations to create a "safe zone" for refugees run by the international body. Plans have yet to come to fruition, and the Turkish public has grown increasingly frustrated with its government's response to the refugee crisis and support for Syrian rebels. With the region in such a precarious state, many Turks express concern that their nation will be dragged deeper into the Syrian conflict.

The United States has been working closely with Turkey to monitor the situation in Syria. Both nations have a lot at stake whether Assad maintains power or his government collapses. The former will likely mean the spread of Hezbollah and Iranian influence in the region. Turkey was at one point allied with Iran, but the relationship continued to crumble in part due to Iran's continued support of Assad. If the Assad regime collapses, it will mean a number of security measures need to be put in place in surrounding countries to aid with a greater influx of refugees and to stop Syria's chemical weapons stockpiles from falling into the wrong hands.

IRAN

In Iran, President Mahmoud Ahmadinejad cast his support of Assad's regime as a move to protect the Middle East from outside incursion. "Enemies are striving to waste Muslim governments and nations' energy and wealth by pushing them to fight one another," Ahmadinejad said. If Assad's government were to fall, not only would Iran lose its only ally in the region, thus reducing its influence, but Syria would also likely put a Sunni government in power, which would operate in direct opposition to Ahmadinejad's Shiite-dominated government. Intelligence officials believe that Iran has been supporting Syria by providing surveillance and communications support. There are questions about whether the country can provide monetary or military assistance, because sanctions from the West have frozen many of Iran's assets and have reduced oil revenues. Hezbollah, however, may be willing to give assistance to Assad on behalf of Iran as it too faces a significant loss of influence if a Sunni government takes over in Syria. Iran's support for Assad raised fears in the Persian Gulf, and specifically in Saudi Arabia, that if the Syrian leader's government would maintain its hold on power, it could mean growing influence for the nuclear-ambitious nation. Both Saudi Arabia and Qatar are thought to be giving military support to the Syrian rebels in the form of weapons.

JORDAN

Syria has long been at odds with its Southern neighbor, Jordan, over power in the region. Recently, the Jordanian government has accused Assad's government of supporting al Qaeda missions on Jordan's soil. However, the countries are deeply dependent on one another, especially given Syria's vital link to trade in Europe. That trade has become almost nonexistent since the start of the civil war in Syria, and Jordan is now facing a daily influx of both refugees and jihadists. On the outside, Jordan has maintained a neutral position on Syria but has quietly helped Western nations equip rebels. Seeking to protect itself from possible military incursion, Jordan asked the United States to leave behind missiles, troops, and warplanes following training exercises with Jordan's military. There are few options for Jordan to come out on top in the Syrian conflict. The Assad regime has not hid its disdain for its neighbor, who has called for Assad's ouster, but if Syria becomes a failed state, Jordan risks both rebel militias and extremists flowing across its border.

WIDESPREAD MIDDLE EASTERN IMPACT

In Iraq, sectarian tension between Sunni and Shiite groups was growing because the Sunni members of al Qaeda put their support behind the Syrian rebels, while the Shiites supported Assad. Western intelligence suggests that al Qaeda militias have frequently entered Syria to fight on behalf of the rebels. Just as thousands of refugees flowed into Syria following the American invasion in 2003, now, more than 200,000 Syrian refugees have entered Iraq, fleeing their own violence.

Israel has been caught in a complex situation with Syria, because the two countries have a long-held animosity that dates to Israel's capture of the Golan Heights in the 1960s. Israel initially expressed concern that a Sunni militant government might overthrow Assad but has recently become increasingly worried about the opposite—if Assad maintains power, it would likely embolden Hezbollah, which has the potential to use its missile stockpile to attack Israel. And if Hezbollah gains power, it will likely align more closely with nuclear-ambitious Iran to target Israel. The best possible outcome for Israel is for an extended conflict that weakens both Assad and the rebels and allows time for a new replacement government to form.

—Heather Kerrigan

Following is the text of a conversation with Lebanese Prime Minister Najib Mikati on February 18, 2013, pertaining to his recent trip to Turkey to discuss the impact of the Syrian civil war on both nations.

PM Mikati on Impact of Syrian Civil War

February 18, 2013

Hürriyet Daily News (Turkey)

We met with Prime Minister Najib Mikati of Lebanon who had visited Ankara two weeks ago at the Grand Serial that was once known to be an Ottoman Palace in the heart of Beirut; Hurriyat discusses with Prime Minister Mikati the political and economic challenges facing Lebanon.

The main theme of interview is the Syrian crisis and its implication on Lebanon. Syria had a direct influence on Lebanon during and after the civil war. Prime Minister Najib Mikati discussed his Government's neutral position towards the Syrian crisis stressing on the importance of this dis-association policy that prevents strife and Syrian crisis spillover to Lebanon.

Prime Minsiter Mikati said that Prime Minister Erdogen understands the Lebanese government's position towards Syria due to the internal divisions in Lebanon associated with the Syrian crisis.

According to Prime Minister Mikati, Turkey is a powerful force in the Middle East, but it is difficult for Turkey to be a model for other countries.

In an exclusive interview with Huriyat Turkish Newspaper, Prime Minister Mikati discusses the Turkish-Lebanese relations, Syrian crisis and the political challenges he is facing.

What were the main topics that you discussed with Turkish PM Erdoğan in your recent visit to Ankara?

My visit to Turkey was successful. I had a productive meeting with Prime Minister Erdogan where we have discussed bilateral cooperation and Turkey's support for Lebanon in the international scene.

We also raised the issue of the displaced Syrians and the challenges that Lebanon is facing due to the increased flow of Syrian migrants, which is burdening Lebanon at all levels; geographic, social, political and economic. Our case is unique due to its complexity and we called upon Turkey and the international community to help in alleviating the agonies of the Syrian displaced migrants.

Furthermore, we discussed thoroughly the issue of the Lebanese hostages in Syria, which is a major concern to us as most Lebanese believe that Turkey can play a major role in liberating the hostages.

How did the Turkish side respond to your request for putting pressure on groups that are allegedly involved in kidnapping of Lebanese nationals in Azez (Syria)?

Irrespective of the complexity of the situation in Syria, and from day one, Turkey has cooperated with Lebanon on this issue and reaffirmed to me that they will do their best to help in liberating the hostages.

What do you make of the blast that targeted General Wissam El Hassan, a major security officer, in your capital last October? Do you agree with the arguments that it had to do with different political stances towards Syria?

We denounced this horrific crime. This crime targeted a major security General and my personal friend General Wissam El Hassan. General Hassan played a vital role in preserving security in Lebanon. Since, we have taken measures such as requesting an international inquiry into this crime.

The ongoing strife in Syria leads to believe that the assassination could be a consequence, but, since there is no clear evidence yet we are awaiting the results of the investigation.

Can Turkey act as a role model for change in the Arab world?

Growth and development experienced by Turkey over the last 10 years is obvious, the same thing can be said regarding Turkey's military power. Turkey is playing a significant role in the region. As for whether it can act as role model in the region, I personally do not think so since I do not believe in standardization, for each country has its own characteristics. In Turkey, civil law is widespread which makes it really difficult for us to adopt the Turkish model.

Do you mean secularism and pertaining laws?

Yes. Regarding that issue, we need more time; we cannot adopt secularism immediately.

There has been recently talks about fundamentalists' actions and influence in the north. Is "al-Qaeda" really influential in Lebanon?

"Al-Qaeda" has become a general denomination to such activities. These factions may not be linked with "Al-Qaeda" whatsoever, and may be they are just "al-Qaeda" sympathizers, but in Lebanon, we are accustomed to such situations that arise from pluralism and that we have the capacity to deal with. But the situation has nothing to do with "Al-Qaeda" and terrorism.

What about the situation on the Syrian-Turkish border? It is said that the "Al-Nosra" faction that is close to "Al-Qaeda" has a significant presence there, do you have information in this regard?

As you have mentioned, these factions are present in northern Syria.

Do you fear that the sectarian clash patterns in Syria might also infect Lebanon which has already suffered a lot from similar clashes in the past?

Because of the political, historical, and geographic connection between Lebanon and Syria, and the deep polarization of the Lebanese between those who support the Syrian uprising and those who support the Syrian regime, we adopted a dis-association policy that aims to safeguard Lebanon from the overspill of the Syrian crisis. Irrespective of our attempts, the consequences of the Syrian crisis have impacted Lebanon mainly with more than 200,000 Syrians fleeing the violence into Lebanon. This forced migration can result in many challenges including political divisions and sectarian tension.

What is your government's take on the situation as a whole in Syria?

We are saddened by the violence that is claiming hundreds of innocent lives each day in Syria. Lebanon reaffirms its dis-association policy on both the political and security levels in order to maintain stability and avoid related consequences and risks. Hence, I always stated that Lebanon did not dis-associate itself from providing humanitarian support to the Syrian refugees in Lebanon in an attempt to alleviate their sufferings.

We hope that the Syrian crisis will be resolved peacefully.

Do you believe a formula which keeps Bashar Assad as part of the solution might work in Syria?

Our dis-association policy towards the ongoing crisis Syria, requires that we don't interfere in the internal affairs of any country and especially that we as Lebanese always been complaining about regional and international interference in our affairs. The answer to this question has to be determined by the Syrian People.

What are your expectations from US President Obama in the second term? Do you believe that he has delivered upon expectations from Islamic world in his first term?

We hope that President Obama's perspective on Arab issues is fundamentally based on preserving peace and justice in the region mainly by ensuring the establishment of a Palestinian State and granting the Palestinians the right of return to their land. In addition to this main concern, we hope that President Obama's administration will deter Israel from its aggressions against the Arab States specifically Lebanon and the Palestinian Territories.

We believe that President Obama's perspective and his Administration's' policy is based on a proper understanding towards the Islamic World. We hope such understanding to be visible in action.

How do you rate the Turkish position in the Syrian crisis?

I am not in a position to evaluate the Turkish stand on this issue. The Turkish officials know better Turkey's interest and accordingly how to deal with the Syrian case. However, there is no doubt that Turkey is a major player and pivotal power in the region.

There is an obvious difference between Turkey's and Lebanon's stance towards the Syrian issue. While you do not support any of the parties, Turkey gives support to Syrian dissidents. Will this affect bilateral relations?

Mr. Erdogan made it clear during the meetings we had, that he was convinced with Lebanon's policy, for he was aware of the Lebanon's social structure and how difficult it is for Lebanon in these circumstances to support any particular party in Syria. Our historical and geographical relations with Syria and divisions in our society compel us to adopt neutrality. The government's support to any of the parties will only deepen the divisions in our country and will not serve any of the parties in Syria even if all Lebanese support the Syrian regime or the opposition. Supporting any of the parties would only further destabilize our society.

What are the conditions of the Syrian refugees in Lebanon? Have you agreed on any means of cooperation on this matter with Turkey?

Our Government is committed to support, within its capacities, the displaced Syrian families awaiting their return to their homes. That goes along acknowledging the right of the Lebanese hosting communities for adequate social services. However, these capacities have reached a deadlock and immediate assistance is needed. With the escalation of violence, massive influx of displaced is expected and that requires extensive resources.

The situation has reached an alarming level that Lebanon cannot handle on its own. Therefore our Government designed a response plan which looks at sustaining the adequate provision of shelter, food and basic commodities in addition to health care and education services of displaced Syrians. Moreover, the plan will assist Lebanese hosting communities to preserve social cohesion, solidarity and prevent conflict and tension.

A such, we have discussed with Turkish counter partners the complexity of the situation and the urgent need for International support in order for Lebanon to be able to sustain its assistance to displaced Syrians and maintain its internal stability and peace.

There has been recent talks about a possible Sunni-Shiite conflict. Will the current controversy turn into a widespread conflict?

This situation started a long time ago, since the occupation of Iraq and even in the eighties during the Iraqi-Iranian war. Wise statesmen are striving to prevent such a conflict, and I hope they will succeed. We, as true Muslims, have transcend Sunni-Shiite divisions and oppose using this issue as an excuse for a conflict.

Do you think it will be possible to keep Iraq unified under current circumstances?

We very much hope that the Iraqis will overcome the ongoing deteriorating situation by maintaining at the minimum level their national solidarity. We hope that such solidarity will crystallize more and more over time since stability in Iraq will positively affect the whole region.

How do you think the developments in Syria and Egypt will affect the Israeli position in the region? Do you think Israel is stronger or weaker than years ago?

Any unfortunate incident and crisis that happens in the Arab world provides an opportunity for Israel to intervene and benefit from the chaos. Therefore, we in Lebanon have been calling for resolving our Arab issues as quickly as possible so as to strengthen our defenses from any hazards.

How do you think the Turkish stance towards Israel is affecting the balances in the region?

Again, I am not in a position to evaluate the Turkish stand towards Israel. This is to be determined by the Turkish Officials.

What do you make of the uprisings of the last two years? Do you believe Islamic countries are undergoing a healthy reform process?

It's too early to discuss and evaluate the consequences of the uprisings. Such transitions need a long time to materialize into any positive change. However, the positive aspect is the increasing participation of the youth in the shaping of the Arab World.

SOURCE: Official Website of Prime Minister Najib Mikati. "Interview With Prime Minister Najib Mikati of Lebanon." February 18, 2013. http://www.najib-mikati.net/en/LatestNews/8503/Interview%20with%20 Prime%20Minister%20Najib%20Mikati%20of%20Lebanon.

OTHER HISTORIC DOCUMENTS OF INTEREST

FROM THIS VOLUME

- Turkish President Remarks on Protests, p. 211
- President Obama Remarks on the Conflict in Syria, p. 411

FROM PREVIOUS *HISTORIC DOCUMENTS*

- United Nations Fails to Take Action in Syria, *2012,* p. 81
- Lebanon Forms New Government, *2011,* p. 40
- Arab Spring: Syrian Government's Violent Crackdown on Protests, *2011,* p. 169
- United Nations on Syrian Troops in Lebanon, *2004,* p. 557

March

President Obama Issues Sequestration Order

MARCH 1, 2013

On March 1, 2013, President Barack Obama signed an executive order setting in motion a series of budget cuts known as the sequester. The $85 billion reduction in federal coffers would impact defense and domestic spending equally. Although federal agencies made clear the impact that such cuts would have—including furloughs, a reduction in welfare benefits, and flight delays—Congress failed to reach an agreement on how to replace all the across-the-board cuts with a more targeted approach. Instead, the only passable bill was one that would shift money around to, among other things, delay furloughs for members of the military.

Debt Ceiling Fix and the Impending Sequester

In May 2011, the United States reached its debt ceiling, a cap set by Congress that limits the amount the government can borrow. The Treasury Department was able to avoid a default until August 2, and before that time Congress needed to reach an agreement on raising the debt ceiling. Failing to do so could result in an inability of the federal government to make necessary payments, such as Social Security benefits. The compromise bill that raised the debt ceiling, known as the Budget Control Act of 2011 (BCA), required the $1.2 trillion raise to be offset by spending cuts in the same amount.

To determine how best to make these cuts, the BCA created the Joint Select Committee on Deficit Reduction, known as the "super committee," which would be responsible for recommending how cuts should be made and proposing legislation to do so. The super committee was given until November 2011 to present its recommendations. As an incentive for them to do so, a stipulation was added to the BCA that failure to meet the deadline would result in $1.2 trillion in automatic, across-the-board spending cuts, known as the sequester. These cuts would be evenly split between defense and domestic spending. In the end, the super committee failed, and the sequester was set to go into effect on January 2, 2013.

The mandatory cuts would begin at the same time as tax cuts passed under former President George W. Bush would expire. The simultaneous increase in tax rates and decrease in government spending became known as the "fiscal cliff." Throughout late 2012, Congress debated how to avoid the situation. The final compromise bill, passed on January 1, 2013, fixed some of the tax increases, but only delayed the sequester until March 1.

When the cuts went into effect, $85 billion came out of federal budgets. This included $43 billion in military cuts, with half coming from national security and military operations. No cuts were made that would affect military personnel. Domestic discretionary spending was cut by $26 billion, and included programs such as national parks, drug enforcement, education, health care, and temporary recovery programs like those for

Hurricane Sandy. No cuts were made to programs run by the Department of Veterans Affairs or certain financial aid programs like Pell Grants. Mandatory spending was cut by a total of $16 billion, with $11 billion in cuts made to Medicare, and the remaining $5 billion in cuts made up mainly in agriculture programs and a reduction in unemployment benefit extensions.

The BCA also put into place discretionary spending caps. Whether or not the super committee reached an agreement on budget control recommendations, these caps would take effect. If at any point the spending caps are exceeded, additional mandatory budget cuts will be made. To date, spending has been kept below this level.

ANTICIPATED IMPACT

When Obama issued the sequestration order on March 1, 2013, it was accompanied by a report from the Office of Management and Budget (OMB) detailing the anticipated impact of the cuts on an agency-by-agency and program-by-program basis. According to OMB, the sequester would require a 7.8 percent reduction in defense discretionary funding, a 5 percent decrease in nondefense discretionary spending, a 2 percent cut to Medicare, a 7.9 percent cut to defense mandatory programs, and a 5.1 percent reduction in nondefense mandatory programs. Obama's budget director, Jeffrey Zients, called the cuts "deeply destructive to national security, domestic investments, and core government functions." He added that the sequester "was never intended to be implemented and does not represent a responsible way for our Nation to achieve deficit reduction."

Although the anticipated impacts were clearly defined, they were not readily noticeable. There was a general misunderstanding about when the sequester actually went into effect on March 1. Technically, OMB was given until 11:59 p.m. to issue the order and set the cuts in motion, but the president had to first issue an order to OMB. This left roughly 4.4 million federal employees questioning when they might receive furlough notices (in the end, almost every agency required furloughs for at least some of its employees). And to that end, federal law prohibited some of the furloughs from going into effect until thirty days until after they were issued. Cutting each agency's budget would be an arduous rather than automatic process as well; some cuts required multiple levels of notification of states or unions. This left few areas where sequester cuts would have an immediate impact. Recognizing this, the president said, "The pain will be real. Many middle-class families will have their lives disrupted in a significant way."

Once in place, however, the impact of the sequester would make its mark. Macroeconomic Advisers, an economic-focused research firm, estimated that U.S. gross domestic product (GDP) would be reduced by more than $150 billion in 2013. The Congressional Budget Office (CBO) stated that 0.6 points would be cut from the GDP in 2013, in addition to impacting the creation or retention of an anticipated 750,000 jobs. In February 2013, Federal Reserve Chair Ben Bernanke appealed to Congress to replace the sequester with more targeted cuts to avoid the anticipated slowing of the economic recovery. "To address both the near- and longer-term [fiscal] issues, the Congress and the Administration should consider replacing the sharp, front-loaded spending cuts required by the sequestration with policies that reduce the federal deficit more gradually in the near term but more substantially in the longer run. Such an approach could lessen the near-term fiscal headwinds facing the recovery while more effectively addressing the longer-term imbalances in the federal budget," Bernanke said.

At the individual level, cuts were made to a variety of public assistance programs, such as emergency unemployment benefit extensions, which, according to the National Employment Law Project, would affect more than 3.8 million people who would face an average $43 per week reduction in unemployment benefits. The Women, Infant, and Children (WIC) program was also reduced, meaning those who rely on the program for things such as formula would be impacted. Head Start, the federal preschool program for lower-income Americans, was cut by more than $400 million, which removed 57,000 children from the program. Public housing assistance also took a hit. Two public assistance programs, Temporary Assistance for Needy Families (TANF) and the Supplemental Nutrition Assistance Program (SNAP), were exempt from cuts.

For air travelers, the cuts would mean longer waits on the ground. The Federal Aviation Administration (FAA) issued furlough notices to air traffic controllers and closed some control towers, which the agency said could cause ground delays of up to ninety minutes. Lawmakers criticized the agency for not seeking a different method for cutting its budget. "The FAA's decision is a dangerous political stunt that could jeopardize the safety and security of air travelers," said Sen. Tom Coburn, R-Okla. The Transportation Security Administration (TSA) trimmed some of its budget by cutting overtime for its agents, meaning that it would be unable to maintain adequate staffing levels during peak travel times.

Varying Proposals

Before the sequester took effect, Congress and the White House worked to determine a method for reducing or stopping its impending impact. House Democrats called for smaller, more targeted cuts to replace the sequester, coupled with restructuring tax programs that would limit tax credits for the wealthiest Americans, and reforming health care programs like Medicare. These targeted cuts would be made mainly to farm subsidies and the national flood insurance program and would be spread out over the next decade. In the Senate, Democrats proposed a similar plan for $110 billion in a combination of tax increases and spending cuts, including a cut to military spending. House Republicans also called for more targeted cuts but refused to make tax hikes a part of any bill. In one of its last attempts to replace the sequester, Republicans passed a bill in December 2012 that replaced reductions in defense spending with cuts to programs like SNAP and the Affordable Care Act. The White House said the Spending Reduction Act of 2012, as it was known, would have a negative impact on middle-class families. The Senate failed to begin debate on the bill.

After March 1, 2013, both parties in Congress floated proposals for sequester relief. Democrats proposed entirely replacing the sequester while subsequently raising federal spending, while Republicans called for deeper cuts to nondefense programs. On March 6, 2013, the House passed a continuing resolution to shift money around to reduce the impact of the sequester to defense and discretionary spending. Although there would still be some reductions, changes were made to add funding for military pay, Food and Drug Administration (FDA) inspections, and research grants. Military furlough days were reduced from twenty-two to fourteen with their start delayed for two months. The Senate passed the bill on March 20, and it was signed by the president on March 26. Both parties attempted to tie subsequent bills to the upcoming budget process without success.

2014 AND BEYOND

The sequester was still in place at the end of 2013. Annual spending cuts of $109 billion will be made be made between 2014 and 2021. Congress is required to determine how these cuts will be made in coming years. They can decide to use an automatic, across-the-board method as in 2013, or they can agree to more targeted cuts.

According to the CBO, by 2021, nondefense discretionary spending will be reduced by nearly $300 billion, while defense will be reduced by more than $450 billion. These cuts would reduce long-term debt; however, the CBO reported in July that ending the sequester would boost the economy by 0.7 percent and add 900,000 jobs through fiscal year 2014. But Congress would be doing so at the risk of increasing the deficit. "Although output would be greater and employment higher in the next few years if the spending reductions under current law were reversed, that policy would lead to greater federal debt, which would eventually reduce the nation's output and income below what would occur under current law," the CBO reported.

—Heather Kerrigan

Following is the text of the sequestration order issued on March 1, 2013, by President Barack Obama.

`DOCUMENT` *Sequestration Order Issued*

March 1, 2013

By the authority vested in me as President by the laws of the United States of America, and in accordance with section 251A of the Balanced Budget and Emergency Deficit Control Act, as amended (the "Act"), 2 U.S.C. 901a, I hereby order that budgetary resources in each non-exempt budget account be reduced by the amount calculated by the Office of Management and Budget in its report to the Congress of March 1, 2013.

Pursuant to sections 250(c)(6), 251A, and 255(e) of the Act, budgetary resources subject to sequestration shall be new budget authority, unobligated balances of defense function accounts carried over from prior fiscal years, direct spending authority, and obligation limitations.

All sequestrations shall be made in strict accordance with the requirements of section 251A of the Act and the specifications of the Office of Management and Budget's report of March 1, 2013, prepared pursuant to section 251A(11) of the Act.

BARACK OBAMA

The White House,
March 1, 2013.

SOURCE: Executive Office of the President. "Sequestration Order for Fiscal Year 2013 Pursuant to Section 251A of the Balanced Budget and Emergency Deficit Control Act, As Amended." March 1, 2013. *Compilation of Presidential Documents* 2013, no. 00132 (March 1, 2013). http://www.gpo.gov/fdsys/pkg/DCPD-201300132/pdf/DCPD-201300132.pdf.

OTHER HISTORIC DOCUMENTS OF INTEREST

FROM THIS VOLUME

FROM PREVIOUS *HISTORIC DOCUMENTS*

International Leaders Respond to Death of Venezuelan Leader Hugo Chavez

MARCH 5, 2013

On March 5, 2013, Venezuelan President Hugo Chavez passed away following a long bout with cancer. A charismatic yet controversial figure who led Venezuela for fourteen years, Chavez left behind not only a complicated legacy marked by expanded social welfare programs and strengthened relationships with neighboring countries, but also economic instability, rising crime rates, internal division, and an increasingly tense relationship with the United States. Venezuela held a new presidential election in April, which pitted Chavez's hand-picked successor, Vice President Nicolás Maduro, against opposition leader Henrique Capriles Radonski. The results, giving Maduro a narrow victory, were contested by Capriles and sparked protests across the country.

Chavez's Rise and Presidency

Hugo Chavez was born in 1954 to two primary school teachers and was the second of seven children. The family lived in poverty in a small mud hut, and Chavez's parents eventually sent him and his older brother to live with his grandmother. Chavez attended Venezuela's military academy when he turned seventeen, and after graduating joined a counterinsurgency unit charged with pursuing a Maoist rebel group. Chavez's study of the rebels and their beliefs had a critical influence on his own political leanings and inspired him to create the Bolivarian Revolutionary Movement, a leftist group that espoused anti-elite, anti-imperial sentiments and was strongly skeptical of the United States and its involvement in Venezuela.

At the time, Venezuela had a system of democracy in place, which the country's elite established in 1958, and which resulted in two major political parties trading the presidency back and forth for forty years. Influential political scientist Samuel Huntington praised this system as "successful democratization," but the government's institutions were accused of lacking accountability, marginalizing the opposition, filling judiciary positions with partisan supporters, corruption, and using oil export revenues to grant favors. By the 1980s, oil prices were falling and more than half of Venezuela's population lived below the poverty line—many in extreme poverty. An announcement of new austerity measures in 1989 resulted in three days of rioting and looting in the capital city of Caracas.

In this environment, Chavez began to emerge as a political figure. In 1992, he led several coconspirators in a failed military coup. Chavez spent two years in prison before being pardoned, but also became a folk hero in the eyes of many Venezuelans. He later relaunched his revolutionary movement as the Movement of the Fifth Republic and was elected president in 1998 on an antiausterity platform.

Once in office, Chavez moved to implement a number of social welfare programs aimed at helping the poor, such as new health clinics, state-run stores that sold subsidized food in impoverished parts of the country, and access to education for all. He continually pushed to increase the president's power, including through a 2009 referendum to abolish term limits for all elected officials. He was a staunch advocate of Latin American unity and led Venezuela's cofounding of the Bolivarian Alliance for the People of Our Americas (ALBA), an organization seeking social, political, and economic integration among the countries of Latin America and the Caribbean. Through ALBA, Venezuela spent billions to support development projects across the continent.

Chavez also sought to limit the influence of the United States and Europe in the region by nationalizing many foreign-owned assets and often blamed the United States for Venezuela's struggles. He maintained a contentious relationship with U.S. officials throughout his presidency, at one point famously calling former President George W. Bush "the devil," and encouraged other energy-exporting Latin American nations to expel U.S. ambassadors.

Following a brief coup in 2002, which removed him from office for forty-eight hours, Chavez became more aggressive in exerting his power as Venezuela's economy struggled. He stripped the Supreme Court of its autonomy in 2004 and used gerrymandering to ensure his supporters retained the majority in the National Assembly in the 2010 elections. He removed opponents from positions within the state-owned oil company, expropriated land, and imprisoned former military officials who spoke out against him. At the same time, the homicide rate skyrocketed, and armed gangs controlled many of the prisons. Public debt rose to $102 billion, poverty and unemployment were widespread, and the country experienced periodic shortages of basic goods. Opposition to Chavez and his policies grew, and the country's political environment became highly charged.

Despite these issues, Chavez maintained strong support among his "Chavistas" and continually won reelection, including what would be his final election in October 2012.

LOSS OF A LEADER

Chavez was diagnosed with an undisclosed form of cancer in June 2011. Many details of his disease and treatment were kept from the public as officials sought to maintain a perception of normality. Chavez did undergo chemotherapy and radiation treatments, but his cancer kept returning. He traveled to Havana four times for various surgeries, the last of which occurred in December 2012 and involved the insertion of a tracheal tube to help him breathe. While Chavez had given speeches, made public appearances, and been active on Twitter throughout most of his treatment, the tube made it difficult for him to speak, and he remained out of the public eye following this final procedure.

Chavez succumbed to his disease on March 5 at the age of fifty-eight. The news was met with a tremendous outpouring of grief among his supporters. Vice President Maduro sought to reassure Venezuelans that Chavez's legacy would live on. "We, your civilian and military companions, Commander Hugo Chavez, assume your legacy, your challenges, your project, accompanied by and with the support of the people," he said. Chavez's opponents, while offering condolences, expressed hope that Chavez's passing would open new opportunities for Venezuela. Some foreign leaders, including U.S. President Barack Obama and Canadian Prime Minister Stephen Harper, shared similar sentiments. "I would like to offer my condolences to the people of Venezuela on the passing of President Chavez," read a statement by Prime Minister Harper. "At this key juncture, I hope the people of Venezuela can now build for themselves a better, brighter future based on the principles of freedom, democracy, the rule of law and respect for human rights."

On March 6, Chavez's body was taken to lie in state at the same military academy where he had been a student. Hundreds of thousands of people gathered in the streets to watch his casket's five-mile procession through Caracas, which was followed by a funeral mass at the academy with his family, close advisors, and the presidents of Argentina, Bolivia, and Uruguay. A formal funeral was held on March 8.

A CONTESTED ELECTION

Since Chavez had just begun a presidential term, the Venezuelan constitution mandated that a new election be held within thirty days of his death. In addition to running for the office, Vice President Maduro, Chavez's chosen political successor, would serve as interim president until the election, even though National Assembly Speaker Diosdado Cabello should have filled this role per the constitution. The National Election Council set the election for April 14, with formal campaigning to begin on April 2.

On March 10, Capriles announced his candidacy in a speech that was highly critical of the existing government, arguing that it had betrayed Venezuelans. He also implied that Maduro might have lied about when Chavez died, and called him incompetent. Maduro responded by calling Capriles a "fascist" who was trying to incite violence. Such insults continued throughout the campaign.

During the campaign, Maduro pledged to continue Chavez's efforts to build "21st century socialism" and leveraged Chavez's endorsement of him to garner further support. "Make the dreams of a giant reality. That's the only thing I want to do," Maduro said. Capriles advocated for a more moderate approach to government, promising more pro-business policies as well as a continuation of strong welfare programs. His aim, Capriles said, was to create a "Venezuela for all" where citizens "eat well," "sleep calmly," and "have money in their pockets." Four other candidates—Reina Sequera, María Bolívar, Eusebio Méndez, and Julio Mora—also entered the race, but none posed a serious challenge to either Capriles or Maduro.

Seventy-eight percent of registered voters turned out on election day. More than 100 foreign election observers were on hand to help monitor the vote, and election officials reported no major incidents. On April 15, the National Election Council announced Maduro as president-elect, with 50.8 percent of the votes to Capriles' 49 percent. Capriles refused to concede and demanded a recount, calling Maduro an "illegitimate" leader. He and his supporters claimed their tally showed Capriles winning by more than 300,000 votes and that it had evidence of approximately 3,200 voting irregularities. By contrast, the official count showed Maduro leading by 265,000 votes. Maduro declared the result "was truly fair, constitutional and popular."

The presidents of Argentina, Bolivia, and Cuba were quick to congratulate Maduro, but others supported a recount. White House Press Secretary Jay Carney said an audit "seems like an important and prudent step to take" given the close margin, and Organization of American States Secretary-General Jose Miguel Insulza offered the use of the group's election experts for a recount "in the context of deep division and political polarization."

The results sparked protests throughout Caracas. Capriles supporters threw rocks and sticks, tried to force entry into a hotel where election observers were meeting, and clashed with government supporters. The government accused protesters of burning Chavez's health clinics and injuring Maduro supporters, but several media outlets published photos showing the health clinics were unharmed, and that the injured citizens were actually Capriles supporters wounded by police or beaten by pro-government thugs. Human rights group Foro Penal Venezolano told the Associated Press they had evidence that the National Guard arrested and beat dozens of opposition supporters inside a barracks for not accepting Maduro's victory, and that troops had used excessive force against other protestors. Chief Prosecutor Luisa Ortega reported that by April 18, 135 people had been arrested in postelection incidents, and 90 had been charged with crimes.

The tension spread to the National Assembly as well. On April 30, Assembly leadership prevented opposition lawmakers from speaking during session unless they recognized Maduro as president. Those lawmakers unfurled a banner reading "Coup in Parliament" in response and interrupted the session with whistles and horns. A physical fight broke out, and several opposition lawmakers were hospitalized.

Despite the contested results, Maduro was sworn in as president on April 19.

AUDITED RESULTS

The same week the election results were announced, the National Election Council agreed to conduct a more complete audit of the votes. The Council had already audited a randomly selected 54 percent of the vote on election day, but said it would review a sample of two-thirds of the remaining votes. Capriles initially agreed to this audit, but withdrew his support on April 25, claiming it was a "joke" and calling the proposed conditions unfair. He demanded that voter signatures and fingerprints be examined as well, but the Council rejected this plan.

While the audit progressed, Capriles took his arguments to the Supreme Court, filing a lawsuit alleging voter irregularities and seeking nullification of the election results. On August 7, the Court dismissed his lawsuit, ruling that the documents he submitted "were inadmissible as they failed to provide sufficient evidence." The Court also fined him $1,500 for making "offensive and disrespectful allegations" against it and other officials and charged public prosecutors with determining whether Capriles should face criminal charges for making unfounded claims.

On June 11, the Council confirmed Maduro's victory, saying its audit found no discrepancy with initial election results. Some speculate that Maduro's slim victory will ultimately lead to internal challenges within the coalition that coalesced around Chavez and question what Venezuela's future will look like without its former charismatic leader.

—Linda Fecteau

Following are statements by U.S. President Barack Obama and Canadian Prime Minister Stephen Harper, delivered on March 5, 2013, in response to the death of Venezuelan president Hugo Chavez.

DOCUMENT

President Obama Remarks on Death of Venezuelan Leader

March 5, 2013

At this challenging time of President Hugo Chavez's passing, the United States reaffirms its support for the Venezuelan people and its interest in developing a constructive relationship with the Venezuelan Government. As Venezuela begins a new chapter in its history, the United States remains committed to policies that promote democratic principles, the rule of law, and respect for human rights.

SOURCE: Executive Office of the President. "Statement on the Death of President Hugo Chavez Frias of Venezuela." March 5, 2013. *Compilation of Presidential Documents* 2013, no. 00137 (March 5, 2013). http://www.gpo.gov/fdsys/pkg/DCPD-201300137/pdf/DCPD-201300137.pdf.

Canadian Prime Minister Stephen Harper on the Death of Hugo Chavez

March 5, 2013

Prime Minister Stephen Harper today issued the following statement on the death of Hugo Chavez Frías, President of the Bolivarian Republic of Venezuela:

"I would like to offer my condolences to the people of Venezuela on the passing of President Chavez.

"Canada looks forward to working with his successor and other leaders in the region to build a hemisphere that is more prosperous, secure and democratic.

"At this key juncture, I hope the people of Venezuela can now build for themselves a better, brighter future based on the principles of freedom, democracy, the rule of law and respect for human rights."

SOURCE: Office of the Prime Minister of Canada. "Statement by the Prime Minister of Canada on the Death of Venezuelan President Hugo Chavez Frías." March 5, 2013. © Her Majesty the Queen in Right of Canada, 2014. http://www.pm.gc.ca/eng/news/2013/03/05/statement-prime-minister-canada-death-venezuelan-president-hugo-chavez-frias.

OTHER HISTORIC DOCUMENTS OF INTEREST

FROM PREVIOUS *HISTORIC DOCUMENTS*

Kenyan President Remarks on Election; New President Sworn In

MARCH 9 AND APRIL 9, 2013

In 2007, Kenya's presidential election was followed by ethnic clashes that killed 1,400 citizens, something political leaders and international observers sought to avoid in the March 2013 election. The two 2013 front runners, Uhuru Kenyatta and Raila Odinga, appealed to their supporters to respect the electoral process and refrain from using violence. Still, armed political gangs threatened to upend the peaceful democratic process, but in the end little violence was reported. Kenyatta was ultimately victorious, becoming the nation's youngest president. His vision for the country is founded on improving the economic vitality of all citizens by expanding Kenya's position in the global marketplace. Whether he can achieve this will be based in part on how the International Criminal Court (ICC) rules in the case against Kenyatta, who was charged with crimes against humanity following the 2007 election.

HISTORY OF ELECTION VIOLENCE

Kenya has a long history of ethnic tension, and since its independence from Great Britain in 1963, the nation's leaders have struggled to balance the interests of competing factions. The country's constitution has been changed at least thirty times, each giving more and more power to the executive, who has generally used the position to benefit himself. The police force has long been corrupt and has worked on behalf of the president to suppress any vocal opposition. Feeling powerless, citizens are often swayed to join ethnic militias and political gangs who threaten or kill their opponents.

The violence came to a head during the 2007 presidential election in which Odinga challenged incumbent Mwai Kibaki. In a majority of opinion polls taken before the vote and as the early votes were tallied, Odinga appeared to be in the lead. Two days after the December 27 election, Odinga declared victory. But on December 30, the election commission announced that Kibaki had closed the gap and had in fact won the election by more than 200,000 votes. Shortly after the announcement, the chairman of the election commission admitted that he remained unsure of who had actually won. The results stood, however, and protests began almost immediately. Kibaki ordered the police to crack down on Odinga supporters. Both sides accused each other of being responsible for the violence, and at one point the justice minister accused Odinga of planning ethnic cleansing, a claim Odinga vehemently denied.

In the aftermath of the 2007 election, up to 1,400 Kenyans were killed, many beheaded or burned alive, while another 600,000 were displaced. The Waki Commission, an international group charged with conducting an inquiry into postelection violence, reported that in various instances, extreme measures were taken by either side to harm its opponents. In one instance, the Commission reported, "mattresses and blankets were set ablaze with petrol and thrown into the building, while mothers and babies who were trying to flee the inferno were pushed back into the church . . . men attempting to defend their church and loved ones were hacked to death with machetes, shot with arrows, or pursued and killed."

In February 2008, in an effort to end the violence and install a credible government, former UN Secretary General Kofi Annan brokered a power sharing agreement between Odinga and Kibaki in which Odinga would assume the newly created position of prime minister. The violence relented, and in 2010, a new constitution was drafted that decentralized the political system, taking a significant amount of power away from both the president and local political leaders in favor of a system of checks and balances.

Citizens and Ethnic Gangs Prepare for Election

From the outset, the 2013 election had two clear front runners: Odinga and Kenyatta, a member of the Kikuyu, Kenya's largest ethnic group and son of Jomo Kenyatta who led the nation to independence and was the first postcolonization leader. At the time of the election, Uhuru Kenyatta was awaiting a court date to stand trial before the ICC, accused of crimes against humanity during the 2007 election.

Given the history of election violence, prior to the March vote, Kenyan citizens, specifically those in the areas hardest hit in 2007, like the slums of Nairobi, began moving their valuables and family members to safe houses outside the city. Wealthy residents of Nairobi increased security or left the city altogether. Charity organizations and embassies operating in Kenya encouraged expatriates to leave the region before the election.

The caution was not without warrant. Political gang members were reported to be buying machetes in bulk and they distributed hate pamphlets in a variety of cities. The Kikuyu militia reportedly sent a letter to Kenya's chief justice admitting to causing the 2007 election violence and noting that the group was better armed than today. International experts said the best way to avoid postelection violence would be for the loser to accept defeat or file a petition with the courts rather than encouraging his supporters to take to the streets, as occurred in 2007.

Kenyatta Victorious

Although the Kenyan central election commission announced a forty-eight-hour turnaround on the vote tally following the March 4 election, technical difficulties delayed the announcement until March 9. Kenyatta was victorious, earning 50.07 percent of the vote to Odinga's 43.31 percent. "We celebrate the triumph of democracy; the triumph of peace; the triumph of nationhood," the president-elect said after the results were announced. "Despite the misgivings of many in the world, we demonstrated a level of political maturity that surpassed expectations." Outgoing president Kibaki praised Kenyans for conducting the election in a peaceful manner. "I heartily commend you for exhibiting a great degree of tolerance and patience. . . . The peaceful conducting of elections is a victory for Kenya," Kibaki said.

Odinga immediately promised to challenge the results with the nation's high court, saying, "We are confident that the court will restore the faith of Kenyans in the democratic role." On March 16, Odinga, along with various civil society organizations, filed a petition calling for a new election. The court issued its ruling on March 30, as Odinga and Kenyatta supporters clashed with police and each other outside the municipal building. In the end, the court upheld the election results and Odinga promised to honor the court's decision. "Although we may not agree with some of [the court's] findings, our belief in constitutionalism remains supreme," Odinga said. Following the ruling, Kenyatta appealed for calm: "I want to assure all Kenyans . . . that my government will work with and serve all Kenyans without any discrimination whatsoever." He continued, "Above all, let us continue to pray for peace in our country."

Compared to the 2007 election, the 2013 vote was relatively peaceful, with only a handful of reports of injury or death. A number of voting irregularities were noted by Kenya's Election Observers Group and other independent election monitors in the country, including unlisted voters being allowed to cast ballots and the secrecy of votes being compromised. Hundreds of thousands of votes were thrown out because they were considered invalid due to the way they were marked. Overall, international election observers maintained that the vote was largely credible.

There was some indication that Kenyatta's indictment may have been what carried him to victory. African nations largely believe the ICC unfairly targets their leaders while ignoring Western nations. "Kenya sent a loud message to the ICC," said Ayo Johnson, director of ViewPoint Africa, an African-focused media group. "Don't interfere. And it does not matter if you brand our leaders as criminals."

CHALLENGES FOR THE NEW LEADER

The biggest challenge facing Kenyatta is Kenya's economy. It is East Africa's largest economy, but annual economic growth had stalled. Still, Kenya has a diversified economy and desires to become a middle-class nation, mainly by harnessing its regional power as a vital trade route.

How any economic growth trickles down to citizens will be critical to Kenyatta's hold on power. Kenyans have been frustrated by past elections, recognizing that candidates differ little from each other and mainly desire profiting from the country's resources as citizens in the slums grow increasingly impoverished. Economic disparity tends to favor the Kikuyu, a holdover from British occupation that placed most economic development and investment along the Mombasa-Kisumu Railway, a majority Kikuyu area. Kenyatta has promised to increase wealth across the board rather than favoring his own political group as have past leaders.

To begin facing the country's economic challenge, Kenyatta promised to ramp up work on Vision 2030, an economic development program started in 2008. Vision 2030 diversifies the means through which all Kenyans can improve their economic livelihoods. This includes access to education and health care, vocational training, and lines of credit to encourage small business growth. Kenya intends to work with its regional and international partners to encourage investment in its small businesses, while subsequently strengthening its manufacturing sector to add value to exported raw materials. In his inaugural address on April 9, Kenyatta noted the importance of achieving the Vision 2030 goals in curbing ethnic unrest. "National unity will only be possible if we deal decisively with some of the issues that continue to hinder our progress. It will come through job creation. It will be founded on economic growth. It will be strengthened by a globally competitive education system," Kenyatta said.

Some portions of Vision 2030 were already in the works before Kenyatta was elected, and it has shown some promise. For example, a program that made primary school free for all children means that 90 percent of those eligible are now enrolled. Less than one third of roads are now considered in disrepair, as compared to more than two thirds in 2003. But while these indicators are positive signs, job creation will be paramount to seeing the rest of the program through. A large portion of Kenya's youth are well educated, but there is a minimal amount of work requiring skilled laborers.

Questions remain about how Kenyatta's hold on power may be threatened while he stands trial, along with his running mate, at the ICC for crimes against humanity. Although Kenyatta agreed to follow through with the trial, the evidence used to bring charges against him has been frequently called into question, and a number of the militia members who were due to testify against Kenyatta have gone missing and are presumed dead. In October, the ICC announced that it would delay the start of the trial until February 2014 to allow the defense more time to develop its case. The outcome of the trial is widely believed to be an important step toward overcoming the mistrust of government that has been pervasive since the 2007 election.

The ongoing trial also brings into question foreign investment, because many countries have policies against funding efforts in nations on trial in The Hague. Western investment in Kenya is hugely important in the effort to find and root out radical Islamists in Africa, and Kenya serves as an important buffer to Sudan and Somalia. International experts believe that if the West fails to deliver continued economic support to the nation, countries like China are poised to gain a foothold. Prior to the vote, Johnnie Carson, the Assistant Secretary of State for African Affairs, made clear his distaste for Kenyatta, noting that while Kenyans can choose their own president, "choices have consequences." However, following Kenyatta's victory, Secretary of State John Kerry said, "We . . . will continue to be a strong friend and ally of the Kenyan people."

—Heather Kerrigan

Following is the text of a statement delivered on March 9, 2013, by outgoing Kenyan President Mwai Kibaki on the presidential election; and a statement on April 9, 2013, by new Kenyan President Uhuru Kenyatta on his inauguration and swearing in.

DOCUMENT

Outgoing Kenyan President on Election Results

MARCH 9, 2013

Fellow Kenyans,

Let me first thank you most sincerely for the peaceful manner in which you conducted yourselves in the just concluded general elections. I thank God for seeing us through one of the most diverse and intense general election in our nations [sic] history.

I heartily commend you for exhibiting a great degree of tolerance and patience. I thank you for heeding to my call that we should conduct ourselves in a manner that shows that our democracy has come of age. The peaceful conducting of elections is a victory for Kenya.

By casting your votes you exercised your democratic right and lived up to your date with destiny. Across our country we have a new crop of leaders who will see to it that we have functional governments at both the county and national levels.

I congratulate all the newly elected leaders. I challenge them to begin the work of serving our people in earnest. Indeed, there are high expectations and a lot of work that lies ahead. That is why every part of this Country must benefit from the governance system that our new constitution has ushered in.

I thank all candidates for urging for peace. Your country still needs you and I am confident that you will continue serving our nation with the enthusiastic zeal that you have always exhibited. My best wishes also go to all those who fought a good battle in the Presidential election.

After the elections, let us all embrace one another in the spirit of one Kenya one nation. Let us immediately get down to the work of entrenching the economic, social and democratic gains that our nation has made.

To Honourable Uhuru Kenyatta who has been declared President Elect by the IEBC, I express my most sincere congratulations. I wish him best wishes, success and God's blessings in the noble duty of governing our great country.

My passionate appeal is that all the new leaders quickly begin the journey of uniting our people and mobilizing resources for the prosperity of our united nation.

I commend the entire Independent Electoral and Boundaries Commission, led by the Chairman Mr. Isaac Hassan for their diligence and commitment. I also salute our security officials and public servants for their vigilance, hard work and sacrifice.

On my part, I commit myself to the management of a smooth transition to the new leadership that the Kenyan people have placed in office. We have credible institutions that should deal with any matter that may have arisen during the electoral process. In the meantime, I appeal to Kenyans to be peaceful and calm and allow for any disputes that may have arisen to be resolved within the legal mechanism.

Once again thank you all and God Bless you and our great country.

SOURCE: Office of the President of the Republic of Kenya. "Statement By His Excellency the President, Hon. Mwai Kibaki, CGH, MP, Following Announcement of Election Results By the Independent Electoral and Boundaries Commission (IEBC)." March 9, 2013. http://www.statehousekenya.go.ke/speeches/kibaki/march2013/2013090301.htm.

New Kenyan President Delivers Inaugural Address

April 9, 2013

Your Excellency Hon. Mwai Kibaki, C.G.H., M.P.;
Your Excellency Daniel arap Moi;
Your Excellencies, Visiting Heads of State & Government;
Chief Justice Willy Mutunga;
All our Invited Guests;
Fellow Kenyans,

Let me begin by thanking all Heads of State present and the representatives of Heads of State for choosing to be here as a symbol of your continued support and goodwill towards Kenyans.

I particularly note, with gratitude, the large presence of our brothers and sisters from across the continent. This is a clear indication of your commitment to the Pan-African agenda. You have bestowed a great honor on me and our country by being here. On behalf of the Kenyan people I welcome all of you to Kenya. Karibuni Sana!

Let me also acknowledge with gratitude and respect the distinguished service of my predecessors. President Mwai Kibaki, a true statesman and a great leader who over the past 10 years has laid a firm foundation for the future prosperity of our country. Asante sana Mzee. Shukrani nyingi sana.

I pay tribute also to former President Moi who is with us today and thank him for his years of leadership and dedication to our nation. Asante Mzee!

With humility and respect, I acknowledge and pay tribute to the memory of my father, the late founding father of our nation, Mzee Jomo Kenyatta. May he and his fellow architects of liberation in Kenya and Africa as a whole rest in peace with the knowledge that this generation is committed to fulfilling their dreams for our nation and our continent.

I would like to thank all my worthy opponents in the recently completed presidential election. Every one of you helped define and make stronger our democracy. Because of you, Kenyans had real choices. Because of you, Kenyans felt free to exercise their sovereign will. Thank you all.

In an open and free democracy, there is a vital role for a vibrant opposition that helps to hold the Government to account. Kenya is such a democracy, and as President I will respect that role just as I will champion the right of every Kenyan to speak their mind free of fear of reprisal or condemnation.

Fellow Kenyans,

Our nation has now successfully navigated the most complex general election in our history. Our journey began three years ago, with the promulgation of a new constitution, and ended eleven days ago, with a landmark Supreme Court decision. Ours has been an unusual story. An unconventional path. We have been praised and criticized in turn—depending on who was telling our story. Yet while some watched the unfolding national events with skepticism, resigned to what they believed was the inevitability of chaos, others, the vast majority, looked upon our nation with a tempered hope; cheering us on not only because they believed in us but because they knew that if Kenya succeeded they too would succeed. For all that has been said of our nation, the records of history will attest to a number of undeniable facts.

They will outline the long queues we made, the long hours we waited to vote and the historic voter turnout of these elections. They will detail the decisions that the Kenyan media made—the professionalism and responsibility with which they acted. They will remind us of the fact that we embarked on a feat that few other countries have attempted, holding six elections simultaneously. They will call our attention to the fact that the youth were meaningfully engaged in the entire electoral period and that the political consciousness of Kenyans was at an all time high. They will list and honor the individuals, institutions and service organizations that played a strong role in this defining chapter of our nation's history. They will contrast our accomplishments, with the fact that Kenya ventured into multi-party politics only 20 years ago further strengthening and entrenching our democracy. When the records remind us of these truths, we will recognize that at the end of the day, it is the indomitable spirit of the Kenyan people; their commitment to peace; their desire for progress and their respect for the rule of law—that was the true headline of this election story.

Where systems failed, Kenyans did not. Where decisions were delayed and ambiguity prevailed, Kenyans were patient—seeking and waiting for clarity. Where contentious issues arose to stir up dissent, Kenyans exercised restraint; peacefully sought redress and submitted themselves again to the constitution and the rule of law—united in the belief that God's judgment would guide that of men.

Today, I am humbled and honouredhonoured [sic] to accept the mantle of leadership that the people of Kenya have bestowed on me. I will lead all Kenyans—those who voted for me—and those who voted for our competitors—towards a national prosperity that is firmly rooted in a rich and abiding peace in which unity can ultimately be realized. Peace is not simply about the absence of violence. It is defined by the presence of fundamental liberties and the prevalence of economic opportunities. We will not settle for a perfunctory peace that is disrupted every five years by an election cycle. Rather, we are calling and working towards a permanent peace, through which democracy is glorified rather than undermined. A peace that fosters unity.

Indeed, national unity will only be possible if we deal decisively with some of the issues that continue to hinder our progress. It will come through job creation. It will be founded on economic growth. It will be strengthened by a globally competitive education system: by the building of more schools across the nation and by ensuring that we have well thought out curricula that prepares our children for the challenges and opportunities of the 21st century. It will be upheld when all citizens are able to access affordable healthcare and protect themselves, and their children, from preventable diseases that still wage war on our populace. It will be strengthened through the promotion of public-private partnerships and through the creation of a friendly and enabling environment for business. It will be reflected in our men and women working side by side as equals to move our country forward. It will be realized when we become a food-secure nation by investing in and modernizing the agricultural sector by equipping it with the relevant information and technology that it needs to grow. It will be confirmed when the rights of all citizens are protected through legislation that upholds the spirit of our constitution. When women and young people are both seen and heard at the decision-making table, at national as well as devolved levels of government. When all communities in Kenya are confident that they have a Government that listens to and addresses their needs.

Achieving peace and strengthening unity will be the goal of my Government. This work begins now. We welcome all Kenyans to hold us to account. Within the first one hundred days—we will ensure that maternity fees are abolished and that all citizens of Kenya are able to access government dispensaries and health centers free of charge. Within the first one hundred days, we will develop a framework to direct the 6 billion Kenya Shillings previously allocated for the election run-off towards establishing a new Youth and Women Fund that will be open to the youth and women from every part of this country. Within the first one hundred days, we will put measures in place to ensure that all students, joining class one next year, within the public school system receive a laptop. We made a promise to our children and we will keep it because we believe that early exposure to technology will inspire future innovation and be a catalyst for growth and prosperity.

Fellow Kenyans,

My government will immediately begin the process of supporting devolution and enabling county leadership to carry out their constitutional mandate and fulfill the pledges they made to the Kenyan people. Let us all be clear—supporting devolution is not a choice, as some claim it to be—it is a duty. A constitutional duty. One that I have sworn to uphold. Our constitution does not suggest devolution, it demands it. I urge all Kenyans to be persistent, pragmatic, patient and non-partisan, as we pursue the promise of devolved governance.

Fellow Kenyans,

Dealing with unemployment will be a priority for my government. We are committed to creating jobs and opportunities for our people—especially our young people. We will do this, by creating an enabling environment for the private sector. We will harness the gifts and talents of our youth, in order to make sports and entertainment providers of profitable livelihood and to make Kenya a global leader in these areas. We will make the procurement process faster, more accessible, and transparent. We will simplify the process of starting and running a business, in order to make it friendly and cost-effective to do business in Kenya. We will expand electricity generation, extend the transmission network and ensure that electricity supply is more consistent and reliable. We will build on the accomplishments of the last administration in infrastructure, by increasing accessibility through roads and rail networks, as well as increasing digital connectivity. To the private sector, my promise to you is that we will create an enabling environment, so that you can play your part in creating employment and fostering economic growth.

Fellow Kenyans,

For too long our nation has exported jobs that should rightly belong to our citizens. We have focused on exporting primary products, instead of promoting value addition and manufacturing finished goods thereby creating jobs and improving our standard of living. Today, I pledge, that my administration will work towards diversifying our economic base. We will support the manufacturing industry and support all enterprises, both local and international, that strive to create finished goods using local labour and materials. I also pledge, that this Government, as the largest buyer of goods and services will take the lead in supporting local industry, by buying Kenyan first.

I have consulted with Parliament and on the 16th of April, I will address both Houses and announce a detailed government program and legislative agenda.

Fellow Kenyans,

One of the biggest challenges to national unity is the feeling of exclusion in the decision making process, hence our desire and need for devolution. That notwithstanding, my commitment to Kenya is that our national Government shall and will reflect the true face of Kenya, with the clear understanding that as we bring decision making and services closer to the people, the integrity and solidarity that binds us as citizens of one nation, must not only remain, but must be strengthened.

I am equally committed to ensuring that interests of women, and the interests of young people are represented in my government. A department in my office will be dedicated to ensuring that the interests of these groups not only inform every decision I make as President, but also those of every department and government ministry. Our doors will always be open. We will never turn a deaf ear to the needs of any person or group. We will leave no community behind.

Fellow Kenyans,

To achieve these goals and to achieve Vision 2030, we must be responsible stewards of our natural resources. In light of this—my commitment and the commitment of the Government will be to support the National Land Commission as they seek to provide the land answer. My government will strive to work with all actors to ensure that the issue of land will never again be a contentious or a divisive subject but rather that land will be seen as what it truly is, a factor of production.

I also promise that we will exploit our natural resources in a way that benefits the current generation while safeguarding the interests of generations to come. I want to assure all Kenyans that we shall use all the money that comes from natural resources for development programs.

Fellow Kenyans,

We will ensure that the harmony we are striving for extends to the environment. It is our heritage. It is our duty as guardians and custodians of that heritage to protect it for future generations. Indeed, my government will strike a decisive blow against all those that threaten it. My fellow Kenyans, poaching and the destruction of our environment has no future in this country. The responsibility to protect our environment belongs not just to the Government, but to each and every one of us. We will do all this, and more. Where there is uncertainty, we will revive confidence in the government's ability to protect its citizens. Where there is disillusion—we will restore hope. Where there is opportunity denied—we will open new frontiers, and through our actions, we will renew our faith in government as an instrument of good.

Let me reiterate that even as we work together to promote inclusion, open new frontiers and create new opportunities, we will not tolerate those who continue to threaten the peace and security of our citizens. Criminals, cattle rustlers, drug barons and agents of terror, who disrupt the peace of our society will be met with the full force of the law and the strength of Kenya's Security Forces. On this matter, we are resolute.

To our men and women in uniform, I say, this nation is indebted to you. You continue to lay down your lives in service, protecting Kenyans from threats both external and internal. My government will continue to work with you and do all that is in its power to support you as you continue in your noble duty.

To our sister countries in the region—we understand that our future is joined to yours. Our peace is linked to the security and stability of the region. We deployed our armed forces to Somalia because terrorism and piracy affects all of us. Indeed in the last two decades, Kenya has invested immense diplomatic energy and resources in the quest for a stable Somalia. Our commitment to fight terrorism and eradicate piracy will remain a central pillar of my government's policy on peace and security.

As President, I will work with, the international community to strengthen its support for IGAD and the AU peace process in Somalia because a stable and prosperous Somalia is in the interest of all nations.

My fellow Kenyans,

The future of Kenya depends not only on our National Unity but also on deepening our bonds with our brothers and sisters in East Africa and Africa as a whole. It is with this unity that we will prosper and truly deliver on the promise of independence and liberation from our colonial past. My administration is therefore committed to regional trade and cooperation and will continue to strengthen ties through the free movement of people, goods and investment, including the removal of tariff and non-tariff barriers to trade within the EAC. My goal is to see the continued growth of our community towards ultimate integration.

As Kenya celebrates its Jubilee year of freedom and independence, Africa too marks slightly over 50 years since the fall of colonialism. The breakaway from colonialism has not been easy. Indeed it has been fraught with great challenges and setbacks. Without fail however, the trajectory of our recent history, in Kenya as in Africa, has been one of great hope, renewed progress and palpable determination. Africa, Ladies and Gentlemen, is on the rise. Kenya sees herself as an integral part of this exciting awakening. The great renaissance spoken of a mere 20 years ago is upon us. Across the continent evidence of renewal and growth is everywhere, built on the bedrock of rising self-confidence, a growing educated, youthful population and God given abundance of natural wealth and resources.

To the Nations of Africa and The African Union—we assure you that in Kenya, you will continue to have a partner and an ally. If we stand together in solidarity I am confident that we will find the strength to thrive and innovate solutions that work for us. Of course, we join you in continuing to insist on relating with all nations as equals—not juniors.

As partners, not subordinates. In our history as nations, we have seen some of the most ardent promoters of ideals of national sovereignty and democracy sometimes fail to live by the principles they espouse, but let us remember that their failure does not justify ours.

To the nations of the world—we acknowledge that in this age of globalization, all of us are interdependent. Our economies are interconnected as indeed are our people. I pledge to continue cultivating the relationships we have had with our traditional partners and I say to all developing and developed nations who desire a deeper and more mutually beneficial relationship with Kenya: we are ready for partnerships, we are open for business and we invite you to invest in our country. I also want to remind the International Community that for the last fifty years, Kenya has been one of the most engaged members and one of the most prolific co-authors of international treaties and instruments.

I assure you again that under my leadership, Kenya will strive to uphold our international obligations, so long as these are founded on the well-established principles of mutual respect and reciprocity.

Central to our continued contribution to the international community, will be the understanding that the world is made up of many countries, cultures, political experiences and world-views. We must remember that no one country or group of countries should have control or monopoly on international institutions or the interpretation of international treaties. While each state has a right to its own view, it must respect the fact that it holds just one view amongst many in the community of nations.

Fellow Kenyans,

Today, work begins. The time has come, not to ask what community we come from but rather what dreams we share. The time has come not to ask what political party we belong to but rather what partnerships we can build.

The time has come to ask, not who we voted for, but what future we are devoted to. Fellow Kenyans we must move forward together. Let us remember that although we are may [sic] not be bound together by ethnicity, or cultural practices or religious conviction—our kinship rests solidly upon the fact that we have all been adopted by Kenya's borders; we are all children of this nation, we are all bound to one constitution which calls us to rise above our individual ideologies and march to our national anthem.

That anthem reminds us of the fundamental principles upon which our prosperity must be built. It calls us to reflect on the power of peace; to the dignity that results from hard work, and to contend for the hope that justice brings.

Brother and sisters; Fellow Kenyans—let us move forward, together, in the spirit of our anthem and in the spirit of our constitution being confident that if we turn neither to the left nor to the right of our national values, we, as a people, will see the promised land of prosperity that our forbearers set out for.

God bless you, God bless the Republic of Kenya and God bless Africa.

SOURCE: Official Website of the President of the Republic of Kenya. "SPEECH BY H.E. HON. UHURU KENYATTA, C.G.H., PRESIDENT AND COMMANDER-IN-CHIEF OF THE DEFENCE FORCES OF THE REPUBLIC OF KENYA DURING HIS INAUGURATION AND SWEARING-IN CEREMONY ON TUESDAY, 9TH APRIL 2013 AT THE MOI INTERNATIONAL SPORTS COMPLEX, NAIROBI." April 9, 2013. http://www.statehousekenya.go.ke/speeches/uhuru/april2013/2013090401.htm.

OTHER HISTORIC DOCUMENTS OF INTEREST

FROM THIS VOLUME

FROM PREVIOUS *HISTORIC DOCUMENTS*

Eurogroup Responds to Cyprus Crisis

MARCH 16 AND MARCH 25, 2013

The eastern Mediterranean island of Cyprus was the focus of world attention in March 2013 when it teetered on the brink of bankruptcy. Following a series of frantic, tense meetings between Cypriot, EU, and International Monetary Fund (IMF) officials, a deal was cobbled together to prevent a financial meltdown of the country. In return for providing €10 billion ($13 billion) in rescue aid—€9 billion from the EU and €1 billion from the IMF—Cyprus agreed to wind up its second largest bank, undertake a raft of painful economic reforms, raise taxes, and lower public spending. The deal was a relative success in economic terms, notably rescuing Cyprus from crashing out of the eurozone, the EU's single currency area. But it left a bitter aftertaste, especially the provisions that require depositors in Cypriot banks—many of them wealthy Russians—to take a big financial hit.

CRISIS IN INFLATED BANK CENTER

The immediate impetus for the Cypriot debt crisis was the severe financial loss the country incurred in early 2012 as a result of the big debt write-downs its neighbor Greece obtained as part of the latter's second bailout deal from the European Union and IMF in early 2012. However, some of the problems by which Cyprus found itself beset were of its own making. The country had inflated its bank sector to dangerous levels, sucking up capital from around the world to the point where the banks were valued at eight times the country's overall economy. It did this by offering interest rates on deposits several percentage points higher than its competitors in other eurozone countries. This turned it into a magnet for rich Russian entrepreneurs wishing to park their money. The return on deposits was so high that some observers argued that depositors in Cypriot banks were really more investors than they were savers. Rumors swirled about the source of that Russian money, with allegations stating that some of it was the proceeds of dubious activities.

All this activity occurred in the Greek Cypriot-populated southern part of the island whose administration is the internationally recognized government. There remains a separatist enclave in northern Cyprus where Turkish Cypriots live, which has been heavily guarded by troops from Turkey since the latter invaded the island in 1974. The United Nations brokered an agreement to reunify the island in 2004, but the Greek Cypriots rejected it in a referendum. Thus, when Cyprus joined the European Union weeks later, only the Greek Cypriot portion of the island enjoyed the benefits of EU membership. Cyprus adopted the euro as its currency in 2008, making the country a more attractive destination for depositors. While Cyprus accounted for a mere 0.2 percent of the eurozone economy, since the euro is so new—introduced into circulation in 2002—EU political leaders were determined to keep Cyprus inside to shore up confidence in the euro.

INITIAL DEAL REACHED

Since the EU's sovereign debt crisis began in 2010, many bailouts had been cobbled together by the European Union and IMF. Greece received €110 billion in May 2010 and a further €130 billion in February 2012; Ireland's bailout, approved in November 2010, was worth €85 billion; Portugal's April 2012 package amounted to €78 billion; and Spain was granted a €100 billion credit line in 2012 for its troubled banking sector, €41 billion of which it actually used. With its financial situation worsening day by day, the Cypriot government decided to apply for a bailout in June 2012. However, the government at the time was led by communists, which made it harder to forge an agreement on the terms of the bailout because it was reluctant to embrace the so-called austerity policies demanded by the European Union.

The political landscape changed following parliamentary and presidential elections in January and February 2013, which resulted in a right-wing government replacing the communists. The new leadership made an agreement with the European Union on March 16 under which the other sixteen eurozone governments agreed to provide a €10 billion lifeline to Cyprus. The price extracted for this was high. A one-off "stability levy" was to be applied to resident and nonresident depositors at a rate of 9.9 percent for deposits above €100,000 and 6.75 percent for deposits below €100,000. The President of the Eurogroup (the Eurogroup is comprised of the meetings of euro area finance ministers), Jeroen Dijsselbloem, who is also a Dutch finance minister, said at the time, "It seems just to ask a contribution of all deposit holders." In addition, capital gains tax rates were to be increased, the corporate tax rate was to go up from 10 percent to 12.5 percent, and bondholders and shareholders in Cyprus' second biggest bank, Laiki, were to incur major losses as part of a "bail-in" deal to shut it down. And a €2.5 billion loan from Russia was to have its maturity extended and interest rates lowered.

The agreement triggered outrage in Cyprus, particularly the clause requiring even smaller depositors to take a financial hit. Cypriots immediately rushed to cash dispensers to remove what funds they could, causing Cypriot banks to close their doors to prevent a run on their deposits. The banks would stay closed for an unprecedented ten days. The Cypriot parliament roundly rejected the deal, and even the government's party refused to vote in favor. In Russia, meanwhile, anger was vented over the high levy being applied to the large depositors, because many of them were Russian.

As fears grew that Cyprus was going to exit the eurozone and slide into bankruptcy, the political leaders went back to the drawing board and put together a more politically palatable deal. On March 25, a day before the European Central Bank (ECB) was set to pull the plug on Cyprus by withdrawing its emergency aid, an agreement was reached on a revised bailout. The most important change made was to exempt depositors of under €100,000 from the stability levy. Welcoming this change, the EU Commissioner responsible for regulating financial services, Michel Barnier, said the €100,000 guarantee should never be questioned. He was referring to an existing EU law that is supposed to protect smaller depositors in cases where banks fail. To compensate for the change, larger depositors, shareholders, and bondholders had to take a bigger hit to make up the €13 billion that Cyprus was asked to come up with in return for the EU-IMF €10 billion package.

Painful public sector reforms were also tacked onto the deal, details of which were finalized on April 2. These included job cuts in the public sector; tax increases; privatizations of electricity and telecommunications companies, the port authority, and government real estate; and caps on wage increases. EU Economic and Monetary Affairs

Commissioner, Olli Rehn, said, "The near future will be very difficult for the country and its people. But [the measures] will be necessary for the Cypriot people to rebuild their economy on a new basis." On April 30, the Cypriot parliament approved the deal 29 to 27. A lawmaker opposed to the bailout, Green Party parliamentarian George Perdikis, commented, "A 'yes' from Cyprus' parliament is by far the biggest defeat in our 8,000-year history. Its democratically-elected representatives have a gun to their head to agree to a deal of enslavement."

In May, the European Union gave the green light for disbursing the first installment, €3 billion, of its bailout fund. By the fall of 2013 the Cypriot government was getting positive report cards from the European Union and IMF. The banking sector was in the process of being dramatically downsized, although this in turn was causing the economy to contract by nearly 9 percent in 2013 with a further contraction of nearly 4 percent forecast for 2014. Instead of relying so much on its banking sector, Cyprus was being urged to develop other sectors, such as tourism, or the natural gas deposits that have been discovered off its coastline.

MORE CENTRALIZED EU EMERGES

The Cyprus bailout came in the wider context of a Europe in grave financial crisis and struggling to adapt to having a single currency despite not being a single state. While everyone claimed the Cyprus deal was exceptional, and the Cypriot crisis certainly had its particularities, the gist of the deal the European Union and IMF concluded was similar to earlier ones they forged with Greece, Ireland, Portugal, and Spain. The bailouts represent one piece of a larger package of reforms that the European Union has been relentlessly implementing since 2010, the net effect of which has been to increase the EU's authority over economic and monetary matters, which national sovereignty has been eroding.

For instance, the European Union paid Cyprus out of a new €500 billion fund called the European Stability Mechanism (ESM), which became operational in 2012. The ESM increasingly resembles a kind of intra-EU IMF, having doled out €240 billion over the past three years, far more than the IMF has disbursed over the same period. The EU partnership with the IMF in the bailout negotiations, called "the troika," has come under growing strain. In part this is because the EU's financial contributions now dwarf those of the IMF, so Europeans bristle when IMF officials start instructing them on what policies to adopt. While most observers believe that Cyprus is now on a path to recovery, there is a good likelihood that the ESM will have to put together a third bailout for Greece in 2014 because it remains mired in debt and economic stagnation. And eurozone member Slovenia is struggling financially, too, due to a glut of nonperforming loans, although its problems are less severe than those of Greece, and its government is determined to weather the crisis without seeking a bailout.

The financial crises that Cyprus and others have experience have also resulted in the adoption of much stricter EU-level regulation of banking. The EU's "banking union" legislative package, still a work in progress, will see the ECB assume sweeping authorities to supervise banks. It will require banks to create "bail-in" funds to which bondholders and shareholders will be asked to contribute to avoid taxpayer-funded bailouts. And it will create an EU-wide insurance scheme to guarantee bank deposits up to a certain level. As Cyprus looks like it will avoid becoming the first country to be forced to exit the euro, the eurozone is preparing to welcome its eighteenth member, Latvia, which will join in January 2014. With the eurozone becoming larger in size and more integrated, a question increasingly being asked by international analysts is how tenable a position it is to be an "out"—a country like the United Kingdom or Sweden that is part of the European Union but not the eurozone.

—Brian Beary

Following are two statements from the European Union—the first, dated March 16, 2013, announces the agreement reached with Cyprus to aid in the bailout of its banking sector, and the second, dated March 25, 2013, supersedes the March 16 agreement and exempts certain deposits from having a levy imposed on them.

DOCUMENT

Eurozone Reaches Agreement on Cyprus

March 16, 2013

The Eurogroup welcomes the political agreement reached with the Cypriot authorities on the cornerstones of the policy conditionality underlying a future macroeconomic adjustment programme. The programme will be based on ambitious measures to ensure the stability of the financial sector, determined action to carry out the required fiscal adjustment and structural reforms to support competitiveness as well as sustainable and balanced growth, allowing for the unwinding of macroeconomic imbalances.

The Eurogroup welcomes the Terms of Reference for an independent evaluation of the implementation of the anti-money laundering framework in Cypriot financial institutions, involving Moneyval alongside a private international audit firm, and is reassured that the launch of the audit is imminent. In the event of problems in the implementation of the framework, problems will be corrected as part of the programme conditionality.

The Eurogroup commends the Cypriot authorities on the steps already taken to adopt fiscal measures agreed with the Commission, in liaison with the ECB, and the IMF. This notably concerns the adoption of consolidation measures amounting to 4½% of GDP. The Eurogroup welcomes the Cypriot authorities' commitment to step up efforts in the area of privatization[.]

The Eurogroup further welcomes the Cypriot authorities' commitment to take further measures mobilising internal resources, in order to limit the size of the financial assistance linked to the adjustment programme. These measures include the introduction of an upfront one-off stability levy applicable to resident and non-resident depositors. Further measures concern the increase of the withholding tax on capital income, a restructuring and recapitalisation of banks, an increase of the statutory corporate income tax rate and a bail-in of junior bondholders. The Eurogroup looks forward to an agreement between Cyprus and the Russian Federation on a financial contribution.

The Eurogroup is confident that these initiatives as well as a strict implementation of the agreed policy conditionality will allow Cyprus' public debt, which is projected to reach 100% of GDP in 2020, to remain on a sustainable path and enhance the economy's growth potential. The current fragile situation of the Cypriot financial sector linked to its very large size relative to the country's GDP will be addressed through an appropriate downsizing, with the domestic banking sector reaching the EU average by 2018, thereby ensuring its long-term viability and safeguarding deposits. Moreover, the Eurogroup welcomes that an agreement could be reached on the Greek branches of the Cypriot banks, which protects the stability of both the Greek and the Cypriot banking systems, and does not burden the Greek debt-to-GDP ratio.

Against this background, the Eurogroup considers that—in principle–financial assistance to Cyprus is warranted to safeguard financial stability in Cyprus and the euro area as a whole by providing a financial envelope which has been reduced to up to EUR 10bn. The Eurogroup would welcome a contribution by the IMF to the financing of the programme.

The Eurogroup calls upon the authorities and the Commission, in liaison with the ECB, and the IMF to swiftly finalise the MoU. The Eurogroup will review the programme documentation prepared by the Commission, in liaison with the ECB, and the IMF as well as the ESM once it becomes available. The relevant national procedures required for the approval of the ESM financial assistance facility agreement will be launched.

The Eurogroup expects that the ESM Board of Governors will be in a position to formally approve the proposal for a financial assistance facility agreement by the second half of April 2013 and subject to completion of national procedures.

SOURCE: Eurozone Portal. "Eurogroup Statement on Cyprus." March 16, 2013. http://eurozone.europa .eu/media/402209/Eurogroup%20statement%20CY_final__16%203%202013%20_2_.pdf.

DOCUMENT

Eurogroup Revises Agreement on Cyprus Bailout

March 25, 2013

The Eurogroup has reached an agreement with the Cypriot authorities on the key elements necessary for a future macroeconomic adjustment programme. This agreement is supported by all euro area Member States as well as the three institutions. The Eurogroup fully supports the Cypriot people in these difficult circumstances.

The programme will address the exceptional challenges that Cyprus is facing and restore the viability of the financial sector, with the view of restoring sustainable growth and sound public finances over the coming years.

The Eurogroup welcomes the plans for restructuring the financial sector as specified in the annex. These measures will form the basis for restoring the viability of the financial sector. In particular, they safeguard all deposits below EUR 100.000 in accordance with EU principles.

The programme will contain a decisive approach to addressing financial sector imbalances. There will be an appropriate downsizing of the financial sector, with the domestic banking sector reaching the EU average by 2018. In addition, the Cypriot authorities have reaffirmed their commitment to step up efforts in the areas of fiscal consolidation, structural reforms and privatisation.

The Eurogroup welcomes the Terms of Reference for an independent evaluation of the implementation of the anti-money laundering framework in Cypriot financial institutions, involving Moneyval alongside a private international audit firm, and is reassured that the launch of the audit is imminent. In the event of problems in the implementation of the framework, problems will be corrected as part of the programme conditionality.

The Eurogroup further welcomes the Cypriot authorities' commitment to take further measures. These measures include the increase of the withholding tax on capital income and of the statutory corporate income tax rate. The Eurogroup looks forward to an agreement between Cyprus and the Russian Federation on a financial contribution.

The Eurogroup urges the immediate implementation of the agreement between Cyprus and Greece on the Greek branches of the Cypriot banks, which protects the stability of both the Greek and Cypriot banking systems.

The Eurogroup requests the Cypriot authorities and the Commission, in liaison with the ECB, and the IMF to finalise the MoU at staff level in early April.

The Eurogroup notes the intention of the Cypriot authorities to compensate potential individual victims of fraudulent practices, in line with established legal and judicial procedures, outside the programme.

The Eurogroup takes note of the authorities' decision to introduce administrative measures, appropriate in view of the present unique and exceptional situation of Cyprus' financial sector and to allow for a swift reopening of the banks. The Eurogroup stresses that these administrative measures will be temporary, proportionate and non-discriminatory, and subject to strict monitoring in terms of scope and duration in line with the Treaty.

Against this background, the Eurogroup reconfirms, as stated already on 16 March, that—in principle—financial assistance to Cyprus is warranted to safeguard financial stability in Cyprus and the euro area as a whole by providing financial assistance for an amount of up to EUR 10bn. The Eurogroup would welcome a contribution by the IMF to the financing of the programme. Together with the decisions taken by Cyprus, this results in a fully financed programme which will allow Cyprus' public debt to remain on a sustainable path.

The Eurogroup expects that the ESM Board of Governors will be in a position to formally approve the proposal for a financial assistance facility agreement by the third week of April 2013 subject to the completion of national procedures.

Annex

Following the presentation by the Cyprus authorities of their policy plans, which were broadly welcomed by the Eurogroup, the following was agreed:

1. Laiki will be resolved immediately—with full contribution of equity shareholders, bond holders and uninsured depositors—based on a decision by the Central Bank of Cyprus, using the newly adopted Bank Resolution Framework.

2. Laiki will be split into a good bank and a bad bank. The bad bank will be run down over time.

3. The good bank will be folded into Bank of Cyprus (BoC), using the Bank Resolution Framework, after having heard the Boards of Directors of BoC and Laiki. It will take 9 bn Euros of ELA with it. Only uninsured deposits in BoC will remain frozen until recapitalisation has been effected, and may subsequently be subject to appropriate conditions.

4. The Governing Council of the ECB will provide liquidity to the BoC in line with applicable rules.

5. BoC will be recapitalised through a deposit/equity conversion of uninsured deposits with full contribution of equity shareholders and bond holders.

6. The conversion will be such that a capital ratio of 9% is secured by the end of the programme.

7. All insured depositors in all banks will be fully protected in accordance with the relevant EU legislation.

8. The programme money (up to 10bn Euros) will not be used to recapitalise Laiki and Bank of Cyprus.

The Eurogroup is convinced that this solution is the best way forward for ensuring the overall viability and stability of the Cyprus financial system and its capability to finance the Cyprus economy.

SOURCE: Eurozone Portal. "Eurogroup Statement on Cyprus." March 25, 2013. http://eurozone.europa .eu/media/404933/EG%20EG%20Statement%20on%20CY%2025%2003%202013.pdf.

OTHER HISTORIC DOCUMENTS OF INTEREST

FROM THIS VOLUME

- European Union Officials on the Addition of Croatia to the EU, p. 341

FROM PREVIOUS *HISTORIC DOCUMENTS*

- European Central Bank Cuts Rates to Record Low, *2012*, p. 320
- European Leaders Agree to New Greek Bailout, *2012*, p. 113
- European Union Agrees to Fiscal Compact, *2011*, p. 656
- European Union Leaders Reach Deal to Save Greece From Financial Collapse, *2011*, p. 397
- EU and IMF Help Stabilize Ireland's Banking System, *2010*, p. 583
- Europeans Protest Austerity Measures and EU Monetary Policy, *2010*, p. 522
- Greek Financial Crisis, *2010*, p. 201
- European Commission President on the "Euro," *1998*, p. 271

April

Iraq Conducts Elections Amid Tenuous Security Environment

APRIL 16 AND 20, 2013

On April 20, 2013, Iraqis went to the polls to choose the representatives for their provincial councils in the first election since U.S. troop withdrawal in 2011. More than 8,100 candidates vied for 447 seats, and did so under the threat of violence from rival candidates and extremist groups, as the level of sectarian violence grew to its highest level in years. The results of the election were noted as an indication of the local level of support for Prime Minister Nouri al-Maliki and his Shiite government. The international community indicated that it will continue closely watching the security situation in Iraq, especially leading up to the April 2014 parliamentary election.

VIOLENCE INCREASES AHEAD OF ELECTION

In the run-up to the first elections being held in Iraq since American troops withdrew in 2011, candidates and their supporters were attacked in increasing numbers. On April 6, a deadly civilian attack took place in a tent in Baquba where a Sunni political rally for the party Azimon was taking place. Two bombs went off, killing twenty and injuring at least fifty of those present. Four candidates were wounded in the attack. Iraqiya, a non-secular political party formed during the 2010 elections, blamed the government's security forces for failing to protect civilians and candidates. "In spite of the repeated targeting, we have not seen any precautionary measures taken to limit the attacks," said group spokesperson Rahim al-Shimari. Muhammed al-Hadlushi, the head of Azimon who was hurt in the April 6 bombing, said his party would not be deterred. "This will not stop us from participating in the election, as we have a message and we will continue with it," he said. The attacks made Iraqi citizens fearful of attending political rallies or even turning out to vote. "Killing candidates means instilling fear," said Hameed Fadhil, a political science professor at Baghdad University. He added that the violence would likely affect turnout, saying, "I don't think that people will want to risk their lives again."

In Anbar and Nineveh provinces, where the preelection violence was centered, the government postponed the vote by two months, citing security concerns. Politicians and citizens in the region criticized the decision, noting that Iraqi elections had always taken place under the threat of violence, and called the delay a tactic by the Shiite-dominated government to prevent Sunnis, who are a minority in the country and oppose the central government, from being elected. "There is killing every day in Iraq," said Jaber al-Jabouri, a leader of the Iraqiya party and Member of Parliament. U.S. Secretary of State John Kerry also criticized the delay imposed on the two provinces and appealed to Maliki to reverse the decision. Maliki declined to do so.

By mid-April, just weeks before the election, at least fifteen Sunni candidates had been assassinated, while others were kidnapped or threatened with death if they did not withdraw from the race. While some of those behind the attacks were rival political parties, Iraqi officials said the attacks bore the hallmarks of al Qaeda in Mesopotamia. The group targets both Shiites as well as Sunnis who support the Shiite government or choose to participate in politics.

Officials for the Independent High Electoral Commission, the body that oversees elections in Iraq, said that the run-up to the 2013 election was marked by more violence than the two previous votes—the 2010 parliamentary and 2009 provincial elections. The security situation was being closely monitored abroad as international analysts wondered whether the Iraqi government could hold a safe, credible election without international assistance.

NEW PROVINCIAL GOVERNMENTS SEATED

Despite the violence experienced prior to the election, on April 20, most Iraqis cast their ballots in relative calm. Some mortar attacks and explosions that resulted in injury were reported, but no major attacks occurred. This evidenced that the country might have some control over its electoral process.

Only slightly more than 50 percent of those eligible turned out to vote, a rate on par with previous elections. While some declared it their duty to vote, others, like Haider al-Mutairy, an Iraqi lawyer, represented the Iraqi public's disenchantment with the problems of the fledgling democracy and its leaders. "I will not be fooled again," he told *The New York Times*. "Nothing changed after I participated in the last elections. My street is still broken and filled with dirt, the electricity and water is still bad, and the terrorists are doing whatever they want."

How effective these new provincial governments will be is up for debate. Those who did vote were reportedly swayed by candidates who gave them calling cards in exchange for a promise sworn on the Koran to cast a favorable vote. Paying for votes, coupled with the threat of death or injury to candidates, raised questions about whether the most qualified were running for office.

The results also rekindled the debate about Maliki's government. The power-sharing agreement that put Maliki in power was intended to give minority Sunnis and Kurds an equal voice in the government. However, much to the dismay of the United States, Maliki has consolidated his power, perhaps most notably that which he holds over the security forces, and marginalized dissent. The way in which the government is currently defined has also led to gridlock and a relative inability to move forward on a variety of pressing issues. Maliki has at times indicated a desire to reform the government to be entirely Shiite-dominated, and his party's showing in the most recent election will certainly give credence to his plans, especially if an increase in power will solidify his victory in the 2014 national election.

DEADLIEST MONTH

In early April, before the election took place, the United Nations raised concerns regarding the security situation in Iraq. According to data from the UN Assistance Mission in Iraq (UNAMI), more than 200 civilians were killed and 800 were wounded in March. These acts of terrorism and armed violence also killed 227 Iraqi security force members and injured 300 more. On April 6, in yet another condemnation of the attacks, the Chief

Human Rights Officer for UNAMI, Francesco Motta, said, "The United Nations deplores the continuing loss of civilian life resulting from acts of terrorism and armed conflict."

One month later, the United Nations marked the deadliest month in Iraq since 2006–2007. In May, more than 1,000 people were killed, which the UN envoy to Baghdad, Martin Kobler, called "a sad record." He added, "Iraqi political leaders must act immediately to stop this intolerable bloodshed." The violence targeted Sunni and Shiite communities in large cities like Baghdad, where locals have responded by closing stores early and staying away from public gathering spots. For his part, Maliki has appealed to Sunnis to work with local militias to fight the militants, but Sunnis have remained wary of such an idea because they despise the Shiite-led security forces that operate in their villages.

The violence in Iraq has yet to reach the fever pitch it did shortly after the U.S. invasion, but the increase has further polarized the various factions within the country's government. There are a variety of issues thought to play a significant role in the increase in violence, including Maliki's continued centralization of power; growing tension between the Shiites, Sunnis, and Kurds; and battles over the nation's oil. The conflict in Syria is also thought to be a driving force behind the violence. Sunni fighters make up the largest opposition to Bashar al-Assad's government, and both Sunni and Shiite Iraqis have crossed the border to fight on opposite sides of the battle.

SLIDE BACK INTO CONFLICT AMID LITTLE ASSISTANCE

Two years before American troop withdrawal, Prime Minister Maliki called Iraq "a peaceful, democratic country." At the time, sectarian violence had fallen to its lowest level in years. But by the end of 2013, that air of calm was a thing of the past, and it turned out to be the most deadly year since 2008. Although accurate data on the number killed is difficult to obtain, the most reliable statistics from the United Nations and IraqBodyCount .org, a volunteer website based in the United Kingdom, somewhere between 7,800 and 9,500 were killed in 2013, approximately double that of past years. The number of deaths per month increased from the beginning to the end of the year and showed no signs of tapering off, sparking fears that the country would slip back into the sectarian warfare that has plagued it for most of its existence.

Some, including Iraqi officials, are urging the United States to recommit itself to Iraq, something the administration of President Barack Obama has been disinclined to do. Sending troops would be politically unpopular with the American public, and that idea seems even less palatable in Iraq itself. White House spokesperson Jay Carney backed the decision to remove all troops from Iraq, leaving not even a residual force in 2012, as the "right decision." He added that the United States does continue to offer security support, but that it is the position of the administration that Iraq must, to a large degree, work internally to solve its problems. "Iraq has to resolve the challenges that face Iraq through intense political effort," Carney said, "aided by the security forces—the troops and police who have been trained by the United States and our allies in that effort—and through the assistance that we provide them and other friends of Iraq provide them going forward." In fiscal year 2012, the United States sent $1.3 billion in foreign aid to Iraq, according to the Stockholm International Peace Research Institute, but that amount was expected to decline moving forward. An additional $316 million in arms and military and surveillance equipment was sent to the Middle Eastern country. Discussions are ongoing with Iraq for the United States to provide elite military training outside of Iraqi soil.

Some, like former White House official Ken Pollack, cautioned that sending weapons would cause Maliki's government to rely on force rather than compromise to work with the Sunnis in an effort to create a more stable government. "Sending weapons isn't going to fix the problem," Pollack said, adding that it would be preferable to make security assistance a condition of other compromises by Maliki to work with the Sunnis. The United States has encouraged Maliki's government to reach out to minority parties to avoid the continuance of sectarian division but has done so cautiously to avoid the appearance that it is taking sides. "This is a fight that belongs to the Iraqis," Secretary Kerry said, adding that while there are no plans to put soldiers back in Iraq, "we're going to help them in their fight."

—Heather Kerrigan

Following is an April 16, 2013, statement from the U.S. Embassy in Baghdad condemning the attacks against political candidates; and a press release from the Embassy of Iraq, issued on April 20, 2013, following peaceful provincial elections.

U.S. Condemns Attacks Against Political Candidates

April 16, 2013

The United States strongly condemns the armed attacks targeting candidates participating in the upcoming elections. These attacks have killed more than a dozen candidates and injured many others. Such terrorist acts are a cowardly and unacceptable attempt to undermine Iraq's democracy and a desperate effort to intimidate Iraqis and deter them from participating in the democratic process. We call on the government of Iraq to investigate these terrorist crimes and on all parties to cooperate with investigations in order to ensure security for electoral candidates and their supporters. The United States is committed to supporting Iraq in successfully conducting credible provincial elections, including in Anbar and Ninewa provinces.

SOURCE: U.S. Embassy in Baghdad, Iraq. "The United States Condemns the Targeting of Election Candidates in Iraq." April 16, 2013. http://iraq.usembassy.gov/pr_april_17_2013.html.

Iraq Holds Provincial Elections

April 20, 2013

On Saturday, April 20, 2013, Iraq held its first elections since the withdrawal of U.S. troops. Voting took place in 12 of Iraq's 18 provinces in which over 6,925 candidates competed for 378 seats in provincial councils. The elections had a participation rate of 51% of eligible voters, similar to the turnout rate in the 2009 local elections.

The peaceful procession of the elections has highlighted the tremendous strides that Iraq has taken in developing its own democratic institutions and undertaking the responsibility for the country's security.

SOURCE: Embassy of the Republic of Iraq. Public Relations Office. "Iraq Holds First Provincial Elections Since U.S. Troop Withdrawal." April 20, 2013. http://www.iraqiembassy.us/article/iraq-holds-first-provincial-elections-since-us-troop-withdrawal.

OTHER HISTORIC DOCUMENTS OF INTEREST

FROM PREVIOUS *HISTORIC DOCUMENTS*

New Zealand, England, and Wales Approve Same-Sex Marriage

APRIL 17 AND JULY 18, 2013

A handful of countries passed new laws in 2013 allowing same-sex couples to marry. In New Zealand, same-sex marriage legislation faced resistance from religious and conservative groups but was backed by the prime minister. France, a typically liberal nation when it comes to social policy, almost failed to pass its law as protests rocked its major cities. In contrast, its more conservative neighbors to the north, England and Wales, passed a law that was approved without much opposition. Other countries passing same-sex marriage laws in 2013 included Brazil and Uruguay. These six countries joined other nations with similar laws on the books including: Argentina (2010), Belgium (2003), Canada (2005), Denmark (2012), Iceland (2010), The Netherlands (2000), Norway (2009), Portugal (2010), Spain (2005), South Africa (2006), and Sweden (2009).

URUGUAY AND BRAZIL ALLOW SAME-SEX COUPLES TO MARRY

On May 3, Uruguay became the second Latin American nation to lift a ban on same-sex marriage. Same-sex couples in Uruguay previously had the option to enter a civil union, after being given that right in 2008. The marriage bill initially passed the nation's congress on April 10, one week after it was approved by the senate. Debate was fierce, with some arguing that it undermined both the institution of marriage as well as family values. Still, the bill was passed by a wide margin, and the law took effect August 5, 2013. Lawmaker Fernando Amado said, "I agree that family is the basis of society but I also believe that love is the basis of family. And love is neither homosexual nor heterosexual." Under the new law, not only do same-sex couples have the freedom to marry, it also gives these couples the freedom to choose the surname order of the children they adopt, and increases the age of consent, from 12 for women and 14 for men, to 16 for everyone.

Before 2013, several Brazilian states allowed and recognized same-sex marriages. However, the central government, pushed by a court ruling in May 2011, only recognized legal cohabitation. While this afforded same-sex couples the same rights as heterosexual married couples, the court did not equalize heterosexual and homosexual marriages.

After multiple Brazilian states came under local court orders to allow same-sex marriage, the Brazilian National Council of Justice ruled on May 14, 2013, that same-sex couples could not be denied marriage licenses. The Social Christian Party has appealed the ruling to the country's Supreme Court, so the fate and staying power of the law could be in jeopardy. Public opinion polls reveal that approximately half of Brazil's citizens support allowing same-sex couples to marry.

New Zealand's Prime Minister Pushes Same-Sex Marriage Bill

New Zealand's path to marriage equalization began in 2005 when the country legalized civil unions. Public opinion on the issue has fluctuated—in 2004, a Herald-DigiPoll showed 40 percent in favor of gay marriage. In 2012, that number rose to more than 59 percent in favor, but has since dropped to slightly less than 50 percent supporting same-sex marriage. Public opposition was largely driven by religious and conservative organizations, while support came from a large swath of New Zealand public life, including Prime Minister John Key and former governor-general Catherine Tizard, the latter of whom appeared in an online video campaign in support of same-sex marriage legislation. In May 2012, a lesbian member of the country's Labour Party, Louisa Wall, sponsored a bill that would give full marriage rights to same-sex couples. The Marriage Amendment Bill was backed by Key, who said he could not see how such a law would undermine the traditional definition of marriage. The bill passed its first two readings in August 2012 and March 2013.

The third reading and final debate of the bill took place on April 17, 2013. During debate, Member of Parliament Maurice Williamson gave a speech in support of the measure that instantly went viral. In giving his reasons of support, Williamson commented on a number of letters he had received regarding why same-sex marriage was wrong and refuted the comments offered. One such letter linked same-sex marriage to the oppressive drought New Zealand was experiencing, to which Williamson replied, "In the Pakuranga electorate this morning it was pouring with rain. We had the most enormous, big, gay rainbow across my electorate. It has to be a sign—it has to be a sign."

The bill won final approval by a 77–44 vote, making New Zealand the first nation in the Asia-Pacific region to legalize same-sex marriage. While Prime Minister Key noted that the bill, which included a provision to allow same-sex couples to adopt children, was "part of equality in modern-day New Zealand," conservative groups continued to speak out against it. Family First NZ called the new law "an arrogant act of cultural vandalism." Even so, the bill received royal assent from the governor-general on April 19, and the law took effect on August 19, 2013.

French Same-Sex Marriage Law Faces Opposition

Shortly after defeating conservative incumbent Nicolas Sarkozy in May 2012, French President François Hollande, a Socialist, followed through on a campaign promise to push a measure legalizing same-sex marriage in France. The bill was not expected to face much resistance, because public opinion polls have long shown broad support for same-sex marriage among French citizens. Public acceptance of the lifestyle extends to the election of a gay mayor of Paris, and civil unions have been permitted since 1999.

However, once the bill was drafted, the most conservative French citizens traveled to Paris to protest. Although the protests drew tens of thousands, the vocal opposition was driven mainly by the small minority of Catholics in the country who rallied against same-sex marriage, the idea that same-sex couples would raise and corrupt future generations, and the tarnishing of the French image around the world. Many of those who joined the opposition movement mainly did so to bring attention to an entirely separate issue: Hollande's handling of the French economy. The largest protests sparked violence, including one in which a far right-wing group charged police and damaged cars along the

Champs-Élysée. Police deterred the crowd from nearing the presidential palace by using tear gas.

Despite the protests, on April 23, 2013, the National Assembly easily passed the same-sex marriage bill, 331–225, led by the Socialist majority party. Speaking to those in opposition, Justice Minister Christiane Taubira said, "We believe that the first weddings will be beautiful and that they'll bring a breeze of joy, and that those who are opposed to them today will surely be confounded when they are overcome with the happiness of the newlyweds and the families."

The first marriages under the new law were expected to take place as early as June 2013, but immediately after the law's passage, the conservative Union for a Popular Movement (UMP) filed a challenge with the Constitutional Council, the nation's highest court, arguing that such a law was unconstitutional. There was little belief that the UMP would be successful because the court had previously ruled that same-sex marriage was an issue to be decided by the legislature. On May 17, the court upheld the law, thus paving the way for its implementation.

One day later, Hollande signed the law, and made France the fourteenth nation to allow same-sex couples to marry. In addition to permitting same-sex marriage, the law also allows same-sex couples to adopt children. The latter provision was sharply criticized by the nation's Catholic Church. Protests continued after passage, despite a growing intolerance among French citizens for such demonstrations. On May 26, an estimated 150,000 protesters marched in Paris. One opposition leader, a former comedian who calls herself Frigide Barjot, said that she intended for the protests to continue and also hoped to field anti-same-sex marriage candidates for regular municipal elections set for 2014.

ENGLAND, WALES APPROVE SAME-SEX MARRIAGE

In 2012, Prime Minister David Cameron proposed the passage of a law legalizing same-sex marriage. Since 2005, same-sex couples had only been allowed to enter into civil partnerships in the United Kingdom. The marriage proposal quickly garnered support from the three leading parties in parliament and was debated and quickly approved 400–175 during the second reading by the House of Commons on February 5, 2013. The bill succeeded 366–161 during the third reading in the House of Commons, followed by passage in the House of Lords. Broad public support for such a measure pushed the law to victory on July 16 when the House of Commons accepted amendments from the House of Lords, despite opposition from the Church of England. Queen Elizabeth II gave her approval of the law, although largely ceremonial, on July 17, 2013. Upon approval, Prime Minister Cameron commented, "I am delighted that the love two people have for each other—and the commitment they want to make—can now be recognised as equal. I have backed this reform because I believe in commitment, responsibility and family. I don't want to see people's love divided by law."

The new law gives same-sex couples the right to begin marrying in March 2014. However, per a prohibition in the law, these marriages cannot be performed within the Church of England, which maintained that it would continue to recognize marriage as between one man and one woman. Only England and Wales are covered under the new law. Because of their semi-autonomous nature, both Scotland and Northern Ireland can pass their own same-sex marriage laws, if they desire. The Northern Ireland parliament rejected a measure in April 2013, but in February 2014, a same-sex marriage bill was approved in Scotland. Marriages could take place there as early as fall 2014.

RECOGNITION OF OTHER UNIONS

In addition to the seventeen countries that recognize same-sex marriage as akin to opposite-sex marriage, some other countries recognize civil unions or other arrangements for same-sex couples. In Kenya, for example, where same-sex marriage has been described as "un-African" by some leaders, certain women in some communities can enter into same-sex partnerships. To qualify, one woman must have never been married, and she takes on the husband role. She then cohabitates with a younger woman and encourages that younger woman to find a male within their clan to have children with. Those children are then considered the offspring of the two females.

Same-sex couples in Andorra, Australia, Colombia, Croatia, the Czech Republic, Finland, Germany, Hungary, Ireland, Israel, Liechtenstein, Luxembourg, parts of Mexico, Slovenia, and Switzerland are afforded some legal rights that apply to their union. However, same-sex couples in these countries argue that they are still treated unfairly under the law and that these benefits are unequal to those afforded to married heterosexual couples.

ONGOING DEBATE

Worldwide, the struggle for same-sex marriage rights continues. In some countries, like the United States, sub-jurisdictions have superseded federal law and now allow same-sex marriage within their borders. This raises a number of legal challenges at both the federal level and for those couples who have married and moved to an area that does not recognize same-sex marriage.

In Australia, same-sex civil partnerships are legal in the Australian Capital Territory; however, there are few other areas in the country that recognize these partnerships, including the Commonwealth government, which has filed a case with the nation's constitutional court to outlaw these partnerships. Tasmania recognizes same-sex marriages but does not allow them to be performed within its borders. Tasmanian citizens, along with those residing in New South Wales, Queensland, and Victoria, are allowed a registered partnership (or civil union). Attempts have been made to make same-sex marriage legal throughout the country, the last of which came in September 2012, but the bill was soundly defeated in the nation's House of Representatives and Senate.

In Vietnam, the government has weighed the option of lifting the prohibition on same-sex marriage. The National Assembly intended to take up the matter in the spring of 2013; however, the Ministry of Justice asked that the body hold off until 2014 to review or propose a law. The National Assembly delayed debate on a proposal only until June 2013. As of November 2013, the government had only taken the step of ending the fine on same-sex marriage ceremonies that can range anywhere from VND100,000 to VND500,000 (USD$5–$25).

In Finland, the Legal Affairs Committee of the nation's parliament rejected a bill proposed in 2012 by the Minister of Justice to allow for same-sex marriage. In March 2013, signatures were gathered on a citizens' petition to force the parliament to take up the issue, which garnered the necessary support on its first day of circulation. The successful petition overturned the rejection by the Legal Affairs Committee, and parliament will now be required to review a same-sex marriage bill.

—Heather Kerrigan

Following is the text of a speech delivered on April 17, 2013, by New Zealand Member of Parliament Maurice Williamson during debate on same-sex marriage legislation; and the text of a statement written by Prime Minister David Cameron on July 18, 2013, upon approval of a same-sex marriage law in England and Wales.

MP Williamson Speaks in Support of Same-Sex Marriage

April 17, 2013

[The remarks of other members of parliament have been omitted.]

. . . I want to, first of all, congratulate Louisa Wall on this bill, the Marriage (Definition of Marriage) Amendment Bill, and I want to say that the good news about spending years in this Parliament is that you learn to deflect all of the dreadful sort of fire and brimstone accusations that people say are going to happen. I have had a reverend in my local electorate call and say that the gay onslaught will start the day after this bill is passed. We are really struggling to know what the gay onslaught will look like. We do not know whether it will come down the Pakuranga Highway as a series of troops, or whether it will be a gas that flows in over the electorate and blocks us all in.

I also had a Catholic priest tell me that I was supporting an unnatural act. I found that quite interesting, coming from someone who has taken an oath of celibacy for his whole life. . . . I have not done it, so I do not know what it is about.

I also had a letter telling me that I would burn in the fires of hell for eternity, and that was a bad mistake because I have got a degree in physics. I used the thermodynamic laws of physics. I put in my body weight and my humidity and so on, I assumed the furnace to be at 5,000 degrees Celsius, and I would last for just on 2.1 seconds. It is hardly eternity—what do you think?

I also heard some more disgusting claims about adoption. Well, I have got three fantastic adopted kids. I know how good adoption is, and I have found some of the claims just disgraceful.

I found some of the bullying tactics really evil. I gave up being scared of bullies when I was at primary school.

However, a huge amount of the opposition was from moderates, from people who were concerned—who were seriously worried—about what this bill might do to the fabric of our society. I respect their concern; I respect their worry. They were worried about what it might to do to their families, and so on. Let me repeat to them now: all we are doing with this bill is allowing two people who love each other to have that love recognised by way of marriage. That is all we are doing. We are not declaring nuclear war on a foreign State. We are not bringing a virus in that could wipe out our agricultural sector for ever. We are allowing two people who love each other to have that recognised, and I cannot see what is wrong with that, for neither love nor money—I just cannot. I cannot understand why someone would be opposed.

I understand why people do not like what it is that others do. That is fine; we are all in that category. But I give a promise to those people who are opposed to this bill right now. I give you a watertight, guaranteed promise. The sun will still rise tomorrow. Your teenage daughter will still argue back at you as if she knows everything. Your mortgage will not grow. You will not have skin diseases or rashes or toads in your bed. The world will just carry on. So do not make this into a big deal. This bill is fantastic for the people it affects, but for the rest of us, life will go on.

Finally, can I say that one of the messages I had was that this bill was the cause of our drought—this bill was the cause of our drought. Well, if any of you follow my Twitter account, you will have seen that in the Pakuranga electorate this morning it was pouring with rain. We had the most enormous, big, gay rainbow across my electorate. It has to be a sign—it has to be a sign. If you are a believer, it is certainly a sign.

Can I finish—for all those who are concerned about this—with a quote from the Bible. It is Deuteronomy. I thought Deuteronomy was a cat out of the musical *Cats*, but never mind. The quote is Deuteronomy 1:29: "Be ye not afraid."

SOURCE: New Zealand Parliament. Volume 689, Week 40. Page 9429. April 17, 2013. http://www.parliament.nz/en-nz/pb/debates/debates/daily/50HansD_20130417/volume-689-week-40-wednesday-17-april-2013.

Prime Minister Cameron on Same-Sex Marriage Law

July 18, 2013

I am proud that we have made same sex marriage happen. I am delighted that the love two people have for each other—and the commitment they want to make—can now be recognised as equal. I have backed this reform because I believe in commitment, responsibility and family. I don't want to see people's love divided by law.

Making marriage available to everyone says so much about the society that we are and the society that we want to live in—one which respects individuals regardless of their sexuality. If a group is told again and again that they are less valuable, over time they may start to believe it. In addition to the personal damage that this can cause, it inhibits the potential of a nation. For this reason too, I am pleased that we have had the courage to change.

I also want to acknowledge those that worked to bring about this moment: the campaigners, groups such as Out4Marriage and Freedom to Marry, and the team in the civil service and Parliament who worked to deliver it.

The UK is rated as the best place in Europe for LGBT equality—but we cannot be complacent. There are subjects we must continue to tackle: not least taking a zero tolerance approach to homophobic bullying, and caring for elderly members of the

LGBT community. Rest assured, this government will work tirelessly to make sure this happens.

As the sun shines this week on our country, the LGBT community now know that the unique bond of marriage is available to them. As Lord Alderdice put it when arguing for civil partnerships in 2004: 'One of the most fundamental rights of all is the right to have close, confiding, lasting, intimate relationships. Without them, no place, no money, no property, no ambition—nothing—amounts to any value. It seems to me a fundamental human right to be able to choose the person with whom you wish to spend your life and with whom you wish to have a real bond.'

I couldn't agree more. Yesterday was an historic day."

SOURCE: Office of the Prime Minister, 10 Downing Street. "Same Sex Marriage: Prime Minister's Statement." July 18, 2013. https://www.gov.uk/government/news/same-sex-marriage-prime-ministers-statement. License: http://www.nationalarchives.gov.uk/doc/open-government-licence/version/2.

OTHER HISTORIC DOCUMENTS OF INTEREST

FROM THIS VOLUME

- Same-Sex Marriage Approved in Hawaii and Illinois, p. 538

FROM PREVIOUS *HISTORIC DOCUMENTS*

- Same-Sex Marriage in the States, *2009*, p. 144

President Obama Remarks on Gun Control Legislation

APRIL 17, 2013

Following a rash of mass shootings that occurred across the United States in 2012, federal policymakers revived the longstanding debate over gun regulations as they considered legislation that would tighten existing gun laws, or in some cases expand gun owners' rights, in the early months of 2013. Despite widespread calls for action, the Senate failed to pass its signature gun legislation, the Safe Communities, Safe Schools Act of 2013, amid partisan disagreement over the most effective solutions to gun violence and the political realities of the looming 2014 midterm elections. Meanwhile, as acts of gun violence continued to make news, President Barack Obama issued a series of new executive orders aimed at strengthening gun regulations, and state lawmakers passed more than 100 new gun-related measures.

SENATE GUN LEGISLATION

In January, lawmakers in both the House and Senate began introducing wide-ranging gun legislation for consideration. Although earlier attempts at passing even modest gun legislation had failed since the expiration of the assault weapons ban in 2004, and lawmakers had been more likely to attempt to expand gun rights, many anticipated that the tragic December 2012 shooting at Sandy Hook Elementary School, in which twenty-six students and teachers were killed, would serve as a catalyst.

Sen. Patrick Leahy, D-Vt., was among the first to act. On January 22, he introduced the Stop Illegal Trafficking in Firearms Act of 2013, which sought to make "straw purchasing" of firearms, or the practice of buying a gun on behalf of another person who is prohibited from making such a purchase, illegal. Two days later, Sen. Dianne Feinstein, D-Calif., introduced the Assault Weapons Ban of 2013, a bill meant to reinstate and strengthen the ban on military-style assault weapons that had expired in 2004. That same day, Sen. Barbara Boxer, D-Calif., introduced the School and Campus Safety Enhancements Act of 2013, which would establish a task force to develop and implement improved safety guidelines for schools. Sen. Chuck Schumer, D-N.Y., later introduced a bill, the Fix Gun Checks Act of 2013, which would require anyone prohibited from purchasing a firearm to be listed on the Federal Bureau of Investigation's (FBI) National Instant Criminal Background Check System and mandate background checks for every gun purchase, except for those between immediate family members.

On March 21, Senate Majority Leader Harry Reid, D-Nev., introduced the Safe Communities, Safe Schools Act of 2013, a single piece of legislation that included language from the bills proposed by Leahy, Schumer, and Boxer. Notably absent from the bill was Feinstein's assault weapons ban renewal. Almost immediately, a group of Republican senators, including Senate Minority Leader Mitch McConnell, R-Ky., said they would block the bill's progress with a filibuster, while others, including Sen. John McCain, R-Ariz., criticized the Republican group's plan. Those opposed to the legislation generally argued that the measures included would represent typical government overreach and would erode constitutionally protected rights to gun ownership. "In my view, we should focus on keeping firearms out of the hands of the criminals and those with mental issues that could cause them to be a threat to our society," said McConnell. "The government should not punish or harass law-abiding citizens in the exercise of their Second Amendment rights." The National Rifle Association (NRA) lobbied particularly hard against the bill, claiming that it would lead to background checks being required for sales and gifts between friends and family, as well as a national registry of gun owners. Supporters of the bill denounced the NRA's claims. "That is simply a lie, and anybody who can read knows that is not factual," said Sen. Joe Manchin, D-W.Va. Proponents also questioned why their colleagues would reject expanded background checks when polls showed that approximately 90 percent of Americans supported such a measure.

Then on April 15, Sen. Pat Toomey, R-Penn., and fifteen other Republicans joined Senate Democrats and voted to allow debate on the bill to begin on April 17. In the week that followed, support for the bill seemed to wane, with odds of passage becoming increasingly slim. Senate leadership agreed to hold successive votes on nine amendments to the bill over the course of April 17 and 18, with each amendment needing to receive sixty votes in order to pass. Among those amendments was a bipartisan proposal put forth by Sens. Toomey and Manchin, which would have extended background checks to purchases made at gun shows and over the Internet but not sales between neighbors and family members. It would also prohibit the creation of a national gun registry, something which gun rights advocates particularly opposed. Many viewed Manchin and Toomey's approach as less expansive than Reid's original background check proposals and speculated that their records as gun owners and defenders of Second Amendment rights could help garner support for their amendment.

Despite appearing to have strong support, the Toomey-Manchin proposal received only fifty-four votes, not enough to pass under the Senate leadership's agreement. Six other amendments failed to meet the sixty-vote threshold. This included an amendment by Sens. Chuck Grassley, R-Iowa, and Ted Cruz, R-Texas, which would have replaced Reid's bill with one that would increase enforcement of existing gun laws, improve mental health records and reporting for gun owners, and fund more school safety measures. Other failed amendments included Sen. Feinstein's assault weapons ban, a ban on high-capacity gun magazines that carry more than ten rounds of ammunition, a proposal to make straw purchasing and gun trafficking a federal crime, an amendment that would only allow a judge to determine whether veterans are not mentally competent enough to own a gun, and an amendment that would have required any state with a concealed-weapons law to recognize the concealed weapons permit of residents from any other state. Only two proposed amendments passed: one reauthorizing and improving mental health programs, and one that would impose penalties on states that release gun ownership data.

Many viewed the Senate's rejection of the Toomey-Manchin amendment in particular as a sign that Congress would not be able to pass any meaningful gun control legislation. The voting records also showed that a number of Democrats from more conservative states, many of whom were expected to face tough reelection campaigns in 2014, voted no to tighter gun regulations. Reid decided to pull the bill from the Senate floor, putting it on hold and moving on to other business, though leadership staff suggested the effort could regain steam if the public demanded it.

President Obama chided Republicans for their votes. "The fact is most of these Senators could not offer any good reason why we wouldn't want to make it harder for criminals and those with severe mental illnesses to buy a gun," Obama said. "It came down to politics: the worry that that vocal minority of gun owners would come after them in future elections. They worried that the gun lobby would spend a lot of money and paint them as anti-Second Amendment." Families who had lost loved ones or otherwise been affected by gun violence and gun control advocates expressed similar sentiments. "This is an insult to the 90 people killed by gun violence every day and the 90 percent of Americans who believe that felons, domestic abusers and the dangerous mentally ill should not be able to buy guns without a background check, no questions asked," said Dan Gross, president of the Brady Campaign to Prevent Gun Violence.

PRESIDENTIAL ACTION

Although Congress was unable to pass gun legislation, President Obama took several steps of his own. On January 16, he released a plan to combat gun violence that included both legislative proposals, a number of which were later considered by Congress, and twenty-three executive actions, such as improving incentives for states to share information with the background check system. The plan was based on recommendations made by a special task force on gun violence that he had established after the Sandy Hook shooting to examine all possible solutions to gun violence, from gun restrictions to improving mental health programs as well as addressing societal factors such as entertainment media.

On August 29, the president announced two new gun-related executive orders. The first sought to close a loophole in the background check system by requiring people associated with trusts or corporations to undergo a background check when purchasing a gun. Some felons had previously evaded background checks by registering their gun to a trust or corporation. The second order declared that the United States would deny all requests from private entities to reimport surplus U.S. military firearms from overseas except in rare cases, such as when a museum requested an item for its collection. White House officials claimed this measure would help prevent some of those weapons from ending up on the streets.

"Even as Congress fails to act on common-sense proposals, like expanding criminal background checks and making gun trafficking a federal crime, the president and vice president remain committed to using all the tools in their power to make progress toward reducing gun violence," the White House said in a statement.

GUN LEGISLATION IN THE STATES

State legislatures across the country were also active on issues related to gun violence. According to the Law Center to Prevent Gun Violence, state lawmakers introduced approximately 1,500 gun-related bills by mid-December, 109 of which became law. Of those, thirty-nine laws tightened gun restrictions and seventy loosened gun regulations.

States that relaxed gun regulations included the Kansas and Arkansas legislatures, which both passed laws nullifying federal gun regulations for guns manufactured and kept within state borders. In other Republican-led states, lawmakers often focused on expanding concealed carry policies, including providing the right to carry concealed weapons in churches and schools. In Texas, lawmakers passed the Protection of Texas Children Act, which allows teachers to serve as armed school marshals, as long as they have a concealed weapon permit, pass a mental health exam, and undergo specific training.

Legislatures in Colorado, Connecticut, Delaware, Maryland, and New York were among those that passed tighter gun laws, and all now require background checks for all online and in-person gun purchases, including those at gun shows. Controversial Colorado, Connecticut, and Maryland laws also ban certain types of high-capacity magazines or assault rifles. Both Connecticut and Maryland officials faced court challenges by firearms manufacturers, and gun rights groups organized a recall of two Democratic state senators in Colorado. Another state senator resigned to avoid a similar recall effort and help keep her seat in Democratic hands. Some sheriffs also refused to enforce the new laws, arguing that they were too vague and violated the Second Amendment. In May, fifty-five of Colorado's sixty-two elected sheriffs signed on to a federal lawsuit challenging the state law's constitutionality. Conversely, some police chiefs and state officials said it was entirely possible to enforce the new laws and that they were already having an effect.

Gun Violence Continues

Mass shootings continued to rack the country as policymakers deliberated over gun legislation. In January, fifteen-year-old Nehemiah Griego shot and killed his parents and three siblings in Albuquerque, New Mexico, and reportedly had also planned a shooting at a nearby Walmart before turning himself in to authorities. In June, John Zawahri shot and killed his father and brother at their home, carjacked a woman, and then shot at passing vehicles (killing three more people) on his way to the Santa Monica College campus, where he was shot in a standoff with police. In July, Pedro Alberto Vargas set fire to his Hialeah, Florida, apartment, shooting and killing the building managers when they came to investigate before shooting another four individuals and taking two tenants hostage. Then in September, former Navy reservist and government subcontractor Aaron Alexis killed twelve people and injured eight others when he opened fire in an office building at the Washington, D.C., Navy Yard. According to a *USA Today* report, there were a total of thirty mass shootings in the United States in 2013.

—Linda Fecteau

Following is the text of a statement delivered by President Barack Obama on April 17, 2013, following the Senate's failure to pass comprehensive gun legislation.

DOCUMENT

President Obama Speaks on Gun Control

April 17, 2013

A few months ago, in response to too many tragedies, including the shootings of a United States Congresswoman, Gabby Giffords, who's here today, and the murder of 20 innocent schoolchildren and their teachers, this country took up the cause of protecting more of our people from gun violence.

Families that know unspeakable grief summoned the courage to petition their elected leaders, not just to honor the memory of their children, but to protect the lives of all of our children. A few minutes ago, a minority in the United States Senate decided it wasn't worth it.

They blocked commonsense gun reforms even while these families looked on from the Senate gallery.

By now, it's well known that 90 percent of the American people support universal background checks that make it harder for a dangerous person to buy a gun. We're talking about convicted felons, people convicted of domestic violence, people with a severe mental illness. Ninety percent of Americans support that idea. Most Americans think that's already the law.

And a few minutes ago, 90 percent of Democrats in the Senate voted for that idea. But it's not going to happen, because 90 percent of Republicans in the Senate just voted against that idea. A majority of Senators voted yes to protecting more of our citizens with smarter background checks. But by this continuing distortion of Senate rules, a minority was able to block it from moving forward.

Now, I'm going to speak plainly and honestly about what's happened here, because the American people are trying to figure out: How can something have 90 percent support and yet not happen? We had a Democrat and a Republican—both gun owners, both fierce defenders of our Second Amendment, with A grades from the NRA—come together and work together to write a commonsense compromise on background checks. And I want to thank Joe Manchin and Pat Toomey for their courage in doing that. That was not easy given their traditional strong support for Second Amendment rights.

As they said, nobody could honestly claim that the package they put together infringed on our Second Amendment rights. All it did was extend the same background check rules that already apply to guns purchased from a dealer to guns purchased at gun shows or over the Internet. So 60 percent of guns are already purchased through a background check system; this would have covered a lot of the guns that are currently outside that system.

Their legislation showed respect for gun owners, and it showed respect for the victims of gun violence. And Gabby Giffords, by the way, is both; she's a gun owner and a victim of gun violence. She is a Westerner and a moderate. And she supports these background checks.

In fact, even the NRA used to support expanded background checks. The current leader of the NRA used to support these background checks. So while this compromise didn't contain everything I wanted or everything that these families wanted, it did represent progress. It represented moderation and common sense. That's why 90 percent of the American people supported it.

But instead of supporting this compromise, the gun lobby and its allies willfully lied about the bill. They claimed that it would create some sort of big brother gun registry, even though the bill did the opposite. This legislation, in fact, outlawed any registry. Plain and simple, right there in the text. But that didn't matter.

And unfortunately, this pattern of spreading untruths about this legislation served a purpose, because those lies upset an intense minority of gun owners, and that in turn intimidated a lot of Senators. And I talked to several of these Senators over the past few weeks, and they're all good people. I know all of them were shocked by tragedies like Newtown. And I also understand that they come from States that are strongly pro-gun. And I have consistently said that there are regional differences when it comes to guns and that both sides have to listen to each other.

But the fact is most of these Senators could not offer any good reason why we wouldn't want to make it harder for criminals and those with severe mental illnesses to buy a gun. There were no coherent arguments as to why we wouldn't do this. It came down to politics: the worry that that vocal minority of gun owners would come after them in future elections.

They worried that the gun lobby would spend a lot of money and paint them as anti–Second Amendment.

And obviously, a lot of Republicans had that fear, but Democrats had that fear too. And so they caved to the pressure, and they started looking for an excuse—any excuse—to vote no.

One common argument I heard was that this legislation wouldn't prevent all future massacres. And that's true. As I said from the start, no single piece of legislation can stop every act of violence and evil. We learned that tragically just 2 days ago. But if action by Congress could have saved one person, one child, a few hundred, a few thousand, if it could have prevented those people from losing their lives to gun violence in the future while preserving our Second Amendment rights, we had an obligation to try. And this legislation met that test.

And too many Senators failed theirs.

I've heard some say that blocking this step would be a victory. And my question is, a victory for who? A victory for what? All that happened today was the preservation of the loophole that lets dangerous criminals buy guns without a background check. That didn't make our kids safer. Victory for not doing something that 90 percent of Americans, 80 percent of Republicans, the vast majority of your constituents wanted to get done? It begs the question, who are we here to represent?

I've heard folks say that having the families of victims lobby for this legislation was somehow misplaced. "A prop," somebody called them. "Emotional blackmail," some outlets said. Are they serious? Do we really think that thousands of families whose lives have been shattered by gun violence don't have a right to weigh in on this issue? Do we think their emotions, their loss is not relevant to this debate? So all in all, this was a pretty shameful day for Washington.

But this effort is not over. I want to make it clear to the American people: We can still bring about meaningful changes that reduce gun violence, so long as the American people don't give up on it. Even without Congress, my administration will keep doing everything it can to protect more of our communities. We're going to address the barriers that prevent States from participating in the existing background check system. We're going to give law enforcement more information about lost and stolen guns so it can do its job. We're going to help to put in place emergency plans to protect our children in their schools.

But we can do more if Congress gets its act together. And if this Congress refuses to listen to the American people and pass commonsense gun legislation, then the real impact is going to have to come from the voters.

To all the people who supported this legislation—law enforcement and responsible gun owners, Democrats and Republicans, urban moms, rural hunters, whoever you are— you need to let your Representatives in Congress know that you are disappointed and that if they don't act this time, you will remember come election time.

To the wide majority of NRA households who supported this legislation, you need to let your leadership and lobbyists in Washington know they didn't represent your views on this one.

The point is, those who care deeply about preventing more and more gun violence will have to be as passionate and as organized and as vocal as those who blocked these commonsense steps to help keep our kids safe. Ultimately, you outnumber those who argued the other way. But they're better organized. They're better financed. They've been at it longer. And they make sure to stay focused on this one issue during election time. And that's the reason why you can have something that 90 percent of Americans support and you can't get it through the Senate or the House of Representatives.

So to change Washington, you, the American people, are going to have to sustain some passion about this. And when necessary, you've got to send the right people to Washington.

And that requires strength, and it requires persistence.

And that's the one thing that these families should have inspired in all of us. I still don't know how they have been able to muster up the strength to do what they've doing over the last several weeks, last several months.

And I see this as just round one. When Newtown happened, I met with these families and I spoke to the community, and I said, something must be different right now. We're going to have to change. That's what the whole country said. Everybody talked about how we were going to change something to make sure this didn't happen again, just like everybody talked about how we needed to do something after Aurora. Everybody talked about, we needed to change something after Tucson.

And I'm assuming that the emotions that we've all felt since Newtown, the emotions that we've all felt since Tucson and Aurora and Chicago—the pain we share with these families and families all across the country who've lost a loved one to gun violence—I'm assuming that's not a temporary thing. I'm assuming our expressions of grief and our commitment to do something different—to prevent these things from happening—are not empty words.

I believe we're going to be able to get this done. Sooner or later, we are going to get this right. The memories of these children demand it. And so do the American people.

Thank you very much, everybody.

SOURCE: Executive Office of the President. "Remarks on Senate Action on Gun Control Legislation." April 17, 2013. *Compilation of Presidential Documents* 2013, no. 00252 (April 17, 2013). http://www.gpo .gov/fdsys/pkg/DCPD-201300252/pdf/DCPD-201300252.pdf.

OTHER HISTORIC DOCUMENTS OF INTEREST

FROM THIS VOLUME

FROM PREVIOUS *HISTORIC DOCUMENTS*

Response to the Boston Marathon Attack

APRIL 18 AND APRIL 22, 2013

On April 15, 2013, as the final groups of runners were crossing the finish line in the iconic Boston Marathon, two bombs exploded in rapid succession, sending shrapnel flying and setting off a mass panic. Runners and spectators scattered, while first responders rushed to help those who had lost limbs or were suffering severe blood loss. Three people, including an eight-year-old boy, were killed in the attack. The manhunt for those responsible ended four days later in a bloody shootout. One of the two suspects was taken into custody and charged with use of a weapon of mass destruction. The other suspect was killed during the search.

CHAOS AT MILE 26

April 15, 2013, marked the 117th running of the Boston Marathon, a race that draws hundreds of thousands of spectators each year who line the streets of Boston to cheer on participants. At approximately 2:49 p.m. Eastern time, two pressure cooker bombs exploded near the finish line, thirteen seconds apart. Approximately three-quarters of the runners had already finished the race, but spectators were still out in full force. Witnesses reported thinking the first blast marked some form of celebration for the race but quickly realized that was not the case after the second bomb went off, and everyone scattered. The bomb blasts shattered windows in nearby buildings and sent nails and ball bearings flying into the air. Those injured by the explosions suffered shrapnel wounds, loss of legs or feet, head injuries, and life-threatening blood loss. Good Samaritans and first responders tried to help as many victims as possible, while ambulances arrived in droves to take the injured to surrounding hospitals. In total, three people were killed—Krystle Campbell, 29; Lingzi Lu, 23, a graduate student from China; and Martin William Richard, 8. More than 200 were wounded.

Police began their investigation immediately following the explosions but were hampered by the fact that spectators dropped their bags as they ran for safety. Given the nature of the attack, police had to treat every bag as if it were an explosive device. The bombings brought the usually bustling urban center to a halt. Public transportation was shut down, and flights coming into and going out of Boston's Logan International Airport were temporarily grounded. Concerts and sporting events were canceled, and police encouraged both tourists and locals alike to remain indoors and refrain from congregating in large groups while they carried out their investigation. The Back Bay neighborhood, the area of the city where the bombings took place, was almost entirely shut down.

Large cities across the country, including New York and Washington, D.C., stepped up security presence at various locations to thwart any potential coordinated attacks. On the day of the attack, President Barack Obama encouraged those in Boston to stay strong.

"Boston is a tough and resilient town. So are its people. I'm supremely confident that Bostonians will pull together, take care of each other, and move forward as one proud city. And as they do, the American people will be with them every single step of the way," Obama said. The president did not immediately label the event as a terrorist attack, encouraging Americans not to jump to conclusions. An anonymous national security official, however, wrote in an email that "any event with multiple explosive devices—as this appears to be—is clearly an act of terror, and will be approached as an act of terror."

Even as Boston came to a standstill, calls rang out across social media networks for residents to be resilient. "Boston Strong" became the motto that soon appeared throughout the country. On April 18, President Obama joined Massachusetts' Governor Deval Patrick for an interfaith prayer service where both echoed this national sentiment. "Boston may be your hometown, but we claim it too. It's one of America's iconic cities. It's one of the world's great cities. And one of the reasons the world knows Boston so well is that Boston opens its heart to the world . . . like you, in this moment of grief, we join you in saying, 'Boston, you're my home.' For millions of us, what happened on Monday is personal," the president said. Governor Patrick promised that the people of his city would recover from this tragedy by supporting each other. "We will recover and repair. We will grieve our losses and heal. We will rise, and we will endure. We will have accountability, without vengeance. Vigilance, without fear. And we will remember . . . that the grace this tragedy exposed is the best of who we are," Governor Patrick said.

SEARCHING FOR THE SUSPECTS

Following the bombing, local and state police began coordinating with the Federal Bureau of Investigation (FBI) to locate those responsible. Due to the large number of people at the crime scene, police had a difficult time identifying who may have been responsible for planting the two bombs. They searched footage of the crowds from photographs and video taken at the race, and received security camera footage from nearby businesses. Police looked specifically for anyone who seemed disinterested in the race. On April 17, CNN cited an unnamed law enforcement source, stating that a suspect had been taken into custody. The Associated Press, Fox News, and *The Boston Globe* subsequently picked up the story, which ran for approximately one hour before the FBI corrected the news outlets. The FBI later issued a statement saying, "Over the past day and a half, there have been a number of press reports based on information from unofficial sources that has been inaccurate. Since these stories often have unintended consequences, we ask the media, particularly at this early stage of the investigation, to exercise caution and attempt to verify information through appropriate official channels before reporting."

On April 18, the FBI took the lead on the investigation and released photographs of the two men suspected of planting the bombs. Law enforcement took to the airwaves and social media to encourage anyone with information about the two suspects to come forward. The FBI call center was overwhelmed with tips, but they eventually led to the identification of both suspects just hours after the pictures were released. The suspects, Dzhokhar and Tamerlan Tsarnaev, aged nineteen and twenty-six, respectively, were brothers of Chechen descent. Dzhokhar was a student at the University of Massachusetts at Dartmouth.

After their photos were identified, the brothers, who had been hiding in the greater Boston area following the bombing, went in search of a vehicle to use to flee. The suspects went to the Massachusetts Institute of Technology (MIT) campus where they shot and killed MIT police officer Sean Collier and subsequently carjacked a Mercedes SUV. The suspects told the driver that they were responsible for the marathon bombings and proceeded to stop at three gas stations to try to use the driver's ATM card to obtain cash. The driver of the vehicle was released without harm in nearby Cambridge, Massachusetts.

By the time the driver had been released, police caught up to the vehicle and pursued it into Watertown; the suspects tossed explosives out the window along the way. With the vehicle cornered by police, the brothers opened fire, hitting a transit officer who sustained severe blood loss. Tamerlan was shot during the firefight after running toward police with what looked like an explosive strapped to his chest, and as Dzhokhar drove the SUV through a line of police officers, he ran over his brother, killing him.

Police lost track of Dzhokhar after he fled in the SUV. On April 19, police issued a "shelter-in-place" advisory for the Watertown area. Public transportation came to a halt, and many businesses closed. Residents reported deserted streets spotted only by heavily armed law enforcement officials. Police searched a twenty-block region throughout the morning and afternoon of April 19, and eventually lifted the advisory around 7 p.m. With the order lifted, a man left his Watertown home to check on a tarp that had come loose on his boat. When he went to investigate, he noticed blood on the tarp and saw a body curled up inside. He immediately called police, who used thermal imaging cameras to determine that there was indeed someone in the boat.

For two hours, gunfire could be heard as police tried to get a badly wounded Dzhokhar Tsarnaev out of the boat. He was eventually taken into custody at approximately 9 p.m. As police left the scene, residents lined the streets cheering for them. Tsarnaev was taken to Boston Beth Israel Deaconess Hospital in serious condition.

The Case Against Tsarnaev

During his initial interrogation by a group known as the High Value Detainee Interrogation Group, which is made up of officials from the FBI, Central Intelligence Agency (CIA), and Department of Defense, Tsarnaev said that his brother had planned the bombing, driven by radical Islamist beliefs. Tsarnaev said that he and Tamerlan were not acting on behalf of, nor were they affiliated with, any terrorist organization. Their plan had been to bomb the marathon and then proceed to Times Square in New York City to set off a bomb there as well.

On April 22, a thirty-count criminal complaint was filed against Tsarnaev, including use of a weapon of mass destruction and malicious destruction of property resulting in death. In June, a federal grand jury returned an indictment charging Tsarnaev on thirty counts. Tsarnaev pleaded not guilty.

At his initial hearing on November 12, federal court judge George O'Toole gave both the prosecutor and defense attorney a deadline of February 28, 2014, to file any motions to dismiss or change the venue. He also set a January 31, 2014, deadline for Attorney General Eric Holder to determine whether he would seek the death penalty; the Attorney General affirmed that he would seek this punishment on January 30, 2014.

During the hearing, federal prosecutors said they wanted the trial to begin in late 2014, but Miriam Conrad, an attorney for the defense, argued that the deadline would not allow them enough time to compile their case. She also argued that without the unlimited resources available to the government, the defense team would not have enough time to research whether it wanted to request a change of venue, or how it might respond to Holder's January decision. As of the end of 2013, no trial date had been set.

Three of Tsarnaev's acquaintances will also face federal charges, including obstructing justice and conspiracy to obstruct justice. Dias Kadyrbayev and Azamat Tazhayakov, both college friends of Tsarnaev, pleaded not guilty to obstructing justice and conspiracy to obstruct justice. Federal prosecutors allege that the pair attempted to get rid of a laptop and backpack located in Tsarnaev's dorm room. If convicted, the two could face a maximum of twenty years in prison on the first count and five years on the second. A third classmate of Tsarnaev, Robel Phillipos, was charged with two counts of making false statements. Prosecutors allege that Phillipos lied about accompanying Tazhayakov and Kadyrbayev to Tsarnaev's dorm room to remove the laptop and backpack. If convicted, Phillipos could receive eight years in prison for each count plus a $250,000 fine. All three will be tried on June 23, 2014.

—Heather Kerrigan

Following is the text of two speeches, one delivered by Massachusetts Governor Deval Patrick and the other by President Barack Obama, at an interfaith prayer service on April 18, 2013; and the edited text of the criminal complaint filed against Dzhokhar Tsarnaev on April 22, 2013.

DOCUMENT

Gov. Patrick Speaks at Interfaith Prayer Service

April 18, 2013

In my faith tradition, scripture teaches: "In <u>every</u> thing give thanks." (I Thessalonians 5:18) That isn't always easy to do. On Monday afternoon, I was not feeling it. What I felt, what so many of us felt then, was shock and confusion and anger.

But the nature of faith, I think, is learning to return to the lessons even when they don't make sense, when they defy logic. And as I returned to those lessons this week, I found a few things to be thankful for.

I'm thankful for the firefighters and police officers and EMTs who ran towards the blasts, not knowing whether the attack was over—and the volunteers and other civilians who ran to help right along side them.

I'm thankful for the medical professionals—from the doctors and trauma nurses to the housekeeping staff, to the surgeon who finished the marathon and kept on running to his operating room—all of whom performed at their very best.

I'm thankful for the agents from the FBI and the ATF, for the officers from the State Police and Boston PD, for the soldiers from the National Guard and all other law enforcement personnel who both restored order and started the methodical work of piecing together what happened and who's responsible.

I'm thankful for Mayor Menino, who started Monday morning frustrated he couldn't be at the finish line this time, as he always is, and then late that afternoon checked himself out of the hospital to help his city, our city, face down this tragedy.

I'm thankful for those who have given blood to the hospitals, money to the OneFund, and prayers and messages of consolation and encouragement from all over the world.

I'm thankful for the presence and steadfast support of the President and First Lady, our many former governors who are here. I'm thankful for the civic and political leaders who are here today, and for the many, many faith leaders who have ministered to us today and in the days since Monday.

I'm thankful for the lives of Krystle and Lingzi and little Martin, and for the lives of the families who survive them, and for the lives of all the people hurt but who still woke up today with the hope of tomorrow.

And I am thankful, maybe most especially, for the countless numbers of people in this proud City and this storied Commonwealth who, in the aftermath of such senseless violence, let their first instinct be kindness. In a dark hour, so many of you showed so many of us that "darkness cannot drive out darkness," as Dr. (Martin Luther) King said. "Only light can do that."

How very strange that the cowardice unleashed on us should come on Marathon day, on Patriots' Day, a day that marks both the unofficial end of our long winter hibernation and the first battle of the American Revolution. And just as we are taught at times like this not to lose touch with our spiritual faith, let us also not lose touch with our civic faith.

Massachusetts invented America. And America is not organized the way countries are usually organized. We are not organized around a common language or religion or even culture. We are organized around a handful of civic ideals. And we have defined those ideals, over time and through struggle, as equality, opportunity, freedom and fair play.

An attack on our civic ritual like the Marathon, especially on Patriots' Day, is an attack on those values. And just as we cannot permit darkness and hate to triumph over our spiritual faith, so we must not permit darkness and hate to triumph over our civic faith. That cannot happen. And it will not.

So, we will recover and repair. We will grieve our losses and heal. We will rise, and we will endure. We will have accountability, without vengeance. Vigilance, without fear. And we will remember, I hope and pray, long after the buzz of Boylston Street is back and the media has turned its attention elsewhere, that the grace this tragedy exposed is the best of who we are.

Fellow citizens, I am honored and humbled to welcome our friend, our leader, our commander in chief, the President of the United States.

SOURCE: Office of the Governor of Massachusetts. "'Healing our City: An Interfaith Service" Remarks. April 18, 2013. http://www.mass.gov/governor/pressoffice/speeches/0418-interfaith-service-remarks.html.

President Obama Addresses Boston Marathon Prayer Service

April 18, 2013

Thank you. Please. Hello, Boston.

Scripture tells us to "run with endurance the race that is set before us." Run with endurance the race that is set before us.

On Monday morning, the Sun rose over Boston. The sunlight glistened off the Statehouse dome. In the Common and the Public Garden, spring was in bloom. On this

Patriot's Day, like so many before, fans jumped onto the "T" to see the Sox at Fenway. In Hopkinton, runners laced up their shoes and set out on a 26.2-mile test of dedication and grit and the human spirit. And across this city, hundreds of thousands of Bostonians lined the streets: to hand the runners cups of water and to cheer them on.

It was a beautiful day to be in Boston, a day that explains why a poet once wrote that this town is not just a capital, not just a place. Boston, he said, "is the perfect state of grace."

And then, in an instant, the day's beauty was shattered. A celebration became a tragedy. And so we come together to pray and mourn and measure our loss. But we also come together today to reclaim that state of grace: to reaffirm that the spirit of this city is undaunted and the spirit of this country shall remain undimmed.

To Governor Patrick; Mayor Menino; Cardinal O'Malley and all the faith leaders who are here; Governors Romney, Swift, Weld, and Dukakis; Members of Congress; and most of all, the people of Boston and the families who've lost a piece of your heart: We thank you for your leadership. We thank you for your courage. We thank you for your grace.

I'm here today on behalf of the American people with a simple message: Every one of us has been touched by this attack on your beloved city. Every one of us stands with you.

Because, after all, it's our beloved city too. Boston may be your hometown, but we claim it too. It's one of America's iconic cities. It's one of the world's great cities. And one of the reasons the world knows Boston so well is that Boston opens its heart to the world. [. . . .]

Like you, Michelle and I have walked these streets. Like you, we know these neighborhoods. And like you, in this moment of grief, we join you in saying, "Boston, you're my home." For millions of us, what happened on Monday is personal. It's personal.

Today our prayers are with the Campbell family of Medford. They're here today. Their daughter Krystle was always smiling. Those who knew her said that with her red hair and her freckles and her ever-eager willingness to speak her mind, she was beautiful, sometimes she could be a little noisy, and everybody loved her for it. She would have turned 30 next month. As her mother said through her tears, "This doesn't make any sense."

Our prayers are with the Lu family of China, who sent their daughter Lingzi to BU so that she could experience all this city has to offer. She was a 23-year-old student, far from home. And in the heartache of her family and friends on both sides of a great ocean, we're reminded of the humanity that we all share.

Our prayers are with the Richard family of Dorchester: to Denise and their young daughter Jane as they fight to recover. And our hearts are broken for 8-year-old Martin, with his big smile and bright eyes. His last hours were as perfect as an 8-year-old boy could hope for: with his family, eating ice cream at a sporting event. And we're left with two enduring images of this little boy, forever smiling for his beloved Bruins and forever expressing a wish he made on a blue poster board: "No more hurting people. Peace." No more hurting people. Peace.

Our prayers are with the injured, so many wounded, some gravely. From their beds, some are surely watching us gather here today. And if you are, know this: As you begin this long journey of recovery, your city is with you. Your Commonwealth is with you. Your country is with you. We will all be with you as you learn to stand and walk and, yes, run again. Of that I have no doubt. You will run again. [*Applause*] You will run again.

Because that's what the people of Boston are made of. Your resolve is the greatest rebuke to whoever committed this heinous act. If they sought to intimidate us, to terrorize us, to shake us from those values that Deval described, the values that make us who we are, as Americans, well, it should be pretty clear by now that they picked the wrong city to do it. Not here in Boston. [*Applause*] Not here in Boston.

You've shown us, Boston, that in the face of evil, Americans will lift up what's good. In the face of cruelty, we will choose compassion. In the face of those who would visit death upon innocents, we will choose to save and to comfort and to heal. We'll choose friendship. We'll choose love.

The Scripture teaches us, "God has not given us a spirit of fear and timidity, but of power, love, and self-discipline." And that's the spirit you've displayed in recent days.

When doctors and nurses, police and firefighters, and EMTs and guardsmen run towards explosions to treat the wounded, that's discipline.

When exhausted runners, including our troops and veterans, who never expected to see such carnage on the streets back home, become first responders themselves, tending to the injured, that's real power.

When Bostonians carry victims in their arms, deliver water and blankets, line up to give blood, open their homes to total strangers, give them rides back to reunite with their families, that's love.

That's the message we send to those who carried this out and anyone who would do harm to our people. Yes, we will find you. And yes, you will face justice. We will find you. We will hold you accountable. But more than that, our fidelity to our way of life—for a free and open society—will only grow stronger. For God has not given us a spirit of fear and timidity, but one of power and love and self-discipline.

Like Bill Iffrig, 78 years old, the runner in the orange tank top who we all saw get knocked down by the blast, we may be momentarily knocked off our feet, but we'll pick ourselves up. We'll keep going. We will finish the race. In the words of Dick Hoyt, who's pushed his disabled son Rick in 31 Boston Marathons, "We can't let something like this stop us." This doesn't stop us.

And that's what you've taught us, Boston. That's what you've reminded us: to push on, to persevere, to not grow weary, to not get faint. Even when it hurts, even when our heart aches, we summon the strength that maybe we didn't even know we had, and we carry on. We finish the race. [*Applause*] We finish the race.

And we do that because of who we are. And we do that because we know that somewhere around the bend, a stranger has a cup of water. Around the bend, somebody is there to boost our spirits. On that toughest mile, just when we think that we've hit a wall, someone will be there to cheer us on and pick us up if we fall. We know that.

And that's what the perpetrators of such senseless violence—these small, stunted individuals who would destroy instead of build and think somehow that makes them important—that's what they don't understand. Our faith in each other, our love for each other, our love for country, our common creed that cuts across whatever superficial differences there may be—that is our power. That's our strength.

That's why a bomb can't beat us. That's why we don't hunker down. That's why we don't cower in fear. We carry on. We race. We strive. We build, and we work, and we love. And we raise our kids to do the same. And we come together to celebrate life and to walk our cities, and to cheer for our teams. When the Sox and Celtics and Patriots or Bruins are champions again—to the chagrin of New York and Chicago fans—[*laughter*]—the crowds will gather and watch a parade go down Boylston Street.

And this time next year, on the third Monday in April, the world will return to this great American city to run harder than ever and to cheer even louder, for the 118th Boston Marathon. Bet on it.

Tomorrow the Sun will rise over Boston. Tomorrow the Sun will rise over this country that we love: this special place, this state of grace.

Scripture tells us to "run with endurance the race that is set before us." As we do, may God hold close those who've been taken from us too soon. May He comfort their families. And may He continue to watch over these United States of America.

SOURCE: Executive Office of the President. "Remarks at an Interfaith Prayer Service for the Victims of the Terrorist Attack in Boston, Massachusetts." April 18, 2013. *Compilation of Presidential Documents* 2013, no. 00253 (April 18, 2013). http://www.gpo.gov/fdsys/pkg/DCPD-201300253/pdf/DCPD-201300253 .pdf.

Justice Department Charges Accused Boston Marathon Bomber

April 22, 2013

[The opening page of the criminal complaint, and a description of the qualifications of Special Agent Daniel R. Genck, has been omitted.]

AFFIDAVIT OF SPECIAL AGENT

3. This affidavit is submitted in support of an application for a complaint charging DZHOKHAR A. TSARNAEV of Cambridge, Massachusetts ("DZHOKHAR TSARNAEV") with using a weapon of mass destruction against persons and property at the Boston Marathon on April 15, 2013, resulting in death. More specifically, I submit this affidavit in support of an application for a complaint charging DZHOKHAR TSARNAEV with (1) unlawfully using and conspiring to use a weapon of mass destruction (namely, an improvised explosive device) against persons and property within the United States used in interstate and foreign commerce and in an activity that affects interstate and foreign commerce, which offense and its results affected interstate and foreign commerce (including, but not limited to, the Boston Marathon, private businesses in Eastern Massachusetts, and the City of Boston itself), resulting in death, in violation of 18 U.S.C. § 2332a; and (2) maliciously damaging and destroying, by means of an explosive, real and personal property used in interstate and foreign commerce and in an activity affecting interstate and foreign commerce, resulting in personal injury and death, in violation of 18 U.S.C. § 844(i). . . .

FACTS AND CIRCUMSTANCES

A. The Boston Marathon Explosions

[Facts about the race have been omitted.]

7. On April 15, 2013, at approximately 2:49 p.m., while the Marathon was still underway, two explosions occurred on the north side of Boylston Street along the Marathon's final stretch. The first explosion occurred in front of 671 Boylston Street and the second occurred approximately one block away in front of 755 Boylston Street. The explosive devices were placed near the metal barriers where hundreds of spectators were watching runners approach the finish line. Each explosion killed at least one person,

maimed, burned and wounded scores of others, and damaged public and private property, including the streets, sidewalk, barriers, and property owned by people and businesses in the locations where the explosions occurred. In total, three people were killed and over two hundred individuals were injured. . . .

B. Surveillance Evidence

9. I have reviewed videotape footage taken from a security camera located on Boylston Street near the corner of Boylston and Gloucester Streets. At approximately 2:38 p.m. (based on the video's duration and timing of the explosions)—i.e., approximately 11 minutes before the first explosion—two young men can be seen turning left (eastward) onto Boylston from Gloucester Street. Both men are carrying large knapsacks. The first man, whom I refer to in this affidavit as Bomber One, is a young male, wearing a dark-colored baseball cap, sunglasses, a white shirt, dark coat, and tan pants. The second man, whom I refer to in this affidavit as Bomber Two, is a young male, wearing a white baseball cap backwards, a gray hooded sweatshirt, a lightweight black jacket, and dark pants. As set forth below, there is probable cause to believe that Bomber One is Tamerlan Tsarnaev and Bomber Two is his brother, DZHOKHAR TSARNAEV.

10. After turning onto Boylston Street, Bomber One and Bomber Two can be seen walking eastward along the north side of the sidewalk towards the Marathon finish line. Bomber One is in front and Bomber Two is a few feet behind him. Additional security camera video taken from a location farther east on Boylston Street, as well as contemporaneous photographs taken from across the street, show the men continuing to walk together eastward along Boylston Street towards Fairfield Street.

11. I have also reviewed video footage taken from a security camera affixed above the doorway of the Forum Restaurant located at 755 Boylston Street, which was the site of the second explosion. This camera is located approximately midway between Fairfield and Exeter Streets and points out in the direction of Boylston and is turned slightly towards Fairfield. At approximately 2:41 p.m. (based on the video's duration and the timing of the explosions), Bomber One and Bomber Two can be seen standing together approximately one half-block from the restaurant.

12. At approximately 2:42 p.m. (i.e., approximately seven minutes before the first explosion), Bomber One can be seen detaching himself from the crowd and walking east on Boylston Street towards the Marathon finish line. Approximately 15 seconds later, he can be seen passing directly in front of the Forum Restaurant and continuing in the direction of the location where the first explosion occurred. His knapsack is still on his back.

13. At approximately 2:45 p.m., Bomber Two can be seen detaching himself from the crowd and walking east on Boylston Street toward the Marathon finishing line. He appears to have the thumb of his right hand hooked under the strap of his knapsack and a cell phone in his left hand. Approximately 15 seconds later, he can be seen stopping directly in front of the Forum Restaurant and standing near the metal barrier among numerous spectators, with his back to the camera, facing the runners. He then can be seen apparently slipping his knapsack onto the ground. A photograph taken from the opposite side of the street shows the knapsack on the ground at Bomber Two's feet.

14. The Forum Restaurant video shows that Bomber Two remained in the same spot for approximately four minutes, occasionally looking at his cell phone and once appearing to take a picture with it. At some point he appears to look at his phone, which is held at approximately waist level, and may be manipulating the phone. Approximately 30 seconds before the first explosion, he lifts his phone to his ear as if he is speaking on his cell

phone, and keeps it there for approximately 18 seconds. A few seconds after he finishes the call, the large crowd of people around him can be seen reacting to the first explosion. Virtually every head turns to the east (towards the finish line) and stares in that direction in apparent bewilderment and alarm. Bomber Two, virtually alone among the individuals in front of the restaurant, appears calm. He glances to the east and then calmly but rapidly begins moving to the west, away from the direction of the finish line. He walks away without his knapsack, having left it on the ground where he had been standing. Approximately 10 seconds later, an explosion occurs in the location where Bomber Two had placed his knapsack. . . .

C. Photographic Identifications

16. I have compared a Massachusetts Registry of Motor Vehicles ("RMV") photograph of DZHOKHAR TSARNAEV with photographic and video images of Bomber Two, and I believe, based on their close physical resemblance, there is probable cause that they arc one and the same person. Similarly, I have compared an RMV photograph of Tamerlan Tsarnaev with photographic and video images of Bomber One, and I likewise believe that they are one and the same person.

D. The Bombers Emerge

. . . 18.   At approximately 5:00 p.m. on April 18, 2013, the FBI published video and photographic images of Bomber One and Bomber Two on its web site. Those images were widely rebroadcast by media outlets all over the country and the world.

19. Near midnight on April 18, 2013, an individual carjacked a vehicle at gunpoint in Cambridge, Massachusetts. A victim of the carjacking was interviewed by law enforcement and provided the following information. The victim stated that while he was sitting in his car on a road in Cambridge, a man approached and tapped on his passenger-side window. When the victim rolled down the window, the man reached in, opened the door, and entered the victim's vehicle. The man pointed a firearm at the victim and stated, "Did you hear about the Boston explosion?" and "I did that." The man removed the magazine from his gun and showed the victim that it had a bullet in it, and then re-inserted the magazine. The man then stated, "I am serious."

20. The man with the gun forced the victim to drive to another location, where they picked up a second man. The two men put something in the trunk of the victim's vehicle. The man with the gun took the victim's keys and sat in the driver's seat, while the victim moved to the front passenger seat. The second man entered the victim's vehicle and sat in the rear passenger seat. The man with the gun and the second man spoke to each other in a foreign language.

21. While they were driving, the man with the gun demanded money from the victim, who gave the man 45 dollars. One of the men compelled the victim to hand over his ATM card and password. They then drove to an ATM machine and attempted to withdraw money from the victim's account. The two men and the victim then drove to a gas station/convenience store in the vicinity of 816 Memorial Drive, Cambridge. The two men got out of the car, at which point the victim managed to escape.

22. A short time later, the stolen vehicle was located by law enforcement in Watertown, Massachusetts. As the men drove down Dexter Street in Watertown, they threw at least two small improvised explosive devices ("IEDs") out of the car. A gun fight ensued between the car's occupants and law enforcement officers in which numerous shots were fired. One

of the men was severely injured and remained at the scene; the other managed to escape in the car. That car was later found abandoned a short distance away, and an intact low-grade explosive device was discovered inside it. In addition, from the scene of the shoot-out on Laurel Street in Watertown, the FBI has recovered two unexploded IEDs, as well as the remnants of numerous exploded IEDs. . . .

F. Preliminary Examination of the Explosives

24. A preliminary examination of the remains of the explosive devices that were used at the Boston Marathon revealed that they were low-grade explosives that were housed in pressure cookers. Both pressure cookers were of the same brand. The pressure cookers also contained metallic BBs and nails. Many of the BBs were contained within an adhesive material. The explosives contained green-colored hobby fuse. . . .

G. DZHOKHAR TSARNAEV is Located

26. On the evening of April 19, 2013, police investigation revealed that there was an individual in a covered boat located at 67 Franklin Street in Watertown. After a stand-off between the boat's occupant and the police involving gunfire, the individual was removed from the boat and searched. . . .

27. On April 21, 2013, the FBI searched DZHOKHAR TSARNAEV's dormitory room at 7341 Pine Dale Hall at the University of Massachusetts at Dartmouth, pursuant to a search warrant. The FBI seized from his room, among other things, a large pyrotechnic, a black jacket and a white hat of the same general appearance as those worn by Bomber Two at the Boston Marathon on April 15, 2013, and BBs.

CONCLUSION

28. Based on the foregoing, there is probable cause to believe that on or about April 15, 2013, DZHOKHAR TSARNAEV violated 18 U.S.C. § 2332a (using and conspiring to use a weapon of mass destruction, resulting in death) and 844(i) (malicious destruction of property by means of an explosive device, resulting in death). Accordingly, I respectfully request that the Court issue a complaint charging DZHOKHAR TSARNAEV with those crimes.

Daniel R. Genck
Special Agent
Federal Bureau of Investigation

[The criminal complaint cover sheet has been omitted.]

Source: U.S. Department of Justice. "Tsarnaev Complaint." April 21, 2013. http://www.justice.gov/iso/opa/resources/363201342213441988148.pdf.

Other Historic Documents of Interest

From previous *Historic Documents*

■ Bush on Terrorist Attacks Against the United States, *2001*, p. 614

Italian President's Address Upon His Reelection

APRIL 22, 2012

Italian citizens voted in February 2013 to choose new members of parliament. However, no party won an outright majority of seats, and the parties failed to work together to form a governing coalition. The fighting both within and among the various political sects became even more pronounced in April when the time came for parliament to choose a new president. After five rounds of balloting failed to produce a winner, the current president, Giorgio Napolitano, agreed to requests from party leaders that he remain in office for a second term. When Napolitano was chosen on the sixth ballot, he became the first Italian president to be elected to serve two terms. Napolitano ordered the creation of a coalition government, but, although one was formed, its hold on power remained tenuous and it had difficulty passing its agenda throughout the year.

Parliamentary Elections Spark Chaos

In late February, Italian citizens went to the polls to elect 630 members of the lower house of parliament, the Chamber of Deputies, and 315 members of the upper house, the Senate of the Republic. The center-right alliance, led by former Prime Minister Silvio Berlusconi, faced off against the center-left alliance, Italy. Common Good (IBS), led by the Pier Luigi Bersani. It was the center-left that bested Berlusconi's alliance in the Chamber of Deputies, winning nearly 55 percent of the seats to the center-right's 19.8 percent of the seats. And in a surprising upset, the new Five Star Movement (M5S), a group led by Beppe Grillo and formed in response to public discontent with the current government, gained the third largest number of seats. In fourth was the centrist coalition headed by outgoing Prime Minister Mario Monti, who took up his seat following the collapse of Berlusconi's government in 2011.

While there were clear winners and losers in the Chamber of Deputies, the Senate was split. No party was able to secure a majority of seats, resulting in a hung parliament. This left Italy without a stable, majority government, which threatened investor confidence in a nation already on shaky financial ground. Italy is the eurozone's third-largest economy, and its politics and finances are closely watched around the world because any crisis in its monetary sector could cause chaos in the European Union.

In these situations, it typically falls to the president to dissolve parliament and hold a new election. But, at the time, President Napolitano had less than six months left in his seven-year term and was constitutionally constrained from taking such action. Instead, Napolitano encouraged the two houses to choose leaders, which they did on March 16, picking Laura Boldrini and Pietro Grasso. Napolitano tapped Bersani to form a new coalition government.

Bersani refused to work with Berlusconi and his center-right coalition. He instead turned to the Five Star Movement, hoping that building a government around it would quell some public discontent. However, Bersani quickly realized that a compromise on how to govern together effectively could not be reached. Following Bersani's failure to form a government, Napolitano announced that the country would move ahead status quo and that, instead of allowing Italy's parliament to take charge of the continuing financial crisis, he would appoint two private sector commissions to determine how to continue Italy's economic recovery through EU-imposed austerity measures in hopes of restoring investor confidence.

Presidential Election Brings Surprise Candidate

With only a few months left in Napolitano's seven-year term, a presidential election was scheduled to take place from April 18 to 20. Italian presidents are elected in a closed meeting, during which members of parliament and regional delegates cast secret ballots. Voting is done in rounds, and if no candidate wins a clear majority in the first round of voting, another round is started, and so on until the president is chosen. In the first three rounds of balloting, a two-thirds majority is required to secure a victory, but beginning with the fourth round, a candidate only needs a simple majority. Although the position is largely ceremonial, it can play a significant role in Italian politics, as it did in November 2011 when Berlusconi's government collapsed, leading Napolitano to appoint a new prime minister. Of the 2013 election, former Italian senator Gianfranco Pasquino said, "This election is extremely important because the president of the republic . . . has the power first to appoint the prime minister and second to dissolve parliament, so he is a very powerful man, especially because the [political] parties are very weak and there is no majority for any party or any single coalition."

In 2013, the first five ballots did not return a successful candidate. This was due in part to the ongoing political division in parliament, even within parties. On April 16, the M5S threw its support to Milena Gabanelli. The party indicated that if their candidate was elected, it might consider working with the center-left coalition. One day later, Gabanelli, a former journalist, withdrew her name from consideration and M5S put forth Stefano Rodotà, a member of the Democratic Party of the Left (PDS). The Democratic Party, led by Bersani, supported various candidates including Franco Marini, a former speaker of the senate. While Marini was Bersani's choice, many key leaders in the party said they would not back him. On the first ballot, more than 200 in the center-left coalition failed to vote for Marini, and his name was not put forward on the second ballot.

On April 19, the Democratic Party (PD) put Romano Prodi, a former prime minister, on the fourth ballot. Berlusconi's coalition refused to back Prodi, and he only garnered 395 votes, well short of the 504 required for victory. Bersani, angered that his preference for Prodi had not earned enough support, said he would resign his post as leader of the Democratic Party effective once a new president was chosen. Bersani accused members of parliament of betraying their own party and said there were "forces trying to destroy the PD." The resignation sparked concern that the potential for snap elections were growing more likely. (Bersani was replaced on May 11 by Guglielmo Epifani, a former trade union leader.)

On April 20, after much negotiation with party leaders, in an unprecedented move, Napolitano was convinced to put his name on the presidential ballot in an effort to end the gridlock. "I believe I must offer my availability as requested," Napolitano said, adding that he would not "shun [his] responsibility toward the nation." Napolitano easily won on the sixth ballot with 738 votes, becoming the first Italian president to be elected to two terms. Napolitano had initially shied away from taking on the position, citing his advanced age (he was eighty-seven years old at the time of his second election). Because each term is seven years long, Italian political analysts do not expect that Napolitano will complete a full term in office.

Napolitano's easy reelection came with backing from Bersani, Monti, Berlusconi, and their respective parties. The only party not involved in discussions with Napolitano was M5S, which following the election called the win a "coup d'état." Grillo wrote on his blog that the election of Napolitano was a backroom deal aimed at preventing change in Italian society. He called on his supporters to join him for a protest in Rome.

DIFFICULT PATH TO COALITION GOVERNMENT

Following his election, Napolitano immediately got to work helping parliament form a governing coalition. On April 24, he appointed Enrico Letta, the deputy secretary of the Democratic Party, to serve as prime minister. Letta, age forty-six, will be one of the nation's youngest prime ministers.

Recognizing the public perception that Italy's current leaders are an elitist group of corrupt individuals, Letta chose a relatively young cabinet with many members who were new to the political spotlight. His coalition cabinet was announced on April 28 and included members of the Democratic Party, People of Freedom (PDL), Civic Choice, the Union of the Centre, and the Radicals. The position of deputy prime minister and interior minister went to Angelino Alfano, the secretary of the PDL, signaling that Berlusconi might be able to exercise significant influence over the new government. Other members of the cabinet include Fabrizio Saccomanni, the new minister of the economy and finances; Emma Bonino, who would serve as foreign minister; and labor minister Enrico Giovannini.

The new ministers officially took office on April 29, after a vote of confidence on April 29, which it won in the Chamber of Deputies 453–153. A second vote in the Senate on April 30, which the right-wing coalition won 233–59, cemented the group's rule. Letta delivered his inaugural address on April 29. In the address he laid out the priorities of his government, chiefly improving the economy. "We will die of fiscal consolidation alone," Letta said. "Growth policies cannot wait." Letta promised to steer away from the European Union's push for austerity and instead implement internal job creation and economic growth measures. He also hoped that postponing a sales tax increase set for June and lowering payroll taxes would encourage companies to begin hiring again. In a nod to the PDL, which has pushed for the abolition of an unpopular housing tax, Letta indicated a willingness to reform tax policy and canceled the June housing tax payment, although he did not immediately end the tax altogether. Letta also promised to set up a commission to review electoral reform in an effort to prevent a political standstill from happening again.

The Italian public, tired of EU-imposed reforms, slow economic growth, and the long 2013 election cycle, remained unconvinced of the coalition's ability to govern effectively. The EMG agency conducted an opinion poll after the new government was seated, which gave the new prime minister a 41 percent approval rating. This was a stark contrast to his predecessor, Monti, who took office with a nearly 70 percent approval rating. Additionally, only 13 percent of those polled said they wanted Letta to be prime minister, sparking concern that he could face difficulty pushing through his various proposals. The markets, however, responded positively to the seating of a new government, and shares began rising while bond yields fell.

BERLUSCONI PULLS OUT OF COALITION, LOSES SEAT

After serving four terms as prime minister, Berlusconi had carved himself a significant position in Italian politics. However, as the nation's economy collapsed in November 2011, he was forced from his position and Napolitano named Monti in his place. While political analysts had written off any chance of future political influence, Berlusconi came roaring back, even despite sex and corruption scandals that surfaced in 2012. His influence was further elevated when his protégé, Alfano, was seated in Letta's cabinet. "Berlusconi can kill the government from one day to the next," said Sergio Romano, a well-known Italian journalist.

Berlusconi tried to exercise this power in late September when he called for new elections and pulled his PDL ministers out of the coalition government. Discouraged by the lack of progress in Letta's government to implement beneficial economic measures, Berlusconi said, "The only way is to proceed with conviction to elections as soon as possible. All the opinion polls tell us that we will win."

Although the move brought the coalition government to a standstill, Berlusconi was quickly losing political capital after being convicted and sentenced on August 1 for tax fraud. Letta called the decision "irresponsible" and said Berlusconi's insinuations that Letta had failed to pass economic measures was a "blatant lie." Letta called for his government to be put to a vote of confidence in parliament. M5S joined Berlusconi's call for new elections. Berlusconi ultimately backed down after it became clear that Letta's government would win its vote.

Berlusconi's decision to leave the coalition came just days before a Senate panel voted to strip the bellicose politician of his seat. On November 27, the full Senate took up the issue, and, although they did not hold a formal vote, motions by Berlusconi supporters were rebuffed. Speaker Grasso announced, "The conclusions of the committee on elections have been approved, abolishing the election of Senator Silvio Berlusconi." Berlusconi is now prohibited from taking part in any general election for the next six years. Alfano called the decision "an ugly day for parliament and for Italy." M5S leader Grillo used the ousting as a call for action for his supporters to remove all current members of the government.

Following the decision, Berlusconi told his supporters, "No political leader has suffered a persecution such as I have lived through." Noting that the decision marked "a bitter day, a day of mourning," he promised to continue pushing for reform in government. "We must stay on the field, we must not despair if the leader of the center-right is not a senator any more. There are leaders of other parties who are not parliamentarians." Berlusconi will likely serve his one-year sentence for tax fraud under house arrest or doing community service. The former senator is also appealing two convictions of breach of confidentiality and paying for sex with a minor.

—Heather Kerrigan

Following is the text of a speech delivered on April 22, 2013, by Italian President Giorgio Napolitano upon his reelection.

President Napolitano Address the Italian Chambers

DOCUMENT

April 22, 2013

Madame Speaker, honourable deputies, honourable senators, delegates from the Regions,

First of all, allow me to express—together with what for me is a very deeply felt tribute to the institutions you represent—the gratitude I owe you for having elected me President of the Republic by such a large vote. It is a sign of renewed trust that I accept with a full understanding of its spirit and meaning, even though it poses a serious challenge to my strengths. And I appreciate, in particular, that it has been extended to me by so many men and women newly elected to Parliament, who belong to a generation so far removed—not just in terms of their date of birth—from my own. . . .

The out-going President has never before, in the history of the Republic, been re-elected for a second mandate, even though the Constitution does not rule out this eventuality but—as was significantly noted—has left "a window ajar for exceptional times." So we found ourselves together taking a fully legitimate, but exceptional, decision. Because the risk that I have just mentioned appeared to be unprecedented: unprecedented, and all the more serious at this time of acute difficulty—emergency, even—that Italy is going through in a most critical, and for us ever more urgent, European and international context.

The need, therefore, was to offer—to the country and the world—evidence of awareness and national cohesion, of institutional vitality, of a will to provide answers to our problems. With a rediscovered sense of self-confidence and a re-awakening of international confidence in Italy.

That is the test I did not back away from. In the knowledge, however, that what has happened here in the past few days was simply the end-point of a long series of omissions and faults, of narrow-mindedness and failings of responsibility. Let me put to you just a rapid summary, a brief overview.

Recent years have seen a failure to provide satisfactory solutions to well-founded needs and urgent calls for institutional reform and a renewal of politics and of the parties, in a situation that became interwoven with an acute financial crisis, a grave recession, and growing social malaise. Confrontation, feet-dragging, hesitations over the choices to be made, calculations of expediency, tactical manoeuvring and instrumentalism ended up prevailing. That is what condemned the dialogue between the political forces and debates in Parliament to remain sterile or achieve just minimal outcomes.

What little success was achieved in terms of adjustments and innovation to reduce the operational costs of our Institutions and increase transparency and morality in public life was easily ignored or undervalued. And dissatisfaction with and protest against politics, the parties, the Parliament, were easily (but also heedlessly) fuelled and magnified by deleterious opinion campaigns, by one-sided, indiscriminate and unilateral representations of the world of politicians and of the organizations and institutions in which they act. . . .

We have simply had enough, in every field, of seeing people shirk their duty to make proposals, to seek practicable solutions, or to take clear and timely decisions on the reforms that Italian democracy and society urgently need if they are to survive and flourish. . . .

I would like to make just two observations on this point. The first concerns the need for the pursuit of certain essential goals—the goals of reforming the political parties and the channels of democratic participation, and of reforming the representative institutions and relations between Parliament and Government and between State and Regions—to be accompanied by a close focus on strengthening and renewing the organs and powers of the State.

I have been very close to these organs in the last seven years, so there is no need for me once again to pay formal tribute to them here today, whether to the armed forces or the forces of law and order, the judiciary or the Court that is the supreme guarantee of the constitutionality of our laws. We must be on our guard, given the need to protect freedom and security from new forms of criminality and the stirring of new subversive pressures, and given the tension and lack of order in relations between various powers of the state and institutions of constitutional significance.

Nor can we ignore the need to react to any misinformation and controversy that strike our military powers, which have rightly embarked on a serious reform. Their focus, however, in the spirit of the Constitution, remains that of safeguarding Italy's participation—with the selfless sacrifice of no small number of our young people—in the international community's stabilisation and peace missions.

The second observation concerns the value of the proposals developed in detail in the document I have just mentioned, "to tackle the recession and grasp any opportunities" that arise, "to influence the European Union in its next options," "to create and support jobs," "to strengthen education and human capital, and to foster research, innovation and the growth of our businesses."

In underscoring these last points, I can observe that I have been—and will continue to be—actively engaged in these matters in every institutional forum and opportunity for discussion. They are crucial points in defining our renewed and vital commitment to take forward a united Europe, by helping to define and respect the constraints of financial sustainability and monetary stability that must bind it. And by helping, together, to rekindle its dynamism and spirit of solidarity and grasp to the full its unique impetus and irreplaceable benefits.

These are also the crucial points—first and foremost, given the distressing growth in unemployment, the creation of jobs and good quality employment opportunities—around which a major social question revolves, a question that has thrust itself onto the agenda in Italy and Europe. The question of the future prospects of an entire generation. The question of the effective and full use of women's resources and energies. We cannot remain indifferent to the plight of entrepreneurs and workers who are forced to take desperate action, young people who lose their way, or women who live in conditions of marginalisation or low status that they view as unacceptable.

A desire for change, with each interpreting the consensus expressed by the voters in his or her own way, says little in itself and does not take us very far if we do not measure ourselves against problems like the ones I have just mentioned and which have recently been described in some detail and in objective and impartial terms. We must measure ourselves against these problems, so that they become a programme of action for the government that must be formed and the subject of deliberation by the Parliament that is preparing to embark on its tasks.

And so that they become the fulcrum of new forms of collective behaviour by forces—firstly in the world of work and business—that "appear to be blocked, afraid, locked into defensive positions and ill at ease with the innovation which is, in fact, the driver of development." We need a new openness, a new impetus in society. We need an intense effort, in southern Italy itself, if we are to lift the south out of a spiral of backwardness and impoverishment.

Parliament recently voted—unanimously, I may add—on its contribution to urgent provisions which the Monti government, still being in power, was responsible for adopting, and which it did indeed adopt. It did so as part of an economic-financial and European policy effort that will certainly merit calmer reflection as we leave behind us the heated and antagonistic election climate and draw up a balance sheet of the role we acquired in the European Union in the course of 2012.

I appreciate the commitment, with respect to its role in the Chamber and Senate, that has been shown by the movement that was amply rewarded by the electorate as a new political-parliamentary actor, earning the weight and influence that are its due. That is the path to a fruitful, yet difficult and rigorous, democratic dialectic. Not the path, adventurous and misleading, of confrontation between Parliament and the streets. Nor can a confrontation between the Web and forms of political organization, such as the parties have historically been, everywhere, for well over a century, hold up and bear fruit.

The Web provides valuable access to the political world, unprecedented opportunities for individual expression and political intervention, and encouragement to bring together and express consensus and dissent. But there can be no truly democratic, representative and effective participation in public decision-making unless it is channelled through organised political movements or parties that are capable of renewing themselves, all of them bound, however, by the constitutional imperative of the "democratic method."

In this crucial period for Italy and Europe, the forces represented in Parliament, without exception, must now provide an input to the decisions that need to be taken for the renewal of our country. Without being afraid to agree on solutions, since the two Chambers have indeed shown recently that they are not afraid to vote unanimously.

And you must all feel—honourable deputies and senators—that you are part of the Parliamentary institution not as members of a faction but as the embodiment of the people's will. Concrete work needs to be done, in a patient and constructive spirit, and expertise needs to be expended and acquired, first and foremost in the Chamber and Senate committees. I hope you will accept these words from someone who entered this Chamber as a deputy at the age of 28 and, day after day, added his own stone to the construction of the edifice of our democratic political life.

The only way to work in Parliament on the burning issues affecting the country is through dialogue with a government that is an essential interlocutor of both the majority and the opposition. 56 days on from the elections of 24–25 February—after which Parliament had to turn its attention to electing the Head of State—the Executive must be formed without delay.

Let us not chase after the formulae or definitions that are giving rise to so much chatter. It is not the President's role to issue mandates, for the formation of the government, that are subject to any constraints other than the one set forth in art. 94 of the Constitution: the government must have the confidence of both Chambers. And it is the government's task to provide itself with a programme, according to the priorities and timescale that it deems fitting.

There is, therefore, only one condition: to take stock of the true forces at play in the recently elected Parliament, in a full awareness of the challenges awaiting the government and the needs and general interest of the country. On the basis of the election results—which must need to be taken into account, like them or not—no one party or coalition (homogeneous or presumed to be so) that asked for votes to govern then received said votes in sufficient numbers to do so under its own steam.

Whatever outlook was presented to the voters, or whatever pact—if that is the preferred expression—each party entered into with its voters—the overall results of the elections must necessarily be taken into account. And those results point in one direction only: to the need for different forces to reach agreement so that a government might come into being and begin its life in Italy today. Without neglecting, at another level, the need for broader understandings, i.e. between majority and opposition, to provide agreed solutions to problems of common institutional responsibility.

After all, not even the United Kingdom—a country with an established democratic tradition—is governed by a single party; governments in Europe normally are formed or are at least supported by two or more parties, parties that may be similar in some way, or traditionally far removed from each other, or even bitter competitors.

In Italy a sort of horror of any suggestion of understandings, alliances, mediation, or convergence between different political forces has taken hold. That is a sign of regression, the spread of an idea that politics can be conducted without knowing or recognising the complex problems involved in governing the res publica and the implications of that in terms, precisely, of political mediation, understandings, and alliances. Or maybe all this is, in more concrete terms, a reflection of a couple of decades of confrontation—to the point where the very idea of civil co-existence has been lost—that have been more partisan and aggressive than ever before. Two decades that have seen a complete breakdown in communication between opposing political ranks.

I said this seven years ago in this chamber, on the same occasion as today, in the hope that "the time is at last almost ripe for a democracy of alternation." Which also means the time for seeking agreed solutions for government when the need arises. Otherwise, we would have to acknowledge a state of ungovernability, at least in the legislature that has just begun.

But it was not to make this point that I accepted your invitation to be sworn in again as President of the Republic. I accepted it so that in the coming days Italy will give itself the government it needs. And to that end I will act according to my remit: going no further than the limits of my constitutional role, and acting at most, to use a technical expression, as a "coagulating factor." But all of the political forces must assume their responsibilities in a spirit of realism: that was the wager implicit in the appeal addressed to me two days ago.

I am about to begin my second mandate, without any illusions, far less any claims for a "redemptive" expansion of my functions. I will, rather, exercise the functions attributed to me by the Constitution with an increased sense of the limits that apply to them and with unchanged impartiality. And I will do so for as long as the situation of the country and of the institutions seems to require of me, and my forces allow. For me today this further, unexpected political commitment begins in what is already a very advanced stage of my life. For you, today sees the beginning of a long road that must be travelled with passion, with rigour and with humility. My encouragement and good wishes for you in this endeavour will not be lacking.

Long live the Parliament! Long live the Republic! Long live Italy!

Source: Office of the President of the Italian Republic. "Speech before the Chambers by the President of the Italian Republic Giorgio Napolitano." April 22, 2013. http://www.quirinale.it/elementi/Continua .aspx?tipo=Discorso&key=2700.

OTHER HISTORIC DOCUMENTS OF INTEREST

Senators Debate Internet Sales Tax Bill

APRIL 25, 2013

Every year, an increasing number of Americans choose to conduct at least a portion of their shopping online, which has given rise to Internet giants like Amazon.com. These online retailers benefit from not being required to collect sales tax, in most cases, from customers who purchase in a state other than the one the retailer is physically located in. Opponents of such a set-up argue that not only do mom-and-pop retailers suffer from loss of business, but also that states lose a significant amount of tax revenue. Some states have attempted to pass laws to require Internet retailers to collect taxes, but in 2013, a large push came from the federal level when the Senate took up the Marketplace Fairness Act. The bill was easily passed, but the House of Representatives failed to debate the bill.

THE STATE OF INTERNET SALES TAX

In 1992, the Supreme Court ruled in *Quill Corp. v. North Dakota* that as long as an Internet retailer does not have a physical presence in the state the customer is making a purchase from, the retailer is not required to charge state and local sales tax. Instead, buyers are responsible for making a tax payment directly to the state for any products purchased online. The reality, however, is that this happens in only a small amount of cases. And with a growing number of individuals choosing to do their shopping online (the Department of Commerce predicts that shopping will be done almost exclusively online by 2023), the practice has a significant impact both on state and local sales tax revenue. Small businesses are also being overrun by major Internet retailers like Amazon.com because purchasers would rather avoid paying the taxes that can range anywhere from 5 percent to upwards of 10 percent of a purchase.

A study conducted by the University of Tennessee in 2009 revealed that state and local governments lose out on $11 billion in tax revenue every year. While noting that noncompliance might still remain, the report concluded, "Changing the law to require remote vendors to collect sales and use taxes would recover a significant portion of the estimated losses." The estimates in this report, however, have been called into question by groups like State Net, a legislative and regulatory information service, which, after reviewing tax data, found that the numbers purported by the University of Tennessee could be off by 75 to 80 percent.

SENATE PASSES BILL

In 2005, Sens. Mike Enzi, R-Wyo., and Byron Dorgan, D-N.D., proposed a bill that would force Internet retailers to collect sales taxes on all purchases. The caveat in the bill was that the taxes could only be collected after a state standardized its tax system to make it easier for online retailers to collect and distribute the taxes. Enzi said that the bill would reduce the variety of sales tax rates across the more than 7,500 tax-collecting jurisdictions in the country and require a "dramatic simplification in almost every aspect of sales and use tax collection and administration." Without passing such a bill, Enzi warned, "Other taxes, such as income or property taxes, will have to be increased to offset the lost revenue to state and local governments. I want to avoid that." The bill was referred to committee but never sent to the Senate floor.

In 2013, Enzi floated a new Internet sales tax bill called the Marketplace Fairness Act, a bill that would require sales and use taxes to be collected by Internet retailers regardless of the physical location of the purchaser. The bill had broad bipartisan support and went directly to the floor without going to committee. Debate on the bill largely revolved around whether it was fair for small retailers to face the burden of collecting sales taxes, distributing them to the states, and being subject to state audits. Sen. Jeanne Shaheen, D-N.H., argued that the bill "is going to put those small businesses at a disadvantage, making it harder for them to compete with large online retailers." These companies "do not need an additional paperwork burden to distract them from running their companies." She went on to say that the bill was specifically harmful for small retailers in states like New Hampshire where no sales tax is collected on any sales, either in person or online.

Those who supported the Marketplace Fairness Act disputed Shaheen's claims, noting the exemption from the bill for any retailer earning less than $1 million in online sales. Sen. Dick Durbin, D-Ill., said the bill would impact the largest online retailers but "does not affect these small retailers." Shaheen said the exemption put "an arbitrary ceiling" on corporate growth "because as they get closer to the $1 million in online revenue . . . they are going to have to ask themselves, is it worth going through the bureaucratic nightmare of complying with forty-six different states' sales taxes? Unfortunately, for them and for too many other businesses, the answer is more than likely to be no." Private companies backing the opposition in the Senate included small companies, prominent conservative groups, some Democrats, and online retailer eBay, the latter of which wanted the small business cap to be raised to $10 million or apply to only those companies with less than fifty employees. Amazon.com was a major supporter of the Marketplace Fairness Act and would likely be unaffected by the provisions of the bill because its rapid growth has led to the building of distribution warehouses in many states, meaning that it is already required to pay a variety of state taxes.

On May 6, 2013, the Senate voted 69–27 to approve the Marketplace Fairness Act. "This bill is about fairness, it's about leveling the playing field for brick-and-mortar shops," said Sen. Enzi. Five Democrats and twenty-two Republicans voted against the bill. Sen. Ted Cruz, R-Texas, was vocal in his distaste and accused those who voted for passage of being heavily influenced by lobbyists. "What we are seeing in this bill is Washington ganging up with the giant corporations—you're seeing Democrats and Republicans arm in arm with the giant corporations," Cruz said.

House Balks

In the House, where conservative support would play a major role in passage, the bill faced an uncertain future. A number of prominent lawmakers said they would not support the Senate's bill because it amounted to little more than a tax increase. Rep. Paul Ryan, R-Wis., chairman of the powerful House Budget Committee said the bill, as passed in the Senate, would increase government taxing authority to an unnecessary level.

In September, the House Judiciary Committee Chairman Bob Goodlatte, R-Va., and Rep. Spencer Bachus, R-Ala., released a list of seven principles that would need to be followed in any Internet sales tax bill if the committee was to approve it and send it to the full House for a vote. These seven principles included: (1) creating a level playing field for all businesses, (2) creating a simpler tax system, (3) preventing unnecessary taxes from being applied, (4) allowing tax competition, (5) leaving state tax activity sovereign, (6) protecting consumer data, and (7) not creating new taxes to apply to Internet sales.

The principles were hailed by a group known as the Marketplace Fairness Coalition, which represents non-online retailers, and the International Council of Shopping Centers. The former hoped that an agreement might be reached on a new bill by the end of 2013; the latter added, "The principles are a good step forward and we will continue to walk with the chairman on this journey." Goodlatte did not say whether he would support the Marketplace Fairness Act, but supporters of the bill have argued that the bill in its current form as sent from the Senate already met a number of those criteria. By the close of 2013, no Internet sales tax bill had been proposed in the House.

UNCERTAIN IMPACT

Even successful passage of a bill would not result in immediate action on the part of states that would be required to make adjustments to their tax systems before out-of-state retailers could properly collect and send taxes to the states. Some states would be required to purchase and use new software to make tax collection easier. Those states with more than one tax agency would need to consolidate down to a single entity, and they would be required to accept a single tax return. Overall, each state would need to simplify its tax system before it could even receive the taxes from online retailers.

A study by the Small Business Administration, released in November, questioned whether an Internet sales tax bill would achieve any of its desired results. According to the study, by exempting small retailers, at least 40 percent of Internet sales will remain untaxed. This would add up to a total loss of billions of dollars in sales tax revenue for state governments each year, according to the study.

STATES TAKE ACTION

Without federal movement on wider enforcement of tax laws on Internet retailers, some states have set up their own regulations. These so-called "Amazon laws" were enacted in Arizona, California, Connecticut, Georgia, Indiana, Kansas, Kentucky, Massachusetts, Nevada, New Jersey, New York, North Dakota, Pennsylvania, Tennessee, Texas, Virginia, Washington, West Virginia, and Wisconsin. States vary on the application of the law—some require retailers to charge the appropriate taxes, while others simply require the retailer to notify a purchaser of the state requirement that a tax payment be made directly to the state. In 2013, the governors of Iowa, Maine, Virginia, and Wisconsin were all working to put measures on the ballot to enact Amazon laws, hoping that action in the states might prompt the House and Senate to reach a compromise and pass a bill. Each governor separately made a push for support by giving examples to the public of what the extra tax revenue might mean. In Virginia, Republican Governor Bob McDonnell said that the extra money could be put toward much-needed transportation and infrastructure projects.

Due to the fact that the laws do not apply in every state, there is a significant amount of confusion among Internet retailers and purchasers, and the laws have been challenged in court. New York's bill was upheld, but Colorado's law, which requires Internet retailers to inform purchasers of the necessity to pay sales tax directly to the state, was struck down in a federal district court.

—Heather Kerrigan

Following is the text of two Senate floor statements delivered on April 25, 2013. The first, by Sen. Dick Durbin, D-Ill., is in support of the Marketplace Fairness Act, while the second, by Sen. Jeanne Shaheen, D-N.H., argues against the act.

Sen. Durbin Floor Statement in Support of Internet Sales Tax

DOCUMENT

April 25, 2013

Mr. DURBIN. Mr. President, pending on the floor is S. 743. This is a bill which, in its simplest terms, will allow the States to ask Internet retailers, when they sell in the State, to collect sales tax.

Currently, every State requires consumers to pay the sales tax, but it is not collected at the point of purchase. So this legislation will respond to a 20-year-old Supreme Court decision that said to Congress: You have to write a law to do this. This is the law.

Senator Enzi and I, Senator HEIDI HEITKAMP, as well as Senator LAMAR ALEXANDER, we have all worked together on this legislation on a bipartisan basis.

This measure was before the Senate last week. It is not a long bill; it is 11 pages. It is certainly within the grasp of any Senator to secure and read it and understand it. It is very straightforward.

We have had efforts made on the Senate floor to delay consideration of this measure. We have taken three votes on it over the past month or so. The first vote under the budget resolution was a generic vote: Do you support the idea or not? Seventy-five Senators voted in the affirmative—a dramatic commitment from the Democratic side and a majority commitment from the Republican side to this measure. We then faced a vote on cloture— in other words, closing down the debate—on the motion to proceed. We had that vote on Monday. Seventy-four Senators voted to proceed. Yesterday, on the actual motion to proceed: 75 Senators. So this is clearly an issue where a substantial majority of the Senate believes we should move forward and pass this legislation.

We have invited our colleagues—Senator ENZI and I have—if they have amendments, to file their amendments. They have had 6 days—6 days—to prepare the amendments and file them. The deadline is an hour and a half from now for filing amendments. So far we have received 31 amendments.

We sat down last night and said: Let's pick a good number of these amendments. Call them. Let's debate them. Let's vote on them. Let's act like the Senate. Let's see how that works.

We started to do that. We came up with a list. Included in that list are amendments being offered by people we know are going to vote against this bill, so they are not friendly amendments. They are adversarial amendments. But that is all right. Isn't that what we are here for—debate it out; express your point of view; we will express ours; let's vote. I think that is fair. No one can criticize us for not being open to that. We are not trying to fix the outcome. We are ready to bring this to full debate. But when we contacted the Senators who are opposed to the bill and said, call your amendments, they said, we are not ready.

I wish those Senators who said they were not ready could meet the Senators we run into in the hall who say, when is this going to end, when can I go home, because the two of them need to get in conversation. We want to do this in a timely, thoughtful way because it is a critically important issue. But we cannot do it unless our colleagues will come to the floor of the Senate and offer their amendments.

Yesterday we had one amendment we thought was simple and easy. It is an amendment that said: We will not impose across America a tax for you to use the Internet—the Internet Freedom Act it is called. It is bipartisan. Senator MARK PRYOR of Arkansas, a Democrat, and Senator BLUNT of Missouri, a Republican, came together and offered to extend the current policy of the United States on Internet freedom.

Senator ENZI and I looked at that and said: We can put that in this bill. That is something with which we agree. We are not imposing any new taxes in this bill—none. So that is certainly a statement of policy with which we would agree.

We brought this to the floor, and a Senator from Oregon came and objected to considering that amendment yesterday. So yesterday, no amendments. Now we are told that as to any amendments we bring to the floor today, there will be more objections.

I do not think this makes the Senate look very good. I do not think this is in the best interests of this institution nor our government. We were elected to roll up our sleeves and go to work and address the problems facing this country. We understand that with 100 people there will be differences of opinion. We are supposed to engage in civil debate on the floor and then vote. But to lunge from one filibuster to the next and have Members coming to the floor and objecting to amendments puts us in a terrible position.

I have served in the minority, as Senator ALEXANDER and Senator ENZI do at this point. The one thing you really want in the minority is a chance to offer an amendment, to express your point of view, even if you lose. Now we are offering that opportunity, and unfortunately there is a resistance to it. Well, we are going to try it. We are going to test it. If the people who are going to continue to try to block any debate on this bill want to come forward, I hope they will face questions from colleagues as to what their intent is.

Ultimately, we will finish this bill before we go home. If it means staying through the weekend—if that satisfies some Members—we will do it. But it is a terrible waste of opportunity. We have gone 2 straight days with no votes on amendments. And Senators ENZI, ALEXANDER, HEITKAMP and I believe it is time for the Senate to be the Senate.

Mr. President, I yield the floor.

SOURCE: Sen. Dick Durbin. "Marketplace Fairness Act of 2013." *Congressional Record* 2013, pt. 159, S2985–2986. April 25, 2013. http://www.gpo.gov/fdsys/pkg/CREC-2013-04-25/pdf/CREC-2013-04-25-pt1-PgS2985-3.pdf.

Sen. Shaheen in Opposition to Internet Sales Tax

DOCUMENT

April 25, 2013

Mrs. SHAHEEN. Madam President, I really came down to the floor today to continue my opposition to the Internet sales tax legislation that is before us.

The proponents of this legislation claim it is about "fairness," but when you really think about it, this bill is anything but fair. In fact, it creates an unfair situation for small businesses in a number of ways.

First, the legislation is particularly unfair for businesses in my State of New Hampshire and in the other four States in this country that do not collect a sales tax.

I filed amendments, as I know a number of my colleagues have—my colleague from New Hampshire, Senator AYOTTE, has filed a number of amendments—that I hope can help address this issue. But I think it is important for everyone here, especially those who are concerned with creating new redtape, to understand how this legislation is going to affect small businesses.

This proposal is going to put new regulatory burdens on small companies across the country, not just in New Hampshire. As a result, it is going to put those small businesses at a disadvantage, making it harder for them to compete with large online retailers.

As a former small business owner myself, I understand how time-consuming regulations and compliance requirements can be. Make no mistake, the bureaucratic nightmare we are going to be creating for small businesses under this legislation is real. I think it is worth talking for a minute about what that process is going to look like for the small online retailers.

In a recent piece for the Daily Beast, writer Megan McArdle went through what the process would be like for a small business. She pointed to the SBA guidebook for small businesses when they collect sales taxes in multiple States. The guidebook tells small businesses:

Generally, states require businesses to pay the sales taxes they collect quarterly or monthly. You'll have to use a special tax return for sales taxes, and report all sales, [all] taxable sales, [all] exempt sales and amount of tax due. Not paying on time can result in penalties. As always, check with your state or local government about the process in your location.

McArdle points out that, despite claims from the proponents of the Marketplace Fairness Act that tax collection will be easy and streamlined, the bottom line for a small business is that "you've still got to keep fifty states worth of records and file 40-odd states worth of returns."

McArdle went on to say:

For Amazon—the actual target of these laws—this is trivial. Their staff of crack accountants can probably roll these things out before their Monday morning coffee break. For a small vendor, however, that's a whole lot of paperwork.

And that is what this legislation is really about—those small business owners who are working hard to grow their companies. They do not need an additional paperwork burden to distract them from running their companies.

Let me provide one example. There is a small company in the town of Epsom, NH. It is called Michele's Sweet Shoppe. Michele's sells popcorn and other gourmet treats both at their brick-and-mortar store in Epsom and online. This is a small business that is growing, and it wants to create jobs. They sell locally in New Hampshire at their brick-and-mortar store, but a big part of their future strategy for growth is taking advantage of new markets through the Internet.

Under this legislation, however, there is an arbitrary ceiling on this company's growth because as they get closer to $1 million in online revenue—as they have said to me—they are going to have to ask themselves, is it worth going through the bureaucratic nightmare of complying with 46 different States' sales taxes? Unfortunately, for them and for too many other businesses, the answer is more than likely to be no.

For Amazon and online retailers, this is not even a question. This is exactly the reason why this bill is good for big businesses and bad for small businesses. It makes it harder for small mom-and-pop stores to compete.

Small businesses—certainly in New Hampshire and in most of the country—are really the economic engine of our economy. Two out of three of the new businesses that are going to be created are going to be created by small business. We should really think twice before we pass this kind of legislation that will keep them from growing and that is really designed to help those big businesses.

I support a number of amendments to this bill. I would like to see them at least voted on. I hope some might be adopted because I think they would make the legislation fairer for small businesses. One of those is a bipartisan amendment we have worked on with Senator Toomey to raise the threshold for small businesses under the legislation. I have also filed an amendment to address a fundamental flaw in the legislation that I think must be addressed because this legislation is anything but fair to States such as New Hampshire, States such as Alaska, Montana, the other States in this country that do not collect a sales tax.

This is a proposal that fundamentally violates State sovereignty. It enables one State to impose the enforcement of its laws on the 49 other States and territories without their approval, and it provides zero benefit for the non-sales tax States while it creates an additional and unnecessary burden on our small businesses. That is why I filed an amendment to create an exemption for businesses in States such as New Hampshire. States will be able to force New Hampshire companies to collect sales taxes—especially when our States get no benefit whatsoever—and this amendment is designed to prevent that.

I am disappointed this evening that it does not look as though we are going to be allowed to vote on any of these amendments, although I am still hopeful that we might get a hearing.

I urge my colleagues, again, to think twice about this legislation. I urge them to look at the amendments when they are filed—if we are able to get an amendment process—and to think about supporting those amendments so the legislation really could live up to its billing as the Marketplace Fairness Act because right now it certainly does not meet that standard for the State of New Hampshire and our small businesses.

Thank you very much, Madam President.

I yield the floor.

SOURCE: Sen. Jeanne Shaheen. "Marketplace Fairness Act of 2013." *Congressional Record* 2013, pt. 159, S3016-3017. April 25, 2013. http://www.gpo.gov/fdsys/pkg/CREC-2013-04-25/pdf/CREC-2013-04-25-pt1-PgS3016.pdf.

May

Bangladeshi Prime Minister and U.S. President on Garment Industry

MAY 1 AND 3, AND JUNE 27, 2013

On April 24, 2013, the eight-story Rana Plaza building collapsed, killing more than 1,000 people. The Rana Plaza housed five garment factories supplying products to major retail outlets in Europe and North America. The disaster highlighted major safety deficiencies in Bangladeshi garment factories, as well as poor wages and a dire lack of adherence to building codes during construction. Bangladesh's garment industry is second only to China's in terms of its size and accounts for around 80 percent of the country's more than $27 billion in export receipts. Subsequent to the disaster, around one hundred primarily North American and European retailers that source garments from Bangladeshi factories signed agreements that commit them to inspect premises and provide financial resources to address safety issues. Meanwhile, some retailers provided ongoing compensation to victims of the disaster and their families to cover lost wages. The Bangladeshi government has also provided financial assistance, although it is limited to families of the deceased and those who have lost at least one limb.

Worst Garment Industry Disaster in History

On April 23, one day before the collapse, workers in the Rana Plaza building in Savar, an industrial suburb of Dhaka, reported structural shaking and cracks in the buildings floors and walls. According to a high-level government report, the building was briefly evacuated and an engineer was brought in to assess the structure. The engineer reportedly warned the building's owner, Sohel Rana, as well as the owners of the garment factories housed in the Rana Plaza, that the building was unsafe for reentry. Despite this, the factory owners urged their employees to return to work the following day. The author of the government's report, Main Uddin Khandaker, a high-ranking bureaucrat in the Home Ministry said that the owners "compelled them to start [working]."

On April 24, the building collapsed, killing upwards of 1,000 people. It was the worst garment industry disaster and one of the deadliest industrial accidents in history. The government report suggested that large power generators located on the top two levels of the building were partially to blame for the collapse. When in use, the heavy generators shook the poorly constructed building where thousands of employees worked in five garment factories. The building had initially been designed to house retail shops and offices and did not meet factory building codes. The Prime Minister, Sheikh Hasina, said that approximately 90 percent of structures in Bangladesh do not meet prescribed building codes. Heavy machinery use on the top floors, cheap construction materials, and land unsuitable for development—Rana Plaza was built over a filled-in pond—were in large part to blame for the collapse.

When the building collapsed at around 9 a.m. local time, an estimated 3,100 people were in the building. The Bangladeshi army led rescue efforts at the site, and some 2,400 people were rescued from the rubble. The Bangladeshi government declined any aid for disaster recovery, including rescue dogs and other search equipment offered by the United Nations. Many of the victims were women, who comprised a large proportion of the factories' workforce. The last survivor was pulled from the rubble seventeen days after the building collapse.

BANGLADESHIS PROTEST

Within days of the disaster, protests broke out in other industrialized areas of the country, with workers demanding safer working conditions, higher pay, and compensation for the victims and their families. Criticism did not come solely from inside Bangladesh. A week after the collapse, Pope Francis referred to the working conditions and pay as "slave labor."

Prior to the collapse, Rana was a powerful local figure and secretary of the local youth wing of the ruling Awami League. He fled after the collapse but was arrested four days later in Benapole, near the Indian border, and charged with criminal negligence. The government recommended a life sentence for Rana and others culpable for the tragedy. Nine months after the disaster, four arrests had been made. As of December 2013, no trial date had been set for Rana.

Bangladesh's clothing industry is critical to the economy, accounting for around 80 percent of the total value of exports (all Bangladeshi exports totaled $27.2 billion in 2013). Around 60 percent of the garments exported are sent to Europe, while around 25 percent are destined for the United States. There are an estimated 5,000 garment factories in Bangladesh, approximately twice that of Indonesia and Vietnam, employing around four million workers. Most of these factory workers are women. Moreover, Bangladeshi labor is some of the cheapest in the world. The minimum wage is just 3,000 taka per month ($39), far below that of Vietnam and China where the average wage is five times that amount. In addition to cheap labor, the Bangladeshi garment industry also enjoys duty-free access to European Union markets, making it a popular location for Western retailers to have their garments stitched.

GLOBAL RESPONSE

Many prominent Western retailers had contracts with the five garment factories in Rana Plaza. U.K.-based Primark, Spain-based Mango, and Italy-based Benetton were just a few retailers buying from the workshops housed in the building. High-profile retailers from the United States, Europe, and Asia, including some that were not directly linked to the Plaza, announced plans to improve factory safety in Bangladesh. The first accord was reached among European firms; the Accord on Fire and Building Safety in Bangladesh was signed by more than 100 European retailers as well as nongovernmental organizations and labor unions in July 2013.

The signatory companies included Sweden-based H&M, U.K.-based Marks & Spencer, the Spanish firm Inditex (which owns Zara), and France's Carrefour. The Accord, which is legally binding, commits to inspecting all Bangladeshi factories utilized by the signatories within nine months and also to "insure that sufficient funds are available to pay for renovations and other safety improvements" when deficiencies are identified. To identify the factories for inspection, retailers are required to disclose which factories they utilize in Bangladesh—an unprecedented commitment given that the list will be made publicly available and most retailers do not disclose this information for fear that their competitors will steal suppliers. Inditex uses around 350 factories in Bangladesh to produce its apparel, while H&M uses nearly 250. Inspection reports will also be made publicly available. The signatories agreed that the funds to fix any safety issues will come from a variety of sources, including direct payments, joint investments, or donor funding.

A separate American plan, called the Alliance for Bangladesh Worker Safety, was announced in July. Retailers including Macy's, Wal-Mart, Gap, and Target made up part of the group of seventeen signatories. The key facet of the American plan is a $42 million commitment to improve safety standards and to set up an anonymous worker tip hotline to report safety concerns at factories. It also commits to $100 million in loans and funding for Bangladeshi factory owners to make necessary safety improvements. Each signatory has a five-year financial commitment based on the amount of business done in Bangladesh. The American plan also calls for inspections of the 500 or so factories used by American retailers to be completed within twelve months. Any issues will be reported to the Bangladeshi government, the factory owner, and a committee of factory workers at the site. The European and American plans differ significantly in that the latter puts the onus on the factory owners to correct safety issues identified during inspections and does not commit retailers to paying for any improvements. Moreover, the American plan is not legally binding for signatories, unlike the European plan. Five labor rights groups, including Worker Rights Consortium, the Clean Clothes Campaign, International Labor Rights Forum, Maquila Solidarity Network, and United Students Against Sweatshops, criticized the American plan, stating that "retailers are not obligated to pay one cent toward the renovation and repair of their factories in Bangladesh."

U.S. President Barack Obama dealt what some considered a knockout blow to the Bangladeshi garment industry when he suspended trade privileges for the nation on June 27, 2013. In a letter to Congress, the president said he was issuing an executive order because Bangladesh was "not taking steps to afford internationally recognized worker rights to workers in that country." The president had been under pressure from labor groups and Democrats to send a tough message to Bangladesh since the Rana Plaza collapse. His executive order will remove the break on tariffs the country receives when it exports goods to the United States. Bangladesh was highly critical of the president's decision.

PIECEMEAL COMPENSATION

In addition to retailers' long-term plans to address safety issues in factories, Primark has developed a compensation plan for those injured and the families of those who died in the disaster. Primark has provided short-term aid equivalent to three months' wages to the injured and families of the deceased, and food aid to 1,300 affected families. Primark called on other retailers who had contracts with garment factories in Rana Plaza to commit to a long-term compensation plan, which would include medical aid. A $40 million compensation fund was agreed to in December 2013. The plan will see that victims and families of the deceased are paid for lost wages on a case-by-case basis. The fund will be chaired by the International Labour Organization.

Meanwhile, the Bangladeshi government has compensated 777 victims of the disaster. However, the funds, totaling less than $2.3 million, have only been provided to those who lost a limb or families of the deceased. Those workers suffering from injuries, such as a fractured spine, have yet to be compensated. There have also been issues with compensation to families of those killed. The government requires DNA testing to confirm victims, but in many cases victims were buried prior to formal identification, leaving families without compensation and no means to prove that their relatives are no longer alive.

—Hilary Ewing

Following is the text of two press releases from the Bangladeshi prime minister's office—the first, on May 1, 2013, calls on industry owners to comply with all welfare and safety regulations; and the second, released on May 3, 2013, details steps being undertaken by the Bangladeshi government to ensure garment factory safety—and the text of an Executive Order issued by U.S. President Barack Obama on June 27, 2013, suspending Bangladesh's trade privileges.

Bangladesh Prime Minister Urges Industry Owners to Comply With Safety Regulations

May 1, 2013

Prime Minister Sheikh Hasina today said the owners of the industries must comply with the rules of principles with regards to labour welfare and their occupational safety for the sake of smooth running of their business.

She also called upon the workers of the mills and factories not to be misguided by false propaganda and get involved in any destructive activities suicidal for country's economy.

The Prime Minister made the call while addressing a discussion organized by Ministry of Labour and Employment marking the historic May Day at Osmani Memorial Auditorium here today.

She said the government has taken massive programmes for welfare of the working class people. Side by side all related laws are being upgraded keeping consistency with international conventions.

The owners of the industries have to obey the laws and ensure highest safety of the workers as well as ensure their fair wages and other allowances, she said.

Presided over by Minister of Labor and Employment Raji Uddin Ahmed Raju, the function was addressed, among others, by State Minister Begum Munnujan Sufian, Chairman of the Parliamentary Standing Committee on the Ministry Israfil Alam and Deputy Director General of ILO Gilbert Fossoun Houngbo.

President of Jatiya Sramik League Sukkur Ahmed, president of Bangladesh Employers Association M Fazlul Haque and Secretary of the Ministry Mikhail Shiffer also spoke on the occasion.

Terming the workers as the lifeline of industries, agriculture and other service sectors, the Prime Minister said mutual cooperation between the labourers and owners is crucial for development of both sides.

The Prime Minister said the government would do everything possible for the workers. But by no means it would accept any unruly activities, she said.

She asked law enforcing agencies to arrest the persons involved in vandalism in the plea of protesting Savar incident verifying the video footages urging the genuine workers to handover the outsider conspirators to the law enforcers for protecting country's industry in their own interest.

Referring to the tragic incident of building collapse in Savar, she said the government has taken prompt action for rescue operation, treatment of the injured persons and their rehabilitation. The government is going with short, mid and long term plans to prevent the recurrence of such incident, she said.

In this context she requested the industrialists and the owners of mills and factories to take necessary measures to implement those plans.

The Prime Minister said, the industries in Bangladesh is suffering from infrastructural lacking as most of them didn't grow in a planned manner.

She said the government has taken plan to set up a garments village with all necessary facilities.

The Prime Minister said her government does not want to see the wails of the workers anymore. The government has raised the wages of the labourers and adopted a labour policy giving the interest of the workers.

The Prime Minister thanked all rescue workers including Army, Fire Service, BGB, Police, RAB and volunteers and termed the engagement of all in such a humanitarian rescue activities as an unprecedented one.

In this regard, she mentioned that despite their life risks, rescue workers retrieved over 2500 people from the debris.

Sheikh Hasina said her government has taken necessary measures to ensure better treatment to every injured worker, made arrangement of jobs for the workers of different RMG factories of Rana Plaza, and rehabilitation of the families of dead and wounded.

The Prime Minister also said the present government has initiated to amend the Labour Act through incorporating some rules on labour union as well as keeping provision of organizing trade union and participatory committee.

Expatriate Welfare Bank has been founded to provide credit facilities to poor workers to go abroad with job, she said.

Sheikh Hasina said, during previous tenure of her government, a good number of steps for welfare of the workers, but those measures didn't continue following the change of the government in 2001, she said.

The Prime Minister thanked the Sramik League, labour front of Bangladesh Awami League, for donating the fund of the organization for Savar victims instead of holding its scheduled May Day rally.

SOURCE: Government of the People's Republic of Bangladesh. Prime Minister's Office. "May 1, 2013." May 1, 2013. http://www.pmo.gov.bd/index.php?option=com_content&task=view&id=842&Itemid=353.

Bangladesh Prime Minister Remarks on Garment Industry Reform

May 3, 2013

Bangladesh is reforming its garment industry: PM

Mentioning that condition now in Bangladesh is good for investment, Prime Minister Sheikh Hasina said her government is moving rapidly to fix the existing problems of the readymade garment (RMG) sector.

"There are some problems in the RMG sector. But, we have been trying our best to improve the situation," she said this in an interview with CNN on Thursday eight days after a nine-storey building collapsed at Savar on the outskirts of Dhaka.

Sheikh Hasina told CNN's Christiane Amanpour that a committee has been formed to ensure the safety of buildings and workers. "This committee will submit the findings to the Cabinet committee," she said.

The Prime Minister expressed little fear that international companies would stop doing business in Bangladesh as a result of the disaster. Investors have tapped into the Bangladeshi market not just because of its high-quality workers, she said. "They get cheap labor. That's why they come here," she said.

Asked about reports that only 18 inspectors are responsible for overseeing safety conditions in more than 100,000 garment factories in and around the capital city, Sheikh Hasina said, "We don't depend on only . . . those inspectors."

Steps to improve conditions were taken before the collapse of the building Rana Plaza at Savar, she said citing passage by the Cabinet of a labor law that will be sent to the Parliament.

The Prime Minister noted that workplace disasters have occurred in the United States, too; she cited last month's explosion of a fertilizer plant in West, Texas, in which 14 people died.

"Anywhere in the world, any accident can take place," she said. "You cannot predict anything."

Amanpour, CNN's chief international correspondent, pointed out that local officials predicted that the building could collapse after cracks appeared on its walls on April 23, and they urged workers not to re-enter it.

"You are very correct," Sheikh Hasina said. "Unfortunately, in the morning, the owners of the factories put pressure to labor to enter."

She praised government officials for trying to prevent the workers at the five garment factories in the building from re-entering on April 24, the morning of the collapse. "It is not true that the government hasn't taken any steps," she said.

The Prime Minister blamed the owners of the five factories as well as Sohel Rana, the building's owner, and disputed the suggestion that their political connections could protect them.

"The law will take its own course," she said. "Criminal is criminal. They will get all the necessary action; that we can assure you. It is our promise to the people."

Sheikh Hasina added, "Any business person, if they commit any kind of crime, our government always takes action."

She pointed to the companies that source their products from such factories, saying they should pay well enough that factory owners can pay good salaries and ensure the business is safely run. "They're partly responsible for it," she said.

And she urged that the disaster be considered in context. "You cannot blame the whole business or whole industry just for one incident," she said.

Sheikh Hasina said officials in her government "are in favor of labor," having increased the minimum wage by 82%, built dormitories and seen to the health care needs of workers.

SOURCE: Government of the People's Republic of Bangladesh. Prime Minister's Office. "May 3, 2013." May 3, 2013. http://www.pmo.gov.bd/index.php?option=com_content&task=view&id=842&Itemid=353.

President Obama Suspends Bangladesh Trade Priviledges

DOCUMENT

June 27, 2013

By the President of the United States of America

A Proclamation

1. Section 502(b)(2)(G) of the Trade Act of 1974, as amended (the "1974 Act") (19 U.S.C. 2462(b)(2)(G)), provides that the President shall not designate any country a beneficiary developing country under the Generalized System of Preferences (GSP) if such country has not taken or is not taking steps to afford internationally recognized worker rights to workers in the country (including any designated zone in that country). Section 502(d)(2) of the 1974 Act (19 U.S.C. 2462(d)(2)) provides that, after complying with the requirements of section 502(f)(2) of the 1974 Act (19 U.S.C. 2462(f)(2)), the President shall withdraw or suspend the designation of any country as a beneficiary developing country if, after such designation, the President determines that as the result of changed circumstances such country would be barred from designation as a beneficiary developing country under section 502(b)(2) of the 1974 Act. Section 502(f)(2) of the 1974 Act requires the President to notify the Congress and the country concerned at least 60 days before terminating its designation as a beneficiary developing country for purposes of the GSP.

2. Having considered the factors set forth in section 502(b)(2)(G) and providing the notification called for in section 502(f)(2), I have determined pursuant to section 502(d) of the 1974 Act, that it is appropriate to suspend Bangladesh's designation as a GSP beneficiary developing country because it has not taken or is not taking steps to afford internationally recognized worker rights to workers in the country. In order to reflect the suspension of Bangladesh's status as a beneficiary developing country under the GSP, I have determined that it is appropriate to modify general notes 4(a) and 4(b)(i) of the Harmonized Tariff Schedule of the United States (HTS).

3. Section 503(c)(2)(A) of the 1974 Act provides that beneficiary developing countries, except those designated as least-developed beneficiary developing countries or beneficiary sub-Saharan African countries as provided in section 503(c)(2)(D) of the 1974 Act (19 U.S.C. 2463(c)(2)(D)), are subject to competitive need limitations on the preferential treatment afforded under the GSP to eligible articles.

4. Pursuant to section 503(c)(2)(A) of the 1974 Act, I have determined that in 2012 certain beneficiary developing countries exported eligible articles in quantities exceeding the applicable competitive need limitations, and I therefore terminate the duty-free treatment for such articles from such beneficiary developing countries.

5. Section 503(c)(2)(F)(i) of the 1974 Act (19 U.S.C. 2463(c)(2)(F)(i)) provides that the President may disregard the competitive need limitation provided in section 503(c)

(2)(A)(i)(II) of the 1974 Act (19 U.S.C. 2463(c)(2)(A)(i)(II)) with respect to any eligible article from any beneficiary developing country, if the aggregate appraised value of the imports of such article into the United States during the preceding calendar year does not exceed an amount set forth in section 503(c)(2)(F)(ii) of the 1974 Act (19 U.S.C. 2463(c)(2)(F)(ii)).

6. Pursuant to section 503(c)(2)(F)(i) of the 1974 Act, I have determined that the competitive need limitation provided in section 503(c)(2)(A)(i)(II) of the 1974 Act should be disregarded with respect to certain eligible articles from certain beneficiary developing countries.

7. Section 503(d)(1) of the 1974 Act (19 U.S.C. 2463(d)(1)) provides that the President may waive the application of the competitive need limitations in section 503(c)(2) of the 1974 Act with respect to any eligible article from any beneficiary developing country if certain conditions are met.

8. Pursuant to section 503(d)(1) of the 1974 Act, I have received the advice of the United States International Trade Commission on whether any industry in the United States is likely to be adversely affected by waivers of the competitive need limitations provided in section 503(c)(2), and I have determined, based on that advice and on the considerations described in sections 501 and 502(c) of the 1974 Act (19 U.S.C. 2462(c)) and after giving great weight to the considerations in section 503(d)(2) of the 1974 Act (19 U.S.C. 2463(d)(2)), that such waivers are in the national economic interest of the United States. Accordingly, I have determined that the competitive need limitations of section 503(c)(2) of the 1974 Act should be waived with respect to certain eligible articles from certain beneficiary developing countries.

9. Section 503(d)(4)(B)(ii) of the 1974 Act (19 U.S.C. 2463(d)(4)(B)(ii)) provides that the President should revoke any waiver of the application of the competitive need limitations that has been in effect with respect to an article for 5 years or more if the beneficiary developing country has exported to the United States during the preceding calendar year an amount that exceeds the quantity set forth in section 503(d)(4)(B)(ii)(I) or section 503(d)(4)(B)(ii)(II) of the 1974 Act (19 U.S.C. 2463(d)(4)(B)(ii)(I) and 19 U.S.C. 2463(d)(4)(B)(ii)(II)).

10. Pursuant to section 503(d)(4)(B)(ii) of the 1974 Act, I have determined that in 2012 certain beneficiary developing countries exported eligible articles for which a waiver has been in effect for 5 years or more in quantities exceeding the applicable limitation set forth in section 503(d)(4)(B)(ii)(I) or section 503(d)(4)(B)(ii)(II) of the 1974 Act, and I therefore revoke said waivers.

11. Section 604 of the 1974 Act (19 U.S.C. 2483) authorizes the President to embody in the HTS the substance of the relevant provisions of that Act, and of other Acts affecting import treatment, and actions thereunder, including removal, modification, continuance, or imposition of any rate of duty or other import restriction.

12. Presidential Proclamation 6763 of December 23, 1994, implemented the trade agreements resulting from the Uruguay Round of multilateral negotiations, including Schedule XX—United States of America, annexed to the Marrakesh Protocol to the General Agreement on Tariffs and Trade 1994 (Schedule XX). In order to maintain the intended tariff treatment for certain products covered in Schedule XX, I have determined that technical corrections to the HTS are necessary.

13. Presidential Proclamation 7011 of June 30, 1997, implemented modifications of the World Trade Organization Ministerial Declaration on Trade in Information Technology Products (the "ITA") for the United States. Products included in Attachment B to the ITA are entitled to duty-free treatment wherever classified. Presidential Proclamation 8840 of June 29, 2012, implemented certain technical corrections are necessary to the HTS in order to maintain the intended tariff treatment for certain products covered in Attachment B. I have determined that certain additional technical corrections are necessary to conform the HTS to the changes made by Presidential Proclamation 8840.

14. Presidential Proclamation 8818 of May 14, 2012, implemented U.S. tariff commitments under the United States-Colombia Trade Promotion Agreement and incorporated by reference Publication 4320 of the United States International Trade Commission, entitled "Modifications to the Harmonized Tariff Schedule of the United States to Implement the United States-Colombia Trade Promotion Agreement." Presidential Proclamation 8894 of October 29, 2012, made modifications to the HTS to correct technical errors and omissions in Annexes I and II to Publication 4320. I have determined that a modification is necessary to correct an additional omission.

Now, Therefore, I, Barack Obama, President of the United States of America, by virtue of the authority vested in me by the Constitution and the laws of the United States of America, including but not limited to title V and section 604 of the 1974 Act, do proclaim that:

(1) The designation of Bangladesh as a beneficiary developing country under the GSP is suspended on the date that is 60 days after the date this proclamation is published in the *Federal Register.*

(2) In order to reflect the suspension of benefits under the GSP with respect to Bangladesh, general notes 4(a) and 4(b)(i) of the HTS are modified as set forth in section A of Annex I to this proclamation by deleting "Bangladesh" from the list of independent countries and least developed countries, effective with respect to articles entered, or withdrawn from warehouse for consumption, on or after the date that is 60 days after the date this proclamation is published in the *Federal Register.*

(3) In order to provide that one or more countries should no longer be treated as beneficiary developing countries with respect to one or more eligible articles for purposes of the GSP, the Rates of Duty 1—Special subcolumn for the corresponding HTS subheadings and general note 4(d) of the HTS are modified as set forth in sections B and C of Annex I to this proclamation.

(4) The modifications to the HTS set forth in sections B and C of Annex I to this proclamation shall be effective with respect to the articles entered, or withdrawn from warehouse for consumption, on or after the dates set forth in the relevant sections of Annex I.

(5) The competitive need limitation provided in section 503(c)(2)(A)(i)(II) of the 1974 Act is disregarded with respect to the eligible articles in the HTS subheadings and to the beneficiary developing countries listed in Annex II to this proclamation.

(6) A waiver of the application of section 503(c)(2) of the 1974 Act shall apply to the articles in the HTS subheadings and to the beneficiary developing countries set forth in Annex III to this proclamation.

(7) In order to provide the intended tariff treatment to certain products as set out in Schedule XX, the HTS is modified as set forth in section A of Annex IV to this proclamation.

(8) In order to conform the HTS to certain technical corrections made to provide the intended tariff treatment to certain products as set out in the ITA, the HTS is modified as set forth in section B of Annex IV to this proclamation.

(9) In order to provide the intended tariff treatment to certain goods from Colombia, the HTS is modified as set forth in section C of Annex IV to this proclamation.

(10) The modifications to the HTS set forth in Annex IV to this proclamation shall be effective with respect to the articles entered, or withdrawn from warehouse for consumption, on or after the dates set forth in the relevant sections of Annex IV.

(11) Any provisions of previous proclamations and Executive Orders that are inconsistent with the actions taken in this proclamation are superseded to the extent of such inconsistency.

In Witness Whereof, I have hereunto set my hand this twenty-seventh day of June, in the year of our Lord two thousand thirteen, and of the Independence of the United States of America the two hundred and thirty-seventh.

BARACK OBAMA

SOURCE: Executive Office of the President. "Proclamation 8997—To Modify Duty-Free Treatment Under the Generalized System of Preferences and for Other Purposes." June 27, 2013. *Compilation of Presidential Documents* 2013, no. 00471 (June 27, 2013). http://www.gpo.gov/fdsys/pkg/DCPD-201300471/pdf/DCPD-201300471.pdf.

Maryland Abolishes the Death Penalty

MAY 2, 2013

The death penalty, which has always been a point of contention in American public life, has become increasingly controversial during the past decade as a growing number of states have attempted to outlaw the practice and the availability of the drugs required for lethal injection has dwindled. On May 2, 2013, Maryland became the latest state to formally outlaw the death penalty, when Governor Martin O'Malley, a Democrat, signed a measure passed by the legislature two months earlier. The new law reignited the debate about whether the United States should join most other Western nations and outlaw the death penalty altogether, or whether the punishment was still an effective crime deterrent.

THE DEATH PENALTY IN THE UNITED STATES

The death penalty has been a legal method of punishment in the United States for most of its history, although it was temporarily outlawed by the Supreme Court from 1972 to 1976. Today, thirty-two states, the federal government, and the military use capital punishment, and it is generally applied to mentally competent adults who are convicted of homicide (the Supreme Court ruled in 2005 in *Roper v. Simmons* that juveniles cannot be put to death). Thirty-nine people were executed in 2013, and as of the end of the year, more than 3,000 remained on death row. Since 1976, 1,362 people have been executed in the United States; the federal government has executed three of those people. Texas leads the nation in the total number of executions conducted.

Although it was once common for felons to be put to death by hanging, burning, or crushing, today, the most common methods of execution used in the United States include lethal injection, firing squad, electrocution, and the gas chamber. The number of those executed and the number of those sentenced to death row have been steadily declining. In 1996, 315 people were sentenced to death row, but by 2013, that number had fallen to 80, one of the lowest since 1976. The number of executions carried out in the United States peaked at ninety-eight in 1999. According to Richard Dieter, the executive director of the Death Penalty Information Center, "The realization that mistakes can be made, and innocent people have been freed who could have been executed—that causes jurors to hesitate. Prosecutors know it is harder to get a death sentence."

MARYLAND OUTLAWS CAPITAL PUNISHMENT

Since reinstating its death penalty in 1978, Maryland put fifty-eight people to death, with the last execution carried out in 2005. When he first came to office in 2007, Governor O'Malley promised to work toward a number of socially liberal policies, including repealing the death penalty. His first attempt came in 2009, but it ended only in an agreement between the House and Senate to limit when the death penalty could be applied. A new bill to repeal the death penalty was circulated in early 2013. It first passed the state Senate 27–20 on March 6, and subsequently passed the House of Delegates on March 15 by a vote of 82–56.

Although there was no question that the governor would sign the bill, he waited until May 2 to give it his final approval. Ahead of the signing, the governor's office released a statement noting that "Maryland has effectively eliminated a policy that is proven not to work." The statement added that not only does the policy not deter crime, but it is also costly, mistake-prone, and racially biased. The governor added, "Over the longer arc of history, I think you'll see more and more states repeal the death penalty. It's wasteful. It's ineffective. It doesn't work to reduce violent crime."

O'Malley was joined at the signing ceremony by Samuel Rosenberg, who has led the charge in the House of Delegates since 2007 to pass a repeal. Of the signing, Rosenberg said, "It was time we all put an end to this unethical, racially discriminatory, wasteful process," adding, "The time and effort that goes into this issue can now go into other criminal justice issues." Ben Jealous, then president of the National Association for the Advancement of Colored People (NAACP), who helped push the bill toward passage, said the signing marked "the day we join the rest of Western civilization by abolishing the death penalty."

With the governor's signature, Maryland joined seventeen other states that have outlawed capital punishment: Alaska, Connecticut, Hawaii, Illinois, Iowa, Maine, Massachusetts, Michigan, Minnesota, New Jersey, New Mexico, New York, North Dakota, Rhode Island, Vermont, West Virginia, and Wisconsin. The practice is also outlawed in the District of Columbia. Maryland, like Connecticut and New Mexico, did not make the prohibition retroactive, meaning that the five men who are currently on death row in the state might still be executed. It is up to Governor O'Malley to decide whether they will be pardoned and have their sentences commuted to life in prison without parole, the new maximum sentence. The governor has not yet decided how to act.

WANING SUPPORT

As a whole, Americans have typically favored the death penalty, according to a variety of public opinion polls, including eighty years worth of polls by the Gallup organization. Gallup first began looking at American opinion of the death sentence in 1936, updating the trends periodically until 1999, when it began annual assessments. In all but one survey, which was conducted in 1966, support for the death penalty has outweighed opposition. This tumultuous period in American history was marked by changes in the way Americans viewed a variety of social issues, and the declining support at that time culminated with the Supreme Court's 1972 ruling in *Furman v. Georgia* when the death penalty was temporarily suspended. The Court failed to rule the practice unconstitutional and executions resumed in 1976, following a separate Supreme Court ruling in *Gregg v. Georgia*.

During the 1980s and 1990s, an overwhelming number of Americans viewed crime as the number one problem facing the United States. Support for capital punishment peaked in 1994 at 80 percent of those surveyed. In the late 1990s and into the 2000s, a number of high-profile cases arose in which death row inmates were exonerated for their crimes after DNA testing proved their innocence (since 1989, 311 people have been exonerated for their crimes based on DNA evidence, eighteen of whom served time on death row).

Gallup's 2013 poll of American opinion on the death penalty revealed a sharp decrease in the number of Americans who support the practice. Overall, only 60 percent of Americans now support the death penalty for convicted murders, the lowest level in four decades. Support varies drastically between Republicans and Democrats—81 percent of Republicans are in favor, while only 47 percent of Democrats support capital punishment. An even slimmer majority of 52 percent believe that the death penalty is applied fairly; 40 percent believe that it is not. Comparatively, in 2004, 61 percent thought it was applied fairly.

DEBATE RAGES

A variety of organizations have protested the use of the death penalty, labeling it an inhumane and ineffective method of punishment that is often racially charged and costly. Of all industrialized democracies in the world, only the United States and Japan still permit capital punishment. Abolition of the death penalty has gained momentum within the past decade, with Connecticut, Illinois, New Mexico, and New Jersey all repealing the practice since 2007. When Governor O'Malley signed the Maryland law, ongoing repeal campaigns in Colorado, Delaware, and New Hampshire gained momentum. "Twenty years ago, use of the death penalty was increasing. Now it is declining by almost every measure," said Dieter. "The recurrent problems of the death penalty have made its application rare, isolated, and often delayed for decades. More states will likely reconsider the wisdom of retaining this expensive and ineffectual practice."

Whether the death penalty is an effective deterrent to crime is a major point of contention. Proponents of abolition argue that it is no more a deterrent than life in prison. But Kent Scheidegger, an advocate for the death penalty who works at the Criminal Justice Legal Foundation, said that when applied appropriately, the penalty is a deterrent. He added that the death penalty still has a place in society because "there are some crimes where a lesser penalty is insufficient."

Capital punishment opponents are also quick to note the racial disparity of those sentenced to death. According to a 2013 study by criminologist Raymond Paternoster, a professor at the University of Maryland, African Americans convicted of a crime in Houston, Texas, are more than three times as likely to face a death penalty sentence than their white counterparts. At the close of 2013, the Death Penalty Information Center released its yearly statistics, which showed that of the thirty-nine executions carried out that year, thirty-two involved a white victim, but only one white person was put to death for killing an African American. Since 1976, across America, most death penalty cases have involved African American defendants and white victims.

Cost is another factor in the debate. Due to the extensive investigations and number of appeals often brought following a death sentence, it is estimated that carrying out the sentence costs three times that of a sentence of life in prison without parole. In Florida, the state with one of the highest numbers of exonerations, Republican Governor Rick Scott signed a measure in June 2013 aimed at reducing the amount of time people can spend on death row. The new law will give the governor thirty days to sign death warrants after a state Supreme Court ruling that the inmate has no further avenue for appeal or review. The state must then execute the convicted felon within six months. While critics argued that the new law would prevent the wrongly convicted from fair appeals, the governor said the new law would ensure that defense attorneys could not work indefinitely on appeals and that those convicted "do not languish on death row for decades."

Since most states now perform executions by lethal injection, the increasing difficulty of obtaining the drugs necessary to carry out the procedure has left many states wondering whether they should change their death penalty laws. The most popular drug, used by itself or in combination, is pentobarbital, and manufacturers of the drug have begun banning its sale for executions. Those states that choose to carry out lethal injections have been forced to look for other possible drug combinations, and in some states, like Ohio, death row inmates have challenged the use of such new drug "cocktails."

Ohio announced in 2013 that it would begin using a new, untested drug combination for its lethal injections. The dose would inject midazolam, a sedative, and hydromorphone, a painkiller. Weeks before his execution, Dennis McGuire filed a lawsuit with the U.S. District Court, arguing that the combination would cause breathing problems that would lead to a terrifying experience prior to his death against his Constitutional rights. McGuire, who was convicted of a 1989 rape and murder, lost his appeal, with Judge Gregory Frost ruling that while the new combination was a human experiment, "the law teaches that Ohio is free to innovate and to evolve its procedures for administering capital punishment." McGuire was put to death on January 16, and is alleged to have gasped for air and convulsed for ten minutes before dying. His family has sued the state for "extreme pain and suffering."

A number of pro-repeal organizations have encouraged the Supreme Court to review the use of capital punishment again. However, the Court has so far not agreed to take on any proposed case regarding repeal.

—Heather Kerrigan

Following is the edited text of the Maryland death penalty repeal, signed by Governor Martin O'Malley on May 2, 2013.

DOCUMENT *Death Penalty Repeal Becomes Law*

May 2, 2013

Chapter 156

(Senate Bill 276)

AN ACT concerning

Death Penalty Repeal ~~and Appropriation from Savings to Aid Survivors of Homicide Victims~~—Substitution of Life Without the Possibility of Parole

FOR the purpose of repealing the death penalty; repealing procedures and requirements related to the death penalty; providing that in certain cases in which the State has filed a notice to seek a sentence of death, the notice shall be considered withdrawn and it shall be considered a notice to seek a sentence of life imprisonment without the possibility of parole under certain circumstances; providing that certain persons serving life sentences are not eligible for Patuxent Institution under certain circumstances; altering the circumstance concerning parole for persons serving life sentences when the State sought a certain penalty; ~~requiring the Governor to include in the annual budget submission for certain fiscal years a certain amount for the State Victims of Crime Fund~~; altering the authorization for the Governor to commute or change a sentence of death into a certain period of confinement; making conforming and clarifying changes; and generally relating to the repeal of the death penalty.

[A listing of the repealed and reenacted articles has been omitted.]

Preamble

WHEREAS, The Maryland Commission on Capital Punishment was created by Chapter 431 of the Acts of the General Assembly of 2008 for the purpose of studying all aspects of capital punishment as currently and historically administered in the State; and

WHEREAS, The Commission comprised 23 appointees representing a broad diversity of views on capital punishment, as well as the racial, ethnic, gender, and geographic diversity of the State; and

WHEREAS, The Commission held five public hearings at which testimony from experts and members of the public was presented and discussed, as well as five additional meetings to discuss the evidence presented at the hearings and in the written submissions; and

WHEREAS, The Commission issued its final report to the General Assembly on December 12, 2008, which included the Commission's strong recommendation that, to eliminate racial and jurisdictional bias, reduce unnecessary costs, lessen the misery that capital cases force family members of victims to endure, and eliminate the risk that an innocent person can be convicted, capital punishment be abolished in Maryland; and

WHEREAS, The Commission, in its final report to the General Assembly, recommended that the savings from repealing the death penalty be used to "increase the services and resources already provided to families of victims"; and

WHEREAS, Repeal of the death penalty in Maryland will result in savings to the General Fund; now, therefore,

SECTION 1. BE IT ENACTED BY THE GENERAL ASSEMBLY OF MARYLAND, That Section(s) 3-901 through 3-909 and the subtitle "Subtitle 9. Death Penalty Procedures" of Article—Correctional Services of the Annotated Code of Maryland be repealed.

SECTION 2. AND BE IT FURTHER ENACTED, That Section(s) 7-201 through 7-204 and the subtitle "Subtitle 2. Proceedings After Death Sentences"; 8-108 and 11-404 of Article—Criminal Procedure of the Annotated Code of Maryland be repealed.

[Section 3, containing the Maryland laws on courts, judicial proceedings, and prisoners, has been omitted.]

SECTION 4. AND BE IT FURTHER ENACTED, That in any case in which the State has properly filed notice that it intended to seek a sentence of death under § 2-202 of the Criminal Law Article in which a sentence has not been imposed, the notice of intention to seek a sentence of death shall be considered to have been withdrawn and it shall be deemed that the State properly filed notice under § 2-203 of the Criminal Law Article to seek a sentence of life imprisonment without the possibility of parole.

SECTION 5. AND BE IT FURTHER ENACTED, That this Act shall take effect October 1, 2013.

Approved by the Governor, May 2, 2013.

Source: Maryland Legislature. Chapter 156. Senate Bill 276. May 2, 2013. http://mgaleg.maryland.gov/2013RS/chapters_noln/Ch_156_sb0276T.pdf.

OTHER HISTORIC DOCUMENTS OF INTEREST

FROM PREVIOUS *HISTORIC DOCUMENTS*

Department of Justice Defends AP Records Subpoena

MAY 14 AND 15, 2013

While the news outlet was working on a story in May 2012 about a covert Central Intelligence Agency (CIA) operation, the Department of Justice secretly subpoenaed the phone records of more than twenty Associated Press (AP) phone lines. The Department said it was trying to determine where the AP had received leaked classified information, but the case set off a firestorm between the media, who accused the Department of Justice of violating First Amendment rights, and federal officials, who defended their move in the name of national security.

CIA ARTICLE SPARKS INVESTIGATION

In the spring of 2012, the AP was working on a story that would reveal a covert CIA operation that prevented a bomb from being planted on a plane leaving Yemen bound for the United States. The CIA received news of the plot, which was set to take place on the anniversary of Osama bin Laden's May 2011 death, from a British intelligence informant. The CIA set up a mission to foil the plot, and British officials responded angrily, noting that the United States had put their intelligence official at risk.

The AP first learned of the story from leaked classified information, and reporters subsequently worked with a number of sources who spoke only on the condition of anonymity. At the request of the White House and CIA, the AP agreed to hold the story until May 8, 2012, when it was assured by intelligence officials that the risk to the American public would have passed. The AP ended up running the story one day earlier, on May 7, which sparked fury among federal officials.

Reuters initially reported that the AP chose to publish one day earlier because the federal government refused to acquiesce to its request that it delay confirming the details of the AP story until one hour after its release. The AP denied that it made such a request. AP spokesperson Erin Madigan said, "[A]t no point did AP offer or propose a deal in relation to this story. We did not publish anything until we were assured by high-ranking officials with direct knowledge of the situation, in more than one part of the government, that the national security risk was over and no one was in danger." AP CEO Gary Pruitt defended the timing of the story as well: "We held that story until the government assured us that the national security concerns had passed," adding, "the White House was preparing to publicly announce that the bomb plot had been foiled." He said that while the White House was planning to note that in May 2012 there was no terrorism threat directed toward America marking the anniversary of bin Laden's death, the AP had learned differently from its anonymous sources, and the news organization felt it necessary to provide that information to the American people.

After the article was published, John Brennan, then the White House counterterrorism adviser, briefed his team on the operation. These advisers then gave accounts to other media organizations on how the plot unfolded and how the CIA had managed to thwart it.

SECRET PHONE RECORD SUBPOENA

It was the AP itself that first announced that the Department of Justice had secretly subpoenaed the April and May 2012 phone records for twenty-one phone lines in five AP offices, five cell phones, three home phones, and two fax lines. The phone lines included those held by five reporters and one editor who worked on the May 7 article. The subpoenas were issued to Verizon and requested information on outgoing calls. The content of the calls was not requested nor was it provided. In providing the data to the Department of Justice, Verizon did not question the motive, nor were the reporters alerted. At the time, the Department of Justice would not reveal details about why it requested such information. In public testimony, the government said only that the Department was undertaking a criminal investigation into the publication of the May 7, 2012, AP article. According to Brennan, the investigation was sparked "when someone informed The Associated Press that the U.S. government had intercepted an IED (improvised explosive device) that was supposed to be used in an attack and that the U.S. government currently had that IED in its possession and was analyzing it."

On May 10, 2013, a letter was sent to Pruitt from Deputy Attorney General James Cole informing him of the subpoena. The one-sentence letter noted "there was a basis to believe" that the information requested was "associated with AP personnel involved in the reporting of classified information." Cole added that the Department of Justice had exhausted all other measures to determine where the leak was coming from before requesting the subpoenas, including interviews and document review. Pruitt told reporters that no further explanation of the latter point was offered. It is typical for the government to negotiate with a news organization for its phone records prior to issuing a subpoena; however, in this case, the government believed that notifying the AP would hamper its investigation.

Pruitt called the subpoenas a "massive and unprecedented intrusion" adding that "these records potentially reveal communications with confidential sources across all of the newsgathering activities undertaken by the AP during a two-month period, provide a road map to AP's newsgathering operations and disclose information about AP's activities and operations that the government has no conceivable right to know." The AP contended that by requesting these records, the government was infringing on the First Amendment right to freedom of the press, noting that sources would now be less likely to speak to AP reporters, perhaps fearful that their information might be sent to the government.

Attorney General Eric Holder maintained that the Department of Justice was well within its rights and that the publication of the AP article "put the American people at risk." He said that the Justice Department only issued the subpoenas after trying other means to determine who had leaked the classified information. "This was a very, very serious leak," Holder said, adding that the Department had to act in the strongest manner possible. Holder further noted, "I've been a prosecutor since 1976—and I have to say that this is among, if not the most serious, in the top two or three most serious leaks that I've ever seen."

SUBPOENA UNITES LEFT, RIGHT, MEDIA

The request for phone records is not unusual for the government, but it was the broad nature of the Department of Justice's 2012 request that sparked controversy. In a protest letter sent from Pruitt to Holder, Pruitt noted that the government was well outside its right. "There can be no possible justification for such an overbroad collection of the telephone communications of The Associated Press and its reporters." Cole responded in a letter dated May 14, 2013, "We understand your position that these subpoenas should have been more narrowly drawn, but in fact, consistent with Department policy, the subpoenas were limited in both time and scope."

Other media organizations were quick to defend the work of the AP. Executive Director of the American Society of News Editors, Arnie Robbins, called the subpoena "a disturbing affront to a free press," adding that the move was "consistent with perhaps the most aggressive administration ever against reporters doing their jobs—providing information that citizens need to know about our government."

In a rare move, even Republican members of Congress came to the AP's defense. The Justice Department "had an obligation to look for every other way to get [the phone records] before they intruded on the freedom of the press," said Rep. Darrell Issa, R-Calif. Sen. Rand Paul, R-Ky., added that the move not only infringed on First Amendment rights, but also the Fourth Amendment right of freedom from unreasonable searches and seizures. The Fourth Amendment, Paul said, "sets a high bar—a warrant—for the government to take actions that could chill exercise of any of those rights. We must guard it with all the vigor that we guard other constitutional protections." Some even compared the decision to subpoena AP records to the Bush administration's intrusive practices used under the umbrella of fighting terrorism. Democrats largely agreed with the Republican position, noting their concern that the Department of Justice may not have met its burden of proof in obtaining the subpoenas. "I think someone from the Justice Department could have gone to the AP and said, 'Will you help us with this?' If they said no, fine, then they could have maybe gone a step further, but I don't think this is fair to just start subpoenaing records," said Senate Majority Leader Harry Reid, D-Nev.

HOLDER FACES QUESTIONING

On May 15, 2013, Holder was called to testify before the House Judiciary Committee on a variety of topics, including the AP subpoena. Holder maintained that he had recused himself from the case and had appointed a James Cole, a deputy attorney general, to conduct the investigation into who was leaking information to the press. Because he was not involved, Holder said he could not answer questions related to the subpoenas or why the Department of Justice had not further negotiated with the AP for information prior to their issue. This raised the ire of those present for questioning, with Rep. James Sensenbrenner, R-Wis., noting, "There doesn't appear to be any acceptance of responsibility for things that have gone wrong."

Holder was also questioned on whether he would charge the journalists related to the case under the Espionage Act. The Attorney General responded, "That is not something that I've ever been involved in, heard of or would think would be a wise policy."

In response to the subpoena, Sen. Chuck Schumer, D-N.Y., and Sen. Lindsey Graham, R-S.C., revived a media shield bill first proposed in 2009. The bill would offer protection to media organizations and journalists and prevent them from being required to reveal their anonymous sources. The bill would include some exceptions for national security, but Schumer said, "At minimum, our bill would have ensured a fairer, more deliberate process in this case." He added that the bill would protect the "right to the free flow of information." President Barack Obama supported the reintroduction, saying, "I think now's the time for us to go ahead and revisit that legislation. I think that's a worthy conversation to have, and I think that's important." If the media shield law had been in place in the case of the AP subpoena, the Department of Justice would have had to prove to a judge why the information was needed, that the reason was valid and supported by a national security threat, and that informing the organization of the subpoenas would hamper the investigation.

FOX NEWS REPORTER ALSO UNDER INVESTIGATION

The AP was not the only media outlet under secret investigation by the Department of Justice. Just days after the AP story came to light, *The Washington Post* reported that James Rosen, a Fox News correspondent, had his calls, e-mail, and visits to the State Department tracked by the Department of Justice. According to the Department of Justice, they considered Rosen a "criminal coconspirator" with Stephen Jin-Woo Kim, a former State Department contractor, as it related to 2009 leaks of classified information on North Korea. To prevent Rosen from being notified, the request for a subpoena noted the journalist as a flight risk. In an article about the subpoena, *Post* reporter Dana Milibank said the Department of Justice treated Rosen "as a criminal for doing his job," which "deprives Americans of the First Amendment freedom on which all other constitutional rights are based."

Despite what he said in his testimony before the House Judiciary Committee, Holder had signed off on the subpoena for Rosen's records. The Congressional committee responded by requesting a full account of Holder's involvement in the case. The Department of Justice stood by the subpoena, stating that it was considered "an appropriately tailored search warrant under the Privacy Protection Act."

—Heather Kerrigan

Following is the text of a letter sent from Deputy Attorney General James Cole to AP CEO Gary Pruitt on May 14, 2013, responding to the AP's concerns about a subpoena issued to gather the phone record information of its reporters; and the edited text of questions and answers between Attorney General Eric Holder and members of the House Judiciary Committee on May 15.

Department of Justice Responds to AP Letter Regarding Subpoenas

May 14, 2013

Gary B. Pruitt
President and CEO
Associated Press
450 W. 33rd Street
New York, NY 10001

Dear Mr. Pruitt:

I am writing in response to your May 13, 2013, letter concerning the Department of Justice's notification on Friday, May 10, 2013, that it is in receipt of subpoenaed toll records for April and May 2012 for certain telephone numbers associated with the Associated Press.

As you know, Department policy provides that we should issue subpoenas for phone records associated with media organizations only in certain circumstances. There should be reasonable grounds to believe that a federal crime has been committed and that the information sought by the subpoena is essential to a successful investigation. The Department should take all reasonable alternative investigative steps before even considering the issuance of a subpoena for toll records related to a media organization. Any subpoena that is issued should be drawn as narrowly as possible, be directed at relevant information regarding a limited subject matter, and should cover a reasonably limited period of time. We are required to negotiate with the media organization in advance of issuing the subpoenas unless doing so would pose a substantial threat to the integrity of the investigation. We take this policy, and the interests that it is intended to protect, very seriously and followed it in this matter.

In May 2012, the Department of Justice opened criminal investigations into the unauthorized disclosure of classified information. Because such disclosures can risk lives and cause grave harm to the security of all Americans, the Department thoroughly investigates cases in which government employees and contractors trusted with our nation's secrets are suspected of willfully disclosing that information to individuals not entitled to them. Even given the significant public interest in enforcing criminal laws that protect our national security, seeking toll records associated with media organizations is undertaken only after all other reasonable alternative investigative steps have been taken. In this case, the Department undertook a comprehensive investigation, including, among other investigative steps, conducting over 550 interviews and reviewing tens of thousands of documents, before seeking the toll records at issue.

We understand your position that these subpoenas should have been more narrowly drawn, but in fact, consistent with Department policy, the subpoenas were limited in both time and scope. As you know, for each of the phone numbers referenced in our May 10, 2013, letter there was a basis to believe the numbers were associated with AP personnel involved in the reporting of classified information. The subpoenas were limited to a reasonable period of time and did not seek the content of any calls. Indeed, although the records do span two months, as we indicated to you last week, they cover only a portion of that two-month period. In addition, these records have been closely held and reviewed solely for the purposes of this ongoing criminal investigation. The records have not been and will not be provided for use in any other investigations.

Given the ongoing nature of this criminal investigation involving highly classified material, I am limited in the information that I can provide to you. Please understand that I appreciate your concerns and that we do not take lightly the decision to issue subpoenas for toll records associated with members of the news media. We strive in every case to strike the proper balance between the public's interest in the free flow of information and the public's interest in the protection of national security and effective enforcement of our criminal laws. We believe we have done so in this matter.

Sincerely,

James M. Cole
Deputy Attorney General

SOURCE: Department of Justice. "DAG Letter to AP President Pruitt." May 14, 2013. http://www.justice.gov/oip/docs/dag-letter-to-ap-president-pruitt.pdf.

Holder Testifies Before House Judiciary Committee

May 15, 2013

[Committee opening remarks, Holder's opening statement, and all questions and answers not pertaining to the AP case, have been omitted.]

Mr. GOODLATTE. It was recently reported by the Justice Department or reported that the Justice Department obtained 2 months of telephone records of more than 20 reporters and editors with the Associated Press, including both work and personal phone lines. There has been a lot of criticism raised about the scope of this investigation, including why the Department needed to subpoena records for 20 people over a lengthy 2-month period. Why was such a broad scope approved?

Attorney General HOLDER. Yes, there's been a lot of the criticism. In fact, the head of the RNC called for my resignation in spite of the fact that I was not the person who was involved in that decision. But be that as it may, I was recused in that matter, as I described, in a press conference that I held yesterday. The decision to issue this subpoena was made by the people who are presently involved in the case. The matter is being supervised by the Deputy Attorney General. I am not familiar with the reasons why the case—why the subpoena was constructed in the way that it was because I'm simply not a part of the case.

Mr. GOODLATTE. It is my understanding that one of the requirements before compelling process from a media outlet is to give the outlet notice. Do you know why that was not done?

Attorney General HOLDER. There are exceptions to that rule. I do not know, however, with regard to this particular case why that was or was not done. I simply don't have a factual basis to answer that question.

Mr. GOODLATTE. And it has also been reported that the Associated Press refrained from releasing this story for a week until the Department confirmed that doing so would not jeopardize national security interests. That indicates that the AP was amenable to working with you on this matter.
    If that is the case, why was it necessary to subpoena the telephone records? Did you seek the AP's assistance in the first place? And if not, why not?

Attorney General HOLDER. Again, Mr. Chairman, I don't know what happened there with the interaction between the AP and the Justice Department. I was recused from the case.

Mr. GOODLATTE. I take it that you or others in the Justice Department will be forthcoming with those answers to those questions as you explore why this was handled what appears to be contrary to the law and standard procedure.

Attorney General HOLDER. Well, again, there are exceptions to some of the rules that you pointed out, and I have faith in the people who actually were responsible for this case that they were aware of the rules and that they followed them. But I don't have a factful basis to answer the questions that you have asked because I was recused. I don't know what has happened in this matter.

Mr. GOODLATTE. Thank you very much. . . .

Mr. SENSENBRENNER. Mr. Attorney General, thank you for coming.

I would like to try to pin down who authorized the subpoenas for the AP. And the Code of Federal Regulations is pretty specific on subpoenas for media. Did Deputy Attorney General Cole do that?

Attorney General HOLDER. Yes, I have to assume he did. I only say assume because you have to understand that recusals are such that I don't have any interaction with the people who are involved in the case. Under the regulations, the Attorney General has to authorize the subpoena. In my absence, the Deputy Attorney General would, in essence, act as the acting Attorney General.

Mr. SENSENBRENNER. Do you know if Deputy Attorney General Cole was also interviewed in the investigation that caused your recusal?

Attorney General HOLDER. I don't know. I don't know. I assume he was, but I don't know.

Mr. SENSENBRENNER. Why were you interviewed? Were you a witness, or was this a part of your official duties as Attorney General?

Attorney General HOLDER. No, I was interviewed as one of the people who had access to the information that was a subject of the investigation. I, along with other members of the National Security Division, recused myself. The head of the National Security Division was left. The present head of the National Security Division, we all recused ourselves.

I recused myself because I thought it would be inappropriate and have a bad appearance to be a person who was a fact witness in the case to actually lead the investigation, given the fact, unlike Mr. Cole, that I have a greater interaction with members of the press than he does.

Mr. SENSENBRENNER. How does that make you a fact witness? If you are getting the work product, the assistant U.S. attorneys and the FBI that are looking into a matter. You would be a policy person in deciding whether or not to proceed with subpoenas or, ultimately, signing off on an indictment.

Attorney General HOLDER. Well, I'm a fact witness in the fact that I am a possessor—I was a possessor, I am a possessor—of the information that was ultimately leaked, and the question then is who of those people who possessed that information, which was a relatively limited number of people within the Justice Department, who of those people, who of those possessors actually spoke in an inappropriate way to members of the Associated Press?

Mr. SENSENBRENNER. Who else had access to that information?

Attorney General HOLDER. Well, this is an ongoing investigation. I would not want to reveal what I know, and I don't know if there are other people who've been developed as possible recipients or possessors of that information during the course of the investigation. I don't know.

Mr. SENSENBRENNER. I am trying to find out who authorized the subpoena. You can't tell me if Deputy Attorney General Cole authorized the subpoena. Somebody had to authorize the subpoena because the Code of Federal Regulations is pretty specific that this is supposed to go as close to the top as possible.

Attorney General HOLDER. Well, no, what I'm saying is that I can't say as a matter of fact. But I have to assume, and I would say I would probably be 95, 99 percent certain, that the Deputy Attorney General, acting in my stead, was the one who authorized the subpoena.

Mr. SENSENBRENNER. Well, okay. The Code of Federal Regulations also is very specific that there should be negotiations prior to the issuance of the subpoena with the news media organization involved, and the AP has said there was no negotiations at all.

Now there are two different parts of the regulation that may be in conflict with each other[.] One is more generic than the other. But there were no negotiations whatsoever. And why weren't there negotiations?

Attorney General HOLDER. That I don't know. There are exceptions to that rule that say that if the integrity of the investigation might be impacted, the negotiations don't have to occur. I don't know why that didn't happen.

Mr. SENSENBRENNER. But hasn't somebody in the Justice Department said that the integrity of the investigation would not be impacted with negotiations either under Subsection C, which is generic, or Subsection D, which is more specific?

Attorney General HOLDER. I don't know. But let me say this, I've just been given a note that we have, in fact, confirmed that the Deputy was the one who authorized the subpoena.

Mr. SENSENBRENNER. Okay. Well, I think we are going to have to talk to him about this. But, Mr. Attorney General, I think that this Committee has been frustrated for at least the last 2½ years, if not the last 4½ years, that there doesn't seem to be any acceptance of responsibility in the Justice Department for things that have gone wrong.

Now may I suggest that you and maybe Mr. Cole and a few other people go to the Truman Library and take a picture of this thing that he had on his desk that said "The buck stops here," because we don't know where the buck stops. And I think to do adequate oversight, we better find out and we better find out how this mess happened. . . .

[The remainder of the session has been omitted.]

Source: House of Representatives Committee on the Judiciary. "Hearing before the Committee on the Judiciary." May 15, 2013. http://judiciary.house.gov/_cache/files/3a578da5-438f-46d5-8be8-6304640505e1/113-43-80973.pdf.

OTHER HISTORIC DOCUMENTS OF INTEREST

Treasury Inspector General Releases IRS Audit on Inappropriate Targeting

MAY 14, 2013

As part of its duties, the Internal Revenue Service (IRS) is responsible for reviewing and making determinations on applications for 501(c)(4) tax-exempt status. These applications must meet a variety of criteria, the most important of which is proof that the group engages in some type of social welfare. In 2013, allegations were raised by various conservative organizations that believed that IRS workers had unfairly targeted them for rigorous screening. Upon investigation, this targeting was directly linked to a 2010 IRS directive on applying additional screening to applications bearing words like "tea party."

TREASURY CONDUCTS REVEALING AUDIT

In 2012, a variety of conservative groups approached the IRS, and subsequently Congress, to determine why their applications for 501(c)(4) tax-exempt status were being held up in processing and why they were being asked to provide information like names of donors, which they considered outside the realm of what the IRS should be reviewing. In response, Sen. Orrin Hatch, R-Utah, wrote to the IRS asking for information on whether conservative groups were being inappropriately targeted. In response to each of the letters he sent, the IRS responded that no such action was taking place.

Driven by Congressional questions raised on the issue, the Treasury Department Inspector General launched an audit investigation into IRS practices on granting tax-exempt status. On May 10, 2013, one day before the release of the audit findings, Lois Lerner, the head of the IRS group that determined tax-exempt status, apologized for what she called "absolutely inappropriate" actions. She added that the targeting was done by a small group of individuals in the IRS Cincinnati office who regularly issued requests for additional information from conservative organizations. However, once the audit report was released, it was learned that officials working at headquarters in Washington, D.C., as well as those in the El Monte and Laguna Niguel, California, offices sent query letters as well. In these queries, the IRS requested information on organization operations, donors, lobbying efforts, and voter outreach, among other things.

The inspector general's audit found that the IRS had created a "Be On the Look Out" (BOLO) list for its employees to use when a group applied for tax-exempt status. Among the things employees were encouraged to look for were the names "Tea Party," "Patriots," and "9/12 Project"; mention of the group wanting to educate the American public about the Constitution or Bill of Rights; criticism from the group of the current government or management of the country; any group stating it wanted to "make America a better place to live"; and any group that included in its application government spending, taxes, or debt as one of its major platform issues. Any group meeting one of these criteria triggered a request for additional information, and subsequent additional scrutiny. Use of the list was discontinued in 2012.

The report concluded, "Whether the inappropriate criterion was shorthand for all potential political cases or not, developing and using criteria that focuses on organization names and policy positions instead of the activities permitted under the Treasury regulations does not promote public confidence that tax-exempt laws are being adhered to impartially." The report found that of the nearly 300 cases reviewed, 202 did not contain any specific reference as noted in the list, seventy-two contained the name "tea party," eleven had the term 9/12 in their titles, and another thirteen contained the word "patriots." The investigation also found that these high-scrutiny reviews were being conducted slowly, leaving some groups waiting years to hear whether they would receive tax-exempt status. The inspector general recommended that the Treasury Department redefine "social welfare activity" to help IRS employees make a determination on whether a group qualifies for tax exempt status, urged the IRS to better train its employees on how and when to choose a case for review, and encouraged the IRS to improve its process for documenting which cases are chosen for review and what material is requested. Regardless of the level of scrutiny, however, no applications for tax-exempt status were actually denied.

Lerner responded to the report, noting that the employees who pulled cases for further review should not be held liable because they were simply the victims of an inefficient process and bad management. "We believe the front-line career employees that made the decisions acted out of a desire for efficiency and not out of any political and partisan viewpoint," she wrote in her response.

Questions Raised About IRS Motive

The report never directly indicated that there was a political motive behind the IRS actions, but that they did give "the appearance that the IRS is not impartial in conducting its mission." The question remained regarding why the IRS began targeting certain groups. According to reports published after the scandal broke, targeting began in early 2010, and carried on for approximately eighteen months. A few months after putting its heightened level of scrutiny in place, the volume of tax exemption applications increased dramatically, following the Supreme Court's ruling in *Citizens United v. Federal Election Commission*. In its decision, the Court ruled that organizations and labor unions could both register for tax-exempt status as long as politics was not their primary purpose and could raise and spend unlimited amounts of money on indirect support of candidates and campaign issues. However, the IRS failed to define what "primary purpose" might actually mean and how much time a group could truly spend on such activities. In absence of such distinctions, some IRS officials argued that the agency was using its "BOLO" criteria in an effort to streamline its workload. "The IRS is required by law to determine if organizations are engaging in a legally permissible level of political activity. Centralizing these cases was necessary to achieve consistent treatment," it said in a statement.

Some members of Congress drew criticism for potentially pushing the IRS to pull certain applications for added scrutiny. A group of Senate Democrats sent a letter to the IRS in 2012 asking why some agencies were receiving tax-exempt status that they were not qualified for because they had not proven that they served a social welfare benefit. Republicans argued that the Democrats' move was in direct response to the *Citizens United* ruling. Democrats had long been frustrated with the ruling, equating it to buying candidates for office and ultimately minimalizing the impact individual citizens can have in choosing their representatives. In their letter, Senate Democrats wrote, "In the absence of clarity in the administration of section 501(c)(4), organizations are tempted to abuse its vagueness, or worse, to organize under section 501(c)(4) so that they may avail themselves of its advantages even though they are not legitimate social welfare organizations."

The 2010–2012 IRS targeting was not the first time the group came under fire for politically motivated actions. President Franklin Delano Roosevelt subjected Andrew Melon, a Treasury secretary under President Herbert Hoover, to tax audits over and above what was traditional. At one point, the IRS alleged that Melon owed more than $3 million in back taxes; Melon was not cleared of the charges until after his death. Other high-profile cases included Martin Luther King Jr., who had a warrant for his arrest issued by the state of Alabama for apparent fraudulent tax returns in 1956 and 1958. The state said that the civil rights leader owed more than $1,000 in back taxes and had failed to properly report his income. King testified on his own behalf in front of an all-white jury, noting that the auditor told King that he had been instructed to find some fault with the tax returns. King was found not guilty. Both the John F. Kennedy and Richard Nixon administrations also used the IRS to target their political enemies. Kennedy targeted conservative groups to stop them from receiving tax-exempt status, while the Nixon administration attempted to target its enemies with audits. In a strange turn of events, tax evasion ended up being one of Nixon's articles of impeachment.

United in Reaction

In the current political environment, there was little for Republicans and Democrats to agree on. However, the two parties were clearly united in their belief that the IRS had overstepped its boundaries in placing special requirements on conservative groups. Sen. Tim Kaine, D-Va., called the IRS actions "un-American," while Sen. Max Baucus, D-Mont., called them "a breach of the public's trust." President Barack Obama, who noted that he had learned of the IRS practices along with the rest of the country, said, "If in fact IRS personnel engaged in the kind of practices that have been reported on, and were intentionally targeting conservative groups, then that's outrageous." The president also called on those responsible "to be held fully accountable."

Republicans were quick to call for the resignation of Steven Miller, the acting IRS commissioner, who was first informed in May 2012 when he was deputy commissioner that a targeting technique was being used for certain tax-exempt applications. A key Republican argument for resignation was that although Miller knew about the targeting, he did not reveal that information in a July 2012 testimony before a House oversight committee. Republicans also called for Lerner to resign. "Heads need to roll today," said Rep. Vern Buchanan, R-Fla. Miller did eventually resign on May 15, telling IRS employees in a letter, "This has been an incredibly difficult time for the IRS given the events of the past few days, and there is a strong and immediate need to restore public trust in the nation's tax agency." Lerner was put on leave in late May and retired from her position in September. Two employees with the IRS office in Cincinnati were singled out as having aggressively applied the standards to a number of tax-exempt cases, and those employees were disciplined. For some, however, the resignations and disciplinary actions were not enough. "Who's going to jail over this scandal," asked Speaker of the House John Boehner, R-Ohio.

Commissions, Bills, and Investigations

As soon as news broke of the IRS scandal, a variety of investigations were launched into what exactly happened, and bills were introduced in the House and Senate to ensure it would never happen again. The Senate Finance Committee and Permanent Subcommittee on Investigations both announced that they would launch separate investigations, as did the House Committee on Ways and Means. The Federal Bureau of Investigation (FBI) launched its own investigation, and in January 2014 determined that it had not found any reason to file federal criminal charges against the individuals involved with the case. The investigation, however, remains ongoing.

Sen. Marco Rubio, R-Fla., and Rep. Mike Turner, R-Ohio, took a different approach to the scandal, introducing bills in their respective bodies to prevent the IRS from ever using such targeting methods again. The bills would require employees who were violating "the constitutional rights of a taxpayer" to be fired and held criminally liable. The bills were assigned to committee in May 2013, but were never sent to the full House and Senate.

—Heather Kerrigan

Following is the edited text from the May 14, 2013, audit on inappropriate IRS targeting released by the Treasury Inspector General.

Audit Report on Inappropriate IRS Review Criteria

May 14, 2013

[The highlights section, an introductory letter, the table of contents, a list of abbreviations, and background on the case have all been omitted. In addition, all footnotes, tables, and appendices have been omitted.]

Results of Review

The Determinations Unit Used Inappropriate Criteria to Identify Potential Political Cases

The Determinations Unit developed and used inappropriate criteria to identify applications from organizations with the words Tea Party in their names. These applications (hereafter referred to as potential political cases) were forwarded to a team of specialists for review. Subsequently, the Determinations Unit expanded the criteria to inappropriately include organizations with other specific names (Patriots and 9/12) or policy positions. While the criteria used by the Determinations Unit specified particular organization names, the team of specialists was also processing applications from groups with names other than those identified in the criteria. The inappropriate and changing criteria may have led to inconsistent treatment of organizations applying for tax-exempt status. For example, we identified some organizations' applications with evidence of significant political campaign intervention that were not forwarded to the team of specialists for processing but should have been. We also identified applications that were forwarded to the team of specialists but did not have indications of significant political campaign intervention. All applications that were forwarded to the team of specialists experienced substantial delays in processing. Although the IRS has taken some action, it will need to do more so that the public has reasonable assurance that applications are processed without unreasonable delay in a fair and impartial manner in the future.

Criteria for selecting applications inappropriately identified organizations based on their names and policy positions

The Determinations Unit developed and began using criteria to identify potential political cases for review that inappropriately identified specific groups applying for tax-exempt status based on their names or policy positions instead of developing criteria based on tax-exempt laws and Treasury Regulations. Soon thereafter, according to the IRS, a Determinations Unit specialist was asked to search for applications with Tea Party, Patriots, or 9/12 in the organization's name as well as other "political-sounding" names. EO [Exempt Organizations] function officials stated that, in May 2010, the Determinations Unit began developing a spreadsheet that would become known as the "Be On the Look Out" listing (hereafter referred to as the BOLO listing), which included the emerging issue of Tea Party applications. In June 2010, the Determinations Unit began training its specialists on issues to be aware of, including Tea Party cases. By July 2010, Determinations Unit management stated that it had requested its specialists to be on the lookout for Tea Party applications.

In August 2010, the Determinations Unit distributed the first formal BOLO listing. The criteria in the BOLO listing were Tea Party organizations applying for I.R.C. § 501(c)(3) or I.R.C. § 501(c)(4) status. Based on our review of other BOLO listing criteria, the use of organization names on the BOLO listing is not unique to potential political cases. EO function officials stated that Determinations Unit specialists interpreted the general criteria in the BOLO listing and developed expanded criteria for identifying potential political cases. Figure 3 shows that, by June 2011, the expanded criteria included additional names (Patriots and 9/12 Project) as well as policy positions espoused by organizations in their applications. . . . Criteria for selecting applications for the team of specialists should focus on the activities of the organizations and whether they fulfill the requirements of the law. Using the names or policy positions of organizations is not an appropriate basis for identifying applications for review by the team of specialists.

We asked the Acting Commissioner, Tax Exempt and Government Entities Division; the Director, EO; and Determinations Unit personnel if the criteria were influenced by any individual or organization outside the IRS. All of these officials stated that the criteria were not influenced by any individual or organization outside the IRS. Instead, the Determinations Unit developed and implemented inappropriate criteria in part due to insufficient oversight provided by management. Specifically, only first-line management approved references to the Tea Party in the BOLO listing criteria before it was implemented. As a result, inappropriate criteria remained in place for more than 18 months. Determinations Unit employees also did not consider the public perception of using politically sensitive criteria when identifying these cases. Lastly, the criteria developed showed a lack of knowledge in the Determinations Unit of what activities are allowed by I.R.C. § 501(c)(3) and I.R.C. § 501(c)(4) organizations. . . .

The team of specialists processed applications by organizations with names other than Tea Party, Patriots, and 9/12

. . . approximately one-third of the applications identified for processing by the team of specialists included Tea Party, Patriots, or 9/12 in their names, while the remainder did not. . . .

- **Applications That the IRS Determined Required Minimal or No Additional Information for Processing**—We reviewed a statistical sample of 94 I.R.C. §

501(c)(4) cases closed from May 2010 through May 2012 from a universe of 2,051 applications that the IRS determined required minimal or no additional information from the organizations (also referred to by the EO function as merit closures). We determined that two (2 percent) of 94 approved applications had indications of significant political campaign intervention and should have been forwarded to the team of specialists. . . .

- **Applications Identified by the IRS That Required Additional Information for Processing**—We reviewed a statistical sample of 244 I.R.C. § 501(c)(4) cases closed from May 2010 through May 2012 or open as of May 31, 2012, from a universe of 2,459 applications that the IRS determined required additional information from the organizations applying for tax-exempt status (also referred to by the EO function as full development applications) but were not forwarded to the team of specialists. For the applications that were available for our review, we found that 14 (6 percent) of 237 applications included indications of significant political campaign intervention and should have been processed by the team of specialists. . . .

- **Applications That the IRS Determined Should Be Processed by the Team of Specialists**—We reviewed all 298 applications that had been identified as potential political cases as of May 31, 2012. In the majority of cases, we agreed that the applications submitted included indications of significant political campaign intervention. However, we did not identify any indications of significant political campaign intervention for 91 (31 percent) of the 296 applications that had complete documentation.

We discussed our results with EO function officials, who disagreed with our findings . . .

Recommendations

The Director, EO, should:

Recommendation 1: Ensure that the memorandum requiring the Director, Rulings and Agreements, to approve all original entries and changes to criteria included on the BOLO listing prior to implementation be formalized in the appropriate Internal Revenue Manual. . . .

Recommendation 2: Develop procedures to better document the reason(s) applications are chosen for review by the team of specialists (*e.g.*, evidence of specific political campaign intervention in the application file or specific reasons the EO function may have for choosing to review the application further based on past experience). . . .

Recommendation 3: Develop training or workshops to be held before each election cycle including, but not limited to, the proper ways to identify applications that require review of political campaign intervention activities. . . .

Potential Political Cases Experienced Significant Processing Delays

Organizations that applied for tax-exempt status and had their applications forwarded to the team of specialists experienced substantial delays. As of December 17, 2012, many organizations had not received an approval or denial letter for more than two years after they submitted their applications. Some cases have been open during two election cycles (2010 and 2012). The *IRS Strategic Plan 2009–2013* has several goals and objectives that involve timely interacting with taxpayers, including enforcement of the tax law in a timely manner while minimizing taxpayer burden. The EO function does not have specific time-liness goals for processing applications, such as potential political cases, that require significant follow-up with the organizations. The time it takes to process an application depends upon the facts and circumstances of the case.

Potential political cases took significantly longer than average to process due to ineffective management oversight. Once cases were initially identified for processing by the team of specialists, the Determinations Unit Program Manager requested assistance via e-mail from the Technical Unit to ensure consistency in processing the cases. However, EO function management did not ensure that there was a formal process in place for initiating, tracking, or monitoring requests for assistance. In addition, there were several changes in Rulings and Agreements management responsible for overseeing the fulfillment of requests for assistance from the Determinations Unit during this time period. This contributed to the lengthy delays in processing potential political cases. As a result, the Determinations Unit waited more than 20 months (February 2010 to November 2011) to receive draft written guidance from the Technical Unit for processing potential political cases.

As a result, the IRS delayed the issuance of letters to organizations approving their tax-exempt status. For I.R.C. § 501(c)(3) organizations, this means that potential donors and grantors could be reluctant to provide donations or grants. In addition, some organizations withdrew their applications and others may not have begun conducting planned charitable or social welfare work. The delays may have also prevented some organizations from receiving certain benefits of the tax-exempt status. For example, if organizations are approved for tax-exempt status, they may receive exemption from certain State taxes and reduced postal rates. For organizations that may eventually be denied tax-exempt status but have been operating while their applications are pending, the organizations will be required to retroactively file income tax returns and may be liable to pay income taxes for, in some cases, more than two years.

To analyze the delays, we: 1) reviewed the events that led to delays in processing potential political cases, 2) compared the amount of time cases assigned to the team of specialists were open to applications that were not assigned to the team of specialists, and 3) determined if organizations were eligible to sue the IRS due to delays in processing certain applications.

Potential political cases experienced long processing delays

The team of specialists stopped working on potential political cases from October 2010 through November 2011, resulting in a 13-month delay, while they waited for assistance from the Technical Unit. Figure 5 illustrates significant events and delays concerning potential political cases. For a comprehensive timeline of events related to potential political cases, see Appendix VII. . . . In April 2010, the Determinations Unit Program Manager requested via e-mail a contact in the Technical Unit to provide assistance with processing the applications. A Technical Unit specialist was assigned this task and began working with the team of specialists. The team of specialists stopped processing cases in October 2010 without closing any of the 40 cases that were begun. However, the Determinations Unit Program Manager thought the cases were being processed. Later, we were informed by the Director, Rulings and Agreements, that there was a miscommunication about processing the cases. The Determinations Unit waited for assistance from the Technical Unit instead of continuing to process the cases. The Determinations Unit Program Manager requested status updates on the request for assistance several times via e-mail. Draft written guidance was not received from the Technical Unit until November 2011, 13 months after the Determinations Unit stopped processing the cases. As of the end of our audit work in February 2013, the guidance had not been finalized because the EO function decided to provide training instead.

Many organizations waited much longer than 13 months for a decision, while others have yet to receive a decision from the IRS. . . . For the 296 potential political cases we reviewed, as of December 17, 2012, 108 applications had been approved, 28 were withdrawn by the applicant, none had been denied, and 160 cases were open from 206 to 1,138 calendar days (some crossing two election cycles).

. . . In April 2012, the Senior Technical Advisor to the Acting Commissioner, Tax Exempt and Government Entities Division, along with a team of EO function Headquarters office employees, reviewed many of the potential political cases and determined that there appeared to be some confusion by Determinations Unit specialists and applicants on what activities are allowed by I.R.C. § 501(c)(4) organizations. We believe this could be due to the lack of specific guidance on how to determine the "primary activity" of an I.R.C. § 501(c)(4) organization. Treasury Regulations state that I.R.C. § 501(c)(4) organizations should have social welfare as their "primary activity"; however, the regulations do not define how to measure whether social welfare is an organization's "primary activity."

As a result of this confusion, the EO function Headquarters employees provided a two-day workshop to the team of specialists in May 2012 to train them on what activities are allowable by I.R.C. § 501(c)(4) organizations, including lobbying and political campaign intervention. After this workshop, potential political cases were independently reviewed by two people to determine what, if any, additional work needed to be completed prior to making a decision to approve or deny the applications for tax-exempt status. This review continued on any newly identified potential political cases. Prior to the hands-on training and independent reviews, the team of specialists had only approved six (2 percent) of 298 applications. After the hands-on training and independent reviews began, the Determinations Unit approved an additional 102 applications by December 2012. In addition, it was decided that applications could be approved, but a referral for follow-up could be sent to another unit, which could review the activities of an organization at a later date to determine if they were consistent with the organization's tax-exempt status.

Potential political cases were open much longer than similar cases that were not identified for processing by the team of specialists

For Fiscal Year 2012, the average time it took the Determinations Unit to complete processing applications requiring additional information from organizations applying for tax-exempt status (also referred to by the EO function as full development cases) was 238 calendar days according to IRS data. In comparison, the average time a potential political case was open as of December 17, 2012, was 574 calendar days (with 158 potential political cases being open longer than the average calendar days it took to close other full development cases). Figure 6 shows that more than 80 percent of the potential political cases have been open more than one year.

Some charitable organizations were eligible to sue the IRS for declaratory judgment due to the delays in processing applications

The Determinations Unit did not always timely approve or deny the applications for I.R.C. § 501(c)(3) tax-exempt status for potential political cases. However, the tax law provides organizations with the ability to sue the IRS to force a decision on their applications if the IRS does not approve or deny their applications within 270 calendar days.

As of May 31, 2012, 32 (36 percent) of 89 I.R.C. § 501(c)(3) potential political cases were open more than 270 calendar days, and the organizations had responded timely to all requests for additional information, as required. As of the end of our fieldwork, none of these organizations had sued the IRS, even though they had the legal right. In another 38 open cases, organizations were timely in their responses to additional information requests, but the 270-calendar-day threshold had not been reached as of May 31, 2012. These 38 organizations may have the right to sue the IRS in the future if determinations are not made within the 270-calendar-day period.

Recommendations

The Director, EO, should:

Recommendation 4: Develop a process for the Determinations Unit to formally request assistance from the Technical Unit and the Guidance Unit. The process should include actions to initiate, track, and monitor requests for assistance to ensure that requests are responded to timely. . . .

Recommendation 5: Develop guidance for specialists on how to process requests for tax-exempt status involving potentially significant political campaign intervention. This guidance should also be posted to the Internet to provide transparency to organizations on the application process. . . .

Recommendation 6: Develop training or workshops to be held before each election cycle including, but not limited to: a) what constitutes political campaign intervention versus general advocacy (including case examples) and b) the ability to refer for follow-up those organizations that may conduct activities in a future year which may cause them to lose their tax-exempt status. . . .

Recommendation 7: Provide oversight to ensure that potential political cases, some of which have been in process for three years, are approved or denied expeditiously. . . .

Recommendation 8: Recommend to IRS Chief Counsel and the Department of the Treasury that guidance on how to measure the "primary activity" of I.R.C. § 501(c)(4) social welfare organizations be included for consideration in the Department of the Treasury Priority Guidance Plan. . . .

The Determinations Unit Requested Unnecessary Information for Many Potential Political Cases

The Determinations Unit sent requests for information that we later (in whole or in part) determined to be unnecessary for 98 (58 percent) of 170 organizations that received additional information request letters. According to the Internal Revenue Manual, these requests should be thorough, complete, and relevant. However, the Determinations Unit requested irrelevant (unnecessary) information because of a lack of managerial review, at all levels, of questions before they were sent to organizations seeking tax-exempt status. We also believe that Determinations Unit specialists lacked knowledge of what activities are allowed by I.R.C. § 501(c)(3) and I.R.C. § 501(c)(4) tax-exempt organizations. This created burden on the organizations that were required to gather and forward information that was not needed by the Determinations Unit and led to delays in processing the applications. These delays could result in potential donors and grantors being reluctant to provide donations or grants to organizations applying for I.R.C. § 501(c)(3) tax-exempt status. In addition, some organizations may not have begun conducting planned charitable or social welfare work.

After receiving draft guidance in November 2011, the team of specialists began sending requests for additional information in January 2012 to organizations that were applying for tax-exempt status. For some organizations, this was the second letter received from the IRS requesting additional information, the first of which had been received more than a year before this date. These letters requested that the information be provided in two or three weeks (as is customary in these letters) despite the fact that the IRS had done nothing with some of the applications for more than one year. After the letters were received, organizations seeking tax-exempt status, as well as members of Congress, expressed concerns about the type and extent of questions being asked. For example, the Determinations Unit requested donor information from 27 organizations that it would be required to make public if the application was approved, even though this information could not be disclosed by the IRS when provided by organizations whose tax-exempt status had been approved. Figure 7 shows an example of requests sent to organizations applying for tax-exempt status regarding donors.

After media attention, the Director, EO, stopped issuance of additional information request letters and provided an extension of time to respond to previously issued letters. The Deputy Commissioner for Services and Enforcement then asked the Senior Technical Advisor to the Acting Commissioner, Tax Exempt and Government Entities Division, to find out how applications were being processed and make recommendations. The Senior Technical Advisor and a team of specialists visited the Determinations Unit in Cincinnati, Ohio, and began reviewing cases. As part of this effort, EO function Headquarters office employees reviewed the additional information request letters prepared by the team of specialists and identified seven questions that they deemed unnecessary. Subsequently, the EO function instituted the practice that all additional information request letters for potential political cases be reviewed by the EO function Headquarters office before they are sent to organizations seeking tax-exempt status. In addition, EO function officials informed us that they decided to destroy all donor lists that were sent in for potential political cases that the IRS determined it should not have requested. Figure 8 lists the seven questions identified as being unnecessary.

We reviewed case file information for all 170 organizations that received additional information request letters and determined that 98 (58 percent) had received requests for information that was later deemed unnecessary by the EO function. Of the 98 organizations:

- 15 were informed that they did not need to respond to previous requests for information and, instead, received a revised request for information.
- 12 either received a letter or a telephone call stating that their application was approved and they no longer needed to respond to information requests they had received from the IRS. . . .

Recommendation

Recommendation 9: The Director, EO, should develop training or workshops to be held before each election cycle including, but not limited to, how to word questions in additional information request letters and what additional information should be requested. . . .

SOURCE: U.S. Department of the Treasury. "Inappropriate Criteria Were Used to Identify Tax-Exempt Applications for Review." May 14, 2013. http://www.treasury.gov/tigta/auditreports/2013reports/20131 0053fr.pdf.

OTHER HISTORIC DOCUMENTS OF INTEREST

FROM PREVIOUS *HISTORIC DOCUMENTS*

- Responses to the 2010 Midterm Elections, *2010*, p. 555
- Supreme Court on Campaign Contributions, *2010*, p. 23

Scientists Successfully Create Human Embryonic Stem Cells

MAY 15, 2013

When Dolly the sheep was born in 1996, the practice of cloning not only raised moral and ethical debates, but it also reinvigorated scientific efforts to continue working to find new methods of putting the cloning process to work for the benefit of humans. In May 2013, after false starts and fraudulent claims by others in the field, scientists at Oregon Health & Science University announced in the journal *Cell* that they had successfully created human embryonic stem cells using the somatic cell nuclear transfer cloning method. Such a breakthrough has the potential to be used to develop human tissue or organs that can be used in life-saving procedures.

DOLLY LEADS THE WAY

In 1996, scientists at the Roslin Institute in Midlothian, Scotland, extracted the nucleus of a cell from one sheep, and injected it into the unfertilized egg of another sheep. The egg was then implanted into a surrogate. Five months later, as scientists around the world waited with bated breath, Dolly was born, and, along with her, a solidified place for cloning technology. While Dolly was not the first cloned animal, she was the first created from an adult somatic cell. This particular method of cloning, known as somatic cell nuclear transfer, paved the way for a variety of other adult cell animal cloning experiments. Scientists hoped that the data they collected from their animal-based procedures would one day lead to the duplication of the technique using human cells, although it was often noted that no one intended to clone a human.

A major goal in the field of cloning was to produce human embryonic stem cells. Unlike adult stem cells, which already have a specific designation, embryonic stem cells have the capacity to become any type of cell. The expectation was that by creating these cells, scientists could develop a more personalized system of medicine where doctors could take tissue cells from a donor and produce healthy cells to replace those causing another person's illness, or even use the cells to produce an entirely new organ. Although scientists could clone animals, for many years following Dolly's birth they were unable to replicate adult cell cloning in humans using the somatic transfer method. In 2004 and 2005, Hwang Woo-suk, a scientist working at Seoul National University in South Korea reported that he had successfully used human eggs to create embryonic stem cells. However, those results were later found to be falsified. The closest anyone came to creating embryonic stem cells via the somatic method was in 2011, when Dieter Egli led a team at the New York Stem Cell Foundation that produced human cells. However, because the transfer method Egli used required that the egg's nucleus be left in the cell, the cell had abnormalities that limited its potential use.

In 2007, scientists developed a new method of cloning cells that changed adult human cells into embryonic-like cells without the nucleus transfer. Instead of extracting DNA, scientists could instead feed molecules to an adult cell. These cells, called *induced pluripotent stem cells*, or iPSCs, became the new model for stem cell research.

Mitalipov's Scientific Breakthrough

Despite breakthroughs occurring in iPSC research, scientists at Oregon Health & Science University and the Oregon National Primate Research Center continued working toward embryonic stem cell creation through the somatic method. These scientists, led by Shoukhrat Mitalipov, first started their work with monkeys, and in 2007, successfully produced monkey stem cells. The team then turned its attention to human cells.

In September 2012, the scientists began working with donated human eggs. The team extracted the DNA from an egg and replaced it almost entirely with the DNA from the skin cells of a separate donor (either a fetus or an eight-month-old with a rare metabolic disorder). Scientists next injected the cells with a chemical combination to encourage the egg cells to attach to body cells, and gave each an electric shock. In theory, the donor egg would then change the DNA in the skin cells back to their original, unassigned embryonic state. Once those cells divide to become blastocysts, the scientists can harvest them to create a cell line that could eventually be programmed to become any type of cell.

The first trials produced little success. The researchers determined that if they could slow down the egg's development prior to DNA transfer, they might have better results. They did this by injecting the cell with caffeine before injecting the DNA. By December 2012, the team had successfully cloned four embryos, which began producing cells and dividing. To ensure the growth was not a fluke, the team sectioned off some of the growing cells, and they still continued to reproduce on their own.

To verify their results, the research team used their process to create a variety of different cell types. In one test, the team was able to create heart cells that mimicked the contraction a heart makes when it beats. Dr. John Gearhart, a stem cell researcher at the University of Pennsylvania, called the announcement "a holy grail that we've been after for years."

Success Reignites Debate

The issue of cloning raises both moral and ethical dilemmas. In the instance of Mitalipov's research, human embryos were used and destroyed in the cloning process. Some argue that this is akin to murder. "This is a case in which one is deliberately setting out to create a human being for the sole purpose of destroying that human being," said Dr. Daniel Sulmasy, a professor of medicine at the University of Chicago. Scientists involved in embryonic stem cell research contend that because the eggs are not naturally fertilized, they are wholly unlike human beings. And Mitalipov said that, based on his past research with monkeys, it is unlikely that the cells created could ever become a viable baby.

Still, others fear that such technology might one day be used to clone a human. "We already know there are people out there who are itching to be able to be the first to bring a cloned human being to birth," said Sulmasy. "And I think it's going to happen." The Conference of Catholic Bishops agreed, saying that "research will be taken up by those who want to produce cloned children as 'copies' of other people." As a whole, the Church views cloning as immoral, specifically that which involves the use of embryos.

Some detractors point to the socioeconomic factors at play. In this particular study, the women who donated their eggs were compensated upwards of $3,000, which some say could eventually lead to scientists exploiting the poor, who are more likely to find the difficult process of egg extraction desirable from a monetary perspective.

Despite pushback, supporters of the technique used by Mitalipov and his team of researchers say that the opportunity to use the embryonic stem cells to cure things like Parkinson's disease, heart disease, diabetes, and a host of other life-altering illnesses far outweighs the ethical and moral concerns. "Where you can improve [a patient's] quality of life tremendously through this kind of technology, I personally believe that it is ethical to use material like this," said Gearhart.

Is the Technology Still Desirable?

Embryonic stem cell research is still in its early stages. Although scientists in the Mitalipov study proved that they could create them and promote them to grow into a variety of different types of cells, the success rate for such creation and the effectiveness of the end product—say, a kidney—is still up in the air. For one, because embryonic stem cells are being created from a fertilized embryo of which the DNA does not match a patient, there is some likelihood that the body would reject any tissue or organ developed from those cells. However, Mitalipov's research proved that when "reprogrammed cells can be generated with nuclear genetic material from a patient, there is no concern of transplant rejection." This type of cloning also depends on the availability of human eggs—should the technique become a viable option for treating a disease like diabetes, there could be a massive need for donor eggs. And although Mitalipov believes only one donation would be necessary for each procedure (his team proved that they could create stem cells using as few as two eggs, whereas previous studies have used many times that amount), the process for a woman to donate her eggs is not simple and can have severe side effects.

And, as iPSC research continues parallel to the work being done by scientists like Mitalipov, there is a chance that iPSC-based work might prove more desirable, especially because it does not involve the use of, or destruction of, embryos. There is also the possibility that adult stem cells might one day be used to regenerate healthy organs or tissue. Both iPSC and the possibility of using adult stem cells are perhaps most promising to a large segment of the population that most often requires significant medical treatment—the elderly.

Researchers do believe that somatic cloning might have some advantages over iPSC, for example, the ability to find genetic flaws that linger in mitochondria. If the technology advances enough, it is possible that in the future scientists could wipe out defective genes. Studies are currently under way to compare the two types of cells. Still, Mitalipov and other scientists involved in researching both embryonic stem cells and iPSC cells admit that it will be many years before the technology advances to the point where it has potential as a therapeutic medicine. Costly embryonic stem cell research will largely be done with private grants and without support by public organizations like the National Institutes of Health (NIH) because the research involves the destruction of embryos, a violation of NIH rules.

—Heather Kerrigan

Following is the text of a press release issued on May 15, 2013, by Oregon Health & Science University, announcing the successful cloning of human embryonic stem cells.

Scientists Successfully Clone Human Embryonic Stem Cells

May 15, 2013

Scientists at Oregon Health & Science University and the Oregon National Primate Research Center (ONPRC) have successfully reprogrammed human skin cells to become embryonic stem cells capable of transforming into any other cell type in the body. It is believed that stem cell therapies hold the promise of replacing cells damaged through injury or illness. Diseases or conditions that might be treated through stem cell therapy include Parkinson's disease, multiple sclerosis, cardiac disease and spinal cord injuries.

The research breakthrough, led by **Shoukhrat Mitalipov, Ph.D.**, a senior scientist at ONPRC, follows previous success in transforming monkey skin cells into embryonic stem cells in 2007. This latest research will be published in the journal *Cell* online May 15 and in print June 6.

The technique used by Drs. Mitalipov, **Paula Amato, M.D.**, and their colleagues in OHSU's Division of Reproductive Endocrinology and Infertility, Department of Obstetrics & Gynecology, is a variation of a commonly used method called somatic cell nuclear transfer, or SCNT. It involves transplanting the nucleus of one cell, containing an individual's DNA, into an egg cell that has had its genetic material removed. The unfertilized egg cell then develops and eventually produces stem cells.

"A thorough examination of the stem cells derived through this technique demonstrated their ability to convert just like normal embryonic stem cells, into several different cell types, including nerve cells, liver cells and heart cells. Furthermore, because these reprogrammed cells can be generated with nuclear genetic material from a patient, there is no concern of transplant rejection," explained Dr. Mitalipov. "While there is much work to be done in developing safe and effective stem cell treatments, we believe this is a significant step forward in developing the cells that could be used in regenerative medicine."

Another noteworthy aspect of this research is that it does not involve the use of fertilized embryos, a topic that has been the source of a significant ethical debate.

The Mitalipov team's success in reprogramming human skin cells came through a series of studies in both human and monkey cells. Previous unsuccessful attempts by several labs showed that human egg cells appear to be more fragile than eggs from other species. Therefore, known reprogramming methods stalled before stem cells were produced.

To solve this problem, the OHSU group studied various alternative approaches first developed in monkey cells and then applied to human cells. Through moving findings between monkey cells and human cells, the researchers were able to develop a successful method.

The key to this success was finding a way to prompt egg cells to stay in a state called "metaphase" during the nuclear transfer process. Metaphase is a stage in the cell's natural division process (meiosis) when genetic material aligns in the middle of the cell before the cell divides. The research team found that chemically maintaining metaphase throughout the transfer process prevented the process from stalling and allowed the cells to develop and produce stem cells.

"This is a remarkable accomplishment by the Mitalipov lab that will fuel the development of stem cell therapies to combat several diseases and conditions for which there are currently no treatments or cures," said **Dr. Dan Dorsa, Ph.D.**, OHSU Vice President for Research. "The achievement also highlights OHSU's deep reproductive expertise across our campuses. A key component to this success was the translation of basic science findings at the OHSU primate center paired with privately funded human cell studies."

One important distinction is that while the method might be considered a technique for cloning stem cells, commonly called therapeutic cloning, the same method would not likely be successful in producing human clones otherwise known as reproductive cloning.

Several years of monkey studies that utilize somatic cell nuclear transfer have never successfully produced monkey clones. It is expected that this is also the case with humans. Furthermore, the comparative fragility of human cells as noted during this study, is a significant factor that would likely prevent the development of clones.

"Our research is directed toward generating stem cells for use in future treatments to combat disease," added Dr. Mitalipov. "While nuclear transfer breakthroughs often lead to a public discussion about the ethics of human cloning, this is not our focus, nor do we believe our findings might be used by others to advance the possibility of human reproductive cloning."

The human studies were funded by OHSU and a grant from Leducq Foundation. The nonhuman primate studies were funded by the following grants from the National Institutes of Health: HD063276, HD057121, HD059946, EY021214 and OD011092. . . .

SOURCE: Oregon Health & Science University. "OHSU research team successfully converts human skin cells into embryonic stem cells." May 15, 2013. http://www.ohsu.edu/xd/about/news_events/news/2013/05-15-ohsu-research-team-succe.cfm.

OTHER HISTORIC DOCUMENTS OF INTEREST

FROM PREVIOUS *HISTORIC DOCUMENTS*

War Crimes Tribunal Acquits Top Serbian Officials

MAY 30, 2013

On May 30, 2013, the United Nations International Criminal Tribunal for the Former Yugoslavia (ICTY) ruled in the cases of two men, Jovica Stanišić and Franko Simatović, accused of war crimes and crimes against humanity during the Bosnian War. The accused were associates of former Serbian leader Slobodan Milošević and headed his secret police. It was expected that these high-ranking officials would be easily convicted; however, when the Tribunal ruled, Stanišić and Simatović were acquitted. Those who were driven from their homes or had family members killed under the direction of Milošević's secret police decried the ruling, accusing the court of failing to administer justice for the victims.

EARLIER JUDGMENTS

Three months prior to the Stanišić ruling, Momčilo Perišić, the Yugoslavian army commander during the wars in Bosnia and Croatia, appeared before the court to appeal his 2011 sentence of twenty-seven years in prison for crimes against humanity. While Perišić was not responsible for the crimes himself, he was found guilty of aiding and abetting those crimes. On February 28, the court ruled to overturn the conviction, thus setting Perišić free. In its ruling, the court used a new set of procedures to determine guilt, which essentially ruled out convicting a person simply for aiding and abetting a crime.

Three months before the Perišić ruling, the conviction of Ante Gotovina and Mladen Markač, two Croatian generals who the court said targeted civilians during the 1995 Operation Storm, was overturned as well. The two judges who voted against acquittal called the majority decision "simply grotesque" and against "any sense of justice." Serbian Croatians decried the ruling, noting that the 2011 trial was the first that saw justice served for their population. The minority Serbs targeted by Gotovina and Markač's troops fled Croatia; many have still not returned and are still suffering. Serbs in Kosovo had the same reaction in November 2012 when their former prime minister, Ramush Haradinaj, had his war crimes conviction overturned as well.

Despite these acquittals, on May 29, 2013, the court voted to convict six leaders of the former statelet of Herceg-Bosna and its army for "crimes against humanity, violations of the laws and customs of war, and grave breaches of the Geneva conventions." The court concluded that the crimes carried out under the direction of the six leaders were targeted at Bosnian Muslims and amounted to ethnic cleansing.

The differing rulings have led many to question the validity of the court. "It is becoming increasingly difficult to see the consistency or logic in the different judgements [sic]," tweeted Carl Bildt, the Swedish foreign minister. Nenad Golcevski, of the Humanitarian Law Center, agreed, noting that the court "has lost credibility, in the region and internationally."

Trial Proceedings

The ICTY, set up in 1993 to prosecute those responsible for the atrocities committed during the conflicts in the former Yugoslavia between 1991 and 1995, heard testimony against Stanišić and Simatović for their roles in supporting paramilitary units that reportedly ethnically cleansed regions of Bosnia, Croatia, and Herzegovina in an effort to drive out non-Serbs. The accused were close aids of Milošević, the former Serbian head of state, who died in 2006 while on trial at The Hague for war crimes. Stanišić and Simatović were two of the highest-ranking Serbian officials to appear before the ICTY. Stanišić was considered the second-in-command to Milošević and headed up his secret police force, while Simatović was in charge of conducting special operations within the secret police. The pair directed paramilitary units known as Arkan's Tigers, the Scorpions, and the Red Berets, who are thought to have pillaged villages, killing the civilians, looting cars, and burning homes.

Over the course of three years, the ICTY heard from approximately 100 witnesses, many of whom testified against the accused under aliases or behind closed doors. Most of the testimonies were delivered by members of the secret units overseen and supported by Stanišić and Simatović. The court also heard recordings of radio and phone conversations during which instructions were given regarding the plans to drive non-Serbs out of Bosnia and Croatia.

Tribunal Votes for Acquittal

After three years of testimony, the three Tribunal judges finally ruled on May 30, 2013. Voting 2–1, the judges voted to acquit Stanišić and Simatović of their charges. While noting that the accused had provided support to the units responsible for committing many of the atrocities during the 1990s conflicts, the two judges voting in favor of acquittal said the pair could not be held criminally liable because they did not commit the acts themselves. "The prosecution had not proven beyond a reasonable doubt that the accused planned or ordered the crimes charged in the indictment," according to the ruling. Although Stanišić and Simatović may have had knowledge that their support could have led the units to commit a number of atrocities, that alone did not make them responsible. Michèle Picard, the lone opponent to the decision, said the majority did "not address the reality" of the case before them. She accused the other judges of failing to review all evidence before them, instead choosing to only pay attention to those facts that supported the conclusion that Stanišić and Simatović were innocent. Picard found that the evidence, as a whole, suggested that the accused intended to establish Serbian control over parts of Croatia and Bosnia by driving out non-Serbs through any means necessary. The accused had a "key role" in ethnic cleansing, she said. Judge Picard said that the failure of the other two judges to reach her conclusion meant the court had reached a "dark place."

Following the ruling, the prosecution, which had hoped for a life imprisonment sentence, vowed to appeal the ruling. By law, they were given thirty days to file an appeal, which they did on June 28, asking for the findings to be reversed and proper sentences to be applied. The prosecution submitted three reasons for appeal including the Tribunal's failure to recognize that the accused had intended to drive non-Serbs from Croatia and Bosnia through any means necessary and failed to include in its judgment that the support given to the units "significantly contributed" to violent acts. The appeal also argued that the court failed to responsibly analyze the data presented and did not apply the proper sentence for the accused's involvement in the atrocities.

The Serbian government celebrated the ruling. Prime Minister Ivica Dacic said that Serbia "has always advocated fair trials to all those accused before the tribunal in The Hague as the only way to establish the truth about the war and make conditions for reconciliation, peace and stability in the region." The Stanišić-Simatović trial was largely believed to be the last chance for prosecutors to prove that Serbia had played a significant role in the atrocities carried out in Bosnia and Croatia during the conflicts in the former Yugoslavia.

CRIES FOR JUSTICE

Those in Bosnia and Croatia who suffered at the hands of the Milošević regime complained that the recent rulings at the ICTY provided them little justice, and instead allowed perpetrators of heinous crimes to walk free. Those who opposed recent court rulings pointed to changes in procedures that would have previously convicted those like Stanišić and Simatović. According to Karijn van der Voort, a lawyer who worked on the case against Simatović, "there has been a shift in the burden of proof required, especially relating to aiding and abetting." In previous cases, the highest ranking military officials and leaders could be sentenced to prison if it could be proved that they were part of a joint criminal enterprise, organizing such a group and providing weapons, training, or other support, even if they did not directly carry out any crimes. But the new procedures were applied in the case of Stanišić and Simatović, and previously in the appeal acquittal of Perišić and Haradinaj. In the case of Perišić, van der Voort says that the appeals chamber "stated that if an organisation committed lawful and unlawful acts, if someone assisted that organisation in any way, you had to prove that the actions of the accused were specifically directed towards the criminal acts of the organisation." She added, "By raising the bar so high, it is making the top people almost impossible to convict."

Legal experts say that the new burden of proof is a threat to the court's legitimacy. In recent years, a number of low-ranking defendants have been prosecuted for much smaller crimes than those with which the highest-ranking officials are being charged. In essence, the new court procedure makes aiding and abetting war crimes no longer a punishable offence.

Chuck Sudetic, a former ICTY analyst, agreed with the notion that top officials are now extremely difficult to convict, noting "if Hitler were being judged for crimes arising out of the Holocaust on the basis of the aiding and abetting standard now being applied by the ICTY, he might well have gotten off." The new court procedure "turns back precedents set at Nuremberg after World War II and does so 20 years after the establishment of the ICTY and might eventually emasculate the capacity of the institutions of international justice to bring to justice the highest-ranking persons responsible for heinous war crimes. Only the actual killers will be punished, not the mass murders," Sudetic said.

—Heather Kerrigan

Following is the edited text of the judgment summary issued on May 30, 2013, by the United Nation's International Tribunal on the Former Yugoslavia, in the case of Jovica Stanišić and Franko Simatović.

The Hague Releases Judgment on Stanišić and Simatović

DOCUMENT

May 30, 2013

This Chamber is sitting today to deliver its Judgement in the case of the Prosecutor versus Jovica Stanišić and Franko Simatović. . . .

This case concerns crimes allegedly committed between 1 April 1991 and 31 December 1995 against Croats, Bosnian Muslims, Bosnian Croats, and other non-Serb civilians in large areas of Croatia and Bosnia-Herzegovina. The areas in Croatia were the Serbian Autonomous Area of Krajina, or the SAO Krajina, and the Serbian Autonomous Area of Slavonia, Baranja, and Western Srem, or the SAO SBWS. The crimes charged by the Prosecution include persecution, murder, deportation, and forcible transfer.

Jovica Stanišić and Franko Simatović stood trial as alleged participants in a joint criminal enterprise. The alleged objective of this enterprise was the forcible and permanent removal of the majority of non-Serbs from large areas of Croatia and Bosnia-Herzegovina. According to the Prosecution, the members of the criminal enterprise sought to accomplish this goal through the commission of the crimes of persecution, murder, deportation, and forcible transfer. Alternatively, the common criminal purpose included the crimes of deportation and forcible transfer, and the crimes of persecution and murder were reasonably foreseeable to the two Accused as a possible consequence of the execution of the joint criminal enterprise. . . .

The Prosecution alleged that Jovica Stanišić and Franko Simatović contributed to the achievement of the objective of the criminal enterprise by their acts or omissions.

According to the Indictment, the Accused shared the intent to further the common criminal purpose.

In addition to the charges of individual criminal responsibility for committing crimes as part of a joint criminal enterprise, the Indictment charged each Accused with having planned, ordered, and/or aided and abetted in the planning, preparation, and/or execution of the alleged crimes.

[A summary of the case presented to the court has been omitted.]

In accordance with an agreement between the parties, the Chamber found that there was an armed conflict in the territories of Croatia and Bosnia-Herzegovina that extended throughout the period relevant to the crimes charged in the Indictment.

Considering that crimes were committed throughout the Indictment area over the course of many years, and that the victims of the crimes were, with few exceptions, non-Serb civilians the Chamber found beyond a reasonable doubt that there was a widespread attack directed against the non-Serb civilian population in the SAO Krajina, the SAO SBWS, and the Indictment municipalities in Bosnia-Herzegovina.

The Chamber has considered evidence on a significant number of specific incidents of deportation and forcible transfer. For instance, two witnesses provided evidence on an incident of 9 April 1992, where members of the SDG and other armed men collected at least 90, primarily elderly, Croats and Hungarians from Erdut and put them on buses to Sarvaš. In Sarvaš, the people were told to walk towards Croat-controlled Osijek, which they did. The Chamber found beyond a reasonable doubt that these perpetrators committed the crime of deportation as a crime against humanity.

The Chamber also received evidence relating to the departure of between 80,000 and 100,000 Croats and other non-Serb civilians from the SAO Krajina in 1991 and 1992. The Chamber found that the people fleeing did so as a result of the situation prevailing in the region, which was created by a combination of the following factors: attacks on villages and towns with Croat population; killings; use of human shields; detention; beatings; forced labour; sexual abuse and other forms of harassment of Croat persons; and looting and destruction of property.

Noting that fear of violence, duress, detention, psychological oppression, and other such circumstances may create an environment where there is no choice but to leave, the Chamber found that those who left the SAO Krajina as a result of the circumstances prevailing there, were forcibly displaced. Based on the foregoing, the Chamber found that members of the SAO Krajina Police, the SAO Krajina territorial defence, and the Yugoslav People's Army, or the JNA, among other forces, in carrying out the aforementioned acts of violence and harassment, committed the crime of deportation as a crime against humanity.

The Chamber also found that the SDG, the Unit, the SAO Krajina Police, and other forces, committed the crimes of deportation and forcible transfer at numerous locations in Croatia and Bosnia-Herzegovina throughout the Indictment period.

The Chamber further received and considered adjudicated facts and evidence on numerous incidents of murder. As an example, the Chamber found that on or about 20 October 1991, members of the SAO Krajina Police rounded up local, mainly Croat civilians and brought them to the fire station in Hrvatska Dubica. The following day, at Krečane near Baćin, members of the SAO Krajina Police shot and killed 39 Croat detainees, many of whom were elderly. The Chamber found that members of the SAO Krajina Police committed the crime of murder as a crime against humanity and as a violation of the laws and customs of war.

The Chamber further found that the SDG, the Unit, the Skorpions, the SAO Krajina Police, and other forces committed a large number of murders against Croats, Muslims, and other non-Serbs in Croatia and Bosnia-Herzegovina.

Having examined the evidence and its findings with regard to the incidents of murder, deportation, and forcible transfer, the Chamber found that they had been carried out with discriminatory intent. The Chamber therefore concluded that they constituted persecution as a crime against humanity.

The Indictment charged the Accused with individual criminal responsibility for the crimes of murder, deportation, forcible transfer, and persecution. These charges were based on the Accused's alleged participation in a joint criminal enterprise, the object of which was the forcible and permanent removal of the majority of non-Serbs from large areas of Croatia and Bosnia-Herzegovina. The Chamber will now address whether the aforementioned crimes can be attributed to the Accused.

The Chamber found that as of 31 December 1991, Jovica Stanišić was the head of the Serbian DB and that Franko Simatović was employed in the Second Administration of the DB throughout the Indictment period.

The Chamber has received a substantial amount of evidence regarding the role of the Accused vis-à-vis the Unit, other alleged special units of the Serbian DB, and other Serb

Forces, often from former members of the same formations or through official DB documentation.

Turning first to the Unit, also known as the Red Berets and later as the JATD, the Chamber found that in the period from May to August 1991, Jovica Stanišić and Franko Simatović formed a Serbian DB unit consisting of around 25 to 30 persons. From late April or early May to July 1991, Franko Simatović cooperated with others in the establishment and operation of a training camp at Golubić, where training commenced in May 1991. Following meetings in Belgrade between Martić and Stanišić and between Simatović and Captain Dragan, instructors Captain Dragan and Dragan Filipović provided training at Golubić, together with, among others, Živojin Ivanović. Upon completion of their training, a number of trainees from Golubić became training instructors themselves.

The Chamber found that the training at Golubić was of a military character and included weapons and ambush training, as well as the treatment of prisoners of war and the treatment of civilians in armed conflict. A total of between 350 and 700 members of the SAO Krajina Police and the SAO Krajina territorial defence were trained at Golubić between April and August 1991. Men who had trained at Golubić set up further units and trained other people in the SAO Krajina. They also participated alongside Simatović, Captain Dragan, and Živojin Ivanović in operations in the SAO Krajina between June and August 1991.

The Chamber found that the Golubić camp was the first of a number of similar camps, where the Unit trained new recruits and other Serb forces. The Unit also deployed its members to various operations of a military character with the support and under the control of the Accused. From late 1991, these camps included the Ležimir camp at Mount Fruška Gora from where the Unit was deployed to operations in the SBWS in September 1991. In 1992, the camps included the Pajzoš camp at Ilok from where members of the Unit were deployed to participate in the take-over of Bosanski Šamac in May 1992, as well as the Mount Ozren and Vila camps, from where members of the Unit were deployed to participate in the Doboj operations in April–July 1992. The Chamber found that members of the Unit committed the crimes of murder, deportation, and forcible transfer in Bosanski Šamac municipality and deportation and forcible transfer in Doboj municipality in 1992.

In 1993, the Unit's training activities continued at the Tara camp and at the Skelani and Bratunac camps from which the Unit took part in combat and mop-up operations in the Skelani area in March and April 1993 and in the Bratunac area in first part of 1993. Training of the Unit continued in 1995 at the Bilje camp, the Sova camp, and the Pajzoš camp.

In 1997, the Accused attended a ceremony marking the anniversary of the Unit's formation, during which Simatović praised the Unit's achievements in, as he put it, protecting national security in circumstances where the existence of the Serbian people was directly jeopardised throughout its entire ethnic area. On this occasion, Stanišić presented awards to several members of the Unit.

In conclusion, the Chamber found that the Accused directed and organized the formation of the Unit, organized its involvement in a number of operations in Croatia and Bosnia-Herzegovina, and directed and organized its financing, logistical support, and other substantial assistance or support, throughout the Indictment period. From at least September 1991, the Accused were in command of the Unit and controlled its deployment and training activities through leading Unit members. As of August 1993, the Unit formally became a part of the Serbian DB, when it was formalized as the JATD.

With regard to the other alleged special units of the DB, the Chamber considered that the ties between these formations and the Accused were less substantial. For example, the

Chamber was unable to conclude that the Accused directed or organised the formation of the SDG or the Skorpions, or directed them in any particular operations. Moreover, the Chamber made only a limited number of findings that the Accused provided support to these two formations.

The Chamber found that the Accused, among others, directed and organized the formation of the SAO Krajina Police, in cooperation with Milan Martić. Furthermore, they contributed to the financing of the SAO Krajina Police in 1990 and 1991, and organized logistical support, in the form of weapons and communication equipment between December 1990 and May or June 1991. The Chamber also found the SAO Krajina Police committed murders in 1991, and deportation in 1991 and 1992, in the SAO Krajina.

The Chamber finally considered the allegations that the Accused provided "channels of communication" between and among the core members of the joint criminal enterprise in Belgrade, in the specific regions, and locally, throughout the Indictment period. Based on the evidence before it, the Chamber found that the Accused were in direct and frequent contact with many of the alleged members of the joint criminal enterprise. It further found that, on occasion, Stanišic acted in a liaison capacity at least in the contacts between Milošević and Martić, as well as Milošević and Karadžić. However, the evidence also indicated that there was regular direct contact between Milošević, Martić, Karadžić, and Babić. The majority, Judge Picard dissenting, did not consider that Jovica Stanišić had acted as a channel of communication. Further, the Chamber could not conclude that Franko Simatović had acted as a channel of communication between and among core members of the joint criminal enterprise.

The Chamber finally considered the question of whether the Accused shared the intent of the alleged joint criminal enterprise to forcibly and permanently remove the majority of non-Serbs from large areas of Croatia and Bosnia-Herzegovina, through the commission of murder, deportation, forcible transfer, and persecution. For both Accused, the Chamber first reviewed direct evidence indicating that they shared the intent. This included evidence on actions taken and words uttered, and in this respect the Chamber paid particular attention to evidence the Prosecution had pointed to in its final trial brief. The Chamber then proceeded to examine what, if anything, could be inferred with regard to the intent from the actions by the Accused.

With regard to Jovica Stanišić, the Prosecution pointed to a few instances of words uttered and actions taken by him that, in its view, would indicate that he shared the intent. For example, according to one witness's testimony, in September 1991 Stanišić arrived at the SAO SBWS government building in Dalj, yelling at people, and berating them because Vukovar had not surrendered yet. Stanišić then called a meeting with among others Hadžić, representatives of the JNA, and territorial defence commanders. Following this meeting Stanišić returned to Belgrade. The Chamber noted that it had not received evidence about what was discussed at the meeting called by Stanišić. The majority, Judge Picard dissenting, considered that Stanišić's action in relation to Vukovar could reasonably be interpreted as support for a successful military takeover of Vukovar.

Having reviewed this, and other, direct evidence regarding Stanišić's intent, the majority, Judge Picard dissenting, did not consider it sufficient to establish Stanišić's intent to further the alleged common criminal purpose through the commission of crimes.

Absent direct evidence, the Chamber examined whether intent could be inferred from Stanišić's actions during the Indictment period. In this respect, the Chamber considered in particular the Accused's actions in relation to the Unit, the SAO Krajina Police, the SDG, and the Skorpions.

With regard to the Unit, the Chamber first recalled its findings that this formation had committed the crimes of murder, deportation, and forcible transfer first in Bosanski Šamac and then of deportation and forcible transfer in Doboj in 1992. The Chamber had further found that the Accused organised the involvement of the Unit in the operations in these municipalities. However, the evidence did not establish that the Accused personally directed the Unit during these operations or that they had issued orders or instructions to commit the aforementioned crimes. Nonetheless, given their role vis-à-vis the Unit and the scope of the crimes, the Chamber found that the Accused must have known that Unit members had committed crimes in Bosanski Šamac and that it may have been reasonably foreseeable to them that Unit members would commit crimes in Doboj. The Chamber further considered the Unit's involvement in other operations, for which the Accused had organized its involvement. These included reconnaissance activities and operations undertaken in response to military attacks by opposing forces. With the exception of the Doboj and Bosanski Šamac operations, the Chamber did not find that Unit members committed crimes during the operations in which they were involved.

In conclusion, the majority, Judge Picard dissenting, did not consider that the only reasonable inference from Stanišić's actions with regard to the Unit was that he shared the intent to further the alleged joint criminal enterprise. Similarly, with regard to Stanišić's actions with regard to training of Serb forces, the majority, Judge Picard dissenting, did not consider that the only reasonable inference from the evidence was that he shared the intent to further the alleged joint criminal enterprise.

With regard to the SAO Krajina police, the Chamber found that the members of this formation committed murders in the SAO Krajina in 1991 and deportation of between 80,000 and 100,000 Croats in the same area in 1991 and 1992. The Chamber further found that the Accused had been closely involved with the formation, logistical, and financial support of the SAO Krajina police. The Accused had also cooperated closely with Milan Martić, who had authority over this formation, and whose intent to deport non-Serbs must have been known to the Accused.

The Chamber found that in continuing to support the SAO Krajina police and cooperate with Milan Martić from April 1991, Stanišić took the risk that the SAO Krajina police would commit crimes when establishing and maintaining Serb control over large areas of Croatia. However, the Chamber found that knowledge and acceptance of such a risk is insufficient for the first form of joint criminal enterprise liability. The majority, Judge Picard dissenting, did not consider that the only reasonable inference from Stanišić's actions with regard to the SAO Krajina Police was that he shared the intent of the alleged joint criminal enterprise.

The majority, Judge Picard dissenting, reached the same conclusion concerning Stanišić's actions with regard to the SDG and the Skorpions.

In making the foregoing findings, the majority, Judge Picard dissenting, allowed for the reasonable possibility that Stanišić's intent in relation to the Unit, including the training of other Serb forces, the SAO Krajina police, the SDG, and the Skorpions, was limited to establishing and maintaining Serb control over large areas of Croatia and Bosnia-Herzegovina.

Based on the foregoing, the majority, Judge Picard dissenting, could not conclude that the only reasonable inference from the evidence on Stanišić's actions was that he shared the intent to further the common criminal purpose of forcibly and permanently removing the majority of non-Serbs from large areas of Croatia and Bosnia-Herzegovina, through the commission of murder, deportation, forcible transfer, and persecution from at least April 1991 through 1995.

With regard to Franko Simatović, the Chamber first considered the evidence with regard to his specific actions or words uttered. In this respect, the Chamber found that Simatović participated in a discussion of the objectives of the attack on Lovinac, which included the objective to have as much of the local population leave as possible in order to establish a purely Serb territory. According to the Chamber, the evidence indicated that Simatović was at least aware of Martić's intent (and may have shared it), to forcibly remove Croat civilians from the village of Lovinac in June 1991, even if the evidence did not establish whether persons actually left Lovinac during or immediately following the attack.

Concerning the Vukovar operations, the Chamber found that Simatović was present at a meeting prior to, and a celebration following, the fall of Vukovar. Considering that the content of the meeting was unknown to the Chamber, and noting that members of the Unit did not participate in the attack, the majority, Judge Picard dissenting, allowed as a reasonable interpretation that Simatović's intent was limited to support for the successful military take-over of Vukovar.

The Chamber further considered evidence on Simatović's acts in relation to other military operations. This evidence indicated that these operations had been military actions directed against opposing forces and it did not indicate that any crimes had been committed during the operations.

Based on the foregoing, the majority, Judge Picard dissenting, was unable to conclude from the evidence on Simatović's actions, that he shared the intent to further the common criminal purpose of forcibly and permanently removing the majority of non-Serbs from large areas of Croatia and Bosnia-Herzegovina, through the commission of murder, deportation, forcible transfer, and persecution from at least April 1991 through 1995.

The Chamber then considered the other modes of criminal liability, charged by the Prosecution.

The Chamber found that the Prosecution had not proven beyond a reasonable doubt that the Accused planned or ordered the crimes charged in the Indictment.

With regard to the allegations of responsibility for aiding and abetting the crimes charged in the Indictment, the Chamber primarily considered whether the Accused's acts vis-à-vis certain formations, in particular the Unit, aided and abetted any crimes.

In this respect, and as stated before, the Chamber found that the Accused directed and organized the formation of the Unit between May and August 1991, and that from at least September 1991, the Accused were in command of the Unit and controlled its deployment and training activities through leading Unit members who acted on behalf of the Accused and were immediately subordinate to them. The Chamber further recalled its findings that the Accused organised the Unit's involvement during the Bosanski Šamac and Doboj operations in 1992, organized the training of its members at the Doboj and Pajzoš camps, and organised their financing. The Chamber found that these contributions of the Accused assisted the commission of the crimes in Bosanski Samač and Doboj.

The majority, Judge Picard dissenting, considered that the Accused's assistance to the Bosanski Šamac and Doboj operations, and to the Unit generally, was not specifically directed towards the commission of the crimes of murder, deportation, forcible transfer, or persecution. Rather, it allowed for the reasonable conclusion that the assistance was specifically directed towards establishing and maintaining Serb control over these areas.

The majority, Judge Picard dissenting, was thus unable to conclude that the assistance rendered to the Unit by the Accused aided and abetted the commission of the crimes in Doboj and Bosanski Šamac.

The Chamber found that there were certain links, albeit looser when compared to the Unit, between the Accused and other groups, for example with the SAO Krajina Police. The Accused's contributions vis-à-vis these other groups were of a similar nature, including financing, supplying, organising involvement, supporting, and training. However, the Chamber recalled that in none of the incidents where members of these other groups committed crimes, did the Accused play any more specific role in providing assistance.

Recalling its finding that the kind of assistance rendered to the Unit was insufficient to incur criminal responsibility as an aider and abettor, the majority, Judge Picard dissenting, was unable to conclude that the Accused aided and abetted crimes perpetrated by the SDG, the SAO Krajina Police, the Skorpions, or other groups.

Mr Stanišić, will you please stand.

For the reasons summarised above, the Chamber by majority, Judge Picard dissenting, having considered all of the evidence and the arguments of the Parties, the Statute and the Rules, and based upon the factual and legal findings as determined in the Judgement, finds you not guilty and therefore acquits you of all Counts against you in the Indictment. The Chamber orders that you be immediately released from the United Nations Detention Unit, after the necessary practical arrangements are made.

You may be seated.

Mr Simatović, will you please stand.

For the reasons summarised above, the Chamber by majority, Judge Picard dissenting, having considered all of the evidence and the arguments of the Parties, the Statute and the Rules, and based upon the factual and legal findings as determined in the Judgement, finds you not guilty and therefore acquits you of all Counts against you in the Indictment. The Chamber orders that you be immediately released from the United Nations Detention Unit, after the necessary practical arrangements are made.

You may be seated.

A dissenting opinion by Judge Picard and a separate opinion by me, Judge Orie, is appended to the Judgement. This concludes the delivery of the Judgement, which will now be made publicly available. The Chamber stands adjourned.

SOURCE: United Nations. International Criminal Tribunal for the Former Yugoslavia. "Judgement Summary for Jovica Stanišić and Franko Simatović." May 30, 2013. http://icty.org/x/cases/stanisic_simatovic/tjug/en/130530_summary.pdf.

OTHER HISTORIC DOCUMENTS OF INTEREST

FROM PREVIOUS *HISTORIC DOCUMENTS*

June

Turkish President Remarks on Protests

JUNE 1, 2013

In late May 2013, protests broke out in Istanbul, Turkey. What started as a sit-in demonstration to contest the development of a park quickly turned into a nationwide movement aimed squarely at the government of Prime Minister Recep Tayyip Erdoğan. Protesters alleged that since first coming to office in 2003, the prime minister had stripped them of their basic rights and imposed Islamic values on their traditionally secular country. Erdoğan remained defiant, even as the demonstrators called for his resignation. By the close of 2013, the prime minister remained in office and the protests, while still ongoing, had dwindled in both size and force.

Erdoğan Takes Power

Erdoğan's Justice and Development Party (AKP) first gained power in 2002, and subsequently won the 2007 and 2011 elections. The party won each election by a wide margin, giving Erdoğan the ability to push through nearly all his policies. This has included both economic changes that have been to the benefit of the nation and helped it recover from its deep recession, as well as more questionable legislation that has infringed on a variety of rights including free speech and a free press. To the latter, the prime minister has aligned himself with "friendly" media organizations that he has largely used as a mouthpiece, while taking legal action against media outlets that speak negatively about his government. The prime minister and his party have also restricted Internet use and heavily filter the content on television.

Of greater concern to some Turkish citizens, however, is the movement of the nation away from secular values to more traditional Islamist beliefs. In 2012, Erdoğan told his countrymen that he wanted to ensure that the next generation would be "pious," and helped pass legislation that added Islamic courses to school curriculum. The prime minister has made this and other changes all while publicly proclaiming the democratization of Turkey, in line with European Union requirements for a successful EU member state bid.

Park Development Sparks Protests

Although Erdoğan's government implemented measures to help pull the country out of its financial crisis, one of the key tenets of the economic growth plan was to encourage more building, some of which has taken place on public land without the support or approval of the Turkish people. One such example is Taksim Gezi Park, located in Istanbul. The government announced that the park was set for redevelopment to include an Ottoman-era barracks replica, angering many environmentalists, approximately fifty of whom started a sit-in to delay the bulldozing of the park. Although the protest was peaceful, on May 28, 2013, police used tear gas and water cannons to remove the protesters from the park and burned down the tent city the protesters had erected. Undeterred, the protesters returned, and on May 31, were again forcefully disbursed.

In response to what they saw as police brutality, an estimated 10,000 people gathered in nearby parks and on Istiklal Avenue. News of what happened in Gezi Park quickly spread around the country, and demonstrations began to take root in other major Turkish cities. The media, which was largely aligned with Erdoğan, downplayed the protests, and the prime minister himself accused extremists of trying to overthrow his government. Without the aid of the mass media, the protesters largely relied on social media outlets to organize themselves and spread the word.

Despite Erdoğan's dismissive attitude toward the protests, Turkey's president, Abdullah Gül, encouraged both the government and the protesters to maintain a level head. Taking direct aim at Erdoğan's assertion that he could rule with absolute power because he was elected by the people, Gül said that true democracy "does not only mean elections." The president added, "There is nothing more natural than various ways of expression other than elections if there are different views, different situations, objections. Peaceful protests are surely a part of that."

PROTESTERS RETURN

On June 1, an even larger encampment of protesters formed in Gezi Park. One day later, while leaving for a three-day trip to North Africa, Erdoğan called the movement little more than "a few looters." The prime minister was heavily criticized for leaving his country at a time when so much resistance was brewing against his government. As the number of protesters joining the movement across the nation grew, so did clashes with police. Protesters in Istanbul were disbursed with tear gas, and one protester was shot in the head and later died. The demonstrators fought back, at one point hijacking a bulldozer destined for Gezi Park and using it to chase police.

On June 4, Taksim Solidarity, the group that led many of the protests in Istanbul and largely served as the only cohesive voice of the demonstrators, delivered a list of demands to Deputy Prime Minister Bulent Arinc. Demands included the release of those who had been arrested during the demonstrations, an end to police brutality, the dismissal of the governors of the country's major cities, the dismissal of some police leaders, and the end of the development plan for Gezi Park. The government said it would review the request.

On June 15, riot police entered Taksim Square near Gezi Park. In an attempt to stave off violence, police informed the protesters camped at the park that it was not their intention to enter the park, but rather to clear the protesters out of the square so that it could be opened back up to traffic. Some of the protesters at the park ignored the statements and threw Molotov cocktails at police, who subsequently entered the park and cleared it. The protesters disbursed and began gathering in other public places, discussing next steps and how to involve more Turks in their protests.

In late June, the protests again gained intensity after police attacked demonstrators in Istanbul who threw carnations at them. A violent protest broke out at the same time in Ankara, Turkey's capital, where the police officer who shot and killed a protester was being released without any punishment.

By mid-summer, the protests had largely died down, with some springing up occasionally, although nowhere near the scope of what was seen in late May and June. This related directly to an announcement during the first week of July that the development plans for Gezi Park had been canceled by court order. The Turkish government had put development plans on hold in mid-June, awaiting the court decision; the government still has the right to appeal the July decision. Smaller demonstrations were revived in September and October when the government proposed building a road through a forest on the campus of Middle East Technical University in Ankara, in violation of Turkish law. The road would require the destruction of approximately 3,000 trees. An occupy protest sprang up but was disbursed by riot police using water cannons, and the city subsequently directed its workers to cut down the trees under the cover of darkness. In response, students and university officials replanted thousands of trees.

In total, an estimated 3.5 million took part in at least one of approximately 5,000 protests conducted in Turkey in 2013. The demographics of the protesters covered a swath of Turkish life, including from both the left and right of the political spectrum. Less than a dozen were killed in the violence, while another 8,000 were injured. An estimated 3,000 protesters were arrested.

Erdoğan Defiant

Throughout the demonstrations, the prime minister remained defiant and gathered his party behind him in a public affairs show of force. On June 8, the AKP held a rally in Ankara where the prime minister told his supporters that police forces would intervene with anyone who refused to leave Gezi Park. The AKP organized a second rally in Istanbul. Each rally drew thousands of supporters.

After meeting with protesters in Ankara, on June 12, the prime minister said that he would hold a public referendum on development of Gezi Park. But at the same time, he called on his interior minister to immediately end all protests. Analysts saw the referendum as an attempt to focus protests on the park rather than on his government as a whole. But regardless of its intent, the move intensified the resolve of protesters who refused the prime minister's proposal. "There are 80-year-old trees in there, it is a public space, and there is an ongoing case in which the court has halted the project," said Taksim Solidarity spokesperson Mucella Yapici.

Late-Year Unrest

In November, Erdoğan again sparked controversy after stating that he wanted to see an end to coed dorms at state universities and surrounding off-campus housing. "Anything can happen," Erdoğan said. "Then parents cry out, saying, 'Where is the state?' These steps are being taken in order to show that the state is there. As a conservative, democratic government, we need to intervene." But Erdoğan's inflammatory November remarks were nothing compared to the growing discontent in December when protesters again took to the streets and called for the downfall of the prime minister's government. The December unrest related to a corruption scandal and investigation involving prominent businessmen, the sons of cabinet ministers, and the chief of a state-owned bank. The probe into these men, who had close ties to the AKP, was thought to reflect growing discontent within Erdoğan's own party.

On December 17, those involved with the corruption scandal were arrested and charged with crimes including bribery, tender rigging, and transferring money to Iran. The three cabinet ministers whose sons were arrested resigned their positions.

Erdoğan called the corruption investigation and subsequent arrests a "dirty operation." He went on to say, "Those who called this operation a corruption operation are themselves the very ones who are corrupt." He refused calls for his resignation, but instead reshuffled his cabinet with ministers considered to be even more loyal to his cause. Erdoğan also removed top justices from their posts, sparking outrage from the public who said they could no longer trust in the judicial system. "This is highly worrying," said Sezgin Tanrikulu, the deputy head of the People's Republican Party, Erdoğan's main opposition. "The little trust that people had left in the Turkish justice system is now gone."

As the corruption scandal wore on, police refused orders from the prosecutor to arrest additional high-ranking government and private sector officials. Prosecutors argued that the failure of the police to aid in the case gave those guilty of major crimes time to tamper with evidence or even flee. Many of the police officials who refused to give arrest orders to their officers had been recently installed after Erdoğan ordered the removal of hundreds of officers and police officials. The public prosecutor was also removed from the corruption probe.

—Heather Kerrigan

Following is the text of a statement delivered on June 1, 2013, by Turkish President Abdullah Gül, responding to the protests in Taksim Square.

DOCUMENT *Turkish President Addresses Protests*

June 1, 2013

It is natural that in our country, which believes in democracy, pluralism and the rule of law and which is resolute to make progress on this path, there are different thoughts, viewpoints, approaches, comments and ideas about important issues. This is the biggest treasure of a democratic people society.

What is important is that we can discuss everything in a civilized fashion and that we can be open to dialogue and to all views. Reactions, in a democratic society, must be shown with common sense and within the framework of the rules and the law and in the way they will not lead to any misuse or abuse. The officials, meanwhile, must make greater efforts to listen to and respect different views and concerns.

The biggest responsibility that falls on us about the ongoing events in Taksim Square which have reached a point that makes us all worried is to have more maturity so that these events cool down.

Our security forces, while performing their duties, must take the utmost care about the issue and they must go easy on people during their interventions, not paving the way for any worrisome and sad sights.

I have discussed this issue with the Prime Minister and the relevant officials this morning. I believe that everyone will do whatever they can so that the issue can be put on track again through dialogue in the way it befits us without delay."

SOURCE: Presidency of the Republic of Turkey. "President Abdullah Gül Issued a Message About the Ongoing Events in Taksim Square." June 1, 2013. http://www.tccb.gov.tr/speeches-statements/344/86279/ preb-statement.html.

OTHER HISTORIC DOCUMENTS OF INTEREST

Supreme Court Rules on
DNA Collection

JUNE 3, 2013

In *Maryland v. King,* the U.S. Supreme Court faced yet another issue arising from the collision of rapidly evolving new technologies and traditional constitutional law. Currently, all fifty states require the DNA testing of anyone who is convicted of a felony. This case, instead, addressed whether the government can collect DNA from those who are merely arrested for a serious crime but not yet convicted of that crime. The case arose in Maryland, which is one of twenty-eight states and the federal government with laws allowing such DNA testing of arrestees. A sharply divided court, with its usual political divisions scrambled, allowed the taking of DNA samples from those arrested in connection with serious crimes in a 5–4 decision. The majority opinion, written by Justice Anthony M. Kennedy, who was joined by Chief Justice John Roberts, Jr., and Justices Clarence Thomas, Stephen Breyer, and Samuel Alito, Jr., described DNA identification as a legitimate part of police booking procedure closely analogous to fingerprinting and photographing. Justice Antonin Scalia disagreed sharply and read from his dissent in open court, a move generally reserved to highlight deep divisions. His dissent was joined by the typically liberal justices Ruth Bader Ginsburg, Sonia Sotomayor, and Elena Kagan.

An Arrest in Maryland

In 2009, Alonzo King of Wicomico County, Maryland, was arrested and charged with felony first- and second-degree assault. As part of Maryland's routine booking procedure for serious offenses, police applied a cotton swab to the inside of his cheek to obtain a DNA sample. Months later, when his DNA was uploaded onto the Maryland DNA database, it was found to match a sample collected six years earlier from the investigation of an unsolved rape and robbery of a fifty-three-year-old woman. King's assault charge was later reduced to a lesser charge of misdemeanor assault and he pled guilty, but he was subsequently charged with the rape. During his trial he tried unsuccessfully to suppress the DNA match on the grounds that it was taken in violation of his Fourth Amendment right to be free of unreasonable searches and seizures. The DNA was the only evidence presented at his trial and the jury found him guilty, sentencing him to life imprisonment.

King appealed his conviction to Maryland's highest court, the Maryland Court of Appeals, which concluded that the testing of an arrested individual's DNA without his consent or a court order was an unconstitutional search in violation of his Fourth Amendment rights. Without the DNA evidence, the Maryland Court vacated the rape conviction. The United States Supreme Court agreed to hear an appeal of this decision.

No Constitutional Problems With DNA Testing

At issue before the Supreme Court was whether the routine DNA testing of everyone arrested for a serious crime violates the Fourth Amendment to the Constitution which holds: "[t]he right of the people to be secure in their persons, houses, papers, and effects, against unreasonable searches and seizures, shall not be violated." Whether a search is unreasonable depends on the balancing of the individual's expectation of privacy against the government's legitimate interest. The majority of the Court did not have much difficulty with this balance, treating the case as if it involved no real extension of existing constitutional principles that allow such routine booking procedures as fingerprinting and photographing.

First, the Court addressed the privacy interest of someone who has been arrested and found that once individuals are arrested and taken into police custody they have greatly reduced expectations of privacy. The police can search an arrestee's possessions, which were on him at the time of arrest as well as perform an extensive search of the body. In a case during the Court's last term, they found no violation when jail officials required detainees to lift their genitals and cough in a squatting position as part of a jailhouse search. By contrast, the DNA swab, according to the Court, is a "gentle rub along the inside of the cheek that does not break the skin," merely a brief and minimal intrusion.

The Court balanced this "minimal intrusion" against the government's "significant" interest in identifying the suspect in custody. This identification is important "not only so that the proper name can be attached to his charges but also so that the criminal justice system can make informed decisions concerning pretrial custody." Knowing as much as possible about the person they have arrested helps the state know more clearly what risks may be posed by introducing the person into the detainee population. Knowledge of previous more serious offenses or a record of violence or mental illness would be relevant to the facility staff. It is also, the Court said, relevant to making bail decisions. If, for example, an individual is arrested for burglary but has also committed a number of sexual assaults, that person may be more likely to flee before trial or to pose a significant danger to the public if released. The Court also referenced that the state's interest in properly identifying the arrestee may lead to the release of someone who is currently wrongly imprisoned for the same offense.

After finding strong government interest in identifying those arrested for serious crimes balanced against only minor intrusions, the Court concluded that the DNA identification of arrestees is a reasonable search under the Fourth Amendment. While acknowledging that the technology enabling DNA identifications represents the most significant advancement for law enforcement of our era, the Court ultimately was not convinced that it poses fundamentally different legal issues than those presented by photographing arrestees to compare with sketch artist depictions of wanted criminals, showing mug shots to potential witnesses, or matching tattoos to known gang signs. The closest analogy to DNA testing referenced in the opinion came from the routine practice of taking all arrestees' fingerprints and running them through an electronic database of known criminals and unsolved crimes. The only relevant difference cited by the Court "between DNA analysis and the accepted use of fingerprint databases is the unparalleled accuracy DNA provides."

Justice Scalia Dissents

In Justice Scalia's colorful language, the majority's assertion that the state took DNA evidence strictly to identify those in custody "taxes the credulity of the credulous." King's identity was never in question; the only thing that was identified by the DNA search was the previously taken sample from the earlier crime. It was clear to the dissenters that the reason the state took arrestees' DNA samples to run through a national database was to search for just this kind of evidence of other unknown criminal wrongdoing; Maryland sought only to solve cold cases that were completely unrelated to the crime for which the individual had been arrested. This is precisely the type of search the Fourth Amendment prohibits, according to Scalia, who explained that the amendment "forbids searching a person for evidence of a crime when there is no basis for believing the person is guilty of the crime." Justice Scalia recognized that "solving unsolved crimes is a noble objective" but not as noble as "the protection of our people from suspicionless law-enforcement searches. The Fourth Amendment must prevail." Clearly more crimes would be solved, he argued, if the state took DNA samples of everyone who applies for a driver's license or attends public school, but, the dissent concluded, "I doubt that the proud men who wrote the charter of our liberties would have been so eager to open their mouths for royal inspection."

The Supreme Court heard several Fourth Amendment cases in the 2013 term, and Justice Scalia argued for a forceful interpretation of the amendment each time. He was on the winning side of the issue when he, as well as the same three liberal-leaning justices from this decision and several other justices, overturned convictions based on the use of drug-sniffing dogs outside of homes and the taking of blood samples in drunk-driving investigations.

Impact Going Forward

The language of the majority opinion allowed DNA testing only for people who were arrested and charged with serious crimes, although it did not define what is meant by "serious." The case reviewed the Maryland statute, which defines serious to include murder, rape, first-degree assault, kidnapping, arson, sexual assault, and a variety of other major crimes. Justice Scalia was skeptical that such a limitation would stand, predicting that as a consequence of this decision "your DNA can be taken and entered into a national DNA database if you are ever arrested, rightly or wrongly, and for whatever reason." In fact, many of the other states which already allow preconviction DNA testing do not have the restriction to "serious" crimes found in the Maryland law. If the Supreme Court's limitation to "serious" crimes does not hold, national DNA databases could grow to hold the DNA of the nearly one-third of Americans arrested for some offense or other by the age of 23. Michael Risher, Staff Attorney for the American Civil Liberties Union (ACLU) of Northern California is pressing ahead with a challenge to the much-broader California law, which currently allows police to DNA test anyone arrested for simple drug possession, joyriding, or intentionally bouncing a check. In his reaction to the Supreme Court's opinion in *Maryland v. King*, he argued that "a single police officer's decision to arrest a person for a minor offense should not justify this intrusion into genetic privacy."

The *Maryland v. King* case did not present the Supreme Court with issues involving government officials searching arrestees' DNA for personal medical information such as genetic diseases or predispositions. Currently the tests run on DNA samples by CODIS, the Combined DNA Index System supervised by the FBI, are from the nonprotein coding junk regions of DNA and do not reveal genetic traits beyond those needed to provide an identification. Recognizing that available technology can change, Justice Kennedy specifically noted in his opinion that "[i]f in the future police analyze samples to determine, for instance, an arrestee's predisposition for a particular disease or other hereditary factors not relevant to identity, that case would present additional privacy concerns not present here."

—Melissa Feinberg

The following are excerpts from the U.S. Supreme Court ruling in Maryland v. King, *in which the Court ruled 5–4 to allow for the taking of DNA samples from those arrested and charged in connection to serious crimes.*

DOCUMENT   *Maryland v. King*

June 3, 2013

No. 12–207

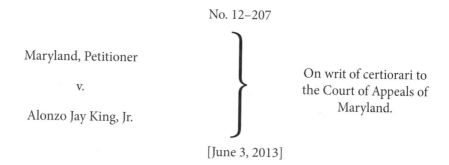

Maryland, Petitioner

v.

Alonzo Jay King, Jr.

On writ of certiorari to the Court of Appeals of Maryland.

[June 3, 2013]

[Footnotes have been omitted.]

JUSTICE KENNEDY delivered the opinion of the Court.

In 2003 a man concealing his face and armed with a gun broke into a woman's home in Salisbury, Maryland. He raped her. The police were unable to identify or apprehend the assailant based on any detailed description or other evidence they then had, but they did obtain from the victim a sample of the perpetrator's DNA.

In 2009 Alonzo King was arrested in Wicomico County, Maryland, and charged with first- and second-degree assault for menacing a group of people with a shotgun. As part of a routine booking procedure for serious offenses, his DNA sample was taken by applying a cotton swab or filter paper—known as a buccal swab—to the inside of his cheeks. The DNA was found to match the DNA taken from the Salisbury rape victim. King was tried and convicted for the rape. Additional DNA samples were taken from him and used in the rape trial, but there seems to be no doubt that it was the DNA from the cheek sample taken at the time he was booked in 2009 that led to his first having been linked to the rape and charged with its commission.

The Court of Appeals of Maryland, on review of King's rape conviction, ruled that the DNA taken when King was booked for the 2009 charge was an unlawful seizure because obtaining and using the cheek swab was an unreasonable search of the person. It set the rape conviction aside. This Court granted certiorari and now reverses the judgment of the Maryland court.

[Sections I and II, containing background on the case and information about DNA testing, have been omitted.]

III

A

Although the DNA swab procedure used here presents a question the Court has not yet addressed, the framework for deciding the issue is well established. The Fourth Amendment, binding on the States by the Fourteenth Amendment, provides that "[t]he right of the people to be secure in their persons, houses, papers, and effects, against unreasonable searches and seizures, shall not be violated." It can be agreed that using a buccal swab on the inner tissues of a person's cheek in order to obtain DNA samples is a search. Virtually any "intrusio[n] into the human body," *Schmerber* v. *California*, 384 U. S. 757, 770 (1966), will work an invasion of "'cherished personal security' that is subject to constitutional scrutiny," *Cupp* v. *Murphy*, 412 U. S. 291, 295 (1973) (quoting *Terry* v. *Ohio*, 392 U. S. 1, 24–25 (1968)). The Court has applied the Fourth Amendment to police efforts to draw blood, see *Schmerber, supra; Missouri* v. *McNeely*, 569 U. S. ___ (2013), scraping an arrestee's fingernails to obtain trace evidence, see *Cupp, supra,* and even to "a breathalyzer test, which generally requires the production of alveolaror 'deep lung' breath for chemical analysis," *Skinner* v. *Railway Labor Executives' Assn.*, 489 U. S. 602, 616 (1989).

A buccal swab is a far more gentle process than a veni-puncture to draw blood. It involves but a light touch on the inside of the cheek; and although it can be deemed a search within the body of the arrestee, it requires no "surgical intrusions beneath the skin." *Winston*, 470 U. S., at 760. The fact than an intrusion is negligible is of central relevance to determining reasonableness, although it is still a search as the law defines that term.

B

To say that the Fourth Amendment applies here is the beginning point, not the end of the analysis. "[T]he Fourth Amendment's proper function is to constrain, not against all intrusions as such, but against intrusions which are not justified in the circumstances, or which are made in an improper manner." *Schmerber, supra,* at 768. "As the text of the Fourth Amendment indicates, the ultimate measure of the constitutionality of a governmental search is 'reasonableness.'" *Vernonia School Dist. 47J* v. *Acton,* 515 U. S. 646, 652 (1995). In giving content to the inquiry whether an intrusion is reasonable, the Court has preferred "some quantum of individualized suspicion . . . [as] a prerequisite to a constitutional search or seizure. But the Fourth Amendment imposes no irreducible requirement of such suspicion." . . .

IV

The legitimate government interest served by the Maryland DNA Collection Act is one that is well established: the need for law enforcement officers in a safe and accurate way to process and identify the persons and possessions they must take into custody. It is beyond dispute that "probable cause provides legal justification for arresting a person suspected of crime, and for a brief period of detention to take the administrative steps incident to arrest." *Gerstein v. Pugh*, 420 U. S. 103, 113–114 (1975). Also uncontested is the "right on the part of the Government, always recognized under English and American law, to search the person of the accused when legally arrested." Weeks v. United States, 232 U. S. 383, 392 (1914), overruled on other grounds, *Mapp v. Ohio*, 367 U. S. 643 (1961). "The validity of the search of a person incident to a lawful arrest has been regarded as settled from its first enunciation, and has remained virtually unchallenged." *United States v. Robinson*, 414 U. S. 218, 224 (1973). Even in that context, the Court has been clear that individual suspicion is not necessary, because "[t]he constitutionality of a search incident to an arrest does not depend on whether there is any indication that the person arrested possesses weapons or evidence. The fact of a lawful arrest, standing alone, authorizes a search." *Michigan v. DeFillippo*, 443 U. S. 31, 35 (1979).

The "routine administrative procedure[s] at a police station house incident to book-ing and jailing the suspect" derive from different origins and have different constitutional justifications than, say, the search of a place, *Illinois v. Lafayette*, 462 U. S. 640, 643 (1983); for the search of a place not incident to an arrest depends on the "fair probability that contraband or evidence of a crime will be found in a particular place," *Illinois v. Gates*, 462 U. S. 213, 238 (1983). The interests are further different when an individual is formally processed into police custody. Then "the law is in the act of subjecting the body of the accused to its physical dominion." *People v. Chiagles*, 237 N. Y. 193, 197, 142 N. E. 583, 584 (1923) (Cardozo, J.). When probable cause exists to remove an individual from the normal channels of society and hold him in legal custody, DNA identification plays a critical role in serving those interests.

First, "[i]n every criminal case, it is known and must be known who has been arrested and who is being tried." *Hiibel v. Sixth Judicial Dist. Court of Nev., Humboldt Cty.*, 542 U. S. 177, 191 (2004). An individual's identity is more than just his name or Social Security number, and the government's interest in identification goes beyond ensuring that the proper name is typed on the indictment. Identity has never been considered limited to the name on the arrestee's birth certificate. In fact, a name is of little value compared to the real interest in identification at stake when an individual is brought into custody. "It is a well recognized aspect of criminal conduct that the perpetrator will take unusual steps to con-ceal not only his conduct, but also his identity. Disguises used while committing a crime may be supplemented or replaced by changed names, and even changed physical features." *Jones v. Murray*, 962 F. 2d 302, 307 (CA4 1992). An "arrestee may be carrying a false ID or lie about his identity," and "criminal history records . . . can be inaccurate or incomplete." *Florence v. Board of Chosen Freeholders of County of Burlington*, 566 U. S. ___, ___ (2012) (slip op., at 16).

A suspect's criminal history is a critical part of his identity that officers should know when processing him for detention. It is a common occurrence that "[p]eople detained for minor offenses can turn out to be the most devious and dangerous criminals. Hours after the Oklahoma City bombing, Timothy McVeigh was stopped by a state trooper who noticed he was driving without a license plate. Police stopped serial killer Joel Rifkin for the same reason. One of the terrorists involved in the September 11 attacks was stopped and ticketed for speeding just two days before hijacking Flight 93." *Id.*, at ___ (slip op., at 14) (citations omitted). Police already seek this crucial identifying information. They use routine and accepted means as varied as comparing the suspect's booking photograph to sketch artists' depictions of persons of interest, showing his mugshot to potential witnesses, and of course making a computerized comparison of the arrestee's fingerprints against electronic databases of known criminals and unsolved crimes. In this respect the only difference between DNA analysis and the accepted use of fingerprint databases is the unparalleled accuracy DNA provides.

The task of identification necessarily entails searching public and police records based on the identifying information provided by the arrestee to see what is already known about him. The DNA collected from arrestees is an irrefutable identification of the person from whom it was taken. Like a fingerprint, the 13 CODIS loci are not themselves evidence of any particular crime, in the way that a drug test can by itself be evidence of illegal narcotics use. A DNA profile is useful to the police because it gives them a form of identification to search the records already in their valid possession. In this respect the use of DNA for iden-tification is no different than matching an arrestee's face to a wanted poster of a previously unidentified suspect; or matching tattoos to known gang symbols to reveal a criminal affil-iation; or matching the arrestee's fingerprints to those recovered from a crime scene. See Tr. of Oral Arg. 19. DNA is another metric of identification used to connect the arrestee with his or her public persona, as reflected in records of his or her actions that are available to the police. Those records may be linked to the arrestee by a variety of relevant forms of identification, including name, alias, date and time of previous convictions and the name then used, photograph, Social Security number, or CODIS profile. These data, found in official records, are checked as a routine matter to produce a more comprehensive record of the suspect's complete identity. Finding occurrences of the arrestee's CODIS profile in outstanding cases is consistent with this common practice. It uses a different form of iden-tification than a name or fingerprint, but its function is the same.

Second, law enforcement officers bear a responsibility for ensuring that the custody of an arrestee does not create inordinate "risks for facility staff, for the existing detainee popula-tion, and for a new detainee." *Florence, supra,* at ___ (slip op., at 10). DNA identification can provide untainted information to those charged with detaining suspects and detaining the property of any felon. For these purposes officers must know the type of person whom they are detaining, and DNA allows them to make critical choices about how to proceed.

> "Knowledge of identity may inform an officer that a suspect is wanted for another offense, or has a record of violence or mental disorder. On the other hand, know-ing identity may help clear a suspect and allow the police to concentrate their ef-forts elsewhere. Identity may prove particularly important in [certain cases, such as] where the police are investigating what appears to be a domestic assault. Of-ficers called to investigate domestic disputes need to know whom they are dealing with in order to assess the situation, the threat to their own safety, and possible danger to the potential victim." Hiibel, *supra,* at 186.

Recognizing that a name alone cannot address this interest in identity, the Court has approved, for example, "a visual inspection for certain tattoos and other signs of gang affili-ation as part of the intake process," because "[t]he identification and isolation of gang mem-bers before they are admitted protects everyone." *Florence, supra,* at ___ (slip op., at 11).

Third, looking forward to future stages of criminal prosecution, "the Government has a substantial interest in ensuring that persons accused of crimes are available for trials." *Bell v. Wolfish*, 441 U. S. 520, 534 (1979). A person who is arrested for one offense but knows that he has yet to answer for some past crime may be more inclined to flee the instant charges, lest continued contact with the criminal justice system expose one or more other serious offenses. For example, a defendant who had committed a prior sexual assault might be inclined to flee on a burglary charge, knowing that in every State a DNA sample would be taken from him after his conviction on the burglary charge that would tie him to the more serious charge of rape. In addition to subverting the administration of justice with respect to the crime of arrest, this ties back to the interest in safety; for a detainee who absconds from custody presents a risk to law enforcement officers, other detainees, victims of previous crimes, witnesses, and society at large.

Fourth, an arrestee's past conduct is essential to an assessment of the danger he poses to the public, and this will inform a court's determination whether the individual should be released on bail. "The government's interest in preventing crime by arrestees is both legitimate and compelling." *United States v. Salerno*, 481 U. S. 739, 749 (1987). DNA identification of a suspect in a violent crime provides critical information to the police and judicial officials in making a determination of the arrestee's future dangerousness. This inquiry always has entailed some scrutiny beyond the name on the defendant's driver's license. For example, Maryland law requires a judge to take into account not only "the nature and circumstances of the offense charged" but also "the defendant's family ties, employment status and history, financial resources, reputation, character and mental condition, length of residence in the community." 1 Md. Rules 4–216(f)(1)(A),(C) (2013). Knowing that the defendant is wanted for a previous violent crime based on DNA identification is especially probative of the court's consideration of "the danger of the defendant to the alleged victim, another person, or the community." Rule 4–216(f)(1)(G); see also 18 U. S. C. §3142 (2006 ed. and Supp. V) (similar requirements).

This interest is not speculative. In considering laws to require collecting DNA from arrestees, government agencies around the Nation found evidence of numerous cases in which felony arrestees would have been identified as violent through DNA identification matching them to previous crimes but who later committed additional crimes because such identification was not used to detain them….

Present capabilities make it possible to complete a DNA identification that provides information essential to determining whether a detained suspect can be released pending trial. See, e.g., States Brief 18, n. 10 ("DNA identification database samples have been processed in as few as two days in California, although around 30 days has been average"). Regardless of when the initial bail decision is made, release is not appropriate until a further determination is made as to the person's identity in the sense not only of what his birth certificate states but also what other records and data disclose to give that identity more meaning in the whole context of who the person really is. And even when release is permitted, the background identity of the suspect is necessary for determining what conditions must be met before release is allowed. If release is authorized, it may take time for the conditions to be met, and so the time before actual release can be substantial. For example, in the federal system, defendants released conditionally are detained on average for 112 days; those released on unsecured bond for 37 days; on personal recognizance for 36 days; and on other financial conditions for 27 days….During this entire period, additional and supplemental data establishing more about the person's identity and background can provide critical information relevant to the conditions of release and whether to revisit an initial release determination. The facts of this case are illustrative. Though the record is not clear, if some thought were being given to releasing the respondent on bail on the gun charge, a release that would take weeks or months in any event, when the DNA report linked him to the prior rape, it would be relevant to the conditions of his release. The same would be true with a supplemental fingerprint report.

Even if an arrestee is released on bail, development of DNA identification revealing the defendant's unknown violent past can and should lead to the revocation of his conditional release. See 18 U. S. C. §3145(a) (providing for revocation of release); see also States Brief 11–12 (discussing examples where bail and diversion determinations were reversed after DNA identified the arrestee's violent history). Pretrial release of a person charged with a dangerous crime is a most serious responsibility. It is reasonable in all respects for the State to use an accepted database to determine if an arrestee is the object of suspicion in other serious crimes, suspicion that may provide a strong incentive for the arrestee to escape and flee.

Finally, in the interests of justice, the identification of an arrestee as the perpetrator of some heinous crime may have the salutary effect of freeing a person wrongfully imprisoned for the same offense. "[P]rompt [DNA] testing . . . would speed up apprehension of criminals before they commit additional crimes, and prevent the grotesque detention of . . . innocent people." J. Dwyer, P. Neufeld, & B. Scheck, Actual Innocence 245 (2000).

Because proper processing of arrestees is so important and has consequences for every stage of the criminal process, the Court has recognized that the "governmental interests underlying a station-house search of the arrestee's person and possessions may in some circumstances be even greater than those supporting a search immediately following arrest." *Lafayette*, 462 U. S., at 645. Thus, the Court has been reluctant to circumscribe the authority of the police to conduct reasonable booking searches. For example, "[t]he standards traditionally governing a search incident to lawful arrest are not . . . commuted to the stricter *Terry* standards." *Robinson*, 414 U. S., at 234. Nor are these interests in identification served only by a search of the arrestee himself. "[I]nspection of an arrestee's personal property may assist the police in ascertaining or verifying his identity." *Lafayette, supra,* at 646. And though the Fifth Amendment's protection against self-incrimination is not, as a general rule, governed by a reasonableness standard, the Court has held that "questions . . . reasonably related to the police's administrative concerns . . . fall outside the protections of *Miranda [v. Arizona,* 384 U. S. 436 (1966)] and the answers thereto need not be suppressed." *Pennsylvania v. Muniz,* 496 U. S. 582, 601–602 (1990).

B

[A portion of Part B, addressing changes in DNA testing, has been omitted.]

In sum, there can be little reason to question "the legitimate interest of the government in knowing for an absolute certainty the identity of the person arrested, in knowing whether he is wanted elsewhere, and in ensuring his identification in the event he flees prosecution." 3 W. LaFave, Search and Seizure §5.3(c), p. 216 (5th ed. 2012). To that end, courts have confirmed that the Fourth Amendment allows police to take certain routine "administrative steps incident to arrest—i.e., . . . book[ing], photograph[ing], and fingerprint[ing]." *McLaughlin*, 500 U. S., at 58. DNA identification of arrestees, of the type approved by the Maryland statute here at issue, is "no more than an extension of methods of identification long used in dealing with persons under arrest." *Kelly*, 55 F. 2d, at 69. In the balance of reasonableness required by the Fourth Amendment, therefore, the Court must give great weight both to the significant government interest at stake in the identification of arrestees and to the unmatched potential of DNA identification to serve that interest.

V

A

By comparison to this substantial government interest and the unique effectiveness of DNA identification, the intrusion of a cheek swab to obtain a DNA sample is a minimal one. True, a significant government interest does not alone suffice to justify a search. The government interest must outweigh the degree to which the search invades an individual's legitimate expectations of privacy. In considering those expectations in this case, however, the necessary predicate of a valid arrest for a serious offense is fundamental. "Although the underlying command of the Fourth Amendment is always that searches and seizures be reasonable, what is reasonable depends on the context within which a search takes place." *New Jersey* v. *T. L. O.*, 469 U. S. 325, 337 (1985). "[T]he legitimacy of certain privacy expectations vis-à-vis the State may depend upon the individual's legal relationship with the State." *Vernonia School Dist. 47J*, 515 U. S., at 654.

The reasonableness of any search must be considered in the context of the person's legitimate expectations of privacy. For example, when weighing the invasiveness of urinalysis of high school athletes, the Court noted that "[l]egitimate privacy expectations are even less with regard to student athletes. . . . Public school locker rooms, the usual sites for these activities, are not notable for the privacy they afford." *Id.,* at 657. Likewise, the Court has used a context-specific benchmark inapplicable to the public at large when "the expectations of privacy of covered employees are diminished by reason of their participation in an industry that is regulated pervasively," *Skinner,* 489 U. S., at 627, or when "the 'operational realities of the workplace' may render entirely reasonable certain work-related intrusions by supervisors and co-workers that might be viewed as unreasonable in other contexts," *Von Raab,* 489 U. S., at 671.

The expectations of privacy of an individual taken into police custody "necessarily [are] of a diminished scope." *Bell,* 441 U. S., at 557. "[B]oth the person and the property in his immediate possession may be searched at the station house." *United States* v. *Edwards,* 415 U. S. 800, 803 (1974). A search of the detainee's person when he is booked into custody may " 'involve a relatively extensive exploration,'" *Robinson,* 414 U. S., at 227, including "requir[ing] at least some detainees to lift their genitals or cough in a squatting position," *Florence,* 566 U. S., at ___ (slip op., at 13).

In this critical respect, the search here at issue differs from the sort of programmatic searches of either the public at large or a particular class of regulated but otherwise law-abiding citizens that the Court has previously labeled as "'special needs'" searches. *Chandler* v. *Miller,* 520 U. S. 305, 314 (1997). When the police stop a motorist at a checkpoint, see *Indianapolis* v. *Edmond,* 531 U. S. 32 (2000), or test a political candidate for illegal narcotics, see *Chandler, supra,* they intrude upon substantial expectations of privacy. So the Court has insisted on some purpose other than "to detect evidence of ordinary criminal wrongdoing" to justify these searches in the absence of individualized suspicion. *Edmond, supra,* at 38. Once an individual has been arrested on probable cause for a dangerous offense that may require detention before trial, however, his or her expectations of privacy and freedom from police scrutiny are reduced. DNA identification like that at issue here thus does not require consideration of any unique needs that would be required to justify searching the average citizen. The special needs cases, though in full accord with the result reached here, do not have a direct bearing on the issues presented in this case, because unlike the search of a citizen who has not been suspected of a wrong, a detainee has a reduced expectation of privacy.

The reasonableness inquiry here considers two other circumstances in which the Court has held that particularized suspicion is not categorically required: "diminished expectations of privacy [and] minimal intrusions." *McArthur,* 531 U. S., at 330. This is not to suggest that any search is acceptable solely because a person is in custody. Some searches, such as invasive surgery, see *Winston,* 470 U. S. 753, or a search of the arrestee's home, see *Chimel* v. *California,* 395 U. S. 752 (1969), involve either greater intrusions or higher expectations of privacy than are present in this case. In those situations, when the Court must "balance the privacy-related and law enforcement-related concerns to determine if the intrusion was reasonable," *McArthur, supra,* at 331, the privacy-related concerns are weighty enough that the search may require a warrant, notwithstanding the diminished expectations of privacy of the arrestee.

Here, by contrast to the approved standard procedures incident to any arrest detailed above, a buccal swab involves an even more brief and still minimal intrusion. A gentle rub along the inside of the cheek does not break the skin, and it "involves virtually no risk, trauma, or pain." *Schmerber,* 384 U. S., at 771. "A crucial factor in analyzing the magnitude of the intrusion . . . is the extent to which the procedure may threaten the safety or health of the individual," *Winston, supra,* at 761, and nothing suggests that a buccal swab poses any physical danger whatsoever. A brief intrusion of an arrestee's person is subject to the Fourth Amendment, but a swab of this nature does not increase the indignity already attendant to normal incidents of arrest.

B

In addition the processing of respondent's DNA sample's 13 CODIS loci did not intrude on respondent's privacy in a way that would make his DNA identification unconstitutional.

First, as already noted, the CODIS loci come from noncoding parts of the DNA that do not reveal the genetic traits of the arrestee. While science can always progress further, and those progressions may have Fourth Amendment consequences, alleles at the CODIS loci "are not at present revealing information beyond identification." Katsanis & Wagner, Characterization of the Standard and Recommended CODIS Markers, 58 J. Forensic Sci. S169, S171 (2013). The argument that the testing at issue in this case reveals any private medical information at all is open to dispute.

And even if non-coding alleles could provide some information, they are not in fact tested for that end. It is undisputed that law enforcement officers analyze DNA for the sole purpose of generating a unique identifying number against which future samples may be matched. This parallels a similar safeguard based on actual practice in the school drug-testing context, where the Court deemed it "significant that the tests at issue here look only for drugs, and not for whether the student is, for example, epileptic, pregnant, or diabetic." *Vernonia School Dist. 47J,* 515 U. S., at 658. If in the future police analyze samples to determine, for instance, an arrestee's predisposition for a particular disease or other hereditary factors not relevant to identity, that case would present additional privacy concerns not present here.

Finally, the Act provides statutory protections that guard against further invasion of privacy. As noted above, the Act requires that "[o]nly DNA records that directly relate to the identification of individuals shall be collected and stored." Md. Pub. Saf. Code Ann. §2–505(b)(1). No purpose other than identification is permissible: "A person may not willfully test a DNA sample for information that does not relate to the identification of individuals as specified in this subtitle." §2–512(c). This Court has noted often that "a 'statutory or regulatory duty to avoid unwarranted disclosures' generally allays . . . privacy concerns." *NASA* v. *Nelson,* 562 U. S. ___, ___ (2011) (slip op., at 20) (quoting *Whalen* v. *Roe,* 429 U. S. 589, 605 (1977)). The Court need not speculate about the risks posed "by a system that did not contain comparable security provisions." *Id.,* at 606. In light of the scientific and statutory safeguards, once respondent's DNA was lawfully collected the STR analysis of respondent's DNA pursuant to CODIS procedures did not amount to a significant invasion of privacy that would render the DNA identification impermissible under the Fourth Amendment.

* * *

In light of the context of a valid arrest supported by probable cause respondent's expectations of privacy were not offended by the minor intrusion of a brief swab of his cheeks. By contrast, that same context of arrest gives rise to significant state interests in identifying respondent not only so that the proper name can be attached to his charges but also so that the criminal justice system can make informed decisions concerning pretrial custody. Upon these considerations the Court concludes that DNA identification of arrestees is a reasonable search that can be considered part of a routine booking procedure. When officers make an arrest supported by probable cause to hold for a serious offense and they bring the suspect to the station to be detained in custody, taking and analyzing a cheek swab of the arrestee's DNA is, like fingerprinting and photographing, a legitimate police booking procedure that is reasonable under the Fourth Amendment.

The judgment of the Court of Appeals of Maryland is reversed.

It is so ordered.

JUSTICE SCALIA, with whom JUSTICE GINSBURG, JUSTICE SOTOMAYOR, and JUSTICE KAGAN join, dissenting.

The Fourth Amendment forbids searching a person for evidence of a crime when there is no basis for believing the person is guilty of the crime or is in possession of incriminating evidence. That prohibition is categorical and without exception; it lies at the very heart of the Fourth Amendment. Whenever this Court has allowed a suspicionless search, it has insisted upon a justifying motive apart from the investigation of crime.

It is obvious that no such noninvestigative motive exists in this case. The Court's assertion that DNA is being taken, not to solve crimes, but to *identify* those in the State's custody, taxes the credulity of the credulous. And the Court's comparison of Maryland's DNA searches to other techniques, such as fingerprinting, can seem apt only to those who know no more than today's opinion has chosen to tell them about how those DNA searches actually work.

[The body of Justice Scalia's dissent has been omitted.]

What DNA adds—what makes it a valuable weapon in the law enforcement arsenal—is the ability to solve unsolved crimes, by matching old crime-scene evidence against the profiles of people whose identities are already known. That is what was going on when King's DNA was taken, and we should not disguise the fact. Solving unsolved crimes is a noble objective, but it occupies a lower place in the American pantheon of noble objectives than the protection of our people from suspicionless law-enforcement searches. The Fourth Amendment must prevail.

* * *

The Court disguises the vast (and scary) scope of its holding by promising a limitation it cannot deliver. The Court repeatedly says that DNA testing, and entry into a national DNA registry, will not befall thee and me, dear reader, but only those arrested for "serious offense[s]." *Ante,* at 28; see also *ante,* at 1, 9, 14, 17, 22, 23, 24 (repeatedly limiting the analysis to "serious offenses"). I cannot imagine what principle could possibly justify this limitation, and the Court does not attempt to suggest any. If one believes that DNA will "identify" someone arrested for assault, he must believe that it will "identify" someone arrested for a traffic offense. This Court does not base its judgments on senseless distinctions. At the end of the day, *logic will out.* When there comes before us the taking of DNA from an arrestee for a traffic violation, the Court will predictably (and quite rightly) say, "We can find no significant difference between this case and *King.*" Make no mistake about it: As an entirely predictable consequence of today's decision, your DNA can be taken and entered into a national DNA database if you are ever arrested, rightly or wrongly, and for whatever reason.

The most regrettable aspect of the suspicionless search that occurred here is that it proved to be quite unnecessary. All parties concede that it would have been entirely permissible, as far as the Fourth Amendment is concerned, for Maryland to take a sample of King's DNA as a consequence of his conviction for second-degree assault. So the ironic result of the Court's error is this: The only arrestees to whom the outcome here will ever make a difference are those who *have been acquitted* of the crime of arrest (so that their DNA could not have been taken upon conviction). In other words, this Act manages to burden uniquely the sole group for whom the Fourth Amendment's protections ought to be most jealously guarded: people who are innocent of the State's accusations.

Today's judgment will, to be sure, have the beneficial effect of solving more crimes; then again, so would the taking of DNA samples from anyone who flies on an airplane (surely the Transportation Security Administration needs to know the "identity" of the flying public), applies for a driver's license, or attends a public school. Perhaps the construction of such a genetic panopticon is wise. But I doubt that the proud men who wrote the charter of our liberties would have been so eager to open their mouths for royal inspection.

I therefore dissent, and hope that today's incursion upon the Fourth Amendment, like an earlier one, will some day be repudiated.

SOURCE: U.S. Supreme Court. *Maryland v. King,* 569 U.S.__(2013). http://www.supremecourt.gov/opinions/12pdf/12-207_d18e.pdf.

OTHER HISTORIC DOCUMENTS OF INTEREST

FROM PREVIOUS *HISTORIC DOCUMENTS*

Federal Leaders Remark on Immigration Reform

JUNE 11 AND JUNE 27, 2013

In June 2013, the U.S. Senate took a major step toward advancing comprehensive immigration reform, passing a bipartisan bill that would create a path to citizenship for the country's approximately 11 million illegal immigrants and create new opportunities for skilled foreign workers while enhancing border security. While many hailed the vote as a major victory in a political battle that had been ongoing for more than a decade, Republican leaders in the House of Representatives refused to take up the Senate's bill for consideration, choosing instead to adopt a piecemeal approach to immigration reform that has yet to result in the passage of any legislation.

A STRUGGLE FOR REFORM

Immigration policy has long been a charged issue in the United States, with ongoing efforts to pass and implement comprehensive immigration reform since at least 2001. Policymakers have struggled to balance economic and social concerns with reasonable regulations and border security measures. Providing a path to citizenship for the millions of illegal immigrants currently living in the United States has proven to be a particular point of contention between Republicans and Democrats, with many claiming such a program would be unfair to those who entered the country legally and could have an adverse effect on the economy.

The last significant effort to pass immigration reform occurred in 2007 under then-President George W. Bush. The Secure Borders, Economic Opportunity and Immigration Reform Act combined various elements of three previously failed immigration bills and sought to provide a path to citizenship for illegal immigrants, while also increasing security along the Mexican border. Yet the bill failed to garner enough votes in the Senate, with opponents claiming it would essentially be an amnesty program for those who had broken the law or that it would result in depressed wages and fewer job opportunities for American workers.

Then in June 2013, President Barack Obama issued an executive order implementing a program called "Consideration of Deferred Action for Childhood Arrivals," which temporarily decriminalized the status of those children of undocumented or illegal immigrants who were raised in the United States and delayed the threat of deportation. Under the program, the Department of Homeland Security would defer any enforcement actions against an individual for a period of two years if that individual arrived in the United States when he or she was younger than sixteen years old and was currently younger than thirty-one; had continuously lived in the United States for at least five years; was in school, had graduated high school, or obtained a GED, or was an honorably discharged U.S. veteran; and had no criminal record and was not perceived as a threat to national security. Obama called on Congress to pass like-minded legislation, which had been introduced several times since 2001 as the Development, Relief, and Education for Alien Minors (DREAM) Act.

"Gang of Eight" Introduces Comprehensive Reform

Following the 2012 presidential election, Republican sentiments about immigration reform began to shift. Latino support for Republican presidential candidates decreased significantly since Bush's reelection in 2004, with Mitt Romney receiving only 27 percent of the Latino vote compared to Obama's 71 percent. Eager to shore up support for future elections, many Republicans became more willing to act on immigration reform.

In the fall of 2012, a bipartisan group of senators formed what would later become known as the "Gang of Eight." Sens. John McCain, R-Ariz., Robert Menendez, D-N.J., Marco Rubio, R-Fla., Chuck Schumer, D-N.Y., Lindsey Graham, R-S.C., Jeff Flake, R-Ariz., Dick Durbin, D-Ill., and Michael Bennet, D-Colo., began developing a package of immigration reform measures. The group first shared their initial proposal publicly in January 2013, but provided only an outline of their proposed policies to allow room for additional debate and rewriting before the bill's official introduction in the Senate. Over the following months, the group negotiated with their congressional colleagues, the Obama administration, and business and labor organizations behind the scenes to broker compromises between competing interests. One such compromise that was viewed by many as critical to the bill's ultimate success was an agreement reached in March between major labor and business groups, including the Chamber of Commerce and the AFL-CIO, to establish a guest worker program for low-skilled immigrants.

The Gang of Eight's months of work culminated on April 16, when Schumer introduced the Border Security, Economic Opportunity, and Immigration Modernization Act of 2013. The bill was referred to the Senate Judiciary Committee, where it underwent an extensive markup. The committee considered more than 300 amendments to the bill over the course of five days. The bill passed out of committee in May with a 13–5 bipartisan vote, but the amendment process was not over. In particular, a number of Republicans and conservative Democrats wanted to add more border security measures to the bill before a full Senate vote. Sens. Bob Corker, R-Tenn., and John Hoeven, R-N.D., proposed creating a "border surge" as part of the bill, which would appropriate billions of dollars over ten years for security measures including an additional 20,000 border patrol agents, 700 additional miles of border fence, and high-tech surveillance equipment. Their proposal helped garner support from more Republicans, giving the bill a much stronger chance of receiving the sixty votes needed to avoid a filibuster.

In addition to the guest worker program and increased border security, the final bill would create a thirteen-year pathway to citizenship for undocumented immigrants currently living in the United States, as long as they met several benchmarks before applying for a green card. Those who came to the United States before age sixteen, graduated from high school, and attended at least two years of college or served four years in the military could apply for registered provisional immigrant status. After five years, those individuals could apply for their green card, then citizenship. Adults would also be able to apply for registered provisional immigrant status if they were eligible, which would enable them to work and travel until they could get a green card.

The bill also included a mandate for employers to use the E-Verify system to ensure they did not hire immigrants who are not authorized to work in the United States. The bill would establish a new INVEST visa for foreign entrepreneurs to enable them to stay in the United States and more easily start companies; add additional visas or green cards for foreign students who have earned a master's degree or higher in science, technology, engineering, and math (STEM) disciplines; increase the number of visas available for high-skilled workers; and shift the overall focus of U.S. immigration policies from being family-based to skills-based by creating a system that awards points for criteria such as professional skills and work history in the United States to help guide decisions on which new immigrants to accept.

On June 27, the Senate voted 68–32 to pass the bill, with fourteen Republicans joining Democrats to vote yes. The senators voted from their desks, a practice typically reserved for historic legislation, and proreform activists sitting in the Senate gallery began chanting, "Yes, we can," as the results became clear. President Obama applauded the vote. "The United States Senate delivered for the American people, bringing us a critical step closer to fixing our broken immigration system once and for all," Obama said in a statement. "Today, the Senate did its job. It's now up to the House to do the same."

Gang of Eight members said they had hoped to receive seventy votes, thinking it would help push the House to act quickly but were pleased with sixty-eight votes. "The strong bipartisan vote we took is going to send a message across the country, it's going to send a message to the other end of the Capitol as well," said Schumer. "The bill has generated a level of support that we believe will be impossible for the House to ignore."

House Action

House leadership, however, proved to be resistant to the Senate's legislation. "The House is not going to take up and vote on whatever the Senate passes," said House Speaker John Boehner, R-Ohio. "We're going to do our own bill, through regular order, and it'll be legislation that reflects the will of our majority and the will of the American people." Boehner said the House would instead adopt a piecemeal approach.

The Senate bill's pathway to citizenship seemed to be a critical issue for House Republicans. Rep. Bob Goodlatte, R-Va., chairman of the House Judiciary Committee, said he instead wanted a "pathway to legalization," which would allow some illegal immigrants to get a green card but not full citizenship. Other Republicans also questioned whether the security measures included in the Senate bill would be strong enough.

In June, the House Judiciary Committee approved four different bills targeting specific immigration-related issues. This included the SAFE Act, which sought to strengthen and fortify enforcement of current immigration law, particularly at the state and local level, through measures such as grants for new security equipment and facilities and immigration-related trainings for state and local personnel. Another bill, the Legal Workforce Act, would require businesses to use the E-Verify system for all new hires and to reverify certain categories of current employees. The third bill, the SKILLS Visa Act, would increase the number of certain visas available to immigrants with degrees in STEM and medical fields, while the fourth bill, the AG Act, would create a new temporary visa program to allow immigrants to come to the United States for agricultural labor. The House Homeland Security Committee also passed the Border Security Results Act, which would increase tech and personnel at the border to try to tighten border security.

At the same time, the House's own "Gang of Seven" was working to develop a bipartisan plan similar to the Senate bill. Their plan would have provided a probationary period for illegal immigrants, during which they'd have to admit their wrongdoings, followed by a longer path to citizenship. Yet in September, Gang of Seven member Rep. Luis Gutierrez, D-Ill., told *The Washington Post* that the process had stalled due to Republican members' resistance and a lack of support from Republican leadership.

On October 2, House Democrats introduced their own bill, which was largely similar to the Senate's legislation but without the border surge proposed by Corker and Hoeven. Instead, their bill would require the Department of Homeland Security to create a detailed plan that would result in the apprehension of 90 percent of illegal border-crossing immigrants in high-traffic areas within thirty-three months and across the U.S.-Mexico border within five years.

KEEPING UP THE PRESSURE

Throughout the year, a wide variety of organizations and individuals sought to encourage lawmakers to pass comprehensive immigration reform. In April, thousands of proreform activists participated in a National Rally for Citizenship on the National Mall in Washington, D.C. In July, leaders of more than 400 companies sent a letter to Boehner and Rep. Nancy Pelosi, D-Calif., in support of immigration reform. During Congress' August recess, a number of organizations lobbied lawmakers in their home districts at town halls and other events. The Alliance for Citizenship organized roughly 360 of its own events across fifty-two congressional districts to pressure lawmakers to act. Some members of Congress even participated in these actions. On October 8, thousands gathered on the National Mall in Washington, D.C., for the March for Dignity and Respect, calling for comprehensive legislation that would give illegal immigrants a path to citizenship. The event moved to the lawn near the Capitol building, where eight Democratic representatives and approximately 200 protesters were arrested for blocking traffic.

POTENTIAL 2014 REFORM EFFORT

Despite mounting pressure, the House did not vote on any proposed immigration measures before the end of 2013. However, some speculate that the House may revisit the immigration debate in early 2014 following Congress' successful brokerage of a bipartisan budget deal that ended a sixteen-day government shutdown in October. Rep. Tom Cole, R-Okla., the deputy whip on Boehner's leadership team, told *The Hill* in December that Boehner may allow votes on one or more of the measures approved by the House Judiciary Committee once congressional primaries are done. "We just saw a budget deal that made progress that brought people together from both sides from very different perspectives and I suspect that can be done on immigration as well," said Cole.

—Linda Fecteau

Following is the edited text of a statement delivered by President Barack Obama on June 11, 2013, on the necessity for immigration reform; and two floor statements delivered on June 27, 2013, one from Sen. Mitch McConnell, R-Ky., in opposition to the immigration reform bill and the other from Sen. Chuck Schumer, D-N.Y., in support of the measure.

President Obama Remarks on Immigration Reform

June 11, 2013

The President. Well, good morning, everybody. Welcome to the White House. It is a pleasure to have so many distinguished Americans today from so many different walks of life. We've got Democrats and Republicans; we've got labor and business leaders up on stage; we have law enforcement and clergy—Americans who don't see eye to eye on every issue, in fact, in some cases, don't see eye to eye on just about any issue—[laughter]—but who are today standing united in support of the legislation that is front and center in Congress this week: a bipartisan bill to fix our broken immigration system. . . .

Throughout our history, the promise we found in those who come from every corner of the globe has always been one of our greatest strengths. It's kept our workforce vibrant and dynamic. It's kept our businesses on the cutting edge. It's helped build the greatest economic engine that the world has ever known.

When I speak to other world leaders, one of the biggest advantages we have economically is our demographics. We're constantly replenishing ourselves with talent from all across the globe. No other country can match that history. . . .

Now, here's the thing: Over the past two decades, our immigration system hasn't kept pace with changing times and hasn't matched up with our most cherished values.

Right now our immigration system invites the best and the brightest from all over the world to come and study at our top universities, and then once they finish—once they've gotten the training they need to build a new invention or create a new business—our system too often tells them to go back home so that other countries can reap the benefits: the new jobs, the new businesses, the new industries. That's not smart. But that's the broken system we have today.

Right now our immigration system keeps families apart for years at a time, even for folks who, technically, under the legal immigration system, should be eligible to become citizens, but it is so long and so cumbersome, so byzantine, that families end up being separated for years. Because of a backlog in visas, people who come here legally—who are ready to give it their all to earn their place in America—end up waiting for years to join their loved ones here in the United States. It's not right. But that's the broken system we have today.

Right now our immigration system has no credible way of dealing with the 11 million men and women who are in this country illegally. And yes, they broke the rules; they didn't wait their turn. They shouldn't be let off easy. They shouldn't be allowed to game the system. But at the same time, the vast majority of these individuals aren't looking for any trouble. They're just looking to provide for their families, contribute to their communities.

They're our neighbors. We know their kids. Too often, they're forced to do what they do in a shadow economy, where shady employers can exploit them by paying less than the minimum wage, making them work without overtime, not giving them any benefits. That pushes down standards for all workers. It's bad for everybody, because all the businesses that do play by the rules, that hire people legally, that pay them fairly, they're at a competitive disadvantage. American workers end up being at a competitive disadvantage. It's not fair. But that's the broken system that we have today.

Now, over the past 4 years, we've tried to patch up some of the worst cracks in the system. We made border security a top priority. Today, we have twice as many border patrol agents as we did in 2004. We have more boots on the ground along our southern border than at any time in our history. And in part, by using technology more effectively, illegal crossings are near their lowest level in decades. . . . [W]e also then took up the cause of the DREAMers, young people like Tolu who were brought to this country as children. We said that if you're able to meet some basic criteria, like pursuing a higher education, then we'll consider offering you the chance to come out of the shadows so you can continue to work here and study here and contribute to our communities legally.

So my administration has done what we can on our own. But the system is still broken. . . .

This week, the Senate will consider a commonsense, bipartisan bill that is the best chance we've had in years to fix our broken immigration system. It will build on what we've done and continue to strengthen our borders. It will make sure that businesses and workers are all playing by the same set of rules, and it includes tough penalties for those who don't. It's fair for middle class families, by making sure that those who are brought into the system pay their fair share in taxes and for services. And it's fair for those who try to immigrate legally by stopping those who try to skip the line. It's the right thing to do.

Now, this bill isn't perfect. It's a compromise. And going forward, nobody is going to get everything that they want: not Democrats, not Republicans, not me. But this is a bill that's largely consistent with the principles that I and the people on this stage have laid out for commonsense reform.

First of all, if passed, this bill would be the biggest commitment to border security in our Nation's history. . . .

Number two, this bill would provide a pathway to earned citizenship for the 11 million individuals who are in this country illegally. So that pathway is arduous. You've got to pass background checks. You've got to learn English. You've got to pay taxes and a penalty. And then you've got to go to the back of the line behind everybody who's done things the right way and have tried to come here legally.

So this won't be a quick process. . . . But it's the only way we can make sure that everyone who's here is playing by the same rules as ordinary families: paying taxes and getting their own health insurance.

That's why, for immigration reform to work, it must be clear from the outset that there is a pathway to citizenship. . . .

Number three, this bill would modernize the legal immigration system so that, alongside training American workers for the jobs of tomorrow, we're also attracting the highly skilled entrepreneurs and engineers from around the world who will ultimately grow our economy. . . .

So that's what immigration reform looks like: smarter enforcement, a pathway to earned citizenship, improvements to our legal system. They're all commonsense steps. They've got bipartisan support. They've got the support of a broad cross-section of leaders from every walk of life. So there's no reason Congress can't get this done by the end of the summer.

Remember, the process that led to this bill was open and inclusive. For months, the bipartisan Gang of Eight looked at every issue, reconciled competing ideas, built a compromise that works. Then the Judiciary Committee held numerous hearings. More than a hundred amendments were added, often with bipartisan support. And the good news is, every day that goes by, more and more Republicans and Democrats are coming out to support this commonsense immigration reform bill. . . .

If you're not serious about it, if you think that a broken system is the best America can do, then I guess it might make sense to try to block it. But if you're actually serious and sincere about fixing a broken system, this is the vehicle to do it. And now is the time to get it done . . .

[The following two pages have been omitted and tell the story of one young immigrant's efforts to get an education and pursue a career in public policy.]

And if you're willing to stand with them—and if you're willing to stand with all these outstanding leaders up here—then now is the time to make your voice heard. You need to call and e-mail and tweet your Senators and tell them, don't kick this problem down the road.

Come together. Work together. Do your job not only to fix a broken immigration system once and for all, but to leave something better for all the generations to come, to make sure we continue to be a nation of laws and a nation of immigrants. Do the right thing.

Thanks. God bless you. God bless America. All right.

Source: Executive Office of the President. "Remarks on Immigration Reform." June 11, 2013. *Compilation of Presidential Documents* 2013, no. 00408 (June 11, 2013). http://www.gpo.gov/fdsys/pkg/ DCPD-201300408/pdf/DCPD-201300408.pdf.

Sen. McConnell in Opposition to Immigration Bill

June 27, 2013

Mr. McCONNELL. Mr. President, at the outset of this debate I expressed my hope that we could do something about our nation's broken immigration system. Millions of men and women are living among us without any documentation or certainty about what the future will bring for themselves or their families. Many of those who come here legally end up staying here illegally. We have no way of knowing who or where they are. And current law simply does not take into account the urgent needs of a modern, rapidly-changing economy.

Beyond all this, it has long been a deep conviction of mine that from our earliest days as a people, immigration has been powerful force of renewal and national strength. . . .

Broad bipartisan majorities agree that our immigration system needs updating. In my view, we had an obligation to our constituents to at least try to do it, together, and, in the process, show the world that we can still solve big national problems around here. And reaffirm the vital role that legal immigration has played in our history. So it is with a great deal of regret—for me at least—that the final bill did not turn out to be something I can support. The reason is fairly simple. As I see it, this bill just does not meet the threshold test for success that I outlined at the start of this debate. It just does not say—to me, at least—that we have learned the lessons of 1986, and that we will not find ourselves right back in the same situation we found ourselves in after that reform.

If you cannot be reasonably certain that the border is secure as a condition of legalization, there is just no way to be sure that millions more won't follow the illegal immigrants who are already here. . . .

It does not give any pleasure to say this, or to vote against this bill. . . .

While I will not be voting for this bill, I think it has to be said that there are real improvements in the bill. . . .

We have learned an important lesson in this debate. One thing I am fairly certain about is that we will never resolve the immigration problem on a bipartisan basis either now or in the future until we can prove—prove—that the border is secure as a condition of legalization. This, to me, continues to be the biggest hurdle to reform. . . .

Hopefully, Democrats now realize that this is the one necessary ingredient for success and they will be a little more willing to accept it as a condition for legalization because until they do, I for one just cannot be confident that we have solved this problem, and I know a lot of others will not be confident either.

So this bill may pass the Senate today but not with my vote. And in its current form, it will not become law. But the good news is this: The path to success, the path to actually making a law is fairly clear at this point. Success on immigration reform runs through the border. Looking ahead, I think it is safe to say that is where our focus should lie.

SOURCE: Sen. Mitch McConnell. "Border Security, Economic Opportunity, and Immigration Modernization Act." *Congressional Record* 2013, pt. 159, S5316-5317. June 27, 2013. http://www.gpo .gov/fdsys/pkg/CREC-2013-06-27/pdf/CREC-2013-06-27-pt1-PgS5315-8.pdf.

Sen. Schumer Floor Statement in Support of Immigration Reform

DOCUMENT

June 27, 2013

Mr. SCHUMER. Madam President, we are now approaching the final hour of this debate on how to fix our broken immigration system—the debate we have been having for 3 weeks here on the Senate floor, for 7 months among the Gang of 8, and for decades in this Nation . . .

There is an unwritten covenant between America and those who immigrate here. It says if you come here with a dream, with a will to work hard, follow the rules and contribute, we will give you a chance to become an American and, in the process, to make America a better place than it was before you got here.

In choosing this country . . . immigrants bring an appreciation for the choices and opportunity that are unique to America. They often love America even more than native-born Americans. We take that appreciation for granted.

It is, therefore, not a surprise that CBO says this bill will grow our economy by 3.3 percent over the next 10 years and 5.4 percent over the next 20. CBO has simply enumerated a concept that many of us already knew: Immigrants have always been the greatest engine of economic growth, innovation and renewal that this country has ever known. . . .

According to CBO, it is a far greater engine for economic growth than any spending program Democrats might traditionally propose or any tax cut Republicans might traditionally propose. . . .

This bill is our best chance, and may be our last chance, to maintain that covenant through the next generation of Americans, and to maintain the greatness of America. This bill includes input from almost every Member of this body. . . .

That is what makes this bill strong; that is what makes this bill good. It has garnered support from the most diverse coalition of groups any bill has ever seen: U.S. Chamber of Commerce; AFL–CIO; the faith community, including Evangelicals and Catholics; the high-tech community; America's farmers and farm workers; the law enforcement community; the immigrant rights community.

Now, what does this bill do? Simply put, it does three simple things: It will prevent future waves of illegal immigration; it will provide a tremendous boost for the American economy by rationalizing future legal immigration; and it will fairly and conclusively address the status of people currently here illegally.

Let's look at the actual facts of what the bill does to end illegal immigration.

If the bill passes, anyone who wants to try to cross the border illegally will have to get over an 18-foot steel pedestrian fence and past border agents standing every 1,000 feet apart from Brownsville to San Diego. . . .

Finally, I do not countenance the way the 11 million undocumented immigrants living in our midst got here. But they are here now, and deporting all of them is unpractical, unrealistic and wrong to consider. Our bill will tell these individuals if they are willing to keep their end of the covenant, their road may be harder and longer than everyone else's road—a 10-year probationary period, no benefits or assistance of any kind—but it too can end with being given the chance to earn American citizenship if they work hard and pay taxes and play by the rules.

So the bill is the right thing to do from top to bottom. It has more deficit reduction than our best deficit-reducing packages. It will stimulate the economy more than any stimulus bill, and it will make our border more secure than it has ever been in our history.

So now there are simply no more legitimate excuses to vote against this bill. Opponents of the bill have given three stated excuses for opposing the bill, each of which has been resoundingly refuted. . . .

Here is what a vote against this bill says: It says it would be nice to reduce the debt, but not if it helps immigrants. It says it would be nice to grow the economy, but not if it helps immigrants. It says it would be nice to end illegal immigration in our security, but not if it helps immigrants. . . .

Make no mistake about it, the support this bill has generated in the Senate will make it impossible to ignore. I believe the support this bill will receive today in the Senate will propel it to pass the House and be placed for signature on the President's desk by the end of the year.

That is because in our hearts we know immigrants have always been part of the fabric of America. While there have always been people who have rejected immigrants—from the know-nothings to the exclusionists—we have always seen the better angels of our nature prevail in the end. . . .

Pass this bill, and let's keep the American covenant alive. Pass this bill, and let the bright torch of Lady Liberty continue to shine brightly as a beacon to those around the globe for generations to come.

I yield the floor.

Source: Sen. Chuck Schumer. "Border Security, Economic Opportunity, and Immigration Modernization Act." *Congressional Record* 2013, pt. 159, S5350–5351. June 27, 2013. http://www.gpo.gov/fdsys/pkg/CREC-2013-06-27/pdf/CREC-2013-06-27-pt1-PgS5329-3.pdf.

Other Historic Documents of Interest

Supreme Court Rules on Gene Patents

JUNE 13, 2013

Generating much publicity and increasing the visibility of genetic testing, movie star Angelina Jolie revealed this year that she had tested positive for genetic mutations that dramatically increased the likelihood she would develop breast or ovarian cancer. With this knowledge, she chose to limit her cancer risk by undergoing an elective double mastectomy. She learned of her genetically high risk of cancer from a test she took provided by Myriad Genetics, a diagnostics company from Salt Lake City, that had identified and isolated and then patented the human BRCA genes, mutations of which are strongly linked to these cancers. Myriad's patent on these genes gave them monopoly protection for any uses of the genes, including the exclusive right to test for them. It had long been the policy of the U.S. Patent and Trademark Office to grant patents on human genes, in fact, according to the National Society of Genetic Counselors, patents have been issued for more than 20 percent of all human genes.

On June 13, 2013, in the case *Association for Molecular Pathology v. Myriad Genetics, Inc.*, the United States Supreme Court had to address the issue of whether human genes such as BRCA genes can be patented at all. Writing for a unanimous court, Justice Clarence Thomas ruled that "naturally occurring" human genes cannot be patented "simply because they have been isolated from the surrounding genetic material." Patent protection, the Court held, requires that something be created and, in this case, the human gene they isolated was unchanged from its natural form; therefore, "Myriad did not create anything." At the same time, the Court ruled that synthetic versions of the genes can be eligible for patent protection if they are a creation not normally present in nature.

PATENT LAW AND MYRIAD GENETICS, INC.

The authorization for American patent laws is found in Article One, Section 8(8) of the Constitution:

> *The Congress shall have power . . . to promote the progress of science and useful arts, by securing for limited times to authors and inventors the exclusive right to their respective writings and discoveries.*

The U.S. Patent Act spelled this out, providing that "whoever invents or discovers any new and useful . . . composition of matter, or any new and useful improvement thereof, may obtain a patent therefor . . ."

The purpose of these laws is to encourage innovation by giving inventors a monopoly over the fruits of their discoveries for a limited period of time. The idea is that a patent creates a financial incentive for people to make the potentially massive investments in research and development necessary for new breakthroughs. But, as Justice Thomas wrote, "patent protection strikes a delicate balance between creating incentives that lead to creation, invention, and discovery," on the one hand, and on the other hand, "impeding the flow of information that might permit, indeed spur, invention."

In this case, Myriad's discovery of the precise location and sequence of the genes now known as BRCA1 and BRCA2 was a medical breakthrough. Mutations in these genes dramatically increase a person's chance of developing breast and ovarian cancer. Myriad's identification of the exact location of these genes allowed it to develop medical tests to detect mutations on the genes, giving the patients knowledge of their increased cancer risk. While women without the mutation have about a 12 percent risk of developing breast cancer, women with mutations on these genes can have as high as a 90 percent chance of developing breast cancer and a 50 percent chance of developing ovarian cancer. Myriad made this discovery first by identifying groups of relatives with a history of breast cancer so that it was more likely their diseases were the result of genetic predisposition and then compared sections of their chromosomes, looking for shared genetic abnormalities not found in the general population. This was a painstaking process that through years of work ultimately enabled Myriad to locate BRCA genes in the genetic sequence.

After receiving its patent, Myriad sent letters to other companies that were providing genetic testing services to women, asserting that their testing infringed Myriad's patents. Myriad then filed patent infringement lawsuits against entities that did not stop performing testing for the BRCA genes. Many of these suits resulted in settlements with the defendants agreeing to cease all allegedly infringing genetic testing. Several years later, a group of geneticists, medical groups, patients, and advocacy groups including the American Civil Liberties Union (ACLU) and the Public Patent Foundation, filed suit seeking a declaration that Myriad's patents were invalid so that other labs could test for the BRCA genes without the fear of facing lawsuits.

The case followed a complicated legal path but ultimately ended up at the Supreme Court.

Unanimous Supreme Court Invalidates Myriad's Patent

Justice Thomas, writing for the Court in a rare unanimous decision, focused on "an important implicit exception" to the patent law. Naturally occurring phenomena, the Court asserted, are simply not patentable. It is not enough to discover something that occurs in nature or figure out a law of nature. Rather, to be patentable, something new must be created. The Court rejected Myriad's argument that the act of locating and isolating the BRCA genes in blood and then extracting them for study was itself an invention of something that did not exist before. It does not matter, Thomas wrote, if the discovery was "groundbreaking, innovative, or even brilliant." It doesn't matter how extensive the research efforts leading to the discovery were. What matters, ultimately, is that "Myriad did not create anything," the Court ruled. "To be sure," Justice Thomas wrote, "it found an important and useful gene, but separating that gene from its surrounding genetic material is not an act of invention."

The case, however, had a split legal outcome for Myriad. The decision ruled out patents for naturally occurring, isolated DNA segments, but, at the same time, the Court did permit patents for synthetically created DNA known as complementary DNA or cDNA. The "cDNA retains the naturally occurring exons of DNA," the Court wrote, "but it is distinct from the DNA from which it was derived." Since these laboratory imitations of genes do not exist in nature, they are not "a product of nature," and can therefore be patented.

Justice Antonin Scalia concurred in the overall judgment in this case but wrote a short separate opinion to emphasize that he was not joining the parts of the decision that went into details concerning molecular biology and genetics, which he wrote were beyond his own knowledge and belief. "It suffices for me to affirm, having studied the opinions below and the expert briefs presented here, that the portion of DNA isolated from its natural state sought to be patented is identical to that portion of the DNA in its natural state; and that complementary DNA (cDNA) is a synthetic creation not normally present in nature," Scalia wrote.

Probable Impact of This Decision

The impact of this decision on the price of a genetic screening test for the BRCA1 and BRCA2 genes was dramatic and immediate. Myriad's test had been popular but priced above the $3,000 to $4,000 range; it priced many women out of learning if they were at an increased risk for breast and ovarian cancers. Within hours of the Supreme Court's decision invalidating Myriad's patents, other bio-tech companies announced competing tests, some advertising prices under $1,000. The Executive Director of Public Patent Foundation, Daniel Ravicher, released a statement celebrating the impact the Court's decision would have on the increased availability of crucial medical information going forward: "Bottom line, diagnostic genetic testing is now free from any patent threat, forever, and the poor can now have their genes tested as freely as the rich." Francis Collins, Director of the National Institutes of Health, also expressed pleasure with the ruling, stating, "Our position all along has been that patenting DNA in its natural state does not provide any benefit to the public." He expressed relief that the decision eliminates the concern that relatively inexpensive advances would be so burdened by the need to pay enormous licensing fees just to use patented genome sequences, that it would "inhibit the progress of DNA research."

Now that researchers no longer need to separate out what genetic tests must be sent to different labs for testing, it opens the door to increased multi-gene testing that may screen for all the mutations implicated for the patient's treatment. Hours after the Court ruling, as just one example, the University of Wisconsin's clinical laboratories announced that they would add testing for mutations in the BRCA1 and BRCA2 genes to their cancer-risk gene panel, which looks for mutations in more than forty genes associated with numerous cancers, including breast, ovarian, colon, pancreatic, throat, and kidney cancers. The ruling also may speed up the development of whole genome sequencing technologies that could test a person's whole DNA sequence all at once.

The decision by the Supreme Court was not, however, all bad news for Myriad. While declaring that "naturally occurring" human genes cannot be patented, at the same time the Court ruled that cDNA or edited forms of genes, whose creation requires actual work in the lab, are eligible to be patented. This is good news for biotech companies, according to Robert Cook-Deegan, a professor at Duke University's Institute for Genome Sciences and Policy, who was quoted in *National Geographic* describing cDNA as "the billion-dollar molecule patents." While not useful for diagnostic tests, Cook-Deegan says that, in the long run, when the science advances beyond discovering and exploiting naturally occurring DNA and into trying to improve upon nature, these cDNA will be crucial for producing protein-based drugs.

Not everyone shares this view of a future of synthetic biology making cDNA patents increasingly valuable. Some analysts believe that these patents will become less relevant in the future in the same way that many software patents became obsolete given the speed with which technological change occurred and the slow bureaucratic pace of the patent application process. TechCrunch.com quoted the head of Cambrian Genomics, Austen Heinz, as he analogized the future of synthetic gene patents with what happened to Windows 95, 98, or Vista. "Like in the software business, synthetic biology companies will need to ship an updated improved OS (i.e. genome) every few years to stay competitive," Heinz said.

—Melissa Feinberg

The following are excerpts from the U.S. Supreme Court ruling in Association for Molecular Pathology v. Myriad Genetics, Inc., *in which the Court ruled unanimously that naturally occurring genes are not eligible for patent protection.*

Association for Molecular Pathology v. Myriad Genetics, Inc.

June 13, 2013

No. 12–398

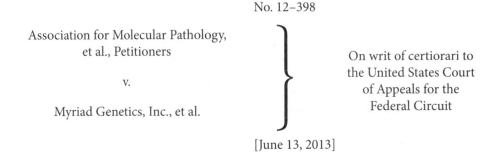

Association for Molecular Pathology,
et al., Petitioners

v.

Myriad Genetics, Inc., et al.

On writ of certiorari to
the United States Court
of Appeals for the
Federal Circuit

[June 13, 2013]

JUSTICE THOMAS delivered the opinion of the Court.

Respondent Myriad Genetics, Inc. (Myriad), discovered the precise location and sequence of two human genes, mutations of which can substantially increase the risks of breast and ovarian cancer. Myriad obtained a number of patents based upon its discovery. This case involves claims from three of them and requires us to resolve whether a naturally occurring segment of deoxyribonucleic acid (DNA) is patent eligible under 35 U. S. C. §101 by virtue of its isolation from the rest of the human genome. We also address the patent eligibility of synthetically created DNA known as complementary DNA (cDNA), which contains the same protein-coding information found in a segment of natural DNA but omits portions within the DNA segment that do not code for proteins. For the reasons that follow, we hold that a naturally occurring DNA segment is a product of nature and not patent eligible merely because it has been isolated, but that cDNA is patent eligible because it is not naturally occurring. We, therefore, affirm in part and reverse in part the decision of the United States Court of Appeals for the Federal Circuit.

I

A

Genes form the basis for hereditary traits in living organisms. See generally Association for *Molecular Pathology v. United States Patent and Trademark Office*, 702 F. Supp. 2d 181, 192–211 (SDNY 2010). The human genome consists of approximately 22,000 genes packed into 23 pairs of chromosomes. Each gene is encoded as DNA, which takes the shape of the familiar "double helix" that Doctors James Watson and Francis Crick first described in 1953. Each "cross-bar" in the DNA helix consists of two chemically joined nucleotides. The possible nucleotides are adenine (A), thymine (T), cytosine (C), and guanine (G), each of which binds naturally with another nucleotide: A pairs with T; C pairs with G. The nucleotide cross-bars are chemically connected to a sugar-phosphate backbone that forms the outside framework of the DNA helix. Sequences of DNA nucleotides contain the information necessary to create strings of amino acids, which in turn are used in the body to build proteins. Only some DNA nucleotides, however, code for amino acids; these nucleotides are known as "exons." Nucleotides that do not code for amino acids, in contrast, are known as "introns."

Creation of proteins from DNA involves two principal steps, known as transcription and translation. In transcription, the bonds between DNA nucleotides separate, and the DNA helix unwinds into two single strands. A single strand is used as a template to create a complementary ribonucleic acid (RNA) strand. The nucleotides on the DNA strand pair naturally with their counterparts, with the exception that RNA uses the nucleotide base uracil (U) instead of thymine (T). Transcription results in a single strand RNA molecule, known as pre-RNA, whose nucleotides form an inverse image of the DNA strand from which it was created. Pre-RNA still contains nucleotides corresponding to both the exons and introns in the DNA molecule. The pre-RNA is then naturally "spliced" by the physical removal of the introns. The resulting product is a strand of RNA that contains nucleotides corresponding only to the exons from the original DNA strand. The exons-only strand is known as messenger RNA (mRNA), which creates amino acids through translation. In translation, cellular structures known as ribosomes read each set of three nucleotides, known as codons, in the mRNA. Each codon either tells the ribosomes which of the 20 possible amino acids to synthesize or provides a stop signal that ends amino acid production.

DNA's informational sequences and the processes that create mRNA, amino acids, and proteins occur naturally within cells. Scientists can, however, extract DNA from cells using well known laboratory methods. These methods allow scientists to isolate specific segments of DNA—for instance, a particular gene or part of a gene—which can then be further studied, manipulated, or used. It is also possible to create DNA synthetically through processes similarly well known in the field of genetics. One such method begins with an mRNA molecule and uses the natural bonding properties of nucleotides to create a new, synthetic DNA molecule. The result is the inverse of the mRNA's inverse image of the original DNA, with one important distinction: Because the natural creation of mRNA involves splicing that removes introns, the synthetic DNA created from mRNA also contains only the exon sequences. This synthetic DNA created in the laboratory from mRNA is known as complementary DNA (cDNA).

Changes in the genetic sequence are called mutations. Mutations can be as small as the alteration of a single nucleotide—a change affecting only one letter in the genetic code. Such small-scale changes can produce an entirely different amino acid or can end protein production altogether. Large changes, involving the deletion, rearrangement, or duplication of hundreds or even millions of nucleotides, can result in the elimination, misplacement, or duplication of entire genes. Some mutations are harmless, but others can cause disease or increase the risk of disease. As a result, the study of genetics can lead to valuable medical breakthroughs.

B

This case involves patents filed by Myriad after it made one such medical breakthrough. Myriad discovered the precise location and sequence of what are now known as the BRCA1 and BRCA2 genes. Mutations in these genes can dramatically increase an individual's risk of developing breast and ovarian cancer. The average American woman has a 12- to 13-percent risk of developing breast cancer, but for women with certain genetic mutations, the risk can range between 50 and 80 percent for breast cancer and between 20 and 50 percent for ovarian cancer. Before Myriad's discovery of the BRCA1 and BRCA2 genes, scientists knew that heredity played a role in establishing a woman's risk of developing breast and ovarian cancer, but they did not know which genes were associated with those cancers. Myriad identified the exact location of the BRCA1 and BRCA2 genes on chromosomes 17 and 13. Chromosome 17 has approximately 80 million nucleotides, and chromosome 13 has approximately 114 million. *Association for Molecular Pathology v. United States Patent and Trademark Office*, 689 F. 3d 1303, 1328 (CA Fed. 2012). Within those chromosomes, the BRCA1 and BRCA2 genes are each about 80,000 nucleotides long. If just exons are counted, the BRCA1 gene is only about 5,500 nucleotides long; for the BRCA2 gene, that number is about 10,200. *Ibid.* Knowledge of the location of the BRCA1 and BRCA2 genes allowed Myriad to determine their typical nucleotide sequence. That information, in turn, enabled Myriad to develop medical tests that are useful for detecting mutations in a patient's BRCA1 and BRCA2 genes and thereby assessing whether the patient has an increased risk of cancer.

Once it found the location and sequence of the BRCA1and BRCA2 genes, Myriad sought and obtained a number of patents. Nine composition claims from three of those patents are at issue in this case. See *id.*, at 1309, and n. 1 (noting composition claims). Claims 1, 2, 5, and 6 from the '282 patent are representative. The first claim asserts a patent on "[a]n isolated DNA coding for a BRCA1 polypeptide," which has "the amino acid sequence set forth in SEQ ID NO:2." App. 822. SEQ ID NO:2 sets forth a list of 1,863 amino acids that the typical BRCA1 gene encodes. See *id.*, at 785–790. Put differently, claim 1 asserts a patent claim on the DNA code that tells a cell to produce the string of BRCA1 amino acids listed in SEQ ID NO:2.

Claim 2 of the '282 patent operates similarly. It claims "[t]he isolated DNA of claim 1, wherein said DNA has the nucleotide sequence set forth in SEQ ID NO:1." *Id.*, at 822. Like SEQ ID NO:2, SEQ ID NO:1 sets forth a long list of data, in this instance the sequence of cDNA that codes for the BRCA1 amino acids listed in claim 1. Importantly, SEQ ID NO:1 lists only the cDNA exons in the BRCA1 gene, rather than a full DNA sequence containing both exons and introns. See *id.*, at 779 (stating that SEQ ID NO:1's "MOLECULE TYPE:" is "cDNA"). As a result, the Federal Circuit recognized that claim 2 asserts a patent on the cDNA nucleotide sequence listed in SEQ ID NO:1, which codes for the typical BRCA1 gene. 689 F. 3d, at 1326, n. 9; *id.*, at 1337 (Moore, J., concurring in part); *id.*, at 1356 (Bryson, J., concurring in part and dissenting in part).

Claim 5 of the '282 patent claims a subset of the data in claim 1. In particular, it claims "[a]n isolated DNA having at least 15 nucleotides of the DNA of claim 1." App. 822. The practical effect of claim 5 is to assert a patent on any series of 15 nucleotides that exist in the typical BRCA1 gene. Because the BRCA1 gene is thousands of nucleotides long, even BRCA1 genes with substantial mutations are likely to contain at least one segment of 15 nucleotides that correspond to the typical BRCA1 gene. Similarly, claim 6 of the '282 patent claims "[a]n isolated DNA having at least 15 nucleotides of the DNA of claim 2." *Ibid.* This claim operates similarly to claim 5, except that it references the cDNA-based claim 2. The remaining claims at issue are similar, though several list common mutations rather than typical BRCA1 and BRCA2 sequences. See *ibid.* (claim 7 of the '282 patent); *id.*, at 930 (claim 1 of the '473 patent); *id.*, at 1028 (claims 1, 6, and 7 of the '492 patent).

C

Myriad's patents would, if valid, give it the exclusive right to isolate an individual's BRCA1 and BRCA2 genes (or any strand of 15 or more nucleotides within the genes)by breaking the covalent bonds that connect the DNA to the rest of the individual's genome. The patents would also give Myriad the exclusive right to synthetically create BRCA cDNA. In Myriad's view, manipulating BRCA DNA in either of these fashions triggers its "right to exclude others from making" its patented composition of matter under the Patent Act. 35 U. S. C. §154(a)(1); see also§271(a) ("[W]hoever without authority makes . . . any patented invention . . . infringes the patent").

But isolation is necessary to conduct genetic testing, and Myriad was not the only entity to offer BRCA testing after it discovered the genes. The University of Pennsylvania's Genetic Diagnostic Laboratory (GDL) and others provided genetic testing services to women. Petitioner Dr. Harry Ostrer, then a researcher at New York University School of Medicine, routinely sent his patients' DNA samples to GDL for testing. After learning of GDL's testing and Ostrer's activities, Myriad sent letters to them asserting that the genetic testing infringed Myriad's patents. App. 94–95 (Ostrer letter). In response, GDL agreed to stop testing and informed Ostrer that it would no longer accept patient samples. Myriad also filed patent infringement suits against other entities that performed BRCA testing, resulting in settlements in which the defendants agreed to cease all allegedly infringing activity. 689 F. 3d, at 1315. Myriad, thus, solidified its position as the only entity providing BRCA testing.

Some years later, petitioner Ostrer, along with medical patients, advocacy groups, and other doctors, filed this lawsuit seeking a declaration that Myriad's patents are invalid under 35 U. S. C. §101. 702 F. Supp. 2d, at 186. Citing this Court's decision in *MedImmune, Inc. v. Genentech, Inc.*, 549 U. S. 118 (2007), the District Court denied Myriad's motion to dismiss for lack of standing. *Association for Molecular Pathology v. United States Patent and Trademark Office*, 669 F. Supp. 2d 365, 385–392 (SDNY 2009). The District Court then granted summary judgment to petitioners on the composition claims at issue in this case based on its conclusion that Myriad's claims, including claims related to cDNA, were invalid because they covered products of nature. 702 F. Supp. 2d, at 220–237. The Federal Circuit reversed, *Association for Molecular Pathology v. United States Patent and Trademark Office*, 653 F. 3d 1329 (2011), and this Court granted the petition for certiorari, vacated the judgment, and remanded the case in light of *Mayo Collaborative Services v. Prometheus Laboratories, Inc.*, 566 U. S. ___ (2012). See *Association for Molecular Pathology v. Myriad Genetics, Inc.*, 566 U. S. ___ (2012).

On remand, the Federal Circuit affirmed the District Court in part and reversed in part, with each member of the panel writing separately. All three judges agreed that only petitioner Ostrer had standing. They reasoned that Myriad's actions against him and his stated ability and willingness to begin BRCA1 and BRCA2 testing if Myriad's patents were invalidated were sufficient for Article III standing. 689 F. 3d, at 1323; *id.*, at 1337 (opinion of Moore, J.); *id.*, at 1348 (opinion of Bryson, J.).

With respect to the merits, the court held that both isolated DNA and cDNA were patent eligible under §101. The central dispute among the panel members was whether the act of isolating DNA—separating a specific gene or sequence of nucleotides from the rest of the chromosome—is an inventive act that entitles the individual who first isolates it to a patent. Each of the judges on the panel had a different view on that question. Judges Lourie and Moore agreed that Myriad's claims were patent eligible under §101 but disagreed on the rationale. Judge Lourie relied on the fact that the entire DNA molecule is held together by chemical bonds and that the covalent bonds at both ends of the segment must be severed in order to isolate segments of DNA. This process technically creates new molecules with unique chemical compositions. See *id.*, at 1328 ("Isolated DNA . . . is a free-standing portion of a larger, natural DNA molecule. Isolated DNA has been cleaved (i.e., had covalent bonds in its backbone chemically severed) or synthesized to consist of just a fraction of a naturally occurring DNA molecule"). Judge Lourie found this chemical alteration to be dispositive, because isolating a particular strand of DNA creates a non-naturally occurring molecule, even though the chemical alteration does not change the information transmitting quality of the DNA. See *id.*, at 1330 ("The claimed isolated DNA molecules are distinct from their natural existence as portions of larger entities, and their informational content is irrelevant to that fact. We recognize that biologists may think of molecules in terms of their uses, but genes are in fact materials having a chemical nature"). Accordingly, he rejected petitioners' argument that isolated DNA was ineligible for patent protection as a product of nature.

Judge Moore concurred in part but did not rely exclusively on Judge Lourie's conclusion that chemically breaking covalent bonds was sufficient to render isolated DNA patent eligible. *Id.*, at 1341 ("To the extent the majority rests its conclusion on the chemical differences between [naturally occurring] and isolated DNA (breaking the covalent bonds), I cannot agree that this is sufficient to hold that the claims to human genes are directed to patentable subject matter"). Instead, Judge Moore also relied on the United States Patent and Trademark Office's (PTO) practice of granting such patents and on the reliance interests of patent holders. *Id.*, at 1343. However, she acknowledged that her vote might have come out differently if she "were deciding this case on a blank canvas." *Ibid.*

Finally, Judge Bryson concurred in part and dissented in part, concluding that isolated DNA is not patent eligible. As an initial matter, he emphasized that the breaking of chemical bonds was not dispositive: "[T]here is no magic to a chemical bond that requires us to recognize a new product when a chemical bond is created or broken." *Id.*, at 1351. Instead, he relied on the fact that "[t]he nucleotide sequences of the claimed molecules are the same as the nucleotide sequences found in naturally occurring human genes." *Id.*, at 1355. Judge Bryson then concluded that genetic "structural similarity dwarfs the significance of the structural differences between isolated DNA and naturally occurring DNA, especially where the structural differences are merely ancillary to the breaking of covalent bonds, a process that is itself not inventive." *Ibid.* Moreover, Judge Bryson gave no weight to the PTO's position on patentability because of the Federal Circuit's position that "the PTO lacks substantive rulemaking authority as to issues such as patentability." *Id.*, at 1357.

Although the judges expressed different views concerning the patentability of isolated DNA, all three agreed that patent claims relating to cDNA met the patent eligibility requirements of §101. *Id.*, at 1326, and n. 9 (recognizing that some patent claims are limited to cDNA and that such claims are patent eligible under §101); *id.*, at 1337 (Moore, J., concurring in part); *id.*, at 1356 (Bryson, J., concurring in part and dissenting in part) ("cDNA cannot be isolated from nature, but instead must be created in the laboratory . . . because the introns that are found in the native gene are removed from the cDNA segment"). We granted certiorari. 568 U. S. ___ (2012).

II

A

Section 101 of the Patent Act provides:

> *"Whoever invents or discovers any new and useful . . . composition of matter, or any new and useful improvement thereof, may obtain a patent therefor, subject to the conditions and requirements of this title."*

35 U. S. C. §101.

We have "long held that this provision contains an important implicit exception[:] Laws of nature, natural phenomena, and abstract ideas are not patentable." *Mayo,* 566 U. S., at ___ (slip op., at 1) (internal quotation marks and brackets omitted). Rather, "'they are the basic tools of scientific and technological work'" that lie beyond the domain of patent protection. *Id.,* at ___ (slip op., at 2). As the Court has explained, without this exception, there would be considerable danger that the grant of patents would "tie up" the use of such tools and thereby "inhibit future innovation premised upon them." *Id.,* at ___ (slip op., at 17). This would be at odds with the very point of patents, which exist to promote creation. *Diamond* v. *Chakrabarty,* 447 U. S. 303, 309 (1980) (Products of nature are not created, and "'manifestations . . . of nature [are] free to all men and reserved exclusively to none'").

The rule against patents on naturally occurring things is not without limits, however, for "all inventions at some level embody, use, reflect, rest upon, or apply laws of nature, natural phenomena, or abstract ideas," and "too broad an interpretation of this exclusionary principle could eviscerate patent law." 566 U. S., at ___ (slip op., at 2). As we have recognized before, patent protection strikes a delicate balance between creating "incentives that lead to creation, invention, and discovery" and "imped[ing] the flow of information that might permit, indeed spur, invention." *Id.,* at ___ (slip op., at 23). We must apply this well-established standard to determine whether Myriad's patents claim any "new and useful . . . composition of matter," §101, or instead claim naturally occurring phenomena.

B

It is undisputed that Myriad did not create or alter any of the genetic information encoded in the BRCA1 and BRCA2 genes. The location and order of the nucleotides existed in nature before Myriad found them. Nor did Myriad create or alter the genetic structure of DNA. Instead, Myriad's principal contribution was uncovering the precise location and genetic sequence of the BRCA1 and BRCA2 genes within chromosomes 17 and 13. The question is whether this renders the genes patentable.

Myriad recognizes that our decision in *Chakrabarty* is central to this inquiry. Brief for Respondents 14, 23–27. In *Chakrabarty,* scientists added four plasmids to a bacterium, which enabled it to break down various components of crude oil. 447 U. S., at 305, and n. 1. The Court held that the modified bacterium was patentable. It explained that the patent claim was "not to a hitherto unknown natural phenomenon, but to a nonnaturally occurring manufacture or composition of matter—a product of human ingenuity 'having a distinctive name, character [and] use.'" *Id.,* at 309–310 (quoting *Hartranft* v. *Wiegmann,* 121 U. S. 609, 615 (1887); alteration in original). The *Chakrabarty* bacterium was new "with markedly different characteristics from any found in nature," 447 U. S., at 310, due to the additional plasmids and resultant "capacity for degrading oil." *Id.,* at 305, n. 1. In this case, by contrast, Myriad did not create anything. To be sure, it found an important and useful gene, but separating that gene from its surrounding genetic material is not an act of invention.

Groundbreaking, innovative, or even brilliant discovery does not by itself satisfy the §101 inquiry. In *Funk Brothers Seed Co.* v. *Kalo Inoculant Co.,* 333 U. S. 127 (1948), this Court considered a composition patent that claimed a mixture of naturally occurring strains of bacteria that helped leguminous plants take nitrogen from the air and fix it in the soil. *Id.,* at 128–129. The ability of the bacteria to fix nitrogen was well known, and farmers commonly "inoculated" their crops with them to improve soil levels. But farmers could not use the same inoculant for all crops, both because plants use different bacteria and because certain bacteria inhibit each other. *Id.,* at 129–130. Upon learning that several nitrogen-fixing bacteria did not inhibit each other, however, the patent applicant combined them into a single inoculant and obtained a patent. *Id.,* at 130. The Court held that the composition was not patent eligible because the patent holder did not alter the bacteria in any way. *Id.,* at 132 ("There is no way in which we could call [the bacteria mixture a product of invention] unless we borrowed invention from the discovery of the natural principle itself"). His patent claim thus fell squarely within the law of nature exception. So do Myriad's. Myriad found the location of the BRCA1 and BRCA2 genes, but that discovery, by itself, does not render the BRCA genes "new . . . composition[s] of matter," §101, that are patent eligible.

Indeed, Myriad's patent descriptions highlight the problem with its claims. For example, a section of the '282 patent's Detailed Description of the Invention indicates that Myriad found the location of a gene associated with increased risk of breast cancer and identified mutations of that gene that increase the risk. See App. 748–749. In subsequent language Myriad explains that the location of the gene was unknown until Myriad found it among the approximately eight million nucleotide pairs contained in a subpart of chromosome 17. See *Ibid.* The '473 and '492 patents contain similar language as well. See *id.,* at 854, 947. Many of Myriad's patent descriptions simply detail the "iterative process" of discovery by which Myriad narrowed the possible locations for the gene sequences that it sought. See, *e.g., id.,* at 750. Myriad seeks to import these extensive research efforts into the §101 patent eligibility inquiry. Brief for Respondents 8–10, 34. But extensive effort alone is insufficient to satisfy the demands of §101.

Nor are Myriad's claims saved by the fact that isolating DNA from the human genome severs chemical bonds and thereby creates a nonnaturally occurring molecule. Myriad's claims are simply not expressed in terms of chemical composition, nor do they rely in any way on the chemical changes that result from the isolation of a particular section of DNA. Instead, the claims understandably focus on the genetic information encoded in the BRCA1 and BRCA2 genes. If the patents depended upon the creation of a unique molecule, then a would-be infringer could arguably avoid at least Myriad's patent claims on entire genes (such as claims 1 and 2 of the '282 patent) by isolating a DNA sequence that included both the BRCA1 or BRCA2 gene and one additional nucleotide pair. Such a molecule would not be chemically identical to the molecule "invented" by Myriad. But Myriad obviously would resist that outcome because its claim is concerned primarily with the information contained in the genetic *sequence*, not with the specific chemical composition of a particular molecule.

Finally, Myriad argues that the PTO's past practice of awarding gene patents is entitled to deference, citing *J. E. M. Ag Supply, Inc.* v. *Pioneer Hi-Bred Int'l, Inc.,* 534 U. S. 124 (2001). See Brief for Respondents 35–39, 49–50. We disagree. *J. E. M.* held that new plant breeds were eligible for utility patents under §101 notwithstanding separate statutes providing special protections for plants, see 7 U. S. C. §2321 *et seq.* (Plant Variety Protection Act); 35 U. S. C. §§161–164 (Plant Patent Act of 1930). After analyzing the text and structure of the relevant statutes, the Court mentioned that the Board of Patent Appeals and Interferences had determined that new plant breeds were patent eligible under §101 and that Congress had recognized and endorsed that position in a subsequent Patent Act amendment. 534 U. S., at 144–145 (citing *In re Hibberd,* 227 USPQ 443 (1985) and 35 U. S. C. §119(f)). In this case, however, Congress has not endorsed the views of the PTO in subsequent legislation. While Myriad relies on Judge Moore's view that Congress endorsed the PTO's position in a single sentence in the Consolidated Appropriations Act of 2004, see Brief for Respondents 31, n. 8; 689 F. 3d, at 1346, that Act does not even mention genes, much less isolated DNA. §634, 118 Stat. 101 ("None of the funds appropriated or otherwise made available under Act may be used to issue patents on claims directed to or encompassing a human organism").

Further undercutting the PTO's practice, the United States argued in the Federal Circuit and in this Court that isolated DNA was *not* patent eligible under §101, Brief for United States as *Amicus Curiae* 20–33, and that the PTO's practice was not "a sufficient reason to hold that isolated DNA is patent-eligible." *Id.,* at 26. See also *id.,* at 28–29. These concessions weigh against deferring to the PTO's determination.

C

cDNA does not present the same obstacles to patentability as naturally occurring, isolated DNA segments. As already explained, creation of a cDNA sequence from mRNA results in an exons-only molecule that is not naturally occurring. Petitioners concede that cDNA differs from natural DNA in that "the non-coding regions have been removed." Brief for Petitioners 49. They nevertheless argue that cDNA is not patent eligible because "[t]he nucleotide sequence of cDNA is dictated by nature, not by the lab technician." *Id.,* at 51. That may be so, but the lab technician unquestionably creates something new when cDNA is made. cDNA retains the naturally occurring exons of DNA, but it is distinct from the DNA from which it was derived. As a result, cDNA is not a "product of nature" and is patent eligible under §101, except insofar as very short series of DNA may have no intervening introns to remove when creating cDNA. In that situation, a short strand of cDNA may be indistinguishable from natural DNA.

III

It is important to note what is *not* implicated by this decision. First, there are no method claims before this Court. Had Myriad created an innovative method of manipulating genes while searching for the BRCA1 and BRCA2 genes, it could possibly have sought a method patent. But the processes used by Myriad to isolate DNA were well understood by geneticists at the time of Myriad's patents "were well understood, widely used, and fairly uniform insofar as any scientist engaged in the search for a gene would likely have utilized a similar approach," 702 F. Supp. 2d, at 202–203, and are not at issue in this case.

Similarly, this case does not involve patents on new *applications* of knowledge about the BRCA1 and BRCA2 genes. Judge Bryson aptly noted that, "[a]s the first party with knowledge of the [BRCA1 and BRCA2] sequences, Myriad was in an excellent position to claim applications of that knowledge. Many of its unchallenged claims are limited to such applications." 689 F. 3d, at 1349.

Nor do we consider the patentability of DNA in which the order of the naturally occurring nucleotides has been altered. Scientific alteration of the genetic code presents a different inquiry, and we express no opinion about the application of §101 to such endeavors. We merely hold that genes and the information they encode are not patent eligible under §101 simply because they have been isolated from the surrounding genetic material.

* * *

For the foregoing reasons, the judgment of the Federal Circuit is affirmed in part and reversed in part.

It is so ordered.

JUSTICE SCALIA, concurring in part and concurring in the judgment.

I join the judgment of the Court, and all of its opinion except Part I–A and some portions of the rest of the opinion going into fine details of molecular biology. I am unable to affirm those details on my own knowledge or even my own belief. It suffices for me to affirm, having studied the opinions below and the expert briefs presented here, that the portion of DNA isolated from its natural state sought to be patented is identical to that portion of the DNA in its natural state; and that complementary DNA (cDNA) is a synthetic creation not normally present in nature.

SOURCE: U.S. Supreme Court. *Association for Molecular Pathology v. Myriad Genetics, Inc.,* 569 U.S.___ (2013). http://www.supremecourt.gov/opinions/12pdf/12-398_1b7d.pdf.

OTHER HISTORIC DOCUMENTS OF INTEREST

FROM PREVIOUS *HISTORIC DOCUMENTS*

Iranian President Remarks on Election

JUNE 18, 2013

On June 14, 2013, Iran held its eleventh presidential election. While none of the candidates vying to succeed President Mahmoud Ahmadinejad represented a clear break from Iran's past leadership, the ultimate victor, Hassan Rouhani, was viewed as a moderate reformer. Rouhani's reputation for shunning extremism and being more open to cooperation within Iran and with other countries led many to believe his presidency could result in eased tensions between the West and Iran and greater personal freedoms for the Iranian people.

A CLOSELY WATCHED ELECTION

Iran's last presidential election occurred in 2009, when then-President Ahmadinejad faced a significant reelection challenge from reform candidate and former Prime Minister Mir-Hossein Mousavi, who supported plans to introduce more freedom and democracy in Iran. Just one hour after polls closed in Iran, the Interior Ministry announced that Ahmadinejad was the winner, with nearly twice as many votes as Mousavi. Immediately, opposition leaders and supporters claimed there was evidence of widespread election fraud, including reports that opposition election observers had been barred from entering voting stations, pro-Mousavi websites and text messages had been blocked, and discrepancies in some regions between the number of eligible voters and the number of votes cast. The opposition also engaged in unprecedented mass protests, prompting a government crackdown that resulted in the arrests of approximately 1,000 Iranians, including some opposition leaders. Mousavi has been under house arrest since 2011. These actions, combined with the government's shutdown of several reformist newspapers, restrictions on access to the Internet and foreign broadcasters, and detention of some journalists in early 2013, raised concerns among many in the international community that the 2013 election could follow a similar course.

In the months leading up to the 2013 election, Iranian officials did amend the country's procedures for tallying the votes. In previous elections, provincial governors would report their region's results to the Executive Election Board, a body comprised of forty-five officials from the Interior Ministry. The Board would then tabulate all votes and send the final results to the Guardian Council for certification. Under the amended procedure, the Board would no longer have this authority. Instead, a new Central Executive Board was established that included the interior minister, a member of parliament's Presiding Board, the attorney general, the minister of intelligence, and seven public trustees, who could be religious, political, cultural, or social figures. The change was meant to address critics' claims that the Executive Election Board had a conflict of interest in overseeing the vote count, as the president directly appoints the interior minister. Independent and international monitors are prohibited from monitoring Iran's elections, but each candidate is allowed to have an agent present at polling stations to observe the voting and the counting.

Beyond these fraud concerns, many speculated that Iran's economic troubles would have a significant impact on the election's outcome. "The central issue of this election is about how to manage the economy better in the face of a debilitating sanctions regime," said Farideh Farhi, an Iranian scholar and member of the National Iranian American Council's Advisory Board. "The main campaign slogans are competence and prudence, I assume developed in reaction to what is deemed as Ahmadinejad's somewhat erratic and bombastic management of the country." By June 2013, the rial had lost roughly 70 percent of its value, inflation hovered at 35 percent, unemployment was rising, and the country's oil revenues had been cut in half due to sanctions imposed by the United States and European Union.

The Campaign

On May 21, 2013, Interior Minister Mostafa Mohammad-Najjar announced eight approved candidates for the presidency. Iran's Guardian Council, a group of six clerics and six lawyers chosen by Supreme Leader Ali Khamenei, selected these eight candidates from 680 Iranians who had registered to be candidates. Ahmadinejad was not allowed to run again due to term limits. Additionally, his supporters and former aides were notably excluded from the list of approved candidates, as were high-profile reform candidates, such as former President Akbar Hashemi Rafsanjani.

The eight men chosen as candidates largely fell into the broad categories of conservative Khamenei loyalists or moderate reformers. Mohammad Bagher Ghalibaf was the mayor of Tehran and previously served as the Iranian Revolutionary Guard Corps' (IRGC) Air Force Commander and chief of Iranian Police Forces. An audio file that surfaced in May described his involvement in the government crackdowns on reformist protests in 1999, 2003, and 2009. Saeed Jalili was the head of Iran's Supreme National Security Council and served as Iran's chief nuclear negotiator. Jalili had overseen a hardening of Iran's stance in the six party talks surrounding the country's nuclear program. Ali Akbar Velayati was a senior advisor to Khamenei on international and diplomatic affairs and a former foreign minister. These three men were considered the top contenders in the election, with Jalili largely viewed as the frontrunner, due to their ultraconservative positions and close ties to Khamenei. Mohsen Rezaei and Mohammad Gharazi were two other conservative candidates. Rezaei was the secretary of Iran's Expediency Discernment Council and a former IRGC commander who had also been on Interpol's wanted list since 2007, following the 1994 bombing of a Jewish center in Buenos Aires. Gharazi had previously served in several ministries and was strongly critical of the United States and other Western nations for their approach to Iran and its nuclear program.

Two of the more moderate candidates, former Vice President Mohammad Reza Aref and former Speaker of Parliament Gholam-Ali Haddad-Adel, both withdrew from the race on June 10 and 11. While it was unclear why Adel withdrew, Aref reportedly did not want to split the reformist vote between himself and Rouhani, the remaining moderate. Rouhani campaigned on a platform of "hope and prudence" and appealed to both conservative and reformist voters. He was a senior cleric and had served in parliament for twenty years. He had also led the Supreme National Security Council for fifteen years and served as Iran's chief nuclear negotiator from 2003 to 2005, during which time he worked with Western countries to negotiate a suspension of Iran's uranium enrichment program. Rouhani promised that he would improve Iran's economy, reduce unemployment, and work to reduce tensions over the country's nuclear program. He also promised greater personal freedoms for Iranians and advocated for greater cooperation with and outreach to the military, civilian politicians, and all parts of Iran's government.

Rouhani was endorsed by Rafsanjani as well as former President Mohammad Khatami. These endorsements helped Rouhani, who was initially viewed as an underdog in the election, gain more public support. His campaign gathered momentum in May following a live interview on state-run television in which Rouhani accused Iran's media of censorship and lying to the public. At a rally a few days later, he criticized levels of security within Iran, asking, "Why does there have to be a securitized atmosphere everywhere? We must crush the securitized atmosphere." He also told Tehran University students that the 2009 opposition protests were not a foreign plot to destabilize Iran, as some government officials had claimed, and that the protestors' concerns should have been addressed.

All eight candidates were given equal time on state broadcast media for their campaign programming and participated in three televised debates. In the final debate on June 7, Rouhani and Jalili got into a heated discussion of Iran's nuclear program. Jalili claimed that Rouhani had been subservient to Western powers in the past and that those countries may try to take advantage of Iran becoming soft under Rouhani's leadership. Rouhani countered that Iran needs to move away from extremism and argued that his efforts at the Supreme National Security Council had helped avert a possible U.S. attack. All the candidates were critical of Ahmadinejad's leadership, particularly with regard to the economy, although the more conservative candidates focused more on improving economic management, increasing privatization and addressing corruption, while the reformists proposed improving relations with the rest of the world and removing economic sanctions.

ELECTION DAY

The election took place on Friday, June 14. Voting was supervised by approximately one million election officers, as well as more than 300,000 security guards. Voting hours were extended three times to accommodate what the interior minister described as a "rush of voters." Officials reported that nearly 73 percent of Iran's roughly fifty million registered voters turned out at the polls.

The following day, the Interior Ministry announced that Rouhani received 18.6 million votes, nearly 51 percent of the total vote, and declared him the winner. Rouhani thanked God "that once again the sun of rationality and moderation is shining over Iran again to send the voice of unity and cohesion of this nation to the world." He described his win as "the victory of wisdom, moderation, growth and awareness, the victory of commitment and religiosity over extremism and ill tempers." Thousands of Iranians took to the street in Tehran and other urban centers to demonstrate in support of their new president, chanting, "Long live reform! Long live Rouhani!"

International officials offered measured reactions to Rouhani's election and urged the new president to work with them. "We call on him to use the opportunity to set Iran on a different course for the future: addressing international concerns about Iran's nuclear program, taking forward a constructive relationship with the international community, and improving the political and human rights situation for the people of Iran," read a statement from the British Foreign Office. A White House spokesperson said President Barack Obama hopes "the Iranian government will heed the will of the Iranian people and make responsible choices that create a better future for all Iranians," adding that the United States "remains ready to engage the Iranian government directly in order to reach a diplomatic solution that will fully address the international community's concerns about Iran's nuclear program." UN Secretary General Ban Ki-moon congratulated Rouhani and similarly called on Iran to take a "constructive role in regional and international affairs."

POST ELECTION

On June 17, Rouhani gave his first press conference as president at the Expediency Council's Center for Strategic Research. He promised to lead a "National Unity" government that would be ultrafactional and promeritocracy, in which everyone would work together and that would focus on the future, not be stuck in the past. He pledged to resolve Iran's domestic problems, saying his top priority would be the economy, and said his government would provide more support to professional guilds, associations, and unions.

Rouhani did defend Iran's nuclear program, stating that it complied with international regulations, and said economic sanctions were both "unfair" and ineffective. He said that more negotiations, transparency—on both sides—and "mutual confidence-building" were the only way to resolve the nuclear dispute with Western countries. "All should know that the new government will not compromise Iranian nation's rights and on the same basis, we are ready for easing tension," he said. Rouhani reiterated that all of Iran's conditions must be met before it would engage in direct talks with the United States, and that any such talks "should be based on mutual respect and on an equal footing."

One week later, the Guardian Council confirmed the election results, and Rouhani took his oath of office before parliament on August 4. Given Rouhani's reputation and his comments on Iran's nuclear program, many expect he will be less aggressive and incendiary than Ahmadinejad in his approach to the West and that he will be more willing to cooperate with others, both within Iran and internationally. However, some project that change will happen slowly and that substantive change may not occur until after Iran's parliamentary elections in 2015.

—Linda Fecteau

Following is the text of a speech delivered by Iranian president-elect Hassan Rouhani released on June 18, 2013, upon his election.

President-Elect Rouhani Addresses the Media After Election

June 18, 2013

Addressing his first press conference after his landslide victory, Rohani said, "Let's learn from the youth, how they exercised jubilation on the streets, forgetting the past and how they are looking for future."

He said that his government will focus on [the] future and will not get entangled with memory of the past. ["]The government will use the experience got from the past to build a bright future."

He advised to get rid of sabotaging one another and develop atmosphere of brotherhood.

Prior to the press conference, he thanked Supreme Leader of Islamic Revolution Ayatollah Seyed Ali Khamenei and all those taking part in the election, especially those respecting national solidarity, ethics and moderation.

President-elect, Hassan Rohani, said on Monday that the new government will develop friendly relations with all the neighboring countries.

Rohani said in response to the question of al-Jazeera TV that his government would have ties with whole the 15 neighboring states, especially Saudi Arabia, to which several hundred thousand Iranians pay Haj pilgrimage annually.

He said the ties would be based on mutual respect, especially with the Persian Gulf littoral states in light of strategic importance of the Persian Gulf.

"I'm proud of being an official from Iran the signatory to a security pact with Saudi Arabia in 1998 and I hope that in the near future, we would have very good relations with our neighbors, especially Saudi Arabia."

As for Syria, he said he believed Syrian people should have the final say in all their country's affairs.

He said that Iranian government is against terrorism, civil war and foreign intervention in Syria, believing in peace based on the will of Syrians.

President-elect, Hassan Rohani, on Monday defended transparency of Iranian nuclear program.

Rohani said Iran's nuclear activities all fall within framework of international regulations and Tehran favors mutual confidence-building.

"Mutual confidence-building, more transparency and abidance by international regulations would be the country's focus in the future," said Rohani.

President-elect, Hassan Rohani, said on Monday that dialogue and mutual confidence-building will solve the nuclear dispute with the western governments.

Rohani said that mutual confidence building is possible.

As for enrichment, he said discussion on the issue would be held in an appropriate time.

"We would God willing follow more actively talks with the G5+1. We believe that negotiations is the sole possible solution to the nuclear problem."

He said sanctions are not effective and in the future, efforts would be made to remove the tyrannical sanctions under the pretext of nuclear dispute.

President-elect Hassan Rohani appreciated Iranian nation for creating a political epic urged by Supreme Leader Ayatollah Ali Khamenei, saying the main winner of the elections is the Iranian nation.

Speaking during his first press conference after landslide victory which is being held at the Expediency Council Center for Strategic Research, Rohani said that he will not forget the promises he gave in presidential campaign.

The recent election was not only an election. It was a vote of confidence, the beginning of a new chapter and active participation, he said.

"After final results were announced, all the Iranians celebrated, because all were winners in the scene of history and before the world public opinion."

He appreciated all those who chose the path of moderation, justice and ethics to meet national interests.

President-elect Hassan Rohani said on Monday that the Islamic Republic of Iran attaches importance to expansion of relations with its neighboring states based on friendship and mutual respect and interests.

Addressing a group of domestic and foreign reporters on his first press conference, the new Iranian president said that the Islamic Republic of Iran favors friendly ties with the Arab states in light of strategic values of the Persian Gulf.

On relations between Iran and Saudi Arabia, Rohani said Saudi Arabia is Iran's brotherly neighbor and the Qibla of the world Muslims is in that country, adding that the two countries have many cultural, historical and regional affinities.

On Syrian developments, he said the Syrian people have the final say in their affairs but the Islamic Republic of Iran is strongly opposing intervention of foreign countries, terrorism as well as civil war in that country.

He expressed the hope that the issue of Syria will be resolved with the assistance of all countries in the region and the globe and the Syrian government would restore peace and tranquility as soon as possible.

The will of Syrian people should be materialized in that country, Rohani underlined.

Rohani promised to resolve the country's problems such as unemployment and inflation step by step to reach the international standard.

President-elect Hassan Rohani said in his first news conference Monday that the government will stop direct interference in everyday affairs of people and will give a boost to the guilds associations and professional unions to bring harmony to the society and businesses.

Asked about the manifestations of moderation as his main motto in the election campaign, Rohani said that moderation is a method which avoids radicalism, extremism and selfish way of government.

Moderation and rationality require consultations with the experts and wisdom, by considering advantages and disadvantages and seeks abidance by law, he added.

Responding to another question, Rohani described his government's main priority as economic issues and livelihood of the people.

On process of taking delivery of administration from the outgoing government, he said that joint committees will be set up with the incumbent government to fulfill the handover and provide the urgent needs of the public.

Underlining the establishment of economic stability in the country, Rohani said that the country's economic capacity for the private sector should be released from monopoly of government and the obstacles should be removed.

On mechanisms to harness inflation, he pointed out that liquidity should be controlled and directed toward manufacturing sector.

Asked about the programs his government will adopt to use the momentum created by the massive turnout in presidential election, he said that the new government feels that a new opportunity has emerged for interaction with the world and it will make optimal use of it.

He hoped that all the countries are expected to seize the opportunity to develop cooperation rather than confrontation.

President-elect Hassan Rohani on Monday criticized the western governments for their unmanly sanctions policy against Iran.

Rohani said that mutual confidence-building by both the western governments and the Islamic Republic of Iran is the only way to put an end to the sanctions.

He defended transparency of Iranian nuclear program.

Calling western sanctions over Iran's nuclear program as "unfair," Rohani said that the western countries are suffering from economic recession, proving that the sanctions harm their economies as well.

He reiterated that for gradual removal of sanctions, two steps should be taken: Mutual confidence-building and more transparency from both sides.

Insisting that Iran's nuclear program is completely transparent, he called for more transparency from both sides.

He made it clear that the Islamic Republic's activities are within the framework of international laws.

Elaborating on the process of lifting sanctions, he said that Iran has to avoid a new sanction and on the other hand should try to reduce sanctions and then remove all of them.

President-elect Hassan Rohani on Monday criticized the western governments for their unmanly sanctions policy against Iran.

Rohani said that mutual confidence-building by both the western governments and the Islamic Republic of Iran is the only way to put an end to the sanctions.

He defended transparency of Iranian nuclear program.

Calling western sanctions over Iran's nuclear program as "unfair," Rohani said that the western countries are suffering from economic recession, proving that the sanctions harm their economies as well.

He reiterated that for gradual removal of sanctions, two steps should be taken: Mutual confidence-building and more transparency from both sides.

Insisting that Iran's nuclear program is completely transparent, he called for more transparency from both sides.

He made it clear that the Islamic Republic's activities are within the framework of international laws.

Elaborating on the process of lifting sanctions, he said that Iran has to avoid a new sanction and on the other hand should try to reduce sanctions and then remove all of them.

Iran President-elect Hassan Rohani said on Monday that the US should meet all conditions and the government will not compromise Iranian nation's rights.

Rohani, addressing his first press conference after election victory, said, "All should know that the new government will not compromise Iranian nation's rights and on the same basis, we are ready for easing tension."

To a question by the US NBC correspondent about his reaction to the US State Department's call for direct talks with Iran, Rohani said, "Any talks with the US should be based on mutual respect and on an equal footing. Definitely, all conditions should be met. Iran's relations with the US is a complicated and difficult issue, not being simple. There is a chronical wound which should be treated by prudence. Of course, we would not favor tension."

As for certain conditions set by Iran for direct talks with the US, the President-elect said, "First of all the US Administration must honor the Algeria Accord it signed with the Islamic Republic of Iran on non-interference in Iran's internal affairs. And that, Americans would officially recognize, all rights, including nuclear rights of Iranian nation."

He said that the US should stop unilateralism and bullying towards Iran.

"Of course, if the conditions are met and the ground prepared and in case of displaying goodwill from the US government, the situation may improve."

To a question on prospect of Iran's relations with the Latin American states, Rohani said, "Our priority would be firstly our neighbors, the Islamic and non-aligned states. We favor expansion of relations with all countries, including the Latin American states."

Elsewhere in the press conference, Rohani said his "National Unity" government would be ultra-factional and pro-meritocracy.

"This means that in the new government all the qualified manpower, including the moderates, reformists and principalists would work together."

Asked about prospect of Iran-China relations, Rohani said Iran-China relations have always been good and cooperation would continue.

Source: Islamic Republic of Iran. Ministry of Foreign Affairs. "President-elect says government will usher in path of cooperation with world." June 18, 2013. http://www.mfa.gov.ir/index.aspx?siteid=3&pageid=2014&newsview=24804.

OTHER HISTORIC DOCUMENTS OF INTEREST

FROM THIS VOLUME

FROM PREVIOUS *HISTORIC DOCUMENTS*

U.S. and Afghanistan on Security Negotiations

JUNE 19 AND JUNE 22, AND NOVEMBER 20, 2013

With the war in Afghanistan drawing to a close and U.S. troops set to leave at the end of 2014, American and Afghan officials worked together throughout 2013 to determine what relationship the two nations would have moving forward, particularly as it related to security. The United States made clear its desire to leave behind a stable Afghan government, which it believed would involve bringing the Taliban peacefully back into the country. Peace talks between Afghanistan and the Taliban stalled before they even started in June when Afghan President Hamid Karzai refused to send his negotiating team to Qatar after the Taliban opened an office there that created the illusion that the Taliban was a formal arm of the government. It fell to U.S. Secretary of State John Kerry to bring Afghanistan back to the peace talks and to restart stalled negotiations on a Bilateral Security Agreement (BSA).

TALIBAN OPENS QATAR OFFICE

For years, officials in Afghanistan and the United States have tried to bring the Taliban to the negotiating table in an effort to start a peace process and rebuild a stable Afghan government. Because the Taliban did not keep an official office or address, a means of protecting its officials from attack, it was difficult to find and contact Taliban representatives. When the Taliban could be reached, meetings would be held in a variety of countries in hotels or other venues. Still, Taliban leaders questioned whether they would be safe traveling to and from the meetings. This opened discussions about finding the group a permanent office.

Some of the countries that initially proposed to host the office included Turkey, Qatar, Saudi Arabia, and the United Arab Emirates. The Taliban preferred Qatar, seeing it as a neutral party on the Afghanistan issue, while Afghanistan preferred Saudi Arabia or Turkey because of close ties with those nations. In the end, Qatar agreed to host an office, and the United States agreed. Many years before it established a permanent presence, the Taliban would come to Qatar to meet with American officials to discuss the U.S. exit from Afghanistan and the Taliban's role in the country moving forward. The talks stalled in 2012 when the United States refused to acquiesce to demands that it turn over prisoners from Guantánamo Bay.

After eighteen months of stalled negotiations, the Taliban officially opened its office on June 19, 2013, after a delay resulting from Karzai's concerns that the group would use the office to recruit members and raise money. The United States gave assurance to the Afghan leader that the office would only be used for activities related to the peace process. The official opening featured a ribbon cutting and the playing of the Taliban anthem. The Taliban said it would use its office "to meet Afghans," which some international analysts saw as a significant change from earlier rhetoric when the Taliban said it would only negotiate with the United States.

The negotiations to create a peace process through which the Taliban will be allowed back into Afghanistan will likely be difficult and time consuming. The Afghan government, U.S. negotiators, and Taliban leaders differ on a number of key issues including women's rights (Afghan women fear that allowing the Taliban back into the country could mean greater limitations on the freedoms they have enjoyed since 2003); the withdrawal of all foreign forces from Afghanistan and the return of some prisoners from Guantánamo Bay (the Taliban wants all troops to leave the country while Afghanistan wants a residual force left); and the promise from the Taliban that it will not use Afghanistan as a staging ground for attacks against other countries. The United States believes it will be difficult to reach a peace agreement with the Taliban if it refuses to sever ties with al Qaeda and rejects the legitimacy of the Afghan government.

Immediately following the office opening, President Karzai suspended planned meetings with the Taliban. Karzai decried the use of the Taliban flag and the nameplate on the door, which read: The Islamic Emirate of Afghanistan. These, he said, gave the office a sense of legitimacy that it did not deserve and that the United States had promised it would not be given. Karzai, perhaps fearful that the United States and Taliban had begun negotiations without the presence of Afghan officials, demanded the removal of both the nameplate and the flag. Kerry promised Karzai that they would be removed. While Secretary Kerry scrambled to bring Afghanistan back to the table, other American officials downplayed the situation. President Barack Obama called it one of the many "areas of friction" that had been anticipated in opening negotiations with the Taliban.

The flag was removed from the office, which was renamed the Political Bureau for Afghan Taliban in Doha. However, Karzai's response to the office opening made Taliban officials even more skeptical about any negotiations moving forward. The Taliban insisted that the Qatari government had given permission for both the nameplate and flag and that no agreement had been made with the United States to the contrary.

DRAFTING A SECURITY AGREEMENT

In 2012, the United States and Afghanistan signed a strategic partnership agreement outlining the relationship between the two countries following the withdrawal of U.S. troops. A section of this document required that the countries complete a BSA that would define the role of U.S. troops after 2014. The aim was to set up a framework regarding how soldiers could still assist and train the Afghan forces while respecting the sovereignty of Afghanistan. Marine Corps General Joseph Dunford, who leads the U.S. coalition in Afghanistan, called the agreement "critical to any post-2014 presence" and said that it "needs to be taken seriously on both sides." Negotiations on the agreement began in November 2012. The United States requested that the document give immunity from an Afghan trial to U.S. soldiers accused of crimes in Afghanistan. The Afghan negotiators requested that the United States not maintain a permanent security base in Afghanistan but would respond with military force to any attack against Afghanistan by an outside country.

Negotiations were on rocky footing from the start because the United States balked at the idea of militarily supporting Afghanistan should it be attacked. This also extended to essentially declaring Pakistan an enemy of the mission of the United States and Afghanistan as they work to fight extremism in the region.

When President Karzai suspended negotiations with the Taliban on June 19, 2013, he also stopped BSA negotiations. "In view of the contradiction between acts and the statements made by the United States of America in regard to the Peace Process, the Afghan government suspended the negotiations, currently underway in Kabul between Afghan and US delegations on the Bilateral Security Agreement," Karzai's office said in a press release. Karzai demanded that the Taliban meet directly with his officials before BSA negotiations would resume. This put the onus on the United States to convince the Taliban to meet with Karzai.

NEGOTIATIONS RESUME, DRAFT AGREEMENT REACHED

Negotiations reopened in late August, and on October 12, a draft agreement was announced. "Tonight we reached some sort of agreement," Karzai said, adding that American troops "will no longer conduct operations by themselves. We have been provided written guarantee for the safety of the Afghan people about invasion. A clear definition has been provided and we accepted it." Kerry added that the draft BSA did not include a resolution on the jurisdiction of Afghan courts to try U.S. troops accused of crimes after 2014. "If the issue of jurisdiction cannot be resolved, then, unfortunately there cannot be a bilateral security agreement," the Secretary of State said.

On November 20, another version of the BSA was released that, although not fully executed, was considered close to final. The draft included a provision that the United States would assist Afghanistan in counterterrorism missions and would continue to train and advise Afghan troops. There was neither a deadline set on when these remaining troops would be required to leave Afghanistan nor an indication of how many troops would remain after 2014. To the latter point, President Karzai called for no more than 15,000 North Atlantic Treaty Organization (NATO) troops, while the United States said they planned for no more than 10,000 American soldiers.

The November 20 release did include an agreement on how to handle U.S. troops accused of crimes after 2014. These troops will be allowed immunity from being tried in Afghan courts and can also not be transferred to another foreign court, other than that in the United States. The United States was authorized "to hold [civil and criminal] trial in such cases, or take other disciplinary action, as appropriate, in the territory of Afghanistan." Afghanistan may not arrest or detain any U.S. troop, although it may make a formal request that a solider be removed from the country. The agreement also resolved the issue of how the United States would respond in the event that Afghanistan was attacked. "The United States shall regard with grave concern any external aggression or threat of external aggression against the sovereignty, independence, and territorial integrity of Afghanistan," the BSA read. No details on how such a compromise was reached were released.

The draft was sent to Afghanistan's loya jirga, the group of elders responsible for making important determinations regarding the nation's governing, and with their approval on November 24, moved to the Afghan parliament. The loya jirga urged Karzai to immediately sign the agreement, and the United States agreed, arguing that without approval by the close of 2013, it could not adequately prepare for postwithdrawal plans. Karzai, however, refused to sign the document until after the 2014 Afghan presidential election but promised to sign it before leaving office. Once signed, the agreement will take effect on

January 1, 2015 and "shall remain in force until the end of 2024 and beyond." Termination is permitted, as long as one nation gives notice to the other at least two years in advance.

—Heather Kerrigan

The following is a June 19, 2013, press release from the President of Iraq announcing the suspension of negotiations on the Bilateral Security Agreement with the United States; the edited text of a press conference held on June 22, 2013, in which Secretary of State John Kerry and the Qatari Prime Minister discussed Qatar's hosting of the Taliban's official office; and the edited text of the draft version of the Bilateral Security Agreement between the United States and Afghanistan, released on November 20, 2013.

President Karzai Suspends Negotiations With United States

June 19, 2013

In view of the contradiction between acts and the statements made by the United States of America in regard to the Peace Process, the Afghan government suspended the negotiations, currently underway in Kabul between Afghan and US delegations on the Bilateral Security Agreement.

SOURCE: Office of the President of the Islamic Republic of Afghanistan. "Afghanistan Suspends Current Afghan-US Talks on Bilateral Security Agreement." June 19, 2013. http://president.gov.af/en/news/afghanistan-suspends-current-afghan-us-talks-on-bilateral-security-agreement.

U.S. Secretary of State and Qatari Prime Minister Remark on Meeting

June 22, 2013

SECRETARY KERRY: Well, thank you very much. It's my privilege to be here with His Excellency the Prime Minister and Foreign Minister Sheikh Hamad bin Jassim. And I also want to thank our overall host here, His Highness the Amir Sheikh Hamad bin Khalifa Al Thani, and look forward to meeting with him, I think, tomorrow morning first thing. And I look forward to meet later today with the Heir Apparent, the Sheikh Tamim.

Qatar has been a very valued partner to the United States of America, and importantly deeply engaged in a number of issues that matter a great deal here in the region. And we seek to—we work on these issues together very, very closely. And I'm very appreciative of the friendship, fortunately, with Hamad bin Jassim, but also for his willingness to step up and lead when it's necessary. And I'm particularly grateful for his leadership as the chairman of the committee within the Arab League, where he has reached out in a visit to Washington with a number of foreign ministers in order to try to help advance the Middle East peace process. We both share a commitment to two states living side by side in peace for two peoples, and that is something that is going to continue, and we will be meeting again later today to talk about that issue and several others in the region that are of importance.

[Secretary Kerry's remarks on the conflict of Syria have been omitted.]

Finally, let me just say I want to thank and express the appreciation of President Obama and all of us working on this issue for Qatar's willingness to host the Taliban office here in Doha in order to facilitate negotiations between the Afghan High Peace Council and the authorized representatives of the Taliban. Now it is obvious from just the early churning around the opening of that office that nothing comes easily in this endeavor, and we understand that. And the road ahead will be difficult, no question about it, if there is a road ahead. Clearly there's been a challenge thus far, but I want to thank our friends in Qatar for having made the effort, having reached out, having gotten far enough to at least have an announcement made that there is an office.

And it is our hope that this could ultimately be an important step in reconciliation if it's possible. We know that that—it may well not be possible, and it's really up to the Taliban to make that choice. The High Peace Council is ready, the United States is ready, the Qataris are ready; all of them have lived up to their obligations thus far, and it remains to be seen in this very first test whether or not the Taliban are prepared to do their part.

So once again, I thank His Highness the Amir, His Highness Sheikh Tamim, and His Excellency the Prime Minister for hosting us here today and being willing to cooperate in these difficult endeavors. Thank you, sir.

PRIME MINISTER HAMAD: Thank you, John. We're going to take some questions. . . .

MODERATOR: Deborah Reichmann from AP.

QUESTION: I'll try to be brief, but (inaudible) two part question for you and the Secretary. The Taliban talks seems to be hold, yet Ambassador Dobbins is here. Is he staying? Is there still a possibility that things could get back together in the next few days as we had thought maybe last week? And secondly, has the Administration actually begun any of the necessary paperwork and notification process that would be needed in order to get authorization for the release of any of the Taliban prisoners at Guantanamo Bay?

And to the Prime Minister, do you think it's possible to bring the Taliban to the table at this time?

SECRETARY KERRY: Well, let me just say with respect to any paperwork or anything like that, that's way ahead of where we are in any process at this point in time, and I'm not going to comment on anything with respect to potential detainees or otherwise because it's just not where the process is.

With respect to Ambassador Dobbins, yes, he is here, and we are waiting to find out whether or not the Taliban will respond in order to follow the sequence, which has been very painstakingly established. And we have performed our part in good faith. Regrettably, the agreement was not adhered to in the early hours, but thanks to our good friends the

Qataris and their efforts, as well as others, the—it's sort of been stepped back from. Now we need to see if we can get it back on track. I don't know whether that's possible or not. If there is not a decision to move forward by the Taliban in short order, then we may have to consider whether or not the office has to be closed.

PRIME MINISTER HAMAD: Well, about Taliban (inaudible), I think the intention of us as a mediator to when the office being open in Qatar is to bring everybody to the table to talk. The Afghanis, the American, they have to talk because we think the only way to get out of this war in Afghanistan is by talking to each other, to have to try to find comprehensive peace and everybody have to live in Afghanistan without (inaudible) any part of the Afghani people. So we hope that is where—that we will do our best as mediators, but all depends on all parties. They have to sit and talk and we will be as the facilitators if they need us (inaudible).

Thank you very much. Thank you.

SECRETARY KERRY: Thank you, all. Thanks very much. Thank you.

Source: U.S. Department of State. Media Center. "Remarks With Qatari Prime Minister and Foreign Minister Sheikh Hamad bin Jassim Al Thani After Their Meeting." June 22, 2013. http://www.state.gov/secretary/remarks/2013/06/211008.htm.

DOCUMENT *Draft Bilateral Security Agreement*

November 20, 2013

SECURITY AND DEFENSE COOPERATION AGREEMENT BETWEEN THE UNITED STATES OF AMERICA AND THE ISLAMIC REPUBLIC OF AFGHANISTAN

Preamble

The United States of America (hereinafter, "the United States") and the Islamic Republic of Afghanistan (hereinafter, "Afghanistan"), hereinafter referred to collectively as "the Parties" and singularly as a "Party;"

Recognizing the *Enduring Strategic Partnership Agreement between the United States of America and the Islamic Republic of Afghanistan,* signed May 2, 2012, (the "Strategic Partnership Agreement") and reaffirming that, as recognized in that Agreement, the Parties are committed to strengthen long-term strategic cooperation in areas of mutual interest, including: advancing peace, security, and stability; strengthening state institutions; supporting Afghanistan's long-term economic and social development; and encouraging regional cooperation;

Confirming the recognition in the Strategic Partnership Agreement that cooperation between the Parties is based on mutual respect and shared interests;

Emphasizing also the Strategic Partnership Agreement's recognition that the Parties will go forward in partnership with confidence because they are committed to seeking a future of justice, peace, security, and opportunity for the Afghan people, as well as the reaffirmation of the Parties' strong commitment to the sovereignty, independence, territorial integrity, and national unity of Afghanistan;

Recognizing the enduring partnership between the United States and Afghanistan, and affirming the mutual intent of the Parties to expand, mature, promote and further elevate their security and defense cooperation based on this Agreement;

Desiring to continue to foster close cooperation concerning defense and security arrangements in order to strengthen security and stability in Afghanistan, contribute to regional and international peace and stability, combat terrorism, achieve a region which is no longer a safe haven for al-Qaida and its affiliates, and enhance the ability of Afghanistan to deter threats against its sovereignty, security, and territorial integrity; and noting that the United States does not seek permanent military facilities in Afghanistan, or a presence that is a threat to Afghanistan's neighbors, and has pledged not to use Afghan territory or facilities as a launching point for attacks against other countries;

Recalling the *Chicago Summit Declaration on Afghanistan,* issued on May 21, 2012, by the Heads of State and Government of Afghanistan and Nations Contributing to the North Atlantic Treaty Organization (NATO)-led International Security Assistance Force (ISAF), and specifically, the participants' renewed firm commitment to a sovereign, secure, and democratic Afghanistan and acknowledgment that ISAF's mission will be concluded by the end of 2014 and that their close partnership will continue beyond the end of the transition period including through NATO and Afghanistan's mutual commitment to work to establish a new NATO-led Mission to train, advise, and assist the Afghan National Defense and Security Forces (ANDSF), and noting here that such a mission will also need to be provided with the necessary authorities, status arrangements, and legal basis;

Reaffirming the continued support of the Parties for regional cooperation and coordination mechanisms, with a goal of increasing security and stability by reducing tensions, uncertainty, and misunderstanding;

Recalling the 2013 Loya Jirga's recognition that this Security and Defense Cooperation Agreement between the United States and Afghanistan is important for the security of Afghanistan;

Desiring to develop further the means of defense and security cooperation between the Parties, based on the principles of full respect for the independence, sovereignty, and integrity of their territories, and non-interference in the domestic affairs of each other, in order to promote security and stability in the region, and to combat terrorism;

Agreeing on the importance of cooperative relationships between Afghanistan and its neighbors conducted on the basis of mutual respect, non-interference, and equality and calling on all nations to respect Afghanistan's sovereignty and territorial integrity, and to refrain from interfering in Afghanistan's internal affairs and democratic processes; and

Affirming also that the Parties' cooperation is based on full respect for the sovereignty of each Party, the purposes of the United Nations Charter, and a shared desire to provide a framework for defense and security cooperation between the Parties; and reaffirming their strong commitment to the sovereignty, independence, territorial integrity, and national unity of Afghanistan, as well as respect for Afghan laws, customs and traditions;

Have agreed as follows:

[Article I, the definitions section, has been omitted.]

ARTICLE 2

Purpose and Scope

1.   The Parties shall continue to foster close cooperation to strengthen security and stability in Afghanistan, counter-terrorism, contribute to regional and international peace and stability, and enhance the ability of Afghanistan to deter internal and external threats against its sovereignty, security, territorial integrity, national unity, and its constitutional order. Unless otherwise mutually agreed, United States forces shall not conduct combat operations in Afghanistan.

2.   To that end, the United States shall undertake supporting activities, as may be agreed, in close cooperation and coordination with Afghanistan, to assist ANDSF in developing capabilities required to provide security for all Afghans including as may be mutually agreed: advising, training, equipping, supporting, and sustaining ANDSF, including in field engineering, countering improvised explosive devices and explosive ordinance disposal; establishing and upgrading ANDSF transportation and logistics systems; developing intelligence sharing capabilities; strengthening Afghanistan's Air Force capabilities; conducting combined military exercises; and other activities as may be agreed. The Parties will continue to work on the details of ANDSF development as set forth in the Afghan Program of Record, at the Chicago Summit in 2012, and in the context of the Security Consultative Forum.

3.   The Parties recognize that ANDSF are responsible for securing the people and territory of Afghanistan. The Parties shall work to enhance ANDSF's ability to deter and respond to internal and external threats. Upon request, the United States shall urgently determine support it is prepared to provide ANDSF in order to respond to threats to Afghanistan's security.

4.   The Parties acknowledge that U.S. military operations to defeat al-Qaida and its affiliates may be appropriate in the common fight against terrorism. The Parties agree to continue their close cooperation and coordination toward those ends, with the intention of protecting U.S. and Afghan national interests without unilateral U.S. military counter-terrorism operations. U.S. military counter-terrorism operations are intended to complement and support ANDSF's counter-terrorism operations, with the goal of maintaining ANDSF lead, and with full respect for Afghan sovereignty and full regard for the safety and security of the Afghan people, including in their homes.

5.   In furtherance of the activities and operations referred to in this Article, and for other purposes and missions as may be mutually agreed, and consistent with the authorizations as detailed in this Agreement, United States forces may undertake transit, support, and related activities, including as may be necessary to support themselves while they are present in Afghanistan under the terms of this Agreement, and such other activities as detailed in this Agreement, or as may be mutually agreed.

6.   This Agreement, including any Annexes and any Implementing Agreements or Arrangements, provides the necessary authorizations for the presence and activities of United States forces in Afghanistan and defines the terms and conditions that describe that presence, and in the specific situations indicated herein, the presence and activities of United States contractors and United States contractor employees in Afghanistan.

ARTICLE 3

Laws

1. It is the duty of members of the force and of the civilian component to respect the Constitution and laws of Afghanistan and to abstain from any activity inconsistent with the spirit of this Agreement and, in particular, from any political activity in the territory of Afghanistan. It is the duty of United States forces authorities to take necessary measures to that end.

2. The Parties' respective obligations under this Agreement, and any subsequent arrangements, are without prejudice to Afghan sovereignty over its territory, and each Party's right of self-defense, consistent with international law. Cooperation and activities relating to implementation of this Agreement shall be consistent with the Parties' respective commitments and obligations under international law.

3.

ARTICLE 4

Developing and Sustaining Afghanistan's Defense and Security Capabilities

1. With full respect for Afghanistan's sovereignty, the Parties recognize Afghanistan's current requirement for continued international security assistance, and share the goal of Afghanistan taking increasing and, ultimately full, responsibility for funding its defense and security needs and sustaining ANDSF.

2. Afghanistan shall make, consistent with its political and economic stability and its general economic condition, the full contribution permitted by its manpower, resources, and facilities to the development and sustainment of its own defense and security forces. Afghanistan shall take all necessary measures to develop and sustain its defense and security capacities.

3. So long as the Strategic Partnership Agreement so provides, and guided by the pledges set forth at the Chicago Summit in 2012, the United States shall have an obligation to seek funds on a yearly basis to support the training, equipping, advising and sustaining of ANDSF, so that Afghanistan can independently secure and defend itself against internal and external threats, and help ensure that terrorists never again encroach on Afghan soil and threaten Afghanistan, the region, and the world. The United States shall consult with Afghanistan regarding the amount of funding needed to accomplish the purposes of this Agreement, keeping in mind pledges made in Chicago, and shall take the results of those consultations into consideration in executing this obligation. Taking into account Afghanistan's annual priorities, the United States shall direct appropriate funds through Afghan Government budgetary mechanisms, to be managed by relevant Afghan institutions implementing financial management standards of transparency and accountability, and procurement, audit, and regulatory oversight in accordance with international best practices.

4. The Parties recognize the importance of ANDSF having the necessary equipment and materiel to secure Afghanistan. To that end, the United States shall continue to cooperate with Afghanistan on providing equipment and materiel for ANDSF.

5.   Afghanistan and the United States may cooperate and coordinate with other countries to strengthen ANDSF, as may be mutually agreed, including on equipping ANDSF.

6.   In order to contribute effectively to the security of Afghanistan and the region, the United States agrees to cooperate with Afghanistan to continue the development of ANDSF capabilities consistent with Afghanistan's status as a Major Non-NATO Ally.

7.   The Parties recognize the benefits for Afghanistan's defense and security to be derived from developing defense capabilities and systems that are consistent with NATO standards and that promote interoperability with NATO. The Parties shall coordinate in the development of Afghanistan's defense and security forces, equipment, materiel, facilities, operational doctrine, and institutions to achieve standardization and interoperability with NATO, in order to promote further the effective utilization and maintenance of defense and security assistance provided to Afghanistan, and to maximize the benefits of cooperation between ANDSF and United States forces. This coordination shall not preclude Afghanistan from procuring independently equipment and material for ANDSF from non-NATO countries with its own resources.

ARTICLE 5

Defense and Security Cooperation Mechanisms

1.   The Parties agree to direct the United States–Afghanistan Working Group on Defense and Security Cooperation, established under the Strategic Partnership Agreement, to:

    a.   Develop appropriate measures of effectiveness for the analysis and strengthening of Afghanistan's use of available defense and security resources, consistent with the purpose and scope of this Agreement;

    b.   Complete semi-annual assessments of actual performance against these measures to inform the Parties' respective resource allocation decisions and their cooperation in developing and sustaining Afghanistan's defense capabilities;

    c.   Develop a process consistent with the purpose and scope of this Agreement, for making timely, accurate, and effective cooperative assessments of internal and external threats to Afghanistan; and

    d.   Make specific recommendations on enhancing information and intelligence sharing and evaluation.

2.   The Parties share the objective of continuing to improve their ability to consult on such threats, including considering how to establish secure or dedicated channels of communication.

ARTICLE 6

External Aggression

1.   Afghanistan has been subject to aggression and other uses of force inconsistent with the United Nations Charter by foreign states and externally based or supported armed groups. In the context of this Agreement, the Parties strongly oppose such uses of armed force or threats thereof against the territorial integrity or political independence

of Afghanistan, including in this regard provision to armed groups of support, such as sanctuary or arms, by any state or other armed groups. The Parties agree to cooperate to strengthen Afghanistan's defenses against such threats to its territorial integrity, sovereignty or political independence.

2.   The United States shall regard with grave concern any external aggression or threat of external aggression against the sovereignty, independence, and territorial integrity of Afghanistan, recognizing that such aggression may threaten the Parties' shared interests in Afghanistan's stability and regional and international peace and stability.

3.   On a regular basis, the Parties shall consult on potential political, diplomatic, military, and economic measures that could form part of an appropriate response in the event of such external aggression or the threat of external aggression against Afghanistan. Consultations shall seek to develop a list of political, diplomatic, military, and economic measures.

4.   In the event of external aggression or the threat of external aggression against Afghanistan, the Parties shall hold consultations on an urgent basis to develop and implement an appropriate response, including, as may be mutually determined, consideration of available political, diplomatic, military, and economic measures on the list developed pursuant to paragraph 3, in accordance with their respective constitutional procedures.

5.   The Parties shall develop comprehensive procedures to promote the effective accomplishment of such regular and urgent consultations.

    a.   Such comprehensive procedures shall recognize consultations involving the participation of the United States Secretary of State and Afghanistan Foreign Minister, the United States Secretary of Defense and Afghanistan Defense Minister, and respective Ambassadors in Kabul and Washington, D.C. as primary channels to initiate urgent consultations in the event of external aggression, or threat of external aggression.

    b.   Such comprehensive procedures shall not, however, limit or prejudice the Parties' ability to consult each other in other channels or through other mechanisms, as urgency or exigency may require.

6.   The Parties agree to direct the United States–Afghanistan Working Group on Defense and Security Cooperation to promote the effective implementation of this Article, including development of such comprehensive procedures, and review on a regular basis the list of measures developed pursuant to paragraph 3.

[Articles 7-12, on the use of facilities, property ownership, storage of equipment and material, movement of vehicles, contracting procedures, and utilities, have been omitted.]

ARTICLE 13

Status of Personnel

1.   Afghanistan, while retaining its sovereignty, recognizes the particular importance of disciplinary control, including judicial and non-judicial measures, by the United States forces authorities over members of the force and of the civilian component. Afghanistan

therefore agrees that the United States shall have the exclusive right to exercise jurisdiction over such persons in respect of any criminal or civil offenses committed in the territory of Afghanistan. Afghanistan authorizes the United States to hold trial in such cases, or take other disciplinary action, as appropriate, in the territory of Afghanistan.

2.   If requested by Afghanistan, the United States shall inform Afghanistan of the status of any criminal proceedings regarding offenses allegedly committed in Afghanistan by the members of the force or of the civilian component involving Afghan nationals, including the final disposition of the investigations, or prosecution. If so requested, the United States shall also undertake efforts to permit and facilitate the attendance and observation of such proceedings by representatives of Afghanistan.

3.   In the interests of justice, the Parties shall assist each other in investigation of incidents, including the collection of evidence. In investigating offenses, United States authorities shall take into account any report of investigations by Afghan authorities.

4.   The United States recognizes the critical role that Afghan law enforcement officials play in the enforcement of Afghan law and order and the protection of the Afghan people. Relevant Afghan authorities shall immediately notify United States forces authorities if they suspect a member of the force or of the civilian component is engaged in the commission of a crime so that United States forces authorities can take immediate action. Members of the force and of the civilian component shall not be arrested or detained by Afghan authorities. Members of the force and of the civilian component arrested or detained by Afghan authorities for any reason, including by Afghan law enforcement authorities, shall be immediately handed over to United States forces authorities.

5.   Afghanistan and the United States agree that members of the force and of the civilian component may not be surrendered to, or otherwise transferred to, the custody of an international tribunal or any other entity or state without the express consent of the United States.

6.   Afghanistan maintains the right to exercise jurisdiction over United States contractors and United States contractor employees.

[Articles 14-26, addressing logistics such as uniforms, weapons, imports and exports, taxation, currency, and the creation of a joint commission to oversee the implantation of the BSA, have been omitted.]

ARTICLE 26

Entry into Force, Amendment, and Termination

1.   This Agreement shall enter into force on January 1, 2015, after the Parties notify one another through diplomatic channels of the completion of their respective internal legal requirements necessary for the entry into force of this Agreement. It shall remain in force until the end of 2024 and beyond, unless terminated pursuant to paragraph 4 of this Article.

2.   This Agreement, upon its entry into force, shall supersede the exchange of notes dated September 26, 2002, December 12, 2002, and May 28, 2003, regarding the status of United States forces in Afghanistan. This Agreement shall also supersede any prior agreements and

understandings which the Parties mutually determine, through a subsequent exchange of diplomatic notes, to be contrary to the provisions of this Agreement.

3.   This Agreement may be amended by written agreement of the Parties through the exchange of diplomatic notes.

4.   This Agreement may be terminated by mutual written agreement or by either Party upon two years' written notice to the other Party through diplomatic channels. Termination of any Annex to or Implementing Arrangement under this Agreement does not result in termination of this Agreement. Termination of this Agreement in accordance with this paragraph shall, without further action, result in termination of all Annexes and Implementing Arrangements.

[The signature lines and annexes have been removed.]

SOURCE: Ministry of Foreign Affairs. Islamic Republic of Afghanistan. "Security and Defense Cooperation Agreement Between the United States of America and the Islamic Republic of Afghanistan." November 20, 2013. http://mfa.gov.af/Content/files/2013-11-18%20BSA%20TEXT.pdf.

OTHER HISTORIC DOCUMENTS OF INTEREST

FROM PREVIOUS *HISTORIC DOCUMENTS*

Supreme Court Rules on Affirmative Action in College Admissions

JUNE 24, 2013

When the U.S. Supreme Court agreed to hear a case challenging the admissions process at the University of Texas, many court-watchers braced for a major decision on affirmative action. Then, after oral arguments, the waiting began while more than eight months passed without a decision. Some thought this long wait meant that a decision of great importance was being carefully crafted; others wondered if intense negotiations were bogging the Court down. When the Court finally released its opinion on June 24, 2013, the result was not the anticipated game-changer. Opponents of affirmative action, who were hoping the Court would take this opportunity to reverse earlier decisions and bar any race-conscious admissions, were disappointed. The Court reaffirmed an earlier precedent acknowledging that the goal of attaining a diverse student body can be a compelling state interest justifying taking race into account in college admissions. But the case was hardly an enthusiastic endorsement of affirmative action. The Court did not rule definitively on whether the University of Texas policy was constitutional but, instead, sent it back to the lower courts to reexamine the policy based on a newly articulated rigorous level of scrutiny. To pass constitutional muster, according to the majority opinion written by Justice Anthony M. Kennedy, the University bears "the ultimate burden of demonstrating, before turning to racial classifications, that available, workable race-neutral alternatives do not suffice." The University will need to show much more than "good faith in its use of racial classifications," because now, under this standard, the courts must closely scrutinize the evidence. So, by continuing to support affirmative action in college admissions, but ordering appeals courts to review them under a demanding standard, this compromise opinion had something for both opponents and supporters of affirmative action in higher education.

APPLICATION REJECTED

Located in Austin, Texas, the University of Texas is one of the nation's leading institutions of higher learning. In 2008, the University received 29,501 applications and accepted 12,843 students, out of which 6,715 enrolled. Students are selected for admission through a unique coupling of two different admissions processes. The Texas State Legislature passed a measure known as the Top Ten Percent Law, which grants automatic admission at any public state college, including the University of Texas, to all students who graduate in the top 10 percent of their class at a Texas high school. Students admitted under this law make up approximately three quarters of the University of Texas's entering class. The rest of the class is chosen through a program called the Personal Achievement Index (PAI) that measures other factors such as a student's leadership and work experience, awards, extra-curricular activities, community service, and other special circumstances giving insight to a student's background. Since 2004, this secondary program has explicitly considered an applicant's race as a meaningful factor. The University adopted race-conscious admissions after an internal study concluded that it was necessary to remedy a deficiency of diversity in undergraduate classes.

Abigail Fisher applied for admission to the University's 2008 entering class. Because she was not in the top 10 percent of her Texas high school class, she missed the cut off for automatic admission. The University rejected her application. Fisher, who is white, then sued the University in federal court, alleging that the school's use of race in the under-graduate admissions process violated the Equal Protection Clause of the Constitution. She argued that she was a victim of racial discrimination because students of color who had less impressive records than hers had been admitted. She lost her lawsuit in the lower courts, but the Supreme Court agreed to hear her appeal, even though by the time the case was argued she had already graduated from another college.

SUPREME COURT PRECEDENTS

The Court quickly reviewed and left in place the holdings of its three past cases addressing the consideration of race in college applications.

The United States Supreme Court first addressed the issue of race-conscious admis-sions decisions in the 1978 landmark case, *Regents v. Bakke*. A white student, Allan P. Bakke, had challenged a special admission program at the Davis campus of the University of California's medical school that set aside sixteen positions for minority students. In reaching its holding that the use of quotas was unconstitutional, this case held that all racial classi-fications, whether to favor or oppress a racial minority, must pass strict scrutiny. It further rejected as a compelling government interest the redressing of past discrimination and held that the only compelling interest would be "the interest in the educational benefits that flow from a diverse student body."

More recently, in two conjoined cases arising out of admissions policies at the University of Michigan, the Supreme Court reaffirmed the conclusion that "student body diversity is a compelling state interest that can justify the use of race in university admis-sions." In *Grutter v. Bollinger* (2003), the Court deferred to the educational judgment of the University of Michigan that such diversity would serve the University's educational goals. It upheld a race conscious admissions policy at the law school, because it regarded race as one factor among many allowing it to "remain flexible enough to ensure that each applicant is evaluated as an individual and not in a way that makes an applicant's race or ethnicity the defining feature of his or her application." Race, the Court reasoned, can be used in college admissions as one of many "plus factors," in a program that considers the overall individual contribution of each applicant. At the same time, the Court, in *Gratz v. Bollinger* (2003), rejected the more doctrinaire policy of University of Michigan's under-graduate admissions, which automatically assigned fixed points to minority status, to be plugged into an admissions points-based formula. This, the Court ruled, was an unconsti-tutional quota system.

COURT RULES ON AFFIRMATIVE ACTION

Though some predicted and others feared that a new coalition of justices on the Supreme Court would take this opportunity for a major reversal of these earlier precedents, instead the Court in *Fisher* reiterated the basic rule that any official action that treats a person differently because of race is inherently suspect and can only be constitutional if (1) the classification serves a compelling governmental interest and (2) is narrowly tailored to serve that interest. This test is referred to as *strict scrutiny* and requires the greatest proof of those seeking to treat people differently based on race. The previous cases had focused primarily on the first prong of this test, with litigants arguing over whether taking race into account as a positive factor in college admissions could ever be a legitimate governmental interest. The Court here left in place the central holding of *Grutter* that if the university, in its judgment, believes that having a diverse student body would serve its educational goals, then the courts should defer to that judgment. This can support the strict scrutiny requirement of a "compelling governmental interest."

The *Fisher* case, by contrast, focused more on the second prong of the "strict scrutiny" analysis. Holding that the appellate courts were correct to give the University deference when it came to the judgment that diversity was necessary to achieve its educational goals, the Supreme Court held that it was inappropriate to have given the University any deference in its judgment about how to go about achieving this diversity. The University must prove to the Court that the means it chose to attain diversity are "narrowly tailored to that goal." In this constitutional requirement, the University receives no deference at all. Part of the court's role in reviewing a race-conscious admissions policy is to determine whether such a policy is necessary to attain the diversity goal. According to *Fisher*, this requires a "careful judicial inquiry into whether a university could achieve sufficient diversity without using racial classifications." Before turning to racial classifications in its admissions, the University bears the ultimate burden of proving to the reviewing court that "available, workable race-neutral alternatives do not suffice." It is unclear how a university will satisfy this requirement, but it may need to prove to a court that it first unsuccessfully tried other methods of encouraging minority enrollment that did not involve considering race in admissions.

Since the appellate court deferred to the University's judgment that its racial classifications were necessary to achieve its diversity goals, the Supreme Court did not rule on whether the University of Texas admissions program was or was not constitutional. Instead, it sent the case back down to the appellate court to make the factual determination of whether the University had proved that its "program is narrowly tailored to obtain the educational benefits of diversity." In the time since this decision, the University has not changed its admissions program because it is continuing to defend it in court arguing that, because they are still short of their diversity goal, they have no other choice but to craft an admissions policy that takes race into account.

This case was decided by eight of the nine Supreme Court justices because Justice Elena Kagan recused herself, likely because of her involvement with the case when she was the Solicitor General. Justice Antonin Scalia agreed with the result but wrote a short separate opinion strongly suggesting that had the challenger in this case asked the Court to overrule *Grutter*'s holding that the goal of achieving the educational benefits of diversity could justify using racial preferences in admissions, he would have done so. Justice

Clarence Thomas wrote a more lengthy concurring opinion, flatly stating that precedent should be overruled and that any use of race in higher education admissions by a state entity "is categorically prohibited by the Equal Protection Clause" of the Fourteenth Amendment to the Constitution. Only Justice Ruth Bader Ginsburg dissented, writing that the University of Texas had already established that it satisfied even this new more rigorous formulation of the "narrowly tailored" standard.

IMPACT OF *FISHER* ON AN UPCOMING CASE

Court observers noted that only eight justices reviewed the *Fisher* case and that it took almost nine months to come to a decision, leading to speculation that the decision crafted a careful compromise necessary to break a stalemate with a number of justices who are willing to ban all forms of affirmative action. Attention is now turning to another case involving race in college admissions that the Court has already agreed to hear for its next term starting in October 2013.

This next case, *Schuette v. Coalition to Defend Affirmative Action*, also involves affirmative action in college admissions but in an entirely different context. In 2006, Michigan voters passed a ballot proposal amending their state constitution to include a flat ban on affirmative action. The amendment reads: "The state shall not discriminate against, or grant preferential treatment to any individual or group on the basis of race, sex, color, ethnicity, or national origin in the operation of public employment, public education or public contracting." The law was challenged by a coalition of groups and individuals interested in continuing the use of affirmative action in the admissions policies of universities in the state. The full Sixth Circuit Court of Appeals heard the case and ruled that the Michigan law was unconstitutional.

Unlike *Fisher*, which asked whether it violates the Equal Protection Clause of the Constitution for a university to use racial classifications in its admissions programs, this new case asks the opposite question. In *Schuette*, the Court will address the question of whether a ban on the use of racial classifications in college admissions can be unconstitutional. As in *Fisher*, the Court will be deciding this case with just eight justices because Justice Kagan will not be participating.

The *Fisher* decision was in many ways a victory for supporters of affirmative action because it continued the precedent of accepting racial diversity on college campuses as an important value, but, at the same time, it articulated a more rigorous standard of proof for universities hoping to use race-conscious admissions. This provided groups hoping to challenge college affirmative action plans with a new roadmap that is likely to trigger a wave of challenges across the country. Likewise, if the Court upholds the Michigan Constitution's ban on state affirmative action that was added through a voter referendum, this would provide another avenue to challenge affirmative action on a state-by-state basis.

—Melissa Feinberg

The following are excerpts from the U.S. Supreme Court ruling in Fisher v. University of Texas, *in which the Court ruled 7–1 to impose a higher level of scrutiny on affirmative action policies and sent the case back to the lower courts for another review.*

Fisher v. University of Texas

June 24, 2013

No. 11–345

Abigail Noel Fisher, Petitioner

v.

University of Texas at Austin et al.

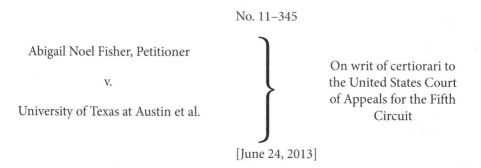

On writ of certiorari to
the United States Court
of Appeals for the Fifth
Circuit

[June 24, 2013]

[Footnotes have been omitted.]

JUSTICE KENNEDY delivered the opinion of the Court.

The University of Texas at Austin considers race as one of various factors in its undergraduate admissions process. Race is not itself assigned a numerical value for each applicant, but the University has committed itself to increasing racial minority enrollment on campus. It refers to this goal as a "critical mass." Petitioner, who is Caucasian, sued the University after her application was rejected. She contends that the University's use of race in the admissions process violated the Equal Protection Clause of the Fourteenth Amendment.

The parties asked the Court to review whether the judgment below was consistent with "this Court's decisions interpreting the Equal Protection Clause of the Fourteenth Amendment, including *Grutter* v. *Bollinger,* 539 U. S. 306 (2003)." Pet. for Cert. i. The Court concludes that the Court of Appeals did not hold the University to the demanding burden of strict scrutiny articulated in *Grutter* and *Regents of Univ. of Cal.* v. *Bakke,* 438 U. S. 265, 305 (1978) (opinion of Powell, J.). Because the Court of Appeals did not apply the correct standard of strict scrutiny, its decision affirming the District Court's grant of summary judgment to the University was incorrect. That decision is vacated, and the case is remanded for further proceedings.

I

A

. . . In recent years the University has used three different programs to evaluate candidates for admission. The first is the program it used for some years before 1997, when the University considered two factors: a numerical score reflecting an applicant's test scores and academic performance in high school (Academic Index or AI), and the applicant's race. In 1996, this system was held unconstitutional by the United States Court of Appeals for the

Fifth Circuit. It ruled the University's consideration of race violated the Equal Protection Clause because it did not further any compelling government interest. *Hopwood* v. *Texas,* 78 F. 3d 932, 955 (1996).

The second program was adopted to comply with the *Hopwood* decision. The University stopped considering race in admissions and substituted instead a new holistic metric of a candidate's potential contribution to the University, to be used in conjunction with the Academic Index. This "Personal Achievement Index" (PAI) measures a student's leadership and work experience, awards, extracurricular activities, community service, and other special circumstances that give insight into a student's background. These included growing up in a single-parent home, speaking a language other than English at home, significant family responsibilities assumed by the applicant, and the general socio-economic condition of the student's family. Seeking to address the decline in minority enrollment after *Hopwood,* the University also expanded its outreach programs.

The Texas State Legislature also responded to the *Hopwood* decision. It enacted a measure known as the Top Ten Percent Law, codified at Tex. Educ. Code Ann. §51.803 (West 2009). Also referred to as H. B. 588, the Top Ten Percent Law grants automatic admission to any public state college, including the University, to all students in the top 10% of their class at high schools in Texas that comply with certain standards.

The University's revised admissions process, coupled with the operation of the Top Ten Percent Law, resulted in a more racially diverse environment at the University. Before the admissions program at issue in this case, in the last year under the post-*Hopwood* AI/PAI system that did not consider race, the entering class was 4.5% African-American and 16.9% Hispanic. This is in contrast with the 1996 pre-*Hopwood* and Top Ten Percent regime, when race was explicitly considered, and the University's entering freshman class was 4.1% African-American and 14.5%Hispanic.

Following this Court's decisions in *Grutter* v. *Bollinger, supra,* and *Gratz* v. *Bollinger,* 539 U. S. 244 (2003), the University adopted a third admissions program, the 2004 program in which the University reverted to explicit consideration of race. This is the program here at issue. In *Grutter,* the Court upheld the use of race as one of many "plus factors" in an admissions program that considered the overall individual contribution of each candidate. In *Gratz,* by contrast, the Court held unconstitutional Michigan's undergraduate admissions program, which automatically awarded points to applicants from certain racial minorities.

The University's plan to resume race-conscious admissions was given formal expression in June 2004 in an internal document entitled Proposal to Consider Race and Ethnicity in Admissions (Proposal). Supp. App. 1a. The Proposal relied in substantial part on a study of a subset of undergraduate classes containing between 5 and 24 students. It showed that few of these classes had significant enrollment by members of racial minorities. In addition the Proposal relied on what it called "anecdotal" reports from students regarding their "interaction in the classroom." The Proposal concluded that the University lacked a "critical mass" of minority students and that to remedy the deficiency it was necessary to give explicit consideration to race in the undergraduate admissions program.

To implement the Proposal the University included a student's race as a component of the PAI score, beginning with applicants in the fall of 2004. The University asks students to classify themselves from among five predefined racial categories on the application. Race is not assigned an explicit numerical value, but it is undisputed that race is a meaningful factor. . . .

B

Among the Court's cases involving racial classifications in education, there are three decisions that directly address the question of considering racial minority status as a positive or favorable factor in a university's admissions process, with the goal of achieving the educational benefits of a more diverse student body: *Bakke*, 438 U. S. 265; *Gratz, supra*; and *Grutter*, 539 U. S. 306. We take those cases as given for purposes of deciding this case. We begin with the principal opinion authored by Justice Powell in *Bakke, supra*. In *Bakke*, the Court considered a system used by the medical school of the University of California at Davis. From an entering class of 100 students the school had set aside 16 seats for minority applicants. In holding this program impermissible under the Equal Protection Clause Justice Powell's opinion stated certain basic premises. First, "decisions based on race or ethnic origin by faculties and administrations of state universities are reviewable under the Fourteenth Amendment." *Id.*, at 287 (separate opinion). The principle of equal protection admits no "artificial line of a 'two-class theory'" that "permits the recognition of special wards entitled to a degree of protection greater than that accorded others." *Id.*, at 295. It is therefore irrelevant that a system of racial preferences in admissions may seem benign. Any racial classification must meet strict scrutiny, for when government decisions "touch upon an individual's race or ethnic background, he is entitled to a judicial determination that the burden he is asked to bear on that basis is precisely tailored to serve a compelling governmental interest." *Id.*, at 299.

Next, Justice Powell identified one compelling interest that could justify the consideration of race: the interest in the educational benefits that flow from a diverse student body. Redressing past discrimination could not serve as a compelling interest, because a university's "broad mission [of] education" is incompatible with making the "judicial, legislative, or administrative findings of constitutional or statutory violations" necessary to justify remedial racial classification. *Id.*, at 307–309.

The attainment of a diverse student body, by contrast, serves values beyond race alone, including enhanced classroom dialogue and the lessening of racial isolation and stereotypes. The academic mission of a university is "a special concern of the First Amendment." *Id.*, at 312. Part of "'the business of a university [is] to provide that atmosphere which is most conducive to speculation, experiment, and creation,'" and this in turn leads to the question of "'who may be admitted to study.'" *Sweezy v. New Hampshire*, 354 U. S. 234, 263 (1957) (Frankfurter, J., concurring in judgment).

Justice Powell's central point, however, was that this interest in securing diversity's benefits, although a permissible objective, is complex. "It is not an interest in simple ethnic diversity, in which a specified percentage of the student body is in effect guaranteed to be members of selected ethnic groups, with the remaining percentage an undifferentiated aggregation of students. The diversity that furthers a compelling state interest encompasses a far broader array of qualifications and characteristics of which racial or ethnic origin is but a single though important element." *Bakke*, 438 U. S., at 315 (separate opinion).

In *Gratz*, 539 U. S. 244, and *Grutter, supra*, the Court endorsed the precepts stated by Justice Powell. In *Grutter*, the Court reaffirmed his conclusion that obtaining the educational benefits of "student body diversity is a compelling state interest that can justify the use of race in university admissions." *Id.*, at 325.

As *Gratz* and *Grutter* observed, however, this follows only if a clear precondition is met: The particular admissions process used for this objective is subject to judicial review.

Race may not be considered unless the admissions process can withstand strict scrutiny. "Nothing in Justice Powell's opinion in *Bakke* signaled that a university may employ whatever means it desires to achieve the stated goal of diversity without regard to the limits imposed by our strict scrutiny analysis." *Gratz, supra,* at 275. "To be narrowly tailored, a race-conscious admissions program cannot use a quota system," *Grutter,* 539 U. S., at 334, but instead must "remain flexible enough to ensure that each applicant is evaluated as an individual and not in a way that makes an applicant's race or ethnicity the defining feature of his or her application," *id.,* at 337. Strict scrutiny requires the university to demonstrate with clarity that its "purpose or interest is both constitutionally permissible and substantial, and that its use of the classification is necessary . . . to the accomplishment of its purpose." *Bakke,* 438 U. S., at 305 (opinion of Powell, J.) (internal quotation marks omitted).

While these are the cases that most specifically address the central issue in this case, additional guidance maybe found in the Court's broader equal protection jurisprudence which applies in this context. "Distinctions between citizens solely because of their ancestry are by their very nature odious to a free people," *Rice v. Cayetano,* 528 U. S. 495, 517 (2000) (internal quotation marks omitted), and therefore "are contrary to our traditions and hence constitutionally suspect," *Bolling v. Sharpe,* 347 U. S. 497, 499 (1954). "'[B]ecause racial characteristics so seldom provide a relevant basis for disparate treatment,'" *Richmond v. J. A. Croson Co.,* 488 U. S. 469, 505 (1989) (quoting *Fullilove v. Klutznick,* 448 U. S. 448, 533–534 (1980) (Stevens, J., dissenting)), "the Equal Protection Clause demands that racial classifications . . . be subjected to the 'most rigid scrutiny.'" *Loving v. Virginia,* 388 U. S. 1, 11 (1967).

To implement these canons, judicial review must begin from the position that "any official action that treats a person differently on account of his race or ethnic origin is inherently suspect." *Fullilove, supra,* at 523 (Stewart, J., dissenting); *McLaughlin v. Florida,* 379 U. S. 184, 192 (1964). Strict scrutiny is a searching examination, and it is the government that bears the burden to prove "'that the reasons for any [racial] classification [are] clearly identified and unquestionably legitimate,'" *Croson, supra,* at 505 (quoting *Fullilove,* 448 *supra,* at 533–535 (Stevens, J., dissenting)).

II

Grutter made clear that racial "classifications are constitutional only if they are narrowly tailored to further compelling governmental interests." 539 U. S., at 326. And *Grutter* endorsed Justice Powell's conclusion in *Bakke* that "the attainment of a diverse student body . . . is a constitutionally permissible goal for an institution of higher education." 438 U. S., at 311–312 (separate opinion). Thus, under *Grutter,* strict scrutiny must be applied to any admissions program using racial categories or classifications.

According to *Grutter,* a university's "educational judgment that such diversity is essential to its educational mission is one to which we defer." 539 U. S., at 328. *Grutter* concluded that the decision to pursue "the educational benefits that flow from student body diversity," *id.,* at 330, that the University deems integral to its mission is, in substantial measure, an academic judgment to which some, but not complete, judicial deference is proper under *Grutter.* A court, of course, should ensure that there is a reasoned, principled explanation for the academic decision. On this point, the District Court and Court of Appeals were correct in finding that *Grutter* calls for deference to the University's conclusion, "'based on its experience and expertise,'" 631 F. 3d, at 230 (quoting 645 F. Supp. 2d 587, 603 (WD Tex. 2009)), that a diverse student body would serve its educational goals.

There is disagreement about whether *Grutter* was consistent with the principles of equal protection in approving this compelling interest in diversity. See *post*, at 1 (SCALIA, J., concurring); *post*, at 4–5 (THOMAS, J., concurring); *post*, at 1–2 (GINSBURG, J., dissenting). But the parties here do not ask the Court to revisit that aspect of *Grutter's* holding.

A university is not permitted to define diversity as "some specified percentage of a particular group merely because of its race or ethnic origin." *Bakke, supra*, at 307 (opinion of Powell, J.). "That would amount to outright racial balancing, which is patently unconstitutional." *Grutter, supra*, at 330. "Racial balancing is not transformed from 'patently unconstitutional' to a compelling state interest simply by relabeling it 'racial diversity.' " *Parents Involved in Community Schools* v. *Seattle School Dist. No. 1*, 551 U. S. 701, 732 (2007).

Once the University has established that its goal of diversity is consistent with strict scrutiny, however, there must still be a further judicial determination that the admissions process meets strict scrutiny in its implementation. The University must prove that the means chosen by the University to attain diversity are narrowly tailored to that goal. On this point, the University receives no deference. *Grutter* made clear that it is for the courts, not for university administrators, to ensure that "[t]he means chosen to accomplish the [government's] asserted purpose must be specifically and narrowly framed to accomplish that purpose." 539 U. S., at 333 (internal quotation marks omitted). True, a court can take account of a university's experience and expertise in adopting or rejecting certain admissions processes. But, as the Court said in *Grutter*, it remains at all times the University's obligation to demonstrate, and the Judiciary's obligation to determine, that admissions processes "ensure that each applicant is evaluated as an individual and not in a way that makes an applicant's race or ethnicity the defining feature of his or her application." *Id.*, at 337.

Narrow tailoring also requires that the reviewing court verify that it is "necessary" for a university to use race to achieve the educational benefits of diversity. *Bakke, supra*, at 305. This involves a careful judicial inquiry into whether a university could achieve sufficient diversity without using racial classifications. Although "[n]arrow tailoring does not require exhaustion of every *conceivable* race-neutral alternative," strict scrutiny does require a court to examine with care, and not defer to, a university's "serious, good faith consideration of workable race-neutral alternatives." See *Grutter*, 539 U. S., at 339–340 (emphasis added). Consideration by the university is of course necessary, but it is not sufficient to satisfy strict scrutiny: The reviewing court must ultimately be satisfied that no workable race-neutral alternatives would produce the educational benefits of diversity. If "'a nonracial approach . . . could promote the substantial interest about as well and at tolerable administrative expense,'" *Wygant* v. *Jackson Bd. of Ed.*, 476 U. S. 267, 280, n. 6 (1986) (quoting Greenawalt, Judicial Scrutiny of "Benign" Racial Preference in Law School Admissions, 75 Colum. L. Rev. 559, 578–579 (1975)), then the university may not consider race. A plaintiff, of course, bears the burden of placing the validity of a university's adoption of an affirmative action plan in issue. But strict scrutiny imposes on the university the ultimate burden of demonstrating, before turning to racial classifications, that available, workable race-neutral alternatives do not suffice.

Rather than perform this searching examination, however, the Court of Appeals held petitioner could challenge only "whether [the University's] decision to reintroduce race as a factor in admissions was made in good faith." 631 F. 3d, at 236. And in considering such a challenge, the court would "presume the University acted in good faith" and place on petitioner the burden of rebutting that presumption. *Id.,* at 231–232. The Court of Appeals held that to "second-guess the merits" of this aspect of the University's decision was a task it was "ill-equipped to perform" and that it would attempt only to "ensure that [the University's] decision to adopt a race-conscious admissions policy followed from [a process of] good faith consideration." *Id.,* at 231. The Court of Appeals thus concluded that "the narrow-tailoring inquiry—like the compelling interest inquiry—is undertaken with a degree of deference to the Universit[y]." *Id.,* at 232. Because "the efforts of the University have been studied, serious, and of high purpose," the Court of Appeals held that the use of race in the admissions program fell within "a constitutionally protected zone of discretion." *Id.,* at 231.

These expressions of the controlling standard are at odds with *Grutter's* command that "all racial classifications imposed by government 'must be analyzed by a reviewing court under strict scrutiny.' " 539 U. S., at 326 (quoting *Adarand Constructors, Inc.* v. *Peña,* 515 U. S. 200, 227 (1995)). In *Grutter,* the Court approved the plan at issue upon concluding that it was not a quota, was sufficiently flexible, was limited in time, and followed "serious, good faith consideration of workable race-neutral alternatives." 539 U. S., at 339. As noted above, see *supra,* at 1, the parties do not challenge, and the Court therefore does not consider, the correctness of that determination.

Grutter did not hold that good faith would forgive an impermissible consideration of race. It must be remembered that "the mere recitation of a 'benign' or legitimate purpose for a racial classification is entitled to little or no weight." *Croson,* 488 U. S., at 500. Strict scrutiny does not permit a court to accept a school's assertion that its admissions process uses race in a permissible way without a court giving close analysis to the evidence of how the process works in practice.

The higher education dynamic does not change the narrow tailoring analysis of strict scrutiny applicable in other contexts. "[T]he analysis and level of scrutiny applied to determine the validity of [a racial] classification do not vary simply because the objective appears acceptable. . . . While the validity and importance of the objective may affect the outcome of the analysis, the analysis itself does not change." *Mississippi Univ. for Women* v. *Hogan,* 458 U. S. 718, 724, n. 9 (1982).

The District Court and Court of Appeals confined the strict scrutiny inquiry in too narrow a way by deferring to the University's good faith in its use of racial classifications and affirming the grant of summary judgment on that basis. The Court vacates that judgment, but fairness to the litigants and the courts that heard the case requires that it be remanded so that the admissions process can be considered and judged under a correct analysis. See *Adarand, supra,* at 237. Unlike *Grutter,* which was decided after trial, this case arises from cross-motions for summary judgment. In this case, as in similar cases, in determining whether summary judgment in favor of the University would be appropriate, the Court of Appeals must assess whether the University has offered sufficient evidence that would prove that its admissions program is narrowly tailored to obtain the educational benefits of diversity. Whether this record—and not "simple . . . assurances of good intention," *Croson, supra,* at 500—is sufficient is a question for the Court of Appeals in the first instance.

* * *

Strict scrutiny must not be "'strict in theory, but fatal in act,'" *Adarand, supra,* at 237; see also *Grutter, supra,* at 326. But the opposite is also true. Strict scrutiny must not be strict in theory but feeble in fact. In order for judicial review to be meaningful, a university must make a showing that its plan is narrowly tailored to achieve the only interest that this Court has approved in this context: the benefits of a student body diversity that "encompasses a . . . broa[d] array of qualifications and characteristics of which racial or ethnic origin is but a single though important element." *Bakke,* 438 U. S., at 315 (opinion of Powell, J.). The judgment of the Court of Appeals is vacated, and the case is remanded for further proceedings consistent with this opinion.

It is so ordered.

JUSTICE KAGAN took no part in the consideration or decision of this case.

JUSTICE SCALIA, concurring.

I adhere to the view I expressed in *Grutter v. Bollinger:* "The Constitution proscribes government discrimination on the basis of race, and state-provided education is no exception." 539 U. S. 306, 349 (2003) (opinion concurring in part and dissenting in part). The petitioner in this case did not ask us to overrule *Grutter*'s holding that a "compelling interest" in the educational benefits of diversity can justify racial preferences in university admissions. Tr. of Oral Arg. 8–9. I therefore join the Court's opinion in full.

JUSTICE THOMAS, concurring.

I join the Court's opinion because I agree that the Court of Appeals did not apply strict scrutiny to the University of Texas at Austin's (University) use of racial discrimination in admissions decisions. *Ante,* at 1. I write separately to explain that I would overrule *Grutter* v. *Bollinger,* 539 U. S. 306 (2003), and hold that a State's use of race in higher education admissions decisions is categorically prohibited by the Equal Protection Clause. . . .

[The remainder of Justice Thomas' opinion has been omitted.]

JUSTICE GINSBURG, dissenting.

. . . I have several times explained why government actors, including state universities, need not be blind to the lingering effects of "an overtly discriminatory past," the legacy of "centuries of law-sanctioned inequality." *Id.,* at 298 (dissenting opinion). See also *Adarand Constructors, Inc.* v. *Peña,* 515 U. S. 200, 272–274 (1995) (dissenting opinion). Among constitutionally permissible options, I remain convinced, "those that candidly disclose their consideration of race [are] preferable to those that conceal it." *Gratz,* 539 U. S., at 305, n. 11 (dissenting opinion).

Accordingly, I would not return this case for a second look. . . . The University's admissions policy flexibly considers race only as a "factor of a factor of a factor of a factor" in the calculus, *id.,* at 608; followed a yearlong review through which the University reached the reasonable, good-faith judgment that supposedly race-neutral initiatives were insufficient to achieve, in appropriate measure, the educational benefits of student body diversity, see 631 F. 3d, at 225–226; and is subject to periodic review to ensure that the consideration of race remains necessary and proper to achieve the University's educational objectives, see *id.,* at 226. Justice Powell's opinion in *Bakke* and the Court's decision in *Grutter* require no further determinations. See *Grutter,* 539 U. S., at 333–343; *Bakke,* 438 U. S., at 315–320.

The Court rightly declines to cast off the equal protection framework settled in *Grutter*. See *ante,* at 5. Yet it stops short of reaching the conclusion that framework warrants. Instead, the Court vacates the Court of Appeals' judgment and remands for the Court of Appeals to "assess whether the University has offered sufficient evidence [to] prove that its admissions program is narrowly tailored to obtain the educational benefits of diversity." *Ante,* at 13. As I see it, the Court of Appeals has already completed that inquiry, and its judgment, trained on this Court's *Bakke* and *Grutter* pathmarkers, merits our approbation.

∗ ∗ ∗

For the reasons stated, I would affirm the judgment of the Court of Appeals.

SOURCE: U.S. Supreme Court. *Fisher v. University of Texas,* 570 U.S.__(2013). http://www.supreme court.gov/opinions/12pdf/11-345_l5gm.pdf.

OTHER HISTORIC DOCUMENTS OF INTEREST

FROM PREVIOUS *HISTORIC DOCUMENTS*

Supreme Court Rules on
Voting Rights Act

JUNE 25, 2013

On June 25, 2013, the United States Supreme Court struck down a central provision of the historic Voting Rights Act of 1965. The Voting Rights Act was a landmark piece of federal legislation designed to end the entrenched resistance of state officials to enforce the right to vote regardless of race. While the Act prohibits racial discrimination in voting in all states, it contains enforcement provisions that require special scrutiny of certain states that were singled out for their deep history of voter suppression. These states were required to get "preclearance" before changing their voting laws, that is, they had to obtain federal permission before enacting any law related to voting. The Supreme Court's divided opinion did not strike down the entire Act, but, instead, gutted the section that determined the nine states and multiple counties and municipalities in other states that were subject to the preclearance requirement. Chief Justice John Roberts, Jr., wrote that singling out some states was a "dramatic departure from the principle that all States enjoy equal sovereignty," but doing so had been nonetheless employed to address "an extraordinary problem." He continued, "Our country has changed and while any racial discrimination in voting is too much, Congress must ensure that the legislation it passes to remedy that problem speaks to current conditions."

This opinion did not explicitly strip the preclearance provision from the Voting Rights Act, but, by voiding the section that determines which states it applies to, the result was to effectively end the requirement. The Court's majority opinion invited Congress to come up with a new formula based on current conditions, but, until that happens, the practical result is an end to a remedy that has proved very successful in blocking discrimination. Within days of the decision, states that had been previously required to seek federal permission to change their voting laws had passed new election laws including stringent voter identification requirements that may, as a practical matter, disproportionately affect minority voters.

THE VOTING RIGHTS ACT

In 1870, in the aftermath of the Civil War, the Fifteenth Amendment to the Constitution was ratified. It guaranteed to all male citizens of the United States that their right to vote could not be denied "on account of race, color, or previous condition of servitude." Nearly one hundred years later, in many parts of the country, the promise of this amendment was unfulfilled. Many states, particularly in the South, had adopted laws specifically designed to prevent African Americans from voting. Discriminatory practices ranged from literacy tests and poll taxes to intimidation, threats, and violence. In the summer of 1964, a voting registration drive was launched in Mississippi, known as Freedom Summer, which sparked intense violence. Three young volunteers, including two college students and a local activist, were abducted and brutally killed by Klansmen in Philadelphia, Mississippi. These murders brought national media attention to the persecution of black voters in the Deep South for the first time. The media was there again the next year to witness the unprovoked attack by state troopers on peaceful voting rights marchers crossing the Edmund Pettus Bridge in Selma, Alabama, en route to the state capitol. National television coverage brought images of what became known as "Bloody Sunday" into living rooms across America. In response to events in Selma, President Lyndon Johnson spoke to the nation and promised to introduce a voting rights bill to Congress in a few days. Johnson said, "Americans everywhere join in deploring the brutality with which a number of Negro citizens of Alabama were treated when they sought to dramatize their deep and sincere interest in attaining the precious right to vote."

On August 6, 1965, President Johnson signed the Voting Rights Act into law. Currently, Section 2 of the Act forbids any "standard, practice, or procedure" that "results in a denial or abridgement of the right of any citizen of the United States to vote on account of race or color." Section 5 of the Act required certain parts of the country to obtain preclearance from the federal government for any changes to their election procedures whether minor changes like moving a polling place or major changes, such as redrawing electoral districts. Section 4 of the Act contained the formula for determining which states or political subdivisions were covered by Section 5. Originally, Section 4 swept in those that had "maintained a test or device as a prerequisite to voting as of November 1, 1964, and had less than 50 percent voter registration or turnout in the 1964 Presidential election." In 1975, Congress reauthorized the Act for seven more years and extended the Act's coverage to include jurisdictions that "had a voting test and less than a 50 percent voter registration or turnout as of 1972." In 1982, Congress reauthorized the Act for twenty-five more years without altering its coverage formula. Most recently, in 2006, Congress again reauthorized the Voting Rights Act for another twenty-five years without making any changes to Section 4's coverage formula. The reauthorization had overwhelming bipartisan backing in Congress where the vote was 98–0 in the Senate and 390–33 in the House. President George W. Bush signed the bill into law describing it as "an example of our continued commitment to a united America where every person is valued and treated with dignity and respect." As of June 2013, the Voting Rights Act required nine states—Alabama, Alaska, Arizona, Georgia, Louisiana, Mississippi, South Carolina, Texas, and Virginia—to get any new voting laws preapproved. A variety of other counties and municipalities in states such as California, Florida, New York, North Carolina, South Dakota, and Michigan were also subject to preclearance.

In 2012, Shelby County, Alabama, a largely white suburb of Birmingham, filed suit in federal court seeking a judgment that Sections 4 and 5 of the Voting Rights Act were unconstitutional. After Shelby County lost in the district and appellate courts, the Supreme Court agreed to hear the appeal of *Shelby County v. Holder*.

COURT INVALIDATES SECTION 4 OF VOTING RIGHTS ACT

The decision in this case divided the Court 5–4, squarely along its ideological divide. Chief Justice Roberts wrote the majority decision, joined by Justices Antonin Scalia, Anthony M. Kennedy, Clarence Thomas, and Samuel Alito, Jr., and ultimately held that it was unfair to continue to treat states differently based on "decades-old data" that references literacy tests and low voter registration and turnout from the 1960s and 1970s.

The Chief Justice agreed that, when it was enacted, the Voting Rights Act was the right response to "entrenched racial discrimination." But, "nearly 50 years later," Justice Roberts wrote, "things have changed dramatically." Discriminatory methods such as literacy tests and poll taxes have been outlawed nationwide for more than forty years, and much has changed in the states covered by Section 5 of the Voting Rights Act. The opinion quotes recent Census data indicating that in the 2012 election "African-American voter turnout exceeded white voter turnout in five of the six states originally covered by Section 5, with a gap in the sixth state of less than one half of one percent." He also cited voter registration rates approaching parity and record numbers of minority candidates holding office in the covered jurisdictions. In fact, both Selma, Alabama, and Philadelphia, Mississippi, the sites of infamous violence during the struggle for voting rights, are now governed by African American mayors. The Court acknowledged that there is "no doubt that these improvements are in large part *because of* the Voting Rights Act," which has "proved immensely successful at redressing racial discrimination and integrating the voting process." Because of these successes, the Court took issue when Congress in 2006 reauthorized the Voting Rights Act for another twenty-five years leaving Section 4's coverage formula untouched "as if nothing had changed." Because Congress instead "reenacted a formula based on 40-year-old facts having no logical relation to the present day," the coverage formula of the Voting Rights Act is no longer constitutional.

Justice Ruth Bader Ginsburg, signaling strong disagreement, read portions of her impassioned dissent from the bench, joined by Justices Stephen Breyer, Sonia Sotomayor, and Elena Kagan. Drawing different lessons from history than those drawn by the majority, she referenced Dr. Martin Luther King Jr. as she argued that justice requires "a steadfast commitment to see the task through to completion." She did not argue that the majority was wrong when it pointed to the success of the Voting Rights Act in eliminating the specific barriers to minority voting that were in use in 1965 but did not think these successes should demand its invalidation. The preclearance requirement has been "particularly effective," the dissent wrote, noting that between 1982 and 2006, the Justice Department had blocked over 700 voting changes in the covered states after determining that they were discriminatory, suggesting "that the state of voting rights in the covered jurisdictions would have been significantly different absent this remedy." The dissent also made the point that success in eliminating direct barriers to registration and turnout does not address "second-generation barriers" to minority voting. These are efforts to reduce the impact of minority votes through various barriers such as redrawing legislative districts to dilute the strength of minority voting, or adoption of at-large voting in cities with a sizable black minority. Congress, according to the dissent, considered these factors when it reauthorized the Voting Rights Act in 2006 after exhaustive evidence gathering and their judgment was due more respect. "The Court errs egregiously," Justice Ginsburg argued, "by overriding Congress' decision."

Consequences from Striking Down Preclearance Requirement

The impact of the *Shelby* decision was swift. Texas was in the process of appealing a federal ruling that rejected its proposed voter ID law, calling it "the most stringent in the country." A court panel also rejected Texas' proposed legislative redistricting maps after finding that they protected white incumbents and altered districts with minority incumbents. However, within hours of the Supreme Court's ruling, Texas Attorney General Greg Abbott announced that the state would enact both measures "immediately." Similarly, Delbert Hosemann, Mississippi's Secretary of State, announced that the Court's decision "removes requirements for Mississippi to travel through the expensive and time-consuming federal application process for any change to state, county, or municipal voting law," and he promised to move forward with his state's new voter ID law. Within a few months of the decision, seven states that previously had to seek preclearance announced new restrictive election laws.

The Justice Department can still sue states over their election practices under Section 2 of the Voting Rights Act, which prohibits racial discrimination in voting wherever it occurs; Section 2 was not impacted by *Shelby*. Before the Supreme Court's decision, states needing preclearance had to demonstrate that a proposed new voting law would not be discriminatory, but that burden has now shifted to the challenger who must prove that an existing law is discriminatory. The Justice Department has been actively pursuing this Section 2 strategy, filing lawsuits against Texas for its strict voter photo identification law and its 2011 redistricting laws and against North Carolina's changes to early voting and same-day registration. Attorney General Eric Holder explained his post-*Shelby* enforcement strategy in an announcement: "We will not allow the Supreme Court's recent decision to be interpreted as open season for states to pursue measures that suppress voting rights. The Department will take action against jurisdictions that attempt to hinder access to the ballot box, no matter where it occurs."

When *Shelby* was first announced, most commentators thought it was extremely unlikely that a highly polarized Congress would take up the Chief Justice's challenge to update the Voting Rights Act, but, on January 16, 2014, a bipartisan group of legislators introduced legislation titled the Voting Rights Amendment Act of 2014. This proposal introduced by Rep. Jim Sensenbrenner, R-Wis., Rep. John Conyers, D-Mich., and Sen. Patrick Leahy, D-Vt., contains a new coverage formula for Section 4, which would tie the preclearance requirement to current data. Among other changes, the new bill would require states with five or more recent Voting Rights Act violations in the past fifteen years to preclear any election changes with the federal government. The future of the bill is unclear, but its backers have expressed optimism. "We need to have hearings immediately, as soon as we can," said Conyers. "That's the best sign of good faith and bipartisanship."

—Melissa Feinberg

The following are excerpts from the U.S. Supreme Court ruling in Shelby County v. Holder, *in which the Court ruled 5–4 to strike down portions of the Voting Rights Act.*

DOCUMENT   *Shelby County v. Holder*

June 25, 2013

No. 12–96

Shelby County, Alabama, Petitioner

v.

Eric H. Holder, Jr., Attorney General, et al.

On writ of certiorari to the United States Court of Appeals for the District of Columbia Circuit

[June 25, 2013]

[Footnotes have been omitted.]

CHIEF JUSTICE ROBERTS delivered the opinion of the Court.

The Voting Rights Act of 1965 employed extraordinary measures to address an extraordinary problem. Section 5 of the Act required States to obtain federal permission before enacting any law related to voting—a drastic departure from basic principles of federalism. And §4 of the Act applied that requirement only to some States—an equally dramatic departure from the principle that all States enjoy equal sovereignty. This was strong medicine, but Congress determined it was needed to address entrenched racial discrimination in voting, "an insidious and pervasive evil which had been perpetuated in certain parts of our country through unremitting and ingenious defiance of the Constitution." *South Carolina* v. *Katzenbach,* 383 U. S. 301, 309 (1966). As we explained in upholding the law, "exceptional conditions can justify legislative measures not otherwise appropriate." *Id.,* at 334. Reflecting the unprecedented nature of these measures, they were scheduled to expire after five years. See Voting Rights Act of 1965, §4(a), 79 Stat. 438.

Nearly 50 years later, they are still in effect; indeed, they have been made more stringent, and are now scheduled to last until 2031. There is no denying, however, that the conditions that originally justified these measures no longer characterize voting in the covered jurisdictions. By 2009, "the racial gap in voter registration and turnout[was] lower in the States originally covered by §5 than it [was] nationwide." *Northwest Austin Municipal Util. Dist. No. One* v. *Holder,* 557 U. S. 193, 203–204 (2009). Since that time, Census Bureau data indicate that African-American voter turnout has come to exceed white voter turnout in five of the six States originally covered by §5, with a gap in the sixth State of less than one half of one percent. See Dept. of Commerce, Census Bureau, Reported Voting and Registration, by Sex, Race and Hispanic Origin, for States (Nov. 2012) (Table 4b).

At the same time, voting discrimination still exists; no one doubts that. The question is whether the Act's extraordinary measures, including its disparate treatment of the States, continue to satisfy constitutional requirements. As we put it a short time ago, "the Act imposes current burdens and must be justified by current needs." *Northwest Austin,* 557 U. S., at 203.

[Section I, containing background on the case and the Voting Rights Act, has been omitted.]

II

In *Northwest Austin,* we stated that "the Act imposes current burdens and must be justified by current needs." 557 U. S., at 203. And we concluded that "a departure from the fundamental principle of equal sovereignty requires a showing that a statute's disparate geographic coverage is sufficiently related to the problem that it targets." *Ibid.* These basic principles guide our review of the question before us.

[Part A, which details states rights contained in the Constitution, has been omitted.]

B

In 1966, we found these departures from the basic features of our system of government justified. The "blight of racial discrimination in voting" had "infected the electoral process in parts of our country for nearly a century." *Katzenbach,* 383 U. S., at 308. Several States had enacted a variety of requirements and tests "specifically designed to prevent" African-Americans from voting. *Id.,* at 310. Case-by-case litigation had proved inadequate to prevent such racial discrimination in voting, in part because States "merely switched to discriminatory devices not covered by the federal decrees," "enacted difficult new tests," or simply "defied and evaded court orders." *Id.,* at 314. Shortly before enactment of the Voting Rights Act, only 19.4 percent of African-Americans of voting age were registered to vote in Alabama, only 31.8 percent in Louisiana, and only 6.4 percent in Mississippi. *Id.,* at 313. Those figures were roughly 50 percentage points or more below the figures for whites. *Ibid.*

In short, we concluded that "[u]nder the compulsion of these unique circumstances, Congress responded in a permissibly decisive manner." *Id.,* at 334, 335. We also noted then and have emphasized since that this extraordinary legislation was intended to be temporary, set to expire after five years. *Id.,* at 333; *Northwest Austin, supra,* at 199.

At the time, the coverage formula—the means of linking the exercise of the unprecedented authority with the problem that warranted it—made sense. We found that "Congress chose to limit its attention to the geographic areas where immediate action seemed necessary." *Katzenbach,* 383 U. S., at 328. The areas where Congress found "evidence of actual voting discrimination" shared two characteristics: "the use of tests and devices for voter registration, and a voting rate in the 1964 presidential election at least 12 points below the national average." *Id.,* at 330. We explained that "[t]ests and devices are relevant to voting discrimination because of their long history as a tool for perpetrating the evil; a low voting rate is pertinent for the obvious reason that widespread disenfranchisement must inevitably affect the number of actual voters." *Ibid.* We therefore concluded that "the coverage formula [was] rational in both practice and theory." *Ibid.* It accurately reflected those jurisdictions uniquely characterized by voting discrimination "on a pervasive scale," linking coverage to the devices used to effectuate discrimination and to the resulting disenfranchisement. *Id.,* at 308. The formula ensured that the "stringent remedies [were] aimed at areas where voting discrimination ha[d] been most flagrant." *Id.,* at 315.

C

Nearly 50 years later, things have changed dramatically. Shelby County contends that the preclearance requirement, even without regard to its disparate coverage, is now unconstitutional. Its arguments have a good deal of force. In the covered jurisdictions, "[v]oter turnout and registration rates now approach parity. Blatantly discriminatory evasions of federal decrees are rare. And minority candidates hold office at unprecedented levels." *Northwest Austin,* 557 U. S., at 202. The tests and devices that blocked access to the ballot have been forbidden nationwide for over 40 years. See §6, 84 Stat. 315; §102, 89 Stat. 400.

Those conclusions are not ours alone. Congress said the same when it reauthorized the Act in 2006, writing that "[s]ignificant progress has been made in eliminating first generation barriers experienced by minority voters, including increased numbers of registered minority voters, minority voter turnout, and minority representation in Congress, State legislatures, and local elected offices." §2(b)(1), 120 Stat. 577. The House Report elaborated that "the number of African-Americans who are registered and who turn out to cast ballots has increased significantly over the last 40 years, particularly since 1982," and noted that "[i]n some circumstances, minorities register to vote and cast ballots at levels that surpass those of white voters." H. R. Rep. No. 109–478, p. 12 (2006). That Report also explained that there have been "significant increases in the number of African-Americans serving in elected offices"; more specifically, there has been approximately a 1,000 percent increase since 1965 in the number of African-American elected officials in the six States originally covered by the Voting Rights Act. *Id.,* at 18 . . . *[table omitted]*

The 2004 figures come from the Census Bureau. Census Bureau data from the most recent election indicate that African-American voter turnout exceeded white voter turnout in five of the six States originally covered by §5, with a gap in the sixth State of less than one half of one percent. See Dept. of Commerce, Census Bureau, Reported Voting and Registration, by Sex, Race and Hispanic Origin, for States (Table 4b). The preclearance statistics are also illuminating. In the first decade after enactment of §5, the Attorney General objected to 14.2 percent of proposed voting changes. H. R Rep. No. 109–478, at 22. In the last decade before reenactment, the Attorney General objected to a mere 0.16 percent. S. Rep. No. 109–295, at 13.

There is no doubt that these improvements are in large part *because of* the Voting Rights Act. The Act has proved immensely successful at redressing racial discrimination and integrating the voting process. See §2(b)(1), 120 Stat. 577. During the "Freedom Summer" of 1964, in Philadelphia, Mississippi, three men were murdered while working in the area to register African-American voters. See *United States* v. *Price,* 383 U. S. 787, 790 (1966). On "Bloody Sunday" in 1965, in Selma, Alabama, police beat and used tear gas against hundreds marching in support of African-American enfranchisement. See *Northwest Austin, supra,* at 220, n. 3 (THOMAS, J., concurring in judgment in part and dissenting in part). Today both of those towns are governed by African-American mayors. Problems remain in these States and others, but there is no denying that, due to the Voting Rights Act, our Nation has made great strides.

Yet the Act has not eased the restrictions in §5 or narrowed the scope of the coverage formula in §4(b) along the way. Those extraordinary and unprecedented features were reauthorized—as if nothing had changed. In fact, the Act's unusual remedies have grown even stronger. When Congress reauthorized the Act in 2006, it did so for another 25 years on top of the previous 40—a far cry from the initial five-year period. See 42 U. S. C. §1973b(a)(8). Congress also expanded the prohibitions in §5. . . .

Respondents do not deny that there have been improvements on the ground, but argue that much of this can be attributed to the deterrent effect of §5, which dissuades covered jurisdictions from engaging in discrimination that they would resume should §5 be struck down. Under this theory, however, §5 would be effectively immune from scrutiny; no matter how "clean" the record of covered jurisdictions, the argument could always be made that it was deterrence that accounted for the good behavior.

The provisions of §5 apply only to those jurisdictions singled out by §4. We now consider whether that coverage formula is constitutional in light of current conditions.

III

A

When upholding the constitutionality of the coverage formula in 1966, we concluded that it was "rational in both practice and theory." *Katzenbach,* 383 U. S., at 330. The formula looked to cause (discriminatory tests) and effect (low voter registration and turnout), and tailored the remedy (preclearance) to those jurisdictions exhibiting both.

By 2009, however, we concluded that the "coverage formula raise[d] serious constitutional questions." *Northwest Austin*, 557 U. S., at 204. As we explained, a statute's "current burdens" must be justified by "current needs," and any "disparate geographic coverage" must be "sufficiently related to the problem that it targets." *Id.,* at 203. The coverage formula met that test in 1965, but no longer does so.

Coverage today is based on decades-old data and eradicated practices. The formula captures States by reference to literacy tests and low voter registration and turnout in the 1960s and early 1970s. But such tests have been banned nationwide for over 40 years. §6, 84 Stat. 315; §102, 89 Stat. 400. And voter registration and turnout numbers in the covered States have risen dramatically in the years since. H. R. Rep. No. 109-478, at 12. Racial disparity in those numbers was compelling evidence justifying the preclearance remedy and the coverage formula. See, *e.g., Katzenbach, supra,* at 313, 329–330. There is no longer such a disparity.

In 1965, the States could be divided into two groups: those with a recent history of voting tests and low voter registration and turnout, and those without those characteristics. Congress based its coverage formula on that distinction. Today the Nation is no longer divided along those lines, yet the Voting Rights Act continues to treat it as if it were.

B

. . . The Government falls back to the argument that because the formula was relevant in 1965, its continued use is permissible so long as any discrimination remains in the States Congress identified back then—regardless of how that discrimination compares to discrimination in States unburdened by coverage. Brief for Federal Respondent 49–50. This argument does not look to "current political conditions," *Northwest Austin, supra,* at 203, but instead relies on a comparison between the States in 1965. That comparison reflected the different histories of the North and South. It was in the South that slavery was upheld by law until uprooted by the Civil War, that the reign of Jim Crow denied African-Americans the most basic freedoms, and that state and local governments worked tirelessly to disenfranchise citizens on the basis of race. The Court invoked that history—rightly so— in sustaining the disparate coverage of the Voting Rights Act in 1966. . . .

But history did not end in 1965. By the time the Act was reauthorized in 2006, there had been 40 more years of it. In assessing the "current need[]" for a preclearance system that treats States differently from one another today, that history cannot be ignored. During that time, largely because of the Voting Rights Act, voting tests were abolished, disparities in voter registration and turnout due to race were erased, and African-Americans attained political office in record numbers. And yet the coverage formula that Congress reauthorized in 2006 ignores these developments, keeping the focus on decades-old data relevant to decades-old problems, rather than current data reflecting current needs.

The Fifteenth Amendment commands that the right to vote shall not be denied or abridged on account of race or color, and it gives Congress the power to enforce that command. The Amendment is not designed to punish for the past; its purpose is to ensure a better future. See *Rice* v. *Cayetano*, 528 U. S. 495, 512 (2000) ("Consistent with the design of the Constitution, the [Fifteenth] Amendment is cast in fundamental terms, terms transcending the particular controversy which was the immediate impetus for its enactment."). To serve that purpose, Congress—if it is to divide the States—must identify those jurisdictions to be singled out on a basis that makes sense in light of current conditions. It cannot rely simply on the past. . . .

C

In defending the coverage formula, the Government, the intervenors, and the dissent also rely heavily on data from the record that they claim justify disparate coverage. Congress compiled thousands of pages of evidence before reauthorizing the Voting Rights Act. The court below and the parties have debated what that record shows—they have gone back and forth about whether to compare covered to noncovered jurisdictions as blocks, how to disaggregate the data State by State, how to weigh §2 cases as evidence of ongoing discrimination, and whether to consider evidence not before Congress, among other issues. Compare, *e.g.,* 679 F. 3d, at 873–883 (case below), with *id.,* at 889–902 (Williams, J., dissenting). Regardless of how to look at the record, however, no one can fairly say that it shows anything approaching the "pervasive," "flagrant," "widespread," and "rampant" discrimination that faced Congress in 1965, and that clearly distinguished the covered jurisdictions from the rest of the Nation at that time. *Katzenbach, supra,* at 308, 315, 331; *Northwest Austin,* 557 U. S., at 201.

But a more fundamental problem remains: Congress did not use the record it compiled to shape a coverage formula grounded in current conditions. It instead reenacted a formula based on 40-year-old facts having no logical relation to the present day. The dissent relies on "second generation barriers," which are not impediments to the casting of ballots, but rather electoral arrangements that affect the weight of minority votes. That does not cure the problem. Viewing the preclearance requirements as targeting such efforts simply highlights the irrationality of continued reliance on the §4 coverage formula, which is based on voting tests and access to the ballot, not vote dilution. We cannot pretend that we are reviewing an updated statute, or try our hand at updating the statute ourselves, based on the new record compiled by Congress. Contrary to the dissent's contention, see *post,* at 23, we are not ignoring the record; we are simply recognizing that it played no role in shaping the statutory formula before us today.

The dissent also turns to the record to argue that, in light of voting discrimination in Shelby County, the county cannot complain about the provisions that subject it to preclearance. *Post,* at 23–30. But that is like saying that a driver pulled over pursuant to a policy of stopping all redheads cannot complain about that policy, if it turns out his license has expired. Shelby County's claim is that the coverage formula here is unconstitutional in all its applications, because of how it selects the jurisdictions subjected to preclearance. The county was selected based on that formula, and may challenge it in court.

[Part D, refuting the defense, has been omitted.]

* * *

Striking down an Act of Congress "is the gravest and most delicate duty that this Court is called on to perform." *Blodgett* v. *Holden,* 275 U. S. 142, 148 (1927) (Holmes, J., concurring). We do not do so lightly. That is why, in 2009, we took care to avoid ruling on the constitutionality of the Voting Rights Act when asked to do so, and instead resolved the case then before us on statutory grounds. But in issuing that decision, we expressed our broader concerns about the constitutionality of the Act. Congress could have updated the coverage formula at that time, but did not do so. Its failure to act leaves us today with no choice but to declare §4(b) unconstitutional. The formula in that section can no longer be used as a basis for subjecting jurisdictions to preclearance.

Our decision in no way affects the permanent, nationwide ban on racial discrimination in voting found in §2. We issue no holding on §5 itself, only on the coverage formula. Congress may draft another formula based on current conditions. Such a formula is an initial prerequisite to a determination that exceptional conditions still exist justifying such an "extraordinary departure from the traditional course of relations between the States and the Federal Government." *Presley*, 502 U. S., at 500–501. Our country has changed, and while any racial discrimination in voting is too much, Congress must ensure that the legislation it passes to remedy that problem speaks to current conditions.

The judgment of the Court of Appeals is reversed.

It is so ordered.

JUSTICE THOMAS, concurring.

I join the Court's opinion in full but write separately to explain that I would find §5 of the Voting Rights Act unconstitutional as well.

[The remainder of Justice Thomas' concurring opinion has been omitted.]

JUSTICE GINSBURG, with whom JUSTICE BREYER, JUSTICE SOTOMAYOR, and JUSTICE KAGAN join, dissenting.

In the Court's view, the very success of §5 of the Voting Rights Act demands its dormancy. Congress was of another mind. Recognizing that large progress has been made, Congress determined, based on a voluminous record, that the scourge of discrimination was not yet extirpated. The question this case presents is who decides whether, as currently operative, §5 remains justifiable, this Court, or a Congress charged with the obligation to enforce the post-Civil War Amendments "by appropriate legislation." With overwhelming support in both Houses, Congress concluded that, for two prime reasons, §5 should continue in force, unabated. First, continuance would facilitate completion of the impressive gains thus far made; and second, continuance would guard against backsliding. Those assessments were well within Congress' province to make and should elicit this Court's unstinting approbation.

I

"[V]oting discrimination still exists; no one doubts that." *Ante*, at 2. But the Court today terminates the remedy that proved to be best suited to block that discrimination. The Voting Rights Act of 1965 (VRA) has worked to combat voting discrimination where other remedies had been tried and failed. Particularly effective is the VRA's requirement of federal preclearance for all changes to voting laws in the regions of the country with the most aggravated records of rank discrimination against minority voting rights.

A century after the Fourteenth and Fifteenth Amendments guaranteed citizens the right to vote free of discrimination on the basis of race, the "blight of racial discrimination in voting" continued to "infec[t] the electoral process in parts of our country." *South Carolina v. Katzenbach*, 383 U. S. 301, 308 (1966). Early attempts to cope with this vile infection resembled battling the Hydra. Whenever one form of voting discrimination was identified and prohibited, others sprang up in its place. This Court repeatedly encountered the remarkable "variety and persistence" of laws disenfranchising minority citizens. *Id.*, at 311. To take just one example, the Court, in 1927, held unconstitutional a Texas law barring black voters from participating in primary elections, *Nixon v. Herndon*, 273 U. S. 536, 541; in 1944, the Court struck down a "reenacted" and slightly altered version of the same law, *Smith v. Allwright*, 321 U. S. 649, 658; and in 1953, the Court once again confronted an attempt by Texas to "circumven[t]" the Fifteenth Amendment by adopting yet another variant of the all-white primary, *Terry v. Adams*, 345 U. S. 461, 469.

During this era, the Court recognized that discrimination against minority voters was a quintessentially political problem requiring a political solution. As Justice Holmes explained: If "the great mass of the white population intends to keep the blacks from voting," "relief from [that] great political wrong, if done, as alleged, by the people of a State and the State itself, must be given by them or by the legislative and political department of the government of the United States." *Giles v. Harris*, 189 U. S. 475, 488 (1903).

Congress learned from experience that laws targeting particular electoral practices or enabling case-by-case litigation were inadequate to the task. In the Civil Rights Acts of 1957, 1960, and 1964, Congress authorized and then expanded the power of "the Attorney General to seek injunctions against public and private interference with the right to vote on racial grounds." *Katzenbach*, 383 U. S., at 313. But circumstances reduced the ameliorative potential of these legislative Acts:

"Voting suits are unusually onerous to prepare, sometimes requiring as many as 6,000 man-hours spent combing through registration records in preparation for trial. Litigation has been exceedingly slow, in part because of the ample opportunities for delay afforded voting officials and others involved in the proceedings. Even when favorable decisions have finally been obtained, some of the States affected have merely switched to discriminatory devices not covered by the federal decrees or have enacted difficult new tests designed to prolong the existing disparity between white and Negro registration. Alternatively, certain local officials have defied and evaded court orders or have simply closed their registration offices to freeze the voting rolls." *Id.*, at 314 (footnote omitted).

Patently, a new approach was needed.

Answering that need, the Voting Rights Act became one of the most consequential, efficacious, and amply justified exercises of federal legislative power in our Nation's history. Requiring federal preclearance of changes in voting laws in the covered jurisdictions—those States and localities where opposition to the Constitution's commands were most virulent—the VRA provided a fit solution for minority voters as well as for States. Under the preclearance regime established by §5 of the VRA, covered jurisdictions must submit proposed changes in voting laws or procedures to the Department of Justice (DOJ), which has 60 days to respond to the changes. 79 Stat. 439, codified at 42 U. S. C. §1973c(a). A change will be approved unless DOJ finds it has "the purpose [or] . . . the effect of denying or abridging the right to vote on account of race or color." *Ibid.* In the alternative, the covered jurisdiction may seek approval by a three-judge District Court in the District of Columbia.

After a century's failure to fulfill the promise of the Fourteenth and Fifteenth Amendments, passage of the VRA finally led to signal improvement on this front. "The Justice Department estimated that in the five years after [the VRA's] passage, almost as many blacks registered [to vote] in Alabama, Mississippi, Georgia, Louisiana, North Carolina, and South Carolina as in the entire century before 1965." Davidson, The Voting

Rights Act: A Brief History, in Controversies in Minority Voting 7, 21 (B. Grofman & C. Davidson eds. 1992). And in assessing the overall effects of the VRA in 2006, Congress found that "[s]ignificant progress has been made in eliminating first generation barriers experienced by minority voters, including increased numbers of registered minority voters, minority voter turnout, and minority representation in Congress, State legislatures, and local elected offices. This progress is the direct result of the Voting Rights Act of 1965." Fannie Lou Hamer, Rosa Parks, and Coretta Scott King Voting Rights Act Reauthorization and Amendments Act of 2006 (hereinafter 2006 Reauthorization), §2(b)(1), 120 Stat. 577. On that matter of cause and effects there can be no genuine doubt.

Although the VRA wrought dramatic changes in the realization of minority voting rights, the Act, to date, surely has not eliminated all vestiges of discrimination against the exercise of the franchise by minority citizens. Jurisdictions covered by the preclearance requirement continued to submit, in large numbers, proposed changes to voting laws that the Attorney General declined to approve, auguring that barriers to minority voting would quickly resurface were the preclearance remedy eliminated. *City of Rome v. United States*, 446 U. S. 156, 181 (1980). Congress also found that as "registration and voting of minority citizens increas[ed], other measures may be resorted to which would dilute increasing minority voting strength." *Ibid.* (quoting H. R. Rep. No. 94–196, p. 10 (1975)). See also *Shaw v. Reno*, 509 U. S. 630, 640 (1993) ("[I]t soon became apparent that guaranteeing equal access to the polls would not suffice to root out other racially discriminatory voting practices" such as voting dilution). Efforts to reduce the impact of minority votes, in contrast to direct attempts to block access to the ballot, are aptly described as "second-generation barriers" to minority voting.

Second-generation barriers come in various forms. One of the blockages is racial gerrymandering, the redrawing of legislative districts in an "effort to segregate the races for purposes of voting." *Id.*, at 642. Another is adoption of a system of at-large voting in lieu of district-by-district voting in a city with a sizable black minority. By switching to at-large voting, the overall majority could control the election of each city council member, effectively eliminating the potency of the minority's votes. Grofman & Davidson, The Effect of Municipal Election Structure on Black Representation in Eight Southern States, in Quiet Revolution in the South 301, 319 (C. Davidson & B. Grofman eds. 1994) (hereinafter Quiet Revolution). A similar effect could be achieved if the city engaged in discriminatory annexation by incorporating majority white areas into city limits, thereby decreasing the effect of VRA-occasioned increases in black voting. Whatever the device employed, this Court has long recognized that vote dilution, when adopted with a discriminatory purpose, cuts down the right to vote as certainly as denial of access to the ballot. Shaw, 509 U. S., at 640–641; *Allen v. State Bd. of Elections*, 393 U. S. 544, 569 (1969); *Reynolds v. Sims*, 377 U. S. 533, 555 (1964). See also H. R. Rep. No.109–478, p. 6 (2006) (although "[d]iscrimination today is more subtle than the visible methods used in 1965," "the effect and results are the same, namely a diminishing of the minority community's ability to fully participate in the electoral process and to elect their preferred candidates").

In response to evidence of these substituted barriers, Congress reauthorized the VRA for five years in 1970, for seven years in 1975, and for 25 years in 1982. *Ante*, at 4–5. Each time, this Court upheld the reauthorization as a valid exercise of congressional power. *Ante*, at 5. As the 1982 reauthorization approached its 2007 expiration date, Congress again considered whether the VRA's preclearance mechanism remained an appropriate response to the problem of voting discrimination in covered jurisdictions.

Congress did not take this task lightly. Quite the opposite. The 109th Congress that took responsibility for the renewal started early and conscientiously. In October 2005, the House began extensive hearings, which continued into November and resumed in March 2006. S. Rep. No. 109–295, p. 2 (2006). In April 2006, the Senate followed suit, with hearings of its own. *Ibid.* In May 2006, the bills that became the VRA's reauthorization were introduced in both Houses. *Ibid.* The House held further hearings of considerable length, as did the Senate, which continued to hold hearings into June and July. H. R. Rep. 109–478, at 5; S. Rep. 109–295, at 3–4. In mid-July, the House considered and rejected four amendments, then passed the reauthorization by a vote of 390 yeas to 33 nays. 152 Cong. Rec. H5207 (July 13, 2006); Persily, The Promise and Pitfalls of the New Voting Rights Act, 117 Yale L. J. 174, 182–183 (2007) (hereinafter Persily). The bill was read and debated in the Senate, where it passed by a vote of 98 to 0. 152 Cong. Rec. S8012 (July 20, 2006). President Bush signed it a week later, on July 27, 2006, recognizing the need for "further work . . . in the fight against injustice," and calling the reauthorization "an example of our continued commitment to a united America where every person is valued and treated with dignity and respect." 152 Cong. Rec. S8781 (Aug. 3, 2006).

In the long course of the legislative process, Congress "amassed a sizable record." *Northwest Austin Municipal Util. Dist. No. One v. Holder,* 557 U. S. 193, 205 (2009). See also 679 F. 3d 848, 865–873 (CADC 2012) (describing the "extensive record" supporting Congress' determination that "serious and widespread intentional discrimination persisted in covered jurisdictions"). The House and Senate Judiciary Committees held 21 hearings, heard from scores of witnesses, received a number of investigative reports and other written documentation of continuing discrimination in covered jurisdictions. In all, the legislative record Congress compiled filled more than 15,000 pages. H. R. Rep. 109–478, at 5, 11–12; S. Rep. 109–295, at 2–4, 15. The compilation presents countless "examples of flagrant racial discrimination" since the last reauthorization; Congress also brought to light systematic evidence that "intentional racial discrimination in voting remains so serious and widespread in covered jurisdictions that section 5 preclearance is still needed." 679 F. 3d, at 866.

After considering the full legislative record, Congress made the following findings: The VRA has directly caused significant progress in eliminating first-generation barriers to ballot access, leading to a marked increase in minority voter registration and turnout and the number of minority elected officials. 2006 Reauthorization §2(b)(1). But despite this progress, "second generation barriers constructed to prevent minority voters from fully participating in the electoral process" continued to exist, as well as racially polarized voting in the covered jurisdictions, which increased the political vulnerability of racial and language minorities in those jurisdictions. §§2(b)(2)–(3), 120 Stat. 577. Extensive "[e]vidence of continued discrimination," Congress concluded, "clearly show[ed] the continued need for Federal oversight" in covered jurisdictions.§§2(b)(4)–(5), *id.,* at 577–578. The overall record demonstrated to the federal lawmakers that, "without the continuation of the Voting Rights Act of 1965 protections, racial and language minority citizens will be deprived of the opportunity to exercise their right to vote, or will have their votes diluted, undermining the significant gains made by minorities in the last 40 years." §2(b)(9), *id.,* at 578.

Based on these findings, Congress reauthorized preclearance for another 25 years, while also undertaking to reconsider the extension after 15 years to ensure that the provision was still necessary and effective. 42 U. S. C. §1973b(a)(7), (8) (2006 ed., Supp. V). The question before the Court is whether Congress had the authority under the Constitution to act as it did.

II

In answering this question, the Court does not write on a clean slate. It is well established that Congress' judgment regarding exercise of its power to enforce the Fourteenth and Fifteenth Amendments warrants substantial deference. The VRA addresses the combination of race discrimination and the right to vote, which is "preservative of all rights." *Yick Wo v. Hopkins*, 118 U. S. 356, 370 (1886). When confronting the most constitutionally invidious form of discrimination, and the most fundamental right in our democratic system, Congress' power to act is at its height....

It cannot tenably be maintained that the VRA, an Act of Congress adopted to shield the right to vote from racial discrimination, is inconsistent with the letter or spirit of the Fifteenth Amendment, or any provision of the Constitution read in light of the Civil War Amendments. Nowhere in today's opinion, or in *Northwest Austin*, is there clear recognition of the transformative effect the Fifteenth Amendment aimed to achieve. Notably, "the Founders' first successful amendment told Congress that it could 'make no law' over a certain domain"; in contrast, the Civil War Amendments used "language [that] authorized transformative new federal statutes to uproot all vestiges of unfreedom and inequality" and provided "sweeping enforcement powers . . . to enact 'appropriate' legislation targeting state abuses.'"...

In summary, the Constitution vests broad power in Congress to protect the right to vote, and in particular to combat racial discrimination in voting. This Court has repeatedly reaffirmed Congress' prerogative to use any rational means in exercise of its power in this area. And both precedent and logic dictate that the rational-means test should be easier to satisfy, and the burden on the statute's challenger should be higher, when what is at issue is the reauthorization of a remedy that the Court has previously affirmed, and that Congress found, from contemporary evidence, to be working to advance the legislature's legitimate objective.

[The remainder of Section III, and most of Section IV, containing a review of Congressional actions and blocked voting laws, and additional discussion about the majority's opinion, have been omitted.]

The sad irony of today's decision lies in its utter failure to grasp why the VRA has proven effective. The Court appears to believe that the VRA's success in eliminating the specific devices extant in 1965 means that preclearance is no longer needed. *Ante*, at 21–22, 23–24. With that belief, and the argument derived from it, history repeats itself. The same assumption—that the problem could be solved when particular methods of voting discrimination are identified and eliminated—was indulged and proved wrong repeatedly prior to the VRA's enactment. Unlike prior statutes, which singled out particular tests or devices, the VRA is grounded in Congress' recognition of the "variety and persistence" of measures designed to impair minority voting rights. *Katzenbach*, 383 U. S., at 311; *supra*, at 2. In truth, the evolution of voting discrimination into more subtle second-generation barriers is powerful evidence that a remedy as effective as preclearance remains vital to protect minority voting rights and prevent backsliding.

Beyond question, the VRA is no ordinary legislation. It is extraordinary because Congress embarked on a mission long delayed and of extraordinary importance: to realize the purpose and promise of the Fifteenth Amendment. For a half century, a concerted effort has been made to end racial discrimination in voting. Thanks to the Voting Rights Act, progress once the subject of a dream has been achieved and continues to be made.

The record supporting the 2006 reauthorization of the VRA is also extraordinary. It was described by the Chairman of the House Judiciary Committee as "one of the most extensive considerations of any piece of legislation that the United States Congress has dealt with in the 27½ years" he had served in the House. 152 Cong. Rec. H5143 (July 13, 2006) (statement of Rep. Sensenbrenner).

After exhaustive evidence-gathering and deliberative process, Congress reauthorized the VRA, including the coverage provision, with overwhelming bipartisan support. It was the judgment of Congress that "40 years has not been a sufficient amount of time to eliminate the vestiges of discrimination following nearly 100 years of disregard for the dictates of the 15th amendment and to ensure that the right of all citizens to vote is protected as guaranteed by the Constitution." 2006 Reauthorization §2(b)(7), 120 Stat. 577. That determination of the body empowered to enforce the Civil War Amendments "by appropriate legislation" merits this Court's utmost respect. In my judgment, the Court errs egregiously by overriding Congress' decision.

* * *

For the reasons stated, I would affirm the judgment of the Court of Appeals.

SOURCE: U.S. Supreme Court. *Shelby County v. Holder,* 570 U.S. __(2013). http://www.supremecourt.gov/opinions/12pdf/12-96_6k47.pdf.

OTHER HISTORIC DOCUMENTS OF INTEREST

FROM PREVIOUS *HISTORIC DOCUMENTS*

Supreme Court Rules on
Same-Sex Marriage

JUNE 26, 2013

On the same day that the Supreme Court struck down a key section of the Defense of Marriage Act (DOMA), it also released another decision with a profound impact on same-sex marriage. In *Hollingsworth v. Perry*, the Court dismissed an appeal to a federal district court ruling that California's Proposition 8 is unconstitutional. The Supreme Court's opinion was based on technical grounds and did not address the constitutionality of the proposition's definition of marriage as the union of a man and woman, deciding instead that private parties did not have the necessary standing to defend the state antigay marriage law in federal court when the state government officials had chosen not to appeal. For same-sex couples in California, however, this was a momentous decision because it meant there was no one who was willing or able to appeal the lower court's invalidation of Proposition 8, leaving that decision in place. Within a few weeks, California was again able to issue marriage licenses to same-sex couples. Although the case created no new sweeping law on gay marriage, after years of litigation during which same-sex couples in California gained and then lost, and then gained and lost again the right to marry, supporters were nonetheless jubilant as California became the thirteenth state to legalize gay marriage.

Like the ruling on DOMA, this decision was 5–4, but with a different makeup of justices. Chief Justice John Roberts, Jr., wrote the decision that the private group that had been behind the voter initiative known as Proposition 8 had no standing to defend it in federal court. He was joined by Justices Antonin Scalia, Ruth Bader Ginsburg, Stephen Breyer, and Elena Kagan. Justice Anthony Kennedy wrote a dissent that was joined by Justices Clarence Thomas, Samuel Alito, Jr., and Sonia Sotomayor, in which he worried that the majority's ruling gave too much power to public officials to nullify the results of voter initiatives with which they disagree.

THE SHIFTING STATUS OF GAY MARRIAGE IN CALIFORNIA

California's supporters and opponents of same-sex marriage alike have celebrated successes and suffered defeats over the past decade as the focus of the debate has ping-ponged from voter initiatives to state court to federal court and back again.

In a series of cases originally arising from a challenge to a voter initiative in 2000, on May 15, 2008, the California Supreme Court declared that limiting marriage to opposite-sex couples while denying it to same-sex couples violated the Equal Protection clause of the California State Constitution. All California counties were required to issue marriage licenses to same-sex couples. The celebration of gay marriage supporters, however, was short-lived. Later that year, after one of the most expensive ballot measure campaigns in U.S. history, California voters passed a voter-initiated referendum banning same-sex marriage with 52.3 percent of the vote. Known as Proposition 8, this referendum amended the

California Constitution for the explicit purpose of overturning the California Supreme Court's finding of a right to gay marriage. Proposition 8 says in its entirety, "Only marriage between a man and a woman is valid or recognized in California." During the almost five months between the California Supreme Court ruling and the passage of Proposition 8, approximately 18,000 same-sex couples had married. On May 26, 2009, the California Supreme Court upheld the validity of Proposition 8 against a procedural challenge. While this ruling left undisturbed the marriages that had taken place during the window in which they were legal, it banned any new same-sex marriages.

A year later, an unlikely pairing of attorneys, David Boies and former U.S. Solicitor General Theodore B. Olson, best known for facing off in *Bush v. Gore*, the ballot recount case that determined the outcome of the 2000 presidential election, brought a federal court challenge to Proposition 8. The case was brought on behalf of two same-sex couples, one male and one female, who wanted to marry and who challenged the constitutionality of the ballot initiative. The complaint named as defendants the California Attorney General, now Governor Jerry Brown, then-Governor Arnold Schwarzenegger, and various other state and local officials responsible for enforcing California's marriage laws. Those officials refused, however, to defend the law in court, although they continued to enforce it. The district court allowed Protect Marriage, the group that had successfully sponsored the voter initiative, to defend it during the trial.

On August 4, 2010, federal District Court Judge Vaughn Walker struck down Proposition 8 after the first trial in federal court examining whether states can legally prohibit same-sex couples from marrying. In a major victory for gay rights supporters, the judge ruled that the voter-enacted ban on same-sex marriage violated both the Due Process and Equal Protection provisions of the Fourteenth Amendment to the U.S. Constitution. His decision ordered California officials not to enforce Proposition 8, but this order was put on hold during the appeal.

California's governor and other officials declined to appeal the district court judgment, so the citizen group Protect Marriage appealed it to the Ninth Circuit Court of Appeals, which in turn sent a single question to the California Supreme Court: "whether official proponents of a ballot initiative have authority to assert the State's interest in defending the constitutionality of the initiative when public officials refuse to do so." The California Supreme Court answered in the affirmative, and the case proceeded in the Ninth Circuit that, relying on that answer, concluded that the petitioner had standing under federal law to defend the constitutionality of Proposition 8.

The Ninth Circuit proceeded to address the merits of the case, and it agreed with the district court judge that Proposition 8 was unconstitutional. In the Court's view, Proposition 8 violated the Equal Protection Clause because it served no purpose "but to impose on gays and lesbians, through the public law, a majority's private disapproval of them and their relationships."

The United States Supreme Court agreed to hear the appeal and asked the parties to also brief and argue "whether the petitioners have standing under Article III of the Constitution."

Case Decided on Jurisdiction Grounds

Article III of the United States Constitution confines the power of the federal courts to decide actual "cases" or "controversies." An important aspect of this requirement is that only people with the standing to do so may bring a case in federal court. To have standing, a litigant must have "suffered a concrete and particularized injury." That injury must be "fairly traceable to the challenged conduct," and a favorable decision by the court must "redress" that injury. The desire to vindicate the constitutional validity of a generally applicable law when the relief sought will not tangibly benefit the seeker any more than anyone else does not state an Article III case or controversy. This standing doctrine serves important interests in our system of separated powers because it prevents the judiciary from weighing in on generalized disputes that belong more properly to the political branches.

Chief Justice Roberts's majority opinion addressed whether the official proponents of Proposition 8 had the standing to defend that measure in court when the state's officials refused to do so. He determined that they do not have the necessary "personal stake" that distinguishes them from "the general interest of every citizen of California." Being merely a concerned bystander, no matter how strong the commitment, cannot satisfy standing requirements. "We have never before upheld the standing of a private party to defend the constitutionality of a state statute when state officials have chosen not to," Chief Justice Roberts concluded. "We decline to do so for the first time here."

The Court's decision vacated the judgments of the Appeals Court, leaving in place the federal district court decision that had invalidated Proposition 8.

When compared to the highly personal underlying issues of marriage and sexuality, this resolution may seem dry and highly technical; however, the decision does establish a new principle of constitutional law that will have an impact well beyond this case. Justice Anthony M. Kennedy, writing in a dissent that was joined by an unusual pairing of conservative Justices Thomas and Alito, and liberal Justice Sotomayor, objects that the majority opinion "has implications for the 26 other States that use an initiative or popular referendum system and which, like California, may choose to have initiative proponents stand in for the State when public officials decline to defend an initiative in litigation." Justice Kennedy accused the majority of failing to grasp the basic premise of initiatives and popular referendums, which provide the people of a state with a mechanism to bypass elected officials and exercise their own inherent sovereign right to govern themselves. According to the dissent, the majority opinion frustrates the very idea of the public referendum by returning the power to state officials who can, by refusing to defend an initiative, render it moot. He would have let the California Supreme Court define, under California law, the authority of a proponent to appear in court and assert the state's interest when public officials have refused to do so.

After the Decision

Within hours of the *Perry* ruling, Governor Brown announced, "I have directed the California Department of Public Health to advise the state's counties that they must begin issuing marriage licenses to same-sex couples in California as soon as the Ninth Circuit confirms the stay is lifted." Seven weeks later, the California Supreme Court, in a brief order with no dissents, refused a motion to reinstate Proposition 8, thus lifting the final legal roadblock to legal same-sex marriage and making California the thirteenth and largest state to legalize gay marriage.

Although it left in place the district court's previous ruling that Proposition 8 was unconstitutional, the Supreme Court's decision expressed no opinion on the ultimate question of whether a ban on same-sex marriage violates the Constitution. This did not stop Boies, one of the attorneys fighting Proposition 8, from reading into the Court's two decisions, *Hollingsworth v. Perry* and *United States v. Windsor*, a willingness to do so in the future. "When that case comes," Boies predicted, "marriage equality will be the law of the land."

—Melissa Feinberg

The following are excerpts from the U.S. Supreme Court ruling in Hollingsworth v. Perry, *in which the Court ruled 5–4 to dismiss a challenge brought against California's Proposition 8, determining that the petitioners had no standing to defend it in federal court.*

DOCUMENT   *Hollingsworth v. Perry*

June 26, 2013

No. 12–144

Hollingsworth, et al., Petitioners

v.

Kristin M. Perry, et al

}

On writ of certiorari to
the United States Court
of Appeals for the Ninth
Circuit

[June 26, 2013]

[Footnotes have been omitted.]

CHIEF JUSTICE ROBERTS delivered the opinion of the Court.

The public is currently engaged in an active political debate over whether same-sex couples should be allowed to marry. That question has also given rise to litigation. In this case, petitioners, who oppose same-sex marriage, ask us to decide whether the Equal Protection Clause "prohibits the State of California from defining marriage as the union of a man and a woman." Pet. for Cert. i. Respondents, same-sex couples who wish to marry, view the issue in somewhat different terms: For them, it is whether California—having previously recognized the right of same-sex couples to marry—may reverse that decision through a referendum.

Federal courts have authority under the Constitution to answer such questions only if necessary to do so in the course of deciding an actual "case" or "controversy." As used in the Constitution, those words do not include every sort of dispute, but only those "historically viewed as capable of resolution through the judicial process." *Flast* v. *Cohen,* 392 U. S. 83, 95 (1968). This is an essential limit on our power: It ensures that we act *as judges,* and do not engage in policymaking properly left to elected representatives.

For there to be such a case or controversy, it is not enough that the party invoking the power of the court have a keen interest in the issue. That party must also have "standing," which requires, among other things, that it have suffered a concrete and particularized injury. Because we find that petitioners do not have standing, we have no authority to decide this case on the merits, and neither did the Ninth Circuit.

[Section I, containing background information on the case, has been omitted.]

II

Article III of the Constitution confines the judicial power of federal courts to deciding actual "Cases" or "Controversies." §2. One essential aspect of this requirement is that any person invoking the power of a federal court must demonstrate standing to do so. This requires the litigant to prove that he has suffered a concrete and particularized injury that is fairly traceable to the challenged conduct, and is likely to be redressed by a favorable judicial decision. *Lujan* v. *Defenders of Wildlife,* 504 U. S. 555, 560–561 (1992). In other words, for a federal court to have authority under the Constitution to settle a dispute, the party before it must seek a remedy for a personal and tangible harm. "The presence of a disagreement, however sharp and acrimonious it may be, is insufficient by itself to meet Art. III's requirements." *Diamond, supra,* at 62.

The doctrine of standing, we recently explained, "serves to prevent the judicial process from being used to usurp the powers of the political branches." *Clapper* v. *Amnesty Int'l USA,* 568 U. S. ___, ___ (2013) (slip op., at 9). In light of this "overriding and time-honored concern about keeping the Judiciary's power within its proper constitutional sphere, we must put aside the natural urge to proceed directly to the merits of [an] important dispute and to 'settle' it for the sake of convenience and efficiency." *Raines* v. *Byrd,* 521 U. S. 811, 820 (1997) (footnote omitted).

Most standing cases consider whether a plaintiff has satisfied the requirement when filing suit, but Article III demands that an "actual controversy" persist throughout all stages of litigation. *Already, LLC* v. *Nike, Inc.,* 568 U. S. ___, ___ (2013) (slip op., at 4) (internal quotation marks omitted). That means that standing "must be met by persons seeking appellate review, just as it must be met by persons appearing in courts of first instance." *Arizonans for Official English* v. *Arizona,* 520 U. S. 43, 64 (1997). We therefore must decide whether petitioners had standing to appeal the District Court's order.

Respondents initiated this case in the District Court against the California officials responsible for enforcing Proposition 8. The parties do not contest that respondents had Article III standing to do so. Each couple expressed a desire to marry and obtain "official sanction" from the State, which was unavailable to them given the declaration in Proposition 8 that "marriage" in California is solely between a man and a woman. App. 59.

After the District Court declared Proposition 8 unconstitutional and enjoined the state officials named as defendants from enforcing it, however, the inquiry under Article III changed. Respondents no longer had any injury to redress—they had won—and the state officials chose not to appeal.

The only individuals who sought to appeal that order were petitioners, who had intervened in the District Court. But the District Court had not ordered them to do or refrain from doing anything. To have standing, a litigant must seek relief for an injury that affects him in a "personal and individual way." *Defenders of Wildlife, supra,* at 560, n. 1. He must possess a "direct stake in the outcome" of the case. *Arizonans for Official*

English, supra, at 64 (internal quotation marks omitted). Here, however, petitioners had no "direct stake" in the outcome of their appeal. Their only interest in having the District Court order reversed was to vindicate the constitutional validity of a generally applicable California law.

We have repeatedly held that such a "generalized grievance," no matter how sincere, is insufficient to confer standing. A litigant "raising only a generally available grievance about government—claiming only harm to his and every citizen's interest in proper application of the Constitution and laws, and seeking relief that no more directly and tangibly benefits him than it does the public at large—does not state an Article III case or controversy." *Defenders of Wildlife, supra,* at 573–574; see *Lance v. Coffman,* 549 U. S. 437, 439 (2007) (*per curiam*) ("Our refusal to serve as a forum for generalized grievances has a lengthy pedigree."); *Allen v. Wright,* 468 U. S. 737, 754 (1984) ("an asserted right to have the Government act in accordance with law is not sufficient, standing alone, to confer jurisdiction on a federal court"); *Massachusetts v. Mellon,* 262 U. S. 447, 488 (1923) ("The party who invokes the [judicial] power must be able to show . . . that he has sustained or is immediately in danger of sustaining some direct injury . . . and not merely that he suffers in some indefinite way in common with people generally.").

Petitioners argue that the California Constitution and its election laws give them a "'unique,' 'special,' and 'distinct' role in the initiative process—one 'involving both authority and responsibilities that differ from other supporters of the measure.'" Reply Brief 5 (quoting 52 Cal. 4th, at 1126, 1142, 1160, 265 P. 3d, at 1006, 1017–1018, 1030). True enough—but only when it comes to the process of enacting the law. Upon submitting the proposed initiative to the attorney general, petitioners became the official "proponents" of Proposition 8. Cal. Elec. Code Ann. §342 (West 2003). As such, they were responsible for collecting the signatures required to qualify the measure for the ballot. §§9607–9609. After those signatures were collected, the proponents alone had the right to file the measure with election officials to put it on the ballot.§9032. Petitioners also possessed control over the arguments in favor of the initiative that would appear in California's ballot pamphlets. §§9064, 9065, 9067, 9069.

But once Proposition 8 was approved by the voters, the measure became "a duly enacted constitutional amendment or statute." 52 Cal. 4th, at 1147, 265 P. 3d, at 1021. Petitioners have no role—special or otherwise—in the enforcement of Proposition 8. See *id.,* at 1159, 265 P. 3d, at 1029 (petitioners do not "possess any official authority . . . to directly enforce the initiative measure in question"). They therefore have no "personal stake" in defending its enforcement that is distinguishable from the general interest of every citizen of California. *Defenders of Wildlife, supra,* at 560–561.

Article III standing "is not to be placed in the hands of 'concerned bystanders,' who will use it simply as a 'vehicle for the vindication of value interests.'" *Diamond,* 476 U. S., at 62. No matter how deeply committed petitioners may be to upholding Proposition 8 or how "zealous [their] advocacy," *post,* at 4 (KENNEDY, J., dissenting), that is not a "particularized" interest sufficient to create a case or controversy under Article III. *Defenders of Wildlife,* 504 U. S., at 560, and n. 1; see *Arizonans for Official English,* 520 U.S., at 65 ("Nor has this Court ever identified initiative proponents as Article-III-qualified defenders of the measures they advocated."); *Don't Bankrupt Washington Committee v. Continental Ill. Nat. Bank & Trust Co. of Chicago,* 460 U. S. 1077 (1983) (summarily dismissing, for lack of standing, appeal by an initiative proponent from a decision holding the initiative unconstitutional).

III

A

Without a judicially cognizable interest of their own, petitioners attempt to invoke that of someone else. They assert that even if *they* have no cognizable interest in appealing the District Court's judgment, the State of California does, and they may assert that interest on the State's behalf. It is, however, a "fundamental restriction on our authority" that "[i]n the ordinary course, a litigant must assert his or her own legal rights and interests, and cannot rest a claim to relief on the legal rights or interests of third parties." *Powers* v. *Ohio*, 499 U. S. 400, 410 (1991). There are "certain, limited exceptions" to that rule. *Ibid.* But even when we have allowed litigants to assert the interests of others, the litigants themselves still "must have suffered an injury in fact, thus giving [them] a sufficiently concrete interest in the outcome of the issue in dispute." *Id.,* at 411 (internal quotation marks omitted).

In *Diamond* v. *Charles*, for example, we refused to allow Diamond, a pediatrician engaged in private practice in Illinois, to defend the constitutionality of the State's abortion law. In that case, a group of physicians filed a constitutional challenge to the Illinois statute in federal court. The State initially defended the law, and Diamond, a professed "conscientious object[or] to abortions," intervened to defend it alongside the State. 476 U. S., at 57–58.

After the Seventh Circuit affirmed a permanent injunction against enforcing several provisions of the law, the State chose not to pursue an appeal to this Court. But when Diamond did, the state attorney general filed a "'letter of interest,'" explaining that the State's interest in the proceeding was "'essentially co-terminous with the position on the issues set forth by [Diamond].'" *Id.,* at 61. That was not enough, we held, to allow the appeal to proceed. As the Court explained, "[e]ven if there were circumstances in which a private party would have standing to defend the constitutionality of a challenged statute, this [was] not one of them," because Diamond was not able to assert an injury in fact of his own. *Id.,* at 65 (footnote omitted). And without "any judicially cognizable interest," Diamond could not "maintain the litigation abandoned by the State." *Id.,* at 71.

For the reasons we have explained, petitioners have likewise not suffered an injury in fact, and therefore would ordinarily have no standing to assert the State's interests.

B

Petitioners contend that this case is different, because the California Supreme Court has determined that they are "authorized under California law to appear and assert the state's interest" in the validity of Proposition 8. 52 Cal. 4th, at 1127, 265 P. 3d, at 1007. The court below agreed: "All a federal court need determine is that the state has suffered a harm sufficient to confer standing and that the party seeking to invoke the jurisdiction of the court is authorized by the state to represent its interest in remedying that harm." 671 F. 3d, at 1072. As petitioners put it, they "need no more show a personal injury, separate from the State's indisputable interest in the validity of its law, than would California's Attorney General or did the legislative leaders held to have standing in *Karcher* v. *May,* 484 U. S. 72 (1987)." Reply Brief 6. . . .

The point of *Karcher* is not that a State could authorize *private parties* to represent its interests; Karcher and Orechio were permitted to proceed only because they were state officers, acting in an official capacity. As soon as they lost that capacity, they lost standing. Petitioners here hold no office and have always participated in this litigation solely as private parties.

[Additional information on the Court's reliance on earlier case decisions has been omitted.]

IV

The dissent eloquently recounts the California Supreme Court's reasons for deciding that state law authorizes petitioners to defend Proposition 8. See *post,* at 3–5. We do not "disrespect[ ]" or "disparage[ ]" those reasons. *Post,* at 12. Nor do we question California's sovereign right to maintain an initiative process, or the right of initiative proponents to defend their initiatives in California courts, where Article III does not apply. But as the dissent acknowledges, see *post,* at 1, standing in federal court is a question of federal law, not state law. And no matter its reasons, the fact that a State thinks a private party should have standing to seek relief for a generalized grievance cannot override our settled law to the contrary.

The Article III requirement that a party invoking the jurisdiction of a federal court seek relief for a personal, particularized injury serves vital interests going to the role of the Judiciary in our system of separated powers. "Refusing to entertain generalized grievances ensures that . . . courts exercise power that is judicial in nature," *Lance,* 549 U. S., at 441, and ensures that the Federal Judiciary respects "the proper—and properly limited—role of the courts in a democratic society," *DaimlerChrysler Corp.* v. *Cuno,* 547 U. S. 332, 341 (2006) (internal quotation marks omitted). States cannot alter that role simply by issuing to private parties who otherwise lack standing a ticket to the federal courthouse.

* * *

We have never before upheld the standing of a private party to defend the constitutionality of a state statute when state officials have chosen not to. We decline to do so for the first time here.

Because petitioners have not satisfied their burden to demonstrate standing to appeal the judgment of the District Court, the Ninth Circuit was without jurisdiction to consider the appeal. The judgment of the Ninth Circuit is vacated, and the case is remanded with instructions to dismiss the appeal for lack of jurisdiction.

It is so ordered.

JUSTICE KENNEDY, with whom JUSTICE THOMAS, JUSTICE ALITO, and JUSTICE SOTOMAYOR join, dissenting.

The Court's opinion is correct to state, and the Supreme Court of California was careful to acknowledge, that a proponent's standing to defend an initiative in federal court is a question of federal law. Proper resolution of the justiciability question requires, in this case, a threshold determination of state law. The state-law question is how California defines and elaborates the status and authority of an initiative's proponents who seek to intervene in court to defend the initiative after its adoption by the electorate. Those state-law issues have been addressed in a meticulous and unanimous opinion by the Supreme Court of California.

Under California law, a proponent has the authority to appear in court and assert the State's interest in defending an enacted initiative when the public officials charged with that duty refuse to do so. The State deems such an appearance essential to the integrity of its initiative process. Yet the Court today concludes that this state-defined status and this state-conferred right fall short of meeting federal requirements because the proponents cannot point to a formal delegation of authority that tracks the requirements of the Restatement of Agency. But the State Supreme Court's definition of proponents' powers is binding on this Court. And that definition is fully sufficient to establish the standing and adversity that are requisites for justiciability under Article III of the United States Constitution.

In my view Article III does not require California, when deciding who may appear in court to defend an initiative on its behalf, to comply with the Restatement of Agency or with this Court's view of how a State should make its laws or structure its government. The Court's reasoning does not take into account the fundamental principles or the practical dynamics of the initiative system in California, which uses this mechanism to control and to bypass public officials—the same officials who would not defend the initiative, an injury the Court now leaves unremedied. The Court's decision also has implications for the 26 other States that use an initiative or popular referendum system and which, like California, may choose to have initiative proponents stand in for the State when public officials decline to defend an initiative in litigation. See M. Waters, Initiative and Referendum Almanac 12 (2003). In my submission, the Article III requirement for a justiciable case or controversy does not prevent proponents from having their day in court.

[Section I, containing background on the case, has been omitted.]

II

A

The Court concludes that proponents lack sufficient ties to the state government. It notes that they "are not elected," "answer to no one," and lack "'a fiduciary obligation'" to the State. *Ante*, at 15 (quoting 1 Restatement (Third) of Agency §1.01, Comments e, f (2005)). But what the Court deems deficiencies in the proponents' connection to the State government, the State Supreme Court saw as essential qualifications to defend the initiative system. The very object of the initiative system is to establish a lawmaking process that does not depend upon state officials. In California, the popular initiative is necessary to implement "the theory that all power of government ultimately resides in the people." 52 Cal. 4th, at 1140, 265 P. 3d, at 1016 (internal quotation marks omitted). The right to adopt initiatives has been described by the California courts as "one of the most precious rights of [the State's] democratic process." *Ibid.* (internal quotation marks omitted). That historic role for the initiative system "grew out of dissatisfaction with the then governing public officials and a widespread belief that the people had lost control of the political process." *Ibid.* The initiative's "primary purpose," then, "was to afford the people the ability to propose and to adopt constitutional amendments or statutory provisions that their elected public officials had refused or declined to adopt." *Ibid.*

The California Supreme Court has determined that this purpose is undermined if the very officials the initiative process seeks to circumvent are the only parties who can defend an enacted initiative when it is challenged in a legal proceeding. See *id.*, at 1160, 265 P. 3d, at 1030; cf. *Alaskans for a Common Language, supra,* at 914 (noting that proponents must be allowed to defend an enacted initiative in order to avoid the perception, correct or not, "that the interests of [the proponents] were not being defended vigorously by the executive branch"). Giving the Governor and attorney general this de facto veto will erode one of the cornerstones of the State's governmental structure. See 52 Cal. 4th, at 1126–1128, 265 P. 3d, at 1006– 1007. And in light of the frequency with which initiatives' opponents resort to litigation, the impact of that veto could be substantial. K. Miller, Direct Democracy and the Courts 106 (2009) (185 of the 455 initiatives approved in Arizona, California, Colorado, Oregon, and Washington between 1900 and 2008 were challenged in court). As a consequence, California finds it necessary to vest the responsibility and right to defend a voter-approved initiative in the initiative's proponents when the State Executive declines to do so.

Yet today the Court demands that the State follow the Restatement of Agency. See *ante*, at 15–16. There are reasons, however, why California might conclude that a conventional agency relationship is inconsistent with the history, design, and purpose of the initiative process. The State may not wish to associate itself with proponents or their views outside of the "extremely narrow and limited" context of this litigation, 52 Cal. 4th, at 1159, 265 P. 3d, at 1029, or to bear the cost of proponents' legal fees. The State may also wish to avoid the odd conflict of having a formal agent of the State (the initiative's proponent) arguing in favor of a law's validity while state officials (e.g., the attorney general) contend in the same proceeding that it should be found invalid.

Furthermore, it is not clear who the principal in an agency relationship would be. It would make little sense if it were the Governor or attorney general, for that would frustrate the initiative system's purpose of circumventing elected officials who fail or refuse to effect the public will. *Id.*, at 1139–1140, 265 P. 3d, at 1016. If there is to be a principal, then, it must be the people of California, as the ultimate sovereign in the State. See *ibid.*, 265 P. 3d, at 1015–1016 (quoting Cal. Const., Art. II, §1) ("'All political power is inherent in the people'"). But the Restatement may offer no workable example of an agent representing a principal composed of nearly 40 million residents of a State. Cf. 1 Restatement (Second) of Agency, p. 2, Scope Note (1957) (noting that the Restatement "does not state the special rules applicable to public officers"); 1 Restatement (First) of Agency, p. 4, Scope Note (1933) (same).

And if the Court's concern is that the proponents are unaccountable, that fear is neither well founded nor sufficient to overcome the contrary judgment of the State Supreme Court. It must be remembered that both elected officials and initiative proponents receive their authority to speak for the State of California directly from the people. The Court apparently believes that elected officials are acceptable "agents" of the State, see *ante*, at 11–12, but they are no more subject to ongoing supervision of their principal—i.e., the people of the State—than are initiative proponents. At most, a Governor or attorney general can be recalled or voted out of office in a subsequent election, but proponents, too, can have their authority terminated or their initiative overridden by a subsequent ballot measure. Finally, proponents and their attorneys, like all other litigants and counsel who appear before a federal court, are subject to duties of candor, decorum, and respect for the tribunal and co-parties alike, all of which guard against the possibility that initiative proponents will somehow fall short of the appropriate standards for federal litigation.

B

Contrary to the Court's suggestion, this Court's precedents do not indicate that a formal agency relationship is necessary. In *Karcher v. May*, 484 U. S. 72 (1987), the Speaker of the New Jersey Assembly (Karcher) and President of the New Jersey Senate (Orechio) intervened in support of a school moment-of-silence law that the State's Governor and attorney general declined to defend in court. In considering the question of standing, the Court looked to New Jersey law to determine whether Karcher and Orechio "had authority under state law to represent the State's interest in both the District Court and Court of Appeals." *Id.*, at 82. The Court concluded that they did. Because the "New Jersey Supreme Court ha[d] granted applications of the Speaker of the General Assembly and the President of the Senate to intervene as parties respondent on behalf of the legislature in defense of a legislative enactment," the *Karcher* Court held that standing had been proper in the District Court and Court of Appeals. *Ibid.* By the time the case arrived in this Court, Karcher and Orechio had lost their presiding legislative offices, without which they lacked the authority to represent the State under New Jersey law. This, the Court held, deprived them of standing. *Id.*, at 81. Here, by contrast, proponents' authority under California law is not contingent on officeholder status, so their standing is unaffected by the fact that they "hold no office" in California's Government. *Ante*, at 12.

Arizonans for Official English v. Arizona, 520 U. S. 43 (1997), is consistent with the premises of this dissent, not with the rationale of the Court's opinion. See *ante*, at 13–14. There, the Court noted its serious doubts as to the aspiring defenders' standing because there was "no Arizona law appointing initiative sponsors as agents of the people of Arizona to defend, in lieu of public officials, the constitutionality of initiatives made law of the State." 520 U. S., at 65. The Court did use the word "agents"; but, read in context, it is evident that the Court's intention was not to demand a formal agency relationship in compliance with the Restatement. Rather, the Court used the term as shorthand for a party whom "state law authorizes" to "represent the State's interests" in court. *Ibid.*

Both the Court of Appeals and the Supreme Court of California were mindful of these precedents and sought to comply with them. The state court, noting the importance of *Arizonans for Official English*, expressed its understanding that "the high court's doubts as to the official initiative proponents' standing in that case were based, at least in substantial part, on the fact that the court was not aware of any 'Arizona law appointing initiative sponsors as agents of the people of Arizona to defend . . . the constitutionality of initiatives made law of the State.'" 52 Cal. 4th, at 1136–1137, 265 P. 3d, at 1013–1014 (quoting 520 U. S., at 65). Based on this passage, it concluded that "nothing in [*Arizonans for Official English*] indicates that if a state's law does authorize the official proponents of an initiative to assert the state's interest in the validity of a challenged state initiative when the public officials who ordinarily assert that interest have declined to do so, the proponents would not have standing to assert the state's interest in the initiative's validity in a federal lawsuit." *Id.*, at 1137, 265 P. 3d, at 1014.

The Court of Appeals, too, was mindful of this requirement. *Perry v. Brown*, 671 F. 3d 1052, 1072–1073 (CA9 2012). Although that panel divided on the proper resolution of the merits of this case, it was unanimous in concluding that proponents satisfy the requirements of Article III. Compare *id.*, at 1070–1075 (majority opinion), with *id.*, at 1096–1097 (N. R. Smith, J., concurring in part and dissenting in part). Its central premise, ignored by the Court today, was that the "State's highest court [had] held that California law provides precisely what the *Arizonans* Court found lacking in Arizona law: it confers on the official proponents of an initiative the authority to assert the State's interests in defending the constitutionality of that initiative, where state officials who would ordinarily assume that responsibility choose not to do so." *Id.*, at 1072 (majority opinion). The Court of Appeals and the State Supreme Court did not ignore *Arizonans for Official English*; they were faithful to it.

C

The Court's approach in this case is also in tension with other cases in which the Court has permitted individuals to assert claims on behalf of the government or others. For instance, Federal Rule of Criminal Procedure 42(a)(2) allows a court to appoint a private attorney to investigate and prosecute potential instances of criminal contempt. Under the Rule, this special prosecutor is not the agent of the appointing judge; indeed, the prosecutor's "determination of which persons should be targets of the investigation, what methods of investigation should be used, what information will be sought as evidence," whom to charge, and other "decisions . . . critical to the conduct of a prosecution, are all made outside the supervision of the court." *Young v. United States ex rel. Vuitton et Fils S. A.*, 481 U. S. 787, 807 (1987). Also, just as proponents have been authorized to represent the State of California, "'[p]rivate attorneys appointed to prosecute a criminal contempt action represent the United States,'" *United States v. Providence Journal Co.*, 485 U. S. 693, 700 (1988). They are "appointed solely to pursue the public interest in vindication of the court's authority," *Young, supra*, at 804, an interest that—like California's interest in the validity of its laws—is "unique to the sovereign," *Providence Journal Co., supra*, at 700. And, although the Court dismisses the proponents' standing claim because initiative proponents "are not elected" and "decide for themselves, with no review, what arguments to make and how to make them" in defense of the enacted initiative, *ante*, at 15, those same charges could be leveled with equal if not greater force at the special prosecutors just discussed. See *Young, supra*, at 807.

Similar questions might also arise regarding *qui tam* actions, see, e.g., *Vermont Agency of Natural Resources v. United States ex rel. Stevens*, 529 U. S. 765, 771–778 (2000); suits involving "next friends" litigating on behalf of a real party in interest, see, e.g., *Whitmore v. Arkansas*, 495 U. S. 149, 161–166 (1990); or shareholder-derivative suits, see, e.g., *Gollust v. Mendell*, 501 U. S. 115, 125–126 (1991). There is no more of an agency relationship in any of these settings than in the instant case, yet the Court has nonetheless permitted a party to assert the interests of another. That *qui tam* actions and "next friend" litigation may have a longer historical pedigree than the initiative process, see *ante*, at 12–13, is no basis for finding Article III's standing requirement met in those cases but lacking here. In short, the Court today unsettles its longtime understanding of the basis for jurisdiction in representative-party litigation, leaving the law unclear and the District Court's judgment, and its accompanying statewide injunction, effectively immune from appellate review.

III

There is much irony in the Court's approach to justiciability in this case. A prime purpose of justiciability is to ensure vigorous advocacy, yet the Court insists upon litigation conducted by state officials whose preference is to lose the case. The doctrine is meant to ensure that courts are responsible and constrained in their power, but the Court's opinion today means that a single district court can make a decision with far-reaching effects that cannot be reviewed. And rather than honor the principle that justiciability exists to allow disputes of public policy to be resolved by the political process rather than the courts, see, e.g., *Allen v. Wright*, 468 U. S. 737, 750–752 (1984), here the Court refuses to allow a State's authorized representatives to defend the outcome of a democratic election. The Court's opinion disrespects and disparages both the political process in California and the well-stated opinion of the California Supreme Court in this case. The California Supreme Court, not this Court, expresses concern for vigorous representation; the California Supreme Court, not this Court, recognizes the necessity to avoid conflicts of interest; the California Supreme Court, not this Court, comprehends the real interest at stake in this litigation and identifies the most proper party to defend that interest. The California Supreme Court's opinion reflects a better understanding of the dynamics and principles of Article III than does this Court's opinion.

Of course, the Court must be cautious before entering a realm of controversy where the legal community and society at large are still formulating ideas and approaches to a most difficult subject. But it is shortsighted to misconstrue principles of justiciability to avoid that subject. As the California Supreme Court recognized, "the question before us involves a fundamental procedural issue that may arise with respect to *any* initiative measure, without regard to its subject matter." 52 Cal. 4th, at 1124, 265 P. 3d, at 1005 (emphasis in original). If a federal court must rule on a constitutional point that either confirms or rejects the will of the people expressed in an initiative, that is when it is most necessary, not least necessary, to insist on rules that ensure the most committed and vigorous adversary arguments to inform the rulings of the courts.

* * *

In the end, what the Court fails to grasp or accept is the basic premise of the initiative process. And it is this. The essence of democracy is that the right to make law rests in the people and flows to the government, not the other way around. Freedom resides first in the people without need of a grant from government. The California initiative process embodies these principles and has done so for over a century. "Through the structure of its government, and the character of those who exercise government authority, a State defines itself as sovereign." *Gregory* v. *Ashcroft*, 501 U. S. 452, 460 (1991). In California and the 26 other States that permit initiatives and popular referendums, the people have exercised their own inherent sovereign right to govern themselves. The Court today frustrates that choice by nullifying, for failure to comply with the Restatement of Agency, a State Supreme Court decision holding that state law authorizes an enacted initiative's proponents to defend the law if and when the State's usual legal advocates decline to do so. The Court's opinion fails to abide by precedent and misapplies basic principles of justiciability. Those errors necessitate this respectful dissent.

SOURCE: U.S. Supreme Court. *Hollingsworth v. Perry*, 570 U.S.__(2013). http://www.supremecourt.gov/opinions/12pdf/12-144_8ok0.pdf.

OTHER HISTORIC DOCUMENTS OF INTEREST

FROM THIS VOLUME

From previous *Historic Documents*

Supreme Court Rules on the Defense of Marriage Act

JUNE 26, 2013

On the final day of the Supreme Court's 2012–2013 term, the Court released two widely anticipated decisions that had a profound impact on the status of gay marriage in the United States. The most far reaching of the two decisions, *United States v. Windsor*, involved a challenge to the federal Defense of Marriage Act (DOMA). The 1996 DOMA, passed by Congress before any states had legalized single-sex marriage, defined the word "marriage" for purposes of all federal law or regulation to mean "only a legal union between one man and one woman as husband and wife." In the ensuing years, twelve states and the District of Columbia had changed their marriage laws to permit same-sex marriage, but because of DOMA, couples who were legally married in their state found that their marriages were not recognized for the purposes of over a thousand federal laws and programs, including Social Security survivor benefits, immigration rights, and family leave. In a vote of 5–4, in an opinion by Justice Anthony M. Kennedy, the Court ruled that DOMA unconstitutionally violates the rights of equal liberty protected by the Fifth Amendment by "creating two contradictory marriage regimes within the same state." According to Justice Kennedy, "DOMA's principal effect [was] to identify a subset of state-sanctioned marriages and make them unequal." The ruling that DOMA is unconstitutional now means that same-sex couples who are legally married in their own states may receive all the federal benefits (and federal responsibilities) that are shared by all married couples, regardless of their sexual orientation.

DOMA Costs Edith Windsor More Than $300,000

Passed in 1996, with broad bipartisan support and signed by President Bill Clinton, Section 3 of DOMA adds a comprehensive definition of marriage for the purposes of all federal statutes and other regulations: "In determining the meaning of any Act of Congress, or of any ruling, regulation, or interpretation of the various administrative bureaus and agencies of the United States, the word 'marriage' means only a legal union between one man and one woman as husband and wife, and the word 'spouse' refers only to a person of the opposite sex who is a husband or a wife." DOMA did not prevent states from enacting laws permitting same-sex marriage, and in the years between its enactment and *United States v. Windsor* twelve states and the District of Columbia passed laws allowing for same-sex marriage and, as of January 2014, that number had climbed to seventeen.

Edith Windsor met Thea Spyer in New York in 1963 and began a long-term relationship. Later, they registered in New York City as domestic partners. In 2007, the couple traveled to Canada where they were legally married. Although the state of New York did not legalize gay marriage until 2011, it did recognize their marriage as valid. In February 2009, Spyer died and left her entire estate to her wife, Windsor. Federal estate law exempts from taxation any property passed to a surviving spouse. Because DOMA denies federal recognition to same-sex spouses, the spousal exemption was held not to apply to Windsor who was forced to pay the Internal Revenue Service (IRS) $363,053 in estate taxes. She filed a refund suit in federal court in New York. The trial court ruled that Section 3 of DOMA was unconstitutional and ordered the Treasury to refund the tax with interest and, on appeal, the Court of Appeals for the Second Circuit agreed. The Supreme Court subsequently said it would hear the final appeal.

Complicating the appeal, the administration of President Barack Obama announced in 2011 that "the President has concluded that given a number of factors, including a documented history of discrimination, classifications based on sexual orientation should be subject to a heightened standard of scrutiny," and, for this reason, the Department of Justice would no longer defend the constitutionality of DOMA in court. In response to this, a group in the House of Representatives known as the Bipartisan Legal Advisory Group (BLAG) voted to intervene in the case to argue in defense of the constitutionality of DOMA.

Court Rules that DOMA is Unconstitutional

The majority opinion, written by Justice Kennedy, focused at some length on the traditional power and authority of states to define marriage. Going back to when the Constitution was adopted, Justice Kennedy, citing earlier case law, asserted that from the beginning "the common understanding was that the domestic relations of husband and wife and parent and child were matters reserved to the states." As long as states don't impede on other constitutional rights, he continued, the regulation of marriage is "an area that has long been regarded as a virtually exclusive province of the States." In the case of same-sex marriage, the states that have adopted it, he continued, made the decision "that same-sex couples should have the right to marry and so live with pride in themselves and their union and in a status of equality with all other married persons."

Characterizing DOMA as a departure from the tradition of relying on state law to define marriage, the Court looked to the purpose and impact of DOMA to evaluate its constitutionality. What it found was evidence that the "avowed purpose and practical effect" of DOMA was "to impose a disadvantage, a separate status, and so a stigma upon all who enter into same-sex marriages made lawful by the unquestioned authority of the States." Where states conferred dignity onto the unions of same-sex couples, the very essence of the federal statute was to interfere with that equal dignity. DOMA, according to the majority, frustrates the objective of state law and "writes inequality into the entire United States Code."

In reaching its conclusion that the principal purpose and effect of the law are "to demean those persons who are in a lawful same-sex marriage," the Court spent some time examining the effect the law had on the children of these legal marriages. Not only does the law demean the same-sex marriages, the Court wrote, but also "it humiliates tens of thousands of children now being raised by same-sex couples" and, in numerous ways, brings those children "financial harm."

Based on its conclusion that DOMA demeans, disparages, and denies equal dignity to a subset of lawful marriages, the Supreme Court ruled that the law violates the Fifth Amendment's guarantees of equality and liberty. Justice Kennedy concluded that "no legitimate purpose overcomes the purpose and effect to disparage and injure those whom the State, by its marriage laws, sought to protect in personhood and dignity."

Joining Justice Kennedy in the majority were Justices Ruth Bader Ginsburg, Stephen Breyer, Sonia Sotamayor, and Elena Kagan. The dissents were divided among three opinions. Justice Antonin Scalia wrote a scathing dissent, joined by Justice Clarence Thomas and in part by Chief Justice John Roberts, Jr., in which he argued that the political branches rather than the courts should make decisions about same-sex marriage, but accused the majority of arrogance and preferring "to buy its stolen moment in the spotlight." He also bitterly described Justice Kennedy's opinion as "a lecture on how superior the majority's moral judgment in favor of same-sex marriage is to the Congress's hateful moral judgment against it." He accused the majority of "real cheek" for their assurances that this opinion was not about the constitutionality of state laws banning same-sex marriage. In Justice Scalia's view, the reasoning of this case will compel future courts to invalidate such state laws.

The Chief Justice also wrote a separate dissent to say that the majority had no evidence that DOMA was motivated by a desire to "codify malice" and that he "would not tar the political branches with the brush of bigotry."

Impact of the Court's Decision on Gay Marriage in the States

This decision had an immediate and profound effect on those same-sex couples who are legally married and who live in one of the states that recognizes their marriages. In the wake of this case, these couples must now receive the same federal benefits that heterosexual couples receive including: health insurance and pension protections for spouses of federal employees, social security survivor's benefits, support and benefits for military spouses, joint income tax filing, and exemption from federal estate taxes, to name just a few. In a statement released shortly after the Court's decision, President Barack Obama applauded the Court for striking down DOMA and stated that he had "directed the Attorney General to work with other members of my Cabinet to review all federal statutes to ensure this decision, including its implications for federal benefits and obligations, is implemented swiftly and smoothly."

One area not mentioned by the Court but likely to be immediately impacted by this decision involves immigration. Under DOMA, federal immigration laws could not recognize the marriages of same-sex couples of different nationalities, leaving American citizens powerless to prevent the deportations of their non-American same-sex spouses. The Senate recently refused to include these same-sex couples in an immigration reform bill, but, now that DOMA has been invalidated, such bi-national same-sex couples would have the same rights as any married couple, without the need for special immigration provisions.

The Court's decision left in place Section 2 of DOMA, which gives states the right to refuse to recognize gay marriages performed in other states, and it gave no guidance on how to treat same-sex couples who legally marry in one state but then live in a state that chooses not to recognize their marriage. Justice Scalia posed this as a practical problem resulting from the majority opinion: Can such a couple file a joint federal tax return? Other questions left open by this opinion involve how states that refuse to recognize same-sex marriage should deal with federal benefits when they administer a federal program.

The majority opinion in *United States v. Windsor* explicitly did not address the question of whether the constitution requires the recognition of gay marriage. However, in an interesting twist, in December 2013, Federal District Judge Robert Shelby struck down Utah's ban on same-sex marriage as an unconstitutional violation of due process and equal protection. In reaching this conclusion, the Utah judge stated that he agreed with "the Honorable Antonin Scalia" when he predicted that legalized gay marriage would be "the logical outcome of the court's ruling in *Windsor*." Over a thousand same-sex couples were married in Utah during the seventeen days following this decision, after which the Supreme Court stayed the decision pending resolution of its appeal. Less than a month later, on January 14, 2014, another federal judge ruled that an anti-gay marriage amendment to Oklahoma's state constitution that had passed by voter referendum with 75 percent of the vote violated the federal constitution. According to James Esseks, who directs the American Civil Liberties Union's Lesbian Gay Bisexual Transgender & AIDS Project, there are currently more than forty cases pending in state and federal courts that challenge bans on same-sex marriage, and he predicts that one of these challenges will reach the Supreme Court "within a couple of years."

—Melissa Feinberg

The following are excerpts from the U.S. Supreme Court ruling in United States v. Windsor, *in which the Court ruled 5–4 to overturn the Defense of Marriage Act, arguing that it violates the Fifth Amendment rights of equal liberty.*

DOCUMENT **United States v. Windsor**

June 26, 2013

No. 12–307

United States, Petitioner

v.

Edith Schlain Windsor, in her capacity as executor of the estate of Thea Clara Spyer, et al.

}

On writ of certiorari to the United States Court of Appeals for the Second Circuit

[June 26, 2013]

[Footnotes have been omitted.]

JUSTICE KENNEDY delivered the opinion of the Court.

Two women then resident in New York were married in a lawful ceremony in Ontario, Canada, in 2007. Edith Windsor and Thea Spyer returned to their home in New York City. When Spyer died in 2009, she left her entire estate to Windsor. Windsor sought to claim the estate tax exemption for surviving spouses. She was barred from doing so, however, by a federal law, the Defense of Marriage Act, which excludes a same-sex partner from the definition of "spouse" as that term is used in federal statutes. Windsor paid the taxes but filed suit to challenge the constitutionality of this provision. The United States District Court and the Court of Appeals ruled that this portion of the statute is unconstitutional and ordered the United States to pay Windsor a refund. This Court granted certiorari and now affirms the judgment in Windsor's favor.

[Sections I and II, offering background on the case, have been omitted.]

III

[A review of the same-sex marriage policies in the states, and states' rights to make such policy, has been omitted.]

The significance of state responsibilities for the definition and regulation of marriage dates to the Nation's beginning; for "when the Constitution was adopted the common understanding was that the domestic relations of husband and wife and parent and child were matters reserved to the States." *Ohio ex rel. Popovici* v. *Agler,* 280 U. S. 379, 383–384 (1930). Marriage laws vary in some respects from State to State. For example, the required minimum age is 16 in Vermont, but only 13 in New Hampshire. Compare Vt. Stat. Ann., Tit. 18, §5142 (2012), with N. H. Rev. Stat. Ann. §457:4 (West Supp. 2012). Likewise the permissible degree of consanguinity can vary (most States permit first cousins to marry, but a handful—such as Iowa and Washington, see Iowa Code §595.19(2009); Wash. Rev. Code §26.04.020 (2012)— prohibit the practice). But these rules are in every event consistent within each State.

Against this background DOMA rejects the long established precept that the incidents, benefits, and obligations of marriage are uniform for all married couples within each State, though they may vary, subject to constitutional guarantees, from one State to the next. Despite these considerations, it is unnecessary to decide whether this federal intrusion on state power is a violation of the Constitution because it disrupts the federal balance. The State's power in defining the marital relation is of central relevance in this case quite apart from principles of federalism. Here the State's decision to give this class of persons the right to marry conferred upon them a dignity and status of immense import. When the State used its historic and essential authority to define the marital relation in this way, its role and its power in making the decision enhanced the recognition, dignity, and protection of the class in their own community. DOMA, because of its reach and extent, departs from this history and tradition of reliance on state law to define marriage. "'[D]iscriminations of an unusual character especially suggest careful consideration to determine whether they are obnoxious to the constitutional provision.'" *Romer* v. *Evans,* 517 U. S. 620, 633 (1996) (quoting *Louisville Gas & Elec. Co.* v. *Coleman,* 277 U. S. 32, 37–38 (1928)).

The Federal Government uses this state-defined class for the opposite purpose—to impose restrictions and disabilities. That result requires this Court now to address whether the resulting injury and indignity is a deprivation of an essential part of the liberty protected by the Fifth Amendment. What the State of New York treats as alike the federal law deems unlike by a law designed to injure the same class the State seeks to protect.

In acting first to recognize and then to allow same-sex marriages, New York was responding "to the initiative of those who [sought] a voice in shaping the destiny of their own times." *Bond* v. *United States,* 564 U. S. ___, ___ (2011) (slip op., at 9). These actions were without doubt a proper exercise of its sovereign authority within our federal system, all in the way that the Framers of the Constitution intended. The dynamics of state government in the federal system are to allow the formation of consensus respecting the way the members of a discrete community treat each other in their daily contact and constant interaction with each other.

The States' interest in defining and regulating the marital relation, subject to constitutional guarantees, stems from the understanding that marriage is more than a routine classification for purposes of certain statutory benefits. Private, consensual sexual intimacy between two adult persons of the same sex may not be punished by the State, and it can form "but one element in a personal bond that is more enduring." *Lawrence* v. *Texas,* 539 U. S. 558, 567 (2003). By its recognition of the validity of same-sex marriages performed in other jurisdictions and then by authorizing same-sex unions and same-sex marriages, New York sought to give further protection and dignity to that bond. For same-sex couples who wished to be married, the State acted to give their lawful conduct a lawful status. This status is a far-reaching legal acknowledgment of the intimate relationship between two people, a relationship deemed by the State worthy of dignity in the community equal with all other marriages. It reflects both the community's considered perspective on the historical roots of the institution of marriage and its evolving understanding of the meaning of equality.

IV

DOMA seeks to injure the very class New York seeks to protect. By doing so it violates basic due process and equal protection principles applicable to the Federal Government. See U. S. Const., Amdt. 5; *Bolling* v. *Sharpe,* 347 U. S. 497 (1954). The Constitution's guarantee of equality "must at the very least mean that a bare congressional desire to harm a politically unpopular group cannot" justify disparate treatment of that group. *Department of Agriculture* v. *Moreno,* 413 U. S. 528, 534–535 (1973). In determining whether a law is motivated by an improper animus or purpose, "'[d]iscriminations of an unusual character'" especially require careful consideration. *Supra,* at 19 (quoting *Romer, supra,* at 633). DOMA cannot survive under these principles. The responsibility of the States for the regulation of domestic relations is an important indicator of the substantial societal impact the State's classifications have in the daily lives and customs of its people. DOMA's unusual deviation from the usual tradition of recognizing and accepting state definitions of marriage here operates to deprive same-sex couples of the benefits and responsibilities that come with the federal recognition of their marriages. This is strong evidence of a law having the purpose and effect of disapproval of that class. The avowed purpose and practical effect of the law here in question are to impose a disadvantage, a separate status, and so a stigma upon all who enter into same-sex marriages made lawful by the unquestioned authority of the States.

The history of DOMA's enactment and its own text demonstrate that interference with the equal dignity of same-sex marriages, a dignity conferred by the States in the exercise of their sovereign power, was more than an incidental effect of the federal statute. It was its essence. The House Report announced its conclusion that "it is both appropriate and necessary for Congress to do what it can to defend the institution of traditional heterosexual marriage. . . . H. R. 3396 is appropriately entitled the 'Defense of Marriage Act.' The effort to redefine 'marriage' to extend to homosexual couples is a truly radical proposal that would fundamentally alter the institution of marriage." H. R. Rep. No. 104–664, pp. 12–13 (1996). The House concluded that DOMA expresses "both moral disapproval of homosexuality, and a moral conviction that heterosexuality better comports with traditional (especially Judeo-Christian) morality." *Id.,* at 16 (footnote deleted). The stated purpose of the law was to promote an "interest in protecting the traditional moral teachings reflected in heterosexual-only marriage laws." *Ibid.* Were there any doubt of this far-reaching purpose, the title of the Act confirms it: The Defense of Marriage.

The arguments put forward by BLAG are just as candid about the congressional purpose to influence or interfere with state sovereign choices about who may be married. As the title and dynamics of the bill indicate, its purpose is to discourage enactment of state same-sex marriage laws and to restrict the freedom and choice of couples married under those laws if they are enacted. The congressional goal was "to put a thumb on the scales and influence a state's decision as to how to shape its own marriage laws." *Massachusetts,* 682 F. 3d, at 12–13. The Act's demonstrated purpose is to ensure that if any State decides to recognize same-sex marriages, those unions will be treated as second-class marriages for purposes of federal law. This raises a most serious question under the Constitution's Fifth Amendment.

DOMA's operation in practice confirms this purpose. When New York adopted a law to permit same-sex marriage, it sought to eliminate inequality; but DOMA frustrates that objective through a system-wide enactment with no identified connection to any particular area of federal law. DOMA writes inequality into the entire United States Code. The particular case at hand concerns the estate tax, but DOMA is more than a simple determination of what should or should not be allowed as an estate tax refund. Among the over 1,000 statutes and numerous federal regulations that DOMA controls are laws pertaining to Social Security, housing, taxes, criminal sanctions, copyright, and veterans' benefits.

DOMA's principal effect is to identify a subset of state sanctioned marriages and make them unequal. The principal purpose is to impose inequality, not for other reasons like governmental efficiency. Responsibilities, as well as rights, enhance the dignity and integrity of the person. And DOMA contrives to deprive some couples married under the laws of their State, but not other couples, of both rights and responsibilities. By creating two contradictory marriage regimes within the same State, DOMA forces same-sex couples to live as married for the purpose of state law but unmarried for the purpose of federal law, thus diminishing the stability and predictability of basic personal relations the State has found it proper to acknowledge and protect. By this dynamic DOMA undermines both the public and private significance of state sanctioned same-sex marriages; for it tells those couples, and all the world, that their otherwise valid marriages are unworthy of federal recognition. This places same-sex couples in an unstable position of being in a second-tier marriage. The differentiation demeans the couple, whose moral and sexual choices the Constitution protects, see *Lawrence,* 539 U. S. 558, and whose relationship the State has sought to dignify. And it humiliates tens of thousands of children now being raised by same-sex couples. The law in question makes it even more difficult for the children to understand the integrity and closeness of their own family and its concord with other families in their community and in their daily lives.

Under DOMA, same-sex married couples have their lives burdened, by reason of government decree, in visible and public ways. By its great reach, DOMA touches many aspects of married and family life, from the mundane to the profound. It prevents same-sex married couples from obtaining government healthcare benefits they would otherwise receive. See 5 U. S. C. §§8901(5), 8905. It deprives them of the Bankruptcy Code's special protections for domestic-support obligations. See 11 U. S. C. §§101(14A), 507(a)(1)(A), 523(a)(5), 523(a)(15). It forces them to follow a complicated procedure to file their state and federal taxes jointly. Technical Bulletin TB–55, 2010 Vt. Tax LEXIS 6 (Oct. 7, 2010); Brief for Federalism Scholars as *Amici Curiae* 34. It prohibits them from being buried together in veterans' cemeteries. National Cemetery Administration Directive 3210/1, p. 37 (June 4, 2008).

For certain married couples, DOMA's unequal effects are even more serious. The federal penal code makes it a crime to "assaul[t], kidna[p], or murde[r] . . . a member of the immediate family" of "a United States official, a United States judge, [or] a Federal law enforcement officer,"18 U. S. C. §115(a)(1)(A), with the intent to influence or retaliate against that official, §115(a)(1). Although a "spouse" qualifies as a member of the officer's "immediate family," §115(c)(2), DOMA makes this protection inapplicable to same-sex spouses.

DOMA also brings financial harm to children of same-sex couples. It raises the cost of health care for families by taxing health benefits provided by employers to their workers' same-sex spouses. See 26 U. S. C. §106; Treas. Reg. §1.106–1, 26 CFR §1.106–1 (2012); IRS Private Letter Ruling 9850011 (Sept. 10, 1998). And it denies or reduces benefits allowed to families upon the loss of a spouse and parent, benefits that are an integral part of family security. See Social Security Administration, Social Security Survivors Benefits 5 (2012) (benefits available to a surviving spouse caring for the couple's child), online at http://www.ssa.gov/pubs/EN-05-10084.pdf.

DOMA divests married same-sex couples of the duties and responsibilities that are an essential part of married life and that they in most cases would be honored to accept were DOMA not in force. For instance, because it is expected that spouses will support each other as they pursue educational opportunities, federal law takes into consideration a spouse's income in calculating a student's federal financial aid eligibility. See 20 U. S. C. §1087nn(b). Same-sex married couples are exempt from this requirement. The same is true with respect to federal ethics rules. Federal executive and agency officials are prohibited from "participat[ing] personally and substantially" in matters as to which they or their spouses have a financial interest. 18 U. S. C. §208(a). A similar statute prohibits Senators, Senate employees, and their spouses from accepting high-value gifts from certain sources, see 2 U. S. C. §31–2(a)(1), and another mandates detailed financial disclosures by numerous high-ranking officials and their spouses. See 5 U. S. C. App. §§102(a), (e). Under DOMA, however, these Government-integrity rules do not apply to same-sex spouses.

* * *

The power the Constitution grants it also restrains. And though Congress has great authority to design laws to fit its own conception of sound national policy, it cannot deny the liberty protected by the Due Process Clause of the Fifth Amendment.

What has been explained to this point should more than suffice to establish that the principal purpose and the necessary effect of this law are to demean those persons who are in a lawful same-sex marriage. This requires the Court to hold, as it now does, that DOMA is unconstitutional as a deprivation of the liberty of the person protected by the Fifth Amendment of the Constitution.

The liberty protected by the Fifth Amendment's Due Process Clause contains within it the prohibition against denying to any person the equal protection of the laws. See *Bolling*, 347 U. S., at 499–500; *Adarand Constructors, Inc.* v. *Peña*, 515 U. S. 200, 217–218 (1995). While the Fifth Amendment itself withdraws from Government the power to degrade or demean in the way this law does, the equal protection guarantee of the

Fourteenth Amendment makes that Fifth Amendment right all the more specific and all the better understood and preserved.

The class to which DOMA directs its restrictions and restraints are those persons who are joined in same-sex marriages made lawful by the State. DOMA singles out a class of persons deemed by a State entitled to recognition and protection to enhance their own liberty. It imposes a disability on the class by refusing to acknowledge a status the State finds to be dignified and proper. DOMA instructs all federal officials, and indeed all persons with whom same-sex couples interact, including their own children, that their marriage is less worthy than the marriages of others. The federal statute is invalid, for no legitimate purpose overcomes the purpose and effect to disparage and to injure those whom the State, by its marriage laws, sought to protect in personhood and dignity. By seeking to displace this protection and treating those persons as living in marriages less respected than others, the federal statute is in violation of the Fifth Amendment. This opinion and its holding are confined to those lawful marriages.

The judgment of the Court of Appeals for the Second Circuit is affirmed.

It is so ordered

[The dissenting opinion of Chief Justice Roberts has been omitted.]

JUSTICE SCALIA, with whom JUSTICE THOMAS joins, and with whom THE CHIEF JUSTICE joins as to Part I, dissenting.

This case is about power in several respects. It is about the power of our people to govern themselves, and the power of this Court to pronounce the law. Today's opinion aggrandizes the latter, with the predictable consequence of diminishing the former. We have no power to decide this case. And even if we did, we have no power under the Constitution to invalidate this democratically adopted legislation. The Court's errors on both points spring forth from the same diseased root: an exalted conception of the role of this institution in America.

I

A

The Court is eager—hungry—to tell everyone its view of the legal question at the heart of this case. Standing in the way is an obstacle, a technicality of little interest to anyone but the people of We the People, who created it as a barrier against judges' intrusion into their lives. They gave judges, in Article III, only the "judicial Power," a power to decide not abstract questions but real, concrete "Cases" and "Controversies." Yet the plaintiff and the Government agree entirely on what should happen in this lawsuit. They agree that the court below got it right; and they agreed in the court below that the court below that one got it right as well. What, then, are we doing here?

The answer lies at the heart of the jurisdictional portion of today's opinion, where a single sentence lays bare the majority's vision of our role. The Court says that we have the power to decide this case because if we did not, then our "primary role in determining the constitutionality of a law" (at least one that "has inflicted real injury on a plaintiff") would "become only secondary to the President's." *Ante*, at 12. But wait, the reader wonders—Windsor won below, and so cured her injury, and the President was glad to see it. True, says the majority, but judicial review must march on regardless, lest we "undermine the clear dictate of the separation-of-powers principle that when an Act of Congress is alleged to conflict with the Constitution, it is emphatically the province and duty of the judicial department to say what the law is." *Ibid.* (internal quotation marks and brackets omitted).

That is jaw-dropping. It is an assertion of judicial supremacy over the people's Representatives in Congress and the Executive. It envisions a Supreme Court standing (or rather enthroned) at the apex of government, empowered to decide all constitutional questions, always and everywhere "primary" in its role.

This image of the Court would have been unrecognizable to those who wrote and ratified our national charter. They knew well the dangers of "primary" power, and so created branches of government that would be "perfectly coordinate by the terms of their common commission," none of which branches could "pretend to an exclusive or superior right of settling the boundaries between their respective powers." The Federalist, No. 49, p. 314 (C. Rossitered. 1961) (J. Madison). The people did this to protect themselves. They did it to guard their right to self-rule against the black-robed supremacy that today's majority finds so attractive. So it was that Madison could confidently state, with no fear of contradiction, that there was nothing of "greater intrinsic value" or "stamped with the authority of more enlightened patrons of liberty" than a government of separate and coordinate powers. *Id.*, No. 47, at 301.

For this reason we are quite forbidden to say what the law is whenever (as today's opinion asserts) "'an Act of Congress is alleged to conflict with the Constitution.'" *Ante*, at 12. We can do so only when that allegation will determine the outcome of a lawsuit, and is contradicted by the other party. The "judicial Power" is not, as the majority believes, the power "'to say what the law is,'" *ibid.*, giving the Supreme Court the "primary role in determining the constitutionality of laws." The majority must have in mind one of the foreign constitutions that pronounces such primacy for its constitutional court and allows that primacy to be exercised in contexts other than a lawsuit. See, e.g., Basic Law for the Federal Republic of Germany, Art. 93. The judicial power as Americans have understood it (and their English ancestors before them) is the power to adjudicate, with conclusive effect, disputed government claims (civil or criminal) against private persons, and disputed claims by private persons against the government or other private persons. Sometimes (though not always) the parties before the court disagree not with regard to the facts of their case (or not only with regard to the facts) but with regard to the applicable law—in which event (and only in which event) it becomes the "'province and duty of the judicial department to say what the law is.'" *Ante*, at 12.

In other words, declaring the compatibility of state or federal laws with the Constitution is not only not the "primary role" of this Court, it is not a separate, freestanding role at all. We perform that role incidentally—by accident, as it were—when that is necessary to resolve the dispute before us. Then, and only then, does it become "'the province and duty of the judicial department to say what the law is.'" That is why, in 1793, we politely declined the Washington Administration's request to "say what the law is" on a particular treaty matter that was not the subject of a concrete legal controversy. Correspondence and Public Papers of John Jay 486–489 (H. Johnston ed. 1893). And that is why, as our opinions have said, some questions of law will never be presented to this Court, because there will never be anyone with standing to bring a lawsuit. See *Schlesinger v. Reservists Comm. to Stop the War*, 418 U. S. 208, 227 (1974); *United States v. Richardson*, 418 U. S. 166, 179 (1974). As Justice Brandeis put it, we cannot "pass upon the constitutionality of legislation in a friendly, non-adversary, proceeding"; absent a "'real, earnest and vital controversy between individuals,'" we have neither any work to do nor any power to do it. *Ashwander v. TVA*, 297 U. S. 288, 346 (1936) (concurring opinion) (quoting *Chicago & Grand Trunk R. Co. v. Wellman*, 143 U. S. 339, 345 (1892)). Our authority begins and ends with the need to adjudge the rights of an injured party who stands before us seeking redress. *Lujan v. Defenders of Wildlife*, 504 U. S. 555, 560 (1992).

That is completely absent here. Windsor's injury was cured by the judgment in her favor. And while, in ordinary circumstances, the United States is injured by a directive to pay a tax refund, this suit is far from ordinary. Whatever injury the United States has suffered will surely not be redressed by the action that it, as a litigant, asks us to take. The final sentence of the Solicitor General's brief on the merits reads: "For the foregoing reasons, the judgment of the court of appeals *should be affirmed*." Brief for United States (merits) 54 (emphasis added). That will not cure the Government's injury, but carve it into stone. One could spend many fruitless afternoons ransacking our library for any other petitioner's brief seeking an affirmance of the judgment against it. What the petitioner United States asks us to do in the case before us is exactly what the respondent Windsor asks us to do: not to provide relief from the judgment below but to say that that judgment was correct. And the same was true in the Court of Appeals: Neither party sought to undo the judgment for Windsor, and so that court should have dismissed the appeal (just as we should dismiss) for lack of jurisdiction. Since both parties agreed with the judgment of the District Court for the Southern District of New York, the suit should have ended there. The further proceedings have been a contrivance, having no object in mind except to elevate a District Court judgment that has no precedential effect in other courts, to one that has precedential effect throughout the Second Circuit, and then (in this Court) precedential effect throughout the United States.

We have never before agreed to speak—to "say what the law is"—where there is no controversy before us. In the more than two centuries that this Court has existed as an institution, we have never suggested that we have the power to decide a question when every party agrees with both its nominal opponent and the court below on that question's answer. The United States reluctantly conceded that at oral argument. See Tr. of Oral Arg. 19–20.

The closest we have ever come to what the Court blesses today was our opinion in *INS v. Chadha*, 462 U. S. 919 (1983). But in that case, two parties to the litigation disagreed with the position of the United States and with the court below: the House and Senate, which had intervened in the case. Because *Chadha* concerned the validity of a mode of congressional action—the one-house legislative veto—the House and Senate were threatened with destruction of what they claimed to be one of their institutional powers. The Executive choosing not to defend that power, we permitted the House and Senate to intervene. Nothing like that is present here.

To be sure, the Court in *Chadha* said that statutory aggrieved-party status was "not altered by the fact that the Executive may agree with the holding that the statute in question is unconstitutional." *Id.*, at 930–931. But in a footnote to that statement, the Court acknowledged Article III's separate requirement of a "justiciable case or controversy," and stated that this requirement was satisfied "because of the presence of the two Houses of Congress as adverse parties." *Id.*, at 931, n. 6. Later in its opinion, the *Chadha* Court remarked that the United States' announced intention to enforce the statute also sufficed to permit judicial review, even absent congressional participation. *Id.*, at 939. That remark is true, as a description of the judicial review conducted in the Court of Appeals, where the Houses of Congress had not intervened. (The case originated in the Court of Appeals, since it sought review of agency action under 8 U. S. C. §1105a(a) (1976 ed.).) There, absent a judgment setting aside the INS order, *Chadha* faced deportation. This passage of our opinion seems to be addressing that initial standing in the Court of Appeals, as indicated by its quotation from the lower court's opinion, 462 U. S., at 939–940. But if it was addressing standing to pursue the appeal, the remark was both the purest dictum (as congressional intervention at that point made the required adverseness "beyond doubt," *id.*, at 939), and quite incorrect. When a private party has a judicial decree safely in hand to prevent his injury, additional judicial action requires that a party injured by the decree seek to undo it. In *Chadha*, the intervening House and Senate fulfilled that requirement. Here no one does.

The majority's discussion of the requirements of Article III bears no resemblance to our jurisprudence. It accuses the amicus (appointed to argue against our jurisdiction) of "elid[ing] the distinction between . . . the jurisdictional requirements of Article III and the prudential limits on its exercise." *Ante*, at 6. It then proceeds to call the requirement of adverseness a "prudential" aspect of standing. Of standing. That is incomprehensible. A plaintiff (or appellant) can have all the standing in the world—satisfying all three standing requirements of *Lujan* that the majority so carefully quotes, *ante*, at 7—and yet no Article III controversy may be before the court. Article III requires not just a plaintiff (or appellant) who has standing to complain but an opposing party who denies the validity of the complaint. It is not the amicus that has done the eliding of distinctions, but the majority, calling the quite separate Article III requirement of adverseness between the parties an element (which it then pronounces a "prudential" element) of standing. The question here is not whether, as the majority puts it, "the United States retains a stake sufficient to support Article III jurisdiction," *ibid.* the question is whether there is any controversy (which requires contradiction) between the United States and Ms. Windsor. There is not.

I find it wryly amusing that the majority seeks to dismiss the requirement of party-adverseness as nothing more than a "prudential" aspect of the sole Article III requirement of standing. (Relegating a jurisdictional requirement to "prudential" status is a wondrous device, enabling courts to ignore the requirement whenever they believe it "prudent"— which is to say, a good idea.) Half a century ago, a Court similarly bent upon announcing its view regarding the constitutionality of a federal statute achieved that goal by effecting a remarkably similar but completely opposite distortion of the principles limiting our jurisdiction. The Court's notorious opinion in *Flast v. Cohen*, 392 U. S. 83, 98–101 (1968), held that standing was merely an element (which it pronounced to be a "prudential" element) of the sole Article III requirement of adverseness. We have been living with the chaos created by that power-grabbing decision ever since, see *Hein v. Freedom From Religion Foundation, Inc.*, 551 U. S. 587 (2007), as we will have to live with the chaos created by this one.

The authorities the majority cites fall miles short of supporting the counterintuitive notion that an Article III "controversy" can exist without disagreement between the parties. In *Deposit Guaranty Nat. Bank v. Roper*, 445 U. S. 326 (1980), the District Court had entered judgment in the individual plaintiff's favor based on the defendant bank's offer to pay the full amount claimed. The plaintiff, however, sought to appeal the District Court's denial of class certification under Federal Rule of Civil Procedure 23. There was a continuing dispute between the parties concerning the issue raised on appeal. The same is true of the other case cited by the majority, *Camreta v. Greene*, 563 U. S. ___ (2011). There the District Court found that the defendant state officers had violated the Fourth Amendment, but rendered judgment in their favor because they were entitled to official immunity, application of the Fourth Amendment to their conduct not having been clear at the time of violation. The officers sought to appeal the holding of Fourth Amendment violation, which would circumscribe their future conduct; the plaintiff continued to insist that a Fourth Amendment violation had occurred. The "prudential" discretion to which both those cases refer was the discretion to deny an appeal even when a live controversy exists— not the discretion to grant one when it does not. The majority can cite no case in which this Court entertained an appeal in which both parties urged us to affirm the judgment below. And that is because the existence of a controversy is not a "prudential" requirement that we have invented, but an essential element of an Article III case or controversy. The majority's notion that a case between friendly parties can be entertained so long as "adversarial presentation of the issues is assured by the participation of *amici curiae* prepared to defend with vigor" the other side of the issue, *ante*, at 10, effects a breathtaking revolution in our Article III jurisprudence.

It may be argued that if what we say is true some Presidential determinations that statutes are unconstitutional will not be subject to our review. That is as it should be, when both the President and the plaintiff agree that the statute is unconstitutional. Where the Executive is enforcing an unconstitutional law, suit will of course lie; but if, in that suit, the Executive admits the unconstitutionality of the law, the litigation should end in an order or a consent decree enjoining enforcement. This suit saw the light of day only because the President enforced the Act (and thus gave Windsor standing to sue) even though he believed it unconstitutional. He could have equally chosen (more appropriately, some would say) neither to enforce nor to defend the statute he believed to be unconstitutional, see Presidential Authority to Decline to Execute Unconstitutional Statutes, 18 Op. Off. Legal Counsel 199 (Nov. 2, 1994)—in which event Windsor would not have been injured, the District Court could not have refereed this friendly scrimmage, and the Executive's determination of unconstitutionality would have escaped this Court's desire to blurt out its view of the law. The matter would have been left, as so many matters ought to be left, to a tug of war between the President and the Congress, which has innumerable means (up to and including impeachment) of compelling the President to enforce the laws it has written. Or the President could have evaded presentation of the constitutional issue to this Court simply by declining to appeal the District Court and Court of Appeals dispositions he agreed with. Be sure of this much: If a President wants to insulate his judgment of unconstitutionality from our review, he can. What the views urged in this dissent produce is not insulation from judicial review but insulation from Executive contrivance.

The majority brandishes the famous sentence from *Marbury v. Madison,* 1 Cranch 137, 177 (1803) that "[i]t is emphatically the province and duty of the judicial department to say what the law is." *Ante*, at 12 (internal quotation marks omitted). But that sentence neither says nor implies that it is always the province and duty of the Court to say what the law is—much less that its responsibility in that regard is a "primary" one. The very next sentence of Chief Justice Marshall's opinion makes the crucial qualification that today's majority ignores: "*Those who apply the rule to particular cases*, must of necessity expound and interpret that rule." 1 Cranch, at 177 (emphasis added). Only when a "particular case" is before us—that is, a controversy that it is our business to resolve under Article III—do we have the province and duty to pronounce the law. For the views of our early Court more precisely addressing the question before us here, the majority ought instead to have consulted the opinion of Chief Justice Taney in *Lord v. Veazie*, 8 How. 251 (1850):

"The objection in the case before us is . . . that the plaintiff and defendant have the same interest, and that interest adverse and in conflict with the interest of third persons, whose rights would be seriously affected if the question of law was decided in the manner that both of the parties to this suit desire it to be.

"A judgment entered under such circumstances, and for such purposes, is a mere form. The whole proceeding was in contempt of the court, and highly reprehensible . . . . A judgment in form, thus procured, in the eye of the law is no judgment of the court. It is a nullity, and no writ of error will lie upon it. This writ is, therefore, dismissed." *Id.*, at 255–256.

There is, in the words of *Marbury*, no "necessity [to] expound and interpret" the law in this case; just a desire to place this Court at the center of the Nation's life. Cranch, at 177.

[Part B, further outlining reasons for the dissent, has been omitted.]

II

For the reasons above, I think that this Court has, and the Court of Appeals had, no power to decide this suit. We should vacate the decision below and remand to the Court of Appeals for the Second Circuit, with instructions to dismiss the appeal. Given that the majority has volunteered its view of the merits, however, I proceed to discuss that as well . . .

[Further discussion of the majority's opinion, specifically as it relates to Equal Protection, has been omitted.]

The majority concludes that the only motive for this Act was the "bare . . . desire to harm a politically unpopular group." *Ante*, at 20. Bear in mind that the object of this condemnation is not the legislature of some once-Confederate Southern state (familiar objects of the Court's scorn, see, *e.g.*, *Edwards* v. *Aguillard*, 482 U. S. 578 (1987)), but our respected coordinate branches, the Congress and Presidency of the United States. Laying such a charge against them should require the most extraordinary evidence, and I would have thought that every attempt would be made to indulge a more anodyne explanation for the statute. The majority does the opposite—affirmatively concealing from the reader the arguments that exist in justification. It makes only a passing mention of the "arguments put forward" by the Act's defenders, and does not even trouble to paraphrase or describe them. See *ante*, at 21. I imagine that this is because it is harder to maintain the illusion of the Act's supporters as unhinged members of a wild-eyed lynch mob when one first describes their views as *they* see them.

To choose just one of these defenders' arguments, DOMA avoids difficult choice-of-law issues that will now arise absent a uniform federal definition of marriage. See, *e.g.*, Baude, Beyond DOMA: Choice of State Law in Federal Statutes, 64 Stan. L. Rev. 1371 (2012). Imagine a pair of women who marry in Albany and then move to Alabama, which does not "recognize as valid any marriage parties of the same sex." Ala. Code §30–1–19(e) (2011). When the couple files their next federal tax return, may it be a joint one? Which State's law controls, for federal-law purposes: their State of celebration (which recognizes the marriage) or their State of domicile (which does not)? (Does the answer depend on whether they were just visiting in Albany?) Are these questions to be answered as a matter of federal common law, or perhaps by borrowing a State's choice-of-law rules? If so, *which* State's? And what about States where the status of an out-of-state same-sex marriage is an unsettled question under local law? See *Godfrey* v. *Spano*, 13 N. Y. 3d 358, 920 N. E. 2d 328 (2009). DOMA avoided all of this uncertainty by specifying which marriages would be recognized for federal purposes. That is a classic purpose for a definitional provision . . .

* * *

. . . It takes real cheek for today's majority to assure us, as it is going out the door, that a constitutional requirement to give formal recognition to same-sex marriage is not at issue here—when what has preceded that assurance is a lecture on how superior the majority's moral judgment in favor of same-sex marriage is to the Congress's hateful moral judgment against it. I promise you this: The only thing that will "confine" the Court's holding is its sense of what it can get away with. . . .

In my opinion, however, the view that *this* Court will take of state prohibition of same-sex marriage is indicated beyond mistaking by today's opinion. As I have said, the real rationale of today's opinion, whatever disappearing trail of its legalistic argle-bargle one chooses to follow, is that DOMA is motivated by " 'bare . . . desire to harm'" couples in same-sex marriages. *Supra,* at 18. How easy it is, indeed how inevitable, to reach the same conclusion with regard to state laws denying same-sex couples marital status. . . .

As to that debate: Few public controversies touch an institution so central to the lives of so many, and few inspire such attendant passion by good people on all sides. Few public controversies will ever demonstrate so vividly the beauty of what our Framers gave us, a gift the Court pawns today to buy its stolen moment in the spotlight: a system of government that permits us to rule *ourselves.* Since DOMA's passage, citizens on all sides of the question have seen victories and they have seen defeats. There have been plebiscites, legislation, persuasion, and loud voices—in other words, democracy. Victories in one place for some . . . are offset by victories in other places for others. . . .

In the majority's telling, this story is black-and-white: Hate your neighbor or come along with us. The truth is more complicated. It is hard to admit that one's political opponents are not monsters, especially in a struggle like this one, and the challenge in the end proves more than today's Court can handle. Too bad. A reminder that disagreement over something so fundamental as marriage can still be politically legitimate would have been a fit task for what in earlier times was called the judicial temperament. We might have covered ourselves with honor today, by promising all sides of this debate that it was theirs to settle and that we would respect their resolution. We might have let the People decide.

But that the majority will not do. Some will rejoice in today's decision, and some will despair at it; that is the nature of a controversy that matters so much to so many. But the Court has cheated both sides, robbing the winners of an honest victory, and the losers of the peace that comes from a fair defeat. We owed both of them better. I dissent.

[The dissenting opinion of Justice Alito, in which Justice Thomas joins in part, has been omitted.]

SOURCE: U.S. Supreme Court. *United States v. Windsor,* 570 U.S.__(2013). http://www.supremecourt.gov/opinions/12pdf/12-307_6j37.pdf.

OTHER HISTORIC DOCUMENTS OF INTEREST

FROM THIS VOLUME

FROM PREVIOUS *HISTORIC DOCUMENTS*

- California and Washington Legalize Same-Sex Marriage, *2012*, p. 90
- Department of Justice Declares Defense of Marriage Act Unconstitutional, *2011*, p. 137
- New York Legalizes Same-Sex Marriage, *2011*, p. 284
- U.S. District Judge Overturns California Ban on Gay Marriage, *2010*, p. 379
- Same-Sex Marriage in the States, *2009*, p. 143
- California Passes Proposition 8 Banning Same-Sex Marriage, *2008*, p. 529
- Clinton on Legislation Barring Same-Sex Marriage, *1996*, p. 687

U.S. and Russian Officials Respond to NSA Leaks

JUNE 26, JUNE 28, AND SEPTEMBER 4, 2013

Americans' sensitivities to the U.S. government's intelligence gathering activities have been at a heightened state since 2005, when *The New York Times* revealed that the National Security Agency (NSA) had secretly been monitoring millions of phone calls, text messages, e-mail, and other communications, including those of U.S. citizens, without warrants. The program was one of several authorized by then-President George W. Bush following the attacks of September 11, 2001, to expand collection of foreign intelligence as part of the War on Terror. Though administration officials argued that the program had been designed to intercept only communications involving at least one individual outside of the United States who was believed to have a link to al Qaeda, the general public was outraged to learn that the program had also intercepted many purely domestic communications, calling it a violation of privacy and expressing concerns that the program could be abused.

While the controversy largely subsided when the program ended in 2007, it was reignited in the summer of 2013 when government contractor Edward Snowden began leaking documents detailing top-secret surveillance programs conducted by the United States and Britain that were collecting electronic communications in bulk, without individual warrants. Described by many as one of the most significant national security leaks in U.S. history, Snowden's actions prompted a renewed debate about the broad reach of the country's surveillance programs, and the appropriate balance between maintaining national security and protecting privacy.

DOCUMENT LEAKS BEGIN

The documents leaked by Snowden first became public on June 5, 2013. *The Guardian's* Glenn Greenwald, citing documents "obtained by" the newspaper, reported that the NSA was collecting the phone records of millions of Verizon's U.S. customers, per an order from the U.S. Foreign Intelligence Surveillance (FISA) Court. The court is charged with reviewing and approving federal law enforcement agencies' requests for surveillance warrants against foreign targets who are suspected of espionage or terrorism. However, Greenwald reported that the court's order to Verizon required the company to provide information on all calls within the United States and between the United States and other countries on an "ongoing, daily basis," regardless of whether the individual callers were suspected of wrongdoing. This included phone numbers, location data, call duration, time of the calls, and any other unique identifiers, although it did not include the contents of phone messages or subscribers' personal information.

Additional documents were published throughout the week. On June 6, both *The Guardian* and *The Washington Post* released a series of PowerPoint slides describing an

NSA program known as PRISM, which indicated that the NSA and the Federal Bureau of Investigation (FBI) were directly tapping into the servers of companies such as Google, Microsoft, and Facebook to collect audio and video chats, photos, e-mail, documents, and other information in bulk. According to their reports, the program focused on foreign communications that were processed through the companies' U.S. servers. The slides also indicated that PRISM was a major source of information for President Barack Obama's daily intelligence briefings, and that PRISM-gathered data accounted for roughly one in seven intelligence reports. Several of the companies named on the slides claimed they did not know about PRISM and that they only gave the government user information in response to specific requests. "We do not provide any government organization with direct access to Facebook servers," said Joe Sullivan, chief security officer for Facebook. "When Facebook is asked for data or information about specific individuals, we carefully scrutinize any such request for compliance with all applicable laws, and provide information only to the extent required by law," he said. Additional slides published later in June showed that PRISM was one of a two-part system for electronic surveillance. The second part, known as Upstream, collected further data from the fiber-optic cable networks that carry Internet and phone data around the world.

On June 7, *The Guardian* reported on Presidential Policy Directive 20. Issued by Obama in October 2012, the directive instructed senior national security and intelligence officials to prepare a list of potential foreign targets on which the United States could launch a cyber attack. It established certain processes for identifying opportunities for a cyber attack, evaluating the risks and consequences of such an attack, and securing approvals for an attack.

Then on June 8, *The Guardian* published more PowerPoint slides, this time describing the NSA's Boundless Informant tool, which provides statistics about the amount and type of data the NSA collects by country. For example, the slides noted that the NSA had collected nearly three billion pieces of intelligence from U.S. computer networks over a thirty-day period in early 2013.

These revelations prompted fears that, once again, the NSA may have collected and searched the records of innocent Americans without first obtaining warrants. U.S. officials were quick to respond to the leaks, defending the NSA's programs and trying to reassure Americans that they did not target U.S. citizens. Director of National Intelligence James Clapper said that information collected through PRISM was "among the most important and valuable foreign intelligence information we collect, and is used to protect our nation from a wide variety of threats. The unauthorized disclosure of information about this important and entirely legal program is reprehensible and risks important protections for the security of Americans." Clapper also argued that the broad collection of data was necessary because a "more narrow collection would limit our ability to screen for and identify terrorism-related communications," and said that "only a small fraction" of phone records are actually examined by analysts for connections to terrorism.

In addition, the White House released a statement reading, in part, that there were "extensive procedures, specifically approved by the court, to ensure that only non-U.S. persons outside the U.S. are targeted, and that minimize the acquisition, retention and dissemination of incidentally acquired information about U.S. persons." The White House also noted that all the NSA surveillance programs had been approved by Congress.

Other officials were critical of the NSA programs. Sens. Tom Udall, D-N.M., and Ron Wyden, D-Ore., issued a joint statement reading, "When Americans call their friends and family, whom they call, when they call, and where they call from is private information. We believe the large-scale collection of this information by the government has a very significant impact on Americans' privacy, whether senior government officials recognize that fact or not."

SNOWDEN'S IDENTITY REVEALED

At Snowden's request, on June 9, *The Guardian* revealed that twenty-nine-year-old Snowden was the source of the leaks. In a video interview with the newspaper, Snowden said that his sole motive for sharing the classified documents was "to inform the public as to that which is done in their name and that which is done against them." He added that he hoped the documents would spark a debate around the world about "what kind of world we want to live in."

Snowden had previously worked as a security guard at the NSA's University of Maryland facilities and later became a technical assistant for the Central Intelligence Agency (CIA), a position that granted him access to classified documents. Snowden said his experience at the CIA and his observation of how the agency conducted its work prompted him to begin questioning the intelligence community. He said he had hoped that things would change once Obama was elected but became disheartened when the president instead expanded the country's intelligence programs. Snowden left the CIA in 2009 and spent the next four years working at NSA facilities as a contractor for various companies. During that time, Snowden said he learned how encompassing the NSA's programs were and came to believe that they were destroying basic privacy and posing "an existential threat to democracy." At the time of the leaks, Snowden was employed by defense contractor Booz Allen Hamilton, a position he later told the *South China Morning Post* that he accepted specifically so that he could collect additional evidence about the NSA's programs.

In May, Snowden requested time off from work under the guise of needing treatment for his epilepsy. On May 20, he flew to Hong Kong, where he stayed through the initial leaks. Snowden said he chose Hong Kong because "they have a spirited commitment to free speech and the right of political dissent" and he believed they would resist U.S. extradition efforts.

On June 14, shortly after Snowden's identity was revealed, the United States filed criminal charges against him, charging him with theft, "unauthorized communication of national defense information," and "willful communication of classified communications intelligence information to an unauthorized person." Officials also requested that Hong Kong arrest Snowden and prepare to extradite him. Then on June 23, the United States revoked Snowden's passport and requested his extradition from Hong Kong. That same day, Hong Kong authorities informed the United States that its extradition request was "insufficient" and Snowden had been allowed to leave and fly to Moscow, reportedly using travel documents issued by the Ecuadorian embassy in London. When Snowden arrived in Moscow, he was not allowed to leave the airport's transit area, because he had no U.S. passport and Ecuadorian President Rafael Correa claimed that Snowden's travel documents were not valid.

According to WikiLeaks, Snowden applied for asylum in more than twenty countries. Brazil, Finland, Germany, India, and Poland rejected his applications, while other countries, including Austria, Ecuador, and Spain said Snowden would have to be in their country before they would consider his application. Snowden remained in the Moscow airport until August 1, when Russia granted him a year of temporary asylum in a move that angered U.S. officials. White House Press Secretary Jay Carney said the United States was "extremely disappointed that the Russian government would take this step despite our very clear and lawful requests in public and in private to have Mr. Snowden expelled to the United States to face the charges against him," adding that the United States was reevaluating a previously planned meeting with Putin during the September Group of 20 (G20) summit in St. Petersburg.

THE LEAKS CONTINUE

Various media outlets around the world continued to publish documents provided by Snowden through the end of the year, some of which generated angry responses from international leaders and strained U.S. relationships with several allies. This included a report by *Der Spiegel* that the NSA had targeted European Union buildings in Washington, D.C., and Brussels as part of its surveillance programs, and that it had infiltrated the EU's computer network. In October, *The Wall Street Journal* and *The Guardian* reported that the NSA had monitored the phone calls of thirty-five world leaders, and another report by *Der Spiegel* suggested that the NSA may have been tapping German Chancellor Angela Merkel's cell phone since 2002. Merkel reacted angrily to the news. "I have made it clear to the president of the United States that spying on friends is not acceptable at all," Merkel said. "We are allies facing challenges together. But such an alliance can only be built on the basis of trust."

It was also reported that the NSA had collected bulk data on approximately sixty million phone calls placed in Spain in December 2012, and that the agency had collected similar records in France and Italy. French President François Hollande demanded that such activity "immediately stop," stating that "there can be no negotiations or transactions in all areas until we have obtained these guarantees, for France but also for all of the European Union." Italian Prime Minister Enrico Letta also denounced the NSA's activities, calling them "inconceivable and unacceptable." The UN later adopted a symbolic resolution declaring a worldwide right of individuals to online privacy.

These and other revelations prompted several governments, including the United States, to begin reviewing their intelligence operations. A number of U.S. organizations, like the American Civil Liberties Union (ACLU) and the Electronic Frontier Foundation, have also filed lawsuits challenging the constitutionality of the NSA programs. Meanwhile, Snowden continues to live in an undisclosed location in Russia and has since received a number of recognitions, including the Sam Adams Award and the German "Whistleblower" prize, from organizations that admire him and regard him as a hero for his actions.

—Linda Fecteau

Following is a press release from the Department of Justice on June 26, 2013, requesting that Hong Kong arrest Edward Snowden; the edited text of a speech delivered by NSA Director Gen. Keith Alexander on June 28, 2013, in regard to the Snowden affair; and the edited text of a September 4, 2013, interview with Russian President Vladimir Putin on the Snowden case.

Justice Department Requests Snowden's Provisional Arrest

June 26, 2013

"The U.S. is disappointed and disagrees with the determination by Hong Kong authorities not to honor the U.S. request for the arrest of the fugitive, Edward J. Snowden.

"The request for the fugitive's arrest for purposes of his extradition complied with all of the requirements of the US/Hong Kong Surrender Agreement. At no point, in all of our discussions through Friday, did the authorities in Hong Kong raise any issues regarding the sufficiency of the U.S's provisional arrest request. In light of this, we find their decision to be particularly troubling.

"Throughout this event, U.S. Department of Justice authorities have been in continual contact with their Hong Kong counterparts starting on June 10, 2013 when we learned that Snowden was in Hong Kong.

"We have had repeated communications with our Hong Kong counterparts at senior levels.

"Attorney General Eric Holder placed a phone call on June 19th EDT, with his counterpart, Hong Kong Secretary for Justice Rimsky Yuen, stressing the importance of the matter and urging Hong Kong to honor our request for Snowden's arrest.

"There have been repeated engagements by the U.S. Department of State and U.S. Consulate General in Hong Kong.

"There have been repeated engagements by the FBI with their law enforcement counterparts.

"And finally, there have been continual communications by the Criminal Division's Office of International Affairs with counterparts at HKSAR's Department of Justice, International Law Division and Mutual Legal Assistance Unit."

BACKGROUND TIMELINE INFORMATION

- On June 14, 2013, the fugitive, Edward J. Snowden, was charged by complaint in the ED VA with violations of:
  - 18 U.S.C. § 793(d) (Unauthorized Disclosure of National Defense Information);
  - 18 U.S.C. § 798(a)(3) (Unauthorized Disclosure of Classified Communication Intelligence); and
  - 18 U.S.C. § 641 (Theft of Government Property).
- On that same date, a warrant was issued for his arrest.
- On June 15, 2013, the United States requested pursuant to the US/HK Surrender Agreement that HKSAR authorities provisionally arrest the fugitive for purposes of extradition.
- The U.S. request complied with all aspects of the treaty in force between the United States and the HKSAR—containing all documents and information required for HKSAR to provisionally arrest Snowden.

- June 17, 2013, Hong Kong authorities acknowledged receipt of our request. Despite repeated inquiries, Hong Kong authorities did not respond with any requests for additional information or documents, stating only that the matter was "under review" and refusing to elaborate;
- On June 21, 2013, Hong Kong authorities requested additional information concerning the U.S. charges and evidence. The U.S. had been in communication with the Hong Kong authorities about their inquiries.
- U.S. authorities were in the process of responding to the request when we learned that Hong Kong authorities had allowed the fugitive to leave Hong Kong.
- On June 23, 2013, Hong Kong authorities notified the U.S. that they had found our request insufficient and had allowed the fugitive to leave Hong Kong without acting on [our] request.

SOURCE: U.S. Department of Justice. Office of Public Affairs. "Justice Department Statement on the Request to Hong Kong for Edward Snowden's Provisional Arrest." June 26, 2013. http://www.justice.gov/opa/pr/2013/June/13-opa-761.html.

DOCUMENT *NSA Director on Snowden Leaks*

June 28, 2013

GENERAL KEITH ALEXANDER: . . . Before I go into my cyber discussion, I thought it was important for me to address some of the media leaks that are going on, and I think it's important that you hear from me some of this. I want to make six key points.

First, our responsibility, my main responsibility is defense of this country. These programs are part of that effort. In 2001, after 9/11, it was determined by the 9/11 Commission that the intelligence community could not connect the dots, foreign and domestic. We set about as a community to figure out how could we connect those dots . . . And we set up these two programs, 215, Section 215 for the business records FISA, and 702, as two of the capabilities look at a methodology to help us connect those dots. These capabilities were approved by the administration—thank you—Congress and the FISA court. With these exceptional authorities came equally exceptional oversight by all three branches of the government. These programs are focused with distinct purposes and oversight mechanisms. We understand and support the need to ensure we protect both civil liberties and national security. It's not one or the other. It must be both. That's why we take oversight of these programs very seriously.

A report issued by the Senate Select Intelligence Committee in June 2012, in support of the reauthorization of the 2008 amendments to FISA, emphasized that the government implements this authority in a responsible manner. And I quote: "Through four year of oversight, the committee has not identified a single case in which a government official engaged in willful effort to circumvent or violate the law—not one case in four years."

I'd like to just give you some insights on the business record FISA first and use an analogy using a lockbox. Under the business record FISA, or Section 215, we take the metadata from the service providers and place it into a virtual lockbox. The only way NSA can go into that lockbox is if we have what is called reasonable, articulable suspicion of a selector that is related to terrorism. In all of 2012, we approved less than 300 selectors—such as telephone numbers—to initiate queries into that virtual lockbox. There has to be a foreign nexus, an association with al-Qaida or other specified terrorist organizations.

[The following two paragraphs have been omitted and provide an example of when the NSA program helped to disrupt a terrorist plot.]

My third point: These programs have helped us connect the dots, as I've just used in Op High Rise, but our allies have benefited, too. On 21 June, last week, last Friday, we provided 54 cases to several congressional committees in which these programs contributed to our understanding, and in many cases, helped enable the disruption of terrorist plots in the U.S. and in over 20 countries throughout the world. It is important to note we are part of a larger government that includes our great partners at FBI, CIA, DHS, the Defense Department, as well as many others. We also partner with our allies in combatting terrorism. Here are some statistics of those 54 events.

Of the 54, 42 involved disruptive plots—disrupted plots. Twelve involved cases of material support to terrorism. Fifty of the 54 cases led to arrests or detentions. Our allies benefited, too. Twenty-five of these events occurred in Europe, 11 in Asia and five in Africa. Thirteen events had a homeland nexus. In 12 of those events, Section 215 contributed to our overall understanding and help to the FBI—twelve of the 13 . . .

Fourth, these programs operate under a rigorous oversight framework from all three branches of our government. FISA provides that in order to target the content of a U.S. persons communications anywhere in the world, NSA and the rest of our government requires a finding of probable cause under a specific court order. This translates into significant information on—these capabilities translate into significant information on ongoing terrorist activities with no willful violations of our law.

Fifty-four terrorist activities disrupted; zero willful violations. When you think about how our government operates and what we've done to bring all three branches together, I think that's something to be proud of. We have defended the nation 54 times, and our allies, and we have ensured the protection of our civil liberties and privacy in oversight by all three forms of our—all three branches of our government. I think that's what the nation expects our government to do, disrupt terrorist activities, defend our civil liberties and privacy . . .

Sixth, my sixth point—I'm getting through this, bear with me—public discussion of NSA's tradecraft or the tools that support its operation provides insights that our adversaries, to include terrorists, can and do use to hide their activities. Those who wish us harm now know how we counter their actions.

These leaks have caused significant and irreversible damage to our nation's security. Historically, every time a capability is revealed, we lose our ability to track those targets. What is going on in these leaks is unconscionable, in my opinion, and it hurts our nation and our allies and it's flat wrong.

There are lawful and legitimate mechanisms to raise concerns about these programs. NSA, DOD and DNI all have whistle-blower programs and investigator generals who are in a position to do this. An individual acting nobly would have chosen one of those as a course of action to reveal his concerns.

I worry that there will be more leaks and that they will attempt to further sensationalize this issue. I'd ask you to remember that context matters, that these authorities are carefully debated and considered across three branches of government and that we only employ these capabilities that we believe are both useful and necessary . . .

So what does that come to? A conclusion: First, the damage is real. I believe the irresponsible release of classified information about these programs will have a long-term detrimental impact on the intelligence community's ability to detect future attacks. These leaks have inflamed and sensationalized for ignoble purposes the work the intelligent (sic) community does lawfully under strict oversight and compliance.

If you want to know who's acting nobly, look at the folks at NSA, FBI, CIA and the Defense Department that defend our nation every day and do it legally and protect our civil liberties and privacy. They take an oath to our Constitution to uphold and defend that Constitution. And they take that oath seriously and they do a great job. They're the heroes that our nation should be looking at. They're the ones that are taking care of us and they're the ones protecting our civil liberties and privacy.

[The following seven pages have been omitted and include Gen. Alexander's remarks on U.S. cybersecurity and a question-and-answer period.]

SOURCE: National Security Agency. "General Keith Alexander Speaks at AFCEA's Conference." June 28, 2013. http://www.nsa.gov/public_info/_files/speeches_testimonies/Transcript_of_GEN_Alexanders_AFCEA_Keynote_Speech_27_June_2013.pdf.

Putin Discusses Russian Position on Snowden

September 4, 2013

On the eve of the G20 Summit, Vladimir Putin gave an interview to Channel One and the Associated Press news agency. The interview was recorded in Novo-Ogaryovo on September 3.

[Text containing discussion of topics including Syria, the G20 Summit, U.S.-Russian relations and Russia's court system has been omitted.]

JOHN DANISZEWSKI: Since we are talking about legal matters, the Edward Snowden case has aroused a lot of unhappiness and frustration. What do you as a former security man think about the actions of a man like Snowden who leaks secret information he was entrusted with?

VLADIMIR PUTIN: If it was really secret information and if such a person caused us some damage, then I would certainly seek his prosecution to the fullest extent permitted by Russian law.

JOHN DANISZEWSKI: In that regard, do you think the US administration is right to seek his return from Russia, to ask you to send him back?

VLADIMIR PUTIN: Probably, yes. You see, the problem is completely different. We do not know if the administration is right or not. The thing is not that we protect Snowden. We do not protect him at all. The problem is that we do not have an agreement with the United States on mutual extradition of criminals. We repeatedly suggested that the United States should conclude such an agreement, but we were refused.

There are certain rules and procedures in the world, according to which a criminal can and must be handed over to the other party if there is an appropriate agreement where many issues are set out and certain guarantees are given. However, the United States refused to sign such an agreement with us. And they do not extradite our criminals who did not reveal just some secrets, but whose hands are stained with blood, who killed people, who traded in human beings, and our American colleagues are aware of it. We cannot judge whether Snowden committed a crime in the United States or not. We simply cannot do that. But as a sovereign country that does not have such agreements with the United States, we cannot do otherwise but to give him the opportunity to live here.

I will now tell you something I have never said before. I have dropped some hints but have never said anything like that directly. Mr Snowden first went to Hong Kong and got in touch with our diplomatic representatives. I was informed that there was such a man, agent of special services. I asked them what he wanted and was told that this man was fighting for human rights and free flow of information, against violations of related human rights and law in the United States, as well as against violations of international law. I said: "So what? If he wants to stay in this country, he is welcome, provided however that he stops any kind of activities that could damage Russian-US relations. This country is not an NGO, it has its own national interests and it does not want to sever Russian-US relations." This information was communicated to him. He said: "No, I am fighting for human rights and I urge you to join me in this fight." I answered: "No, Russia will not join him, let him fight alone." And he left, just like this.

Then he took a flight to Latin America. I learned that Mr Snowden was on the way to our country two hours before his plane landed. What happened next? Information was leaked. No offence, but I think that US special services' agents along with diplomats should have acted with greater professionalism. After they learnt that he was on the way to our country on a transit flight, they put all possible destination countries under pressure, all countries in Latin American and Europe. But they could have allowed him to get to a country where his security could not be guaranteed or intercepted him along the way—they did the same, by the way, with the plane carrying the president of one Latin American country, which, to my opinion, was absolutely unacceptable, done in a rude fashion inappropriate for the United States or your European partners. That was humiliating. The United States could have done the same with respect to Snowden. What stopped them? Instead, they scared everyone; the man quickly decided to stay in Russia's transit zone and got stuck in our country. What were we to do after that? Hand him over to the United States? In this case we need to sign an agreement. You do not want to? All right, hand our criminals to us instead. You do not want that either? Good. Why would you then request extradition on a unilateral basis? Why so snobbish? Both sides need to take into account each other's interests, work together and look for professional solutions.

So, we are defending specific norms governing state-to-state relations rather than Mr Snowden. I really hope that in the future, Russia and the United States will reach the relevant arrangements and formalise them as legally binding instruments.

JOHN DANISZEWSKI: Has Edward Snowden offered Russia any information, any confidential information and if he did, would you say what?

VLADIMIR PUTIN: No, he didn't offer us any information. We didn't receive anything from him and we do not intend to. We are professionals as well, and we believe that everything he could tell us is already known to our US colleagues from special services. They have minimised all possible risks in this regard, they have altered, destroyed, changed everything. He is of no use to us. We did not even want to get involved into all this, you see. He is a man of a completely different type; of course he can be presented as anyone. I understand that US special services are interested in portraying him as a traitor, but he sees things differently—he calls himself a fighter for human rights. He may well be denied this characteristic but that is already the business of those who make judgments. He calls himself like this and behaves just like this. We have no desire to involve him in any kind of cooperation or get any information from him. He has never tried to give us anything, and we have never tried to get anything out of him.

JOHN DANISZEWSKI: So, theoretically, he could live to a ripe old age in Russia?

VLADIMIR PUTIN: You know, I sometimes think about him, he is a strange type. He is a young man, just over 30, I cannot even imagine what he thinks. How is he going to live his future life? In fact, it is a hard life that awaits him. I cannot even imagine what he will do afterwards. It is clear, though, that we will not hand him over, he can feel safe here. But what is next? As time passes, the United States will probably understand that it has been dealing with a person who has certain beliefs that can be judged differently, rather than with a traitor or a spy. And some compromises might be found in this case. Do not ask me. It is his life and he has opted for it by himself. He believes this is noble and justified and that such sacrifices are necessary—it is his choice.

[The following text has been omitted, and contains discussion of topics including Russia's economy, domestic crime, and the 2014 Olympics.]

SOURCE: President of Russia. "Interview to Channel One and Associated Press news agency." September 4, 2013. http://eng.kremlin.ru/news/5935.

OTHER HISTORIC DOCUMENTS OF INTEREST

FROM THIS VOLUME

- Federal Review of NSA Surveillance Program Issued, p. 633

FROM PREVIOUS HISTORIC DOCUMENTS

- WikiLeaks Founder Denied Stay of Extradition, *2012*, p. 228
- U.S. Department of State Responds to WikiLeaks, *2010*, p. 596

July

European Union Officials on the Addition of Croatia to the EU

JULY 1, 2013

Supporters of the European Union (EU) saw the year 2013 as a recovery period for the bloc, following hot on the heels of years of severe stress caused by a deep economic recession and consequent sovereign debt crisis. Two notable bright spots appeared on the horizon. On July 1, the Western Balkan nation of Croatia became the EU's 28th member state and its first new member since the economic crisis began in 2008. The event was greeted with enthusiasm in Croatia and the European Union, albeit tempered somewhat by the continuing stiff headwinds that Croatia faces economically with high debt and unemployment. At the same time, the small Baltic nation of Latvia got the green light to join the EU's single currency area, the eurozone. Latvia joined the EU back in 2004, which is a necessary step countries must take before they can join the eurozone. These two events were modest signs that, despite its ongoing economic challenges, the EU retains some attraction for countries. As Andris Spruds, director of the Latvian Institute of International Affairs, said, "Croatia and Latvia are keeping the European dream alive."

CROATIA OPENS A NEW CHAPTER

With a population of 4.3 million, Croatia emerged as an independent country in 1991 during the violent break-up of the former Yugoslavia, a multiethnic, multireligious nation in southeast Europe. Prior to disintegration, communist Yugoslavia had been a frontrunner to join the EU, since it was more developed economically than many of its Balkan neighbors, and had long pursued an independent foreign policy unlike its easterly communist neighbors. But a surge in nationalist sentiment from the late 1980s triggered ethnic tensions that split the country apart. Croatia seceded from Yugoslavia in 1991, but then was forced to fight a war of independence in which 20,000 Croats were killed. As bloody as that war was, it paled in comparison to the fighting in neighboring Bosnia, which, after seceding from Yugoslavia in 1992, was devastated by a three-year civil war. Croatia's President, Franjo Tudjman, wanted to annex the area of Bosnia where ethnic Croats lived, but he failed and Croatia's borders remained what they were in the Yugoslav era.

The destruction wreaked by multiple Yugoslav wars in the 1990s hampered Croatia in advancing its bid to join the EU. So did the authoritarian leadership of President Tudjman, which was incompatible with the democratic standards that aspiring EU members had to meet. Croatia began to turn a new page in 2003 when a new leader, Ivo Sanader, made it clear that his top priority was to secure EU membership for Croatia. Sanader was willing to do whatever it took to reach that goal, including carrying out tough reforms to root out corruption and forge an independent judiciary. While Croatia officially became a candidate to join the EU in 2003, it took a couple more years for the accession negotiations to begin. This was largely because it was some time before the EU was convinced that Croatia was doing all it could to hand over suspects to the International Criminal Tribunal for the Former Yugoslavia (ICTY) in The Hague. This was the court responsible for prosecuting war crimes committed during the Yugoslav Wars. But the arrest of General Ante Gotovina in Spain's Canary Islands in 2005 and his subsequent extradition to The Hague satisfied the EU that the time was ripe to start accession talks.

The negotiations proceeded at a steady pace as Croatia showed itself eager to implement the tens of thousands of pages of EU laws and regulations as required before joining. However, just as Croatia was approaching the finishing line, its neighbor and fellow former Yugoslav republic, Slovenia, blocked its path to membership over a bilateral dispute about where their mutual border lay. Slovenia had escaped the Yugoslav wars relatively unscathed, and in May 2004, it had become the first of the former Yugoslav republics to join the EU. This meant that it now had a veto over Croatia joining the bloc. Croatia made the concessions necessary to resolve their border dispute, and a path was cleared for accession. A referendum on membership passed in Croatia in January 2012, with 66 percent voting in favor. Even though enthusiasm for taking in new members had greatly diminished from the heady days of the early 2000s when EU membership nearly doubled from fifteen to twenty-seven, existing members were generally supportive of Croatia joining. Croatia's accession fits in with the EU's wider strategy to integrate all the Western Balkan countries into the EU to stabilize and pacify the region.

CROATIA GAINS BENEFITS OF MEMBERSHIP WHILE ITS NEIGHBORS CONTINUE TO STRUGGLE

Two of the EU's presidents, Commission President José Manuel Barroso and Council President Herman Van Rompuy, traveled to the Croatian capital Zagreb to attend celebratory events. "You will discover that membership is not just about respecting and shaping rules, but as much about sharing the responsibility for our common endeavour. In weather fair and foul, 'for better and for worse,' we must remain united as a Union," said Van Rompuy. Croatia "is a fundamentally different place than 20 years ago," said Barroso. "There is full respect for fundamental rights, the rule of law, non-discrimination, and a more modern economy," he added.

The benefits of EU membership for Croatia include financial support of around €1 billion a year until 2020 and full access to the EU's single market of more than 500 million people, including free movement of people, goods, labor, and capital. For the time being, Croatia is not part of the eurozone, which is a group of more than half the EU member states who have adopted a common currency. Croatia is legally obliged to join the eurozone once it meets the macroeconomic criteria for euro membership, which include limits on public debt, deficits, and inflation. Neither is Croatia yet part of the EU's so-called Schengen Area that permits citizens to travel between other EU countries without having to go through border controls. But this too should follow once Croatia meets certain standards of border controls as well as police and judicial cooperation.

Most of Croatia's neighbors are trying to emulate its example and accede to full EU membership. Some are closer to achieving this goal than others. The small state of Montenegro is widely seen as having the best chance of joining within a few years. But others face more serious obstacles, many of which are a legacy of the wars of the 1990s. For instance, Bosnia's inability to put in place a functional, unitary federal government as a result of the poor relations between Bosnian Muslims, Serbs, and Croats has held back its bid. Serbia and Kosovo were hindered by Serbia's refusal to recognize Kosovo's secession from Serbia in 2008, although the two nations reached an important agreement in April

2013 that is helping both advance their bids. Macedonia is hampered by the refusal of its neighbor, Greece—which joined the EU in 1981—to recognize the name of the country as "Macedonia" because a region in northern Greece is also called Macedonia. And Albania is slowly advancing, but it will need to make greater inroads in tackling corruption if it is to be admitted. The other two countries that are in the midst of negotiations to join the EU are Iceland and Turkey. Iceland's banking and fishing sectors have dominated its membership negotiations, whereas Turkey faces a multitude of obstacles to advancing its candidacy, not least of which is its support for the separatist Turkish Republic of Northern Cyprus occupied by Turkish troops since 1974.

LATVIA BECOMES THE EUROZONE'S NEWEST MEMBER

The decision taken by EU finance ministers on July 9 to allow Latvia join the eurozone starting in January 2014 was an important milestone both for Latvia and the euro. The EU's single currency first entered circulation in 2002 in eleven member states. By 2013, eurozone membership had grown to seventeen. Some EU countries, such as Sweden, Denmark, and the United Kingdom, have chosen to stay out of the eurozone, while others such as Poland plan to join but have not yet met the macroeconomic standards required for membership. Latvia, a country of 2.2 million people, has only been independent since 1990 when it seceded from the Soviet Union shortly before the Soviet Union split into fifteen independent countries. Latvians became full members of the EU in May 2004 along with nine other countries, most of whom were formerly communist nations behind the Iron Curtain separating Western from Eastern Europe. Like their Baltic neighbors and their fellow former Soviet republics Lithuania and Estonia, Latvians are keen to integrate themselves as fully as possible into the EU. In part this is because they harbor great residual resentment of their easterly neighbor, Russia, and view EU membership as a bulwark against potential Russian interference in their affairs.

Latvia's efforts to join the eurozone suffered a temporary setback when the economic recession of 2008–2009 hit hard. The Latvian government responded to the crisis by adopting austerity policies that included cutting public sector employees' wages in half to slash deficits and regain the country's competitiveness in global markets. This sudden drop in living standards was a big shock for Latvians, but it did enable them to rebound relatively quickly, and their economy grew by nearly 6 percent in 2010. Welcoming the EU's decision to admit Latvia to the eurozone, Prime Minister Valdis Dombrovskis explained his support, saying: "It becomes ever more clear that two-speed Europe is emerging. Do we want to belong to core Europe?" He was referring to the widening chasm in the EU between members who use the euro as their currency (the "ins") and those who do not (the "outs"). As eurozone members forge ahead with ever closer economic integration—for instance, introducing a common regulatory regime for banks—the "outs" are unsure whether or not they should apply such measures. Eurozone membership is likely to continue expanding. With Latvia's neighbor, Estonia, having joined in January 2011, the only country part of the Baltic trio that remains outside is Lithuania. The Lithuanians are similarly eager to join and this may happen as early as 2015.

—Brian Beary

Following are two statements given July 1, 2013, by the presidents of the European Council and European Commission upon Croatia's ascension to the European Union.

Economic Council President on Croatia's Inclusion in the EU

July 1, 2013

Mr. President, Mr. Prime-Minister, Excellencies, Ladies and gentlemen, and above all: you, Citizens of Zagreb, People of Croatia! To all of you I say: Čestitam Hrvatska! Congratulations Croatia!

As midnight struck, your country crossed an important threshold. It will change the life of this nation for good. You have always been Europeans—and you are now members of the Union. On behalf of the leaders of the 27 member states, many of whom are here, I welcome you wholeheartedly.

Your country has worked hard for it—with success. As of tomorrow your representatives will sit side-by-side with all other member states. Together shaping decisions for the benefit of all citizens across the Union—from Zagreb to Zaragoza, from Split to Stockholm.

As new challenges arise, you will discover that membership is not just about respecting and shaping rules, but as much about sharing the responsibility for our common endeavour. In weather fair and foul, "for better and for worse," we must remain united as a Union.

The European Union is one of peace, built on the spirit of reconciliation. In the recent history of the Western Balkans, your country's entry marks a milestone towards a shared future: living together, in peace and prosperity. Over the past months, jointly with Slovenia, you have courageously overcome hurdles; also with Bosnia Herzegovina.

Following the same path, Belgrade and Priština have also reached a historic agreement. I am confident that more positive steps will follow. As a trailblazer for the region, your country, now as a member state, has a vitally important role to play.

I'm proud to be here tonight for this historical moment. Hvala, thank you.

SOURCE: European Council. "Speech by President of the European Council Herman Van Rompuy on the occasion of the entry of Croatia into the European Union." July 1, 2013. http://europa.eu/rapid/press-release_PRES-13-309_en.htm.

President of the European Commission Congratulates Croatia

July 1, 2013

Prime Minister Milanović,
President Schulz,
Deputy Prime Minister Pusić,
Vice-President Reding,
Vice-President Karas,
Vice-President Miguel Angel Martínez,

Minister Thierry Repentin,
Colleagues from the Commission—Štefan Füle, Neven Mimica,
Distinguished guests,
Excellencies,
Ladies and Gentlemen,
Dear friends,

Dobro jutro Hrvatska. Dobro došla u Europsku Uniju!

This morning Croatians have woken up for the first time as citizens of the European Union—after a fantastic celebration last night!

As the famous Croatian poet Petar Preradović once said: "In this world only change is constant." And Croatia has changed, to the better! It is a fundamentally different place than 20 years ago, a proud and confident member of the European family. There is full respect for fundamental rights, the rule of law, non-discrimination, and a more modern economy. It's the efforts of all Croatians who have made this change possible.

Just as Croatians have changed Croatia, so your country can help change this part of Europe. Your accession to the European Union is a signal. You have shown that it is not only possible to overcome the burdens of the past, to work towards reconciliation and a better future for all—but that it is in everybody's own interest. This is the spirit that Europe is about!

These positive changes are not the end, they are a new beginning. Every day, we must all work to defend and uphold these values, the European values. Every day, we must all work to enjoy the benefits of the European Union.

Ladies and gentlemen,

The European Union is not simply an end in itself. The European Union, for all the challenges it faces today, is a tool that enables you—its citizens—to shape your own futures for the better.

This new Representation which we are opening today—this truly European house—is here to help you do that: to provide information about the European Union, to answer your questions, and to act as your advocate.

On your path to the European Union, the European Commission stood by your side. We provided support and assistance. We will continue to do so.

We will support you in Brussels and right here in the heart of your beautiful capital city Zagreb. There will be significant financial support, over €1 billion a year until 2020. But more than this, we offer the support that a family gives to any of its members.

This will be for the benefit of Croatia, for the benefit of Europe and above all for the benefit of you, the citizens of our newest Member State. This is of course a way of waiting for your contribution to our very important European project.

Let me conclude with a personal remark. When some time ago, together with the President of the European Parliament, Martin Schulz, and the President of the European Council, Herman Van Rompuy, we were receiving, on behalf of the European Union, the Nobel peace prize, it was precisely about this idea of a reconciled, united Europe that we were thinking. How big, how important is this project that is able to unite a continent that before was divided? How actual are indeed our commitments to the great goals of peace, of freedom, solidarity and justice?

I thank you for your attention.

SOURCE: European Commission. "Speech by President Barroso at the opening ceremony of the EU Representation in Zagreb." July 1, 2013. http://europa.eu/rapid/press-release_SPEECH-13-590_en.htm.

OTHER HISTORIC DOCUMENTS OF INTEREST

FROM PREVIOUS *HISTORIC DOCUMENTS*

U.S. Leaders Remark on Egyptian Coup

JULY 3 AND 27, 2013

In February 2011, after eighteen days of widespread protests, Egypt's long-time leader, Hosni Mubarak, resigned his position, setting in motion a period of instability in the Arab world's most populous nation. Power was initially handed to the military, and in June 2012, a new leader was democratically elected. From the outset, Mohamed Morsi faced many challenges, perhaps most significant of which was overseeing the process of drafting and approving a new constitution, which he did successfully by early 2013. Citizens across the nation, unhappy with the resulting governing law, continued to protest the new president, claiming that he intended to enforce Islamic Sharia law and give himself absolute power. On July 3, after days of violent protests, Morsi was removed by Egypt's military, leaving the fledgling democracy again without a leader.

2011 Arab Spring Protests Set Stage for Uncertainty

Former president Mubarak first came to power in 1981 after the assassination of Anwar el-Sadat. He immediately gave himself virtually absolute power, quieting his dissenters by governing under emergency law. This gave his powerful police force the ability to make arrests without reason, detain prisoners without charges or trials, and prevent any form of assembly. Mubarak grew increasingly unpopular, but there was little cohesive opposition in place to challenge his government.

In early 2011, unrest began brewing across the Middle East and a handful of leaders were deposed, starting with Tunisian ruler Zine al-Abidine Ben Ali. Ben Ali's ouster rang through Egyptian society, and soon protesters took to the streets in an attempt to make radical changes in their own country. On January 25, protesters began gathering in Cairo's Tahrir Square demanding greater democratic freedom and accountability for government leaders. Initially, Mubarak refused to step down, instead making lackluster promises for government reform. But on February 11, 2011, having lost the support of his military, Mubarak could no longer withstand the demands of the protesters and resigned his position.

The protests had little cohesive leadership that could effectively take charge of the nation's government. Upon resigning, Mubarak handed power to Egypt's military, the Armed Forces Supreme Council (SCAF). The military kept emergency law in place to prevent continuing demonstrations and did little to open up the government as protesters had hoped. In October 2011, the SCAF announced that it would not fully hand over executive power following an election in 2012, but would instead give the new president and parliament a subordinate role in the government. Additionally, the prime minister and cabinet would be chosen by the SCAF. The 2012 elections did proceed as planned; members of the Muslim Brotherhood gained a majority of the seats in parliament, but the SCAF retained broad control.

Morsi Elected and Challenged

With a parliament installed, presidential elections were set for May 2012. The Muslim Brotherhood initially promised not to seek the presidency, but instead it put forward Morsi, a conservative American-educated Islamist. Morsi was one of the top two candidates following the first round of voting, and heading into the June 2012 runoff, the SCAF dissolved parliament and gave itself control over all legislative activities and further limited the power of the presidency. The election still went ahead as planned, and Morsi won with 52 percent of the vote.

Morsi, who was largely a figurehead when he took office, promised to continue the Egyptian renaissance started by protesters in 2011 and install a firmly democratic government. Unwilling to accept such limited powers, on July 8, he ordered parliament back into session, and later that month appointed his own prime minister, Hesham Qandil. The SCAF did not relent in its decision to retain almost all military, legislative, and budgetary power until a new constitution could be drafted. Morsi refused to give in, and in August he forced the resignation of senior military officials including the army chief of staff. Morsi subsequently repealed the SCAF decree that took power away from the president, thus awarding himself far-reaching executive and legislative powers. Morsi said that by doing so he was protecting the will of the Egyptian people.

On November 22, Morsi made another power grab, giving himself new sweeping powers and putting any of his past and future decisions above judicial review. He also made the Islamist-dominated group charged with drafting the new constitution free from fear of legal challenges. According to the president, such a decision was necessary in an effort to move the country swiftly into a constitutional democracy. The public largely saw Morsi's announcement as a plan to cement authoritarian rule. Demonstrations began almost immediately after Morsi's announcement, and at one point an estimated 200,000 were gathered in Tahrir Square. Morsi supporters in the Muslim Brotherhood staged counter protests, and both sides clashed with police who used tear gas to disperse the crowds. As protests grew increasingly violent in the first week of December, Morsi relented and said he would immediately annul his decree, although it would not be retroactive, meaning that the group drafting the constitution could proceed with strong legal protection.

A referendum was set on a draft constitution for December 15 and 16. Morsi's opponents and some in the international community raised concerns that the 234-article document did not do much to protect minority religious groups and women, and that the Sharia law instated under Mubarak was maintained. Despite the concerns, the draft was passed with 64 percent of the public vote, and Morsi officially approved it on December 25.

Renewed Protests

On January 25, 2013, protesters returned to Tahrir Square to mark the second anniversary of the start of the revolution that brought Mubarak's reign to an end. The gatherings quickly evolved into a challenge to Morsi's leadership and his handling of the constitutional process. The president declared states of emergency in three cities and deployed the armed forces to help local police manage the violence; he also began attempting to work with opposition groups to find a way to end the demonstrations. These actions were largely dismissed as being without substance by groups such as the National Salvation Front (NSF), a political organization that rose out of the 2012 protests in opposition to Morsi's rule.

In April, the NSF, along with the April 6 Youth Movement and the Strong Egypt Party, started a grassroots effort to increase momentum to force Morsi out of office. The goal of the group was to collect enough signatures to remove the president by the end of June. The movement gained traction on June 15 when Morsi called for foreign intervention in Syria. The army refused to take any action, stating that it would do nothing more than protect Egypt's borders. Morsi's announcement brought protesters back to Tahrir Square where they clashed with Morsi supporters. Those opposed to Morsi demanded that he step down, frustrated by the president's authoritarian rule and his inability to shore up the economy, combat energy shortages, provide public security, and rebuild the nation's crumbling infrastructure. Protesters also accused Morsi's Muslim Brotherhood of imposing strict Sharia law.

On July 1, with the June 30 deadline for Morsi's removal past and violent protests still raging across the country, the SCAF issued the president a forty-eight hour ultimatum, which Morsi rejected saying that he would instead work through his own channels toward national reconciliation. Accusing his opponents of trying to overthrow his government, in a televised address Morsi called on Egyptian citizens to respect the constitution and his power as president, calling it the "only guarantee against further bloodshed." On July 3, Morsi reached out to the SCAF to persuade it to work with him to help form a consensus government, but one that would leave him in power. Rejecting the offer, the SCAF instead arrested the president and top Muslim Brotherhood leaders, suspended the constitution, and called for new elections to be held and new constitutional amendments drafted. Morsi offered little physical resistance to his arrest. Chief Justice Adly Mansour was appointed as interim president and tasked with forming a caretaker government until new elections could be held. In a televised address, military leader General Abdel-Fattah el-Sisi said that the military had no intention of becoming involved in politics but instead had to remove the president because he failed to meet the expectations of the Egyptian public; the ouster was, according to the general, the only chance for "national reconciliation."

Around the world, leaders called on the military to follow through on the intent to hold a new round of elections, expressing concern that the nation could devolve back into violence. "We are deeply concerned by the decision of the Egyptian Armed Forces to remove President Morsi and suspend the Egyptian Constitution," said President Barack Obama, who refrained from calling the situation a coup.

EGYPT STRUGGLES TO MOVE FORWARD

The overthrow of Morsi was met with cheers in Tahrir Square, but Morsi's supporters condemned what they called a coup d'état. After the military took power, it cracked down on Morsi supporters who held daily protests and set up camps around Egypt, deploying tanks and troops to the streets. The SCAF tried to work with the protesters to clear the camps, but, unable to do so, on August 14, the military entered two of the largest camps in Cairo, and forcibly expelled the protesters there. Tents were burned with their occupants still in them, as was a mosque. The Egyptian Health Ministry estimated that nearly 600 civilians were killed in the raid, but groups like the Muslim Brotherhood and National Coalition for Supporting Legitimacy put the death toll at closer to 2,500. International human rights organizations urged an investigation into the raid and subsequent killings. Gasser Abdel-Razek, the associate director at the Egyptian Initiative for Personal Rights, said there could "be no hope for the rule of law and political stability in Egypt . . . without accountability for what may be the single biggest incident of mass killing in Egypt's recent history." Any investigation was thought to be paramount to moving Egypt forward and restarting the democratic process.

In September, an Egyptian court ordered the disbanding of the Muslim Brotherhood, which forced the group back underground where it had operated during Mubarak's reign when it was banned from participating in public life. In November, Morsi went on trial for inciting murder. The trial was ultimately postponed to a date to be announced later while the court determined whether the case had merit to move forward. The trial coincided with a visit by Secretary of State John Kerry, who was in the country to encourage the Egyptian leaders to continue pressing for unity. Just two months after his visit, Kerry dismissed as unfair the results of a referendum in which voters approved a new draft constitution by an overwhelming 98 percent. According to Kerry, the process of drafting the new document was not inclusive and the military kept dissenters from voting. Despite his concern, Kerry urged the interim government to make its commitment to a democratic society a reality. Sisi is largely expected to be elected president when elections are held in the spring of 2014, which has raised concern in the international community that the army chief would further consolidate his power and continue limiting Egyptian rights.

—Heather Kerrigan

Following is a statement by President Barack Obama on July 3, 2013, regarding the overthrow of Egyptian President Mohamed Morsi; and a statement by Secretary of State John Kerry on July 27, 2013, regarding the continuing unrest in Egypt.

President Obama Remarks on the Situation in Egypt

July 3, 2013

As I have said since the Egyptian revolution, the United States supports a set of core principles, including opposition to violence, protection of universal human rights, and reform that meets the legitimate aspirations of the people. The United States does not support particular individuals or political parties, but we are committed to the democratic process and respect for the rule of law. Since the current unrest in Egypt began, we have called on all parties to work together to address the legitimate grievances of the Egyptian people, in accordance with the democratic process and without recourse to violence or the use of force.

The United States is monitoring the very fluid situation in Egypt, and we believe that ultimately, the future of Egypt can only be determined by the Egyptian people. Nevertheless, we are deeply concerned by the decision of the Egyptian Armed Forces to remove President Mursi and suspend the Egyptian Constitution. I now call on the Egyptian military to move quickly and responsibly to return full authority back to a democratically elected civilian government as soon as possible through an inclusive and transparent process and to avoid any arbitrary arrests of President Mursi and his supporters. Given today's developments, I have also directed the relevant departments and agencies to review the implications under U.S. law for our assistance to the Government of Egypt.

The United States continues to believe firmly that the best foundation for lasting stability in Egypt is a democratic political order with participation from all sides and all political parties: secular and religious, civilian and military. During this uncertain period, we expect the military to ensure that the rights of all Egyptian men and women are protected, including the right to peaceful assembly, due process, and free and fair trials in civilian courts. Moreover, the goal of any political process should be a government that respects the rights of all people, majority and minority; that institutionalizes the checks and balances upon which democracy depends; and that places the interests of the people above party or faction. The voices of all those who have protested peacefully must be heard, including those who welcomed today's developments and those who have supported President Mursi. In the interim, I urge all sides to avoid violence and come together to ensure the lasting restoration of Egypt's democracy.

No transition to democracy comes without difficulty, but in the end it must stay true to the will of the people. An honest, capable, and representative government is what ordinary Egyptians seek and what they deserve. The longstanding partnership between the United States and Egypt is based on shared interests and values, and we will continue to work with the Egyptian people to ensure that Egypt's transition to democracy succeeds.

SOURCE: Executive Office of the President. "Statement on the Situation in Egypt." July 3, 2013. *Compilation of Presidential Documents* 2013, no. 00488 (July 3, 2013). http://www.gpo.gov/fdsys/pkg/DCPD-201300488/pdf/DCPD-201300488.pdf.

Secretary of State Kerry on the Violence in Egypt

July 27, 2013

I spoke this morning with Interim Vice President Mohamed ElBaradei, Interim Foreign Minister Nabil Fahmy, and European Union High Representative Catherine Ashton and expressed our deep concern about the bloodshed and violence in Cairo and Alexandria over the past 24 hours that has claimed the lives of scores of Egyptian demonstrators and injured more than 1,000 people.

I want to convey our deepest sympathies to the families of those who lost their lives as well as those who were injured.

This is a pivotal moment for Egypt.

Over two years ago, a revolution began. Its final verdict is not yet decided, but it will be forever impacted by what happens right now.

In this extremely volatile environment, Egyptian authorities have a moral and legal obligation to respect the right of peaceful assembly and freedom of expression. Both are essential components of the inclusive democratic process they have publicly embraced.

Violence not only further sets back the process of reconciliation and democratization in Egypt, but it will negatively impact regional stability.

At this critical juncture, it is essential that the security forces and the interim government respect the right of peaceful protest, including the ongoing sit-in demonstrations.

The United States urges an independent and impartial inquiry into the events of the last day, and calls on all of Egypt's leaders across the political spectrum to act immediately to help their country take a step back from the brink.

An inclusive political process is needed that achieves as soon as possible a freely and fairly elected government committed to pluralism and tolerance.

The Egyptians who poured into Tahrir Square in 2011 and 2013 themselves called for this outcome for their country's future and for their aspirations.

A meaningful political dialogue, for which interim government officials have themselves called, requires participants who represent all the political parts of Egyptian society.

To enable such a dialogue, the United States reiterates our call for an end to politicized detentions and the release of political leaders consistent with the law.

SOURCE: U.S. Department of State. Media Center. "Situation in Egypt." July 27, 2013. http://www.state.gov/secretary/remarks/2013/07/212498.htm.

OTHER HISTORIC DOCUMENTS OF INTEREST

FROM PREVIOUS *HISTORIC DOCUMENTS*

- Egypt Announces Presidential Decree, Acceptance of Draft Constitution, *2012*, p. 567
- New Egyptian President Delivers Victory Speech, *2012*, p. 269
- Arab Spring: International Response to Mubarak's Resignation (Egypt), *2011*, p. 95

EU and U.S. Open Free
Trade Discussions

JULY 8 AND 12, 2013

On July 8, the European Union (EU) and the United States started negotiating a free trade agreement, holding a first round of talks in Washington, D.C. The planned trade pact, which is called the Transatlantic Trade and Investment Partnership (TTIP) would, if concluded, be the world's largest bilateral free trade agreement, covering 40 percent of the world's economic output. The initiative came about in part because of the failure of the World Trade Organization (WTO) to significantly advance trade liberalization since being established in 1995. It is also the U.S. and EU response to the remarkable economic growth that Asian economies, especially China, have enjoyed in recent years. The old transatlantic allies believe that their new agreement will increase growth, create more jobs, and make them leaders in setting global regulatory standards.

ECONOMIC DOWNTURN SPURS ACTION

Since the end of World War II, the United States and the European Union have been consistent advocates of a more liberalized world trading system. However, since the early 2000s, they have grown increasingly frustrated with what they had thought would become the main vehicle to advance this agenda, the Geneva-based WTO. The WTO launched the Doha round of trade liberalization talks in 2001, but it has so far failed to deliver much. This has been partly because the advanced economies like the United States and the EU have clashed often with emerging economies like Brazil, China, and India, and their positions in the talks have diverged greatly. The economic crisis of 2008 did not help matters because the world leaders were focused on preventing a resurgence of economic protectionism rather than actively advancing further trade liberalization.

Faced with deadlock at the WTO, in the late 2000s, the European Union opted for a new strategy: to forge ahead with as many bilateral and regional trade agreements as possible. The United States, however, was much slower to follow this path. This was mainly because President Barack Obama, who took office in January 2009, was more sympathetic to the widespread public hostility toward free trade pacts that has developed in the United States since the 1990s. Many Americans believe that more liberalized global trade has hurt the U.S. economy by causing U.S. markets to be flooded by cheap imports of Chinese goods and triggering outsourcing of U.S. jobs as companies move their factories to lower-wage countries. Opposition has been especially strong among the U.S. labor unions, which retain close ties to President Obama's Democratic Party. Consequently, Obama did not start talks on any new bilateral trade agreement during his first term.

However, the calls, especially from the business community, for the European Union and the United States to do something ambitious to increase their mutual trade began to grow stronger. The Great Recession of 2007–2009, followed by the eurozone debt crisis from 2010 to 2012, caused both economies to lose further ground to emerging economies like Brazil, China, and India. At a U.S.–EU summit hosted by President Obama at the White House on November 28, 2011, the leaders decided to create a high-level working group to explore what might be possible in the way of a new trade deal. That working group returned with a clear recommendation in early 2013 to start talks on a comprehensive agreement that eliminated tariffs, removed barriers to investment, increased access to procurement markets, and brought about greater regulatory convergence.

Talks Get Political Green Light

The process was transformed from a technocratic one to a political one when President Obama announced in his State of the Union speech to Congress in February 2013 that he would launch negotiations with the European Union on the TTIP. The next step was to adopt negotiating mandates. The procedures for this differed between the two partners. In March 2013, the European Commission, the EU executive arm that leads trade negotiations, proposed a negotiating mandate to the EU's twenty-seven member state governments (twenty-eight as of July 1, when Croatia joined the bloc). The countries that were most supportive of granting the Commission a broad negotiating mandate were Germany and the United Kingdom, two traditionally pro-free trade nations. France, however, was less enthusiastic. Keen to protect its heavily-subsidized film industry, France demanded that audio-visual services be excluded from the agreement. Reluctantly, the others agreed to the French request, and the mandate was adopted in June. On the U.S. side, the procedure involved President Obama notifying Congress that he was going to start the negotiations, with Congressional consent not required at this stage. At the G-8 leaders' summit hosted by the United Kingdom on June 17 and 18, President Obama, U.K. Prime Minister David Cameron, EU Commission President José Manuel Barroso, and EU Council President Herman Van Rompuy announced the launch of negotiations.

The first round was hosted by the U.S. Trade Representative (USTR). Opening proceedings on July 8, USTR Michael Froman said, "We have the opportunity to complement one of the greatest alliances of all time with an equally compelling economic relationship." Keen to maintain the momentum created earlier in the year, Froman said he wanted to get this deal concluded "on one tank of gas," although he did not give a specific target timetable. The European Union was even more ambitious, with the Commission indicating that it would like to clinch a deal by the end of 2014. Froman also told the negotiators: "We need to resist the temptation to downsize our ambitions or avoid tough issues just for the sake of getting a deal." At the close of the first round on July 12, an upbeat chief EU negotiator from the Commission, Ignacio Garcia-Bercero, said, "It's been a very productive week."

NSA Spy Revelations Threaten to Derail Talks

Transatlantic trade negotiators were glad to get through this initial round given the major political storm that was brewing. Early in June 2013, the first revelations emerged from Edward Snowden, a former contractor at the U.S. National Security Agency (NSA), of mass U.S. government surveillance of allies and ordinary citizens' e-mail and phone calls. Europeans were among those targeted, with German Chancellor Angela Merkel reputed to have had her mobile phone monitored by the NSA. Many Europeans are especially sensitive about the issue of government use of their personal data due to negative experiences they had with fascist and communist dictatorships in the twentieth century. Thus, many in Europe were deeply shocked by the revelations, and some demanded that the TTIP talks be suspended. Ultimately, these calls did not prevail, but it became obvious to all that, even if the scandal did not delay the launch, the issue of data privacy would have to be addressed sooner rather than later. For instance, the European Parliament, which would need to ratify any future TTIP agreement, made clear that it would only approve the deal if it received clear guarantees on data privacy issues.

Despite the shadow that the NSA scandal cast on transatlantic relations, the United States and the European Union have so far maintained the momentum in the trade talks. One glitch occurred when the U.S. government partly shut down in October over the Republican Party's efforts—ultimately unsuccessful—to repeal President Obama's signature healthcare law. The shutdown occurred just as the second round of the TTIP negotiations was due to take place in Brussels. The talks were postponed until November, by which time the U.S. government was fully operational again. A third round took place from December 16 to 20 in Washington, D.C. In February 2014, the talks entered a new phase when the United States and the European Union made their first exchange of offers where they indicated to each other what tariff reductions and eliminations they were willing to contemplate for agricultural and industrial goods. The stakes are high; in 2012, the United States exported €205 billion in goods to the European Union, while the European Union exported €292 billion in goods to the United States.

But trade analysts agree that, with import tariffs between the European Union and United States already relatively low (around 4 percent on average), the biggest sticking points to concluding an agreement are likely to be so-called nontariff barriers. These include notably the multitude of Sanitary and Phytosanitary measures that the European Union and United States have adopted to protect their consumers and environment, which often cause headaches for exporters. For instance, the European Union has banned the administering of growth-promoting hormones to animals whose meat is intended for human consumption. This has irked the United States where use of such hormones is commonplace and—the United States claims—safe. Similarly, the European Union has a lengthy process for approving genetically modified foods, which has frustrated U.S. producers of these products who would like to expand into the European market.

Another issue generating some heat is a proposed investor-state dispute-settlement mechanism. This would allow companies to sue governments at specially established trade panels if they feel their investment rights have been flouted. Should investors win a case on these panels, the government that loses could be forced to pay out hefty compensation sums. Consumer groups are unhappy about including such a provision, raising the specter, for instance, of tobacco producers having to be compensated for losses incurred due to mandatory health warnings on cigarette packets. The consumer groups say that such a mechanism is unnecessary given that both the United States and the European Union have strong, independent judiciaries, which they argue is a more appropriate—and citizen-friendly—forum to address any grievances investors may have. One common goal that the negotiators have with this agreement is to agree on common regulatory standards that they hope will globalize standards, given what a large share of the world economy they comprise. They would like to set, for instance, global standards in areas like Intellectual Property rights, and rules for supporting State-Owned Enterprises, which remain major bones of contention in their relations with China.

Perhaps the biggest obstacle of all to a future TTIP ever coming into force may be the U.S. Congress. While the European Parliament has specific issues it wants addressed at some point in the TTIP negotiations—for instance, data privacy—Parliament is still generally pro-free trade in orientation. Thus, as long as those concerns are addressed, Parliament can be expected to sign off on a final deal. However, the White House will have to do heavier political lifting to persuade Capitol Hill to approve TTIP. In early 2014, President Obama asked Congress to grant him a power called Trade Promotion Authority that allows him to send to Congress a trade agreement for approval by a simple yes or no vote rather than having Congress vote on it article by article. The granting of this so-called fast track presidential authority is deemed vital to persuading a partner like the EU to sign off on a deal. But many in Congress, mainly from President Obama's own party, are opposed to granting him that authority because they dislike free trade agreements. Meanwhile, President Obama is also trying to conclude negotiations on a Transpacific Partnership (TPP) trade agreement between the United States, Canada, and ten other Pacific and Asian countries. Opposition to the TPP in Congress is stronger than for TTIP, the latter having not yet registered as prominently on their radar. But should the atmosphere in Congress turn decisively against TPP, it could also hurt the TTIP's chances of being passed.

—Brian Beary

Following is a statement by the United States Trade Representative on July 8, 2013, upon opening free trade negotiations with the European Union; and a press release from the European Commission issued on July 12, 2013, on the conclusion of the first round of trade negotiations.

U.S. Trade Representative Opens EU Free Trade Negotiations

July 8, 2013

As Prepared for Delivery

"I want to welcome everyone to USTR on an important day in transatlantic relations—the first round of negotiations of the Transatlantic Trade and Investment Partnership, the first step toward making T-TIP a reality.

"Although negotiations are just beginning, this day has been a long time coming. From the evolution of the Transatlantic Economic Council to the work of the U.S.-EU High Level Working Group for Jobs and Growth, our teams have been laying the foundation for today's negotiations by identifying the opportunities to bring our two economies closer together and the mechanisms for doing so.

"In TTIP, we have the opportunity to accomplish something very significant for our economies, for our relationship, and for the global trading system as a whole.

"We have an opportunity to spur growth and to generate significant increases in the already substantial number of jobs supported by transatlantic trade and investment.

"We have the opportunity to complement one of the greatest alliances of all time with an equally compelling economic relationship.

"And we have the opportunity to work together to establish and enforce international norms and standards that will help inform and strengthen the multilateral, rules-based trading system.

"We go into this exercise with eyes wide open. We know there will be challenges. But we also know that there is strong political will at the highest levels on both sides of the Atlantic determined to stay focused and get this done on one tank of gas. I have every confidence that we can achieve this goal.

"Promoting growth, creating jobs, strengthening the middle class—these are the principles that animate President Obama's economic policies, including this Administration's trade policy.

"As President Obama said in Northern Ireland last month, T-TIP can be a success if "we can achieve the kind of high-standard, comprehensive agreement that the global trading system is looking to us to develop."

"European Leaders have expressed similar hopes and support for T-TIP as one component of an overall strategy to return Europe to a path of growth.

"In view of this leader-level attention, Commissioner De Gucht and I intend to stay very much involved in these negotiations.

"We will give our teams the space they need to move forward and find solutions, but we will stay very closely engaged to ensure that we are finding those solutions. We want you to avoid unnecessary delays, but we also recognize that the most important thing is to get the substance right. We need to resist the temptation to downsize our ambitions or avoid tough issues just for the sake of getting a deal.

"So, be creative, be flexible, and think outside of the box as necessary to make progress.

"When you have difficulties working through issues, know that you will have my support to help reach a mutually beneficial and comprehensive outcome—an outcome that meets the economic priorities of both the United States and the European Union.

"I wish you all a productive and enjoyable week and I look forward to hearing of your progress over the course of this week.

"Thanks again for all the work you've done to get us to this point.

"And thank you for the work still to come."

SOURCE: U.S. Trade Representative. "Remarks by United States Trade Representative Michael Froman at the Transatlantic Trade and Investment Partnership First Round Opening Plenary." July 8, 2013. http://www.ustr.gov/about-us/press-office/speeches/transcripts/2013/july/amb-froman-ttip-opening-plenary.

DOCUMENT *EU on First Round of TTIP Discussions*

July 12, 2013

"It's been a very productive week," said EU Chief Negotiator Ignacio Garcia-Bercero coming out of the talks. "We have been striving already for many months to prepare the ground for an ambitious trade and investment deal that will boost the transatlantic economy, delivering jobs and growth for both European and Americans. This week we have been able to take this negotiation to the next step. The main objective has been met: we had a substantive round of talks on the full range of topics that we intend to cover in this agreement. This paves the way to for a good second round of negotiations in Brussels in October."

Working throughout the week, the negotiating groups have set out respective approaches and ambitions in as much as twenty various areas that the TTIP—the biggest bilateral trade and investment negotiation ever undertaken—is set to cover. They included: market access for agricultural and industrial goods, government procurement, investment, energy and raw materials, regulatory issues, sanitary and phytosanitary measures, services, intellectual property rights, sustainable development, small- and medium-sized enterprises, dispute settlement, competition, customs/trade facilitation, and state-owned enterprises.

Negotiators identified certain areas of convergence across various components of the negotiation and—in areas of divergence—begun to explore possibilities to bridge the gaps.

The talks have been based on a thorough review of the stakeholders views expressed to date. The negotiators met also in the middle of the week with approximately 350 stakeholders from academia, trade unions, the private sector, and non-governmental organisations to listen to formal presentations and answer questions related to the proposed agreement.

The next round of TTIP negotiations will take place during the week of 7 October in Brussels.

BACKGROUND

The first round of talks follows the official launch of the negotiations that was announced by US President Barack Obama, President of the European Commission José Manuel Barroso, President of the European Council Herman Van Rompuy and UK Prime Minister David Cameron at the G8 Summit held on 17 June 2013. Beforehand, EU Member States agreed to give the European Commission 'the green light' to start negotiations with the United States and defined their negotiating guidelines. The initiative of a transatlantic agreement is based on the recommendations of the EU-US High Level Working Group on Jobs and Growth that steered the reflection on future EU-US relations since late 2011.

The aim of the ambitious Transatlantic Trade and Investment Partnership is to liberalise as much as possible trade and investment between the two blocs. The trade agreement with the US is expected to result in more jobs and more growth on both sides. That will help boost economic growth and would be a very good message for the whole world economy.

The EU and the US make up 40% of global economic output and their bilateral economic relationship is already the world's largest. According to an independent study by the Centre for Economic Policy Research, based in London, an ambitious and comprehensive trans-Atlantic trade and investment partnership could bring the EU economic gains of €119 billion a year once fully implemented. The final agreement could see EU exports to the US rise by 28%, earning its exporters of goods and services an extra €187 billion every year. Consumers will benefit too: on average, the agreement could offer an extra €545 in disposable income each year for a family of four living in the EU.

The European Union and the United States have their eyes on more than just removing tariffs. Tariffs between them are already low (on average only 4%) so the main hurdles to trade lie 'behind the border' in regulations, non-tariff barriers and red tape. Estimates show that 80% of the overall potential wealth gains of a trade deal will come from cutting administrative costs, as well as from liberalising trade in services and public procurement.

That's why the two trading giants will reinforce their regulatory cooperation, so as to create converging regulations rather than have to try to adapt them at a later stage. The aim is to build a more integrated transatlantic marketplace, while respecting each side's right to regulate in a way that ensures the protection of health, safety and the environment at a level it considers appropriate. Both sides hope that by aligning their domestic standards, they will be able to set the benchmark for developing global rules. Such a move would be clearly beneficial to both EU and US exporters, but it would also strengthen the multilateral trading system.

SOURCE: European Commission. "EU and US conclude first round of TTIP negotiations in Washington." July 12, 2013. http://trade.ec.europa.eu/doclib/press/index.cfm?id=941.

OTHER HISTORIC DOCUMENTS OF INTEREST

FROM THIS VOLUME

- State of the Union Address and Republican Response, p. 35
- U.S. and Russian Officials Respond to NSA Leaks, p. 329

FROM PREVIOUS *HISTORIC DOCUMENTS*

- The London Summit on Global Economic Recovery, *2009*, p. 157

Detroit Files for Bankruptcy

JULY 18, 2014

In March 2013, Michigan Governor Rick Snyder announced that the city of Detroit was in a state of financial emergency. He appointed an emergency manager to recommend methods for helping the city avoid bankruptcy. On July 18, however, the plan failed and Detroit became the largest city in the nation to file for Chapter 9 bankruptcy protection. At the time of its filing, the city's debt was estimated between $18 billion and $20 billion. A judge approved the filing on December 3, 2013, paving the way for Detroit to begin working on a plan to restructure its finances.

Manufacturing Meltdown and Urban Flight Precede Financial Meltdown

Detroit did not reach the point of bankruptcy overnight—its financial failings were long in the making. In 1950, the city's population reached a peak of 1.8 million residents and it was the hub of blue-collar manufacturing jobs in the United States. Led by auto giants, Detroit was upheld as the portrait of middle-class America. Automobile manufacturers, including Ford, General Motors, Packard, and Chrysler, provided good paying jobs to almost all interested applicants. "It was the Silicon Valley of America," said Kevin Boyle, a history professor at Northwestern University. He added, "It was home to the most innovative, cutting-edge dominant industry in the world. The money there at that point was just staggering."

But even as the city grew to the nation's fifth largest urban area, automakers were working to set up plants in the suburbs, the South, and even overseas where labor was cheaper and the labor unions weren't as strong. By 1963, Detroit had lost 140,000 of its nearly 300,000 auto manufacturing jobs. By the 1970s, the automakers that remained were quickly losing business to their Japanese competitors and cut even more jobs. While the contracting of Detroit's auto base contributed to the decline of America's once great city, its leaders also played a major part in the overall financial collapse. Even while recognizing that tax revenue was quickly declining, city leaders continued to increase public employee pay and pensions, essentially punting difficult financial decisions to another day.

Today, Detroit is home to abandoned buildings, vacant lots, and crumbling infrastructure. Auto manufacturers have closed, moved operations, or significantly cut their workforces, and those jobs that are available no longer come with the pay and benefits enjoyed five decades ago. Between 2000 and 2012, Detroit lost more than a quarter million of its residents, and today is home to only 700,000. The decline in population and subsequent decline in tax revenue hurt city finances and city services. Notably, Detroit is no longer able to consistently cover pensions or health insurance for its retired workers; any payments it can make come from the sale of debt. The city has done some recent downtown and midtown redevelopment work, but it still has an estimated 80,000 abandoned or blighted buildings and nearly half of the streetlights do not work.

Detroit is now also well known for having one of the highest rates of violent crime in the country. Even its police chief has reported nearly being carjacked while riding in an unmarked car. Because the city has been forced to cut back, it takes police nearly an hour to respond to a call (the national average is eleven minutes). Recently, Detroit has relied on donors to provide new ambulances and police cars, which it cannot afford itself.

STATE GOVERNMENT INCREASES OVERSIGHT

Acknowledging its dire financial situation, in April 2012, Governor Snyder and Detroit Mayor David Bing reached an agreement to give the state's government additional financial oversight of the city. In return, the state promised to provide financial assistance. After a financial review, in February 2013, the governor announced that the state would assume complete control of the city's finances. It was the opinion of the state that Detroit had not followed through on key tenets of the earlier agreement, including some basic financial restructuring. According to Snyder, the city was in a state of financial emergency. That declaration gave him the authority to appoint an emergency financial manager who would be tasked with liquidating assets and rewriting standing contracts, such as those with public employee unions, in an effort to avoid filing for bankruptcy protection.

Kevyn Orr, a lawyer who formerly represented Chrysler in its 2009 bankruptcy restructuring, was appointed to the position of emergency financial manager. He commissioned a report on the city's financial health, which was released to the public in May 2013, and found the city "clearly insolvent on a cash flow basis." Without some form of restructuring, the city would have a budget deficit of $386 billion within two months. In June 2013, Orr released a financial plan to move the city forward. It included an end to some unsecured debt payments and a proposal to negotiate with the city's creditors, offering 10 percent of the amount they were owed. Altogether, the unsecured debt payments, including pensions, made up an estimated one-third of the city's total budget. To protect retirees, the city's two municipal pension funds, which account for $9.2 billion in unfunded pension and retiree health care liabilities, sued on July 17 to prevent any cuts to benefits.

After releasing his plan, Orr warned that if debtors and pension fund managers were unwilling to come to the table and work with the city, bankruptcy might be the only choice. If the city had to take that drastic measure, it would likely mean far more dire outcomes for past and current city employees and debtors. Still, few were willing to negotiate.

DETROIT FILES FOR BANKRUPTCY

On July 18, 2013, with the approval of the governor, Detroit filed for Chapter 9 bankruptcy protection in the U.S. Bankruptcy Court in the Eastern District of Michigan. Calling the filing a "difficult step," Governor Snyder said, "The fiscal realities confronting Detroit have been ignored for too long. I'm making this tough decision so the people of Detroit will have the basic services they deserve and so we can start to put Detroit on a solid financial footing that will allow it to grow and prosper in the future." He added, "The City's financial emergency cannot be satisfactorily rectified in a reasonable period of time absent this filing." Orr's spokesperson, Bill Nowling, scolded those who were unwilling to work with the city to avoid the bankruptcy filing: "Pension boards, insurers, it's clear that if you're suing us, your response is 'no.' We still have other creditors we continue to have meetings with, other stakeholders who are trying to find a solution here, because they recognize that, at the end of the day, we have to have a city that can provide basic services to its 700,000 residents."

Following the filing, up to three months could be used to decide whether the city was eligible to apply for bankruptcy. This determination would also include information on which creditors would be allowed to claim any settlement resources if Detroit's filing were successfully approved. Throughout the process, Orr promised to "negotiate with creditors until and unless we find that the negotiations won't bear fruit, with the understanding that the city has a limited amount of time."

The filing sparked another lawsuit brought on behalf of the 30,000 city workers and retirees, seeking to stop the bankruptcy action. Coupled with the suit from the two pension funds, the groups collectively argued that state law prevents a bankruptcy filing from proceeding if it includes a reduction in pension benefits. The lawsuit put an automatic stay on the bankruptcy proceedings. On July 19, Judge Rosemarie Aquilina of the Ingham County Circuit Court ruled that the bankruptcy filing was a violation of Michigan law because it would impact city pensions. The bankruptcy proceedings were stayed on July 23 by the Michigan Court of Appeals pending the outcome of the state's challenge to Aquilina's ruling. One day later, Michigan Bankruptcy Judge Steven Rhodes ordered the cases currently pending in state court to be halted.

Detroit was not the first U.S. city to file for bankruptcy, but it was the largest. More than 600 municipalities and special-purpose districts have filed for bankruptcy protection since 1937 when Congress revised the Municipal Bankruptcy Act. Recent bankruptcy filings included Jefferson County, Alabama, which had $4 billion in debt in 2011. Prior to the Detroit filing, Jefferson County was the largest municipal bankruptcy in history. Stockton, California, filed for bankruptcy in June 2012, and was the largest municipality by population to do so before Detroit. Given its size, legal experts expected that the ultimate determination in the Detroit case would be used as a model for other governments that are struggling financially.

JUDGE APPROVES BANKRUPTCY ORDER

Despite the lawsuits, the bankruptcy filing moved forward, and a nine-day trial was held in October and November presided over by Judge Rhodes, who gave unions the opportunity to argue why the case should be rejected. Those who appeared before the court tried to put a human face on the crisis and said that the city made no "good faith" effort to negotiate.

On December 3, Judge Rhodes ruled that Detroit would in fact be allowed to proceed with its bankruptcy filing. Rhodes summarized his 140-page ruling during a ninety-minute speech noting that the ruling was "an opportunity for a fresh start" for Detroit. "The court finds that Detroit was and is insolvent," Rhodes said, adding that the filing was a "foregone conclusion for a very long time."

Although he approved the case to move forward, Rhodes was highly critical of the state's handling of negotiations prior to its bankruptcy protection filing. Typically, such a failure to negotiate in good faith would derail a bankruptcy case, but Rhodes noted in his decision that it would have been nearly impossible for the city to negotiate with its unions and creditors because of the lawsuits that had been filed. He also criticized the unions for being a "stone wall" in the process.

Rhodes also ruled that the city would be allowed to take pension cuts into consideration when outlining its financial restructuring plan. However, he noted that he was only making that decision to help move bankruptcy proceedings along and might not necessarily accept pension cuts in the final plan if they were not fair. In opposition to the filings by the city's unions, Rhodes indicated that the state protection of pensions did not necessarily apply in cases of bankruptcy.

After the ruling, Detroit was given time to begin working with unions, creditors, and retirees to reach agreements on how to restructure the city's debt. It would also begin reviewing its assets, including valuable pieces of art, to determine what could be sold during the bankruptcy proceedings. "Time is of the essence, and we will continue to move forward as quickly and efficiently as possible," said Orr, who hoped to file a final restructuring plan by January 2014. "We hope all parties will work together to help us develop a realistic restructuring plan that improves the financial condition of Detroit and the lives of its 700,000 citizens," Orr continued. Detroit Mayor Bing said that there would "be a lot of pain for a lot of different people," but that "in the long run, the future will be bright."

Unions Vow to Continue the Fight

Public employee unions promised that they would continue to challenge Rhodes's decision in an effort to prevent pension funds from being cut to shore up city finances. "The only thing we can do is challenge this ruling legally and question the morality of attacking pensions that have been earned by these workers," said Lee Saunders, president of the American Federation of State, County, and Municipal Employees (AFSCME). He continued, "Pensions in Detroit average $19,000 a year, and there is a good possibility that they will be reduced. That is dead-ass wrong and morally corrupt." The union filed lawsuits asking the courts to review both the city's eligibility to file for bankruptcy and to ask that the city be blocked from restructuring pensions as a means to shoring up its finances. Judge Rhodes gave the AFSCME case the right to appeal directly to the Sixth Circuit.

—Heather Kerrigan

Following is the text of a speech given on July 18, 2013, by Michigan Governor Rick Snyder authorizing the City of Detroit to file for bankruptcy.

Gov. Snyder Authorizes Detroit Bankruptcy Filing

July 18, 2013

Today I authorized Detroit's emergency manager to seek federal bankruptcy protection for the City of Detroit.

This is a difficult, painful step, and it is one I would not be authorizing if I felt any other viable option remained.

I'd like to take a moment to explain why I made that decision and what it means for the city—and for the State of Michigan.

In many respects, this day has been six decades in the making. Detroit is buried under $18 billion in debt and unfunded liabilities. In fact, 38 cents of every city dollar goes toward debt repayment, legacy costs and other obligations. By 2017, that figure will go up to 65 cents per dollar.

That level of debt is unsustainable.

Meanwhile, the people of Detroit already pay the highest taxes per capita in Michigan. And the city's 700,000 residents don't receive the city services they deserve.

For Michigan to be a great state, Detroit needs to be a great city. And the simple fact is, Detroit is broke. By filing for bankruptcy, Detroit can get back on the right path. It can fix its finances. And it can focus on investing in city services so that Detroiters have a better quality of life. Better police and fire protection, trash pickup and street lighting.

We've been reinventing Michigan so it can be the comeback state of the nation. Now it's time to move Detroit forward, too.

SOURCE: State of Michigan. Office of Governor Rick Snyder. "Governor Snyder Authorizes Detroit Bankruptcy Filing." July 18, 2013. http://www.michigan.gov/snyder/0,4668,7-277-60279-308596-,00 .html.

OTHER HISTORIC DOCUMENTS OF INTEREST

FROM PREVIOUS *HISTORIC DOCUMENTS*

- Aid to New York City, *1975*, p. 860

Bradley Manning Convicted for Classified U.S. Document Leaks

JULY 30, 2013

In 2010, the website known as WikiLeaks caused an international stir when it published thousands of confidential government documents revealing controversial and politically damaging information about key elements of U.S. foreign policy, particularly the Iraq and Afghanistan Wars. Army Pfc. Bradley Manning, a low-level Army intelligence analyst deployed in Iraq, was later identified as the alleged source of the leaked information and was charged with twenty-two violations of the Uniform Code of Military Justice and the Espionage Act of 1917. In 2013, Manning was tried by court martial, found guilty of nearly all charges, and sentenced to more than thirty years in prison.

WikiLeaks Publishes Classified Documents

WikiLeaks, which describes itself as a "non-profit media organization dedicated to bringing important news and information to the public," has been publishing reports about U.S. foreign policy since at least 2007. Such reports have included an operations manual for the U.S. military's Guantánamo Bay detention facility and the confidential Rules of Engagement for the U.S. war in Iraq, both of which exposed the United States to criticism and embarrassment.

In 2010, however, WikiLeaks began publishing secret U.S. information with greater frequency. In April, the organization released a military video of a group of civilians being shot down in Baghdad by a U.S. Apache helicopter in 2007, in which American soldiers could be heard congratulating themselves and mocking the dead. In July, WikiLeaks began releasing a series of roughly 92,000 internal records of U.S. military action in Afghanistan from 2004 to 2009, followed by the October release of more than 390,000 similar reports on the War in Iraq. Finally, in November, WikiLeaks released an initial set of more than 250,000 diplomatic cables collected from approximately 250 embassies around the world, several of which suggested that U.S. diplomats were encouraged to gather extensive personal information about other diplomats, beyond standard practice.

U.S. officials decried each release, claiming the publication of such sensitive information was a threat to national security, and launched a criminal investigation to determine how WikiLeaks had obtained the documents.

Manning Arrested and Charged

Twenty-two-year-old Army Pfc. Manning was widely suspected to be WikiLeaks' source. Manning was arrested on May 29, 2010, after confiding in former computer hacker Adrian Lamo in an online chat that "someone he knew" had been downloading and encrypting confidential data and uploading it to WikiLeaks, and, in some instances, admitted to leaking the material himself. Lamo in turn shared this information with the FBI and the Army. At the time, Manning was stationed at a forward operating base in Iraq and was responsible for monitoring security threats in a section of Baghdad. As a low-level intelligence analyst, he had access to a classified computer network from which he had downloaded confidential documents and videos. Manning reportedly gave an initial set of documents to WikiLeaks in February 2010, and continued to submit material until his arrest.

On July 6, 2010, U.S. officials charged Manning with violating the Uniform Code of Military Justice for disobeying an order and general misconduct—in this case, breaking federal laws against disclosing classified information. He was also accused of illegally downloading and submitting defense information to an "unauthorized source."

Following a further investigation of Manning's communications with WikiLeaks, officials announced a second round of charges on March 1, 2011. The charges read in part that Manning did, "without proper authority, knowingly give intelligence to the enemy, through indirect means" and that he did "wrongfully and wantonly cause to be published on the internet intelligence belonging to the United States government, having knowledge that intelligence published on the internet is accessible to the enemy." Manning was also charged with theft of public property, transmitting defense information, and computer fraud.

DETENTION AT QUANTICO

Manning was held at the U.S. Marine Brig at Marine Corps Base Quantico following his arrest. He was placed in maximum custody under a "prevention of injury" watch, which meant, among other things, that his cell featured a mattress with a built-in pillow, no sheets, and a blanket that could not be shredded, and that he could sleep in boxer shorts only. He was later required to sleep naked after commenting to the guards that he could harm himself with just an elastic band or a flip flop. Manning's attorney, David Coombs, described this action as overly punitive, but 1st Lt. Brian Villiard, a spokesperson for the brig, claimed it was meant "to ensure the safety and security of the detainee and make sure he is able to stand trial." Coombs continued to argue that the conditions of Manning's detention were too harsh. He was reportedly confined to a six-by-twelve foot cell with a bed, water fountain, and toilet for twenty-three hours a day. No other detainees were being held in the neighboring cells, and Manning had no window or source of natural light. When he was allowed outside, he was always kept by himself. Coombs claimed that he was essentially being held in solitary confinement and requested that Manning be removed from maximum custody and prevention of injury watch, which the government denied.

Descriptions of Manning's experience at Quantico angered his supporters, many of whom viewed him as a hero, and others who were sympathetic to his plight, including Rep. Dennis Kucinich, D-Ohio, who lobbied U.S. officials for better conditions. In January 2011, Juan Mendez, the UN special rapporteur on torture, began a fourteen-month investigation into Manning's detention, which concluded in March 2012. He accused the United States of cruel, inhuman, and degrading treatment, and said that "imposing seriously punitive conditions of detention on someone who has not been found guilty of any crime is a violation of his right to physical and psychological integrity as well as of his presumption of innocence." Manning was transferred from Quantico to the prison at Fort Leavenworth, Kansas, in April 2011, and was held in more open conditions.

TRIAL AND SENTENCING

Coombs attempted to have the charges against Manning dismissed during a pretrial hearing in April 2012, claiming the prosecution was intentionally withholding evidence. But the presiding judge, Army Col. Denise Lind, rejected his arguments, ruling there was "no evidence of prosecutorial misconduct" and set an initial court martial date in September 2012. Manning's trial was ultimately postponed for several months and rescheduled for February 2013.

On February 28, Manning appeared before the court and pled guilty to ten of the twenty-two charges against him. He did not deny that he had sent WikiLeaks most of the material that led to the charges. Manning said he took "full responsibility" for the leaks and that no one associated with WikiLeaks had "pressured me into sending any more information." He said he had carefully considered the information he was sharing and that he believed releasing the documents "would not damage the United States," although he "did believe the release of the cables might be embarrassing." Manning went on to say that he "believed if the public—in particular the American public—had access to the information" in the reports, it "could spark a debate about foreign policy in relation to Iraq and Afghanistan." He claimed the military was "obsessed with capturing or killing" people on a list and was indifferent to civilian casualties.

Despite Manning's guilty pleas, military prosecutors announced on March 1 that they would still try him on the remaining charges, with a trial date set for June 3. Throughout the trial, prosecutors argued that Manning had betrayed the United States and was guilty of communicating with the enemy, although indirectly, because he knew that the information he had shared with WikiLeaks could be read by terrorists. In defending Manning, Coombs sought to portray him as a well-intentioned whistleblower. He also argued that a number of stresses, including working in a combat zone, had impacted Manning's mental health but that military officials had ignored signs that he was struggling.

A verdict was issued in the case on July 30. Lind found Manning not guilty of knowingly aiding the enemy and of sending WikiLeaks a video of an airstrike in Afghanistan in which dozens of civilians were killed. She did find him guilty of the other twenty charges, including six violations of the Espionage Act "related to the misappropriation of hundreds of thousands of intelligence documents." Manning's sentencing hearing began the following day. Because he had been found not guilty of aiding the enemy, he could not receive a life sentence or the death penalty but could face a maximum of ninety years in prison. On August 21, Lind sentenced Manning to thirty-five years in prison, minus nearly 1,300 days of credit for time already served and for a 112-day period during that Lind ruled that he had been mistreated at Quantico. Lind also reduced Manning's rank to private, ordered him to forfeit military pay and benefits, and said he would be dishonorably discharged.

Even with the credit, Manning's sentence was the longest one handed down in a case involving the leak of U.S. government information for the purpose of having that information reported to the public. Some denounced his punishment as extreme. "It is a dangerous precedent and an example of national security extremism," said WikiLeaks founder Julian Assange. Assange continued, "It is a short sighted judgment that cannot be tolerated and must be reversed. It can never be that conveying true information to the public is 'espionage.'" Some civil liberties organizations agreed. "When a soldier who shared information with the press and public is punished far more harshly than others who tortured prisoners and killed civilians, something is seriously wrong with our justice system," said Ben Wizner, director of the American Civil Liberties Union's Speech, Privacy and

Technology Project. However, others characterized Manning's sentence as appropriate for the crimes he committed. "Justice has been served today," said House Intelligence Committee Chairman Mike Rogers, R-Mich., and ranking member Dutch Ruppersberger, D-Md., in a statement. "Pfc. Manning harmed our national security, violated the public's trust, and now stands convicted of multiple serious crimes," Ruppersberger continued.

Manning's court martial will automatically be reviewed by the Army Court of Criminal Appeals to decide whether the verdict and sentence can be appealed. The government is also required to compile a complete record of the case, review all transcripts and findings, and submit a final report to Maj. Gen. Jeffrey S. Buchanan, who oversees the Military District of Washington. Buchanan could potentially reduce Manning's sentence if he sees fit.

CHELSEA MANNING APPLIES FOR PARDON

On August 22, one day after receiving his sentence, Manning announced that he wanted to live as a woman named Chelsea and requested that the Army provide him with hormone therapy while he served time at Fort Leavenworth. Manning reportedly had experienced gender identity confusion since childhood, and his lawyers argued that such confusion had also impacted his mental health while deployed. The announcement immediately raised questions about whether the Army would provide the requested therapy and how Manning would fare as a transgender inmate at the all-male Leavenworth prison. An Army spokesperson later said Manning would have the same access to mental health professionals as all other Leavenworth detainees but that the Army does not provide hormone therapy or gender reassignment surgery.

Shortly thereafter, on September 3, Manning's attorney filed a request for a presidential pardon. In a related statement, Manning said he had done what he did "out of a love for my country and a sense of duty" to expose what he believed to be abuses committed during the Iraq and Afghanistan wars, but that if his request was denied, he would "serve my time knowing that sometimes you have to pay a heavy price to live in a free society." A White House spokesperson said Manning's pardon application would receive routine consideration, and a decision is still pending.

—Linda Fecteau

Following is a news article from the United States Army dated July 30, 2013, announcing the charges against Bradley Manning.

DOCUMENT   *Manning Convicted of Twenty Counts*

July 30, 2013

Army Pfc. Bradley Manning was found not guilty of the most serious charge of knowingly aiding the enemy, but was convicted on 20 other specifications related to the misappropriation of hundreds of thousands of intelligence documents sent to WikiLeaks.

"Right now, he still faces a possibility of 136 years" of confinement, said Manning's defense attorney, David Coombs, speaking outside the courtroom minutes after the verdict was read by Army Col. Denise Lind, the presiding judge. She said sentencing phase of the trial will begin July 31.

Manning and his defense team were encouraged at the first "not guilty" count, Coombs said, but added that there will be "no celebrating tonight."

"We won the battle, per se, but the war is going to be tomorrow," Coombs said. "Sentencing is what really matters at the end of the day."

Aiding the enemy held a maximum penalty of life in prison, so Coombs said beating that specification was a boost to the defense. Manning was also found not guilty of specification 11 of count 2, involving the alleged unauthorized release of a video.

He pled guilty, however, at the beginning of the trial to 10 specifications involving the unauthorized release of classified information, and was found guilty of another 10 specifications. These include theft of government records, violating lawful regulations and wrongfully storing classified information.

CLOSING ARGUMENTS

Manning's release of classified material did immeasurable harm to national security and put lives at risk, the prosecutor said in his closing arguments, July 25.

The next day though, Manning's defense attorney argued the accused was a young, naïve but well-intentioned Soldier who wanted to make a difference in this world for the better by bringing to light the wrongs that were done during the wars in Iraq and Afghanistan.

Manning, now 25, was an intelligence analyst in Iraq in 2009 and 2010, working in a tactical-sensitive compartmented information facility, or T-SCIF, at Forward Operating Base Hammer near Baghdad. A SCIF is a restricted facility where secret materials are transmitted, collected and analyzed.

The prosecutor, Maj. Ashden Fein, stated that the facts clearly pointed to Manning's culpability, while the defense, led by Coombs, argued that the prosecution's charges amounted to "diatribes not based in facts."

At the start of the trial on June 3, 2013, Manning pled guilty to 10 charges related to leaking classified information to the organization WikiLeaks, which then made the documents accessible to the public on the Internet and through media outlets like the New York Times, the United Kingdom-based The Guardian and the Germany-based Der Spiegel.

Even the term "media" was argued during the trial, with the prosecution saying the WikiLeaks organization was not a legitimate news outlet and the defense arguing that it was.

Manning chose to have a trial by the judge alone, rather than a trial by a panel, which is the military's version of a jury. Following his sentencing, Manning's verdict will be reviewed by the Military District of Washington commander, Maj. Gen. Jeffery S. Buchanan.

PROSECUTION'S CASE

Manning's very rigorous and thorough training as an intelligence analyst instilled in him the importance significant activities, or SIGACTS, have on whether Soldiers succeed in battle, fail or are killed, said the prosecutor, Fein.

Yet despite this knowledge, Manning downloaded some 470,000 SIGACTS from the SIPRNET to an SD card, which he later transferred to his home computer. Some 380,000 were from Iraq and 90,000 from Afghanistan.

The SIPRNET is the military's classified section of the Internet and an SD card is a memory card used to store data that can be transferred from one computer to another.

In addition to SIGACTS, there were Apache attack helicopter videos and thousands of State Department cables Manning released, Fein said.

A SIGACT, he said, could include anything from where an attack or improvised explosives device detonated to how an attack helicopter engages the enemy and numbers of casualties resulting from an ambush or IED.

He said commanders decide their main supply routes, plan their battles and base other tactical decisions on SIGACTS, which are even plotted on maps to provide a clear picture of where dangers, as well as where opportunities lie.

If the enemy gets these SIGACTS, they will have access to the Army's "playbook" and can then deduce the tactics, techniques and procedures, or TTP, used and can devise effective countermeasures or adjust fires, Fein said.

A number of foreign governments would gladly pay millions of dollars to have this sort of information, Fein added.

Having released the information soon after deploying to Iraq, Manning "basked in the amount of press he was receiving" and even posed and smiled in a photo he had taken of himself, holding his memory card containing the data, Fein said.

He was clearly on an ego trip and knew the information he'd released would harm U.S. national security, Fein said, adding that Manning even wiped his machine seven times during a three-hour period to ensure his tracks were covered.

Wiping a machine means deleting everything on it. Traces of information often remain so multiple wipes are preferred as a more effective scrub.

In short, Fein said, Manning "wanted to be hailed as famous" without regard for the lives of his fellow Soldiers. "The flag meant nothing to him."

Defense's Case

Manning had access to the entire SIPRNET, which contains millions of documents, said Coombs. He could have probably downloaded and released the entire SIPRNET.

Yet, he selectively chose to download and pass on only those secret documents that he felt would show how U.S. policy exploited third-world countries and harmed a lot of innocent lives, he said.

If Americans learned about what their government was doing, Coombs continued, then Manning truly believed they'd see the light and demand changes.

Coombs argued as well that classified documents were arbitrarily labeled "secret" and most released by Manning could arguably be deemed appropriate for declassification by any reasonable person.

Far from being a traitor, Manning was acting in a way he thought was patriotic, Coombs said, citing recorded conversations Manning had with his friend, Lauren McNamara and Adrian Lamo, the man who ultimately turned Manning in to the FBI.

As for wiping his computer seven times, Coombs said that was normal procedure as the software often got corrupted and had to be reinstalled. Additionally, he continued to use his computer to gain classified materials for several months and never subsequently wiped it.

As to TTPs, playbook and SIGACTS, Coombs said those and other terms are "buzzwords" designed to cast aspersions on Manning. In fact, the enemy already was adjusting fires and adapting based on their own observations, and doing so effectively.

As to WikiLeaks itself, Coombs said it was a legitimate news organization, having been recognized with journalistic awards, vetting its sources and publishing information that turned out to be highly accurate.

The press, including WikiLeaks, has a responsibility to provide government oversight as part of its Constitutional 1st Amendment rights, Coombs said. He added that the Watergate scandal would have never been brought to light had it not been for the intrepid journalists.

Coombs concluded that there is absolutely zero proof Manning ever even hinted that he was knowingly aiding the enemy. "He really did care what happened to people and hoped to spark a worldwide debate with discussions and reforms."

The small courtroom at Fort Meade was packed and others had to attend the trial at a nearby trailer, which was considered an annex of the courtroom where no audio or photos were allowed.

Dozens were there and it appeared they were sympathetic to Manning. Most clapped to show their solidarity with Manning when the defense rested its case. The judge warned them that such outbursts were not appropriate or tolerated in a court of law.

The remainder of the trial attendees were from various media outlets. Those interviewed said they were committed to being "neutral" in their reporting, but that Manning definitely violated the law by leaking classified material and should receive at least some level of punishment commensurate with his crimes.

Source: U.S. Army. Army News Service. "Manning guilty of 20 specifications, but not 'aiding enemy.'" July 30, 2013. http://www.army.mil/article/108143/Closing_arguments_heard_in_Pfc__Manning_trial.

Other Historic Documents of Interest

From this volume

- U.S. and Russian Officials Respond to NSA Leaks, p. 329

From previous *Historic Documents*

- WikiLeaks Founder Denied Stay of Extradition, *2012*, p. 228
- U.S. Department of State Responds to Wikileaks, *2010*, p. 595

August

Amazon.com Founder Purchases *The Washington Post*

AUGUST 5, 2013

The increasing digitization of the modern world has left many media outlets fighting for revenue and questioning their paths moving forward. One such iconic publication is *The Washington Post*, a stronghold in the national newspaper marketplace. However, like its counterparts, the paper faced years of declining readership, which in turn led to a dwindling number of advertisers. Although staffing levels were reduced in an effort to keep pace with falling revenue, the paper was unable to keep up. In August 2013, after months of behind-the-scenes deal making, *Washington Post* Publisher Katharine Weymouth announced that the paper would be sold to Amazon.com founder Jeff Bezos.

A SHINING HISTORY

The Washington Post was founded in 1877, and three years later became Washington, D.C.'s first and only newspaper that was published seven days per week. The paper was sold in 1899 to a former Congressman from Ohio and a former postmaster general who sought to increase national awareness of the paper. To do so, they called on famous composer John Philip Sousa to write a march that was used during an essay award ceremony run by the paper. The newspaper exchanged hands multiple times during the following two decades, and at one point the son of a former owner took power and all but ran the newspaper into the ground.

In 1933, the paper was purchased in a bankruptcy auction by Eugene Meyer, a former Chairman of the Federal Reserve. Although he did not have experience in the industry, Meyer invested heavily in the paper, intent on building it into the nation's greatest newspaper. He devised a set of principles by which the paper would function, including telling all the truth on a story that its reporters can learn, remaining loyal to the public and not to the owners, and not becoming beholden to special interests. Meyer's policies were successful. In the first decade following his takeover, circulation tripled and advertising revenue skyrocketed.

In 1946, the paper was taken over by Philip Graham, Meyer's son-in-law. Graham aimed at making the *Post* D.C.'s number one newspaper. To do this, he acquired a number of media holdings including radio station WTOP, a local television station, a television station in Florida, and the *Post*'s competitor, the *Washington Times-Herald*. Graham died in 1963, and the newspaper's ownership was passed on to his wife, Katharine Graham. As one of the few women at the helm of a newspaper, Katharine faced an uphill battle.

It was during Katharine Graham's tenure that the *Post* finally rose to the national prominence its earlier owners had desired. Graham turned the paper's focus to in-depth investigative reporting and made it the best newspaper for political coverage. Well-known reporters like Bob Woodward and Carl Bernstein became household names during Graham's tenure and helped the paper increase its stature in the media world when they broke the story about the Watergate Scandal, which would eventually bring down then-President Richard Nixon. Their reporting would go on to win a Pulitzer Prize in 1973. Graham served as publisher from 1969 to 1979, and the paper won numerous Pulitzer Prize awards (including one that was later returned when it was found out that the story about an eight-year-old heroin addict was fabricated).

When Graham resigned as publisher, she was replaced by her son, Donald E. Graham, who in 1991 also took over as CEO of the company and chairman of the board in 1993. In 2000, Boisfeuillet Jones, Jr., took over as publisher and CEO, leaving Graham in the chairman position. In 2013, Graham's niece, Katharine Graham Weymouth, took over as publisher and CEO.

The *Washington Post* Hits Hard Times

Under Graham's direction, in 1996, the newspaper set up its first website, offering limited content that also appeared in its print publication. As the Internet became a more widely used tool, the *Post* expanded its online presence by adding custom content to the website, and thus drew in additional advertisers.

But the days of climbing revenue were short lived. Shortly before the recession hit in 2007/2008, the number of *Post* subscribers was quickly declining; a situation similarly experienced in newsrooms across the country. Newsreaders moved toward more free, online content, and while the website brought the possibility of new advertising revenue, a model was not yet well-established enough to prove as profitable as a hard copy paper. In an online environment, advertising space is almost infinite, and because readers can quickly click through stories or even click through to external websites, advertisers have less of a guarantee that their information will be seen. The advent of new delivery formats like the iPad have piqued the interest of advertisers, who have reportedly paid up to five times more per ad in the e-reader version than they would have on a newspaper website because space is more limited. Still, the profitability is nowhere near what newspapers could expect when only a hard copy was available. In 2012, the *Post* had $582 million in revenue, but a $53.7 million operating loss. By 2013, *The Washington Post* was facing an estimated $40 million loss, even though it had managed to maintain a positive cash flow in the few years prior.

Well aware of the pressures facing the newspaper, Weymouth met with Graham to discuss options for moving forward. The *Post* was facing its seventh year in which it would post a loss in revenue, so Weymouth presented three options: they could move forward status quo, basically ensuring the paper's continued decline; continue cutting staff in hopes they might be able to turn a profit in the future; or sell the paper. It had long been Graham's intent to ensure that each of the *Post*'s holdings could stand on its own, and with the namesake newspaper not pulling its weight, difficult decisions needed to be made. Graham would later say that Weymouth made the gravity of the situation clear: "She was saying the decline in revenue was going to go on, so, you know, the only choice was lose money or cut costs. . . . It's certainly an option to lose money for three or four years. The question was what would happen in three or four years." Weymouth maintained a neutral position on how to proceed, leaving the ultimate decision to Graham, who concluded that a sale would be the only viable option.

Over a period of eight months, Weymouth and Graham met privately to determine the best way to find a buyer. In the end, after speaking to less than a dozen potential owners, Graham turned to his long-time friend Jeff Bezos, the billionaire founder of Amazon .com. Bezos agreed to purchase the paper and some of The Washington Post Company's other holdings for $250 million. Graham's long-term relationship with Bezos reportedly made him comfortable that the paper's new owner would treat the business with the utmost respect it deserved.

Post Sold to Amazon.com Founder

On August 5, 2013, Weymouth announced to *Post* staff that The Washington Post Company intended to sell the newspaper to Bezos. Upon finalization of the sale, The Washington Post Company would transfer the paper and its assets to Bezos's investment company, Nash Holdings. The Washington Post Company would continue to operate independently. Other portions of the company not included in the sale were the company's office building in Washington, D.C. (which was sold in November to Carr Properties for $159 million), media assets like Slate Group and *Foreign Policy*, Post-Newsweek Stations, and the Kaplan education company. As expected, on November 29, The Washington Post Company changed its name to Graham Holdings Company.

The *Post* was not the first newspaper to decide to take drastic measures to keep itself afloat. In 2007, the *Cincinnati Post* closed its doors, ending both its 126-year print run and its website. In 2009, the 146-year-old *Seattle Post Intelligencer* announced that it would move to an online-only format. In an effort to remain afloat, a number of small- to mid-sized newspapers have been sold to both private investors and large media conglomerates, like the Hearst Corporation. But the sale of *The Washington Post* came with the biggest price tag; when the New York Times Company decided to sell the *Boston Globe* to the owner of the Red Sox in 2013, it went for $70 million, and *Newsweek* was sold in 2011 to billionaire Sidney Harman for a symbolic $1.

Bezo's Plan for the Future

The sale was officially completed on October 1, 2013, ending eight decades of ownership by the Graham family. "We are officially under new ownership, and a new era for *The Washington Post* begins," Weymouth wrote in a memo to staff. She added that under Bezos's leadership "we will build on [the foundation built by my uncle] and take *The Post* to new heights."

Bezos told *Post* staff and the public that he had no intention of becoming involved with the day-to-day editorial decisions being made by the newspaper. Bezos left in place the *Post*'s leaders Weymouth and executive editor Martin Baron. Bezos intended to keep his primary focus on Amazon.com but said he would visit the Washington offices from time to time. Instead, it was his intent to continue the paper's investigative excellence by developing a long-term plan to ensure the economic vitality of the paper for years to come. Bezos did not immediately announce a plan for the newspaper, but during meetings with staff, he indicated that he wanted to give the paper the leeway to experiment with different ideas that might become the next big money maker for the *Post*. "There is no map, and charting a path ahead will not be easy," Bezos said, adding that the paper "will need to invent, which means we will need to experiment."

—Heather Kerrigan

Following is the text of a press release from Graham Holdings Company (formerly The Washington Post Company), released on August 5, 2013, announcing the sale of The Washington Post to the founder of Amazon.com.

The Washington Post Company Announces Sale of Namesake Newspaper

August 5, 2013

The Washington Post Company (NYSE: WPO) announced today that it has signed a contract to sell its newspaper publishing businesses, including The Washington Post newspaper, to Jeffrey P. Bezos.

The purchaser is an entity that belongs to Mr. Bezos in his individual capacity and is not Amazon.com, Inc.

"Everyone at the Post Company and everyone in our family has always been proud of The Washington Post—of the newspaper we publish and of the people who write and produce it," said Donald E. Graham, Chairman and CEO of The Washington Post Company. "I, along with Katharine Weymouth and our board of directors, decided to sell only after years of familiar newspaper-industry challenges made us wonder if there might be another owner who would be better for the Post (after a transaction that would be in the best interest of our shareholders). Jeff Bezos' proven technology and business genius, his long-term approach and his personal decency make him a uniquely good new owner for the Post."

"I understand the critical role the Post plays in Washington, DC and our nation, and the Post's values will not change," said Mr. Bezos. "Our duty to readers will continue to be the heart of the Post, and I am very optimistic about the future."

Mr. Bezos has asked Katharine Weymouth, CEO and Publisher of The Washington Post; Stephen P. Hills, President and General Manager; Martin Baron, Executive Editor; and Fred Hiatt, Editor of the Editorial Page to continue in those roles.

"With Mr. Bezos as our owner, this is the beginning of an exciting new era," said Ms. Weymouth. "I am honored to continue as CEO and Publisher. I have asked the entire senior management team at all of the businesses being sold to continue in their roles as well."

The transaction covers The Washington Post and other publishing businesses, including the Express newspaper, The Gazette Newspapers, Southern Maryland Newspapers, Fairfax County Times, El Tiempo Latino and Greater Washington Publishing.

Slate magazine, TheRoot.com and Foreign Policy are not part of the transaction and will remain with The Washington Post Company, as will the WaPo Labs and SocialCode businesses, the Company's interest in Classified Ventures and certain real estate assets, including the headquarters building in downtown Washington, DC. The Washington Post Company, which also owns Kaplan, Post–Newsweek Stations and Cable ONE, will be changing its name in connection with the transaction; no new name has yet been announced.

The purchase price is $250 million, subject to normal working capital adjustments, payable at closing later this year.

Allen & Co. assisted the Post Company in the sale process.

ABOUT THE WASHINGTON POST COMPANY

The Washington Post Company (NYSE:WPO) is a diversified education and media company. The Company's Kaplan subsidiary provides a wide variety of educational services, both domestically and outside the United States, including programs to prepare students for careers in healthcare and many other fields. Its media operations include newspaper publishing (principally The Washington Post), television broadcasting (through the ownership and operation of six television broadcast stations) and cable television systems. The Company also owns Celtic Healthcare, a multistate provider of Medicare-certified home healthcare and hospice services, and Forney Corporation, a global supplier of products and systems that control and monitor combustion processes in electric utility and industrial applications.

SOURCE: Graham Holdings Company. "Jeffrey P. Bezos to Purchase The Washington Post." August 5, 2013. http://www.ghco.com/phoenix.zhtml?c=62487&p=irol-pressArticle&ID=1844731&highlight=.

OTHER HISTORIC DOCUMENTS OF INTEREST

FROM PREVIOUS *HISTORIC DOCUMENTS*

- Changes in the Publishing Industry, *2010*, p. 344

Department of Justice Issues Revised Drug Sentencing Guidelines

AUGUST 12, 2013

On August 12, 2013, in a speech before the American Bar Association (ABA), Attorney General Eric Holder announced a policy shift that would allow some low-level, nonviolent drug offenders to avoid mandatory minimum sentences. This, Holder anticipated, would begin freeing up law enforcement and court officials to deal with more serious offenders, and would also alleviate some overcrowding of America's jails and prisons.

MANDATORY SENTENCING MINIMUMS

In 1971, then-President Richard Nixon called for a "War on Drugs," an all-out effort that increased the size and force of drug control agencies and heavily target marijuana, crack, and cocaine users and distributors. Subsequent presidents, including Ronald Reagan and Bill Clinton, continued to encourage the movement and passed large law enforcement spending increases to back them up. The War on Drugs created mandatory minimum sentencing guidelines aimed at imposing long sentences on any drug offender, no matter how little drugs he or she was caught in possession of. States joined the movement as well, enacting their own laws that restricted the ability of prosecutors to use their own judgment about how harsh a penalty should be.

Such mandatory minimum sentences disproportionately affected the black and Hispanic populations as well as impoverished communities. Approximately 30 percent of those sentenced every year for drug offenses are African American, while 40 percent are Hispanic, says Marc Mauer of The Sentencing Project. According to the Drug Policy Alliance, usage and sale rates are equal across racial lines, but law enforcement entities have traditionally focused their drug efforts on impoverished and urban communities.

Since the War on Drugs began, crime has fallen in the United States, but its prison population has continued to increase. Although the United States accounts for only 5 percent of the world's population, it makes up 25 percent of the total global jail population. Federal prisons are 40 percent over capacity, at approximately 220,000 inmates, around half of whom were sentenced for drug-related crimes, and 60 percent of those were sentenced under mandatory minimums. Federal and state prisoners cost taxpayers upwards of $80 billion annually. Of the 25,000 sentenced to prison each year for drug offenses, nearly half are low-level offenders or are being charged for minimum amounts. For example, someone convicted of conspiring to sell 5 gm of crack can expect to receive a ten-year sentence.

"SMART ON CRIME"

As crime has fallen, the public's appetite for tougher prison sentences has waned. Mandatory minimum sentences leave little leeway for prosecutors when determining sentences for drug offenders. With the War on Drugs, entering its fifth decade, in a speech before the ABA, Holder said it was only prudent to evaluate whether it has "been truly effective." Indicating his own opinion that the War on Drugs is unsustainable, Holder said, "Twentieth century criminal justice solutions are not adequate to overcome our 21st century challenges. And, again, it is well past time to implement common-sense changes that will foster safer communities from coast to coast." Holder made it clear that he had no intention of waiting for Congress to change sentencing guidelines to give U.S. attorneys more prosecutorial discretion. "Today, a vicious cycle of poverty, criminality, and incarceration traps too many Americans and weakens too many communities," Holder said. "However, many aspects of our criminal justice system may actually exacerbate this problem, rather than alleviate it," he continued.

Holder said he would direct federal prosecutors to seek tough sentences only for high-level or violent drug offenders. This approach, called "Smart on Crime," would leave state and local governments more in control of their own sentencing guidelines that better applied to their own realities. This would allow U.S. attorneys to decide when federal charges should be filed and when other, lesser punishments would suffice. "By reserving the most severe penalties for serious, high-level, or violent drug traffickers, we can better promote public safety, deterrence, and rehabilitation—while making our expenditures smarter and more productive," Holder said.

Such new prosecutorial guidelines will also help significantly decrease the federal prison population. "Too many Americans go to too many prisons for far too long, and for no good law enforcement reason," Holder said. "While the aggressive enforcement of federal criminal statutes remains necessary, we cannot simply prosecute or incarcerate our way to becoming a safer nation," Holder said, adding, "We need to ensure that incarceration is used to punish, deter and rehabilitate—not merely to convict, warehouse and forget." To avoid the requirement of charging drug offenders under mandatory minimum sentences, prosecutors would not include in the official charging documents the amount of drugs the defendant had in his or her possession. This change would not require Congressional approval; however, fully breaking the mandatory minimum sentencing guidelines would need to be approved by Congress. It will still be left to the ninety-four U.S. Attorneys' offices to determine how to use Holder's guidelines in sentencing drug offenders.

Not everyone supported Holder's decision. In a letter to the Attorney General, the National Association of Assistant United States Attorneys wrote: "Mandatory minimum sentences are a critical tool in persuading defendants to cooperate, thereby enabling law enforcement to dismantle large drug organizations and violent gangs." The letter goes on to note that the group believes the current mandatory minimum sentencing system has played an important role in reducing crime rates and keeping Americans safe. "We believe our current sentencing laws . . . should be preserved, not weakened," the letter concludes. Others took issue with how Holder went about attempting to change sentencing guidelines. House Judiciary Committee Chairman Rep. Bob Goodlatte, R-Va., urged Holder to let Congress make laws regarding sentencing. "If Attorney General Holder wants to reform our criminal justice system, he should work with Congress to do so," Goodlatte said.

Justice Department Encourages Inmates to Seek Clemency

On January 30, 2014, Deputy Attorney General James Cole called on lawyers and prison officials for assistance to help find drug offenders who were sentenced under much harsher laws in the 1980s and 1990s and assist them in applying for clemency. Those sentencing guidelines, part of the War on Drugs, primarily targeted crack users, imposing harsher sentences than on those who used powdered cocaine. Given the demographics of the users of each drug, these strict sentencing regulations put a disproportionate number of black men in prison. At the end of 2011, the Bureau of Justice Statistics reported that 30,000 inmates were charged on crack violations.

The Obama administration began seeking to reduce this disparity in 2010 when the president commuted the federal crack cocaine sentences of eight black men. A bill in the Senate, known as the Smarter Sentencing Act, would quicken the pace of the Obama goal by allowing the new drug sentencing guidelines to be retroactive. "There are more low-level, nonviolent drug offenders who remain in prison, and who would likely have received a substantially lower sentence if convicted of precisely the same offenses today," said Cole. "This is not fair, and it harms our criminal justice system," he added. If passed, the bill could help up to 12,000 prisoners. The bill moved out of committee in early 2014 and is awaiting debate by the full Senate. It is likely that the Justice Department will wait for the outcome of the bill before placing further emphasis on its intent to seek out individuals to offer clemency. There is hope that the legislation will pass and thus avoid a deluge of applications from hitting the Justice Department's pardon unit, which already has a significant backlog.

States Act; Congress Looks Toward Possible New Laws

Prior to Holder's Smart on Crime initiative, at least seventeen states were already working toward reducing jail sentences and offering rehabilitative treatment or community service instead of jail time for low-level drug offenses. The states, led by both Republican and Democratic governors, included Arkansas, California, Georgia, Hawaii, Kentucky, New York, North Carolina, Ohio, Pennsylvania, and Texas. Each state has worked in a variety of different ways to redirect resources away from jails and into treatment programs and probation. State level changes could have a significant impact on prison populations. According to the U.S. Bureau of Justice Statistics, approximately 225,000 people are currently incarcerated in state prisons for drug offenses.

In Kentucky, the state is on track to save $400 million during the next decade by reducing its prison population by more than 3,000 by sentencing only the most violent and dangerous offenders to prison. Texas has invested additional funds in drug treatment programs, and in 2012 reduced its prison population by more than 5,000 by making changes to the parole and treatment programs. The state of California has made some adjustments to its sentencing system for drug offenders, but because the changes have not had enough impact, California had been ordered by a court to reduce its number of inmates by 10,000 in 2013.

In Congress, a bipartisan group of senators are fighting to bring the Smarter Sentencing Act to a floor vote. The bill would not only make Holder's guidelines retroactive but would also reduce the likelihood that a court will use the mandatory minimum sentencing guidelines. Sens. Rand Paul, R-Ky., Patrick Leahy, D-Vt., Dick Durbin, D-Ill., Jeff Flake, R-Ariz., Ted Cruz, R-Texas, Carl Levin, D-Mich., Sheldon Whitehouse, D-R.I., Angus King, I-Maine, Martin Heinrich, D-N.M., and Mike Lee, R-Utah, are the driving forces behind the bill. Holder called the legislation a "very promising" move that could "save our country billions of dollars," but federal prosecutors remain opposed to such legislation.

—Heather Kerrigan

Following is the edited text of Attorney General Eric Holder's August 12, 2013, remarks before the American Bar Association on revised sentencing guidelines; the text of the guidelines issued by the Department of Justice on August 12, 2013, on developing and implementing a revised criminal justice system; and a statement in response to the proposal by Rep. Bob Goodlatte, chairman of the House Judiciary Committee, also on August 12, 2013.

Attorney General Remarks on Revised Sentencing Guidelines

August 12, 2013

[Holder's introductory remarks have been omitted.]

It's time—in fact, it's well past time—to address persistent needs and unwarranted disparities by considering a fundamentally new approach. As a prosecutor; a judge; an attorney in private practice; and now, as our nation's Attorney General, I've seen the criminal justice system firsthand, from nearly every angle. While I have the utmost faith in—and dedication to—America's legal system, we must face the reality that, as it stands, our system is in too many respects broken. The course we are on is far from sustainable. And it is our time—and our duty—to identify those areas we can improve in order to better advance the cause of justice for all Americans.

Even as most crime rates decline, we need to examine new law enforcement strategies—and better allocate resources—to keep pace with today's continuing threats as violence spikes in some of our greatest cities. As studies show that six in ten American children are exposed to violence at some point in their lives—and nearly one in four college women experience some form of sexual assault by their senior year—we need fresh solutions for assisting victims and empowering survivors. As the so-called "war on drugs" enters its fifth decade, we need to ask whether it, and the approaches that comprise it, have been truly effective—and build on the Administration's efforts, led by the Office of National Drug Control Policy, to usher in a new approach. And with an outsized, unnecessarily large prison population, we need to ensure that incarceration is used to punish, deter, and rehabilitate—not merely to warehouse and forget.

Today, a vicious cycle of poverty, criminality, and incarceration traps too many Americans and weakens too many communities. And many aspects of our criminal justice system may actually exacerbate these problems, rather than alleviate them.

It's clear—as we come together today—that too many Americans go to too many prisons for far too long, and for no truly good law enforcement reason. It's clear, at a basic level, that 20th-century criminal justice solutions are not adequate to overcome our 21st-century challenges. And it is well past time to implement common sense changes that will foster safer communities from coast to coast.

These are issues the President and I have been talking about for as long as I've known him—issues he's felt strongly about ever since his days as a community organizer on the South Side of Chicago. . . .

That's why, over the next several months, the President will continue to reach out to Members of Congress from both parties—as well as governors, mayors, and other leaders—to build on the great work being done across the country to reduce violent crime and reform our criminal justice system. We need to keep taking steps to make sure people feel safe and secure in their homes and communities. And part of that means doing something about the lives being harmed, not helped, by a criminal justice system that doesn't serve the American people as well as it should . . . .

Particularly in these challenging times—when budgets are tight, federal sequestration has imposed untenable and irresponsible cuts, and leaders across government are being asked to do more with less—coordination between America's federal, state, local, and tribal law enforcement agencies has never been more important. It's imperative that we maximize our resources by focusing on protecting national security; combating violent crime; fighting against financial fraud; and safeguarding the most vulnerable members of our society.

This means that federal prosecutors cannot—and should not—bring every case or charge every defendant who stands accused of violating federal law. Some issues are best handled at the state or local level. And that's why I have today directed the United States Attorney community to develop specific, locally-tailored guidelines—consistent with our national priorities—for determining when federal charges should be filed, and when they should not.

I've also issued guidance to ensure that every case we bring serves a substantial federal interest and complements the work of our law enforcement partners. I have directed all U.S. Attorneys to create—and to update—comprehensive anti-violence strategies for badly-afflicted areas within their districts. And I've encouraged them to convene regular law enforcement forums with state and local partners to refine these plans, foster greater efficiency, and facilitate more open communication and cooperation.

By targeting the most serious offenses, prosecuting the most dangerous criminals, directing assistance to crime "hot spots," and pursuing new ways to promote public safety, deterrence, efficiency, and fairness—we in the federal government can become both smarter and tougher on crime. By providing leadership to all levels of law enforcement—and bringing intelligence-driven strategies to bear—we can bolster the efforts of local leaders, U.S. Attorneys, and others in the fight against violent crime . . . .

As we come together this morning, this same promise must lead us all to acknowledge that—although incarceration has a significant role to play in our justice system—widespread incarceration at the federal, state, and local levels is both ineffective and unsustainable. It imposes a significant economic burden—totaling $80 billion in 2010 alone—and it comes with human and moral costs that are impossible to calculate.

As a nation, we are coldly efficient in our incarceration efforts. While the entire U.S. population has increased by about a third since 1980, the federal prison population has grown at an astonishing rate—by almost 800 percent. It's still growing—despite the fact that federal prisons are operating at nearly 40 percent above capacity. Even though this country comprises just 5 percent of the world's population, we incarcerate almost a quarter of the world's prisoners. More than 219,000 federal inmates are currently behind bars. Almost half of them are serving time for drug-related crimes, and many have substance use disorders. Nine to 10 million more people cycle through America's local jails each year. And roughly 40 percent of former federal prisoners—and more than 60 percent of former state prisoners—are rearrested or have their supervision revoked within three years after their release, at great cost to American taxpayers and often for technical or minor violations of the terms of their release.

As a society, we pay much too high a price whenever our system fails to deliver outcomes that deter and punish crime, keep us safe, and ensure that those who have paid their debts have the chance to become productive citizens. Right now, unwarranted disparities are far too common. As President Obama said last month, it's time to ask tough questions about how we can strengthen our communities, support young people, and address the fact that young black and Latino men are disproportionately likely to become involved in our criminal justice system—as victims as well as perpetrators.

We also must confront the reality that—once they're in that system—people of color often face harsher punishments than their peers. One deeply troubling report, released in February, indicates that—in recent years—black male offenders have received sentences nearly 20 percent longer than those imposed on white males convicted of similar crimes. This isn't just unacceptable—it is shameful. It's unworthy of our great country, and our great legal tradition. And in response, I have today directed a group of U.S. Attorneys to examine sentencing disparities, and to develop recommendations on how we can address them.

In this area and many others—in ways both large and small—we, as a country, must resolve to do better. The President and I agree that it's time to take a pragmatic approach. And that's why I am proud to announce today that the Justice Department will take a series of significant actions to recalibrate America's federal criminal justice system.

We will start by fundamentally rethinking the notion of mandatory minimum sentences for drug-related crimes. Some statutes that mandate inflexible sentences—regardless of the individual conduct at issue in a particular case—reduce the discretion available to prosecutors, judges, and juries. Because they oftentimes generate unfairly long sentences, they breed disrespect for the system. When applied indiscriminately, they do not serve public safety. They—and some of the enforcement priorities we have set—have had a destabilizing effect on particular communities, largely poor and of color. And, applied inappropriately, they are ultimately counterproductive.

This is why I have today mandated a modification of the Justice Department's charging policies so that certain low-level, nonviolent drug offenders who have no ties to large-scale organizations, gangs, or cartels will no longer be charged with offenses that impose draconian mandatory minimum sentences. They now will be charged with offenses for which the accompanying sentences are better suited to their individual conduct, rather than excessive prison terms more appropriate for violent criminals or drug kingpins. By reserving the most severe penalties for serious, high-level, or violent drug traffickers, we can better promote public safety, deterrence, and rehabilitation—while making our expenditures smarter and more productive. We've seen that this approach has bipartisan support in Congress—where a number of leaders, including Senators Dick Durbin, Patrick Leahy, Mike Lee, and Rand Paul have introduced what I think is promising legislation aimed at giving federal judges more discretion in applying mandatory minimums to certain drug offenders. Such legislation will ultimately save our country billions of dollars while keeping us safe. And the President and I look forward to working with members of both parties to refine and advance these proposals.

Secondly, the Department has now updated its framework for considering compassionate release for inmates facing extraordinary or compelling circumstances—and who pose no threat to the public. In late April, the Bureau of Prisons expanded the criteria which will be considered for inmates seeking compassionate release for medical reasons. Today, I can announce additional expansions to our policy—including revised criteria for elderly inmates who did not commit violent crimes and who have served significant portions of their sentences. Of course, as our primary responsibility, we must ensure that the American public is protected from anyone who may pose a danger to the community. But considering the applications of nonviolent offenders—through a careful review process that ultimately allows judges to consider whether release is warranted—is the fair thing to do. And it is the smart thing to do as well, because it will enable us to use our limited resources to house those who pose the greatest threat.

Finally, my colleagues and I are taking steps to identify and share best practices for enhancing the use of diversion programs—such as drug treatment and community service initiatives—that can serve as effective alternatives to incarceration.

Our U.S. Attorneys are leading the way in this regard—working alongside the judiciary to meet safety imperatives while avoiding incarceration in certain cases. In South Dakota, a joint federal-tribal program has helped to prevent at-risk young people from getting involved in the federal prison system—thereby improving lives, saving taxpayer resources, and keeping communities safer. This is exactly the kind of proven innovation that federal policymakers, and state and tribal leaders, should emulate. And it's why the Justice Department is working—through a program called the Justice Reinvestment Initiative—to bring state leaders, local stakeholders, private partners, and federal officials together to comprehensively reform corrections and criminal justice practices.

In recent years, no fewer than 17 states—supported by the Department, and led by governors and legislators of both parties—have directed funding away from prison construction and toward evidence-based programs and services, like treatment and supervision, that are designed to reduce recidivism. In Kentucky, for example, new legislation has reserved prison beds for the most serious offenders and re-focused resources on community supervision and evidence-based alternative programs. As a result, the state is projected to reduce its prison population by more than 3,000 over the next 10 years—saving more than $400 million.

In Texas, investments in drug treatment for nonviolent offenders and changes to parole policies brought about a reduction in the prison population of more than 5,000 inmates last year alone. The same year, similar efforts helped Arkansas reduce its prison population by more than 1,400. From Georgia, North Carolina, and Ohio, to Pennsylvania, Hawaii, and far beyond—reinvestment and serious reform are improving public safety and saving precious resources. Let me be clear: these measures have not compromised public safety. In fact, many states have seen drops in recidivism rates at the same time their prison populations were declining. The policy changes that have led to these welcome results must be studied and emulated. While our federal prison system has continued to slowly expand, significant state-level reductions have led to three consecutive years of decline in America's overall prison population—including, in 2012, the largest drop ever experienced in a single year.

Clearly, these strategies can work. They've attracted overwhelming, bipartisan support in "red states" as well as "blue states." And it's past time for others to take notice.

I am also announcing today that I have directed every U.S. Attorney to designate a Prevention and Reentry Coordinator in his or her district—to ensure that this work is, and will remain, a top priority throughout the country. And my colleagues and I will keep working closely with state leaders, agency partners, including members of the Federal Interagency Reentry Council—and groups like the American Bar Association—to extend these efforts.

In recent years, with the Department's support, the ABA has catalogued tens of thousands of statutes and regulations that impose unwise and counterproductive collateral consequences—with regard to housing or employment, for example—on people who have been convicted of crimes. I have asked state attorneys general and a variety of federal leaders to review their own agencies' regulations. And today I can announce that I've directed all Department of Justice components, going forward, to consider whether any proposed regulation or guidance may impose unnecessary collateral consequences on those seeking to rejoin their communities.

The bottom line is that, while the aggressive enforcement of federal criminal statutes remains necessary, we cannot simply prosecute or incarcerate our way to becoming a safer nation. To be effective, federal efforts must also focus on prevention and reentry. We must never stop being tough on crime. But we must also be smart and efficient when battling crime and the conditions and the individual choices that breed it.

Ultimately, this is about much more than fairness for those who are released from prison. It's a matter of public safety and public good. It makes plain economic sense. It's about who we are as a people. And it has the potential to positively impact the lives of every man, woman, and child—in every neighborhood and city—in the United States. After all, whenever a recidivist crime is committed, innocent people are victimized. Communities are less safe. Burdens on law enforcement are increased. And already-strained resources are depleted even further.

Today—together—we must declare that we will no longer settle for such an unjust and unsustainable status quo. To do so would be to betray our history, our shared commitment to justice, and the founding principles of our nation. Instead, we must recommit ourselves—as a country—to tackling the most difficult questions, and the most costly problems, no matter how complex or intractable they may appear. We must pledge—as legal professionals—to lend our talents, our training, and our diverse perspectives to advancing this critical work. And we must resolve—as a people—to take a firm stand against violence; against victimization; against inequality—and for justice.

This is our chance—to bring America's criminal justice system in line with our most sacred values.

This is our opportunity—to define this time, our time, as one of progress and innovation.

This is our promise—to forge a more just society.

And this is our solemn obligation, as stewards of the law, and servants of those whom it protects and empowers: to open a frank and constructive dialogue about the need to reform a broken system. To fight for the sweeping, systemic changes we need. And to uphold our dearest values, as the ABA always has, by calling on our peers and colleagues not merely to serve their clients, or win their cases—but to ensure that—in every case, in every circumstance, and in every community—justice is done.

This, after all, is the cause that has been our common pursuit for more than two centuries, the ideal that has guided the ABA since its inception, and the goal that will drive additional actions by President Obama—and leaders throughout his Administration—in the months ahead. Of course, we recognize—as you do—that the reforms I've announced today, and others that we must consider, explore, and implement in the coming years, will not take hold overnight. There will be setbacks and false starts. We will encounter resistance and opposition.

But if we keep faith in one another, and in the principles we've always held dear; if we stay true to the ABA's history as a driver of positive change; and if we keep moving forward together—knowing that the need for this work will outlast us, but determined to make the difference that we seek—then I know we can all be confident in where these efforts will lead us. I look forward to everything that we will undoubtedly achieve. And I will always be proud to stand alongside you in building the brighter, more just, and more prosperous future that all of our citizens deserve.

SOURCE: U.S. Department of Justice. "Attorney General Eric Holder Delivers Remarks at the Annual Meeting of the American Bar Association's House of Delegates." August 12, 2013. http://www.justice.gov/iso/opa/ag/speeches/2013/ag-speech-130812.html.

Department of Justice Guidelines for a Revised Criminal Justice System

August 12, 2013

INTRODUCTION

At the direction of the Attorney General, in early 2013 the Justice Department launched a comprehensive review of the criminal justice system in order to identify reforms that would ensure federal laws are enforced more fairly and—in an era of reduced budgets—more efficiently. Specifically, this project identified five goals:

- To ensure finite resources are devoted to the most important law enforcement priorities;
- To promote fairer enforcement of the laws and alleviate disparate impacts of the criminal justice system;
- To ensure just punishments for low-level, nonviolent convictions;
- To bolster prevention and reentry efforts to deter crime and reduce recidivism;
- To strengthen protections for vulnerable populations.

As part of its review, the Department studied all phases of the criminal justice system—including charging, sentencing, incarceration and reentry—to examine which practices are most successful at deterring crime and protecting the public, and which aren't. The review also considered demographic disparities that have provoked questions about the fundamental fairness of the criminal justice system.

The preliminary results of this review suggest a need for a significant change in our approach to enforcing the nation's laws. Today, a vicious cycle of poverty, criminality, and incarceration traps too many Americans and weakens too many communities. However, many aspects of our criminal justice system may actually exacerbate this problem, rather than alleviate it.

The reality is, while the aggressive enforcement of federal criminal statutes remains necessary, we cannot prosecute our way to becoming a safer nation. To be effective, federal efforts must also focus on prevention and reentry. In addition, it is time to rethink the nation's system of mass imprisonment. The United States today has the highest rate of incarceration of any nation in the world, and the nationwide cost to state and federal budgets was $80 billion in 2010 alone. This pattern of incarceration is disruptive to families, expensive to the taxpayer, and may not serve the goal of reducing recidivism. We must marshal resources, and use evidence-based strategies, to curb the disturbing rates of recidivism by those reentering our communities.

These findings align with a growing movement at the state level to scrutinize the cost-effectiveness of our corrections system. In recent years, states such as Texas and Arkansas have reduced their prison populations by pioneering approaches that seek alternatives to incarceration for people convicted of low-level, nonviolent drug offenses.

It is time to apply some of the lessons learned from these states at the federal level. By shifting away from our over-reliance on incarceration, we can focus resources on the most important law enforcement priorities, such as violence prevention and protection of vulnerable populations.

The initial package of reforms described below—dubbed the Justice Department's "Smart on Crime" initiative—is only the beginning of an ongoing effort to modernize the criminal justice system. In the months ahead, the Department will continue to hone an approach that is not only more efficient, and not only more effective at deterring crime and reducing recidivism, but also more consistent with our nation's commitment to treating all Americans as equal under the law.

We of course must remain tough on crime. But we must also be smart on crime.

FIVE PRINCIPLES OF "SMART ON CRIME"

I. PRIORITIZE PROSECUTIONS TO FOCUS ON MOST SERIOUS CASES

Given scarce resources, federal law enforcement efforts should focus on the most serious cases that implicate clear, substantial federal interests. Currently, the Department's interests are:

1. Protecting Americans from national security threats

2. Protecting Americans from violent crime

3. Protecting Americans from financial fraud

4. Protecting the most vulnerable members of society

Based on these federal priorities, the Attorney General is, for the first time, requiring the development of district-specific guidelines for determining when federal prosecutions should be brought. This necessarily will mean focusing resources on fewer but the most significant cases, as opposed to fixating on the sheer volume of cases.

The Attorney General's call for the creation of district-specific guidelines recognizes that each U.S. Attorney is in the best position to articulate the priorities that make sense for that area. A particular district's priorities will often depend on local criminal threats and needs.

In the coming months, the U.S. Attorneys' Manual will be updated to reflect the requirement that U.S. Attorneys develop district-specific guidelines for the prioritization of cases.

II. REFORM SENTENCING TO ELIMINATE UNFAIR DISPARITIES AND REDUCE OVERBURDENED PRISONS.

Our prisons are over-capacity and the rising cost of maintaining them imposes a heavy burden on taxpayers and communities. At the state level, costs for running corrections facilities have roughly tripled in the last three decades, making it the second-fastest rising expense after Medicaid. At the federal level, the Bureau of Prisons comprises one-third of the Justice Department's budget.

This requires a top-to-bottom look at our system of incarceration. For many non-violent, low-level offenses, prison may not be the most sensible method of punishment. But even for those defendants who do require incarceration, it is important to ensure a sentence length commensurate with the crime committed. Our policies must also seek to eliminate unfair sentencing disparities.

It is time for meaningful sentencing reform. As a start, the Attorney General is announcing a change in Department of Justice charging policies so that certain people who have committed low-level, nonviolent drug offenses, who have no ties to large-scale organizations, gangs, or cartels will no longer be charged with offenses that impose draconian mandatory minimum sentences. Under the revised policy, these people would instead receive sentences better suited to their individual conduct rather than excessive prison terms more appropriate for violent criminals or drug kingpins. Reserving the most severe penalties for serious, high-level, or violent drug traffickers will better promote public safety, deterrence, and rehabilitation—while making our expenditures smarter and more productive.

The Attorney General also plans to work with Congress to pass legislation that would reform mandatory minimum laws. A number of bipartisan proposals—including bills by Senators Dick Durbin (D-IL) and Mike Lee (R-UT), as well as Senators Patrick Leahy (D-VT) and Rand Paul (R-KY)—show the emerging consensus in favor of addressing this issue.

Sentencing reform also entails considering reductions in sentence for inmates facing extraordinary and compelling circumstances—and who pose no threat to public safety. In late April, the Bureau of Prisons (BOP) expanded the medical criteria that will be considered for inmates seeking compassionate release. In a new step, the Attorney General is announcing revised criteria for other categories of inmates seeking reduced sentences. This includes elderly inmates and certain inmates who are the only possible caregiver for their dependents. In both cases, under the revised policy, BOP would generally consider inmates who did not commit violent crimes and have served significant portions of their sentences. The sentencing judge would ultimately decide whether to reduce the sentence.

III. PURSUE ALTERNATIVES TO INCARCERATION FOR LOW-LEVEL, NON-VIOLENT CRIMES.

Incarceration is not the answer in every criminal case. Across the nation, no fewer than 17 states have shifted resources away from prison construction in favor of treatment and supervision as a better means of reducing recidivism. In Kentucky, new legislation has reserved prison beds for the most serious offenders and re-focused resources on community supervision and evidence-based programs. As a result, the state is projected to reduce its prison population by more than 3,000 over the next 10 years—saving more than $400 million.

Federal law enforcement should encourage this approach. In appropriate instances involving non-violent offenses, prosecutors ought to consider alternatives to incarceration, such as drug courts, specialty courts, or other diversion programs. Accordingly, the Department will issue a "best practices" memorandum to U.S. Attorney Offices encouraging more widespread adoption of these diversion policies when appropriate.

In its memorandum, the Department will endorse certain existing diversion programs as models. In the Central District of California, the USAO, the court, the Federal Public Defender, and the Pretrial Services Agency (PSA) have together created a two-track specialty court/post-plea diversion program, known as the Conviction and Sentence Alternatives (CASA) program. Selection for the program is not made solely by the USAO, but by the program team, comprised of the USAO, the Public Defender, PSA, and the court. Track one is for candidates with minimal criminal histories whose criminal conduct appears to be an aberration that could appropriately be addressed by supervision, restitution and community service. Examples of potential defendants include those charged with felony, though relatively minor, credit card or benefit fraud, mail theft, and narcotics offenses. Track two is for those defendants with somewhat more serious criminal histories whose conduct appears motivated by substance abuse issues. Supervision in these cases includes intensive drug treatment. Examples of eligible defendants are those charged with non-violent bank robberies, or mail and credit card theft designed to support a drug habit.

The Department will also recommend the use of specialty courts and programs to deal with unique populations. Examples include a treatment court for veterans charged with misdemeanors in the Western District of Virginia, and the Federal/Tribal Pretrial Diversion program in the District of South Dakota, which is designed specifically for juvenile offenders in Indian country.

IV. IMPROVE REENTRY TO CURB REPEAT OFFENDERS AND RE-VICTIMIZATION

After prison, recidivism rates are high. A reduction in the recidivism rate of even one or two percentage points could create long-lasting benefits for formerly incarcerated individuals and their communities.

To lead these efforts on a local level, the Department is calling for U.S. Attorneys to designate a prevention and reentry coordinator within each of their offices to focus on prevention and reentry efforts. As part of this enhanced commitment, Assistant U.S. Attorneys will be newly encouraged to devote time to reentry issues in addition to casework. The Executive Office of U.S. Attorneys will report periodically on the progress made in USAOs on the reentry front.

Other efforts to aid reentry are also being launched. It is well documented that the consequences of a criminal conviction can remain long after someone has served his or her sentence. Rules and regulations pertaining to formerly incarcerated people can limit employment and travel opportunities, making a proper transition back into society difficult. Currently, the Justice Department is working with the American Bar Association to publish a catalogue of these collateral consequences imposed at the state and federal level. To address these barriers to reentry, the Attorney General will issue a new memorandum to Department of Justice components, requiring them to factor these collateral consequences into their rulemaking. If the rules imposing collateral consequences are found to be unduly burdensome and not serving a public safety purpose, they should be narrowly tailored or eliminated.

The Attorney General's Reentry Council has published helpful materials on reentry efforts related to employment, housing, and parental rights. In an update to these materials, the Department will publish new fact sheets on ways to reduce unnecessary barriers to reentry in two areas: (1) to connect the reentering population with legal services to address obstacles such as fines and criminal records expungement when appropriate; and (2) to highlight efforts to reduce or eliminate fines at the local level.

V. 'SURGE' RESOURCES TO VIOLENCE PREVENTION AND PROTECTING MOST VULNERABLE POPULATIONS.

Even as crime levels have fallen, many of our communities still suffer from alarming rates of homicides, shootings and aggravated assaults. Confronting this problem and its root causes with a holistic approach remains a priority for the Department of Justice.

By exploring cost-effective reforms to our prison system, it will allow law enforcement to redirect scarce federal resources towards the priority of violence prevention.

Under a new memorandum issued by the Deputy Attorney General, U.S. Attorneys will put in place updated anti-violence strategies that are specific to their district. As an initial step, they will be urged to lead anti-violence forums to include Special Agents-in-Charge, Assistant Special Agents-in-Charge, U.S. Marshals and Chief Deputy Marshals, and State and Local Police Chiefs, Commanders, and Captains. With multiple federal, state, and local agencies involved in the fight against violent crime, strong relationships and robust information sharing are critical to achieve common goals and to avoid the unnecessary duplication of competing resources and efforts.

To monitor the success of these district-based anti-violence strategies, the Department will, in the coming months, implement new information-sharing techniques to share data from high-crime communities across Justice Department components.

The Department will also stress efforts to reduce and respond to violence, particularly violence against women and youth violence.

Within the Department, the Office of Community Oriented Policing Services (COPS), the Office of Victims of Crimes (OVC), and the Office of Violence Against Women (OVW) have partnered together to provide law enforcement agencies with the resources, technical assistance, and support they need to combat gender bias and sexual assault.

In April, the Department issued a revised Sexual Assault Forensic Examinations (SAFE) Protocol to standardize up-to-date approaches to victim-centered forensic medical examinations. In a new step, OVW will release a companion document that applies the protocol's recommendations for use in correctional facilities. A similar document will be released in the coming weeks for tribal communities.

In the coming months, the Department will also work with the Federal Bureau of Investigation to support states' implementation of the revised Uniform Crime Report definition of "rape."

In the effort to further protect children, the Department envisions several new steps:

- As part of the Attorney General's Defending Childhood Initiative:
  - This fall, the Department will launch a public awareness and community action campaign to stem youth violence.
  - The Department will establish a Task Force on American Indian/Alaska Native Children Exposed to Violence.

- ○ The Department will partner with select states to form "State Commissions" that will implement model public policy initiatives at the state and local level to reduce the impact of children's exposure to violence, including the adaptation and implementation of recommendations of the Attorney General's Task Force on Children Exposed to Violence.
- The Department will prioritize School Resource Officer requests in its COPS Hiring grant awards this year.
- The Department and the Department of Education will jointly issue guidance to public elementary and secondary schools on their federal civil rights obligations to administer student discipline without discrimination on the basis of race, color, or national origin, and the Department will continue to vigorously enforce civil rights laws to ensure that school discipline is fair and equitable.
- In September, the Department will host the National Forum Youth Violence Prevention Summit, which, for the first time, will convene stakeholders from the Forum, Defending Childhood, Community-Based Grant Programs, and youth violence prevention initiatives at other federal agencies to collaborate on innovative strategies and comprehensive solutions to end youth violence, protect the children that are exposed to it, and create safer and healthier communities.

In addition to these violence prevention efforts, the Department also remains focused on serving victims of crime. In June, the Justice Department issued the *Vision 21* report that offers an unprecedented snapshot of the current state of victim services and calls for sweeping, evidence-based changes to bring these services into the 21st century. It will empower survivors by closing research gaps and developing new ways to reach those who need our assistance the most.

SOURCE: U.S. Department of Justice. "Smart on Crime: Reforming the Criminal Justice System for the 21st Century." August 12, 2013. http://www.justice.gov/ag/smart-on-crime.pdf.

Rep. Goodlatte Responds to Smart on Crime Proposal

August 12, 2013

"Unfortunately, the Obama Administration has a pattern of overstepping its constitutional bounds by selectively enforcing our laws and attempting to change them through executive fiat in blatant disregard for the limitations the U.S. Constitution places on the Executive Branch.

"I agree with many of the policy issues Attorney General Holder outlined today. In fact, months ago the House Judiciary Committee created the Overcriminalization Task Force to broadly address these as well as other issues with our nation's criminal justice system. Over the past few decades, the federal criminal code has expanded dramatically, often duplicating state efforts and creating an ever-increasing labyrinth of federal regulations, many of which impose criminal penalties without requiring that criminal intent be shown to establish guilt. This Task Force is in the process of taking a broad look at our criminal code, allowing for input from experts, and is already considering sentencing and prison reform issues. The Committee will continue its work on this critical issue in the fall. If Attorney General Holder wants to reform our criminal justice system, he should work with Congress to do so. We welcome his input on this important issue.

"However, Attorney General Holder cannot unilaterally ignore the laws or the limits on his Executive powers. While the Attorney General has the ability to use prosecutorial discretion in individual cases, that authority does not extend to entire categories of people. We will be closely monitoring his efforts to ensure that the Obama Administration does not attempt to exceed its constitutional powers once again."

SOURCE: House of Representatives Committee on the Judiciary. "Goodlatte: If Administration Wants to Reform Criminal Justice System, Work With Congress." August 12, 2013. http://judiciary.house.gov/index.cfm/2013/8/goodlatte-if-administration-wants-to-reform-criminal-justice-system-work-with-congress.

OTHER HISTORIC DOCUMENTS OF INTEREST

FROM THIS VOLUME

FROM PREVIOUS *HISTORIC DOCUMENTS*

Department of Justice Issues Guidelines on Enforcement of Marijuana Laws

AUGUST 29, 2013

In 2012, Colorado and Washington approved the nation's first two laws to legalize recreational marijuana use. The laws were a clear violation of federal statute, but the Justice Department was slow to indicate how it would proceed. On August 29, 2013, Attorney General Eric Holder announced that he would allow the laws to continue without federal intervention as long as the states developed clear regulation and enforcement policies. The Justice Department would still retain the right to sue the states if implementation was carried out in a fashion deemed inappropriate and would also still be permitted to conduct operations against illegal drug traffickers.

COLORADO AND WASHINGTON APPROVE MARIJUANA LAWS

According to polling data, Americans are becoming increasingly more tolerant of decriminalizing recreational marijuana use. A 2013 Gallup poll found 58 percent of Americans in support of legalization, and only 39 percent opposed. This was an increase from 2011, when only 50 percent of Americans supported legalization. Supporters of such a law argue that states could increase tax revenue by allowing recreational marijuana use, free up law enforcement, offer some relief to overcrowded jails and prisons, and put a damper on drug trafficking operations. Opponents argue that legalization would hamper economic productivity while increasing the number of traffic and workplace accidents. By 2013, twenty states and Washington, D.C., had laws allowing the use of medical marijuana.

On November 6, 2012, Colorado and Washington became the first two states in the country to legalize marijuana for recreational use. Both states already had laws on the books to allow for controlled use of the substance for medical purposes, but the two referenda opened the doors for anyone over the age of twenty-one to use the drug so long as they complied with certain regulations.

In Colorado, Amendment 64 was officially signed by Governor John Hickenlooper on December 10, 2012, and went into effect on January 1, 2014. The new law allowed both residents and nonresidents to possess up to one ounce of marijuana for personal, recreational use. Residents were also allowed to grow up to six marijuana plants for personal use, as long as only three were mature and flowering at one time. Any marijuana produced by the plants was not allowed to leave the grower's property. Those found in possession of more than one ounce or more than three flowering plants would face stiff penalties. In addition, anyone caught driving with more than 5 nanograms of Delta-9-tetrahydrocannabinol (THC) in their blood could be found guilty of driving under the influence of drugs (DUID). In 2014, Colorado businesses will be allowed to apply for state licenses to sell recreational marijuana, but cities will have leeway to ban stores and cultivation farms within their borders.

In Washington, voters passed Initiative 502 with 56 percent of the vote. It became law on December 6 and, like Colorado, would allow for the possession of one ounce of marijuana for personal use. However, residents of Washington would not be allowed to grow marijuana for personal use—only state-licensed farmers would be allowed to grow the product. Marijuana consumption in public remained illegal, and those driving with more than 5 nanograms of THC in their blood could receive a DUI. Starting in 2014, state businesses will be allowed to apply for licenses to sell marijuana for recreational use.

CONFLICT WITH FEDERAL LAW

Both the Colorado and Washington ballot initiatives were in violation of the 1970 Controlled Substances Act, which classifies marijuana as a Schedule I controlled substance, meaning that it has no accepted medical use. This meant that even users cooperating with Colorado and Washington laws could still face federal fines and jail time. However, after the laws were passed, President Barack Obama's administration did not appear poised to make an all-out effort to track down individual users in the two states. In November 2012, the Department of Justice noted that it would review the initiatives but was not yet ready to make a determination on how to proceed. In December, President Obama told Barbara Walters, "We've got bigger fish to fry. It would not make sense for us to see a top priority as going after recreational users in states that have determined that it's legal." Kevin Sabet, a former senior adviser at the White House Office of National Drug Control Policy said that while the Obama administration might not target individual users, "you're going to see efforts by the Justice Department against large commercial grows or retail sales or states making money off the new laws."

In the past, the federal government has given a mixed response to state-based medical marijuana policy, but no individual has been prosecuted under federal law in any state that has legalized its medical use, so long as that person is acting within the bounds of the state law. This might be due in part to how tough in-state regulations are. In California, for example, cities are left to determine how to enforce the state's medical marijuana law, which has resulted in lackluster enforcement in which even those with minor aches and pains can receive a medical marijuana permit. In 2012, Los Angeles asked the state to step in and offer additional guidance on how to enforce the law after the city was sued during its attempt to shut down 1,000 dispensaries that it deemed too difficult to regulate. Because California's law does not have strict enforcement guidelines, the federal government has made a concerted effort to crack down on dispensaries and greenhouses thought to be a front for the illegal drug trade.

JUSTICE DEPARTMENT ALLOWS STATE LAWS TO PROCEED

On August 29, 2013, the Justice Department announced that it would allow the Colorado and Washington laws to be implemented under state regulation. In a conference call with Governor Hickenlooper and Washington Governor Jay Inslee, Holder said the department would follow a "trust but verify" approach to tracking activity related to recreational marijuana use in the two states, and that it would also maintain its right to sue either state under the Controlled Substances Act.

To provide guidance to all fifty states, Deputy Attorney General James Cole issued a memo outlining eight priorities for federal prosecutors to use in marijuana cases. Each priority was intended to prevent drug use outside the bounds of state or federal law and included preventing the following: the distribution of marijuana to minors, revenue from going to drug cartels or gangs, sending marijuana from a state where it is legal to a place where it is still illegal, drug trafficking or other illegal drug activity, violence or firearms use in marijuana cultivation and distribution, drugged driving, marijuana grown on public lands, and possession or use of marijuana on federal property. "The Department's guidance in this memorandum rests on its expectation that states and local governments that have enacted laws authorizing marijuana-related conduct will implement strong and effective regulatory and enforcement systems that will address the threat those state laws could pose to public safety, public health and other law enforcement interests," Cole wrote.

Enforcement of these regulations is unlikely to be lenient. In the past, federal prosecutors have aggressively gone after drug traffickers, distributors, and cultivators who have tried to hide under state medical marijuana laws. At one point, the Justice Department asked federal prosecutors to focus more on large, illegal drug trafficking operations or cartels rather than individual users. Several attorneys general refused to comply with what they saw as a lax interpretation of drug policy.

Washington and Colorado officials welcomed the Justice Department's decision, because it made clear how the states could proceed. "This is a critical first step in providing much-needed certainty for Colorado's residents and businesses who have been left in limbo since the voters decriminalized marijuana in 2012," said Sen. Mark Udall, D-Colo. John Walsh, the District of Colorado's lead prosecutor, said, "Because the Department of Justice's guidance emphasizes the central importance of strong and effective state marijuana regulatory systems, the U.S. Attorney's Office will continue to focus on whether Colorado's system, when it is implemented, has the resources and tools necessary to protect those key federal public safety interests . . . we look forward to closely working with our federal, state and local partners."

Debate Continues

Legalization advocates hailed the Justice Department's decision. "Today's announcement demonstrates the sort of political vision and foresight from the White House we've been seeking for a long time," said Ethan Nadelmann, the executive director of the Drug Policy Alliance. "This is politically and historically significant," he continued. Sen. Patrick Leahy, D-Vt., the chairman of the Senate Judiciary Committee, also welcomed the announcement: "The Justice Department should focus on countering and prosecuting violent crime, while respecting the will of the states whose people have voted to legalize small amounts of marijuana for personal and medical use." Sen. Leahy had scheduled a hearing to take place in September 2013 if the Justice Department failed to reach a decision on how to handle the Washington and Colorado laws.

The reaction was not all favorable. Calvina Fay, executive director of the Drug Free America Foundation, expressed disappointment at the guidelines, noting that Holder "should be fired" for failing to enforce federal law. "He has created what will become a tsunami that will most likely result in far too many young people becoming victims of chemical slavery," she said.

The Department's new guidelines will likely serve as the template for states seeking to legalize recreational marijuana use in their own states. White House spokesperson Josh Earnest said that the Obama administration intended to continue targeting drug traffickers but that "the administration believes that targeting individual marijuana users . . . is not the best allocation of federal government resources." California, Maine, and Rhode Island have all recently explored methods for legalizing personal, recreational marijuana use, and the new guidelines may be the impetus for expanding discussions on the issue.

—Heather Kerrigan

Following is the text of a memorandum issued to United States Attorneys by the Department of Justice on August 29, 2013, on revised marijuana enforcement guidelines.

Department of Justice Revises Marijuana Law Enforcement Policy

August 29, 2013

[The footnote has been omitted.]

MEMORANDUM FOR ALL UNITED STATES ATTORNEYS

FROM: James M. Cole

Deputy Attorney General

SUBJECT: Guidance Regarding Marijuana Enforcement

In October 2009 and June 2011, the Department issued guidance to federal prosecutors concerning marijuana enforcement under the Controlled Substances Act (CSA). This memorandum updates that guidance in light of state ballot initiatives that legalize under state law the possession of small amounts of marijuana and provide for the regulation of marijuana production, processing, and sale. The guidance set forth herein applies to all federal enforcement activity, including civil enforcement and criminal investigations and prosecutions, concerning marijuana in all states.

As the Department noted in its previous guidance, Congress has determined that marijuana is a dangerous drug and that the illegal distribution and sale of marijuana is a serious crime that provides a significant source of revenue to large-scale criminal enterprises, gangs, and cartels. The Department of Justice is committed to enforcement of the CSA consistent with those determinations. The Department is also committed to using its limited investigative and prosecutorial resources to address the most significant threats in the most effective, consistent, and rational way. In furtherance of those objectives, as several states enacted laws relating to the use of marijuana for medical purposes, the

Department in recent years has focused its efforts on certain enforcement priorities that are particularly important to the federal government:

- Preventing the distribution of marijuana to minors;
- Preventing revenue from the sale of marijuana from going to criminal enterprises, gangs, and cartels;
- Preventing the diversion of marijuana from states where it is legal under state law in some form to other states;
- Preventing state-authorized marijuana activity from being used as a cover or pretext for the trafficking of other illegal drugs or other illegal activity;
- Preventing violence and the use of firearms in the cultivation and distribution of marijuana;
- Preventing drugged driving and the exacerbation of other adverse public health consequences associated with marijuana use;
- Preventing the growing of marijuana on public lands and the attendant public safety and environmental dangers posed by marijuana production on public lands; and
- Preventing marijuana possession or use on federal property.

These priorities will continue to guide the Department's enforcement of the CSA against marijuana-related conduct. Thus, this memorandum serves as guidance to Department attorneys and law enforcement to focus their enforcement resources and efforts, including prosecution, on persons or organizations whose conduct interferes with any one or more of these priorities, regardless of state law.

Outside of these enforcement priorities, the federal government has traditionally relied on states and local law enforcement agencies to address marijuana activity through enforcement of their own narcotics laws. For example, the Department of Justice has not historically devoted resources to prosecuting individuals whose conduct is limited to possession of small amounts of marijuana for personal use on private property. Instead, the Department has left such lower-level or localized activity to state and local authorities and has stepped in to enforce the CSA only when the use, possession, cultivation, or distribution of marijuana has threatened to cause one of the harms identified above.

The enactment of state laws that endeavor to authorize marijuana production, distribution, and possession by establishing a regulatory scheme for these purposes affects this traditional joint federal-state approach to narcotics enforcement. The Department's guidance in this memorandum rests on its expectation that states and local governments that have enacted laws authorizing marijuana-related conduct will implement strong and effective regulatory and enforcement systems that will address the threat those state laws could pose to public safety, public health, and other law enforcement interests. A system adequate to that task must not only contain robust controls and procedures on paper; it must also be effective in practice. Jurisdictions that have implemented systems that provide for regulation of marijuana activity must provide the necessary resources and demonstrate the willingness to enforce their laws and regulations in a manner that ensures they do not undermine federal enforcement priorities.

In jurisdictions that have enacted laws legalizing marijuana in some form and that have also implemented strong and effective regulatory and enforcement systems to control the cultivation, distribution, sale, and possession of marijuana, conduct in compliance with those laws and regulations is less likely to threaten the federal priorities set forth above. Indeed, a robust system may affirmatively address those priorities by, for example, implementing effective measures to prevent diversion of marijuana outside of the regulated system and to other states, prohibiting access to marijuana by minors, and replacing an illicit marijuana trade that funds criminal enterprises with a regulated market in which revenues are tracked and accounted for. In those circumstances, consistent with the traditional allocation of federal-state efforts in this area, enforcement of state law by state and local law enforcement and regulatory bodies should remain the primary means of addressing marijuana-related activity. If state enforcement efforts are not sufficiently robust to protect against the harms set forth above, the federal government may seek to challenge the regulatory structure itself in addition to continuing to bring individual enforcement actions, including criminal prosecutions, focused on those harms.

The Department's previous memoranda specifically addressed the exercise of prosecutorial discretion in states with laws authorizing marijuana cultivation and distribution for medical use. In those contexts, the Department advised that it likely was not an efficient use of federal resources to focus enforcement efforts on seriously ill individuals, or on their individual caregivers. In doing so, the previous guidance drew a distinction between the seriously ill and their caregivers, on the one hand, and large-scale, for-profit commercial enterprises, on the other, and advised that the latter continued to be appropriate targets for federal enforcement and prosecution. In drawing this distinction, the Department relied on the common-sense judgment that the size of a marijuana operation was a reasonable proxy for assessing whether marijuana trafficking implicates the federal enforcement priorities set forth above.

As explained above, however, both the existence of a strong and effective state regulatory system, and an operation's compliance with such a system, may allay the threat that an operation's size poses to federal enforcement interests. Accordingly, in exercising prosecutorial discretion, prosecutors should not consider the size or commercial nature of a marijuana operation alone as a proxy for assessing whether marijuana trafficking implicates the Department's enforcement priorities listed above. Rather, prosecutors should continue to review marijuana cases on a case-by-case basis and weigh all available information and evidence, including, but not limited to, whether the operation is demonstrably in compliance with a strong and effective state regulatory system. A marijuana operation's large scale or for-profit nature may be a relevant consideration for assessing the extent to which it undermines a particular federal enforcement priority. The primary question in all cases—and in all jurisdictions—should be whether the conduct at issue implicates one or more of the enforcement priorities listed above.

As with the Department's previous statements on this subject, this memorandum is intended solely as a guide to the exercise of investigative and prosecutorial discretion. This memorandum does not alter in any way the Department's authority to enforce federal law, including federal laws relating to marijuana, regardless of state law. Neither the guidance herein nor any state or local law provides a legal defense to a violation of federal law, including any civil or criminal violation of the CSA. Even in jurisdictions with strong and effective regulatory systems, evidence that particular conduct threatens federal priorities will subject that person or entity to federal enforcement action, based on the circumstances. This memorandum is not intended to, does not, and may not be relied upon to create any rights, substantive or procedural, enforceable at law by any party in any matter civil or criminal. It applies prospectively to the exercise of prosecutorial discretion in future cases and does not provide defendants or subjects of enforcement action with a basis for reconsideration of any pending civil action or criminal prosecution. Finally, nothing herein precludes investigation or prosecution, even in the absence of any one of the factors listed above, in particular circumstances where investigation and prosecution otherwise serves an important federal interest.

[All cc's have been omitted.]

Source: U.S. Department of Justice. "Memorandum for all United States Attorneys." August 29, 2013. http://www.justice.gov/iso/opa/resources/3052013829132756857467.pdf.

Other Historic Documents of Interest

From this volume

- Department of Justice Issues Revised Drug Sentencing Guidelines, p. 380

From previous *Historic Documents*

- Colorado and Washington State Officials Respond to Marijuana Referenda, *2012*, p. 523
- Justice Department Announces Medical Marijuana Policy, *2009*, p. 494

September

Southern Philippines
Continuing Conflict

SEPTEMBER 9, 12, AND 25 2013

The long history of violent insurgencies in the Philippines, combined with a series of devastating natural disasters, has led to the internal displacement of millions of Filipinos. Often those worst affected by conflicts, particularly in the southern region of Mindanao, are also impacted by natural disasters, undermining the economic and social recovery process and pushing some further into poverty. Three major natural disasters struck the nation from late 2012 through the end of 2013: typhoon Bopha in December 2012, an earthquake in Bohol in October 2013, and typhoon Haiyan in November 2013. While some progress has recently been made to end the violence led by the Moro Islamic Liberation Front (MILF), other Muslim insurgent groups and the communist/socialist New People's Army (NPA) continue to undertake destructive and sometimes deadly attacks in the southern Philippines. The conflict in Zamboanga City in September 2013 is one notable example. The impact of terrorist activities and conflict in the region is profound, with an estimated 3.5 million people internally displaced between 2000 and 2013.

Ongoing Muslim Insurgencies

Internal conflicts have devastated affected regions of the Philippines and displaced millions of people in the past three decades. The largely Muslim southern Philippines region of Mindanao has been particularly affected by the violence. The region is the poorest in the country, and the economic underdevelopment, ineffective governance, and income inequality have exacerbated issues around the marginalization of the Muslim and indigenous inhabitants. The Muslims are known locally as *Moros*, and the indigenous people are known as *Lumads*.

The Moro National Liberation Front (MNLF) was born from an advocacy group called the Mindanao Independence Movement in the late 1960s. In the 1950s, the central government encouraged Christian citizens to settle in the region and tensions arose between the relatively poorer Muslims and the newly arrived Christians who, by the 1960s, represented a majority of the population. By the early 1970s, the MNLF was a powerful terrorist organization with tens of thousands of members and control over large swathes of Mindanao and neighboring Sulu. The government responded with force, committing around 80 percent of the country's military forces to fighting the MNLF.

In 1976, the government and the MNLF agreed to an accord and a referendum was called for a vote on the creation of an autonomous southern region. With a Christian majority, the referendum predictably failed. This failure damaged the MNLF's membership, and splinter groups formed. Two decades later a peace accord was signed with the government, which saw the creation of the Autonomous Region of Muslim Mindanao (ARMM) that encompassed four provinces. However, not all Muslim nationalists were satisfied with the agreement, and they subsequently joined other terrorist organizations in the region, namely the MILF and the Abu Sayyaf Group.

MILF was responsible for terrorist attacks throughout the 1980s and 1990s, but by 2001 had signed a peace agreement with then-president of the Philippines, Gloria Arroyo. Nevertheless, the group claimed responsibility for subsequent terrorist attacks. In mid-2008 negotiations between the MILF and the government on an autonomous Moro region, known as the Memorandum of Agreement on Ancestral Domain, collapsed, leading to a revival in armed clashes between rebels and government forces. The Philippines Department of Social Welfare and Development estimated that the renewed conflict caused the displacement of around 750,000 people, mostly inhabitants of the ARMM. A cease-fire was called a year later, allowing many, but not all, of those displaced to return home.

After months of negotiations, the government and the MILF signed a framework peace agreement in October 2012. The agreement calls for the MILF to gradually lay down its arms in exchange for the replacement of the Autonomous Region of Muslim Mindanao. The final annex to the agreement was signed in January 2014. The new region will have a Basic Law, which will be drafted with input from Muslim rebel leaders, and will be compatible with the country's constitution. Previous agreements were unsuccessful in large part because questions were raised over their constitutionality. Nevertheless, despite an agreement in place, significant hurdles remain. Extremist elements and other third parties oppose the agreement and have staged armed attacks, apparently in an effort to reignite conflict between the MILF and the government.

A MAJOR ATTACK

The MNLF staged an armed protest in the southern city of Zamboanga in September 2013. The group's leader, Nur Misuari, claimed that his group had been sidelined in the government's peace negotiations with the MILF. In a statement to journalists, MNLF National Security Commander Asamin Hussin said, "We want to establish our own Bangsamoro government, not an autonomous government but we want an independent Mindanao as Bangsamoro nation." *Bangsamoro* is the term for Muslims in the southern Philippines.

According to local police, the conflict began when around three hundred armed men marched into the city with the intention of raising a flag of independence in City Hall. The rebels countered that it was a peaceful march and that government forces attacked first. The rebels subsequently took control over part of the city, grinding commercial activities and transport (including the local airport) to a halt. Civilian hostages were taken by the MNLF but were subsequently freed. The conflict, which lasted nearly three weeks, was resolved through military and police action. The United Nations designated the conflict as a humanitarian disaster. Around 120,000 people in the Zamboanga area were initially displaced, and three months later more than half were still displaced.

THE THREAT OF THE NEW PEOPLE'S ARMY

In addition to the Muslim insurgency in the southern Philippines, various other ongoing conflicts have wreaked havoc on civilian populations. In particular, the communist insurgency, which was begun by the armed wing of the Communist Party, the NPA, has cost more than 40,000 lives since the conflict began forty-five years ago, according to the International Crisis Group. The NPA is considered a significant security threat, particularly in its stronghold in Mindanao. According to the National Consortium for the Study of Terrorism and Responses to Terrorism, the NPA aims to overthrow the Filipino government and implement a communist/socialist state in its place.

To do this, the NPA employs a two-pronged approach. The first tactic is to remove and deter all foreign investment in the country. To this end it engages in attacks on foreign-owned assets and also extorts foreign-owned firms for protection money. Second, the group undertakes assassinations of Filipino politicians, security officials, and members of the media. The reasoning behind the NPA's approach is that it will force the Filipino government to act decisively to suppress the NPA, and in so doing will also be forced to suppress the rights and freedoms of average Filipinos, who will then rise up against the government. Although the government engaged in several rounds of negotiations with the NPA in the 1990s, no significant progress has been made in curtailing the group's violent activities.

CIVILIANS AFFECTED BY NATURAL DISASTERS AND ONGOING CONFLICT

Conflict-induced displacement affected around 200,000 civilians in Mindanao alone in 2013. Fighting between government forces and insurgent groups, and indeed even among insurgent groups, led to ongoing and widespread displacement in the region. In addition to Zamboanga, major incidents include clashes between the MNLF and MILF between May and September 2013 in the North Cotabato province and government action against the Bangsamoro Islamic Freedom Fighters in August and September, the latter of which saw around 30,000 civilians displaced. Approximately 1,500 people were displaced throughout 2013 as a result of government counterinsurgency operations against the NPA. Although the displacement is typically short term, some Filipinos are affected for prolonged periods. For example, by mid-2011 there were still around 25,000 displaced by the clashes between the MILF and government forces nearly two years prior.

The threats faced by Filipinos are not limited to the country's insurgencies. Within the span of a year, the country was devastated by three major natural disasters. Typhoon Bopha wreaked havoc in Mindanao and part of the Visayas region in December 2012, followed by an earthquake on the island of Bohol in Visayas in October 2013, and finally the Category 5 typhoon Haiyan in early November 2013 that devastated large swathes of Visayas. According to estimates from aid groups, these natural disasters in concert with internal conflicts led to the displacement of up to eight million people.

In some cases there is an overlap between those people affected (and even displaced) by violent conflict and those who are impacted by natural disasters. Indeed, some typhoon Bopha victims were already negatively impacted by economic and social conditions arising from the region's insurgencies. According to a December 2013 report by the Internal Displacement Monitoring Center, between 2000 and 2010, 40 percent of families in central Mindanao were displaced by conflict or violence on at least one occasion; 25 percent were affected two or more times. The situation was even more dire in Maguindanao in southern Mindanao, where 80 percent of families were displaced at least once, and 75 percent were displaced two or more times.

There are safety and security concerns for those displaced by conflict and natural disasters, both prior to and after their return. According to the Internal Displacement Monitoring Center, these include "abuses by armed groups, unexploded ordnance and gender-based violence. . . . Large-scale disasters such as those brought about by typhoons

Bopha and Haiyan not only result in widespread devastation and displacement, but also in worsening security conditions."

—Hilary Ewing

Following is the text of two statements on September 9 and 12 from the office of the President of the Philippines regarding the attacks in Zamboanga City; and the text of a press release issued by the United Nations on September 25, 2013, in response to the crisis in Zamboanga City.

Presidential Spokesperson Condemns Zamboanga City Attack

September 9, 2013

Statement of Secretary Edwin Lacierda:

We condemn the attack on Zamboanga City in the strongest possible terms. It is incumbent on all people of goodwill to reject the violence that has erupted.

The ongoing attack of armed individuals in Zamboanga City, including initial reports of the possible use of civilians as human shields, is a cause for great concern. The authorities are responding to the situation in a manner that will reduce the risk to innocent civilians and restore peace and order to Zamboanga City at the soonest possible time.

The City government has appealed for the national government to help; the President is being briefed on the situation and is receiving updates as new information comes in. We ask our fellow citizens to refrain from spreading speculation: fear and alarm spread by disinformation will only help those intent on disrupting the lives of residents of Zamboanga City.

SOURCE: Official Gazette of the Republic of the Philippines. "Statement: The Presidential Spokesperson on the attack in Zamboanga City." September 9, 2013. http://www.gov.ph/2013/09/09/statement-the-presidential-spokesperson-on-the-attack-in-zamboanga-city.

Statement on the Ongoing Situation in Zamboanga City

September 12, 2013

Statement of Secretary Edwin Lacierda:

Groups opposed to the peace process, or who want to impose a peace solely from their viewpoint and on their terms, have sought to create disturbances. We have witnessed the bombing of Cagayan de Oro City and other similar events.

There have been a lot of text messages circulating, causing confusion and alarm among our people. Let us set the record straight.

Alleged MNLF members wanted to proceed to Zamboanga City bearing arms, supposedly to exercise their right to peaceful assembly. But the right to peaceful assembly cannot be exercised while bearing arms. In fact, when they tried to conduct a "peace rally" in Sulu, they were prevented from doing so because they were armed. Allegedly, they attempted to do the same in Zamboanga City, where some of their members were arrested by the PNP; others were caught in a firefight in the waters off Zamboanga City by elements of the Philippine Navy. And those seeking safety inside coastal barangays have had to disperse.

The forces of the state are ready to exercise the resolve of the government. While the government is exhausting all avenues for a peaceful resolution to the situation, let it be clear to those defying us that they should not entertain the illusion that the state will hesitate to use its forces to protect our people.

Instead, it is time for you to cooperate to resolve this situation peacefully at the soonest possible time.

As for others who seek to take advantage of the situation, you will fail. There has been an encounter in Basilan today when members of the BIFF and ASG, estimated at around 150, ostensibly tried to attack Lamitan City. The armed forces stopped them, and after a two hour firefight, are now in hot pursuit. The BIFF and ASG assumed they could take advantage of the situation. They were wrong. As others who will also make similar attempts will be proven wrong.

To the people of Zamboanga City, your government stands in solidarity with you and is working to ensure your needs are met. The President has directed national government agencies to attend to the needs of the people of Zamboanga City and the BASULTA by providing basic supplies through the DOTC and DTI. We have asked the BSP to ensure sufficient supplies of currency.

We ask further cooperation from the people of Zamboanga City: we reiterate that there are people relishing this situation and who seek to inflame passions for various reasons. Please understand that rumors of abductions of religious leaders and firefights that did not take place, which are spread through anonymous text messages, aim to take advantage of you. Instead, listen to the authorities, who will give you the truth all the time.

We are very pleased with the performance of the Zamboanga City government: Mayor Beng Climaco, despite being new to the job, has demonstrated true leadership. We appeal to those eyeing the coming barangay elections to set aside politics when we are all busy ensuring the safety of our fellow citizens in Zamboanga City.

SOURCE: Official Gazette of the Republic of the Philippines. "Statement: The Presidential Spokesperson on the situation in Zamboanga City." September 12, 2013. http://www.gov.ph/2013/09/12/statement-the-presidential-spokesperson-on-the-situation-in-zamboanga-city.

UN Remarks on Humanitarian Crisis in Zamboanga City

September 25, 2013

The situation in Zamboanga City in the southern Philippines is now a humanitarian crisis, as tens of thousands of people remain forcibly displaced, the United Nations said today, calling for support to the victims of the recent wave of violence in the country.

"We are increasingly alarmed by the situation and the growing needs of people caught up with violence," said the UN Resident and Humanitarian Coordinator in the Philippines, Luiza Carvalho. "We are particularly concerned for the most vulnerable, especially the well-being of women and children."

Earlier this month, armed clashes erupted between Government forces and non-State actors in Zamboanga City. Some 132 people have died as a result of the standoff and the UN Office for the Coordination of Humanitarian Affairs (OCHA) estimates that some 158,000 people have been affected by the violence and more than 10,000 homes have been destroyed. In addition, over 109,000 people are now displaced in Zamboanga City and nearly 19,000 are displaced in the Basilan province.

Ms. Carvalho expressed concern over the plight of those displaced, many of whom are struggling to survive. Some 70,000 people are currently staying in the main sports complex in Zamboanga City in overcrowded conditions and insufficient sanitation facilities. OCHA warned there is a real risk of a disease outbreak and an urgent need for food, drinking water, health services, cooking utensils, tents and other necessities.

"We are particularly concerned that aid is delivered in an impartial manner, with the needs of the most vulnerable met and those outside the evacuation centres not forgotten," Ms. Carvalho said.

"We expect that all humanitarian workers providing support to the victims of violence are protected and respected, and their safety is ensured by all actors."

She also reiterated OCHA's commitment to the humanitarian response as well as its support for Government efforts to respond and provide assistance to civilians.

SOURCE: United Nations. News Centre. "Humanitarian crisis in southern Philippines as violence uproots tens of thousands—UN." September 25, 2013. http://www.un.org/apps/news/story.asp/story.asp?NewsID=45996&Cr=Philippines&Cr1=#.U0LtVdzDRkg.

OTHER HISTORIC DOCUMENTS OF INTEREST

FROM PREVIOUS HISTORIC DOCUMENTS

President Obama Remarks on the Conflict in Syria

SEPTEMBER 10 AND 24, 2013

As the civil war in Syria continued into its third year, the international community still could not reach a consensus on whether to intervene in the Middle Eastern nation. As it grew increasingly more evident that President Bashar al-Assad had used chemical weapons against civilians in an attempt to end the rebel incursion, the likelihood that the United States might take unilateral action grew. On September 10, 2013, U.S. President Barack Obama addressed the nation on the conflict, saying that he would reserve the right to intervene militarily in Syria, but he first wanted to explore the option of working with the Russians toward a diplomatic solution that would remove all chemical weapons from Syria.

ARAB SPRING EVOLVES INTO CIVIL WAR

The 2011 Arab Spring uprisings that swept across the Middle East reached Syria on March 15, 2011, when residents in a southern city protested the torture of students who had been accused of antigovernment graffiti. Assad quickly ordered his police forces to crack down, and this strong response from the president sparked demonstrations across the country. The protesters demanded that Assad open up the government, end the nation's state of emergency, and halt all violence directed at the demonstrations. In the early days of the protest movement, Assad wavered between offering reform and continuing the use of force to dispel protesters. As the conflict entered the summer of 2011, Assad's own soldiers began joining the rebel cause. The conflict grew increasingly violent in late 2011, and Assad seemed willing to stop at nothing to maintain his stranglehold on power. The skyrocketing number of civilian deaths, coupled with the humanitarian crisis springing up in the region as refugees fled the violence, led the United Nations to declare that the country had fallen into a civil war.

As the opposition movement organized itself into rebel groups, the government security forces blindly targeted any area thought to be a rebel stronghold. Attacks included the bombing of entire towns as well as the kidnapping, rape, torture, and murder of civilians, including children. The rebels gained momentum throughout 2012, and at varying points took control of key Syrian cities. The rebels were aided in their cause by fighters who entered from other nations and by weapons and monetary support from a variety of countries including Saudi Arabia. At one point, in an effort to bring some organization to the anti-Assad movement, an opposition government was formed in exile.

The Syrian National Council, as the opposition government became known, was plagued from the beginning by infighting and a lack of a cohesive agenda. The second attempt at a representative body was known as the National Council, which suffered the same internal disagreements. The group was also infiltrated by jihadists who were in direct opposition to the secular nature of the Syrian population. The National Council was absorbed into the National Coalition of Syrian Revolutionary and Opposition Forces in November 2012, and, as opposed to its predecessors, gained recognition from foreign governments as the legitimate representative of the Syrian people.

Former UN Secretary General Kofi Annan had an apparent breakthrough when he negotiated a cease-fire with Assad's government set to go into effect in April 2012. However, the six-point plan that Assad agreed to was quickly disregarded by the president and his security forces, and the United Nations ended its cease-fire observer mission in June 2012.

As the conflict has worn on, the Assad government stopped trying to regain control of cities and towns, and instead shifted its focus to destroying rebel areas. This included waging a massive air assault that leveled cities and killed thousands. By 2013, the United Nations estimated that more than 100,000 had been killed in the Syrian conflict, with hundreds of thousands more fleeing the country.

UN Announces Use of Chemical Weapons

In late 2012, the United States and United Kingdom announced that they had intelligence indicating that Assad had moved his chemical weapons in what they expected to be a precursor to creating sarin gas. Assad is thought to have one of the world's largest stockpiles of chemical weapons, which include mustard gas, cyanide, and a nerve agent. The Syrian leader said in 2012 that he would never use these weapons unless a foreign nation attempted to intervene in the crisis. Russia fiercely denied that there was any evidence of such weapons being moved, and said that direct talks with the Syrian leader backed up this assessment.

Speculation grew in early 2013, as an increasing number of social media reports showed what appeared to be Syrian citizens suffering from effects of nerve gas. Not only was this apparent use of chemical weapons viewed as a gross violation of the rules of war, but it was also a "red line" of sorts for international intervention. In August 2012, President Barack Obama said that he would consider U.S. military action if there was any evidence of Assad moving or using his chemical weapons stockpiles. "We cannot have a situation in which chemical or biological weapons are falling into the hands of the wrong people," Obama said at the time, adding that chemical weapons aren't only of concern to Syria but rather are an issue that "concerns our close allies in the region."

In September 2013, the United Nations released a report confirming that Assad had used chemical weapons against civilians. The report, which detailed when and to what extent chemical weapons were used, was accompanied by a letter from UN Secretary General Ban Ki-moon who called the use of such weapons "a war crime." The Secretary General went on to note that "the international community has a moral responsibility to hold accountable those responsible and for ensuring that chemical weapons can never re-emerge as an instrument of warfare." The investigators involved in producing the report cited finding traces of sarin gas in blood, urine, and hair samples. The report concluded that chemical weapons were used "against civilians, including children, on a relatively large scale." In December, the United Nations Mission released a final report on the use of chemical weapons, again concluding that there was "clear and convincing evidence" that the weapons were used.

On September 24, 2013, President Obama appeared before the United Nations General Assembly to address the existence of chemical weapons in Syria. The president called on the body to pass a resolution that would ensure that the weapons were secured and destroyed. If the body could not act on such a matter, the president said, it would "show that the U.N. is incapable of enforcing the most basic of international laws."

INTERNATIONAL RESPONSE

By the end of 2013, there was little international intervention in Syria. Reasons for remaining out of the violence vary, from a desire to protect the delicate political balance in the Middle East, which would surely be threatened if Assad were removed from power, to the risk of losing allies. Many countries have looked to the United Nations hoping that the international body might intervene, or at least encourage its members to do so. However, the group has been hampered by the unwillingness of Russia and China, two of Syria's supporters, to vote for action. Russia has been the leading opponent of intervention in Syria for a number of reasons including its strategically significant naval base in Syria, a strong military alliance, and the cash infusion it receives from sales of weapons to Syria. Russia and China are permanent members of the Security Council, and therefore hold veto power, so any resolution to take action would require their approval. So far, the two countries have managed to thwart any attempts, arguing that it is not the place of the United Nations to intervene in a country's internal matters. Despite pressure from the Secretary General, by the close of 2013, the United Nations had done nothing more than issue resolutions strongly condemning the actions of the Assad regime.

In the United States, a number of Members of Congress, led by Sens. John McCain, R-Ariz., and Lindsey Graham, R-S.C., led the call for the United States to arm the Syrian rebels. This, they argued, would weaken other influences in the region like Iran. The Obama administration has shied away from such an option, arguing that it could embolden jihadists in the Middle East. And as bad as the current situation was, toppling Assad would create a power vacuum in the region that could be even worse.

President Obama addressed the nation on September 10, 2013, making the case that the United States needed to do something to try to lessen the bloodshed in Syria. The president made clear that he had no intention of putting American troops in Syria: "I will not put American boots on the ground in Syria. I will not pursue an open-ended action like Iraq or Afghanistan. I will not pursue a prolonged air campaign like Libya or Kosovo." Instead, the president proposed using targeted airstrikes that he said would "achieve a clear objective: deterring the use of chemical weapons and degrading Assad's capabilities." If Obama were to fire missiles at Syria, they would be unlikely to topple the Assad regime or end the civil war. The main intent of this response would be to discourage Assad from using chemical weapons in the future and also to discourage world leaders who have chemical weapons stocks from using them in any future war. Obama said airstrikes would protect American troops from chemical weapons in future wars and "make clear to the world that we will not tolerate their use."

Despite his announcement, the president called on Congress to delay a vote on whether such strikes should be launched against Syria until the United States determined whether a diplomatic solution proposed by Russia would prove effective. The proposal offered by Russia would not take down the Assad regime, but rather would allow international experts to enter Syria to find and dismantle the nation's chemical weapons. An agreement was reached in October 2013 to begin dismantling the weapons, with a deadline set for their removal by February 2014. In December, the Organisation for the Prohibition of Chemical Weapons, the group tasked with removing the weapons from the country, announced that it would likely miss the deadline.

THE NEAR FUTURE IN SYRIA

Given the forces at play in the region and the limited options for international intervention, it is likely that the civil war in Syria will continue on for years. There are no signs that the Assad regime wants to relent, or that it has any desire to come to the table and work out a peace agreement with the rebels. Even if it did, the rebels have no cohesive leadership that could represent them at such negotiations. And the rebel cause, supported by a number of foreign governments, is likely to keep fighting on because the alternative could be worse—a growing number of refugees in surrounding nations and an even more severe crackdown on those who oppose the Assad regime.

Some international experts have looked to Lebanon as a parallel to what is happening in Syria today. There, the civil war lasted for fifteen years, ending with a shaky peace agreement in 1990. Even today, citizens are subject to crackdowns on government dissenters and bombings, although infrequent. What is a near certainty at this point is that the ongoing war in Syria will further fracture the delicate political balance in the Middle East, pitting ethnic groups as well as supporters and opponents of Assad against each other. Surrounding nations like Lebanon, Turkey, Israel, Jordan, and Iraq will feel the most pressure from the conflict as refugees continue to flood their borders and deepen the humanitarian crisis.

—Heather Kerrigan

Following is the text of an address delivered by President Barak Obama on September 10, 2013, on the situation in Syria and a plan for U.S. involvement in the conflict; and the edited text of a speech delivered by President Obama on September 24, 2013, before the United Nations on the conflict in Syria.

President Obama Addresses the Nation on Syria

September 10, 2013

My fellow Americans, tonight I want to talk to you about Syria: why it matters and where we go from here.

Over the past 2 years, what began as a series of peaceful protests against the repressive regime of Bashar al-Asad has turned into a brutal civil war. Over 100,000 people have been killed. Millions have fled the country. In that time, America has worked with allies to provide humanitarian support, to help the moderate opposition, and to shape a political settlement. But I have resisted calls for military action because we cannot resolve someone else's civil war through force, particularly after a decade of war in Iraq and Afghanistan.

The situation profoundly changed, though, on August 21, when Asad's Government gassed to death over a thousand people, including hundreds of children. The images from this massacre are sickening: men, women, children lying in rows, killed by poison gas; others foaming at the mouth, gasping for breath; a father clutching his dead children, imploring them to get up and walk. On that terrible night, the world saw in gruesome detail the terrible nature of chemical weapons and why the overwhelming majority of humanity has declared them off limits: a crime against humanity and a violation of the laws of war.

This was not always the case. In World War I, American GIs were among the many thousands killed by deadly gas in the trenches of Europe. In World War II, the Nazis used gas to inflict the horror of the Holocaust. Because these weapons can kill on a mass scale; with no distinction between soldier and infant, the civilized world has spent a century working to ban them. And in 1997, the United States Senate overwhelmingly approved an international agreement prohibiting the use of chemical weapons, now joined by 189 Governments that represent 98 percent of humanity.

On August 21, these basic rules were violated, along with our sense of common humanity. No one disputes that chemical weapons were used in Syria. The world saw thousands of videos, cell phone pictures, and social media accounts from the attack, and humanitarian organizations told stories of hospitals packed with people who had symptoms of poison gas.

Moreover, we know the Asad regime was responsible. In the days leading up to August 21, we know that Asad's chemical weapons personnel prepared for an attack near an area where they mix sarin gas. They distributed gasmasks to their troops. Then they fired rockets from a regime-controlled area into 11 neighborhoods that the regime has been trying to wipe clear of opposition forces. Shortly after those rockets landed, the gas spread, and hospitals filled with the dying and the wounded. We know senior figures in Asad's military machine reviewed the results of the attack, and the regime increased their shelling of the same neighborhoods in the days that followed. We've also studied samples of blood and hair from people at the site that tested positive for sarin.

When dictators commit atrocities, they depend upon the world to look the other way until those horrifying pictures fade from memory. But these things happened. The facts cannot be denied. The question now is what the United States of America—and the international community—is prepared to do about it. Because what happened to those people—to those children—is not only a violation of international law, it's also a danger to our security.

Let me explain why. If we fail to act, the Asad regime will see no reason to stop using chemical weapons. As the ban against these weapons erodes, other tyrants will have no reason to think twice about acquiring poison gas and using them. Over time, our troops would again face the prospect of chemical warfare on the battlefield. And it could be easier for terrorist organizations to obtain these weapons and to use them to attack civilians.

If fighting spills beyond Syria's borders, these weapons could threaten allies like Turkey, Jordan, and Israel. And a failure to stand against the use of chemical weapons would weaken prohibitions against other weapons of mass destruction and embolden Asad's ally Iran, which must decide whether to ignore international law by building a nuclear weapon or to take a more peaceful path.

This is not a world we should accept. This is what's at stake. And that is why, after careful deliberation, I determined that it is in the national security interests of the United States to respond to the Asad regime's use of chemical weapons through a targeted military strike. The purpose of this strike would be to deter Asad from using chemical weapons, to degrade his regime's ability to use them, and to make clear to the world that we will not tolerate their use.

That's my judgment as Commander in Chief. But I'm also the President of the world's oldest constitutional democracy. So even though I possess the authority to order military strikes, I believed it was right, in the absence of a direct or imminent threat to our security, to take this debate to Congress. I believe our democracy is stronger when the President acts with the support of Congress. And I believe that America acts more effectively abroad when we stand together.

This is especially true after a decade that put more and more war-making power in the hands of the President and more and more burdens on the shoulders of our troops, while sidelining the people's representatives from the critical decisions about when we use force.

Now, I know that after the terrible toll of Iraq and Afghanistan, the idea of any military action, no matter how limited, is not going to be popular. After all, I've spent 4½ years working to end wars, not to start them. Our troops are out of Iraq. Our troops are coming home from Afghanistan. And I know Americans want all of us in Washington—especially me—to concentrate on the task of building our Nation here at home: putting people back to work, educating our kids, growing our middle class.

It's no wonder, then, that you're asking hard questions. So let me answer some of the most important questions that I've heard from Members of Congress and that I've read in letters that you've sent to me.

First, many of you have asked, won't this put us on a slippery slope to another war? One man wrote to me that we are "still recovering from our involvement in Iraq." A veteran put it more bluntly: "This nation is sick and tired of war." My answer is simple: I will not put American boots on the ground in Syria. I will not pursue an open-ended action like Iraq or Afghanistan. I will not pursue a prolonged air campaign like Libya or Kosovo. This would be a targeted strike to achieve a clear objective: deterring the use of chemical weapons and degrading Asad's capabilities.

Others have asked whether it's worth acting if we don't take out Asad. As some Members of Congress have said, there's no point in simply doing a "pinprick" strike in Syria. Let me make something clear: The United States military doesn't do pinpricks. Even a limited strike will send a message to Asad that no other nation can deliver. I don't think we should remove another dictator with force; we learned from Iraq that doing so makes us responsible for all that comes next. But a targeted strike can make Asad—or any other dictator—think twice before using chemical weapons.

Other questions involve the dangers of retaliation. We don't dismiss any threats, but the Asad regime does not have the ability to seriously threaten our military. Any other retaliation they might seek is in line with threats that we face every day. Neither Asad nor his allies have any interest in escalation that would lead to his demise. And our ally Israel can defend itself with overwhelming force, as well as the unshakeable support of the United States of America.

Many of you have asked a broader question: Why should we get involved at all in a place that's so complicated and where, as one person wrote to me, "those who come after Asad may be enemies of human rights"? It's true that some of Asad's opponents are extremists. But Al Qaida will only draw strength in a more chaotic Syria if people there see the world doing nothing to prevent innocent civilians from being gassed to death. The majority of the Syrian people—and the Syrian opposition we work with—just want to live in peace, with dignity and freedom. And the day after any military action, we would redouble our efforts to achieve a political solution that strengthens those who reject the forces of tyranny and extremism.

Finally, many of you have asked: Why not leave this to other countries or seek solutions short of force? As several people wrote to me, "We should not be the world's policeman." I agree, and I have a deeply held preference for peaceful solutions. Over the last 2 years, my administration has tried diplomacy and sanctions, warnings and negotiations, but chemical weapons were still used by the Asad regime.

However, over the last few days, we've seen some encouraging signs. In part because of the credible threat of U.S. military action, as well as constructive talks that I had with President Putin, the Russian Government has indicated a willingness to join with the international community in pushing Asad to give up his chemical weapons. The Asad regime has now admitted that it has these weapons and even said they'd join the Chemical Weapons Convention, which prohibits their use.

It's too early to tell whether this offer will succeed, and any agreement must verify that the Asad regime keeps its commitments. But this initiative has the potential to remove the threat of chemical weapons without the use of force, particularly because Russia is one of Asad's strongest allies.

I have therefore asked the leaders of Congress to postpone a vote to authorize the use of force while we pursue this diplomatic path. I'm sending Secretary of State John Kerry to meet his Russian counterpart on Thursday, and I will continue my own discussions with President Putin. I've spoken to the leaders of two of our closest allies, France and the United Kingdom, and we will work together in consultation with Russia and China to put forward a resolution at the U.N. Security Council requiring Asad to give up his chemical weapons and to ultimately destroy them under international control. We'll also give U.N. inspectors the opportunity to report their findings about what happened on August 21. And we will continue to rally support from allies from Europe to the Americas, from Asia to the Middle East, who agree on the need for action.

Meanwhile, I've ordered our military to maintain their current posture to keep the pressure on Asad and to be in a position to respond if diplomacy fails. And tonight I give thanks again to our military and their families for their incredible strength and sacrifices.

My fellow Americans, for nearly seven decades, the United States has been the anchor of global security. This has meant doing more than forging international agreements. It has meant enforcing them. The burdens of leadership are often heavy, but the world is a better place because we have borne them.

And so to my friends on the right, I ask you to reconcile your commitment to America's military might with a failure to act when a cause is so plainly just. To my friends on the left, I ask you to reconcile your belief in freedom and dignity for all people with those images of children writhing in pain and going still on a cold hospital floor. For sometimes, resolutions and statements of condemnation are simply not enough.

Indeed, I'd ask every Member of Congress—and those of you watching at home tonight—to view those videos of the attack and then ask: What kind of world will we live in if the United States of America sees a dictator brazenly violate international law with poison gas and we choose to look the other way?

Franklin Roosevelt once said, "Our national determination to keep free of foreign wars and foreign entanglements cannot prevent us from feeling deep concern when ideals and principles that we have cherished are challenged." Our ideals and principles, as well as our national security, are at stake in Syria, along with our leadership of a world where we seek to ensure that the worst weapons will never be used.

America is not the world's policeman. Terrible things happen across the globe, and it is beyond our means to right every wrong. But when, with modest effort and risk, we can stop children from being gassed to death—and thereby make our own children safer over the long run—I believe we should act. That's what makes America different. That's what makes us exceptional. With humility, but with resolve, let us never lose sight of that essential truth.

Thank you. God bless you, and God bless the United States of America.

SOURCE: Executive Office of the President. "Address to the Nation on the Situation in Syria." September 10, 2013. *Compilation of Presidential Documents* 2013, no. 00615 (September 10, 2013). http://www.gpo .gov/fdsys/pkg/DCPD-201300615/pdf/DCPD-201300615.pdf.

President Obama Addresses the United Nations on Syria

September 24, 2013

[The President's opening remarks have been omitted.]

. . . [T]he world is more stable than it was five years ago. But even a glance at today's headlines indicates that dangers remain. In Kenya, we've seen terrorists target innocent civilians in a crowded shopping mall, and our hearts go out to the families of those who have been affected. In Pakistan, nearly 100 people were recently killed by suicide bombers outside a church. In Iraq, killings and car bombs continue to be a terrible part of life. And meanwhile, al Qaeda has splintered into regional networks and militias, which doesn't give them the capacity at this point to carry out attacks like 9/11, but does pose serious threats to governments and diplomats, businesses and civilians all across the globe.

Just as significantly, the convulsions in the Middle East and North Africa have laid bare deep divisions within societies, as an old order is upended and people grapple with what comes next. Peaceful movements have too often been answered by violence—from those resisting change and from extremists trying to hijack change. Sectarian conflict has reemerged. And the potential spread of weapons of mass destruction continues to cast a shadow over the pursuit of peace.

Nowhere have we seen these trends converge more powerfully than in Syria. There, peaceful protests against an authoritarian regime were met with repression and slaughter. In the face of such carnage, many retreated to their sectarian identity—Alawite and Sunni; Christian and Kurd—and the situation spiraled into civil war.

The international community recognized the stakes early on, but our response has not matched the scale of the challenge. Aid cannot keep pace with the suffering of the wounded and displaced. A peace process is stillborn. America and others have worked to bolster the moderate opposition, but extremist groups have still taken root to exploit the crisis. Asad's traditional allies have propped him up, citing principles of sovereignty to shield his regime. And on August 21st, the regime used chemical weapons in an attack that killed more than 1,000 people, including hundreds of children.

Now, the crisis in Syria, and the destabilization of the region, goes to the heart of broader challenges that the international community must now confront. How should we respond to conflicts in the Middle East and North Africa—conflicts between countries, but also conflicts within them? How do we address the choice of standing callously by while children are subjected to nerve gas, or embroiling ourselves in someone else's civil war? What is the role of force in resolving disputes that threaten the stability of the region and undermine all basic standards of civilized conduct? What is the role of the United Nations and international law in meeting cries for justice?

Today, I want to outline where the United States of America stands on these issues. With respect to Syria, we believe that as a starting point, the international community must enforce the ban on chemical weapons. When I stated my willingness to order a limited strike against the Asad regime in response to the brazen use of chemical weapons, I did not do so lightly. I did so because I believe it is in the security interest of the United States and in the interest of the world to meaningfully enforce a prohibition whose origins are older than the United Nations itself. The ban against the use of chemical weapons, even in war, has been agreed to by 98 percent of humanity. It is strengthened by the searing memories of soldiers suffocating in the trenches; Jews slaughtered in gas chambers; Iranians poisoned in the many tens of thousands.

The evidence is overwhelming that the Asad regime used such weapons on August 21st. U.N. inspectors gave a clear accounting that advanced rockets fired large quantities of sarin gas at civilians. These rockets were fired from a regime-controlled neighborhood, and landed in opposition neighborhoods. It's an insult to human reason—and to the legitimacy of this institution—to suggest that anyone other than the regime carried out this attack.

Now, I know that in the immediate aftermath of the attack there were those who questioned the legitimacy of even a limited strike in the absence of a clear mandate from the Security Council. But without a credible military threat, the Security Council had demonstrated no inclination to act at all. However, as I've discussed with President Putin for over a year, most recently in St. Petersburg, my preference has always been a diplomatic resolution to this issue. And in the past several weeks, the United States, Russia and our allies have reached an agreement to place Syria's chemical weapons under international control, and then to destroy them.

The Syrian government took a first step by giving an accounting of its stockpiles. Now there must be a strong Security Council resolution to verify that the Asad regime is keeping its commitments, and there must be consequences if they fail to do so. If we cannot agree even on this, then it will show that the United Nations is incapable of enforcing the most basic of international laws. On the other hand, if we succeed, it will send a powerful message that the use of chemical weapons has no place in the 21st century, and that this body means what it says.

Agreement on chemical weapons should energize a larger diplomatic effort to reach a political settlement within Syria. I do not believe that military action—by those within Syria, or by external powers—can achieve a lasting peace. Nor do I believe that America or any nation should determine who will lead Syria; that is for the Syrian people to decide. Nevertheless, a leader who slaughtered his citizens and gassed children to death cannot regain the legitimacy to lead a badly fractured country. The notion that Syria can somehow return to a pre-war status quo is a fantasy.

It's time for Russia and Iran to realize that insisting on Asad's rule will lead directly to the outcome that they fear: an increasingly violent space for extremists to operate. In turn, those of us who continue to support the moderate opposition must persuade them that the Syrian people cannot afford a collapse of state institutions, and that a political settlement cannot be reached without addressing the legitimate fears and concerns of Alawites and other minorities.

We are committed to working this political track. And as we pursue a settlement, let's remember this is not a zero-sum endeavor. We're no longer in a Cold War. There's no

Great Game to be won, nor does America have any interest in Syria beyond the well-being of its people, the stability of its neighbors, the elimination of chemical weapons, and ensuring that it does not become a safe haven for terrorists.

I welcome the influence of all nations that can help bring about a peaceful resolution of Syria's civil war. And as we move the Geneva process forward, I urge all nations here to step up to meet humanitarian needs in Syria and surrounding countries. America has committed over a billion dollars to this effort, and today I can announce that we will be providing an additional $340 million. No aid can take the place of a political resolution that gives the Syrian people the chance to rebuild their country, but it can help desperate people to survive.

What broader conclusions can be drawn from America's policy toward Syria? I know there are those who have been frustrated by our unwillingness to use our military might to depose Asad, and believe that a failure to do so indicates a weakening of American resolve in the region. Others have suggested that my willingness to direct even limited military strikes to deter the further use of chemical weapons shows we've learned nothing from Iraq, and that America continues to seek control over the Middle East for our own purposes. In this way, the situation in Syria mirrors a contradiction that has persisted in the region for decades: the United States is chastised for meddling in the region, accused of having a hand in all manner of conspiracy; at the same time, the United States is blamed for failing to do enough to solve the region's problems and for showing indifference toward suffering Muslim populations.

I realize some of this is inevitable, given America's role in the world. But these contradictory attitudes have a practical impact on the American people's support for our involvement in the region, and allow leaders in the region — as well as the international community sometimes — to avoid addressing difficult problems themselves.

[An outline of U.S. policy in the Middle East and North Africa has been omitted.]

. . . We will not stop asserting principles that are consistent with our ideals, whether that means opposing the use of violence as a means of suppressing dissent, or supporting the principles embodied in the Universal Declaration of Human Rights.

We will reject the notion that these principles are simply Western exports, incompatible with Islam or the Arab World. We believe they are the birthright of every person. And while we recognize that our influence will at times be limited, although we will be wary of efforts to impose democracy through military force, and although we will at times be accused of hypocrisy and inconsistency, we will be engaged in the region for the long haul. For the hard work of forging freedom and democracy is the task of a generation.

And this includes efforts to resolve sectarian tensions that continue to surface in places like Iraq, Bahrain and Syria. We understand such longstanding issues cannot be solved by outsiders; they must be addressed by Muslim communities themselves. But we've seen grinding conflicts come to an end before—most recently in Northern Ireland, where Catholics and Protestants finally recognized that an endless cycle of conflict was causing both communities to fall behind a fast-moving world. And so we believe those same sectarian conflicts can be overcome in the Middle East and North Africa.

To summarize, the United States has a hard-earned humility when it comes to our ability to determine events inside other countries. The notion of American empire may be useful propaganda, but it isn't borne out by America's current policy or by public opinion. Indeed, as recent debates within the United States over Syria clearly show, the danger for the world is not an America that is too eager to immerse itself in the affairs of other countries or to take on every problem in the region as its own. The danger for the world is that the United States, after a decade of war—rightly concerned about issues back home, aware of the hostility that our engagement in the region has engendered throughout the Muslim world—may disengage, creating a vacuum of leadership that no other nation is ready to fill.

I believe such disengagement would be a mistake. I believe America must remain engaged for our own security. But I also believe the world is better for it. Some may disagree, but I believe America is exceptional—in part because we have shown a willingness through the sacrifice of blood and treasure to stand up not only for our own narrow self-interests, but for the interests of all . . . .

This leads me to a final point. There will be times when the breakdown of societies is so great, the violence against civilians so substantial that the international community will be called upon to act. This will require new thinking and some very tough choices. While the United Nations was designed to prevent wars between states, increasingly we face the challenge of preventing slaughter within states. And these challenges will grow more pronounced as we are confronted with states that are fragile or failing—places where horrendous violence can put innocent men, women and children at risk, with no hope of protection from their national institutions.

I have made it clear that even when America's core interests are not directly threatened, we stand ready to do our part to prevent mass atrocities and protect basic human rights. But we cannot and should not bear that burden alone. In Mali, we supported both the French intervention that successfully pushed back al Qaeda, and the African forces who are keeping the peace. In Eastern Africa, we are working with partners to bring the Lord's Resistance Army to an end. And in Libya, when the Security Council provided a mandate to protect civilians, America joined a coalition that took action. Because of what we did there, countless lives were saved, and a tyrant could not kill his way back to power.

I know that some now criticize the action in Libya as an object lesson. They point to the problems that the country now confronts—a democratically elected government struggling to provide security; armed groups, in some places extremists, ruling parts of a fractured land. And so these critics argue that any intervention to protect civilians is doomed to fail—look at Libya. No one is more mindful of these problems than I am, for they resulted in the death of four outstanding U.S. citizens who were committed to the Libyan people, including Ambassador Chris Stevens—a man whose courageous efforts helped save the city of Benghazi. But does anyone truly believe that the situation in Libya would be better if Qaddafi had been allowed to kill, imprison, or brutalize his people into submission? It's far more likely that without international action, Libya would now be engulfed in civil war and bloodshed.

We live in a world of imperfect choices. Different nations will not agree on the need for action in every instance, and the principle of sovereignty is at the center of our international order. But sovereignty cannot be a shield for tyrants to commit wanton murder, or an excuse for the international community to turn a blind eye. While we need to be modest in our belief that we can remedy every evil, while we need to be mindful that the world is full of unintended consequences, should we really accept the notion that the world is powerless in the face of a Rwanda or Srebrenica? If that's the world that people want to live in, they should say so and reckon with the cold logic of mass graves.

But I believe we can embrace a different future. And if we don't want to choose between inaction and war, we must get better—all of us—at the policies that prevent the breakdown of basic order. Through respect for the responsibilities of nations and the rights of individuals. Through meaningful sanctions for those who break the rules. Through dogged diplomacy that resolves the root causes of conflict, not merely its aftermath. Through development assistance that brings hope to the marginalized. And yes, sometimes—although this will not be enough—there are going to be moments where the international community will need to acknowledge that the multilateral use of military force may be required to prevent the very worst from occurring.

Ultimately, this is the international community that America seeks—one where nations do not covet the land or resources of other nations, but one in which we carry out the founding purpose of this institution and where we all take responsibility. A world in which the rules established out of the horrors of war can help us resolve conflicts peacefully, and prevent the kinds of wars that our forefathers fought. A world where human beings can live with dignity and meet their basic needs, whether they live in New York or Nairobi; in Peshawar or Damascus.

These are extraordinary times, with extraordinary opportunities. Thanks to human progress, a child born anywhere on Earth today can do things today that 60 years ago would have been out of reach for the mass of humanity. I saw this in Africa, where nations moving beyond conflict are now poised to take off. And America is with them, partnering to feed the hungry and care for the sick, and to bring power to places off the grid.

I see it across the Pacific region, where hundreds of millions have been lifted out of poverty in a single generation. I see it in the faces of young people everywhere who can access the entire world with the click of a button, and who are eager to join the cause of eradicating extreme poverty, and combating climate change, starting businesses, expanding freedom, and leaving behind the old ideological battles of the past. That's what's happening in Asia and Africa. It's happening in Europe and across the Americas. That's the future that the people of the Middle East and North Africa deserve as well—one where they can focus on opportunity, instead of whether they'll be killed or repressed because of who they are or what they believe . . . .

I know what side of history I want to the United States of America to be on. We're ready to meet tomorrow's challenges with you—firm in the belief that all men and women are in fact created equal, each individual possessed with a dignity and inalienable rights that cannot be denied. That is why we look to the future not with fear, but with hope. And that's why we remain convinced that this community of nations can deliver a more peaceful, prosperous and just world to the next generation.

Thank you very much.

Source: Executive Office of the President. "Remarks to the United Nations General Assembly in New York City." September 24, 2013. *Compilation of Presidential Documents* 2013, no. 00655 (September 24, 2013). http://www.gpo.gov/fdsys/pkg/DCPD-201300655/pdf/DCPD-201300655.pdf.

Other Historic Documents of Interest

From this volume

- Lebanese Prime Minister on the Impact of Syrian Civil War, p. 69
- Organization for the Prohibition of Chemical Weapons Awarded 2013 Nobel Peace Prize, p. 616

From previous *Historic Documents*

- United Nations Fails to Take Action in Syria, *2012*, p. 81
- Arab Spring: Syrian Government's Violent Crackdown on Protests, *2011*, p. 168

NASA's *Voyager 1* Reaches Interstellar Space

SEPTEMBER 12, 2013

On September 12, 2013, the National Aeronautics and Space Administration (NASA) announced that its unmanned *Voyager 1* spacecraft had officially entered interstellar space. *Voyager 1* reached a location that was more than 12 billion miles from the sun—approximately 130 times farther than Earth—and was the first human-made object to travel this far. What began in the 1970s as a historic mission to study Jupiter and Saturn now presents NASA with a unique opportunity to map the previously uncharted outer boundaries of our solar system.

THE VOYAGE BEGINS

The *Voyager* program evolved from a 1960s proposal for NASA to embark on a "Grand Tour" of the solar system that would explore the planets from Jupiter to Pluto. The Grand Tour was ultimately scaled back due to NASA budget cuts, but some elements were preserved and formed the foundation of the *Voyager* program. The program involved two spacecraft, *Voyager 1* and *Voyager 2,* both of which would explore Jupiter and Saturn. It was later decided that *Voyager 2* would also travel on to Uranus and Neptune.

These missions were preceded by the *Pioneer* program, which performed first-of-its-kind explorations of the sun and several outer planets, and helped inform the NASA engineers' design of the *Voyager* program and spacecraft. Six of the eight *Pioneer* spacecraft launched prior to the *Voyager* missions, gathering information about the general interplanetary environment and the effects of solar activity on Earth. *Pioneer 10* was the first to pass through the Asteroid Belt and study Jupiter up close, charting the planet's radiation belts, studying its magnetic field, and discovering that it was a predominantly liquid planet. *Pioneer 11* also examined Jupiter, making the first observation of the planet's polar regions, before traveling on to Saturn where it identified three new moons and an additional ring around the planet. Neither *Pioneer* spacecraft has returned a signal to Earth since 2002 and 1995, respectively.

The *Voyager* missions were approved in 1972 and scheduled to launch in 1977 at a time when they could leverage a special planetary alignment to effectively slingshot from one planet to the next, aided by the planets' gravitational pull. Each spacecraft would follow its own flight path and travel at a different speed. NASA's Jet Propulsion Lab built and continues to operate both *Voyager* spacecraft, which feature a variety of instruments ranging from television cameras and ultraviolet sensors to plasma detectors and cosmic-ray and charged-particle sensors. Both spacecraft were also equipped with a special gold-plated record that featured sounds and images from Earth in case they were found by intelligent life forms in other planetary systems. The records' audio not only included natural sounds such as whale song and volcano eruptions, but also music by artists from

Mozart to Chuck Berry and greetings in fifty-five different languages. The records were also engraved with pictorial instructions on how to use them and a pulsar map to show where the spacecraft had come from.

Voyager 1 launched on September 5, 1977, sixteen days after Voyager 2 launched. Although it launched later, Voyager 1 reached Jupiter and Saturn first, taking iconic images that have appeared in textbooks, magazines, and newspapers for decades. It was the first spacecraft to return detailed images of these planets and their moons, and made a number of new discoveries. In March 1979, the spacecraft spotted a never-before-seen ring around Jupiter. It also discovered two new moons, Thebe and Metis, and took detailed pictures of other moons including Callisto, Ganymede, Europa, and Io. In fact, Voyager 1's pictures of Europa's surface led scientists to believe there may be ice or an ocean underneath. One of the spacecraft's more notable findings was that Io had active volcanoes and a mottled yellow-brown-orange surface that proved the moon had an active interior like Earth's. This was the first time active volcanoes had been seen on another body within the solar system. The following year, Voyager 1 traveled on to Saturn where it discovered three new moons—Prometheus, Pandora, and Atlas. It also found a new Saturnian ring, labeled the "G" ring.

Once Voyager I completed its primary mission in 1980, NASA focused on tracking it as it moved to exit the solar system. In 1988, Voyager 1 passed the last known distance of Pioneer 10, becoming the farthest machine ever sent from Earth. The spacecraft transmitted its last images on February 14, 1990, sending a series of images used to create the "Solar System Family Portrait"—a mosaic of sixty individual frames showing six of the planets in relation to each other. Together, Voyager 1 and Voyager 2 returned a total of 5 trillion bits of scientific data, enough to fill more than 7,000 audio CDs, to Earth during their primary missions.

LEAVING THE HELIOSPHERE

NASA officially announced that Voyager 1 had crossed into interstellar space on September 12, 2013, stating that the spacecraft was "in a transitional region immediately outside the solar bubble, where some effects from our sun are still evident." The same day, Voyager's plasma wave science team, led by University of Iowa physics and astronomy professor, Don Gurnett, published a report proving Voyager 1's location in the journal Science. Scientists speculated several times over the preceding year that Voyager 1 had achieved this milestone, causing some to be skeptical that NASA was correct this time. Yet Gurnett's team provided an analysis of data that indicated the spacecraft had actually reached interstellar space in August 2012.

The sun's influence on our solar system can be felt well beyond the planets and into an area of space called the heliosphere. Within that area, charged particles and plasma coming from the sun constantly swirl in the form of a solar wind. That wind begins to slow down and interact with interstellar space at a point called the heliosheath. From this point on, the plasma flowing through space becomes cooler and denser than the solar wind, and it is this distinction that scientists used to confirm Voyager 1's location. The spacecraft's plasma detector, which specifically measures plasma density, temperature, and speed, stopped working more than thirty years ago, but the Voyager team was able to use vibrations picked up by the spacecraft's antennas to calculate the density of the surrounding space.

In April 2013, Voyager 1 transmitted data indicating it had detected a coronal mass ejection, or "a massive burst of solar wind and magnetic fields," which scientists determined had actually occurred in March 2012. The burst of solar material had plowed into interstellar plasma, causing it to oscillate. Those oscillations were in turn picked up by *Voyager 1*'s antenna and translated into measurements of plasma density. Those measurements, and the fact that it took more than a year for the solar particles to reach *Voyager 1,* led scientists to believe that the spacecraft had indeed left the heliosphere and entered interstellar space. The Voyager team discovered further proof of the spacecraft's location while reviewing earlier data for comparable measurements. They found that *Voyager 1* had registered similar information in late fall of 2012 following another solar flare, and that in 2004 the spacecraft had crossed the "termination shock," or the point in space at which the solar wind's speed drops abruptly, slowed by wind coming from interstellar space. Further calculations showed that *Voyager 1*'s instruments first detected a change in particle density on August 25, 2012 that was characteristic of interstellar space, and that subsequent density measures had not changed significantly since then. Taken together, these findings gave scientists the proof they needed to announce that the spacecraft had entered interstellar space.

"We have been cautious because we're dealing with one of the most important milestones in the history of exploration," said Ed Stone, *Voyager* project lead scientist. He continued, "Only now do we have the data—and the analysis—we needed." Stone said he had called three meetings of the Voyager team to discuss the data before making a final determination. "In the end, there was general agreement that *Voyager 1* was indeed outside in interstellar space," Stone said. "But that location comes with some disclaimers— we're in a mixed, transitional region of interstellar space. We don't know when we'll reach interstellar space free from the influence of our solar bubble."

NASA officials hailed the announcement as a major achievement. "*Voyager* has boldly gone where no probe has gone before, marking one of the most significant technological achievements in the annals of the history of science, and adding a new chapter in human scientific dreams and endeavors," said John Grunsfeld, NASA's associate administrator for science in Washington, D.C. "Perhaps some future deep space explorers will catch up with *Voyager,* our first interstellar envoy, and reflect on how this intrepid spacecraft helped enable their journey," Grunsfeld added. On December 3, Stone was presented with NASA's Distinguished Public Service Medal in recognition of his work for the *Voyager* program. The citation accompanying the award commended Stone "for a lifetime of extraordinary scientific achievement and outstanding leadership of space science missions, and for his exemplary sharing of the exciting results with the public."

The Mission Continues

Voyager mission control personnel still communicate with and receive data from both spacecraft every day, though the signals are very dim. NASA officials say that *Voyager 1* has enough battery power to continue operating its fields and particles instruments through at least 2020. NASA will begin turning those instruments off one by one to conserve power, with the last one expected to power down in 2025. *Voyager 1* is expected to continue sending engineering data for several years after that, but then will go silent.

In the meantime, its continued operation provides NASA with an opportunity to collect information about previously unexplored regions of our solar system. The spacecraft's current mission, the Voyager Interstellar Mission, is to "extend the NASA exploration of the solar system beyond the neighborhood of the outer planets to the outer limits of the Sun's sphere of influence, and possibly beyond." It will seek to characterize the environment of the farthest parts of our solar system and define its outermost boundary, known as the heliopause, which no spacecraft has ever reached. The spacecraft is also tasked with taking measurements of the interstellar fields, particles, and waves.

Voyager 1 is expected to reach the Oort Cloud, viewed by many as the edge of our solar system, in approximately 300 years.

—Linda Fecteau

Following is a press release from the National Aeronautics and Space Administration (NASA) from September 12, 2013, on the Voyager *spacecraft's mission into interstellar space.*

NASA Announces Voyager 1 *Reaches Interstellar Space*

DOCUMENT

September 12, 2013

Whether and when NASA's *Voyager 1* spacecraft, humankind's most distant object, broke through to interstellar space, the space between stars, has been a thorny issue. For the last year, claims have surfaced every few months that *Voyager 1* has "left our solar system." Why has the Voyager team held off from saying the craft reached interstellar space until now?

"We have been cautious because we're dealing with one of the most important milestones in the history of exploration," said *Voyager* Project Scientist Ed Stone of the California Institute of Technology in Pasadena. "Only now do we have the data—and the analysis—we needed."

Basically, the team needed more data on plasma, which is ionized gas, the densest and slowest moving of charged particles in space. (The glow of neon in a storefront sign is an example of plasma.) Plasma is the most important marker that distinguishes whether *Voyager 1* is inside the solar bubble, known as the heliosphere, which is inflated by plasma that streams outward from our sun, or in interstellar space and surrounded by material ejected by the explosion of nearby giant stars millions of years ago. Adding to the challenge: they didn't know how they'd be able to detect it.

"We looked for the signs predicted by the models that use the best available data, but until now we had no measurements of the plasma from *Voyager 1*," said Stone.

Scientific debates can take years, even decades to settle, especially when more data are needed. It took decades, for instance, for scientists to understand the idea of plate tectonics, the theory that explains the shape of Earth's continents and the structure of its sea floors. First introduced in the 1910s, continental drift and related ideas were controversial for years. A mature theory of plate tectonics didn't emerge until the 1950s and 1960s. Only after scientists gathered data showing that sea floors slowly spread out from mid-ocean ridges did they finally start accepting the theory. Most active geophysicists accepted plate tectonics by the late 1960s, though some never did.

Voyager 1 is exploring an even more unfamiliar place than our Earth's sea floors—a place more than 11 billion miles (17 billion kilometers) away from our sun. It has been sending back so much unexpected data that the science team has been grappling with the question of how to explain all the information. None of the handful of models the Voyager team uses as blueprints have accounted for the observations about the transition between our heliosphere and the interstellar medium in detail. The team has known it might take months, or longer, to understand the data fully and draw their conclusions.

"No one has been to interstellar space before, and it's like traveling with guidebooks that are incomplete," said Stone. "Still, uncertainty is part of exploration. We wouldn't go exploring if we knew exactly what we'd find."

The two *Voyager* spacecraft were launched in 1977 and, between them, had visited Jupiter, Saturn, Uranus and Neptune by 1989. *Voyager 1*'s plasma instrument, which measures the density, temperature and speed of plasma, stopped working in 1980, right after its last planetary flyby. When *Voyager 1* detected the pressure of interstellar space on our heliosphere in 2004, the science team didn't have the instrument that would provide the most direct measurements of plasma. Instead, they focused on the direction of the magnetic field as a proxy for source of the plasma. Since solar plasma carries the magnetic field lines emanating from the sun and interstellar plasma carries interstellar magnetic field lines, the directions of the solar and interstellar magnetic fields were expected to differ.

Most models told the Voyager science team to expect an abrupt change in the magnetic field direction as *Voyager* switched from the solar magnetic field lines inside our solar bubble to those in interstellar space. The models also said to expect the levels of charged particles originating from inside the heliosphere to drop and the levels of galactic cosmic rays, which originate outside the heliosphere, to jump.

In May 2012, the number of galactic cosmic rays made its first significant jump, while some of the inside particles made their first significant dip. The pace of change quickened dramatically on July 28, 2012. After five days, the intensities returned to what they had been. This was the first taste of a new region, and at the time Voyager scientists thought the spacecraft might have briefly touched the edge of interstellar space.

By Aug. 25, when, as we now know, *Voyager 1* entered this new region for good, all the lower-energy particles from inside zipped away. Some inside particles dropped by more than a factor of 1,000 compared to 2004. The levels of galactic cosmic rays jumped to the highest of the entire mission. These would be the expected changes if *Voyager 1* had crossed the heliopause, which is the boundary between the heliosphere and interstellar space. However, subsequent analysis of the magnetic field data revealed that even though the magnetic field strength jumped by 60 percent at the boundary, the direction changed less than 2 degrees. This suggested that *Voyager 1* had not left the solar magnetic field and had only entered a new region, still inside our solar bubble, that had been depleted of inside particles.

Then, in April 2013, scientists got another piece of the puzzle by chance. For the first eight years of exploring the heliosheath, which is the outer layer of the heliosphere, Voyager's plasma wave instrument had heard nothing. But the plasma wave science team, led by Don Gurnett and Bill Kurth at the University of Iowa, Iowa City, had observed bursts of radio waves in 1983 to 1984 and again in 1992 to 1993. They deduced these bursts were produced by the interstellar plasma when a large outburst of solar material would plow into it and cause it to oscillate. It took about 400 days for such solar outbursts to reach interstellar space, leading to an estimated distance of 117 to 177 AU (117 to 177 times the distance from the sun to the Earth) to the heliopause. They knew, though, that they would be able to observe plasma oscillations directly once *Voyager 1* was surrounded by interstellar plasma.

Then on April 9, 2013, it happened: *Voyager 1*'s plasma wave instrument picked up local plasma oscillations. Scientists think they probably stemmed from a burst of solar activity from a year before, a burst that has become known as the St. Patrick's Day Solar Storms. The oscillations increased in pitch through May 22 and indicated that Voyager was moving into an increasingly dense region of plasma. This plasma had the signatures of interstellar plasma, with a density more than 40 times that observed by *Voyager 2* in the heliosheath.

Gurnett and Kurth began going through the recent data and found a fainter, lower-frequency set of oscillations from Oct. 23 to Nov. 27, 2012. When they extrapolated back, they deduced that Voyager had first encountered this dense interstellar plasma in August 2012, consistent with the sharp boundaries in the charged particle and magnetic field data on August 25.

Stone called three meetings of the Voyager team. They had to decide how to define the boundary between our solar bubble and interstellar space and how to interpret all the data *Voyager 1* had been sending back. There was general agreement *Voyager 1* was seeing interstellar plasma, based on the results from Gurnett and Kurth, but the sun still had influence. One persisting sign of solar influence, for example, was the detection of outside particles hitting Voyager from some directions more than others. In interstellar space, these particles would be expected to hit *Voyager* uniformly from all directions.

"Now that we had actual measurements of the plasma environment—by way of an unexpected outburst from the sun—we had to reconsider why there was still solar influence on the magnetic field and plasma in interstellar space," Stone said. "The path to interstellar space has been a lot more complicated than we imagined."

Stone discussed with the Voyager science group whether they thought *Voyager 1* had crossed the heliopause. What should they call the region were *Voyager 1* is?

"In the end, there was general agreement that *Voyager 1* was indeed outside in interstellar space," Stone said. "But that location comes with some disclaimers—we're in a mixed, transitional region of interstellar space. We don't know when we'll reach interstellar space free from the influence of our solar bubble."

So, would the team say *Voyager 1* has left the solar system? Not exactly—and that's part of the confusion. Since the 1960s, most scientists have defined our solar system as going out to the Oort Cloud, where the comets that swing by our sun on long timescales originate. That area is where the gravity of other stars begins to dominate that of the sun. It will take about 300 years for *Voyager 1* to reach the inner edge of the Oort Cloud and possibly about 30,000 years to fly beyond it. Informally, of course, "solar system" typically means the planetary neighborhood around our sun. Because of this ambiguity, the Voyager team has lately favored talking about interstellar space, which is specifically the space between each star's realm of plasma influence.

"What we can say is *Voyager 1* is bathed in matter from other stars," Stone said. "What we can't say is what exact discoveries await Voyager's continued journey. No one was able to predict all of the details that *Voyager 1* has seen. So we expect more surprises."

Voyager 1, which is working with a finite power supply, has enough electrical power to keep operating the fields and particles science instruments through at least 2020, which will mark 43 years of continual operation. At that point, mission managers will have to start turning off these instruments one by one to conserve power, with the last one turning off around 2025.

Voyager 1 will continue sending engineering data for a few more years after the last science instrument is turned off, but after that it will be sailing on as a silent ambassador. In about 40,000 years, it will be closer to the star AC +79 3888 than our own sun. (AC +79 3888 is traveling toward us faster than we are traveling towards it, so while Alpha Centauri is the next closest star now, it won't be in 40,000 years.) And for the rest of time, Voyager 1 will continue orbiting around the heart of the Milky Way galaxy, with our sun but a tiny point of light among many.

The *Voyager* spacecraft were built and continue to be operated by NASA's Jet Propulsion Laboratory, in Pasadena, Calif. Caltech manages JPL for NASA. The *Voyager* missions are a part of NASA's Heliophysics System Observatory, sponsored by the Heliophysics Division of the Science Mission Directorate at NASA Headquarters in Washington.

SOURCE: National Aeronautics and Space Administration. Jet Propulsion Laboratory. "How Do We Know When *Voyager* Reaches Interstellar Space?" September 12, 2013. http://www.jpl.nasa.gov/news/news .php?release=2013-278.

OTHER HISTORIC DOCUMENTS OF INTEREST

FROM PREVIOUS *HISTORIC DOCUMENTS*

Federal Leaders Remark on the Navy Yard Shooting and Mental Health Care in America

SEPTEMBER 16 AND 19, 2013

On September 16, 2013, the United States was shaken once again by another mass shooting in which twelve people were killed at the Washington, D.C., Navy Yard. While some called for a return to the stalled gun control debate following this tragedy, the shooter's troubled history instead reignited a national conversation about the state of mental health care in the United States, particularly the care provided to veterans.

THE SHOOTING

Just after 8:00 a.m. on September 16, shots were fired at office building 197 at the Washington, D.C., Navy Yard. The shooter killed twelve people and injured eight more before law enforcement officials located and killed him in a shootout. All the victims were civilians or contractors. Officials initially suspected that there could be two other shooters involved based on security camera footage, but confirmed later that evening that there had been just one.

President Barack Obama ordered that all American flags be flown at half-staff to honor the victims, and commented briefly on the tragedy before a planned speech on the economy. "These are men and women who were going to work, doing their job, protecting all of us," Obama said. "They're patriots, and they know the dangers of serving abroad, but today they faced the unimaginable violence that they wouldn't have expected here at home." He added, "We will do everything in our power to make sure whoever carried out this cowardly act is held responsible."

The shooter was later identified as thirty-four-year-old Aaron Alexis, a former Navy reservist who was working at the Navy Yard for a military subcontractor called The Experts, an IT company affiliated with Hewlett Packard Enterprise Services. The Experts later drew criticism for not recognizing Alexis as a threat, but CEO Thomas Hoshko told the Associated Press that Alexis had "no personal issues" and the company said that his background check "revealed no issues other than one minor traffic violation."

Law enforcement officials said Alexis had driven a rental car to the base and used his access card to enter the building. Investigators said he entered the building with a bag, in which they believed he carried a disassembled shotgun. They said Alexis reassembled the shotgun in a bathroom before opening fire on employees who were eating breakfast in the building's atrium. Alexis reportedly also used a handgun during the shooting, which he took from a security guard whom he killed. Officials said the killings appeared to be random. "We have not determined there to be any previous relationship between Alexis and any of the victims," said Valerie Parlave, assistant director for the FBI's D.C. field office.

A Troubled Mind

An investigation into Alexis and his motives revealed a man who was troubled but not seen by his employers as a major concern. Alexis had a history of aggressive behavior. In 2004, he was arrested for shooting the tires of a construction worker's vehicle. Alexis later told police that the man had disrespected him and characterized the incident as an anger-fueled "blackout." In 2008, he was arrested in Georgia on a disorderly conduct charge after he damaged property at an Atlanta night club and refused to stop cursing at police officers. Two years later, he was arrested in Fort Worth, Texas, after shooting a gun through his ceiling into a neighbor's apartment. The neighbor said the incident occurred shortly after Alexis had confronted her about making too much noise, but Alexis told police he accidentally fired the gun while cleaning it. Alexis's father reportedly told police that his son's aggression was caused by post-traumatic stress disorder (PTSD), which he said Alexis suffered after working as "an active participant in rescue attempts" on September 11.

Alexis enlisted as a Navy reservist in 2007 and received "secret" security clearance. He was honorably discharged in 2011 after a "pattern of misbehavior," which included insubordination, disorderly conduct, unauthorized absences, and at least one instance of intoxication. Naval officials initially sought a general discharge, but they did not have sufficient evidence to warrant it, and Alexis had not been convicted of any charges. After the shooting, Navy spokesman Rear Adm. John Kirby said Alexis "wasn't a stellar sailor," but his offenses were not "grievously serious" and would not suggest that "he was capable of this sort of brutal, vicious violence."

Investigating authorities also obtained documents that raised questions about Alexis's mental health. Material pulled from thumb drives, phones, and computers belonging to Alexis included a message reading, "Ultra low frequency attack is what I've been subject to for the last 3 months, and to be perfectly honest, that is what has driven me to this." He had reportedly also written "My ELF weapon" on the shotgun he used at the Navy Yard. "ELF" refers to low-frequency electromagnetic waves, a technology used in submarine communications that is also often described by conspiracy theorists as a tool the government used to monitor and manipulate citizens.

This also appeared to be connected to an incident that occurred in Newport, Rhode Island, on August 7 after Alexis filed a harassment complaint with local police. According to the police report, Alexis said that someone he argued with three days before at a Norfolk, Virginia, airport "sent three people to follow him and to talk, keep him awake and send vibrations to his body." Alexis claimed these people had followed him to three different hotels in the area and were using "some sort of microwave machine" to send vibrations through him. He also said he was hearing voices coming through the walls and floor. Police notified Navy officials in Rhode Island, but they took no action. The Exports reportedly suspended Alexis's access to classified material for two days, but quickly restored it.

Roughly two weeks later, on August 23, Alexis went to the emergency room at Providence Veterans Affairs (VA) Medical Center in Rhode Island saying that he could not sleep. Doctors said his speech and thoughts seemed "clear and focused" and that he "denies flashbacks, denies recent stress" as well as any suicidal or homicidal thoughts. They prescribed a low dose of an antidepressant and anti-anxiety medication to help him sleep. Five days later, Alexis went to another VA facility, this time in D.C., again complaining of insomnia. Doctors provided a similar analysis of his condition and gave him more of the same medication.

The Department of Veterans Affairs released a statement after the shooting acknowledging that Alexis had been treated twice for insomnia at VA hospitals. "On both occasions, Mr. Alexis was alert and oriented, and was asked by VA doctors if he was struggling with anxiety or depression, or had thoughts about harming himself or others, which he denied," the statement read. The VA also said Alexis had never sought care from a mental health specialist.

Alexis's past led many to question how he was able to get a job as a contractor with security clearance. On September 17, Navy Secretary Ray Mabus ordered two security reviews of how the Navy protects its bases and screens its workers, and President Obama ordered the Office of Management and Budget to review security standards for government contractors and employees across federal agencies. The Defense Department and Congress also launched investigations into the shooting, looking in part at security clearance procedures for any flaws that enabled Alexis to get and keep his job.

REEXAMINING MENTAL HEALTH IN THE UNITED STATES

In the wake of the shooting, some politicians saw an opportunity to revive the gun control legislation that failed to pass Congress earlier in the year, but many on Capitol Hill were skeptical that such efforts would be successful. "We don't have the votes," said Senate Majority Leader Harry Reid, D-Nev. Instead, lawmakers refocused their attention on the quality and accessibility of mental health care in the United States, an issue that had been debated in part following the 2012 Sandy Hook Elementary School shooting. "The mental health component seems to be the place where the Congress could do the most good," said Sen. Lindsey Graham, R-S.C. In an impassioned floor speech on September 19, 2013, Rep. Timothy Murphy, R-Pa., called on Congress to review the assistance offered to mental health agencies and the VA, linking the declining availability of treatment for those suffering from mental illnesses to the 1,000 homicides committed by these people each year. "What America has done in dealing with people with mental illness is so far short of what we should be doing, it's not surprising we are still failing the system," Murphy said.

In particular, the Navy Yard shooting prompted many to reexamine the state of veterans' mental health care. Reports indicate that approximately 20 percent of Iraq and Afghanistan war veterans screen positive for PTSD or depression, and nearly 250,000 veterans have been diagnosed with a traumatic brain injury since September 11, 2001. According to a 2013 VA analysis, an estimated twenty-two veterans commit suicide each day. The government has set a goal of counseling veterans seeking mental health assistance within two weeks of first requesting care, but a report by *USA Today*, citing VA data, found that in 2013 one third of new patient appointments occurred after that fourteen-day window had passed. The report stated that veterans seeking a VA psychiatrist for therapy or someone who can assess psychiatric conditions for disability compensation typically have to wait for more than a month before they begin seeing someone. Furthermore, the Government Accountability Office issued a report in April 2013 that found that only 39 percent of civilian mental health care providers were accepting new patients with veterans' TRICARE health insurance coverage. Mary Schohn, director of VA mental health operations, told *USA Today* that new patient wait times had improved by 6 percent over 2012 and that any suicidal patient gets immediate treatment. The VA had also increased its mental health staff by 10 percent over 2012 and reported a 96 percent success rate of seeing repeat patients on a timely basis once they start therapy. Some legislators said this was not enough. "It is unacceptable that even after the hiring of 1,600 new mental health staff, certain VA facilities remain unable to . . . treat veterans in a timely manner," said Sen. Bernard Sanders, I-Vt. "Consequences of leaving mental health conditions untreated can be dire. Such failures cannot continue," Sanders stated.

The National Alliance on Mental Illness was among those who called on the president and Congress to act on mental health legislation that had been stalled since the collapse of the Senate's gun control bill. "Congress has bills introduced that are about mental health. They are not about guns," said the alliance's executive director, Mike Fitzpatrick, adding, "They are modest proposals that will at least begin to make a difference."

These proposals included the Mental Health First Aid Act, introduced by Rep. Ron Barber, D-Ariz., in June 2013, which would authorize $20 million in grants for mental health training for law enforcement, emergency officials, teachers, primary care doctors, and others. Also introduced in June and sponsored by Sen. Jon Tester, D-Mont., the Rural Veterans Mental Health Care Improvement Act would give the VA authority to allow veterans to be seen by licensed mental health counselors, including marriage and family therapists, and would strengthen the requirement for the VA to work with and educate veterans' immediate families about mental health. The bill would also encourage the use of telemedicine to help increase access to care for those living in rural areas. Rep. Jeff Miller, R-Fla., had also been working on draft legislation called the Veterans Integrated Mental Health Care Act of 2013, which would require the VA to provide mental health care to any eligible veteran who chooses to receive such care at a non-VA facility, using a care coordination contract with a qualified third-party entity. The bill would also require that third party to meet specific performance metrics regarding quality and timeliness of care and to exchange relevant clinical information with the VA. During a May House Committee on Veterans' Affairs hearing on the draft bill, Miller said it had become clear that the VA "cannot cope with the magnitude of mental health needs our veterans experience in a bureaucratic vacuum with the normal VA business-as-usual approach. . . . And, the time to act is now."

Miller had yet to introduce his bill by the end of 2013. All other proposed mental health legislation is pending committee approval or a vote.

—Linda Fecteau

Following is a statement by President Barack Obama on September 16, 2013, on the shootings at Washington Navy Yard; and a September 19, 2013, floor statement by Rep. Tim Murphy, R-Pa., on mental health care in the United States.

President Obama Addresses the Navy Yard Shootings

September 16, 2013

Good afternoon, everybody. Please have a seat. Before I begin, let me say a few words about the tragedy that's unfolding not far away from here at the Washington Navy Yard. Now, that's part of why our event today was delayed.

I've been briefed by my team on the situation. We still don't know all the facts, but we do know that several people have been shot and some have been killed. So we are confronting yet another mass shooting, and today it happened on a military installation in our Nation's Capital.

It's a shooting that targeted our military and civilian personnel. These are men and women who were going to work, doing their job, protecting all of us. They're patriots, and they know the dangers of serving abroad, but today they faced the unimaginable violence that they wouldn't have expected here at home.

So we offer our gratitude to the Navy and local law enforcement, Federal authorities, and the doctors who have responded with skill and bravery. I've made it clear to my team that I want the investigation to be seamless so that Federal and local authorities are working together. And as this investigation moves forward, we will do everything in our power to make sure whoever carried out this cowardly act is held responsible.

In the meantime, we send our thoughts and prayers to all at the Navy Yard who have been touched by this tragedy. We thank them for their service. We stand with the families of those who have been harmed. They're going to need our love and support. And as we learn more about the courageous Americans who died today—their lives, their families, their patriotism—we will honor their service to the Nation they helped to make great. And obviously, we're going to be investigating thoroughly what happened, as we do so many of these shootings, sadly, that have happened, and do everything that we can to try to prevent them.

[The following six pages have been omitted and contain remarks about the use of chemical weapons in Syria and President Obama's plan for economic growth.]

SOURCE: Executive Office of the President. "Remarks on the National Economy." September 16, 2013. *Compilation of Presidential Documents* 2013, no. 00631 (September 16, 2013). http://www.gpo.gov/fdsys/pkg/DCPD-201300631/pdf/DCPD-201300631.pdf.

Rep. Murphy Floor Statement on Mental Health Care in America

September 19, 2013

Mr. MURPHY of Pennsylvania. Mr. Speaker, this week America was once again shocked by the tragic shootings at the Navy Yard in Washington, D.C., and once again, it raised the issue of how we're handling mental health to stop this terrible violence.

When you look at the background that was reported in the general media about Aaron Alexis, who is responsible for the shooting at the Navy Yard, we see a record of being arrested multiple times; receiving treatment at a veterans hospital; law enforcement officials in Rhode Island were called upon because he had been hearing voices in his head; he was worried and "had sent three people to follow him to keep him awake by talking to him and sending vibrations to his body"; he checked into multiple hotels to avoid the voices; he also had episodes of shooting firearms.

Recently, there was also a case in Georgia where Michael Brandon Hill clutched a butcher knife over his parents' bed; attempted to set the home on fire; made deadly threats through social media; was bipolar, had attention disorder, was schizophrenic; told police he was off medication; had stolen a firearm; had 498 rounds of ammunition when he entered a school. Luckily, no one was harmed.

What America has done in dealing with people with mental illness is so far short of what we should be doing, it's not surprising we are still failing the system. America has replaced its psychiatric hospitals with prisons and bridges for homelessness. Pennsylvania some years ago had 20 psychiatric hospitals and 8 jails. Now we have 20 jails and 8 psychiatric hospitals. One out of five men has mental illness, and one out of every two women in those jails has a mental illness.

Why don't we use such things as considered background checks for those to obtain guns? In 2010, when 14 million attempts were made to purchase weapons, there were 72,000 denials because those folks had pinged positive because they had an arrest record or had an inpatient obligatory stay. Of those, 34,000 had felony conviction indictments and 13,000 were fugitives. But there were only 44 prosecutions, and only a few of those were found guilty. Background checks don't even begin to deal with the millions of people who have a psychiatric illness and go untreated. There is a lack of inpatient and outpatient treatment options, and we need to finally begin dealing with these problems.

What we need are several aspects, and in the next couple of weeks I'll be offering a package of legislation that finally works towards dealing with these so we do not continue to say our primary methods of treatment for Americans with mental illness are jails and homelessness.

First, we need to recognize that we have a lack of inpatient treatment options. There were 500,000 psychiatric beds in 1955; now there are less than 40,000. What we need to do is increase the options that are available for people with inpatient and outpatient treatment.

Two, we need to get serious on research for those with mental illness. NIMH has a paltry little over $1 billion in money it can spend on research, and very little of that is spent on those with serious mental illness. Indeed, most with mental illness are not violent, but when you see someone with a selective set of symptoms with serious mental illness, we know that they may be at a more increased risk, particularly those who have a history of delusion, paranoia, and interest in violence. What happens in general, from the time of onset of first symptoms, a person may wait an average of 110 weeks before they get into treatment.

In addition, we need more research on medications. There are 11.4 million American adults that suffer from serious mental illness, including schizophrenia, bipolar disorder, and major depression, but 2 million are not being treated. We need more effective research.

Three, Federal laws, which are meant to protect confidentiality, such as HIPAA and FERPA, otherwise known as the Family Educational Rights and Privacy Act, have frustrated the efforts of physicians and family to share information. Many times doctors and other officials cannot get to the very people who can prevent problems and get the person in treatment. Colleges and high schools do not share information with parents because they're afraid of getting sued. Mental health professionals hold on to information, and they wish they could talk more with parents. We need to clarify these boundaries.

Four, law enforcement officials need more training. Police officers are on the frontline of dealing with the violent mentally ill. They need to understand how to identify and handle mental health emergencies. In addition, the primary responders to these ought to be paramedics, those who are trained to deal with health issues. We need to remove the stigma. From the very beginning, we need to be dealing with this as a health issue.

One thousand homicides a year are committed by those with serious mental illness. It's only 5 percent to 10 percent of homicides, but we need to make sure we have that help. We also need to make sure we have integrated care at community mental health centers. Unfortunately, there are barriers to billing with Medicare. We need incentives for pediatricians to get additional training. We need to review what SAMHSA does with its spending, and VA hospitals need to have more help.

Overall, there are many areas that we can engage in, and we will continue to do this to make sure we effectively treat mental illness.

SOURCE: Rep. Timothy Murphy. "Dealing with Mental Health Issues." *Congressional Record* 2013, pt. 159, H5657-H5658. September 19, 2013. http://www.gpo.gov/fdsys/pkg/CREC-2013-09-19/pdf/CREC-2013-09-19-pt1-PgH5657-5.pdf.

OTHER HISTORIC DOCUMENTS OF INTEREST

FROM THIS VOLUME

FROM PREVIOUS *HISTORIC DOCUMENTS*

Census Bureau Reports on Poverty in the United States

SEPTEMBER 17 AND NOVEMBER 6, 2013

The 2012 U.S. poverty rate did not record a statistically significant change over the 2011 rate, according to a U.S. Census Bureau report released on September 17, 2013. The official poverty rate, or the percentage of Americans falling below the poverty line, was 15 percent in 2012, or 46.5 million Americans, marking the first time since 1965 that the poverty rate has remained at or above 15 percent for three years in a row. Although there was no significant overall change, the report did indicate that the nation is recovering at an uneven rate—the most impoverished Americans, and even those in the middle class, are still struggling to get back to where they were in 2007 before the recession.

NO SIGNIFICANT CHANGE IN THE POVERTY LEVEL

Since then-Federal Reserve Chair Ben Bernanke reported that the recession officially came to an end in 2009, the United States as a whole has been on a gradual economic upswing. Unemployment had fallen from a peak of 10 percent in October 2009, to 6.7 percent in December 2013. As companies hired, more Americans injected money into the economy, investors gained confidence, and the stock market rose alongside tax revenue. The annual *Income, Poverty, and Health Insurance Coverage in the United States* report echoed the improvement, because no statistically significant year-over-year increase in the poverty rate was reported. The 2012 percentage of those in poverty, set at an income level below $23,492 for a family of four, was 2.5 percentage points higher than the number recorded in 2007. Income, however, was still 8.3 percent below 2007 levels. "The poverty rate is still very high by historical standards," said Isabel Sawhill, a senior fellow at the Brookings Institution. "The good news," she added, "is that it is likely to decline as the economy recovers over the next decade. The bad news is that it's unlikely to get back to its 2007 level—12.5 percent—until the middle of the next decade, according to our projections."

The number and type of families in poverty did not show a significant change from 2011. By age group, those under 18 had a 21.8 percent poverty rate, the 18 to 64 group was 13.7 percent, and those 65 and older were 9.1 percent. By region, only the West showed a statistically significant difference from 2011, declining from 15.8 percent to 15.1 percent. In the South, the percentage of those in poverty did not change, but the number did, rising from 18.4 million to 19.1 million. In Mississippi, the nation's poorest state, the poverty rate increased from 22.6 percent to 24.2 percent; California and New Hampshire also posted increases. Minnesota and Texas were the only two states that reported a decline in poverty.

The poverty rate was varied between racial groups: non-Hispanic whites had a poverty rate of 9.7 percent, while blacks had a rate of 27.2 percent, Hispanics of 25.6 percent, and Asians of 11.7 percent. Shared households increased again in 2012, from 17 percent of all households in 2011 to 19 percent in 2012. The Census Bureau indicated in its report that it is difficult to determine what impact shared households have on poverty rates because those aged 25 to 34 who live with their parents had an official poverty rate of 9.7 percent, but if only their own finances are taken into account, young people who live with their parents had a poverty level of 43.3 percent.

CHILDREN REMAIN HARDEST HIT

Of the more than 46 million Americans living in poverty, 16.1 million were children, according to the official Census report. Of these, nearly one in ten were living in extreme poverty, defined as being less than half of the poverty line. The Census data showed that the younger a child is, the more dire the child's financial state—those under the age of five have a poverty rate of 25.1 percent. The disparity continues between ethnic groups with 37.9 percent of black children living in poverty, 33.8 percent of Hispanic children, and 12.3 percent of non-Hispanic white children. California had the largest number of children in poverty, at 2.2 million, but Mississippi had the highest rate of impoverished children at more than one in three. "Stubbornly high child poverty rates in the wake of the Great Recession suggest we have not yet turned the corner three years after its official end," said Marybeth Mattingly, of the University of New Hampshire's Carsey Institute.

Although bleak, according to the National Center for Children in Poverty at Columbia University, the Census measure fails to fully capture the portrait of child poverty in America. The Center found that to cover basic expenses, a family of four would require twice the poverty threshold. Impoverished children face a variety of challenges, many of which are related to educational outcomes. According to the American Psychological Association, children living in poverty tend to have poor memory and concentration, a higher high school dropout rate, behavioral and emotional problems, low self-esteem, anxiety, depression, poor social skills, health problems, some tendency toward violence (if the child is living in an impoverished, unsafe neighborhood), and a higher likelihood of eventually entering the criminal justice system.

As displayed in the Census official and supplemental poverty reports, the inability of lower class Americans to break the cycle of poverty has an impact on future generations. Those communities that are heavily affected by poverty consistently fail to meet the educational needs of students, making it more difficult for them to lift themselves out of poverty as adults.

SUPPLEMENTAL POVERTY MEASURE ALSO REMAINS UNCHANGED

When the supplemental poverty measure was first released in 2010, it was hailed as a more accurate method for determining the number of Americans living in poverty. The official Census estimate of poverty does not take into account food stamps, cash assistance, tax credits, and a variety of other governmental support systems in its calculations, all of which can have a significant impact on the number of Americans deemed to be impoverished. The calculations in the official measure are the only ones used to determine allocations for government aid programs.

On November 6, the Census released its third annual supplemental poverty estimate, a report meant to take into account both government assistance and expenses like health insurance, child care, housing, and job expenses such as transportation. The supplemental poverty rate remained unchanged from 2011 to 2012 at 16 percent, or 50 million Americans. What the supplemental report did show was the importance of government programs in keeping Americans out of poverty. Social Security was the number one program for this reason, and the supplemental report estimated that without it 54.7 percent of Americans over the age of 65 would be impoverished, as compared to the actual rate of 14.8 percent. Tax credits, like the earned income tax credit and child tax credit, were also helpful in lowering the poverty rate by 3 percentage points. Food stamps (known as the Supplemental Nutrition Assistance Program, or SNAP), used by a near record of more than 47 million people in June 2013, helped keep five million people out of poverty in 2012, according to Sheldon Danziger, the president of the Russell Sage Foundation, a social science research company. The latter assistance program has sparked major debate over the past couple of years as lawmakers wrangle over whether the program should be restructured, eliminated, or face significant cuts. According to Danziger, cuts to any of these programs could prove detrimental. "The report shows that programs, particularly like refundable tax credits, housing subsidies, school lunch subsidies and food stamps, take people out of poverty," Danziger said, adding "that the safety net works."

ECONOMIC DISPARITY CONTINUES

As evidenced in earlier Census reports, the income gap between those at the low and high ends of the economic spectrum continued into 2012. According to the Economic Policy Institute, since June 2009, only the top five percent of income earners have made gains. "The growth of the stock market shows that the recovery is even more unbalanced than what the Census Bureau numbers show," said Lawrence Mishel, the president of the Economic Policy Institute. "But the Census Bureau numbers definitely do show a pretty unbalanced pattern of income growth," Mishel added. In 2012, more than 24 percent of households made less than $24,999, an increase from 2008, while those households earning between $50,000 and $99,000 declined from 31.2 percent to 29.9 percent.

A study by University of California at Berkeley economist Emmanuel Saez reached a similar conclusion. According to its preliminary 2012 data, the top 1 percent of income earners has increased its earnings by 31.4 percent between 2009 and 2012, while the remainder of the country experienced economic growth of only 0.4 percent. "We're in a selective recovery," said William H. Frey of the Brookings Institution.

President Barack Obama's 2012 reelection campaign was predicated on the notion that building America's middle class was the best way to move the country forward and keep it on an economic path of success. Following his election, and throughout the start of his second term, the president continued to press Congress to work with him to eliminate economic disparity. "Even though our businesses are creating new jobs and have broken record profits, the top 1 percent of Americans took home 20 percent of the nation's income last year, while the average worker isn't seeing a raise at all," the president said. "Most of the gains have gone to the top one-tenth of 1 percent. So in many ways, the trends that have taken hold over the past few decades of a winner-take-all economy, where a few do better and better and better, while everybody else just treads water or loses ground, those trends have been made worse by the recession."

—Heather Kerrigan

Following are excerpts from the U.S. Census Bureau report on the poverty level in the United States, released on September 17, 2013; and a press release detailing the findings of a supplemental poverty report released by the U.S. Census Bureau on November 6, 2013.

Census Bureau Report on Poverty in the United States

September 17, 2013

[All portions of the report not corresponding to poverty have been omitted.]

[Tables, graphs, and footnotes, and references to them, have been omitted.]

POVERTY IN THE UNITED STATES

Highlights

- In 2012, the official poverty rate was 15.0 percent. There were 46.5 million people in poverty.
- For the second consecutive year, neither the official poverty rate nor the number of people in poverty at the national level were statistically different from the previous year's estimates.
- The 2012 poverty rate was 2.5 percentage points higher than in 2007, the year before the most recent recession.
- In 2012, the poverty rate for people living in the West was statistically lower than the 2011 estimate.
- For most groups, the number of people in poverty did not show a statistically significant change. However, between 2011 and 2012, the number of people in poverty did increase for people aged 65 and older, people living in the South, and people living outside metropolitan statistical areas.
- The poverty rate in 2012 for children under age 18 was 21.8 percent. The poverty rate for people aged 18 to 64 was 13.7 percent, while the rate for people aged 65 and older was 9.1 percent. None of these poverty rates were statistically different from their 2011 estimates.

RACE AND HISPANIC ORIGIN

The poverty rate for non-Hispanic Whites was 9.7 percent in 2012, lower than the poverty rates for other racial groups. Non-Hispanic Whites accounted for 62.8 percent of the total population and 40.7 percent of the people in poverty. For non-Hispanic Whites, neither the poverty rate nor the number of people in poverty experienced a statistically significant change between 2011 and 2012.

For Blacks, the 2012 poverty rate was 27.2 percent and there were 10.9 million people in poverty. For Asians, the 2012 poverty rate was 11.7 percent, which represented 1.9 million people in poverty. Among Hispanics, the 2012 poverty rate was 25.6 percent, and there were 13.6 million people in poverty. None of these estimates were statistically different from their 2011 values.

AGE

Between 2011 and 2012, the number of people aged 65 and older in poverty increased to 3.9 million in 2012, up from 3.6 million in 2011, while the poverty rate for this age group was not statistically different at 9.1 percent. Neither the poverty rate nor the number in poverty for people aged 18 to 64 were statistically different from 2011, at 13.7 percent and 26.5 million.

In 2012, for children under age 18, the survey found no statistically significant change in the poverty rate or the number in poverty (21.8 percent and 16.1 million). The poverty rate for children was higher than the rates for people aged 18 to 64 and those aged 65 and older. Children represented 23.7 percent of the total population and 34.6 percent of the people in poverty.

Related children are people under age 18 related to the householder by birth, marriage, or adoption who are not themselves householders or spouses of householders. The poverty rate and the number in poverty for related children under age 18 were 21.3 percent and 15.4 million in 2012, not statistically different from the 2011 estimates. For related children in families with a female householder, 47.2 percent were in poverty, compared with 11.1 percent of related children in married-couple families.

The poverty rate and the number in poverty for related children under age 6 were 24.4 percent and 5.8 million in 2012, not statistically different from the 2011 estimates. About 1 in 4 of these children were in poverty in 2012. More than half (56.0 percent) of related children under age 6 in families with a female householder were in poverty. This was four-and-a-half times the rate for children in married couple families (12.5 percent).

SEX

In 2012, 13.6 percent of males and 16.3 percent of females were in poverty. Neither poverty rate showed a statistically significant change from its 2011 estimate.

Gender differences in poverty rates were more pronounced for the age group 65 and older. The poverty rate for women aged 65 and older was 11.0 percent, while the poverty rate for men aged 65 and older was 6.6 percent. The poverty rate for women aged 18 to 64 was 15.4 percent, while the poverty rate for men aged 18 to 64 was 11.9 percent. For children under age 18, the poverty rate for girls was 22.3 percent and for boys 21.3 percent.

NATIVITY

Of all people, 87.1 percent were native born, 5.9 percent were foreign born naturalized citizens, and 7.0 percent were foreign-born noncitizens. The poverty rate and the number in poverty for the native born and the foreign born were not statistically different from 2011 (14.3 percent and 38.8 million for the native born and 19.2 percent and 7.7 million for the foreign born in 2012).

Within the foreign-born population, 45.4 percent were naturalized citizens, while the remaining were not citizens of the United States. The poverty rates in 2012 were 12.4 percent for foreign-born naturalized citizens and 24.9 percent for those who were not citizens, neither statistically different from 2011.

REGION

The poverty rate in the West fell from 15.8 percent in 2011 to 15.1 percent in 2012, while the number in poverty remained unchanged at 11.0 million. For the South, the poverty rate remained unchanged at 16.5 percent in 2012, while the number in poverty increased to 19.1 million, up from 18.4 million in 2011. In 2012, the poverty rate and the number in poverty for the Northeast (13.6 percent and 7.5 million) and the Midwest (13.3 percent and 8.9 million) were not statistically different from 2011 estimates.

RESIDENCE

Inside metropolitan statistical areas, the poverty rate and the number of people in poverty were 14.5 percent and 38.0 million in 2012, not statistically different from 2011. The number in poverty increased for those living outside metropolitan statistical areas to 8.5 million in 2012, from 8.0 million in 2011, while their poverty rate was not statistically different at 17.7 percent in 2012.

The 2012 poverty rate and the number of people in poverty for those living inside metropolitan areas but not in principal cities were 11.2 percent and 18.1 million. Among those who lived in principal cities, their 2012 poverty rate and the number in poverty were 19.7 percent and 19.9 million. Neither estimate was statistically different from 2011.

Within metropolitan areas, people in poverty were more likely to live in principal cities in 2012. While 38.5 percent of all people living in metropolitan areas lived in principal cities, 52.4 percent of poor people in metropolitan areas lived in principal cities.

WORK EXPERIENCE

In 2012, 7.3 percent of workers aged 18 to 64 were in poverty. The poverty rate for those who worked full time, year round was 2.9 percent, while the poverty rate for those working less than full time, year round was 16.6 percent. None of these rates were statistically different from the 2011 poverty rates.

Among those who did not work at least 1 week in 2012, the poverty rate and the number in poverty were 33.1 percent and 15.8 million in 2012, not statistically different from the 2011 estimates. Those who did not work in 2012 represented 24.7 percent of all people aged 18 to 64, compared with 59.7 percent of people aged 18 to 64 in poverty.

DISABILITY STATUS

In 2012, for people aged 18 to 64 with a disability, the poverty rate and number in poverty were 28.4 percent and 4.3 million. For people aged 18 to 64 without a disability, the poverty rate and number in poverty were 12.5 percent and 22.2 million. None of these estimates were statistically different from the 2011 estimates. Among people aged 18 to 64, those with a disability represented 7.7 percent of all people in this age group compared with 16.1 percent of people in poverty.

FAMILIES

In 2012, the family poverty rate and the number of families in poverty were 11.8 percent and 9.5 million, neither statistically different from the 2011 estimates.

In 2012, 6.3 percent of married-couple families, 30.9 percent of families with a female householder, and 16.4 percent of families with a male householder lived in poverty. Neither the family poverty rates nor the estimates of the number of families in poverty for these three family types showed any statistically significant change between 2011 and 2012.

DEPTH OF POVERTY

Categorizing a person as "in poverty" or "not in poverty" is one way to describe his or her economic situation. The income-to-poverty ratio and the income deficit or surplus describe additional aspects of economic well-being. While the poverty rate shows the proportion of people with income below the relevant poverty threshold, the income-to-poverty ratio gauges the depth of poverty and shows how close a family's income is to its poverty threshold. The income-to-poverty ratio is reported as a percentage that compares a family's or an unrelated person's income with the applicable poverty threshold. For example, a family with an income-to-poverty ratio of 125 percent has income that is 25 percent above its poverty threshold.

The income deficit or surplus shows how many dollars a family's òr an individual's income is below (or above) their poverty threshold. For those with an income deficit, the measure is an estimate of the dollar amount necessary to raise a family's or a person's income to their poverty threshold.

Ratio of Income to Poverty

. . . In 2012, 20.4 million people reported an income below one-half of their poverty threshold. They represented 6.6 percent of all people and 43.9 percent of those in poverty. One in 5 people (19.7 percent) had income below 125 percent of their threshold, 1 in 4 people (24.6 percent) had income below 150 percent of their poverty threshold, while approximately 1 in 3 (34.2 percent) had income below 200 percent of their threshold.

Of the 20.4 million people with income below one-half of their poverty threshold, 7.1 million were children under age 18, 12.1 million were aged 18 to 64, and 1.2 million were aged 65 years and older. The percentage of people aged 65 and older with income below 50 percent of their poverty threshold was 2.7 percent, less than one-half the percentage of the total population at this poverty level (6.6 percent).

The demographic makeup of the population differs at varying degrees of poverty. In 2012 children represented:

- 23.7 percent of the overall population.
- 35.0 percent of the population below 50 percent of their poverty threshold.
- 27.0 percent of people with income between 100 percent and 200 percent of their poverty threshold.
- 20.3 percent of the people with income above 200 percent of their poverty threshold.

By comparison, people aged 65 and older represented:

- 13.9 percent of the overall population.
- 5.8 percent of people below 50 percent of their poverty threshold.
- 17.8 percent of the people between 100 percent and 200 percent of their poverty threshold.
- 14.0 percent of the people with income above 200 percent of their poverty threshold.

Income Deficit

The income deficit for families in poverty (the difference in dollars between a family's income and its poverty threshold) averaged $9,785 in 2012, which was not statistically different from the inflation-adjusted 2011 estimate. The average income deficit was larger for families with a female householder ($10,361) than for married-couple families ($9,348).

For families in poverty, the average income deficit per capita for families with a female householder ($3,112) was higher than for married-couple families ($2,443). The income deficit per capita is computed by dividing the average deficit by the average number of people in that type of family. Since families with a female householder were smaller on average than married-couple families, the larger per capita deficit for female householder families reflects their smaller average family size as well as their lower average family income.

For unrelated individuals, the average income deficit for those in poverty was $6,542 in 2012. The $6,279 deficit for women was lower than the $6,873 deficit for men.

SHARED HOUSEHOLDS

While poverty estimates are based on income in the previous calendar year, estimates of shared households reflect household composition at the time of the survey, which is conducted during the months of February, March, and April of each year. In 2013, the number and percentage of shared households was higher than in 2007, prior to the recession. In 2007, there were 19.7 million shared households, representing 17.0 percent of all households; by 2013, there were 23.2 million shared households, representing 19.0 percent of all households. The number of adults in shared households grew from 61.7 million (27.7 percent) in 2007 to 71.5 million (30.2 percent) in 2013.

Between 2012 and 2013, the number and percentage of shared households increased by an estimated 889,000 households (0.5 percentage points). However, change in the number and percentage of additional adults residing in shared households between 2012 and 2013 was not statistically significant. Indeed, there has been no change in the number or proportion of additional adults living in shared households since 2010.

In 2013, an estimated 10.1 million adults aged 25 to 34 (24.1 percent) were additional adults in someone else's household. Of these young adults, 5.8 million (13.9 percent) lived with their parents. The change between 2012 and 2013 in the number and percentage of additional adults in this age group living in their parents' household was not statistically significant. Further, there has been no change since 2011 in the number and percent of adults aged 25 to 34 living with their parents.

It is difficult to assess the precise impact of household sharing on overall poverty rates. In 2012, adults aged 25 to 34 living with their parents had an official poverty rate of 9.7 percent (when the entire family's income is compared with the threshold that includes the young adult as a member of the family). However, if poverty status were determined using only the additional adult's own income, 43.3 percent of those aged 25 to 34 would have been below the poverty threshold for a single person under age 65.

SOURCE: U.S. Census Bureau. "Income, Poverty, and Health Insurance Coverage in the United States: 2012." September 17, 2013. https://www.census.gov/prod/2013pubs/p60-245.pdf.

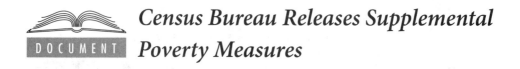

Census Bureau Releases Supplemental Poverty Measures

November 16, 2013

The nation's poverty rate was 16.0 percent in 2012, unchanged from 2011, according to the supplemental poverty measure released today by the U.S. Census Bureau. The 2012 rate was higher than the official measure of 15.0 percent. The official poverty rate in 2012 was also not significantly different from the corresponding rate in 2011.

Unlike the official poverty rate, the supplemental poverty measure takes into account the impact of different benefits and necessary expenses on the resources available to families, as well as geographic differences in housing costs. For example, the measure adds refundable tax credits (the Earned Income Tax Credit and the refundable portion of the child tax credit) to cash income, which reduces the supplemental poverty rate for all people by three percentage points (19.0 percent to 16.0 percent). For children, the supplemental poverty rate of 18.0 percent would rise to 24.7 percent if refundable tax credits were excluded.

The supplemental poverty measure deducts various necessary expenses from income; these include medical out-of-pocket expenses, income and payroll taxes, child care expenses and work-related expenses. These expenses reduce income available for necessary basic goods purchases including food, clothing, shelter and utilities (FCSU) and a small additional amount to allow for other needs. Deducting medical out-of-pocket expenses increases the supplemental poverty rate by 3.4 percentage points. Without accounting for medical out-of-pocket expenses, the number of people living below the poverty line would have been 39.2 million rather than the 49.7 million people classified as poor with the supplemental poverty measure.

Without adding Social Security benefits to income, the supplemental poverty rate overall would have been 8.6 percentage points higher (or 24.5 percent rather than 16.0 percent). People 65 and older had a supplemental poverty rate of 14.8 percent, equating to 6.4 million. Excluding Social Security would leave the majority of this population (54.7 percent or 23.7 million) in poverty.

The supplemental poverty measure's poverty thresholds vary by geography, family size and whether a family pays a mortgage, rents or owns their home free and clear. For example, the 2012 thresholds for families with two adults and two children were around $18,000 for homeowners without a mortgage living outside metropolitan areas in North Dakota, Kentucky, West Virginia, Alabama, Arkansas, South Dakota, Tennessee and Missouri, but around $35,500 for homeowners with a mortgage in the San Jose-Sunnyvale-Santa Clara, Calif., and San Francisco-Oakland-Fremont, Calif., metro areas. The $23,283 official poverty threshold for a family of four was the same no matter where a family lives.

These findings are contained in the Census Bureau's annual report, The Research Supplemental Poverty Measure, released with support from the Bureau of Labor Statistics and describing research showing different ways of measuring poverty in the United States.

"The important contribution that the supplemental poverty measure provides is allowing us to gauge the effectiveness of tax credits and transfers in alleviating poverty," said Kathleen Short, a Census Bureau economist and the report's author. "We can also examine the effect of necessary expenses that families face, such as paying taxes or work-related and medical-out-of-pocket expenses."

ESTIMATES FOR STATES

The differences between the official and supplemental poverty measures varied considerably by state. The supplemental rates were higher than the official statewide poverty rates in 13 states and the District of Columbia. The states were California, Colorado, Connecticut, Florida, Hawaii, Illinois, Maryland, Massachusetts, Nevada, New Hampshire, New Jersey, New York and Virginia.

For another 28 states, supplemental rates were lower than the official statewide poverty rates. The states were Alabama, Arkansas, Idaho, Indiana, Iowa, Kansas, Kentucky, Louisiana, Maine, Michigan, Minnesota, Mississippi, Missouri, Montana, Nebraska, New Mexico, North Carolina, North Dakota, Ohio, Oklahoma, South Carolina, South Dakota, Tennessee, Texas, Vermont, West Virginia, Wisconsin and Wyoming. Rates in the remaining nine states were not statistically different using the two measures.

Comparing Poverty Rates for Different Demographic Groups

The supplemental poverty measure can show the effects of tax and transfer policies on various subgroups, unlike the current official poverty measure. According to the report:

- Including tax credits and noncash benefits results in lower poverty rates for some groups. For instance, the supplemental poverty rate was lower for children than the official rate: 18.0 percent compared with 22.3 percent.
- Subtracting necessary expenses from income results in higher poverty rates for other groups. The supplemental poverty rate for those 65 and older was 14.8 percent compared with only 9.1 percent using the official measure. Medical out-of-pocket expenses were a significant element for this group.
- Even though supplemental poverty rates were lower than the official rates for children and higher for those 65 and older, the rates for children were still higher than the rates for both 18- to 64-year-olds and people 65 and older.
- Supplemental poverty rates were higher than the official measure for all race groups and for Hispanics, with one exception: blacks, whose 25.8 percent supplemental poverty rate was lower than the official rate of 27.3 percent.
- Supplemental poverty rates differed by region primarily because the supplemental poverty rate has thresholds that vary geographically. The rates were higher than official rates for the Northeast and West, lower in the Midwest and not statistically different from the official measure in the South. These results reflect differences in housing costs, which are not captured by the official poverty measure.

Background

The supplemental poverty measure is an effort to take into account many of the government programs designed to assist low-income families and individuals that were not included in the current official poverty measure, released Sept. 17.

While the official poverty measure includes only pretax money income, the supplemental measure adds the value of in-kind benefits, such as the Supplemental Nutrition Assistance Program, school lunches, housing assistance and refundable tax credits. Additionally, the supplemental poverty measure deducts necessary expenses for critical goods and services from income. Expenses that are deducted include taxes, child care and commuting expenses, out-of-pocket medical expenses and child support paid to another household.

Today's report compares 2012 supplemental poverty estimates to 2012 official poverty estimates for numerous demographic groups at the national level. In addition, the report presents supplemental poverty estimates for states using three-year averages. At the national level, the report also compares 2011 supplemental poverty estimates with 2012 estimates.

There has been a continuing debate about the best approach to measure income and poverty in the United States since the publication of the first official U.S. poverty estimates in 1964. In 2009, an interagency group asked the Census Bureau, in cooperation with the Bureau of Labor Statistics, to develop a new, supplemental measure to allow for an improved understanding of the economic well-being of American families and the way that federal policies affect those living in poverty.

The measures presented in this report used the 2013 Current Population Survey Annual Social and Economic Supplement with income information that referred to calendar year 2012 to estimate supplemental poverty measure resources, including the value of various in-kind benefits beyond cash income. (The official poverty measure is based solely on cash income.)

SOURCE: U.S. Census Bureau. "Supplemental Measure of Poverty Remains Unchanged." November 6, 2013. https://www.census.gov/newsroom/releases/archives/poverty/cb13-183.html.

OTHER HISTORIC DOCUMENTS OF INTEREST

FROM THIS VOLUME

- State of the Union Address and Republican Response, p. 35

FROM PREVIOUS HISTORIC DOCUMENTS

- Census Bureau Reports on Poverty in the United States, *2012*, p. 413
- President Obama and Former Gov. Romney Meet in Second Presidential Debate, *2012*, p. 482

African Union Condemns Mall Shooting

SEPTEMBER 21, 2013

A four-day siege of a mall in Nairobi, Kenya, by the terrorist group al-Shabaab claimed the lives of at least seventy-two people and wounded upwards of 200. The Kenyan government came under fire for its response to the attack, with claims that Kenyan forces had looted the mall and that they lied about the deaths of the four attackers. According to a report released by the New York Police Department (NYPD), the forces sent in to end the siege had extended it by two days and had allowed the attackers to escape.

A Warning Before a Deadly Attack

In late 2011, the al-Shabaab terrorist organization threatened to carry out attacks in Kenya after the Kenyan military in cooperation with the Somali military launched an attack against al-Shabaab strongholds in Somalia. Although nothing came to be in 2012, in 2013, the United Nations began warning of a likely attack in Kenya and even members of the Kenyan National Intelligence Service (NIS) said they had evidence that an attack would soon be carried out. Reportedly, the NIS members were told where the attack would take place and reported the information to their superiors, who failed to take action.

On September 21, a number of gunmen entered the Westgate mall in Nairobi, located in an area of the city frequented by Westerners. The attackers reportedly entered from three different areas in an attempt to stop anyone trying to flee the mall. Shoppers who tried to run were shot or had grenades thrown at them. Reports from the Kenyan government indicated that the attackers rounded up hostages, specifically seeking non-Muslims, and held them in various locations: a casino, basement, and movie theater located in the mall. Local security forces did not enter the mall until approximately one hour after the attack began. The attackers and security forces began to battle one another, and the attackers had the upper hand because they had apparently stashed weapons around the mall and were able to reload or rearm with ease. The security forces who entered the mall focused on trying to secure hostages and anyone still trapped and hiding in the building. A few hours into the attack, the Kenya Defense Forces (KDF) took over control from local security. Eyewitnesses said the attackers used this power handover to begin shooting at random with high-caliber machine guns. The KDF responded with a barrage of fire. At the end of the first day of the siege, fifty-nine were reported killed.

The standoff continued into a second day, and the Kenyan Interior Ministry reported that there were still up to fifteen attackers that they knew of inside the mall. They noted, however, that the KDF had gained control of the CCTV room and were able to now monitor the militants' movements. In an effort to wipe out the attackers and take control of the mall, two KDF helicopters landed on the roof of the mall, but another KDF assault did not take place until September 23. Following the assault, the Interior Ministry announced that a majority of the hostages had been rescued, but sixty-two people were now thought to have been killed. At this point, the ministry said, KDF was in control of the entire facility. It was now to be the job of the KDF to clear the remaining militants. On September 24, the Kenyan government reported that the mall had been cleared and the operation was complete.

A number of allegations and questions were raised immediately following the attack. Some of the mall shop owners alleged that the KDF officers had looted stores because products and money were missing. There were conflicting reports about how many attackers were in the mall—it was initially believed to be ten to fifteen, but later reports showed that it may have been as few as four. There was also no early indication about whether all those responsible were accounted for—at least two were initially thought to have been killed when a portion of the mall roof collapsed, but Interior Minister Joseph Ole Lenku said that he "could not rule out the possibility that when we were evacuating people in the first stages of the operation, it is possible some [of the attackers] could have slipped out."

The biggest question facing the Kenyan government was why it took so long for its elite group of antiterrorism forces to end the siege. One possible reason was the hand-off from police to KDF, during which confusion ensued and the terrorists were able to regroup. Another possible reason is that, despite their training, the group had never dealt with a hostage situation before. Some suggested that the KDF stalled in an effort to loot shops before ending the attack.

TERRORIST GROUP CLAIMS RESPONSIBILITY

The Kenyan government released information on those thought to be the four primary attackers: Abu Baara al-Sudani, Omar Nabhan, Khattab al-Kene, and Umayr. According to the Kenyan government, all four were thought to have been killed. Al-Shabaab, an Islamist extremist group that operates out of Somalia, immediately claimed responsibility for the attack. The group was once in control of wide swaths of Somali cities and towns, even controlling portions of the capital of Mogadishu until 2012. Today, it operates mainly in rural areas, where it imposes strict sharia law on the residents. After more than two decades of civil war, al-Shabaab has operated without significant intervention from the Somali government, which has very little authority or credibility.

Al-Shabaab, officially recognized by the United States and United Kingdom as a terrorist organization, is led by Ahmed Abdi Godane who is also known as Mukhtar Abu Zubair. The group forged formal ties with al Qaeda in 2012, and it is believed that al Qaeda members have sought refuge in Somalia because they have been driven out of Afghanistan and Pakistan. Questions have been raised about whether al-Shabaab is affiliated with other terrorist organizations like Boko Haram, which operates primarily out of Nigeria, and al Qaeda in the Islamic Maghreb (AQIM).

The Kenyan mall assault was not al-Shabaab's first attack. The group is believed by some in the United States to be responsible, at least in part, for the 1998 attacks on the U.S. embassies in Nairobi and Dar es Salaam and the 2002 attacks on Israeli targets in Kenya. The group claimed responsibility for a twin suicide bombing in Uganda in 2010 that killed seventy-six people.

As it has increasingly lost its hold in Somalia, al-Shabaab has placed a new focus on Kenya. Al-Shabaab fighters cross the Somali border into Kenya frequently and often undetected. It has been reported that their wounded fighters often seek treatment in Nairobi. A senior official familiar with the investigation into the mall attack, who spoke to the BBC on the condition of anonymity, said that information following the Nairobi mall attack indicated that the four people responsible came to Kenya months earlier, likely in June, and had remained in the country. "They were in Somalia prior to the attack being carried out" to receive training, the source said, and "they were in Kenya for some time together." The attack raised concerns that al-Shabaab would strengthen its presence in Kenya and use the nation as a recruiting base. "An attack like this gives them the capability to recruit, it shows off their abilities, and it demonstrates to Al Qaeda central that they are not dead," said Rudy Atallah, the former director of the Pentagon's African counterterrorism unit.

Report Brings Light to Questions Surrounding the Attack

The New York Police Department (NYPD) was tasked with putting together a report on the attack to evaluate the response and whether the impact could have been lessened. It sent detectives and terrorism task force members to Nairobi after the assault to reconstruct the events. The results of the investigation were compiled into a report released on December 10, 2013. The report, based on evidence collected by NYPD officers after the assault, found that there were only four gunmen in the mall, and that it was likely that they escaped the attack and are still at large, despite the Kenyan government's assertion to the contrary. The report also found that no hostages were held by the gunmen and that the attackers only used light weapons, not high-caliber machine guns as claimed by the Egyptian government based on eyewitness accounts. The NYPD report also found a high likelihood that the Kenyan military had looted the mall.

According to the NYPD, the four attackers split into teams of two, throwing three grenades as they entered the mall. The attackers carried AK-47s, which they used to shoot their victims. More than one-third of those killed were in a mall parking structure and were attacked during the first fifteen minutes of the siege. The attackers killed as many people as they could, but spared some who could recite Muslim prayers. The response to the siege was slow because the police forces thought they were responding to an armed robbery. Private security guards, local police, and military units did not wear identifying badges or uniforms; this caused confusion and the various response units fired on each other. The response teams also had little knowledge of what the mall looked like and were not aware of how to get to the CCTV equipment.

Based on footage available to the NYPD from the mall, the attackers were last seen on camera at 12:15 p.m. on the second day of the siege. This led the NYPD to reach the conclusion that after that point, the attackers had left and the mall was no longer under threat. The Kenyan government claimed that the attackers had set fire to mattresses and collapsed a portion of the building, which in turn killed two of the attackers, but the NYPD investigation found that the cause of the fire and collapse was unknown and more likely may have been fires caused by rocket-propelled grenades and antitank missiles used by Kenyan forces.

Arrests and Charges

Despite conflicting claims about whether the attackers had escaped alive or were killed, dozens were arrested following the attack, but none were thought to have been responsible for carrying out the actual assault. Four Somalis living in Kenya were charged in November with harboring the suspected gunmen. They pleaded not guilty and are currently awaiting trial.

—Heather Kerrigan

Following is a statement by the African Union on September 21, 2013, condemning the Westgate mall attacks in Nairobi, Kenya.

African Union Condemns Deadly Mall Attack

September 21, 2013

The Chairperson of the Commission of the African Union (AU), Dr. Nkosazana Dlamini-Zuma, condemns in the strongest possible terms the dastardly terrorist attacks today against innocent civilians in a Nairobi shopping mall, which caused the loss of many lives.

The Chairperson of the Commission states that this cowardly attack, for which the al Qaeda-linked Al Shabaab group has claimed responsibility, once again underlines the imperative for renewed and reinvigorated efforts to combat terrorism throughout the continent. She reiterates the AU's commitment to continue working with its Member States and partners to this end.

The Chairperson of the Commission expresses the solidarity of the AU with the government and peoples of Kenya. She presents the AU's heartfelt condolences to the families of the victims, and wishes a speedy recovery to the injured.

The Chairperson of the Commission reiterates the AU's commitment to sustain its efforts to counter terrorism throughout the continent, as well as to pursue its efforts to stabilize the situation in Somalia and the fight against Al Shabaab, through its Mission in Somalia (AMISOM).

SOURCE: African Union. "The African Union Strongly Condemns the Dastardly Terrorist Attacks Against Innocent Civilians in Nairobi." September 21, 2013. http://cpauc.au.int/en/sites/default/files/au-statement-on-nairobikenya-attacks.pdf.

OTHER HISTORIC DOCUMENTS OF INTEREST

FROM PREVIOUS HISTORIC DOCUMENTS

Germany Holds Federal Elections

SEPTEMBER 23, OCTOBER 9, AND DECEMBER 17, 2013

The party of German Chancellor Angela Merkel won a decisive victory in parliamentary elections on September 22, 2013, giving Merkel a historic third term as Chancellor. The convincing electoral win for her center-right alliance of Christian Democrats was a sure sign that the voters approved of Merkel's handling of Germany and the EU's severe economic challenges. In particular, it was seen as an endorsement of her actions in addressing the eurozone debt crisis, including arranging EU-funded bailouts for the most indebted eurozone countries like Greece and Portugal. Merkel's party fell just short of an overall majority, which required her to form a coalition government. She eventually decided to partner with the second largest party in the parliament, the center-left Social Democratic Party (SPD). A new so-called grand coalition government took office by the end of the year.

HANDLING OF THE ECONOMIC CRISIS AIDS MERKEL

Merkel has been Germany's Chancellor since 2005. In her first term, she led a grand coalition of the two largest parties in the Bundestag, the lower house of Germany's parliament. Her own party is an alliance of two sister parties, the Christian Democratic Union (CDU) and the Bavarian-based Christian Social Union (CSU), both of which have a center-right political ideology. Her coalition partner from 2005 to 2009 was the SPD, which won four seats fewer than the CDU-CSU alliance's 226 seats in the Bundestag.

She won a second term in the 2009 elections, with her party increasing slightly their number of seats. On this occasion, she chose as her coalition partner the smaller, Free Democrat Party (FDP), which espouses free market policies and has strong support within the business community. Political analysts noted how Merkel's coalition partners, both in her first and second terms, hemorrhaged popular support over the course of their four-year term and lost a lot of seats in subsequent elections. By contrast, Merkel's own CDU-CSU alliance has steadily increased its representation during her eight years as leader. Merkel's detractors have half-jokingly dubbed this phenomenon the "vampire effect," an allusion to her metaphoric "sucking the life-blood" out of coalition partners, often by "stealing" their more popular policies and then gaining credit for them. As the 2013 election campaign got into full swing, the FDP watched with dismay and alarm as opinion polls showed them in danger of winning less than 5 percent of the vote, the threshold that political parties must exceed to win seats in the Bundestag.

Merkel's CDU-CSU bloc led in the polls throughout the 2013 campaign. However, it was unclear by how much they would win and in particular whether they would win an absolute majority of seats, a feat only achieved once before in post-war Germany by Chancellor Konrad Adenauer in 1957. Merkel's popularity was attributed to the calm, methodic way in which she navigated Germany through both the economic recession that hit Europe in 2008–2009 and the eurozone sovereign debt crisis that followed from 2010 to 2012. Although she was initially reluctant to bail out the most indebted countries like Greece and Portugal when they risked defaulting on their debts, she ultimately decided that bailouts were in Germany and Europe's best interests and that the euro had to be saved at all costs. She was a pivotal figure in pushing through major structural changes to the EU's institutional architecture such as the creation of a permanent EU bailout fund, the European Stability Mechanism. While she received criticism at home for approving taxpayer funded bailouts of foreign nations—and she was also unpopular in bailout recipient nations like Greece due to the austerity policies that were tied to the bailout—her strategy seemed to have paid off by 2013. None of the eurozone countries had defaulted on their debts or left the eurozone, while Germany was experiencing modest but steady economic growth. This was largely on the back of a surge in German exports of manufactured goods, a trend facilitated by Germany's membership of the eurozone. A survey conducted of 7,000 firms in Germany in late 2013 showed that in general the business community was increasingly optimistic about the prospects for continued economic growth. Domestic demand for German goods, in particular, was on the rise, and inflation was at a manageable level, while Germany continued to run a hefty trade surplus due to its goods exports.

MERKEL CRUISES TO VICTORY

On election day, 71.5 percent of Germany's electorate of 62 million people turned out to vote—a slight increase on the turnout of 70.8 percent in the 2009 ballot. To nobody's surprise, Merkel's CDU-CSU alliance emerged as clear winners, winning 41.5 percent of the poll. This translated into 311 seats in the 631-member Bundestag, leaving it tantalizingly a few seats short of an overall majority. Coming in second place with a very disappointing score of 25.7 percent of the vote and 193 seats was the SPD. This was the party's second worst performance since World War II. Only two other parties cleared the 5 percent threshold that allowed them to take seats in parliament: the Green Party, which won 8.4 percent and 63 seats, and The Left (*Die Linke*), which won 8.6 percent and 64 seats. The biggest shock of the night was the failure of the FDP to clear the threshold—they won 4.7 percent—meaning that they lost all their 93 seats in parliament. This was the first time that the FDP was unable to secure parliamentary representation in the Bundestag since World War II. Another important outcome was the failure of a new anti-EU party called Alternative for Germany to clear the threshold, having won only 4.7 percent. This party had created a policy platform based on opposition to the eurozone bailouts and the euro currency generally. The total share of the vote for all the parties who failed to clear the threshold was 14.6 percent, which was unusually high.

A jubilant Merkel proclaimed, "This is a super result. Together we will do all we can to make the next four years successful ones for Germany." The daughter of a Protestant pastor, Merkel grew up in communist East Germany. She joined the center-right CDU after East Germany was united with West Germany in 1990. She gradually worked her way up to the top of the party echelons, succeeding Helmut Kohl as leader of the CDU in 1998. Failing narrowly to win the Chancellorship in the 2002 elections, Merkel finally acceded to the job following snap elections called by the SPD Chancellor Gerhard Schroder in 2005. Merkel is the first ever female Chancellor of Germany. During her 2013 reelection campaign, her supporters donned "Angie" T-shirts, a sign of her personal popularity, which stemmed from her down-to-earth style that seemed to appeal to German voters.

The CDU-CSU's performance in the 2013 elections was its best since German unification. Only two other former Chancellors, Adenauer and Kohl, have equaled Merkel's achievement of winning three successive elections (they each won four elections).

COALITION AGREEMENT WITH SOCIAL DEMOCRATS

At the start of her third term, Merkel needed to find a coalition partner given that the CDU-CSU had fallen short of the overall majority required to pass legislation comfortably. Of the three other parties in parliament with which she could potentially partner, *Die Linke*, many of whose members support communist policies, was never a viable option given how far apart their political ideologies were. A CDU-CSU coalition with the Greens was a possibility. However, the Greens were wary of entering such a partnership given what had just happened to the FDP, the small coalition partner that was eviscerated at the polls after four years of coalition government with Merkel. It soon became apparent that the only workable option was a grand coalition of the CDU-CSU and the SPD.

The negotiations between these two parties to agree on a policy agenda for the next four years took five weeks, longer than for any government formed since World War II. Merkel's main interlocutor from the SPD was the party's chair, Sigmar Gabriel. One of the most debated topics was the SPD's demand that a nationwide minimum wage of €8.50 be introduced. In the end, Merkel agreed to this demand and the minimum wage is due to take effect from January 2015. Another important area where Merkel gave ground was pensions, where she agreed to lower the retirement age from sixty-five to sixty-three years for those Germans who had paid social security contributions for forty-five years. However, she resisted the SPD's calls for tax increases. The coalition agreement maintained some policies from the previous government, notably the commitment to phase out the use of nuclear energy and to increase the amount of renewable energy that Germany produces, in particular solar energy. In addition, the new government pledged to maintain Germany's broadly pro-EU stance, including supporting the euro and bailouts for the troubled eurozone members. On immigration policy, the parties agreed to offer dual citizenship for Turks and other immigrants who were born and raised in Germany. The Prime Minister of Bavaria, Horst Seehofer, got a commitment that the new government would institute a highway toll on foreign motorists, with the proviso that the toll had to be compatible with EU law.

The grand coalition deal, which ran to 185 pages, was signed by the party leaders on November 27. It received the final necessary stamp of approval when the members of the SPD voted on December 14 to endorse the deal. Merkel was confirmed as German Chancellor on December 17 by the Bundestag, with 462 parliamentarians out of 631 voting for her. Her new cabinet consisted of ten CDU-CSU members and six SPD members. It contained some familiar faces. The incumbent finance minister Wolfgang Schauble kept his job. Schauble was the architect of the so-called austerity policies that reduced public spending during the economy crisis to keep the deficit and debt under control. The new foreign minister was the SPD's Frank-Walter Steinmeier, who had previously held this post in the 2005–2009 grand coalition government. Other prominent appointees included Ursula von der Leyen as defense minister—the first time a woman in Germany has held this office—and Thomas de Maiziere as interior minister. The coalition agreement was welcomed by the German labor unions, although there were some grumblings from the business community, which was not so surprising given that the new government is more left-leaning than its predecessor.

—Brian Beary

Following are two press releases from the German Federal Returning Officer: the first, issued on September 23, 2013, includes information on the provisional result of the federal election, and the second, issued on October 9, 2013, includes the final election results; and the text of a German Federal Government press release dated December 17, 2013, announcing the reelection of Angela Merkel as chancellor.

Germany Releases Provisional Election Results

September 23, 2013

On 23 September 2013 at 3.15 a.m., the Federal Returning Officer released the official provisional result of the election to the 18th German Bundestag, which was held on 22 September 2013.

With a voter turnout of 71.5 percent (2009: 70.8 percent), the parties obtained the following shares of the total number of valid second votes:

- CDU	34.1 percent	(2009: 27,3 percent)
- SPD	25.7 percent	(2009: 23,0 percent)
- DIE LINKE	8.6 percent	(2009: 11,9 percent)
- GRÜNE	8.4 percent	(2009: 10,7 percent)
- CSU	7.4 percent	(2009: 6,5 percent)
- Sonstige [other]	15.7 percent	(2009: 6,0 percent)
darunter [among them]:		
FDP	4.8 percent	(2009: 14,6 percent)
AfD	4.7 percent	

The share of invalid second votes in the 2013 Bundestag election was 1.3 percent (2009: 1.4 percent).

The share of invalid first votes in the 2013 Bundestag election was 1.6 percent (2009: 1.7 percent).

Pursuant to Section 1 (1) of the Federal Elections Act and subject to deviations resulting from the calculation method laid down in Section 6 of the Federal Elections Act, the Bundestag consists of 598 members. The newly elected Bundestag will comprise 630 members (2009: 622 members), including 28 additional seats.

According to the official provisional election result, the parties listed below have received the following numbers of mandates (including additional seats) in the 18th German Bundestag:

- CDU	255 seats	(2009: 194),	including 191 (2009: 173)	(2009: 173) constituency seats
- SPD	192 seats	(2009: 146),	including 58 (2009: 64)	(2009: 64) constituency seats
- DIE LINKE	64 seats	(2009: 76),	including 4 (2009: 16)	(2009: 16) constituency seats
- GRÜNE	63 seats	(2009: 68),	including 1 (2009: 1)	(2009: 1) constituency seats
- CSU	56 seats	(2009: 45),	including 45 (2009: 45)	(2009: 45) constituency seats

According to the official provisional election result, the 28 additional seats resulting from the provisions in Section 6 of the Federal Elections Act are distributed among the parties as follows:

- CDU	13 seats
- SPD	9 seats
- DIE LINKE	4 seats
- GRÜNE	2 seats
- CSU	0 seats

. . . The Federal Returning Officer expresses his warmest thanks to the more than 600,000 voluntary workers in the electoral boards. "Your work has been a significant contribution to the successful conduct of the 2013 Bundestag election and you have done a good service to democracy." Special thanks also go to the several thousand workers in the electoral offices, administrative agencies and in the Deutsche Post AG postal services who kept the election process running smoothly.

The Federal Electoral Committee will presumably determine and announce the official final result of the 2013 Bundestag election on Wednesday, 9 October 2013, at a public meeting in the German Bundestag in Berlin.

Source: German Federal Returning Officer. "Official provisional result of the 2013 Bundestag election." September 23, 2013. http://www.bundeswahlleiter.de/en/bundestagswahlen/BTW_BUND_13/ presse/031p13_Vorlaeufiges_amtliches_Ergebnis.html.

Final German Election Results Released

October 9, 2013

In its meeting today, the Federal Electoral Committee has determined the final result of the election to the 18th German Bundestag. Then the Federal Returning Officer has announced the final election result in the Europasaal of the Paul-Löbe building of the German Bundestag in Berlin.

With voter turnout at 71.5 percent (2009: 70.8 percent), the political parties obtained the following shares in the total number of valid second votes:

- CDU:	34.1 percent	(2009: 27.3 percent)
- SPD:	25.7 percent	(2009: 23.0 percent)
- DIE LINKE:	8.6 percent	(2009: 11.9 percent)
- GRÜNE:	8.4 percent	(2009: 10.7 percent)
- CSU:	7.4 percent	(2009: 6.5 percent)
- Sonstige mit [others with] FDP:	15.7 percent	
- FDP:	4.8 percent	(2009: 14.6 percent)
- Sonstige ohne [others without] FDP:	10.9 percent	(2009: 6.0 percent)

The share of invalid second votes was 1.3 percent (2009: 1.4 percent) and the share of invalid first votes was 1.5 percent (2009: 1.7 percent). Compared with the provisional election result, only the share of invalid first votes was down by 0.1 percentage points.

The other parties (not including the FDP) obtained the following shares of second votes (order by number of votes obtained):

- AfD:	4.7 percent	(2009: did not participate)
- Piraten:	2.2 percent	(2009: 2.0 percent)
- NPD:	1.3 percent	(2009: 1.5 percent)
- FREIE Wähler:	1.0 percent	(2009: did not participate)
- Tierschutzpartei:	0.3 percent	(2009: 0.5 percent)
- ÖDP:	0.3 percent	(2009: 0.3 percent)
- REP:	0.2 percent	(2009: 0.4 percent)

(Continued)

(Continued)

- DIE PARTEI:	0.2 percent	(2009: did not participate)
- pro Deutschland:	0.2 percent	(2009: did not participate)
- BP:	0.1 percent	(2009: 0.1 percent)
- Volksabstimmung:	0.1 percent	(2009: 0.1 percent)
- RENTNER:	0.1 percent	(2009: 0.1 percent)
- PARTEI DER VERNUNFT:	0.1 percent	(2009: did not participate)
- MLPD:	0.1 percent	(2009: 0.1 percent)
- PBC:	0.0 percent	(2009: 0.1 percent)
- BIG:	0.0 percent	(2009: did not participate)
- BüSo:	0.0 percent	(2009: 0.1 percent)
- DIE FRAUEN:	0.0 percent	(2009: did not participate)
- Partei der Nichtwähler:	0.0 percent	(2009: did not participate)
- Bündnis 21/RRP:	0.0 percent	(2009: 0.2 percent)
- DIE VIOLETTEN:	0.0 percent	(2009: 0.1 percent)
- FAMILIE:	0.0 percent	(2009: 0.3 percent)
- PSG:	0.0 percent	(2009: 0.0 percent)
- DIE RECHTE:	0.0 percent	(2009: did not participate)

Pursuant to Section 1 subsection 1 in conjunction with Section 6 of the Federal Elections Act, the newly elected Bundestag will have a total of 631 members (2009: 622).

In accordance with the official final election result, the parties listed below will be represented with the following numbers of mandates in the 18th German Bundestag:

- CDU:	255 seats	(2009: 194)	including 64	(2009: 21)	national list seats
- SPD:	193 seats	(2009: 146)	including 135	(2009: 82)	national list seats
- DIE LINKE:	64 seats	(2009: 76)	including 60	(2009: 60)	national list seats
- GRÜNE:	63 seats	(2009: 68)	including 62	(2009: 67)	national list seats
- CSU:	56 seats	(2009: 45)	including 11	(2009: 0)	national list seats

Compared with the provisional result, the SPD wins another seat.

[Websites and information on how to obtain a printed copy of results have been omitted.]

SOURCE: German Federal Returning Officer. "Official final result of the 2013 Bundestag Election." October 9, 2013. http://www.bundeswahlleiter.de/en/bundestagswahlen/BTW_BUND_13/presse/034w13_Endgueltiges_amtliches_Ergebnis.html.

DOCUMENT   *Angela Merkel Reelected*

December 17, 2013

. . . Angela Merkel has now been elected Chancellor for her third consecutive term of office, after her previous elections in 2005 and 2009. 621 of the 631 members of the German Bundestag cast their vote. Angela Merkel was the choice of the so-called 'chancellor majority,' i.e. the absolute majority of members of the German Bundestag, in the first round of voting.

Letter of appointment from the Federal President

At Schloss Bellevue, the Chancellor received her letter of appointment from Federal President Joachim Gauck.

Thereafter she was sworn in by Bundestag President Norbert Lammert in the Bundestag in line with Article 56 of the German Basic Law or constitution.

The Chancellor took the following oath, "I swear that I will dedicate my efforts to the well-being of the German people, promote their welfare, protect them from harm, uphold and defend the Basic Law and the laws of the Federation, perform my duties conscientiously, and do justice to all. So help me God."

Following the swearing in, the new Cabinet ministers will also receive their letters of appointment at the Office of the Federal President and will be sworn in before the German Bundestag. SPD Party Chair Sigmar Gabriel will be Vice-Chancellor and Federal Minister of Economics and Energy . . .

Source: The Press and Information Office of the German Federal Government. "Angela Merkel re-elected Chancellor." December 17, 2013. http://www.bundesregierung.de/Content/EN/Artikel/2013/12/2013-12-17-bundeskanzlerin-wiedergewaehlt.html?nn=393830.

OTHER HISTORIC DOCUMENTS OF INTEREST

From this volume

From previous *Historic Documents*

Intergovernmental Panel on Climate Change Releases Report on Greenhouse Gases

SEPTEMBER 27, 2013

Every four or five years, the United Nations' climate change group releases a new report on the worsening state of the atmosphere and how climate change impacts our world. The report serves as a basis for international climate change and carbon emission negotiations. In 2013, the group increased the likelihood that humans are the key culprit behind climate change to "extremely likely." Such a declaration, coupled with the scientific data showing rising sea levels, increasing global temperatures, and the extinction of animal and plant species, served as a call-to-action for a number of environment-oriented organizations and Western countries, while climate change skeptics poked holes in the data in an attempt to prove that climate change is not as dire as the United Nations predicts.

IPCC RELEASES NEW CLIMATE CHANGE REPORT

When the United Nation's Intergovernmental Panel on Climate Change (IPCC) publishes its regular study on global warming, its data is the work of thousands of researchers and scientists from around the world. The study looks at the causes of climate change, the impact on global temperatures, sea levels, and carbon levels, among other things. The 2013 study was the fifth of its kind. The first portion of the report was released on September 27, 2013, with an abbreviated handbook for policymakers intended to be used to help drive global environmental decisions in the coming years. The remaining three sections of the report will be released in March, April, and October 2014, and will cover the impact of climate change and attempts at mitigating its impact.

The first IPCC report was released in 1990 and was used as a starting point for the United Nations Framework Convention on Climate Change (UNFCCC), which was charged with developing a global emissions framework. The first report noted with great certainty that carbon dioxide emissions contribute to the greenhouse effect and that human activities can increase the level of carbon dioxide in the atmosphere. The fourth report, released in 2007, noted a 90 percent, or "very likely," chance that humans were the leading cause of climate change. According to that report, activities like driving cars, increasing industrial production, deforestation, and running coal- and oil-fired power plants were to blame for a 1° Fahrenheit rise in global temperatures since preindustrial times and an increasing number of extreme weather events.

The 2,500 page 2013 report raised the opinion of scientists that humans are behind global temperature increases from "very likely" to "extremely likely" stating that there is a 95 to 100 percent chance that people are responsible for the climate change that has been occurring since the 1950s. "Human influence has been detected in warming of the atmosphere and the ocean, in changes in the global water cycle, in reductions in snow and ice, in global mean sea level rise, and in changes in some climate extremes," according to the report. "It is extremely likely that human influence has been the dominant cause of the observed warming since the mid-20th century." The new estimates made in the 2013 report were significant. "At 90 percent it means there is a 10 percent probability that it's not entirely correct," said Christopher Field who is a leader at the IPCC, but who was not involved with this report. He continued, "Now that's 5 percent. So it's a doubling of our confidence. That's actually a consequential change in our level of understanding." According to the IPCC, it is not surprising that their estimate of the human impact has grown with each report because the science of studying climate change is constantly changing as new and better techniques and analysis are available.

Of the overall 2013 report, co-chair Qin Dahe said, "Our assessment of the science finds that the atmosphere and ocean have warmed, the amount of snow and ice has diminished, the global mean sea level has risen and the concentrations of greenhouse gases have increased." Some of the predictions in the 2013 report included a rise in sea levels of between ten and thirty-two inches by 2100, marking an increase from the seven to twenty-three inches predicted in the 2007 report. The sea level increase will be led by the near complete melting of the Arctic ice cap. The report also predicted a global temperature rise of somewhere between 2.7 to 8.1 degrees Fahrenheit by 2100, a decrease from the 2007 prediction of 3.6 to 8.1 degrees. The latter point is highly debated by scientists who think that the panel that developed the report was too conservative in their estimate of temperature rise if the carbon dioxide level in the atmosphere doubles, as it is expected to on its current trajectory.

REPORT SERVES AS ANOTHER CALL TO ACTION

The IPCC reports are intended to be used by the UNFCCC, the international group charged with creating a new UN climate change deal by 2015. "This new report will be essential for Governments as they work to finalize an ambitious, legal agreement on climate change in 2015," said UN Secretary General Ban Ki-moon. "The goal is to generate the political commitment to keep global temperature rise below the agreed 2-degree Celsius threshold." After a 2 degrees Celsius rise over preindustrial temperatures, climate scientists believe the worst impacts of climate change will begin to kick in—more intense hurricanes, severe drought and wildfires, and deadly storms.

The panel working on the agreement will use both the IPCC report to determine how significantly carbon dioxide emissions should be cut and where national emission targets should be set. The necessity of forming a global climate change agreement was hastened by the expiration of the Kyoto Protocol in 2011. That agreement was temporarily extended to allow a new one to be drafted, but negotiations have been slow and it remains to be seen whether nations like the United States, which was not a Kyoto Protocol signatory, will join the new agreement. (The United States failed to join Kyoto in 1997, because it did not believe the carbon limits on newly developing nations were strong enough.) The approval of the United States is considered key to bringing rapidly industrializing nations like China onboard. Currently, the increase in global emissions is led by nations like China that, as they have grown, have not put their own internal caps on carbon emissions, arguing that such a cap would hinder development. China has also been vocal in its opinion that Western nations should bear greater responsibility for cutting emissions because they have emitted carbon for a longer period of time.

The scientists tasked with developing the 2013 IPCC report recommended that a global "carbon budget" be created, possibly as a portion of the new UNFCCC agreement. This budget would put a cap on how much carbon dioxide can be produced. To keep global warming below the 2 degrees Celsius target outlined by the United Nations, no more than one trillion metric tons of carbon dioxide could be burned. Since the start of the Industrial Revolution in the 18th Century, more than a half trillion tons have been burned. If energy usage were to continue on its current upward trajectory, the trillionth ton will be burned around 2040. After this point, the IPCC report authors suggest that companies that continue burning fossil fuels must come up with a method for trapping and storing the carbon dioxide byproduct underground.

The administration of President Barack Obama has already suggested a plan that would mimic the IPCC recommendations, which has attracted backlash from Republicans and energy companies that accuse the president of a "war on coal." Secretary of State John Kerry said the report should serve as a call to action. "Those who deny the science or choose excuses over action are playing with fire," Kerry said. "Once again, the science grows clearer, the case grows more compelling, and the costs of inaction grow beyond anything that anyone with conscience or common sense should be willing to even contemplate."

REMAINING QUESTIONS AND DOUBTS

In the environmental science world, "extremely likely" is considered the gold standard of probability, but the scientists working on the report admitted that their opinion is not conclusive and that there are still some uncertainties surrounding climate change. The remaining questions include how quickly the human aspect of climate change might impact things like rising ocean levels, global temperature, and the extinction of plants and animals. Regardless, the IPCC said the best method for overcoming these uncertainties was to find ways to reduce carbon emissions.

Climate change skeptics disagreed and used the uncertainties of the report to embolden their cause. For example, the 2013 report showed a slowdown of global temperature rise over the past fifteen years. Despite the scientific evidence proving that the past ten years have been the warmest on record, skeptics consider the slowdown as proof that the concept of climate change might not be iron clad. Even a slow increase of a few tenths of a degree "would not represent a climate crisis," said The Heartland Institute, a conservative and libertarian think tank. Because temperatures can vary widely from year to year, the 2013 report did not focus too much on this piece of data. "An old rule says that climate-relevant trends should not be calculated for periods less than around 30 years," said the report's co-chair, Thomas Stocker. Climate scientists—both those who did and did not work on the report—said that there are a number of reasons why the 2013 report showed a slowing of temperature rise, including a temporary settling of ocean temperatures and a baseline year (1998) that was unusually high. "People think that global warming means every year is going to be warmer than the year before," said Gerald Meehl, an American scientist who worked on the IPCC report. But, Meehl said, "It's more like a stair-step kind of thing."

DEEPENING IMPACT OF CLIMATE CHANGE

The head of the World Meteorological Organization (WMO), Michel Jarraud, said the IPCC report "should serve as yet another wake-up call that our activities today will have a profound impact on society, not only for us, but for many generations to come." The WMO has been a leading voice in the climate change debate, using the increasing number of extreme weather events as proof that it is time for the world to take action to limit carbon emissions.

According to the report, the extreme weather events that used to be considered "storms of the century" are now happening more frequently, less than every twenty years. If carbon emissions continue status quo, the situation will worsen, meaning the world will experience more deadly typhoons like that in the Philippines in late 2013, EF5 tornadoes like those that have ripped through the Midwestern United States over the past few years, and worsening droughts and stronger floods like those experienced in the Western United States.

—Heather Kerrigan

The following is an edited version of the report released on September 27, 2013, by the Intergovernmental Panel on Climate Change regarding the human impact on climate change and the necessity for a ceiling on global emissions.

IPCC Releases
Climate Change Findings

September 27, 2013

[A listing of report authors has been omitted.]

[All charts and graphs, and references to them, have been omitted; all footnotes have been omitted as well.]

A. INTRODUCTION

The Working Group I contribution to the IPCC's Fifth Assessment Report (AR5) considers new evidence of climate change based on many independent scientific analyses from observations of the climate system, paleoclimate archives, theoretical studies of climate processes and simulations using climate models. It builds upon the Working Group I contribution to the IPCC's Fourth Assessment Report (AR4), and incorporates subsequent new findings of research. As a component of the fifth assessment cycle, the IPCC Special Report on Managing the Risks of Extreme Events and Disasters to Advance Climate Change Adaptation (SREX) is an important basis for information on changing weather and climate extremes.

This Summary for Policymakers (SPM) follows the structure of the Working Group I report. The narrative is supported by a series of overarching highlighted conclusions which, taken together, provide a concise summary. Main sections are introduced with a brief paragraph in italics which outlines the methodological basis of the assessment.

The degree of certainty in key findings in this assessment is based on the author teams' evaluations of underlying scientific understanding and is expressed as a qualitative level of confidence (from *very low* to *very high*) and, when possible, probabilistically with a quantified likelihood (from *exceptionally unlikely* to *virtually certain*). Confidence in the validity of a finding is based on the type, amount, quality, and consistency of evidence (e.g., data, mechanistic understanding, theory, models, expert judgment) and the degree of agreement. Probabilistic estimates of quantified measures of uncertainty in a finding are based on statistical analysis of observations or model results, or both, and expert judgment. Where appropriate, findings are also formulated as statements of fact without using uncertainty qualifiers . . .

B. Observed Changes in the Climate System

Observations of the climate system are based on direct measurements and remote sensing from satellites and other platforms. Global-scale observations from the instrumental era began in the mid-19th century for temperature and other variables, with more comprehensive and diverse sets of observations available for the period 1950 onwards. Paleoclimate reconstructions extend some records back hundreds to millions of years. Together, they provide a comprehensive view of the variability and long-term changes in the atmosphere, the ocean, the cryosphere, and the land surface.

> Warming of the climate system is unequivocal, and since the 1950s, many of the observed changes are unprecedented over decades to millennia. The atmosphere and ocean have warmed, the amounts of snow and ice have diminished, sea level has risen, and the concentrations of greenhouse gases have increased.

B.1 Atmosphere

> Each of the last three decades has been successively warmer at the Earth's surface than any preceding decade since 1850. In the Northern Hemisphere, 1983–2012 was *likely* the warmest 30-year period of the last 1400 years (*medium confidence*).

- The globally averaged combined land and ocean surface temperature data as calculated by a linear trend, show a warming of 0.85 [0.65 to 1.06] °C, over the period 1880 to 2012, when multiple independently produced datasets exist. The total increase between the average of the 1850–1900 period and the 2003–2012 period is 0.78 [0.72 to 0.85] °C, based on the single longest dataset available.
- For the longest period when calculation of regional trends is sufficiently complete (1901 to 2012), almost the entire globe has experienced surface warming.
- In addition to robust multi-decadal warming, global mean surface temperature exhibits substantial decadal and interannual variability. Due to natural variability, trends based on short records are very sensitive to the beginning and end dates and do not in general reflect long-term climate trends. As one example, the rate of warming over the past 15 years (1998–2012; 0.05 [−0.05 to 0.15] °C per decade), which begins with a strong El Niño, is smaller than the rate calculated since 1951 (1951–2012; 0.12 [0.08 to 0.14] °C per decade).
- Continental-scale surface temperature reconstructions show, with *high confidence,* multi-decadal periods during the Medieval Climate Anomaly (year 950 to 1250)

that were in some regions as warm as in the late 20th century. These regional warm periods did not occur as coherently across regions as the warming in the late 20th century (*high confidence*).

- It is *virtually certain* that globally the troposphere has warmed since the mid-20th century. More complete observations allow greater confidence in estimates of tropospheric temperature changes in the extratropical Northern Hemisphere than elsewhere. There is *medium confidence* in the rate of warming and its vertical structure in the Northern Hemisphere extra-tropical troposphere and *low confidence* elsewhere.

- *Confidence* in precipitation change averaged over global land areas since 1901 is *low* prior to 1951 and *medium* afterwards. Averaged over the mid-latitude land areas of the Northern Hemisphere, precipitation has increased since 1901 (*medium confidence* before and *high confidence* after 1951). For other latitudes area-averaged long-term positive or negative trends have *low confidence.*

- Changes in many extreme weather and climate events have been observed since about 1950. It is *very likely* that the number of cold days and nights has decreased and the number of warm days and nights has increased on the global scale. It is *likely* that the frequency of heat waves has increased in large parts of Europe, Asia and Australia. There are *likely* more land regions where the number of heavy precipitation events has increased than where it has decreased. The frequency or intensity of heavy precipitation events has *likely* increased in North America and Europe. In other continents, *confidence* in changes in heavy precipitation events is at most *medium.*

B.2 Ocean

> Ocean warming dominates the increase in energy stored in the climate system, accounting for more than 90% of the energy accumulated between 1971 and 2010 (*high confidence*). It is *virtually certain* that the upper ocean (0–700 m) warmed from 1971 to 2010, and it *likely* warmed between the 1870s and 1971.

- On a global scale, the ocean warming is largest near the surface, and the upper 75 m warmed by 0.11 [0.09 to 0.13] °C per decade over the period 1971 to 2010. Since AR4, instrumental biases in upper-ocean temperature records have been identified and reduced, enhancing confidence in the assessment of change.

- It is *likely* that the ocean warmed between 700 and 2000 m from 1957 to 2009. Sufficient observations are available for the period 1992 to 2005 for a global assessment of temperature change below 2000 m. There were *likely* no significant observed temperature trends between 2000 and 3000 m for this period. It is *likely* that the ocean warmed from 3000 m to the bottom for this period, with the largest warming observed in the Southern Ocean.

- More than 60% of the net energy increase in the climate system is stored in the upper ocean (0–700 m) during the relatively well-sampled 40-year period from 1971 to 2010, and about 30% is stored in the ocean below 700 m. The increase in upper ocean heat content during this time period estimated from a linear trend is *likely* 17 [15 to 19] $\times 10^{22}$ J.

- It is *about as likely* as not that ocean heat content from 0–700 m increased more slowly during 2003 to 2010 than during 1993 to 2002. Ocean heat uptake from

700–2000 m, where interannual variability is smaller, *likely* continued unabated from 1993 to 2009.

- It is *very likely* that regions of high salinity where evaporation dominates have become more saline, while regions of low salinity where precipitation dominates have become fresher since the 1950s. These regional trends in ocean salinity provide indirect evidence that evaporation and precipitation over the oceans have changed (*medium confidence*).
- There is no observational evidence of a trend in the Atlantic Meridional Overturning Circulation (AMOC), based on the decade-long record of the complete AMOC and longer records of individual AMOC components.

B.3 Cryosphere

Over the last two decades, the Greenland and Antarctic ice sheets have been losing mass, glaciers have continued to shrink almost worldwide, and Arctic sea ice and Northern Hemisphere spring snow cover have continued to decrease in extent (*high confidence*).

- The average rate of ice loss from glaciers around the world, excluding glaciers on the periphery of the ice sheets, was *very likely* 226 [91 to 361] Gt yr^{-1} over the period 1971 to 2009, and *very likely* 275 [140 to 410] Gt yr^{-1} over the period 1993 to 2009.
- The average rate of ice loss from the Greenland ice sheet has *very likely* substantially increased from 34 [–6 to 74] Gt yr^{-1} over the period 1992 to 2001 to 215 [157 to 274] Gt yr^{-1} over the period 2002 to 2011.
- The average rate of ice loss from the Antarctic ice sheet has *likely* increased from 30 [–37 to 97] Gt yr^{-1} over the period 1992–2001 to 147 [72 to 221] Gt yr^{-1} over the period 2002 to 2011. There is *very high confidence* that these losses are mainly from the northern Antarctic Peninsula and the Amundsen Sea sector of West Antarctica.
- The annual mean Arctic sea ice extent decreased over the period 1979 to 2012 with a rate that was *very likely* in the range 3.5 to 4.1% per decade (range of 0.45 to 0.51 million km^2 per decade), and *very likely* in the range 9.4 to 13.6% per decade (range of 0.73 to 1.07 million km^2 per decade) for the summer sea ice minimum (perennial sea ice). The average decrease in decadal mean extent of Arctic sea ice has been most rapid in summer (*high confidence*); the spatial extent has decreased in every season, and in every successive decade since 1979 (*high confidence*). There is *medium confidence* from reconstructions that over the past three decades, Arctic summer sea ice retreat was unprecedented and sea surface temperatures were anomalously high in at least the last 1,450 years.
- It is *very likely* that the annual mean Antarctic sea ice extent increased at a rate in the range of 1.2 to 1.8% per decade (range of 0.13 to 0.20 million km^2 per decade) between 1979 and 2012. There is *high confidence* that there are strong regional differences in this annual rate, with extent increasing in some regions and decreasing in others.
- There is *very high confidence* that the extent of Northern Hemisphere snow cover has decreased since the mid-20th century. Northern Hemisphere snow cover extent decreased 1.6 [0.8 to 2.4] % per decade for March and April, and 11.7 [8.8 to 14.6] % per decade for June, over the 1967 to 2012 period. During this period, snow cover extent in the Northern Hemisphere did not show a statistically significant increase in any month.

- There is *high confidence* that permafrost temperatures have increased in most regions since the early 1980s. Observed warming was up to 3°C in parts of Northern Alaska (early 1980s to mid-2000s) and up to 2°C in parts of the Russian European North (1971 to 2010). In the latter region, a considerable reduction in permafrost thickness and areal extent has been observed over the period 1975 to 2005 (*medium confidence*).
- Multiple lines of evidence support very substantial Arctic warming since the mid-20th century.

B.4 Sea Level

The rate of sea level rise since the mid-19th century has been larger than the mean rate during the previous two millennia (*high confidence*). Over the period 1901 to 2010, global mean sea level rose by 0.19 [0.17 to 0.21] m.

- Proxy and instrumental sea level data indicate a transition in the late 19th to the early 20th century from relatively low mean rates of rise over the previous two millennia to higher rates of rise (*high confidence*). It is *likely* that the rate of global mean sea level rise has continued to increase since the early 20th century.
- It is very likely that the mean rate of global averaged sea level rise was 1.7 [1.5 to 1.9] mm yr^{-1} between 1901 and 2010, 2.0 [1.7 to 2.3] mm yr^{-1} between 1971 and 2010, and 3.2 [2.8 to 3.6] mm yr^{-1} between 1993 and 2010. Tide-gauge and satellite altimeter data are consistent regarding the higher rate of the latter period. It is *likely* that similarly high rates occurred between 1920 and 1950.
- Since the early 1970s, glacier mass loss and ocean thermal expansion from warming together explain about 75% of the observed global mean sea level rise (*high confidence*). Over the period 1993 to 2010, global mean sea level rise is, with *high confidence,* consistent with the sum of the observed contributions from ocean thermal expansion due to warming (1.1 [0.8 to 1.4] mm yr^{-1}), from changes in glaciers (0.76 [0.39 to 1.13] mm yr^{-1}), Greenland ice sheet (0.33 [0.25 to 0.41] mm yr^{-1}), Antarctic ice sheet (0.27 [0.16 to 0.38] mm yr^{-1}), and land water storage (0.38 [0.26 to 0.49] mm yr^{-1}). The sum of these contributions is 2.8 [2.3 to 3.4] mm yr^{-1}.
- There is *very high confidence* that maximum global mean sea level during the last interglacial period (129,000 to 116,000 years ago) was, for several thousand years, at least 5 m higher than present, and *high confidence* that it did not exceed 10 m above present. During the last interglacial period, the Greenland ice sheet *very likely* contributed between 1.4 and 4.3 m to the higher global mean sea level, implying with *medium confidence* an additional contribution from the Antarctic ice sheet. This change in sea level occurred in the context of different orbital forcing and with high-latitude surface temperature, averaged over several thousand years, at least 2°C warmer than present (*high confidence*).

B.5 Carbon and Other Biogeochemical Cycles

The atmospheric concentrations of carbon dioxide, methane, and nitrous oxide have increased to levels unprecedented in at least the last 800,000 years. Carbon dioxide concentrations have increased by 40% since pre-industrial times, primarily from fossil fuel emissions and secondarily from net land use change emissions.

> The ocean has absorbed about 30% of the emitted anthropogenic carbon dioxide, causing ocean acidification.

- The atmospheric concentrations of the greenhouse gases carbon dioxide (CO_2), methane (CH_4), and nitrous oxide (N_2O) have all increased since 1750 due to human activity. In 2011 the concentrations of these greenhouse gases were 391 ppm, 1803 ppb, and 324 ppb, and exceeded the pre-industrial levels by about 40%, 150%, and 20%, respectively.
- Concentrations of CO_2, CH_4, and N_2O now substantially exceed the highest concentrations recorded in ice cores during the past 800,000 years. The mean rates of increase in atmospheric concentrations over the past century are, with *very high confidence*, unprecedented in the last 22,000 years.
- Annual CO_2 emissions from fossil fuel combustion and cement production were 8.3 [7.6 to 9.0] GtC[12] yr^{-1} averaged over 2002–2011 (*high confidence*) and were 9.5 [8.7 to 10.3] GtC yr^{-1} in 2011, 54% above the 1990 level. Annual net CO_2 emissions from anthropogenic land use change were 0.9 [0.1 to 1.7] GtC yr^{-1} on average during 2002 to 2011 (*medium confidence*).
- From 1750 to 2011, CO_2 emissions from fossil fuel combustion and cement production have released 375 [345 to 405] GtC to the atmosphere, while deforestation and other land use change are estimated to have released 180 [100 to 260] GtC. This results in cumulative anthropogenic emissions of 555 [470 to 640] GtC.
- Of these cumulative anthropogenic CO_2 emissions, 240 [230 to 250] GtC have accumulated in the atmosphere, 155 [125 to 185] GtC have been taken up by the ocean and 160 [70 to 250] GtC have accumulated in natural terrestrial ecosystems (i.e., the cumulative residual land sink).
- Ocean acidification is quantified by decreases in pH. The pH of ocean surface water has decreased by 0.1 since the beginning of the industrial era (*high confidence*), corresponding to a 26% increase in hydrogen ion concentration.

C. Drivers of Climate Change

. . . Total radiative forcing [RF] is positive, and has led to an uptake of energy by the climate system. The largest contribution to total radiative forcing is caused by the increase in the atmospheric concentration of CO_2 since 1750.

- The total anthropogenic RF for 2011 relative to 1750 is 2.29 [1.13 to 3.33] W m^{-2}, and it has increased more rapidly since 1970 than during prior decades. The total anthropogenic RF best estimate for 2011 is 43% higher than that reported in AR4 for the year 2005. This is caused by a combination of continued growth in most greenhouse gas concentrations and improved estimates of RF by aerosols indicating a weaker net cooling effect (negative RF).
- The RF from emissions of well-mixed greenhouse gases (CO_2, CH_4, N_2O, and Halocarbons) for 2011 relative to 1750 is 3.00 [2.22 to 3.78] W m^{-2}. The RF from changes in concentrations in these gases is 2.83 [2.26 to 3.40] W m^{-2}.
- Emissions of CO_2 alone have caused an RF of 1.68 [1.33 to 2.03] W m^{-2}. Including emissions of other carbon-containing gases, which also contributed to the increase in CO_2 concentrations, the RF of CO_2 is 1.82 [1.46 to 2.18] W m^{-2}.

- Emissions of CH_4 alone have caused an RF of 0.97 [0.74 to 1.20] W m^{-2}. This is much larger than the concentration-based estimate of 0.48 [0.38 to 0.58] W m^{-2} (unchanged from AR4). This difference in estimates is caused by concentration changes in ozone and stratospheric water vapour due to CH_4 emissions and other emissions indirectly affecting CH_4.

- Emissions of stratospheric ozone-depleting halocarbons have caused a net positive RF of 0.18 [0.01 to 0.35] W m^{-2}. Their own positive RF has outweighed the negative RF from the ozone depletion that they have induced. The positive RF from all halocarbons is similar to the value in AR4, with a reduced RF from CFCs but increases from many of their substitutes.

- Emissions of short-lived gases contribute to the total anthropogenic RF. Emissions of carbon monoxide (CO) are *virtually certain* to have induced a positive RF, while emissions of nitrogen oxides (NO_x) are *likely* to have induced a net negative RF.

- The RF of the total aerosol effect in the atmosphere, which includes cloud adjustments due to aerosols, is –0.9 [–1.9 to –0.1] W m^{-2} (*medium confidence*), and results from a negative forcing from most aerosols and a positive contribution from black carbon absorption of solar radiation. There is *high confidence* that aerosols and their interactions with clouds have offset a substantial portion of global mean forcing from well-mixed greenhouse gases. They continue to contribute the largest uncertainty to the total RF estimate.

- The forcing from stratospheric volcanic aerosols can have a large impact on the climate for some years after volcanic eruptions. Several small eruptions have caused an RF of –0.11 [–0.15 to –0.08] W m^{-2} for the years 2008 to 2011, which is approximately twice as strong as during the years 1999 to 2002.

- The RF due to changes in solar irradiance is estimated as 0.05 [0.00 to 0.10] W m^{-2}. Satellite observations of total solar irradiance changes from 1978 to 2011 indicate that the last solar minimum was lower than the previous two. This results in an RF of –0.04 [–0.08 to 0.00] W m^{-2} between the most recent minimum in 2008 and the 1986 minimum.

- The total natural RF from solar irradiance changes and stratospheric volcanic aerosols made only a small contribution to the net radiative forcing throughout the last century, except for brief periods after large volcanic eruptions.

D. Understanding the Climate System and its Recent Changes

... Human influence on the climate system is clear. This is evident from the increasing greenhouse gas concentrations in the atmosphere, positive radiative forcing, observed warming, and understanding of the climate system.

[The sections on evaluating climate models and quantifying climate system responses have been omitted.]

D.3 Detection and Attribution of Climate Change

Human influence has been detected in warming of the atmosphere and the ocean, in changes in the global water cycle, in reductions in snow and ice, in global mean sea level rise, and in changes in some climate extremes. This evidence for human influence has grown since AR4. It is *extremely likely* that human influence has been the dominant cause of the observed warming since the mid-20th century.

- It is *extremely likely* that more than half of the observed increase in global average surface temperature from 1951 to 2010 was caused by the anthropogenic increase in greenhouse gas concentrations and other anthropogenic forcings together. The best estimate of the human-induced contribution to warming is similar to the observed warming over this period.

- Greenhouse gases contributed a global mean surface warming *likely* to be in the range of 0.5°C to 1.3°C over the period 1951 to 2010, with the contributions from other anthropogenic forcings, including the cooling effect of aerosols, *likely* to be in the range of −0.6°C to 0.1°C. The contribution from natural forcings is *likely* to be in the range of −0.1°C to 0.1°C, and from natural internal variability is *likely* to be in the range of −0.1°C to 0.1°C. Together these assessed contributions are consistent with the observed warming of approximately 0.6°C to 0.7°C over this period.

- Over every continental region except Antarctica, anthropogenic forcings have *likely* made a substantial contribution to surface temperature increases since the mid-20th century. For Antarctica, large observational uncertainties result in low *confidence* that anthropogenic forcings have contributed to the observed warming averaged over available stations. It is *likely* that there has been an anthropogenic contribution to the very substantial Arctic warming since the mid-20th century.

- It is *very likely* that anthropogenic influence, particularly greenhouse gases and stratospheric ozone depletion, has led to a detectable observed pattern of tropospheric warming and a corresponding cooling in the lower stratosphere since 1961.

- It is *very likely* that anthropogenic forcings have made a substantial contribution to increases in global upper ocean heat content (0–700 m) observed since the 1970s. There is evidence for human influence in some individual ocean basins.

- It is *likely* that anthropogenic influences have affected the global water cycle since 1960. Anthropogenic influences have contributed to observed increases in atmospheric moisture content in the atmosphere (*medium confidence*), to global-scale changes in precipitation patterns over land (*medium confidence*), to intensification of heavy precipitation over land regions where data are sufficient (*medium confidence*), and to changes in surface and sub-surface ocean salinity (*very likely*).

- There has been further strengthening of the evidence for human influence on temperature extremes since the SREX. It is now *very likely* that human influence has contributed to observed global scale changes in the frequency and intensity of daily temperature extremes since the mid-20th century, and *likely* that human influence has more than doubled the probability of occurrence of heat waves in some locations.

- Anthropogenic influences have *very likely* contributed to Arctic sea ice loss since 1979. There is *low confidence* in the scientific understanding of the small observed increase in Antarctic sea ice extent due to the incomplete and competing scientific explanations for the causes of change and *low confidence* in estimates of natural internal variability in that region.

- Anthropogenic influences *likely* contributed to the retreat of glaciers since the 1960s and to the increased surface mass loss of the Greenland ice sheet since 1993. Due to a low level of scientific understanding there is *low confidence* in attributing the causes of the observed loss of mass from the Antarctic ice sheet over the past two decades.

- It is *likely* that there has been an anthropogenic contribution to observed reductions in Northern Hemisphere spring snow cover since 1970.
- It is *very likely* that there is a substantial anthropogenic contribution to the global mean sea level rise since the 1970s. This is based on the *high confidence* in an anthropogenic influence on the two largest contributions to sea level rise, that is thermal expansion and glacier mass loss.
- There is *high confidence* that changes in total solar irradiance have not contributed to the increase in global mean surface temperature over the period 1986 to 2008, based on direct satellite measurements of total solar irradiance. There is *medium* confidence that the 11-year cycle of solar variability influences decadal climate fluctuations in some regions. No robust association between changes in cosmic rays and cloudiness has been identified.

E. Future Global and Regional Climate Change

Projections of changes in the climate system are made using a hierarchy of climate models ranging from simple climate models, to models of intermediate complexity, to comprehensive climate models, and Earth System Models. These models simulate changes based on a set of scenarios of anthropogenic forcings. A new set of scenarios, the Representative Concentration Pathways (RCPs), was used for the new climate model simulations carried out under the framework of the Coupled Model Intercomparison Project Phase 5 (CMIP5) of the World Climate Research Programme. In all RCPs, atmospheric CO_2 concentrations are higher in 2100 relative to present day as a result of a further increase of cumulative emissions of CO_2 to the atmosphere during the 21st century. Projections in this Summary for Policymakers are for the end of the 21st century (2081–2100) given relative to 1986–2005, unless otherwise stated. To place such projections in historical context, it is necessary to consider observed changes between different periods. Based on the longest global surface temperature dataset available, the observed change between the average of the period 1850– 1900 and of the AR5 reference period is 0.61 [0.55 to 0.67] °C. However, warming has occurred beyond the average of the AR5 reference period. Hence this is not an estimate of historical warming to present.

> Continued emissions of greenhouse gases will cause further warming and changes in all components of the climate system. Limiting climate change will require substantial and sustained reductions of greenhouse gas emissions.

- Projections for the next few decades show spatial patterns of climate change similar to those projected for the later 21st century but with smaller magnitude. Natural internal variability will continue to be a major influence on climate, particularly in the near-term and at the regional scale. By the mid-21st century the magnitudes of the projected changes are substantially affected by the choice of emissions scenario.
- Projected climate change based on RCPs is similar to AR4 in both patterns and magnitude, after accounting for scenario differences. The overall spread of projections for the high RCPs is narrower than for comparable scenarios used in AR4 because in contrast to the SRES emission scenarios used in AR4, the RCPs used in AR5 are defined as concentration pathways and thus carbon cycle uncertainties affecting atmospheric CO_2 concentrations are not considered in the concentration-driven CMIP5 simulations. Projections of sea level rise are larger than in the AR4, primarily because of improved modelling of land-ice contributions.

E.1 ATMOSPHERE: TEMPERATURE

Global surface temperature change for the end of the 21st century is *likely* to exceed 1.5°C relative to 1850 to 1900 for all RCP scenarios except RCP2.6. It is *likely* to exceed 2°C for RCP6.0 and RCP8.5, and *more likely than not* to exceed 2°C for RCP4.5. Warming will continue beyond 2100 under all RCP scenarios except RCP2.6. Warming will continue to exhibit interannual-to-decadal variability and will not be regionally uniform.

- The global mean surface temperature change for the period 2016–2035 relative to 1986–2005 will *likely* be in the range of 0.3°C to 0.7°C (*medium confidence*). This assessment is based on multiple lines of evidence and assumes there will be no major volcanic eruptions or secular changes in total solar irradiance. Relative to natural internal variability, near-term increases in seasonal mean and annual mean temperatures are expected to be larger in the tropics and subtropics than in mid-latitudes (*high confidence*).
- Increase of global mean surface temperatures for 2081–2100 relative to 1986–2005 is projected to *likely* be in the ranges derived from the concentration-driven CMIP5 model simulations, that is, 0.3°C to 1.7°C (RCP2.6), 1.1°C to 2.6°C (RCP4.5), 1.4°C to 3.1°C (RCP6.0), 2.6°C to 4.8°C (RCP8.5). The Arctic region will warm more rapidly than the global mean, and mean warming over land will be larger than over the ocean (*very high confidence*).
- Relative to the average from year 1850 to 1900, global surface temperature change by the end of the 21st century is projected to *likely* exceed 1.5°C for RCP4.5, RCP6.0 and RCP8.5 (*high confidence*). Warming is *likely* to exceed 2°C for RCP6.0 and RCP8.5 (*high confidence*), *more likely than not* to exceed 2°C for RCP4.5 (*high confidence*), but *unlikely* to exceed 2°C for RCP2.6 (*medium confidence*). Warming is *unlikely* to exceed 4°C for RCP2.6, RCP4.5 and RCP6.0 (*high confidence*) and is *about as likely as not* to exceed 4°C for RCP8.5 (*medium confidence*).
- It is *virtually certain* that there will be more frequent hot and fewer cold temperature extremes over most land areas on daily and seasonal timescales as global mean temperatures increase. It is *very likely* that heat waves will occur with a higher frequency and duration. Occasional cold winter extremes will continue to occur . . . .

E.3 ATMOSPHERE: AIR QUALITY

- The range in projections of air quality (ozone and PM2.5 in near-surface air) is driven primarily by emissions (including CH_4), rather than by physical climate change (*medium confidence*). There is *high confidence* that globally, warming decreases background surface ozone. High CH_4 levels (as in RCP8.5) can offset this decrease, raising background surface ozone by year 2100 on average by about 8 ppb (25% of current levels) relative to scenarios with small CH_4 changes (as in RCP4.5 and RCP6.0) (*high confidence*).
- Observational and modelling evidence indicates that, all else being equal, locally higher surface temperatures in polluted regions will trigger regional feedbacks in

chemistry and local emissions that will increase peak levels of ozone and PM2.5 (*medium confidence*). For PM2.5, climate change may alter natural aerosol sources as well as removal by precipitation, but no confidence level is attached to the over-all impact of climate change on PM2.5 distributions.

E.4 OCEAN

> The global ocean will continue to warm during the 21st century. Heat will penetrate from the surface to the deep ocean and affect ocean circulation.

- The strongest ocean warming is projected for the surface in tropical and Northern Hemisphere subtropical regions. At greater depth the warming will be most pronounced in the Southern Ocean (*high confidence*). Best estimates of ocean warming in the top one hundred meters are about 0.6°C (RCP2.6) to 2.0°C (RCP8.5), and about 0.3°C (RCP2.6) to 0.6°C (RCP8.5) at a depth of about 1000 m by the end of the 21st century.
- It is *very likely* that the Atlantic Meridional Overturning Circulation (AMOC) will weaken over the 21st century. Best estimates and ranges for the reduction are 11% (1 to 24%) in RCP2.6 and 34% (12 to 54%) in RCP8.5. It is likely that there will be some decline in the AMOC by about 2050, but there may be some decades when the AMOC increases due to large natural internal variability.
- It is *very unlikely* that the AMOC will undergo an abrupt transition or collapse in the 21st century for the scenarios considered. There is *low confidence* in assessing the evolution of the AMOC beyond the 21st century because of the limited number of analyses and equivocal results. However, a collapse beyond the 21st century for large sustained warming cannot be excluded.

E.5 CRYOSPHERE

> It is very likely that the Arctic sea ice cover will continue to shrink and thin and that Northern Hemisphere spring snow cover will decrease during the 21st century as global mean surface temperature rises. Global glacier volume will further decrease.

- Year-round reductions in Arctic sea ice extent are projected by the end of the 21st century from multi-model averages. These reductions range from 43% for RCP2.6 to 94% for RCP8.5 in September and from 8% for RCP2.6 to 34% for RCP8.5 in February (*medium confidence*).
- Based on an assessment of the subset of models that most closely reproduce the climatological mean state and 1979 to 2012 trend of the Arctic sea ice extent, a nearly ice-free Arctic Ocean in September before mid-century is *likely* for RCP8.5 (*medium confidence*). A projection of when the Arctic might become nearly ice-free in September in the 21st century cannot be made with confidence for the other scenarios.
- In the Antarctic, a decrease in sea ice extent and volume is projected with *low confidence* for the end of the 21st century as global mean surface temperature rises.

- By the end of the 21st century, the global glacier volume, excluding glaciers on the periphery of Antarctica, is projected to decrease by 15 to 55% for RCP2.6, and by 35 to 85% for RCP8.5 (*medium confidence*)..
- The area of Northern Hemisphere spring snow cover is projected to decrease by 7% for RCP2.6 and by 25% in RCP8.5 by the end of the 21st century for the model average (*medium confidence*).
- It is *virtually certain* that near-surface permafrost extent at high northern latitudes will be reduced as global mean surface temperature increases. By the end of the 21st century, the area of permafrost near the surface (upper 3.5 m) is projected to decrease by between 37% (RCP2.6) to 81% (RCP8.5) for the model average (*medium confidence*).

E.6 SEA LEVEL

Global mean sea level will continue to rise during the 21st century. Under all RCP scenarios, the rate of sea level rise will *very likely* exceed that observed during 1971 to 2010 due to increased ocean warming and increased loss of mass from glaciers and ice sheets.

- Confidence in projections of global mean sea level rise has increased since the AR4 because of the improved physical understanding of the components of sea level, the improved agreement of process-based models with observations, and the inclusion of ice-sheet dynamical changes.
- Global mean sea level rise for 2081–2100 relative to 1986–2005 will likely be in the ranges of 0.26 to 0.55 m for RCP2.6, 0.32 to 0.63 m for RCP4.5, 0.33 to 0.63 m for RCP6.0, and 0.45 to 0.82 m for RCP8.5 (*medium confidence*). For RCP8.5, the rise by the year 2100 is 0.52 to 0.98 m, with a rate during 2081 to 2100 of 8 to 16 mm yr^{-1} (*medium confidence*). These ranges are derived from CMIP5 climate projections in combination with process-based models and literature assessment of glacier and ice sheet contributions.
- In the RCP projections, thermal expansion accounts for 30 to 55% of 21st century global mean sea level rise, and glaciers for 15 to 35%. The increase in surface melting of the Greenland ice sheet will exceed the increase in snowfall, leading to a positive contribution from changes in surface mass balance to future sea level (*high confidence*). While surface melting will remain small, an increase in snowfall on the Antarctic ice sheet is expected (*medium confidence*), resulting in a negative contribution to future sea level from changes in surface mass balance. Changes in outflow from both ice sheets combined will *likely* make a contribution in the range of 0.03 to 0.20 m by 2081–2100 (*medium confidence*).
- Based on current understanding, only the collapse of marine-based sectors of the Antarctic ice sheet, if initiated, could cause global mean sea level to rise substantially above the *likely* range during the 21st century. However, there is *medium confidence* that this additional contribution would not exceed several tenths of a meter of sea level rise during the 21st century.
- The basis for higher projections of global mean sea level rise in the 21st century has been considered and it has been concluded that there is currently insufficient evidence to evaluate the probability of specific levels above the assessed *likely* range. Many semi-empirical model projections of global mean sea level rise are higher

than process-based model projections (up to about twice as large), but there is no consensus in the scientific community about their reliability and there is thus *low confidence* in their projections.

- Sea level rise will not be uniform. By the end of the 21st century, it is *very likely* that sea level will rise in more than about 95% of the ocean area. About 70% of the coastlines worldwide are projected to experience sea level change within 20% of the global mean sea level change. . . .

[The remainder of the predictions section has been omitted.]

SOURCE: IPCC, 2013: Summary for Policymakers. In: Climate Change 2013: The Physical Science Basis. Contribution of Working Group I to the Fifth Assessment Report of the Intergovernmental Panel on Climate Change [Stocker, T.F., D. Qin, G.-K. Plattner, M. Tignor, S.K. Allen, J. Boschung, A. Nauels, Y. Xia, V. Bex and P.M. Midgley (eds.)]. Cambridge University Press, Cambridge, United Kingdom and New York, NY, USA. http://www.climatechange2013.org/images/report/WG1AR5_SPM_FINAL.pdf.

OTHER HISTORIC DOCUMENTS OF INTEREST

FROM PREVIOUS *HISTORIC DOCUMENTS*

October

President Obama Remarks on the Government Shutdown

OCTOBER 1, 7, AND 17, 2013

In October 2013, the federal government shut down for sixteen days because Congress could not reach an agreement on a budget to keep the government running. The impact was felt across the country where vacationers were kept out of national parks, school groups arrived in Washington, D.C., only to find "closed" signs on museums, and home-buyers could not receive federally backed loans. The shutdown was brought to an end on October 16 when Democrats and Republicans reached an agreement that would keep the government funded at its current level through January 15, 2014.

IMPENDING SHUTDOWN

The fight in Congress that led to the 2013 shutdown was predicated on a fundamental disagreement between Republicans and Democrats about the Affordable Care Act (ACA), President Barack Obama's landmark health care legislation that was passed in 2010. Since its passage, Republicans have worked unsuccessfully to overturn the bill, even appealing to the Supreme Court. Although a Republican win in the 2012 presidential election might have been a death sentence for the ACA, also known as Obamacare, President Obama held on to his seat, and a large portion of the Republican Party backed down from its challenge to the law. This did not include the most conservative members of the party, those backed by the tea party, who vowed to fight on.

The tea party's work to put an end to the ACA culminated in the budget debate at the end of 2013. Each year, Congress is supposed to pass twelve appropriations bills that make up the coming year's budget and keep the federal government funded. Stymied by gridlock, over the past few years there has not been enough consensus to pass an overarching budget. Instead, Congress has passed stop-gap funding measures known as continuing resolutions (CR). The last CR was passed on March 28, and kept the government funded through September 30, at which point Congress would either have to agree to a budget, a new CR, or shut down the government.

On September 20, Republicans in the House led passage of a vote that would keep the government funded until December 15, but would entirely defund the ACA, a major portion of which was set to go into effect on October 1. The Senate took up debate on the bill, although it was clear the Democratic-led body would not pass it in its current form. On September 24, Sen. Ted Cruz, R-Texas, gave a twenty-one-hour speech against the ACA and called for a government shutdown unless the president and Democrats would change certain portions of the law. Although he spent a majority of his time speaking about the health care law, Cruz also did a Darth Vader impersonation, read Dr. Seuss's *Green Eggs and Ham* to his children, recited passages from Ayn Rand, and even commented on

White Castle hamburgers. The filibuster did not stop the Senate from invoking cloture to pass the revised bill back to the House with a simple majority.

On September 27, the Senate sent the bill back to the House with the ACA provision removed. The House sent a new version back to the Senate that did not defund the health care law but instead delayed its implementation for a year and voided a tax on medical devices. The Senate rejected this on September 30, and the House sent back yet another new version that delayed only the requirement for all Americans to purchase health insurance, known as the individual mandate, by one year. The new version also called on the president to require members of Congress and Congressional staff to cover unsubsidized health insurance costs. The Senate again refused to make any changes to the health care law, well aware that the president would likely veto such a motion.

Shutdown Commences

Without a compromise, on October 1, more than 800,000 federal employees received furlough notices, marking the seventeenth lapse in government funding in history. Not all funding lapses are considered shutdowns—six times during the 1970s, the government went on without funding. In the 1980s, the attorney general at the time ruled that the government was required to shut down if it did not have adequate funding in place. The longest shutdown in history lasted for twenty-one days between 1995 and 1996.

The 2013 shutdown did not impact all federal government functions, but rather only those deemed "nonessential." For example, military families continued to be paid, as were Social Security, unemployment, and food stamp recipients, and those functions related to national security and public safety kept running. As a self-funded entity, the U.S. Postal Service also continued delivering mail.

A number of other federal agencies were at least partially, if not fully, shut down. This included the Centers for Disease Control and Prevention (CDC) no longer being able to run its seasonal flu and other similar programs, which it said would cause a "reduced capacity to respond to outbreak investigations." Employers were not able to use the Department of Homeland Security's e-Verify system to check legal employment status, and national parks and museums run by the National Park Service were closed to visitors. Veterans still had access to VA hospitals, but the agency was unable to process education and rehabilitation payments. Funding for the Women, Infants, and Children (WIC) program, which is used by approximately nine million Americans, was cut off, meaning reduced access to items like formula and nutritious foods for pregnant women and new moms. Air traffic controllers remained in their jobs, but inspections conducted by the Department of Transportation at most airports stopped.

One day after the shutdown began, both parties in Congress started working on a plan to open the government entirely; Republicans also began putting together piecemeal legislation that would fund some of the most popular government programs such as national parks, the Federal Emergency Management Agency (FEMA), and Head Start, a preschool program for low-income families. These one-off efforts were rejected by Democrats who insisted that Republicans could not pick and choose what federal programs were most important.

On October 10, Republican Congressional leaders met with the president at the White House to come up with a plan that would keep the government funded temporarily and delay a debt limit debate for six weeks so long as the president agreed to discuss some spending cuts. The meeting produced no consensus, so new negotiations began between

Senate Majority Leader Harry Reid, D-Nev., and Senate Minority Leader Mitch McConnell, R-Ky. The deal they reached would reopen the government and require that members of Congress pay more for their own health insurance coverage. The deal was pushed aside when Speaker of the House John Boehner, R-Ohio, said he could not muster enough votes for passage.

Outside of Congress, debate was heated. Democrats and Republicans took to the airwaves, blasting their counterparts for failing the American people by not passing a budget. While no one was ready to take responsibility, a Pew poll conducted during the first week of October found that 38 percent of Americans blamed Republicans for the shutdown, while only 30 percent blamed the president and Democrats. The rising tenor of the debate became personal on October 3, when Rep. Randy Neugebauer, R-Texas, confronted a Park Ranger at the World War II memorial in Washington, D.C. The Park Ranger was allowing veterans into the memorial, which was technically closed due to the shutdown, but was keeping other tourists out. Neugebauer was caught on camera telling the Ranger that "the Park Service should be ashamed of themselves." The Ranger replied, "I'm not ashamed." The crowd became involved, yelling to the congressman that it was Congress that should be ashamed of its behavior and inability to, as one crowd member put it, "do its job and pass a budget."

It wasn't until October 16, shortly before midnight, that the two houses passed a compromise bill that funded the government until January 15, 2014, and extended the debt limit until February 7, 2014. The bill also made a change to the ACA to require income verification for those who apply for insurance subsidies and created a House/Senate budget conference that was tasked with developing recommendations for the new budget that would need to be passed come January. The conference was to report back to Congress by December 13.

The president signed the compromise bill, known as the Continuing Appropriations Act of 2014, once it arrived on his desk. In a speech after the signing, the president chastised members of Congress for yet again failing to work toward consensus for the American people. "There are no winners here," the president said. "These last few weeks have inflicted completely unnecessary damage on our economy. We don't know yet the full scope of the damage, but every analyst out there believes it slowed our growth."

COST OF THE SHUTDOWN

On October 17, just one day after federal workers were back on the job, Standard & Poor's estimated that the shutdown had cost the country approximately $24 billion and would impact fourth-quarter gross domestic product (GDP) growth by up to 0.6 percent. "The bottom line is the government shutdown has hurt the U.S. economy," Standard & Poor's said. The White House Council of Economic Advisers estimated that 120,000 fewer private sector jobs were created during the shutdown, negatively impacting the economy and harming business confidence.

The Congressional Budget Office (CBO) released its own assessment of the impact of the shutdown in November. The report included an estimation that the shutdown significantly hurt the economy by delaying energy and transportation projects that would likely create jobs; negatively impacted trade by delaying review of import and export license applications; delayed consideration of federal loans to homeowners and small businesses; disrupted private sector lending by stopping access to Social Security and government income verification networks; and dramatically reduced travel and tourism, thus hurting local economies, specifically that in the District of Columbia. The report went on to state that Americans who relied on critical services like tax refunds were impacted, and safety programs like the Food and Drug Administration (FDA) inspections and National Transportation Safety Board (NTSB) investigations were put on hold. While federal employees had their pay withheld during the shutdown, they did receive retroactive checks after the budget agreement was reached.

—Heather Kerrigan

Following is the text of three statements by President Barack Obama. The first, on October 1, 2013, details the start of the federal government shutdown; the second, on October 7, 2013, discusses the effects of the continuing shutdown; and the third, dated October 17, 2013, announces the signing of a budget agreement to reopen the government.

President Obama Remarks on Day One of the Federal Government Shutdown

DOCUMENT

October 1, 2013

Good morning, everybody. At midnight last night, for the first time in 17 years, Republicans in Congress chose to shut down the Federal Government. Let me be more specific: One faction of one party in one House of Congress in one branch of Government shut down major parts of the Government, all because they didn't like one law.

This Republican shutdown did not have to happen. But I want every American to understand why it did happen. Republicans in the House of Representatives refused to fund the Government unless we defunded or dismantled the Affordable Care Act. They've shut down the Government over an ideological crusade to deny affordable health insurance to millions of Americans. In other words, they demanded ransom just for doing their job.

And many Representatives, including an increasing number of Republicans, have made it clear that had they been allowed by Speaker Boehner to take a simple up-or-down vote on keeping the Government open, with no partisan strings attached, enough votes from both parties would have kept the American people's Government open and operating.

Now, we may not know the full impact of this Republican shutdown for some time. It will depend on how long it lasts. But we do know a couple of things. We know that the last time Republicans shut down the Government in 1996, it hurt our economy. And unlike 1996, our economy is still recovering from the worst recession in generations.

We know that certain services and benefits that America's seniors and veterans and business owners depend on must be put on hold. Certain offices, along with every national park and monument, must be closed. And while last night, I signed legislation to make sure our 1.4 million Active Duty military are paid through the shutdown, hundreds of thousands of civilian workers—many still on the job, many forced to stay home—aren't being paid, even if they have families to support and local businesses that rely on them. And we know that the longer this shutdown continues, the worse the effects will be. More families will be hurt. More businesses will be harmed.

So, once again, I urge House Republicans to reopen the Government, restart the services Americans depend on, and allow the public servants who have been sent home to return to work. This is only going to happen when Republicans realize they don't get to hold the entire economy hostage over ideological demands.

As I've said repeatedly, I am prepared to work with Democrats and Republicans to do the things we need to do to grow the economy and create jobs and get our fiscal house in order over the long run. Although I should add, this shutdown isn't about deficits or spending or budgets. After all, our deficits are falling at the fastest pace in 50 years. We've cut them in half since I took office. In fact, many of the demands the Republicans are now making would actually raise our deficits.

So no, this shutdown is not about deficits. It's not about budgets. This shutdown is about rolling back our efforts to provide health insurance to folks who don't have it. It's all about rolling back the Affordable Care Act. This, more than anything else, seems to be what the Republican Party stands for these days. I know it's strange that one party would make keeping people uninsured the centerpiece of their agenda, but that apparently is what it is.

And of course, what's stranger still is that shutting down our Government doesn't accomplish their stated goal. The Affordable Care Act is a law that passed the House; it passed the Senate. The Supreme Court ruled it constitutional. It was a central issue in last year's election. It is settled, and it is here to stay. And because of its funding sources, it's not impacted by a Government shutdown.

[The remainder of the president's remarks, on the Affordable Care Act, has been omitted.]

SOURCE: Executive Office of the President. "Remarks on the Federal Government Shutdown and the Patient Protection and Affordable Care Act." October 1, 2013. *Compilation of Presidential Documents* 2013, no. 00683 (October 1, 2013). http://www.gpo.gov/fdsys/pkg/DCPD-201300683/pdf/DCPD-201300683.pdf.

President Obama on the Continuing Government Shutdown

October 7, 2013

Okay. I'm here at FEMA for a couple of reasons. First of all, I want to thank Craig Fugate, his entire team, and the incredible workers who are here at FEMA. They are having to, under less than optimal situations, still respond to Mother Nature, which doesn't stop just because the Government has shut down.

I wanted to get initially a briefing on what had happened with Hurricane Karen, became Tropical Storm Karen, and then fortunately dissipated, so we dodged a bullet there. In the meantime, we're on tornado watch here in the Mid-Atlantic States because of severe weather patterns. And we've got blizzards up north; we've got some weather patterns in the middle of the country that we're still monitoring. And so I just want to say thank you to all of you for the incredible work that you're doing.

I think it's important to understand that the people here at FEMA have been doing everything they can to respond to potential events. Here at FEMA, they're in touch with their State and local partners in case resources are needed. FEMA remains prepared for natural disasters year around, with supplies prepositioned in distribution centers across the country.

But their job has been made more difficult. Thanks to the folks at FEMA, we were prepared for what might have happened down in Florida. Nevertheless, the Government is still shut down, services are still interrupted, and hundreds of thousands of hard-working public servants, including many FEMA professionals, are still furloughed without pay, or they're not allowed to work at all.

So Craig was just explaining to me, here at FEMA, about 86 percent of the FEMA workforce is furloughed. In response to the potential event that might have happened down in Florida and along the coasts, Craig called back 200 of those workers. Keep in mind, calling them back doesn't mean they were getting paid, it just means they had the privilege of working without pay to make sure that they were doing everything they can to respond to the potential needs of their fellow citizens.

Now that this particular storm has dissipated, Craig is going to have to refurlough at least a hundred of those folks who were called back. So think about that. Here you are, somebody who's a FEMA professional dedicated to doing your job; at a moment's notice, you're willing to show up here in case people got in trouble and respond to them, even though you're not getting paid, even though you don't have certainty. And now you're being put back on furlough because the Government is shut down. That's no way of doing business.

That, by the way, just speaks to the day-to-day emergencies that may come up and that is FEMA's job to respond to. Craig was also explaining the fact that when it comes to training first responders, for example, we have on a weekly basis already scheduled training for first responders that now have to be rescheduled. It will probably end up ultimately costing the Government more money for us to put those things back together again. And so not only is this shutdown hurting FEMA workers, not only is it making it more difficult for us to respond to potential natural disasters, but it may actually end up costing taxpayers more than it should.

Right now Congress should do what's in the best interests of the economy and the American people, and that's move beyond this manufactured crisis and work together to focus on growth, jobs, and providing the vital services that Americans all across the country depend on, including the services that FEMA provides.

I heard a lot of talk over the weekend that the real problem is, is that the President will not negotiate. Well, let me tell you something: I have said from the start of the year that I'm happy to talk to Republicans about anything related to the budget. There's not a subject that I am not willing to engage in, work on, negotiate, and come up with commonsense compromises on.

What I've said is that I cannot do that under the threat that if Republicans don't get a hundred percent of their way, they're going to either shut down the Government or they are going to default on America's debt, so that America for the first time in history does not pay its bills. That is not something I will do. We're not going to establish that pattern.

We're not going to negotiate under the threat of further harm to our economy and middle class families. We're not going to negotiate under the threat of a prolonged shutdown until Republicans get a hundred percent of what they want. We're not going to negotiate under the threat of economic catastrophe that economists and CEOs increasingly warn would result if Congress chose to default on America's obligations.

Now, the other thing I heard over the weekend was this notion that Congress doesn't have the capacity to end this shutdown. The truth of the matter is, there are enough Republican and Democratic votes in the House of Representatives right now to end this shutdown immediately with no partisan strings attached. The House should hold that vote today. If Republicans and Speaker Boehner are saying there are not enough votes, then they should prove it. Let the bill go to the floor and let's see what happens. Just vote. Let every Member of Congress vote their conscience, and they can determine whether or not they want to shut the Government down.

My suspicion is—my very strong suspicion is—that there are enough votes there. And the reason that Speaker Boehner hasn't called a vote on it is because he doesn't, apparently, want to see the Government shutdown end at the moment unless he's able to extract concessions that don't have anything to do with the budget. Well, I think the American people simply want Government to work. And there's no reason that there has to be a shutdown in order for the kinds of negotiations Speaker Boehner says he wants to proceed. Hold a vote. Call a vote right now, and let's see what happens.

The second thing Congress needs to do is to raise the debt ceiling next week so the Treasury can pay the bills that Congress has already spent. That's what most Americans do if they buy something. If they buy a car or if they buy a house, if they put something on a credit card, they understand they've got to pay the bills.

This is something routine. It's been done more than 40 times since Ronald Reagan was President. It has never before been used in the kind of ways that the Republicans are talking about using it right now. We can't threaten economic catastrophe in the midst of budget negotiations.

So authorize the Treasury to pay America's bills. Pass a budget, end the Government shutdown, pay our bills, and prevent an economic shutdown.

And as soon as that happens, I am eager and ready to sit down and negotiate with Republicans on a whole range of issues: How do we create more jobs? How do we grow the economy? How do we boost manufacturing? How do we make sure our kids are getting a first-class education? All those things will be on the table. I'm happy to talk about health care, happy to talk about energy policy, how do we deal with our long-term fiscal situation.

All those things I've been eager and anxious to talk to Republicans about for the last 7 months, and I've put out a budget that specifically lays out my vision for how we're going to grow this economy. And I expect the Republicans should do the same, and we can negotiate it. But we shouldn't hurt a whole bunch of people in order for one side to think that they're going to have a little more leverage in those negotiations.

Last point I'm going to make: The bill that is being presented to end the Government shutdown reflects Republican priorities. It's the Republican budget. The funding levels of this short-term funding bill, called the CR, is far lower than what Democrats think it should be. Nevertheless, Democrats are prepared to put the majority of votes on to reopen the Government. So when you hear this notion that Democrats aren't compromising, we're compromising so much we're willing to reopen the Government at funding levels that reflect Republican wishes, don't at all reflect our wishes.

For example, here at FEMA, they're still subject to the sequester, so even before the shutdown, they were having trouble making sure that everybody was staying on the job and fulfilling all of their various functions.

We need to get that sequester lifted that's been hanging over the head of the economy and Federal agencies during the course of this entire year. This short-term legislation to reopen the Government doesn't even address that. That has to be done in a broader budget framework.

So Democrats have said we are willing to pass a bill that reflects the Republicans' priorities in terms of funding levels. That's a pretty significant compromise. What we're not willing to do is to create a permanent pattern in which unless you get your way, the Government is shut down or America defaults. That's not how we do business in this country, and we're not going to start now.

So again, I want to thank everybody at FEMA here for the extraordinary work that we're—that you're doing. You show each and every day that you take your responsibilities seriously. You do your jobs with consummate professionalism. And hopefully, you're setting a good example for Members of Congress. They need to be doing the same thing. And if they do, then there's no reason why we all can't move forward and make sure that we're taking care of America's business. All right?

Thank you very much, everybody.

SOURCE: Executive Office of the President. "Remarks on the Federal Government Shutdown." October 7, 2013. *Compilation of Presidential Documents* 2013, no. 00690 (October 7, 2013). http://www.gpo.gov/fdsys/pkg/DCPD-201300690/pdf/DCPD-201300690.pdf.

President Obama on Reopening the Federal Government

DOCUMENT

October 17, 2013

Good morning, everybody. Please have a seat.

Last night I signed legislation to reopen our Government and pay America's bills. Because Democrats and responsible Republicans came together, the first Government shutdown in 17 years is now over. The first default in more than 200 years will not happen. These twin threats to our economy have now been lifted. And I want to thank those Democrats and Republicans for getting together and ultimately getting this job done.

Now, there's been a lot of discussion lately of the politics of this shutdown. But let's be clear: There are no winners here. These last few weeks have inflicted completely unnecessary damage on our economy. We don't know yet the full scope of the damage, but every analyst out there believes it slowed our growth.

We know that families have gone without paychecks or services they depend on. We know that potential home buyers have gotten fewer mortgages and small-business loans have been put on hold. We know that consumers have cut back on spending and that half of all CEOs say that the shutdown and the threat of shutdown set back their plans to hire over the next 6 months. We know that just the threat of default, of America not paying all the bills that we owe on time, increased our borrowing costs, which adds to our deficit.

And of course, we know that the American people's frustration with what goes on in this town has never been higher. That's not a surprise that the American people are completely fed up with Washington. At a moment when our economic recovery demands more jobs, more momentum, we've got yet another self-inflicted crisis that set our economy back. And for what?

There was no economic rationale for all of this. Over the past 4 years, our economy has been growing, our businesses have been creating jobs, and our deficits have been cut in half. We hear some Members who pushed for the shutdown say they were doing it to save the American economy, but nothing has done more to undermine our economy these past 3 years than the kind of tactics that create these manufactured crises.

And you don't have to take my word for it. The agency that put America's credit rating on watch the other day explicitly cited all of this, saying that our economy "remains more dynamic and resilient" than other advanced economies and that the only thing putting us at risk is—and I'm quoting here—"repeated brinksmanship." That's what the credit rating agency said; that wasn't a political statement; that was an analysis of what's hurting our economy by people whose job it is to analyze these things.

That also happens to be the view of our diplomats who've been hearing from their counterparts internationally. Some of the same folks who pushed for the shutdown and threatened default claim their actions were needed to get America back on the right track, to make sure we're strong. But probably nothing has done more damage to America's credibility in the world, our standing with other countries, than the spectacle that we've seen these past several weeks. It's encouraged our enemies, it's emboldened our competitors, and it's depressed our friends, who look to us for steady leadership.

Now, the good news is we'll bounce back from this. We always do. America is the bedrock of the global economy for a reason. We are the indispensable nation that the rest of the world looks to as the safest and most reliable place to invest, something that's made it easier for generations of Americans to invest in their own futures. We have earned that responsibility over more than two centuries because of the dynamism of our economy and our entrepreneurs, the productivity of our workers, but also because we keep our word and we meet our obligations. That's what full faith and credit means: You can count on us.

And today I want our people and our businesses and the rest of the world to know that the full faith and credit of the United States remains unquestioned. But to all my friends in Congress, understand that how business is done in this town has to change, because we've all got a lot of work to do on behalf of the American people. And that includes the hard work of regaining their trust. Our system of self-government doesn't function without it. And now that the Government is reopened and this threat to our economy is removed, all of us need to stop focusing on the lobbyists and the bloggers and the talking heads on radio and the professional activists, who profit from conflict, and focus on what the majority of Americans sent us here to do. And that's, grow this economy, create good jobs, strengthen the middle class, educate our kids, lay the foundation for broad-based prosperity, and get our fiscal house in order for the long haul. That's why we're here; that should be our focus.

Now, that won't be easy. We all know that we have divided Government right now. There's a lot of noise out there, and the pressure from the extremes affect how a lot of Members of Congress see the day-to-day work that's supposed to be done here. And let's face it: The American people don't see every issue the same way. But that doesn't mean we can't make progress. And when we disagree, we don't have to suggest that the other side doesn't love this country or believe in free enterprise—or all the other rhetoric that seems to get worse every single year. If we disagree on something, we can move on and focus on the things we agree on and get some stuff done.

Let me be specific about three places where I believe we can make progress right now. First, in the coming days and weeks, we should sit down and pursue a balanced approach to a responsible budget, a budget that grows our economy faster and shrinks our long-term deficits further.

At the beginning of this year, that's what both Democrats and Republicans committed to doing. The Senate passed a budget; House passed a budget; they were supposed to come together and negotiate. And had one side not decided to pursue a strategy of brinksmanship, each side could have gotten together and figured out, how do we shape a budget that provides certainty to businesses and people who rely on Government, provides certainty to investors in our economy? And we'd be growing faster right now.

Now, the good news is the legislation I signed yesterday now requires Congress to do exactly that, what it could have been doing all along. And we shouldn't approach this process of creating a budget as an ideological exercise, just cutting for the sake of cutting. The issue is not growth versus fiscal responsibility: We need both. We need a budget that deals with the issues that most Americans are focused on, creating more good jobs that pay better wages.

And remember, the deficit is getting smaller, not bigger. It's going down faster than it has in the last 50 years. The challenge we have right now are not short-term deficits, it's the long-term obligations that we have around things like Medicare and Social Security. And we want to make sure those are there for future generations.

So the key now is a budget that cuts out the things that we don't need, closes corporate tax loopholes that don't help create jobs, and frees up resources for the things that do help us grow, like education and infrastructure and research. And these things historically have not been partisan. And this shouldn't be as difficult as it's been in past years because we already spend less than we did a few years ago. Our deficits are half of what they were a few years ago. The debt problems we have now are long term, and we can address them without shortchanging our kids or shortchanging our grandkids or weakening the security that current generations have earned from their hard work. So that's number one.

Number two, we should finish fixing the job of our—let me say that again. Number two, we should finish the job of fixing a broken immigration system. There's already a broad coalition across America that's behind this effort of comprehensive immigration reform, from business leaders to faith leaders, to law enforcement. In fact, the Senate has already passed a bill with strong bipartisan support that would make the biggest commitment to border security in our history; would modernize our legal immigration system; make sure everyone plays by the same rules; make sure that folks who came here illegally have to pay a fine, pay back taxes, meet their responsibilities. That bill has already passed the Senate. And economists estimate that if that bill becomes law, our economy would be 5 percent larger two decades from now. That's $1.4 trillion in new economic growth.

The majority of Americans think this is the right thing to do. And it's sitting there waiting for the House to pass it. Now, if the House has ideas on how to improve the Senate bill, let's hear them. Let's start the negotiations. But let's not leave this problem to keep festering for another year or 2 years or 3 years. This can and should get done by the end of this year.

Number three, we should pass a farm bill, one that American farmers and ranchers can depend on, one that protects vulnerable children and adults in times of need, one that gives rural communities opportunities to grow and the long-term certainty that they deserve.

Again, the Senate's already passed a solid bipartisan bill. It's got support from Democrats and Republicans. It's sitting in the House waiting for passage. If House Republicans have ideas that they think would improve the farm bill, let's see them. Let's negotiate. What are we waiting for? Let's get this done.

So passing a budget, immigration reform, farm bill—those are three specific things that would make a huge difference in our economy right now. And we could get them done by the end of the year if our focus is on what's good for the American people. And that's just the big stuff. There are all kinds of other things that we could be doing that don't get as much attention.

I understand we will not suddenly agree on everything now that the cloud of crisis has passed. Democrats and Republicans are far apart on a lot of issues. And I recognize there are folks on the other side who think that my policies are misguided—that's putting it mildly. That's okay; that's democracy; that's how it works. We can debate those differences vigorously, passionately, in good faith, through the normal democratic process.

And sometimes, we'll be just too far apart to forge an agreement. But that should not hold back our efforts in areas where we do agree. We shouldn't fail to act on areas that we do agree or could agree just because we don't think it's good politics, just because the extremes in our party don't like the word compromise.

I will look for willing partners wherever I can to get important work done. And there's no good reason why we can't govern responsibly, despite our differences, without lurching from manufactured crisis to manufactured crisis. In fact, one of the things that I hope all of us have learned these past few weeks is that it turns out, smart, effective Government is important. It matters. I think the American people during this shutdown had a chance to get some idea of all the things, large and small, that Government does that make a difference in people's lives.

We hear all the time about how Government is the problem. Well, it turns out we rely on it in a whole lot of ways. Not only does it keep us strong through our military and our law enforcement, it plays a vital role in caring for our seniors and our veterans, educating our kids, making sure our workers are trained for the jobs that are being created, arming our businesses with the best science and technology so they can compete with companies from other countries. It plays a key role in keeping our food and our toys and our workplaces safe. It helps folks rebuild after a storm. It conserves our natural resources. It finances startups. It helps to sell our products overseas. It provides security to our diplomats abroad.

So let's work together to make Government work better, instead of treating it like an enemy or purposely making it work worse. That's not what the Founders of this Nation envisioned when they gave us the gift of self-government. You don't like a particular policy or a particular President? Then argue for your position, go out there and win an election, push to change it, but don't break it. Don't break what our predecessors spent over two centuries building. That's not being faithful to what this country is about.

And that brings me to one last point. I've got a simple message for all the dedicated and patriotic Federal workers who've either worked without pay or been forced off the job without pay these past few weeks, including most of my own staff: Thank you. Thanks for your service. Welcome back. What you do is important. It matters.

You defend our country overseas. You deliver benefits to our troops who've earned them when they come home. You guard our borders. You protect our civil rights. You help businesses grow and gain footholds in overseas markets. You protect the air we breathe and the water our children drink. And you push the boundaries of science and space, and you guide hundreds of thousands of people each day through the glories of this country. Thank you. What you do is important. And don't let anybody else tell you different. Especially the young people who come to this city to serve believe that it matters. Well, you know what, you're right. It does.

And those of us who have the privilege to serve this country have an obligation to do our job as best we can. And we come from different parties, but we are Americans first. And that's why disagreement cannot mean dysfunction. It can't degenerate into hatred. The American people's hopes and dreams are what matters, not ours. Our obligations are to them. Our regard for them compels us all, Democrats and Republicans, to cooperate and compromise and act in the best interests of our Nation—"one Nation under God, indivisible, with liberty and justice for all."

Thanks very much.

SOURCE: Executive Office of the President. "Remarks on the Continuing Appropriations Act, 2014." October 17, 2013. *Compilation of Presidential Documents* 2013, no. 00706 (October 17, 2013). http://www.gpo.gov/fdsys/pkg/DCPD-201300706/pdf/DCPD-201300706.pdf.

OTHER HISTORIC DOCUMENTS OF INTEREST

FROM THIS VOLUME

FROM PREVIOUS *HISTORIC DOCUMENTS*

Treasury Secretary on the Debt Ceiling

OCTOBER 1 AND 16, 2013

Congress's political brinksmanship continued into late 2013, when the nation faced the dual crisis of both a government shutdown due to the lack of a budget agreement to keep the government funded, and the impending government default if Congress failed to act to raise the debt ceiling. On the latter, Democrats refused to allow a bill to be passed that would require additional spending cuts, while Republicans demanded that at least some concessions be made. In the end, the two parties came together to raise the debt ceiling, but only until February 2014, when they would again have to take up the issue. The Treasury Department expressed concern that the continuing debt ceiling crisis would hurt America's image abroad and deal a serious blow to consumer and investor confidence.

HISTORY OF THE DEBT CEILING

Congress first set the debt ceiling at $11.5 billion in 1917 in an effort to help fund the war effort and allow the Treasury to issue bonds. Before that point, if the government wanted to issue debt, it had to receive Congressional authorization. By 2013, the debt ceiling had reached $17.1 trillion. Debt has risen under every president in the past three decades, after remaining relatively stable for the twenty-five-year period following World War II. Since 1960, Congress has voted to raise the debt ceiling seventy-eight times—forty-nine of these votes were under Republican presidents and twenty-nine were under Democratic presidents. In traditional party politics fashion, if a Democrat holds the presidency, Republicans in Congress will vote to oppose the increase, and vice versa. In its history, the United States has only technically defaulted once, in 1979, when negotiations in Congress to raise the debt ceiling came down to the wire. The default, however, was actually caused by a glitch at the Treasury that resulted in some Treasury notes not being paid in full. This is typically not considered a true default because the Treasury paid the notes in full once it realized its mistake.

The money that the federal government can borrow under the debt ceiling covers previously incurred debts like Social Security payments, payments to contractors, interest on bonds, and spending allocated in budget bills. If Congress does not vote to raise the debt ceiling when necessary, the government would default on its payments. The potential impact of a default could include anything from stopping Social Security payments and military benefits, to an overall loss of confidence in the United States and a decrease in foreign investment.

In 2011, the Treasury announced that the nation would officially default on May 16, although payments could be shifted and other financial steps taken to keep payments flowing on time until August 2. The two parties in Congress bickered throughout the year, time and time again failing to agree on how to raise the debt ceiling. Republicans wanted to see spending offsets to cover the increase, but Democrats were adamant that the issue of budget cuts be dealt with outside of debt ceiling negotiations, perhaps instead during the appropriations and budgeting process. With the clock ticking, Republicans and Democrats met with Vice President Joe Biden for a series of meetings at the White House. On July 31, 2011, negotiations resulted in a deal in which the debt ceiling would rise but the increase would be offset by $2.4 trillion in spending cuts over the following decade. To determine how these cuts should be made, a congressional super committee was formed and tasked with finding the best places to make the spending cuts. If the committee failed or if Congress failed to enact the committee's recommendations, automatic, across-the-board reductions would be made to military spending, education, transportation, and Medicare payments. The committee failed in November 2011 to produce any recommendations, and the cuts, known as the sequester, went into effect in 2013.

As the sequester went into effect, the United States was already facing another debt ceiling crisis, and had technically breeched the debt ceiling on December 31, 2012, but the Treasury Department was operating under what it called "extraordinary measures" to keep the nation from default. On February 4, 2013, the president signed a bill to suspend the debt ceiling and allow for additional debate on the issue. The bill kept the debt ceiling at its current level until May 19, when it rose to a level "necessary to fund commitment incurred by the Federal Government that required payment," which amounted to approximately $16.7 trillion. By August, the Treasury said it would be forced to default by sometime in October if Congress could not reach another agreement to again raise the debt ceiling.

October Debt Ceiling Debate

In October, while Congress debated how to reopen the federal government, it also began to take note of the looming default the nation would face on October 17 if the debt ceiling did not rise. If a deal was not finalized by then, the Treasury would still have approximately $30 billion to pay some obligations, but the larger worry was what would happen to financial markets as well as consumer and investor confidence.

During debate on the issue, Republicans asked for a variety of concessions from the Democrats in order to raise the debt ceiling. These ranged from privatization of Medicare or Social Security to food stamp reductions, tax reform, Medicaid block-grants, the end to agricultural subsidies, and an increase in the retirement age. Democrats, backed by the president, refused to negotiate, saying that they had already agreed to the budget cuts that were made under the sequester. The president said that if Congress would pass a clean debt ceiling bill, he would open up negotiations on the other issues Republicans had presented.

The first House bill was put on the table in September 2013 and would raise the debt ceiling for twelve months while also delaying the implementation of the Affordable Care Act (ACA). The bill called for votes to be held on tax reform by the end of the year and a start to Keystone XL pipeline construction. The bill never made it to a vote. A second bill was drafted in the House that would raise the debt ceiling for a little more than one month, to November 22, but keep the shutdown in place. This bill also did not have enough support to come before the House for a vote.

The final agreement, the Continuing Appropriations Act, ended the government shutdown by funding the government at its current levels through January 15, 2014, and also increased the debt ceiling until February 7, 2014. The bill created a budget conference between the two houses to discuss long-term spending and also strengthened the income verification portion of the ACA. The Senate passed the bill 81–18, while the House voted, without amendment, 285–144. With the bill passed, Treasury Secretary Jack Lew applauded the move, saying that he welcomed "the bipartisan action Congress is taking to resolve this crisis, re-open the government, and lift the cloud of uncertainty hanging over the economy. . . . Because of today's efforts, we will continue to honor all of our commitments—a core American value—and preserve the full faith and credit of the United States."

The agreement was largely viewed as a win for President Obama, who had been asking for a clean debt limit increase for months. The agreement would stave off the next debt ceiling fight until February 7, 2014, when Congress again would need to raise the debt ceiling. The Treasury said it had some methods at its disposal for extending its borrowing authority beyond that time, but that the political brinksmanship would ultimately be what hurt the nation's prestige and would stop current and potential creditors from seeing the United States as a stable financial center for investment.

Ongoing Debate

In December, Treasury Secretary Lew sent a letter to Congressional leaders, urging them to act responsibly and raise the debt ceiling when they returned from recess. "The creditworthiness of the United States is an essential underpinning of our strength as a nation; it is not a bargaining chip to be used for partisan political ends," Lew wrote. He added, "Increasing the debt limit does not authorize new spending commitments. It simply allows the government to pay for expenditures Congress has already approved."

Rep. Paul Ryan, R-Wis., chairman of the powerful House Budget Committee, said in December that Republicans did not want to pass a clean debt limit increase, but instead wanted to bargain with Democrats. "We don't want nothing out of this debt limit," he said in an interview. "We are going to decide what it is we can accomplish out of this debt limit fight." The White House had already announced that it would not approve a debt limit increase that was attached to other budgetary measures.

On February 12, 2014, Congress approved a clean debt ceiling increase, the first since 2009, which included no riders or requirements for spending cuts. Final approval came after a hard-fought debate between Republicans and Democrats, the former of whom pleaded with members to support the end of a filibuster that had held up the bill. Republican leadership in Congress largely believed that the blame for an inability to pass a debt limit increase would be squarely placed on their party. In the end, the Senate passed the clean bill 55–43, giving the United States reprieve from a debt crisis until March 2015.

—Heather Kerrigan

Following is a the text of a letter sent by Treasury Secretary Jack Lew to Congressional leaders on October 1, 2013, asking them to raise the debt ceiling; and a statement by Lew on October 16, 2013, on the vote to raise the debt ceiling.

Secretary Lew Calls on Congress to Raise Debt Ceiling

DOCUMENT

October 1, 2013

The Honorable John A. Boehner
Speaker
U.S. House of Representatives
Washington, DC 20515

Dear Mr. Speaker:

I am writing to follow up on my previous letters regarding the Department of the Treasury's responsibility to finance the government and to protect the full faith and credit of the United States.

In May of this year, the U.S. government reached the statutory debt limit, and Treasury began taking certain extraordinary measures to be able to continue, on a temporary basis, to pay the nation's bills. Today, I am writing to inform Congress that as of today Treasury has begun using the final extraordinary measures. There are no other legal and prudent options to extend the nation's borrowing authority. The impact of these measures was incorporated into the forecast that I shared with you last week, and Treasury continues to believe that extraordinary measures will be exhausted no later than October 17, 2013.

Each of these measures is authorized by law, and each has been used by previous Secretaries of the Treasury during past debt limit impasses:

- Treasury will suspend, as necessary, the daily reinvestment of the portion of the Exchange Stabilization Fund that is invested in Treasury securities.
- Treasury will enter into a debt swap with the Federal Financing Bank and the Civil Service Retirement and Disability Fund (CSRDF), which will lead to the elimination of a limited amount of debt that counts against the debt limit. Although this measure is of limited value, I have determined that it should be used given the urgency of the situation.
- With regard to the CSRDF, I have previously determined that a "debt issuance suspension period" exists through October 11. I have now determined that, by reason of the statutory debt limit, I will continue to be unable to fully invest the portion of the CSRDF not immediately required to pay beneficiaries, and that the debt issuance suspension period will continue through October 17.

As previously noted, all of these measures were incorporated into the estimate that I provided last week and do not provide Congress with more time to act. It is important to note that once the final extraordinary measures are exhausted, no later than October 17, we will be left to meet our country's commitments at that time with only approximately $30 billion. This amount would be far short of net expenditures on certain days, which can be as high as $60 billion. Although the current lapse in appropriations creates some additional uncertainty, we do not believe it will impact our projections materially unless it continues for an extended period of time. If we have insufficient cash on hand, it would be impossible for the United States of America to meet all of its obligations for the first time in our history. For this reason, I respectfully urge Congress to act immediately to meet its responsibility by extending the nation's borrowing authority.

Sincerely,

Jacob J. Lew

Identical letter sent to:
 The Honorable Nancy Pelosi, House Democratic Leader
 The Honorable Harry Reid, Senate Majority Leader
 The Honorable Mitch McConnell, Senate Republican Leader

cc: The Honorable Dave Camp, Chairman, House Committee on Ways and Means
 The Honorable Sander M. Levin, Ranking Member, House Committee on Ways and Means
 The Honorable Max Baucus, Chairman, Senate Committee on Finance
 The Honorable Orrin G. Hatch, Ranking Member, Senate Committee on Finance
 All other Members of the 113th Congress

SOURCE: U.S. Department of the Treasury. "Secretary Lew Sends Debt Limit Letter to Congress." October 1, 2013. http://www.treasury.gov/initiatives/Documents/Treasury%20Letter%20to%20Congress_100113.pdf.

Secretary Lew Responds to Debt Ceiling Raise

DOCUMENT

October 16, 2013

"We welcome the bipartisan action Congress is taking to resolve this crisis, re-open the government, and lift the cloud of uncertainty hanging over the economy. Over 224 years, the United States has established our credit as the strongest in the world. The United States is the anchor of the international financial system and the world's reserve currency. We are the world's largest economy with the deepest and most liquid financial markets. When risk rises, the flight to safety and to quality brings investors to U.S. markets. Because of today's efforts, we will continue to honor all of our commitments—a core American value—and preserve the full faith and credit of the United States.

"At the same time, we remain committed to reaching agreement on a balanced fiscal package that will create jobs, grow our economy, and put us on a path toward long-term fiscal sustainability. Without question, it will require difficult choices. We stand ready to find that common ground with both Republicans and Democrats so we can sustain the recovery the American people have so painstakingly fought for and ensure we remain the most powerful economy in the world for generations to come."

SOURCE: U.S. Department of the Treasury. Press Center. "Statement of Secretary Lew." October 16, 2013. http://www.treasury.gov/press-center/press-releases/Pages/jl2187.aspx.

OTHER HISTORIC DOCUMENTS OF INTEREST

Al Qaeda Operative Captured in Tripoli

OCTOBER 8, 2013

On October 5, 2013, U.S. Special Forces successfully captured a high-level al Qaeda leader in Tripoli, Libya. In a departure from the Obama administration's liberal use of drone strikes in pursing terrorists abroad, the use of U.S. Special Forces has gained appeal for its ability to obtain actionable intelligence from suspected terrorists and to deliver these suspects for civilian trials in the United States, though the legality of such military actions has been questioned. However, instability in the Middle East has continued to plague diplomatic efforts to pursue such suspects.

Two Missions, Two Results

On the morning of October 5, 2013, U.S. Special Forces attempted simultaneous strikes against alleged terrorists in both Libya and Somalia. The two targeted missions to capture and detain alleged high-level leaders of known terrorist groups produced mixed results. The team in Tripoli, Libya, successfully apprehended Nazih Abdul-Hamed al-Ruqai, who uses the alias Abu Anas al-Libi, in a rapidly executed strike with no shots fired. Al-Libi is suspected of conspiring with al Qaeda leaders in the planning of the 1998 bombings of U.S. embassies in Kenya and Tanzania, as well as additional terrorist activity. In contrast, Navy SEAL Team 6, known for the role that it played in the raid leading to the death of Osama bin Laden, failed in an attempt to capture Abdikadir Mohamed Abdikadir, better known as Ikrima, who is believed to be a top planner of al-Shabaab attacks and who has links to al Qaeda and other extremist groups in the area. SEAL Team 6 retreated after sustaining heavy fire from militants in the area amid concerns regarding possible civilian casualties if it returned fire with matching force. Initial reports claimed that the target may have been among the casualties of the strike, but later reports denied that the mission was successful in eliminating Ikrima.

It is reported that al-Libi was captured by a team of highly trained operatives after returning to his home in Tripoli after morning prayer. The suspect's car was surrounded, and he was forced into another vehicle, which promptly departed. Al-Libi was taken to the U.S.S. *San Antonio* in the Mediterranean and remained on the ship in custody for approximately one week during which he was interrogated by an elite team of terrorism experts from the United States. Concerns regarding his chronic health condition prompted a transfer to New York, where al-Libi would face an indictment from 2000 related to his alleged role in al Qaeda's conspiracy to kill U.S. nationals, including al Qaeda plans to attack U.S. forces stationed in Saudi Arabia, Yemen, and Somalia as well as the two U.S. embassies in Dar es Salaam, Tanzania, and Nairobi, Kenya.

It is unclear what knowledge the Libyan government had of the U.S. capture mission. Shortly after al-Libi was taken into custody, there was speculation that the Libyan government may have been involved. In an exclusive CNN interview with al-Libi's wife, she alluded to the fact that the captors were Libyan, though this claim was promptly disavowed publicly by the government of Libya. In a statement to the press, Department of Defense spokesperson, George Little, conveyed that the Libyan government "tacitly approved" the mission. However, Little also remarked that Libyan officials were not forewarned about the timing of the mission, nor did they have a role in the actual operation.

The operation in Somalia not only failed to apprehend Ikrima, but is purported to have bolstered the morale of al-Shabaab fighters, the group suspected to be behind the attack on a shopping mall in Nairobi, Kenya, in September 2013. With the backlash from this failed attempt, further missions to apprehend suspects related to the 2012 attacks on the American diplomatic mission in Benghazi, Libya, which resulted in the death of U.S. Ambassador Chris Stevens and three additional American citizens, seem unlikely to proceed. Some have questioned the timing of the strikes and their implication for further action in the region. Intelligence suggests that another suspect in the Benghazi attacks, who was known at the time to the dual Special Forces missions to be living in Libya, is unlikely to remain in his last known location, negating the possibility that this suspect could be swiftly apprehended in a similarly designed strike in the near future. Little stated that the timing of the October 5 attacks was based on intelligence that led somewhat coincidentally to the strikes having been carried out nearly simultaneously, but also stated that the Department of Defense did not have reason to believe that the success or failure of these military actions would prevent the United States from seeking out other insurgents using similar means. Marie Harf, Deputy Spokesperson for the Department of State, expressed that it is the preference of the United States "to capture terrorists as opposed to taking lethal action" to obtain intelligence to pursue other threats.

INSTABILITY IN LIBYA

Since the ousting of Muammar el-Qaddafi in 2011, the fledgling Libyan government has relied heavily on various regional militias for security and protection. These regional militias, often loyal to their leaders rather than to the elected government, offer little stability, and the government remains weak in the absence of a centralized national defense or police force. After the capture of al-Libi by U.S. Special Forces, one such militia faction sought action against the prime minister of Libya, Ali Zeidan, because it was believed by the group that he was involved in al-Libi's capture. The militia kidnapped the prime minister from his hotel and held him captive for several hours until other militia groups intervened and called for him to be released.

Upon his release, in a public statement on October 11, 2013, Zeidan denied any government involvement in the operation in Tripoli that led to the capture of al-Libi. The prime minister did, in a statement to reporters, express that he did not expect the incident to cause a permanent rift in U.S.-Libyan relations and that the government remains committed to working with the United States to seek out those suspected of terrorist activity. As a result of the mission in Tripoli, it has been reported that militant groups, including those affiliated with al Qaeda, have threatened retaliation against both the United States and the Libyan government, suggesting abductions of American citizens and blockades to prevent oil production. The Department of State maintains that these threats are uncorroborated. Even prior to the capture of al-Libi, Libyan oil production had been curbed by blockades coordinated by militias demanding more autonomy from the government. In an interview with CNN's Christiane Amanpour that aired just a week prior to the al-Libi raid, Prime Minister Zeidan stated that oil production was at approximately 40 to 50 percent and that the government hoped to increase this production to 100 percent. Attempts to raise production have had little success.

LEGAL MATTERS

Libya called for al-Libi to be returned to face justice in the Libyan justice system. On October 7, 2013, U.S. Ambassador to Libya Deborah Jones met with Libyan Minister of Justice Salah al-Marghani at the request of the Libyan government about concerns regarding a perceived violation of Libya's sovereignty. The detention of al-Libi was discussed during the meeting, as was his treatment during detention. The Department of State restated during an October 8, 2013, press briefing that al-Libi was "still in United States custody" and that the United States had "reiterated to the ICRC that we [the U.S. government] are treating him humanely." The International Committee of the Red Cross (ICRC) had not been allowed direct access to the detainee at the time of the briefing. During al-Libi's detention on board the U.S.S. *San Antonio,* humanitarian groups continued to demand access to assess his living conditions and to ensure that the detainee was being held in accordance with international standards and law. Though the Department of State maintained that al-Libi was being treated humanely, it was hesitant to go into detail regarding al-Libi's confinement.

Questions regarding the legality of the seizure and detention of al-Libi continue to loom. Both the capture of al-Libi and the failed action in Somalia were undertaken, reportedly, with authority from the Authorization to Use Military Force (AUMF), a U.S. law enacted just after the attacks of September 11, 2001. The application of this law to military action beyond the borders of the United States is not clear; however, some interpretations of the AUMF have been expanded to include action beyond U.S. borders in cases of imminent threats. Though the government of Libya remains weak and seems ill-equipped to pursue terrorism within its own borders, the continued liberal application of the AUMF to authorize U.S. military action abroad has raised concerns from the international community regarding sovereignty. By the same token, the International Criminal Court (ICC) has requested that members of the ousted Qaddafi regime be handed over to be tried by the ICC, due in part to concerns about the capabilities of the Libyan justice system. Despite these requests from the ICC, the government of Libya intends to try top aides and officials from the toppled regime within the Libyan justice system.

In addition to any authority that may be conferred by the AUMF, during the October 8, 2013, press briefing Harf stated that al-Libi had been designated a global terrorist under authority from Executive Order 13224 and named on the al Qaeda sanction list of UN Security Council Resolution 12671/1989. Signed by President George W. Bush on September 23, 2001, Executive Order 13224 gives the U.S. government the authority to impede terrorist funding as part of an international effort to stop the activities of terrorist groups such as al Qaeda. The order provides authorization to block the assets of those who provide assistance or associate with persons or groups designated under the order. The broader reach of this order is defensible, according to some, due to the global nature of financial networks. UN 12671/1989 requires member states to freeze assets and prevent financial transactions of any persons or entities contained on the sanction list. It is unclear, however, what legal authority would be conferred upon the United States to pursue a listed designee beyond its own borders and whether this financial authority can be interpreted to authorize military action against a designee.

FUTURE IMPLICATIONS

There remains some uncertainty about the legality of the continued use of U.S. Special Forces operations to target suspected terrorists abroad. In the October 8, 2013, briefing, the Obama administration's commitment to seeking civilian trials for terrorism suspects and condemnation of the use of torture during interrogation was reiterated. The wider ramifications of continued targeted military action in areas of Africa and the Middle East are unclear, and the effect of these military strikes regarding the stability of the region is so far unknown. Opponents of such operations are alarmed by the potential for human rights violations. Even among proponents of these targeted actions, there is concern that legal technicalities may prevent justice from being served. In the case of al-Libi, it remains to be seen whether his detention at sea will influence the ability of prosecutors to hold him fully accountable to the indictment with which he is charged. Others, including some members of Congress, contend that the use of such U.S. military operations should be expanded further to include possible action in Syria.

—Sarah Gall

Following is the edited text of a State Department press conference held on October 8, 2013, discussing the capture of an al Qaeda operative in Iraq.

State Department Discusses al Qaeda Operative Capture

DOCUMENT

October 8, 2013

[Opening statements have been omitted.]

Ms. Harf: So I can confirm that on Monday, Ambassador Jones met with Libyan Justice Minister Salah al-Marghani. They discussed matters related to the detention of Abu Anas al-Libi as well as other issues. Ambassador Jones conveyed that al-Libi is being treated humanely, that we have been in touch with the ICRC. And as we've repeatedly said, we consult regularly with the Government of Libya on a range of security and counterterrorism issues, certainly continuing to do so. We value our relationship and strategic partnership with the government and people of Libya.

Question: So did they have a heads up or not?

Ms. Harf: I'm sorry. About what? The meeting?

Question: Yeah. The government. No. Did the government have a heads up on–

Ms. Harf: I am not going to get into more specifics about our diplomatic conversations. We have a close partnership with them on counterterrorism issues, and we'll continue to do so going forward.

Question: Do you stand by your position that you did not violate their sovereignty?

Ms. Harf: Yes.

Question: So is there a way to not violate their sovereignty by abducting one of their citizens without giving them a heads up?

Ms. Harf: I am just not going to get into more details about discussions with them, about the operation, about any of those issues.

Question: I just don't see how you cannot violate somebody's sovereignty by arresting and abducting one of their citizens unless you gave them a heads up.

Ms. Harf: I'm just not going to go any further.

Question: Can I ask about the ICRC involvement? Does that mean that you're giving them access to Mr. Libi wherever he may be?

Ms. Harf: We've been in touch with the ICRC. He's still in United States custody, as we've talked about. I don't have anything further than that. We'll continue talking with the ICRC going forward.

Question: So you haven't given the ICRC access. Why have you been in touch with them?

Ms. Harf: Again, we reiterated to the ICRC that we are treating him humanely. We're going to continue to be in touch with them, but I don't have anything to announce or updates about further involvement of the ICRC at this time.

Question: And has he been giving an access to any legal advice, to a lawyer, or has he been read any kind of rights or charges?

Ms. Harf: I don't have any more details for you about the process that's ongoing right now about sort of where he is and what he's doing other than what we've already talked about, but nothing further.

Question: Why should the ICRC take your word that he is being treated humanely if they are not given an opportunity to actually check on his conditions of containment?

Ms. Harf: I didn't say that they weren't going to be given that opportunity. I didn't comment any further, I believe. We're going to continue talking to them about his case.

Question: Was the call partly about the possibility that they might be given access?

Ms. Harf: What call? I'm sorry.

Question: You said you contacted him.

Ms. Harf: Oh, we—yes, I'm sorry.

Question: Was the contact about the possibility that they might be given access?

Ms. Harf: We have—we're going to keep discussing his case with them, including possible access, and I just don't have any additional details for you at this point.

Question: Okay. But just so we're clear, you said we're going to continue, including possible access.

Ms. Harf: Mm-hmm.

Question: Was possible access part of the contact that you have had thus far?

Ms. Harf: I can check on the specifics. . . .

Question: More about the access. And the Libyans are saying that they specifically are asking. Can you confirm that they are asking–

Ms. Harf: Asking?

Question: —for al-Libi to be returned to Libya? And also, have you discussed issues of access for the Libyans? Are they going to have consular access to him?

Ms. Harf: These are all good questions. Again, I—Elise, just because you weren't here at the very beginning and some other folks just walked in, on Monday, Ambassador Jones did meet with the Libyan Justice Minister Salah al-Marghani. They discussed his case as well as other issues. She assured them that he's being treated humanely and that we've been in touch with the ICRC. I just don't have further details for you on any of these issues, on any of those discussions, or what this is going to look like going forward. If we do, I'm happy to provide them as we can.

Question: I understand. But if I—

Ms. Harf: Mm-hmm.

Question: But I'm—I can't remember exactly what, since the government has taken office, what parties and conventions they're a party to. But I mean, isn't it typical that a foreign national who's arrested by the United States would have consular access—or detained?

Ms. Harf: I can certainly check on that issue.

. . .

Question: It also would help to know if he's actually charged. I mean, I know he's facing indictment.

Ms. Harf: He's facing indictment, correct.

Question: But whether those have been read to him and whether he's been given any of his rights, whether he's had access to a lawyer. . . . these are all questions that I think if an American citizen was held in similar circumstances you guys would be seeking to find out from that government who was holding him.

Ms. Harf: Absolutely, and I am happy to take those questions. Also, I'm sure the Department of Justice is happy to talk about some of this as well. But I'll see what I can do, and we can continue the conversation.

. . .

Question: Libyan National Conference has asked the U.S. to return Abu Anas al-Libi to Libya. What can you answer that?

Ms. Harf: . . . we're going to continue talking to the Government of Libya. We value their partnership on counterterrorism. I'd also point you to the statements that the Prime Minister of Libya made today which focused on the relationship moving forward, so I think that's what we're focused on as well. And beyond that, no further comment on his whereabouts or what's going to happen next.

Question: The Prime Minister also asked that he be returned and tried in Libya. So, seeing as we have a good relationship with that country, do you think that—is that the plan?

Ms. Harf: I think we've made it clear that he's in our custody, that there's a process that will happen from here. . . . I'm not going to go any further about what might happen next. We said he's being detained lawfully. We said that we've talked to the ICRC about his case. We've said he's being treated humanely. I just don't have additional details. . . .

Question: Because their [the ICRC] report alleges that as long as you keep him there, then he's a treasure trove of information that you can talk to him without the President's Council, without having . . . to read him his rights and so on, and that would actually give a great deal of information that you might need.

Ms. Harf: . . . I don't want to misspeak about anything certainly involving some of those issues that you mentioned. . . . We have said, of course, that our preference, where possible, is to capture terrorists as opposed to taking lethal action because we do get a great deal of intelligence from them when we are able to capture them.

. . .

Question: . . . Is there any likely point of disembarkation for him, I mean, like New York or elsewhere?

Ms. Harf: He is, as we know, under indictment in the Southern District of New York. I just don't have further details for you on where he may end up next.

Question: Since al-Libi's detention, there's been some chatter among terrorist groups. Has there been any initiative from the State Department—message, communiques—about strengthening security at the consulars and embassies?

Ms. Harf: . . . we, of course, always remain vigilant about potential threats to American citizens, about our diplomats working overseas. I think many of you know that our last Travel Warning for Libya was June 7th. That still remains in effect, warns U.S. citizens about traveling to Libya. And of course, the protection of our folks overseas is of great concern to us. We spend a lot of effort making sure they're protected, and of course, we'll evaluate any potential threats. And if we have to take any specific security action, we will.

Question: On the subject of humane treatment, are there halal meals available for al-Libi aboard the vessel?

Ms. Harf: I don't know the answer to that.

Question: . . . as I think you know, Amnesty International issued a report today about al-Libi, and they specifically call on the U.S. Government to immediately confirm his whereabouts and provide him access to legal counsel, medical care, and his family members. What is your response to their call for you to do those four things?

Ms. Harf: Well, I think a couple points. First, we've said that he's being treated humanely . . . I haven't actually seen that report so I don't have a specific comment on it. If there. . . . are more details to share in terms of his location and his treatment and his situation, I'm happy to do so. I would also encourage you to check in with my colleagues in other places around town. We've talked a lot about Department of Defense's role here. I think they can speak to some of these issues directly as well. But again, if there's more to share about this, I'm happy to throughout the rest of the week.

. . .

Question: What does "being treated humanely" mean to you, though?

Ms. Harf: I'm not going to get into a definition from here.

. . .

Question: Could I ask you on the list that came out after September 11, there were like 22 people and so on. I think a number of them have been eliminated, maybe 10 or 12. Do you have a—could you give us a breakdown of who still remains on the list? . . . there was a list like of the al-Qaida leaders at the time.

Ms. Harf: . . . without getting into numbers is that al-Qaida core in Afghanistan and Pakistan, who, of course, was responsible for 9/11, that almost all of their leadership has been taken off the battlefield. I mean, if you think about their leadership on September 11th, all of them are no longer able to threaten the U.S. except, of course, for Ayman al-Zawahiri. So as the core of al-Qaida has been decimated in this region, they have been replaced with younger, less capable, certainly less experienced operatives. So we've seen that happen, I think, over the last years since 2001, but certainly since 2009 as well when we really ramped up our counterterrorism operations there.

So look, we've been clear that the group that attacked us on 9/11 is a very different group today. But at the same time, as they've weakened there, they've spread other places, places like Yemen, Somalia, North Africa. We've talked about this a lot in this room. I talked about it yesterday. So we've kept up the pressure in these other places as they've tried to disperse in other ways, in other places, and establish strongholds there as well.

Question: . . . did you say or do you have any information about Abu Anas al-Libi being involved in the murder of Ambassador Chris Stevens last year?

. . .

Ms. Harf: He's under indictment specifically for being linked to al-Qaida, also for the '98 bombings, but not to my knowledge on Benghazi. . . . He is indicted in the Southern District of New York in connection with his alleged role in al-Qaida's conspiracy to kill U.S. nationals and to conduct attacks against U.S. interests worldwide, which included al-Qaida plots to attack U.S. forces stationed in Saudi Arabia, Yemen, and Somalia, as well as the two U.S. Embassies in Dar es Salaam, Tanzania and Nairobi, Kenya . . . not just for the embassy bombings.

. . . He's also been designated as a specially designated global terrorist under Executive Order 13224. He's listed as a subject on the U.S. Rewards for Justice Program. He's also listed on the UN 1267/1989 al-Qaida sanctions list.

Question: Does to "treat him humanely" mean that he is not being subjected to any forms of physical or mental duress?

Ms. Harf: . . . I don't have more detail for you on his situation right now. I think the President was very clear when he came into office that some of the tactics that had been used in the previous years in terms of talking to suspected terrorists weren't going to be done anymore. He was very clear on I think his second or third day in office when he signed an executive order banning torture. So I don't have more details for you about the current state of Mr. al-Libi, other than to say that I think this Administration has been very clear about what we do and do not do.

Question: The problem is that . . . if no one answers questions about how a prisoner is being treated, and if respected international bodies such as the ICRC do not at least as yet have access to them, it's very hard to know whether they are being treated humanely. And if you can't say yes, humanely means that someone is not being subjected to physical or mental duress, then it leaves open the possibility that your definition of humane treatment includes subjecting people to duress.

Ms. Harf: I understand the question. I will endeavor to get a definition for you about what "being treated humanely" means . . . Because I understand it's an important question . . . and the reason I brought up the principles that the President outlined when he came into office is because I think they underpin everything we've done since then when it comes to this topic. But it's a fair question, and I'll try to get you a definition.

. . .

Question: On the issue of security . . . like the Embassy in Tripoli and others throughout North Africa, have you strengthened security since al-Libi was detained?

Ms. Harf: Well, our security at our embassies, particularly in places like Tripoli, are always on an incredibly high footing, so I'm not going to get into specifics about what the security looks like. Obviously, we'll take steps if we need to.

. . .

Question: Libyan militant groups called for revenge attacks on strategic targets, including gas export pipelines, airplanes and ships, as well as for the kidnappings of Americans in Tripoli and in Libya. How do you take this threat?

Ms. Harf: . . . we always, of course, remain vigilant against potential threats and take them seriously, and our folks are looking at them every single day to make sure we do everything we can to protect our people. But I would stress that these are, at this point, uncorroborated.

Question: Can we go back to the question of legality? . . . I understand that under the U.S. Authorization to Use Military Force, you believe that he's been lawfully detained. . . . that's a U.S. domestic law. Is it also your contention that internationally, under international law, he's being lawfully detained?

Ms. Harf: I can certainly take the question and see if there's a legal guidance I can give on that. . . . but an authorization to use military force—and you were kind of getting at this yesterday—applies to our conduct overseas. So the Authorization to Use Military Force talks about things we can and can't do legally under U.S. law overseas to protect U.S. interests.

Question: But similarly, you couldn't have—I mean, if France has a law or Britain has a law, and they wanted to do something within America, they wouldn't be able to do it without your permission because that would be encroaching onto your sovereignty.

Ms. Harf: And I think I answered the sovereignty question, and I'm happy to take the international law question and see if our legal experts have an answer for you.

. . .

Question: When was the Ambassador asked to go see the government? And was she able to share anything with them? . . .

Ms. Harf: Well, they met on Monday, and this meeting did take place at the request of the Libyans. I don't know when it was requested, but they did meet on Monday. And she—yes, they had a good, productive discussion. Yes, I think these diplomatic discussions are very open and very frank. Obviously, we don't read out all of the details of them for good diplomatic reasons, but I think that—obviously, they talked about al-Libi, but other issues as well.

Question: Has the Libyan Government been cooperative in this particular case on al-Libi?

. . . I mean, are they understanding of your position?

Ms. Harf: Again, we've been in contact with them about it. I think you saw the Prime Minister's comments today. And we're going to continue working with them on counter-terrorism and security issues going forward because they are a very valued partner in this shared fight. And obviously, one of our goals here is to work with them as our partner to help improve their capabilities as well. So that's part of the longer-term goal here. We've talked about this some in the past . . .

Question: Because . . . there's been some anger publicly expressed by Tripoli about what happened over the weekend. But, I mean, I suppose the question is: Is this just a misunderstanding that they thought they were not told something that they should have been told? Or is it that they're playing a publicity game and that they, in fact, helped you with what you—what was carried out, but then publicly can't be seen to be doing that?

Ms. Harf: I think what we're focused on, and what I think they're focused on, quite frankly at this point, is how we move forward and where we go from here. And that's—I think you saw some of that in the statements today, and I think you'll see more of that going forward.

[Duplicate questions and answers about Amnesty International and the definition of humane treatment have been omitted.]

Question: But you say that he was taken and detained because he's indicted in a U.S. court.

Ms. Harf: . . . let's step back for a second. The operation was undertaken under the AUMF, so under our 2001 law that allows us to go after terrorists who might—who have in the past or are attempting to harm the United States. It wasn't undertaken for the purposes of law enforcement.

He is indicted; you're right. That will be a part of this going forward, but that's not the reason it was undertaken.

Question: So did you see him as an imminent threat to U.S. interests? And that's why he was taken?

Ms. Harf: I'm not going to characterize him that way. He is a well-known senior al-Qaida figure in the past who has been associated with attacking the United States.

Clearly, we believed he was a lawful target under the AUMF so under our 2001 law that allows us to go after terrorists who might—who have in the past or are attempting to harm the United States. It wasn't undertaken for the purposes of law enforcement. He is indicted; you're right. That will be a part of this going forward, but that's not the reason it was undertaken.

Question: So did you see him as an imminent threat to U.S. interests? And that's why he was taken?

Ms. Harf: I'm not going to characterize him that way. He is a well-known senior al-Qaida figure in the past who has been associated with attacking the United States. Clearly, we believed he was a lawful target under the AUMF, and I think that's all I have for you.

Question: This guy has been living in the open in Libya, though, for several years. So why, all of a sudden, was it so important to take him?

Ms. Harf: Well, I would maybe disagree a little bit with your characterization that he's been living in the open. I'm not sure exactly what that's based on. But look, timing of operations is driven by operational concerns, by the intelligence, by the situation on the ground, by all of these things, and this was the right time operationally to undertake it. And beyond that, I just don't have any more details for you about the timing.

Question: But you know it was his family that came out and said he's been living a normal life.

Ms. Harf: I've seen some of those comments, and I'm just not going to fact-check all of them for you.

Question: Just a point of clarification: Is the same law that applied here is applied when this—the other operation done in Somali?

Ms. Harf: . . . both under the AUMF, correct.

. . .

Question: You listed Somalia, Yemen, and northern Africa. How about northern Syria? How the Administration is—how much the Administration is concerned about the existence of al-Qaida factions in northern Syria?

Ms. Harf: . . . we've said that we're concerned about extremist elements there. We've talked a lot about al-Nusrah in this room, we've talked about ISIS, we've talked about others. I think—and this is an important point to make—I know we talked a little bit about extremism yesterday—but that the reason there are these terrorists in Syria today creating so many problems is because the Assad regime created an environment for them to flourish, to plan, to plot, and indeed to undertake attacks there. So I think yesterday we were talking about some of this, and I think that's an important point to make. We're certainly concerned about it. That's why we've called on the opposition to reject this extremism, to coalesce around a moderate group and leadership, and that's the conversation we're going to continue with them going forward.

Question: . . . I asked this question to understand what is the exact position of the Administration when it comes to the . . . fight against al-Qaida? . . . You are conducting Special Forces operations in Yemen, Northern Africa, or Somalia . . . but in northern Syria, it's out of question right now. It's not on the table, I think, right?

Ms. Harf: . . . Every situation is different. The threat picture everywhere is different and the operational picture everywhere is different. So wherever al-Qaida plots and plans against the U.S., there are different considerations you take into place in terms of how you counter it.

So in Syria—when we talk about the extremists in Syria, we're working with the opposition to encourage them to reject this extremism. We're also working with our partners in the region to do so as well.

[Questions and answers unrelated to al Qaeda have been omitted.]

Ms. Harf: . . . the security situation in Syria today that is a direct result of the Assad regime's brutal crackdown on its people, the civil war that the Assad regime has been waging against the legitimate, moderate opposition, has created a climate and a security atmosphere where groups like al-Qaida can flourish—al-Qaida-affiliated groups can flourish. So we've said repeatedly that the security vacuum in Syria hasn't just let extremists flourish in Syria, but around the region. We've talked a lot about Iraq in here, and it's certainly been the case that Iraq has seen some of this terrorist violence because of the situation in Syria.

. . . . I think that the regime today has a lot of incentives . . . to move towards a Geneva 2 process where everybody comes to the table, and indeed, we can get passed what's happening there and hopefully move towards a democratic political transition. I think that's what's in the best interest of the Syrian people and will help the security situation in the country moving forward.

[Information provided regarding humanitarian aid in Syria; questions and answers related to guidelines for Americans attending the Olympics in Sochi, Russia; and discussion regarding the government shutdown have been omitted.]

SOURCE: U.S. Department of State. IIP Digital. "State Department Daily Briefing." October 8, 2013. http://translations.state.gov/st/english/texttrans/2013/10/20131008284221.html#axzz2vEoVPnuq.

OTHER HISTORIC DOCUMENTS OF INTEREST

FROM THIS VOLUME

FROM PREVIOUS *HISTORIC DOCUMENTS*

WHO Determines Air Pollution to Be a Leading Environmental Cause of Cancer Deaths

OCTOBER 17, 2013

On October 17, the World Health Organization's (WHO) International Agency for Research on Cancer (IARC) announced that it had classified outdoor air pollution as a carcinogen and declared it to be a leading environmental cause of cancer. The announcement followed the release of several reports pointing to particularly high levels of air pollution and increased risk of disease in Asian countries, particularly in China, and occurred as Chinese cities struggled with record levels of hazardous air pollution.

WHO EVALUATES AIR POLLUTION

The IARC seeks to promote international collaboration in cancer research, and its Monographs Section is regarded as an authoritative source for scientific evidence on environmental causes of cancer. Prior to IARC's October announcement, the Monographs Section had convened a group of experts to conduct an independent review of more than 1,000 existing scientific studies involving millions of people from across five continents that evaluated various air pollutants' link to cancer. Based on this review, the group concluded that "there is sufficient evidence that exposure to outdoor air pollution causes lung cancer" and classified such pollution as a "Group 1" carcinogen, or a definite cause of cancer. They also concluded that exposure to outdoor air pollution has a positive association with increased risk of bladder cancer. Additionally, the research team conducted a separate evaluation of particulate matter (PM), a combination of very small solid particles and liquid droplets of substances such as dust or chemicals that are found in the air, and classified that as a carcinogen as well.

Air pollution was already known to increase the risk for heart and respiratory disease, asthma attacks, and other lung conditions. Common forms of air pollution include nitrogen dioxide, sulfur dioxide, ozone gas, and carbon monoxide, and primary sources include transportation, power plants, industrial and agricultural emissions, and residential heating and cooking. The IARC had previously classified several specific substances found within air pollution as carcinogens, such as diesel engine exhaust, solvents, metals, and dust, but its October announcement marked the first time it has declared air pollution as a whole to be a carcinogen.

Dr. Kurt Straif, Head of the IARC's Monographs Section, said, "The air we breathe has become polluted with a mixture of cancer-causing substances. We now know that outdoor air pollution is not only a major risk to health in general, but also a leading environmental cause of cancer deaths." The exact contents of air pollution vary by location, time of year, and weather, among other factors, and Straif told reporters that in some parts of the world the cancer risks of air pollution exposure are similar to that of breathing secondhand tobacco smoke. IARC's announcement acknowledged that studies have shown significant increases in air pollution exposure levels in recent years, "particularly in rapidly industrializing countries with large populations." IARC Director Dr. Christopher Wild said the agency's report "should send a strong signal to the international community to take action without further delay."

Air Quality in Asia

Indeed, several recent reports had found evidence of particularly high levels of air pollution and related health concerns in developing Asian countries. In December 2012, *The Lancet* published findings from the WHO's 2010 Global Burden of Disease study, which analyzes the most important risk factors contributing to diseases around the world. It includes a list of the most significant risk factors by region; the higher a particular factor's position on the list, the greater the associated risk of disease and the greater the number of people it affects in that region. According to this most recent analysis, outdoor air pollution contributed to more than 3.2 million premature deaths worldwide each year, and more than 76 million years of healthy life lost. It estimated that two-thirds of all deaths caused by PM pollution occurred in the developing countries of South, East, and Central Asia, and stated that air pollution levels in these countries are the highest in the world. The analysis further concluded that household air pollution, caused by people burning solid fuel for heat and cooking, was a significant contributor to overall pollution and risk of disease in low- and middle-income countries. In China, the report estimated that outdoor air pollution contributed to approximately 1.2 million premature deaths and 25 million healthy years of life lost in 2010, which represents a 33 percent increase since the first Global Burden of Disease study in 1990. Outdoor air pollution ranked fourth among the report's list of all risk factors contributing to disease in China.

Another 2012 study conducted by Greenpeace East Asia and Peking University's School of Public Health found that small particle air pollution caused more than 8,500 premature deaths in four Chinese cities that year, and that those same cities lost a combined $1.08 billion due to pollution-related expenses. Other studies pointed to growing rates of cancer in China. In the spring of 2013, Shanghai's Health and Family Planning Commission released a report showing that 98 Shanghai residents die of cancer each day, or approximately 36,000 people each year. Further, the report found that roughly 54,000 city residents had been diagnosed with cancer in 2012, up from 48,000 in 2010. According to a report by the *Los Angeles Times*, lung cancer deaths have risen by 465 percent in China during the past thirty years while cigarette smoking has declined.

China's "Airpocalypse"

Global public awareness of China's air quality issues rose precipitously during the 2008 Olympic Games as the world was exposed to images of thick smog over Beijing, and many speculated about the pollution's impact on visiting athletes and spectators. Shortly thereafter, China's State Environment Protection Agency began providing daily reports of air pollution levels in 86 major cities using the Air Pollution Index. The index measured five atmospheric pollutants, including PM less than 10 micrometers in diameter. Also known as PM10, this material poses a health concern because it can be easily inhaled and accumulates in the respiratory system. Around the same time, the U.S.

Embassy in Beijing installed its own pollution monitor and reported data hourly via Twitter. In addition to PM10, the United States also measured PM2.5. These particles are much finer and are believed to pose the greatest health risk among particulate matter because they can lodge deeply into the lungs. Discrepancies between the U.S. embassy's data and the Chinese government's data caused some to question whether Chinese officials had falsified their numbers, and ultimately led to a public campaign that caused the government to change their reporting methods. Beginning in January 2012, China's Ministry of Environmental Protection began using an enhanced Air Quality Index to measure pollutants, including PM2.5, in 163 cities. The government also issued hourly reports for seventy-four of those cities.

China had been struggling to manage severe air pollution in a number of its cities for months before IARC's announcement. On January 12, 2013, air quality monitors measured PM2.5 levels of 755 in Beijing, nearly forty times higher than the WHO's maximum daily level of 20. PM2.5 levels of 300 or more are considered hazardous to human health. Similar conditions continued for roughly one week in what became known as China's "airpocalypse." Smog affected more than thirty cities across China, and PM2.5 levels reached 900 at one point in Beijing—the highest measured concentration of toxic smog since record-keeping began. More than half of the seventy-four cities receiving hourly pollution readings showed severe air pollution levels during this period.

The extreme levels of pollution were attributed to a number of factors, especially the country's fast development. China has been the world's largest vehicle market since 2009, and thousands of new cars take to the road each day. According to China National Radio, vehicle emissions account for 23 percent of PM2.5 in the air in Beijing. The 2012–2013 winter season was also particularly cold, prompting more people to burn coal to stay warm. The weather patterns reportedly also made the atmosphere above China very stable, causing air pollution to accumulate closer to the ground.

Beijing officials warned citizens to stay inside and to make sure their windows were tightly closed to avoid the thick smog. They temporarily closed some construction sites and factories, banned sales of lower-quality gasoline, and took nearly one-third of official cars off the road. The high volume of harmful particles continued through January and February, prompting many to leave Beijing for fear of increased risk of emphysema and lung cancer. Indeed, Agence France-Presse (AFP) reported in late January that hospital admissions for respiratory complaints rose by 20 percent during the airpocalypse.

As cold weather began to set in again in October, Beijing officials released a color-coded alert system to help manage air pollution emergencies. Different levels of alert called for varied responses, such as temporarily halting construction, factory production, outdoor BBQs, and the setting off of fireworks. On October 21, air pollution soared again, this time in the northeastern city of Harbin. PM2.5 levels reached 1,000, surpassing the record set by Beijing earlier in the year. City officials closed schools, the airport, and a number of bus routes in response. By December, air pollution had decreased across the country, but was still nearly 20 times higher than the WHO's recommended maximum levels..

Chinese media and the general public were critical of how the government handled these issues. One *South China Morning Post* editorial read, "It is sad to note that despite the severity of the smog and its hazardous impact on people's lives, neither the central government leaders nor the officials from those affected cities have come out publicly to apologise and discuss ways to address the issue." Others argued the government should have done more to prevent the pollution. "The air quality in big cities could have been better had more attention been paid to the density of high rises, had more trees been planted in proportion to the number of residential areas, and had the number of cars been strictly controlled," read a *China Daily* editorial.

Some state-controlled outlets tried to deflect blame for the crisis from the government to the Chinese people, while others claimed the pollution had its benefits. A *Global Times* article, for example, argued that the smog could give China a "defensive advantage in military operations" because it could hinder missile strikes. In December, a journalist with CCTV published an editorial called "Five Unexpected Gains the Haze Has Brought" that claimed the air pollution was bringing "major benefits" to China, even if it was also an "enemy." The purported benefits included making people more united; more sober, because it was prompting the Chinese to reflect on the consequences of their country's economic boom; more equal, because it was affecting both the rich and the poor; and more humorous, because people were using comedy to keep "light hearts." Finally, the editorial argued, the pollution was improving Chinese minds. "Our knowledge of meteorology, geography, physics, chemistry and history has grown and the standard of our English has improved too," the journalist argued. "Without this haze, would you know what PM2.5 was? Would you know that 60 years ago the haze claimed 12,000 lives in London? Would you even know the words 'haze' and 'smog'?"

This commentary infuriated the Chinese, drawing more than 80,000 online comments within two hours of being published. Such reactions were indicative of an important shift among the Chinese. While many had previously believed government propaganda that the air quality was fine and improving, or that the smog was just fog or mist, the airpocalypse prompted them to challenge the government and demand solutions.

Chinese officials in Beijing have since pledged to cut air pollution by 15 percent by 2016. The Ministry of Environmental Protection will also require enhanced real-time air pollution reporting for 161 cities, increased from seventy-four, beginning January 1, 2014. Additionally, China's National Health and Family Planning Commission said it will establish a nationwide network to begin monitoring the health effects of air pollution in cities and provinces including Beijing and Shanghai within the next three to five years.

—Linda Fecteau

Following is the text of a press release from the World Health Organization's International Agency for Research on Cancer, issued on October 17, 2013, announcing findings that air pollution is a leading environmental cause of cancer deaths.

WHO Releases Findings on Outdoor Air Pollution

October 17, 2013

[All footnotes have been omitted.]

The specialized cancer agency of the World Health Organization, the International Agency for Research on Cancer (IARC), announced today that it has classified outdoor air pollution as *carcinogenic to humans* (Group 1).

After thoroughly reviewing the latest available scientific literature, the world's leading experts convened by the IARC Monographs Programme concluded that there is *sufficient evidence* that exposure to outdoor air pollution causes lung cancer (Group 1). They also noted a positive association with an increased risk of bladder cancer.

Particulate matter, a major component of outdoor air pollution, was evaluated separately and was also classified as *carcinogenic to humans* (Group 1).

The IARC evaluation showed an increasing risk of lung cancer with increasing levels of exposure to particulate matter and air pollution. Although the composition of air pollution and levels of exposure can vary dramatically between locations, the conclusions of the Working Group apply to all regions of the world.

A major environmental health problem

Air pollution is already known to increase risks for a wide range of diseases, such as respiratory and heart diseases. Studies indicate that in recent years exposure levels have increased significantly in some parts of the world, particularly in rapidly industrializing countries with large populations. The most recent data indicate that in 2010, 223,000 deaths from lung cancer worldwide resulted from air pollution.

The most widespread environmental carcinogen

"The air we breathe has become polluted with a mixture of cancer-causing substances," says Dr Kurt Straif, Head of the IARC Monographs Section. "We now know that outdoor air pollution is not only a major risk to health in general, but also a leading environmental cause of cancer deaths."

The IARC Monographs Programme, dubbed the "encyclopaedia of carcinogens," provides an authoritative source of scientific evidence on cancer-causing substances and exposures. In the past, the Programme evaluated many individual chemicals and specific mixtures that occur in outdoor air pollution. These included diesel engine exhaust, solvents, metals, and dusts. But this is the first time that experts have classified outdoor air pollution as a cause of cancer.

"Our task was to evaluate the air everyone breathes rather than focus on specific air pollutants," explains Dr Dana Loomis, Deputy Head of the Monographs Section. "The results from the reviewed studies point in the same direction: the risk of developing lung cancer is significantly increased in people exposed to air pollution."

IARC Monographs evaluations

Volume 109 of the IARC Monographs is based on the independent review of more than 1000 scientific papers from studies on five continents. The reviewed studies analyse the carcinogenicity of various pollutants present in outdoor air pollution, especially particulate matter and transportation-related pollution. The evaluation is driven by findings from large epidemiologic studies that included millions of people living in Europe, North and South America, and Asia.

The predominant sources of outdoor air pollution are transportation, stationary power generation, industrial and agricultural emissions, and residential heating and cooking. Some air pollutants have natural sources, as well.

"Classifying outdoor air pollution as carcinogenic to humans is an important step," stresses IARC Director Dr Christopher Wild. "There are effective ways to reduce air pollution and, given the scale of the exposure affecting people worldwide, this report should send a strong signal to the international community to take action without further delay."

[IARC contact information has been omitted.]

Annexes

Evaluation groups—Definitions

Group 1: The agent is carcinogenic to humans.
This category is used when there is sufficient evidence of carcinogenicity in humans. Exceptionally, an agent may be placed in this category when evidence of carcinogenicity in humans is less than sufficient but there is sufficient evidence of carcinogenicity in experimental animals and strong evidence in exposed humans that the agent acts through a relevant mechanism of carcinogenicity.

Group 2.
This category includes agents for which, at one extreme, the degree of evidence of carcinogenicity in humans is almost *sufficient,* as well as those for which, at the other extreme, there are no human data but for which there is evidence of carcinogenicity in experimental animals. Agents are assigned to either Group 2A (*probably carcinogenic to humans*) or Group 2B (*possibly carcinogenic to humans*) on the basis of epidemiological and experimental evidence of carcinogenicity and mechanistic and other relevant data. The terms *probably carcinogenic* and *possibly carcinogenic* have no quantitative significance and are used simply as descriptors of different levels of evidence of human carcinogenicity, with *probably carcinogenic* signifying a higher level of evidence than *possibly carcinogenic.*

- Group 2A: The agent is probably carcinogenic to humans.

This category is used when there is limited evidence of carcinogenicity in humans and *sufficient evidence of carcinogenicity* in experimental animals. In some cases, an agent may be classified in this category when there is *inadequate evidence of carcinogenicity* in humans and *sufficient evidence of carcinogenicity* in experimental animals and strong evidence that the carcinogenesis is mediated by a mechanism that also operates in humans. Exceptionally, an agent may be classified in this category solely on the basis of *limited evidence of carcinogenicity* in humans. An agent may be assigned to this category if it clearly belongs, based on mechanistic considerations, to a class of agents for which one or more members have been classified in Group 1 or Group 2A.

- Group 2B: The agent is possibly carcinogenic to humans.

This category is used for agents for which there is *limited evidence of carcinogenicity* in humans and less than *sufficient evidence of carcinogenicity* in experimental animals. It may also be used when there is *inadequate evidence of carcinogenicity* in humans but there is *sufficient evidence of carcinogenicity* in experimental animals. In some instances, an agent for which there is *inadequate evidence of carcinogenicity* in humans and less than *sufficient evidence of carcinogenicity* in experimental animals together with supporting evidence from mechanistic and other relevant data may be placed in this group. An agent may be classified in this category solely on the basis of strong evidence from mechanistic and other relevant data.

Group 3: The agent is not classifiable as to its carcinogenicity to humans.

This category is used most commonly for agents for which the evidence of carcinogenicity is *inadequate* in humans and *inadequate* or *limited* in experimental animals. Exceptionally, agents for which the evidence of carcinogenicity is *inadequate* in humans but *sufficient* in experimental animals may be placed in this category when there is strong evidence that the mechanism of carcinogenicity in experimental animals does not operate in humans. Agents that do not fall into any other group are also placed in this category. An evaluation in Group 3 is not a determination of non-carcinogenicity or overall safety. It often means that further research is needed, especially when exposures are widespread or the cancer data are consistent with differing interpretations.

Group 4: The agent is probably not carcinogenic to humans.

This category is used for agents for which there is *evidence suggesting lack of carcinogenicity* in humans and in experimental animals. In some instances, agents for which there is *inadequate evidence of carcinogenicity* in humans but *evidence suggesting lack of carcinogenicity* in experimental animals, consistently and strongly supported by a broad range of mechanistic and other relevant data, may be classified in this group.

Evidence for studies in humans—Definition

As shown previously, the evidence relevant to carcinogenicity is evaluated using standard terms. For studies in humans, evidence is defined into one of the following categories:

Sufficient evidence of carcinogenicity: The Working Group considers that a causal relationship has been established between exposure to the agent and human cancer. That is, a positive relationship has been observed between the exposure and cancer in studies in which chance, bias and confounding could be ruled out with reasonable confidence. A statement that there is *sufficient evidence* is followed by a separate sentence that identifies the target organ(s) or tissue(s) where an increased risk of cancer was observed in humans. Identification of a specific target organ or tissue does not preclude the possibility that the agent may cause cancer at other sites.

Limited evidence of carcinogenicity: A positive association has been observed between exposure to the agent and cancer for which a causal interpretation is considered by the Working Group to be credible, but chance, bias or confounding could not be ruled out with reasonable confidence.

Inadequate evidence of carcinogenicity: The available studies are of insufficient quality, consistency or statistical power to permit a conclusion regarding the presence or absence of a causal association between exposure and cancer, or no data on cancer in humans are available.

Evidence suggesting lack of carcinogenicity: There are several adequate studies covering the full range of levels of exposure that humans are known to encounter, which are mutually consistent in not showing a positive association between exposure to the agent and any studied cancer at any observed level of exposure. The results from these studies alone or combined should have narrow confidence intervals with an upper limit close to the null value (e.g. a relative risk of 1.0). Bias and confounding should be ruled out with reasonable confidence, and the studies should have an adequate length of follow-up. A conclusion of *evidence suggesting lack of carcinogenicity* is inevitably limited to the cancer sites, conditions and levels of exposure, and length of observation covered by the available studies. In addition, the possibility of a very small risk at the levels of exposure studied can never be excluded.

In some instances, the above categories may be used to classify the degree of evidence related to carcinogenicity in specific organs or tissues.

SOURCE: From IARC. "Outdoor air pollution a leading environmental cause of cancer deaths." Press release n 221, 17 October 2013. http://www.iarc.fr/en/media-centre/iarcnews/pdf/pr221_E.pdf.

OTHER HISTORIC DOCUMENTS OF INTEREST

FROM THIS VOLUME

- Intergovernmental Panel on Climate Change Releases Report on Greenhouse Gases, p. 460

FROM PREVIOUS *HISTORIC DOCUMENTS*

- 2011 Durban Climate Change Conference; Canada Leaves Kyoto, *2011*, p. 670
- Concerns over the 2008 Beijing Summer Olympic Games, *2008*, p. 296

President Obama Remarks on the Affordable Care Act

OCTOBER 21, 2013

The long-anticipated start of the Affordable Care Act (ACA) individual mandate, under which all Americans were required to purchase some form of health insurance, came on October 1, 2013, after Democrats thwarted Republican efforts to delay the mandate's implementation. The federal health exchange through which Americans could purchase health coverage opened to much fanfare, but it was instantly criticized because of the system's inability to handle the volume of users. States that opened their own exchanges had a bit more success, with Kentucky as the leading example of how to enroll its uninsured in cost-effective health plans.

THE AFFORDABLE CARE ACT

The Patient Protection and Affordable Care Act (ACA) was debated for nearly a year in Congress before it came before the president to sign. The Democrats in the House and Senate worked on separate versions of a bill, partly because of internal disagreements within the party about exactly what the bill would do. The House version of the bill included the public option (the creation of a government-run health insurance agency), a tax on high-income earners, and penalties for companies that did not comply with the requirement to insure their employees. Some exemptions to the latter point were included in an effort to garner support from more conservative members of the Democratic Party. The House version also included an amendment that prohibited public option coverage of abortion, except in the instances of rape, incest, or if the mother's life was in danger. The Senate bill was developed by Sen. Max Baucus, D-Mont., and excluded the public option because of its unpopularity with Republicans, who saw it as a means to increase government bureaucracy. The Baucus bill also included a provision that would tax insurance companies that offered so-called Cadillac plans, or plans with an unusually high premium and low deductible, and increased the Medicare payroll tax on high-income earners. Additionally, his bill would not require employers to provide insurance to their employees, but would instead require any employer choosing not to provide coverage to pay a fee to the government to help cover the cost to employees who would have to buy their own coverage from a health insurance exchange. The House passed its version of the bill in November 2009, while the Senate passed its bill on Christmas Eve 2009.

With two different versions moving forward, lawmakers met in February 2010 with President Barack Obama to discuss options for combining the two bills. Republicans were critical of the passage of any bill, arguing that it was not in line with the will of the American people, nor had it been fully vetted. They also believed it would be yet another large entitlement for the federal government to cover that would add more to the federal deficit. During the marathon seven-hour meeting, Democrats threatened to use a controversial reconciliation bill tactic that would ensure the bill could be passed by simple majority vote in the Senate because the rules do not allow for a filibuster on this type of bill.

In the end, it was the Democrats in the House who decided to pass the Senate version of the bill with a separate changes bill, fearful that the Senate would not be able to hold a successful vote on the House version, especially in light of the election of Sen. Scott Brown, R-Mass., to fill the late Sen. Ted Kennedy's seat. The House passed the Senate version 219–212 on March 10. After a long debate in the Senate, Democrats were able to pass the changes bill 56–43, after making some minor adjustments of their own. The changes went back to the House, which gave the bill final approval 220–207. No Republicans voted in favor of the bill. The ACA was signed into law on March 23, 2010, and guaranteed access to medical insurance for tens of millions of uninsured Americans and gave additional coverage guarantees to those already insured. As passed, the act was expected to cost $940 billion during the next decade, and it would be fully implemented by 2014.

Without Republican support, it was clear that implementation of the law would be difficult. The first provisions, including a ban on dropping sick or otherwise costly patients from insurance coverage after finding technical mistakes on applications, and a requirement to allow dependents to remain on their parents' health insurance until age twenty-six, went into effect in September 2010. There was an instant backlash from health insurers, who vowed to leave certain markets or refuse to sell certain policies. In an effort to stop any long-term damage, the Obama administration made concessions, including a one-year extension on adhering to certain rules for nearly thirty insurers.

Republicans used the health care reform law as one of the cornerstones of their 2010 midterm election campaigns. Republicans across the country promised that, if elected, they would challenge the law through any means necessary with the ultimate goal of repealing it. A new conservative movement was born out of the debate, the tea party (tea standing for "taxed enough already"), and its members were able to garner enough support to put in office candidates who fought hard for the act's repeal, like Sen. Ted Cruz, R-Texas, who held a twenty-one hour marathon filibuster speech against the ACA during budget negotiations in September 2013. The 2010 midterm election put Republicans in control of the House and they closed in on the Democratic majority in the Senate.

The biggest blow to Republican efforts to repeal the ACA to date was the June 28, 2012, ruling by the Supreme Court in *National Federation of Independent Business v. Sebelius*. The case was a challenge to the ACA, specifically whether the individual mandate had been constitutionally enacted, and whether the act's Medicaid expansion provisions were legal. Four justices voted to strike down the ACA in its entirety, while four of the more liberal justices wanted to uphold the act. Chief Justice John Roberts was the deciding vote to uphold the individual mandate, arguing that it was a constitutionally sound use of Congress's taxing power.

FEDERAL EXCHANGE OPENS

A key provision of the ACA was the individual mandate, which required all Americans to have health insurance coverage. Those who did not receive coverage from an employer or a government program like Medicare or Medicaid could purchase insurance through state insurance exchanges or the Health Insurance Marketplace, the federal insurance exchange that offered certain cost-effective health care plans for individuals to choose from based on their own needs.

Under the federal exchange, there are four primary insurance tiers: bronze, silver, gold, and platinum, ranging from lowest to highest premiums, respectively. There is a fifth high-deductible plan available for those under age thirty or those with a special exemption. The cap on out-of-pocket expenses under each of the plans is set at $6,350 for individuals and $12,700 for families. For those with an income between 133 percent and 400 percent of the federal poverty line, subsidies are available to help offset costs. These subsidies are given as refundable tax credits.

Enrollment began on October 1, 2013, when HealthCare.gov opened, a website intended to give interested individuals access to an application for health insurance and plan choices. Those without access to a computer could also visit certain community centers that were able to assist with enrollment or call an insurance hotline. During the first few weeks of operation, the website either timed out or crashed for many users. According to Todd Park, the government's Chief Technology Officer, the problem was the volume of users trying to access the website. The site had been developed to support 50,000 to 60,000 visitors at any one time, but it was drawing approximately 250,000. In the first four days of operation, more than eight million Americans attempted to log in to HealthCare.gov. President Obama responded to criticism of the website in a speech on October 21. "The problem has been that the web site that's supposed to make it easy to apply for and purchase the insurance is not working the way it should for everybody. And there's no sugar-coating it. The web site has been too slow, people have been getting stuck during the application process. And I think it's fair to say that nobody is more frustrated by that than I am. . . . And there's no excuse for the problems, and . . . these problems are getting fixed," Obama said. Despite the difficulties, Obama said, "Thousands of people are signing up and saving money as we speak. Many Americans with a preexisting condition . . . are discovering that they can finally get health insurance like everybody else."

Given the difficulties Americans experienced trying to sign up for health care, in late October, the enrollment deadline was moved back six weeks to March 31, 2014. At that point, anyone who did not have coverage would face a penalty. Some groups were given an extension into April, including those who claimed through a checkbox on the website that they had attempted to sign up prior to the deadline, those who were seeking coverage under the Pre-Existing Condition Insurance Plan, and those who had received special exemption under the rules of the law and were not required to enroll in the plan.

STATES HAVE MORE SUCCESS

Eighteen states—Arkansas, California, Colorado, Connecticut, Hawaii, Idaho, Illinois, Kentucky, Maryland, Massachusetts, Minnesota, Nevada, New Mexico, New York, Oregon, Rhode Island, Vermont, and Washington—and the District of Columbia opted out of the federal exchange, in favor of setting up their own state-based insurance exchanges for their citizens. The go-live date on some of these exchanges was October 1, and by and large the states experienced greater success than the federal exchange in their first months of operation. Some states chose to delay their go-live until early 2014.

During the first week of activity, California enrolled more than 28,000 individuals and more than 40,000 signed up in New York. Overall, according to federal data, for the month of October, even though the fifteen exchanges up and running as of October 1 accounted for less than one-third of the nation's population, they made up 75 percent of private insurance enrollments and more than half of all Medicaid sign-ups.

One reason cited for the success in state exchanges was that many allow consumers to browse available coverage options without creating an account first, something the federal exchange does not permit. Alan Weil, executive director at the National Academy for State Health Policy, also cited the adaptability of the smaller exchanges. "They can respond more quickly to solve problems as they arise," Weil said. A few states, like Minnesota and Nevada, faced early glitches because their systems communicate with the federal exchange for certain processes like identity proofing. Hawaii and Vermont used the federal government's IT vendor CGI and had start-up problems of their own.

Kentucky has been touted as a national health care model. The state has approximately 640,000 uninsured residents, and in its first week of operation, enrolled 17,300 in health insurance plans. During the first month, 29,000 people signed up for Medicaid, making it the most successful state, per capita, in registering people for private insurance and Medicaid. Success in Kentucky has been linked to a few different factors, including three months of exhaustive testing (as compared to two weeks of full testing for the federal exchange) and a very basic design. "Our system doesn't have a lot of bells and whistles," said Carrie Banahan, the executive director of the state's exchange, known as Kynect. "There aren't a lot of graphics that would take a lot of bandwidth," she continued. Kentucky's governor, Steve Beshear, applauded his state's efforts, saying, "We're incredibly proud of the continued success of Kynect, which has helped thousands of Kentuckians find affordable health coverage, many of them for the first time."

—Heather Kerrigan

Following is the text of a speech delivered by President Barack Obama on October 21, 2013, in defense of the Affordable Care Act and the health insurance exchange website, HealthCare.gov.

President Obama Remarks on the Opening of the Federal Health Insurance Exchange

DOCUMENT

October 21, 2013

. . . About 3 weeks ago, as the Federal Government shut down, the Affordable Care Act's health insurance marketplaces opened for business across the country. Well, we've now gotten the Government back open for the American people, and today I want to talk about how we're going to get the marketplaces running at full steam as well. And I'm joined today by folks who have either benefited from the Affordable Care Act already or who are helping their fellow citizens learn about what this law means for them and how they can get covered.

Of course, you've probably heard that healthcare.gov—the new web site where people can apply for health insurance and browse and buy affordable plans in most States—hasn't worked as smoothly as it was supposed to work. And the number of people who have visited the site has been overwhelming, which has aggravated some of these underlying problems.

Despite all that, thousands of people are signing up and saving money as we speak. Many Americans with a preexisting condition, like Janice [a beneficiary of the Patient Protection and Affordable Care Act], are discovering that they can finally get health insurance like everybody else.

So today I want to speak to every American who's looking to get affordable health insurance. I want you to know what's available to you and why it may be a good deal for you. And for those who've had some problems with the web site, I want to tell you what we're doing to make it work better and how you can sign up to get covered in other ways.

But before I do that, let me remind everybody that the Affordable Care Act is not just a web site. It's much more. For the vast majority of Americans—for 85 percent of Americans who already have health insurance through your employer or Medicare or Medicaid—you don't need to sign up for coverage through a web site at all. You've already got coverage. What the Affordable Care Act does for you is to provide you with new benefits and protections that have been in place for some time. You may not know it, but you're already benefiting from these provisions in the law.

For example, because of the Affordable Care Act, young people like Jasmine Jennings and Jessica Ugalde and Ezra Salop—all of whom are here today—they've been able to stay on their parents' plans until they're 26. Millions of other young people are currently benefiting from that part of the law. Another part of the Affordable Care Act is providing seniors with deeper discounts on their prescription medicine. Billions of dollars have been saved by seniors already. That's part of the law. It's already in place. It's happening right now.

Already, because of the Affordable Care Act, preventive care like mammograms and birth control are free through your employers. That's part of this law. So there are a wide range of consumer protections and benefits that you already have if you've got health insurance. You may not have noticed them, but you've got them, and they're not going anywhere. And they're not dependent on a web site.

Here's another thing that the Affordable Care Act does. In States where Governors and legislatures have wisely allowed it, the Affordable Care Act provides the opportunity for many Americans to get covered under Medicaid for the first time. So in Oregon, for example, that's helped cut the number of uninsured people by 10 percent just in the last 3 weeks. Think about that. That's 56,000 more Americans who now have health care. That doesn't depend on a web site.

Now, if you're one of the 15 percent of Americans who don't have health insurance—either because you can't afford it or because your employer doesn't offer it or because you're a small-businessperson and you have to go out on the individual market and buy it on your own and it's just too expensive—October 1 was an important date. That's when we opened the new marketplaces where people without health insurance or who can't afford health insurance or who aren't part of a group plan can finally start getting affordable coverage.

And the idea is simple. By enrolling in what we're calling these marketplaces, you become part of a big group plan, as if you were working for a big employer: a Statewide group plan that spreads risk between sick people and healthy people, between young and old, and then bargains on your behalf for the best deal on health care. What we've done is essentially created competition where there wasn't competition before. We created these big group plans, and now insurers are really interested in getting your business. And so insurers have created new health care plans with more choices to be made available through these marketplaces.

And as a result of this choice and this competition, prices have come down. When you add the new tax credits that many people are eligible for through the law, then the prices come down even further. So one study shows that through new options created by the Affordable Care Act, nearly 6 in 10 uninsured Americans will find that they can get covered for less than a hundred dollars a month. Think about that. Through the marketplaces, you can get health insurance for what may be the equivalent of your cell phone bill or your cable bill, and that's a good deal.

So the fact is, the product of the Affordable Care Act for people without health insurance is quality health insurance that's affordable. And that product is working. It's really good. And it turns out, there's a massive demand for it. So far, the national web site, healthcare.gov, has been visited nearly 20 million times. [*Applause*] Twenty million times. And there's great demand at the State level as well, because a lot—there are a bunch of States that are running their own marketplaces.

We know that nearly one-third of the people applying in Connecticut and Maryland, for example, are under 35 years old. They understand that they can get a good deal at low costs, have the security of health care, and this is not just for old folks like me, that everybody needs good quality health insurance. And all told, more than half a million consumers across the country have successfully submitted applications through Federal and State marketplaces. And many of those applications aren't just for individuals, it's for their entire families. So even more people are already looking to potentially take advantage of the high quality, affordable insurance that is provided through the Affordable Care Act.

So let me just recap here. The product is good. The health insurance that's being provided is good. It's high quality, and it's affordable. People can save money, significant money, by getting insurance that's being provided through these marketplaces. And we know that the demand is there. People are rushing to see what's available. And those who've already had a chance to enroll are thrilled with the result. Every day, people who were stuck with sky-high premiums because of preexisting conditions are getting affordable insurance for the first time or finding, like Janice did, that they're saving a lot of money. Every day, women are finally buying coverage that doesn't charge them higher premiums than men for the same care. Every day, people are discovering that new health insurance plans have to cover maternity care, mental health care, free preventive care

. . . . The point is, the essence of the law—the health insurance that's available to people—is working just fine. In some cases, actually, it's exceeding expectations: The prices are lower than we expected, the choice is greater than we expected.

But the problem has been that the web site that's supposed to make it easy to apply for and purchase the insurance is not working the way it should for everybody. And there's no sugarcoating it. The web site has been too slow, people have been getting stuck during the application process. And I think it's fair to say that nobody is more frustrated by that than I am. Because—precisely because the product is good, I want the cash registers to work. I want the checkout lines to be smooth. So I want people to be able to get this great product. And there's no excuse for the problems, and it's—these problems are getting fixed.

But while we're working out the kinks in the system, I want everybody to understand the nature of the problem. First of all, even with all the problems at healthcare.gov, the web site is still working for a lot of people, just not as quick or efficient or consistent as we want.

And although many of these folks have found that they had to wait longer than they wanted, once they complete the process, they're very happy with the deal that's available to them, just like Janice is.

Second, I want everybody to remember that we're only 3 weeks into a 6-month open enrollment period, when you can buy these new plans. Keep in mind, the insurance doesn't start until January 1; that's the earliest that the insurance can kick in. No one who decides to purchase a plan has to pay their first premium until December 15. And unlike the day after Thanksgiving sales for the latest PlayStation or flat-screen TVs, the insurance plans don't run out. They're not going to sell out. They'll be available through the marketplace throughout the open enrollment period. The prices that insurers have set will not change. So everybody who wants insurance through the marketplace will get insurance, period. [*Applause*] Everybody who wants insurance through the marketplace will get insurance.

Third, we are doing everything we can possibly do to get the web sites working better, faster, sooner. We've got people working overtime, 24/7, to boost capacity and address the problems. Experts from some of America's top private sector tech companies who, by the way, have seen things like this happen before, they want it to work. They're reaching out. They're offering to send help. We've had some of the best IT talent in the entire country join the team. And we're well into a tech surge to fix the problem. And we are confident that we will get all the problems fixed.

Number four, while the web site will ultimately be the easiest way to buy insurance through the marketplace, it isn't the only way. And I want to emphasize this. Even as we redouble our efforts to get the site working as well as it's supposed to, we're also redoubling our efforts to make sure you can still buy the same quality, affordable insurance plans available on the marketplace the old-fashioned way: offline, either over the phone or in person.

And by the way, there are a lot of people who want to take advantage of this who are more comfortable working on the phone anyway or in person. So let me go through the specifics as to how you can do that if you're having problems with the web site or you just prefer dealing with a person.

Yesterday we updated the web site's home page to offer more information about the other avenues to enroll in affordable health care until the online option works for everybody. So you'll find information about how to talk to a specialist who can help you apply over the phone or to receive a downloadable application you can fill out yourself and mail in.

We've also added more staff to the call centers where you can apply for insurance over the phone. Those are already—they've been working. But a lot of people have decided first to go to the web site. But keep in mind, these call centers are already up and running. And you can get your questions answered by real people, 24 hours a day, in 150 different languages. The phone number for these call centers is 1-800-318-2596. I want to repeat that: 1-800-318-2596. Wait times have averaged less than 1 minute so far on the call centers, although I admit that the wait times probably might go up a little bit now that I've read the number out loud on national television. [*Laughter*]

But the point is, the call centers are available. You can talk to somebody directly, and they can walk you through the application process. And I guarantee you, if one thing is worth the wait, it's the safety and security of health care that you can afford or the amount of money that you can save by buying health insurance through the marketplaces.

Once you get on the phone with a trained representative, it usually takes about 25 minutes for an individual to apply for coverage, about 45 minutes for a family. Once you apply for coverage, you will be contacted by mail—by e-mail or postal mail about your coverage status.

But you don't have to just go through the phone. You can also apply in person with the help of local navigators. These are people specially trained to help you sign up for health care, and they exist all across the country. Or you can go to community health centers and hospitals. Just visit localhelp.healthcare.gov to find out where in your area you can get help and apply for insurance in person.

And finally, if you've already tried to apply through the web site and you've been stuck somewhere along the way, do not worry. In the coming weeks, we will contact you directly, personally, with a concrete recommendation for how you can complete your application, shop for coverage, pick a plan that meets your needs, and get covered once and for all.

So here's the bottom line. The product, the health insurance, is good. The prices are good. It is a good deal. People don't just want it, they're showing up to buy it. Nobody is madder than me about the fact that the web site isn't working as well as it should, which means it's going to get fixed. [*Laughter*]

And in the meantime, you can bypass the web site and apply by phone or in person. So don't let problems with the web site deter you from signing up or signing your family up or showing your friends how to sign up, because it is worth it. It will save you money. If you don't have health insurance, if you've got a preexisting condition, it will save you money, and it will give you the security that your family needs.

In fact, even with the web site issues, we've actually made the overall process of buying insurance through the marketplace a lot smoother and easier than the old way of buying insurance on your own. Part of the challenge here is that a lot of people may not remember what it's like to buy insurance the traditional way.

The way we've set it up, there are no more absurdly long application forms. There's no medical history questionnaire that goes on for pages and pages. There's no more getting denied because you've had a preexisting condition. Instead of contacting a bunch of different insurers once—one at a time, which is what Janice and a lot of people who are shopping on the individual market for health insurance had to do, there's one single place you can go shop and compare plans that have to compete for your business. There's one single phone number you can call for help. And once the kinks in the web site have been ironed out, it will be even smoother and even easier. But in the meantime, we will help you sign up, because consumers want to buy this product and insurance companies want to sell it to you.

[President Obama's remarks on Republican efforts to repeal the Affordable Care Act, and additional anecdotes about those seeking out health insurance, have been omitted.]

. . . Our goal has always been to declare that in this country the security of health care is not a privilege for a fortunate few, it's a right for all to enjoy. That's what the Affordable Care Act is all about. That's its promise. And I intend to deliver on that promise.

Thank you very much, everybody. God bless you.

SOURCE: Executive Office of the President. "Remarks on the Patient Protection and Affordable Care Act." October 21, 2013. *Compilation of Presidential Documents* 2013, no. 00716 (October 21, 2013). http://www.gpo.gov/fdsys/pkg/DCPD-201300716/pdf/DCPD-201300716.pdf.

OTHER HISTORIC DOCUMENTS OF INTEREST

International Organizations Respond to Violence in Mozambique

OCTOBER 23, 2013

Sporadic violence and simmering political tensions dominated Mozambique's political scene in 2013. The conflict between the Mozambique Liberation Front (Frelimo), the dominant political party in the country, and the main opposition Mozambican National Resistance (Renamo), which fought a bloody and prolonged civil war that ended in 1992, raised concerns that the country could again dissolve into a crisis. An attack by Renamo on a police station in April, reportedly in retaliation for the arrest of fifteen of its members, resulted in the deaths of five police officers. The crisis worsened in October when government forces took control of Renamo's bush camp (and former war-time headquarters), causing its long-time leader, Afonso Dhlakama, to flee. The main opposition party responded by stating in the press that the 1992 peace accord that ended the civil war was annulled. Chief among Renamo's complaints was electoral reform, and in particular greater participation on the part of Renamo in the country's highly politicized National Electoral Commission (CNE). Subsequent negotiations between the two sides on electoral reform cooled tensions, and in February 2014 significant changes to the CNE were unanimously passed by the legislature. Nevertheless, concerns over long-term political stability remain ahead of the October 2014 presidential election.

Sixteen-Year Civil War Devastates Country

Mozambique declared its independence from Portugal in 1975 after the colonialist government was forced to relinquish the territory after a military coup in Lisbon, the Portuguese capital, in 1974. The anticolonialist Frelimo, a coalition of three banned political groups that had previously engaged in a guerilla war against colonialist forces in the north of the country, was handed power by the Portuguese in July 1975. The new government, led by Samora Machel, faced significant economic and political hurdles, not least of which was the mass exodus of the country's Portuguese managers and technicians, leaving behind a largely unskilled labor force. Faced with severe economic woes, the government centralized the economy, nationalizing the former colonial businesses and properties. Just two years after independence, the government declared Mozambique a single-party Marxist state.

In the two years that followed, the government's development program stifled private activity, while its class enemies, broadly defined, were sidelined or sent to re-education camps. The economic mismanagement, coupled with Frelimo's tight grip on power and lack of accountability, resulted in the emergence of disaffected groups. Renamo was established by the Rhodesian security services as a counter-revolutionary force, and soon posed an armed threat to Frelimo. In 1977, civil war erupted, leading to the displacement of five million civilians and the death of approximately one million as a result of the conflict and starvation.

In 1986, then-president Machel was killed in a plane crash in South Africa. He was succeeded in office by Joaquim Chissano, who was considered to be a pragmatist. Owing to a confluence of factors, including the end of the Cold War and of the Apartheid regime in South Africa, which had provided financial support to Renamo, and a new, more pragmatic president, the political situation evolved, leading the two sides to come together for protracted negotiations to end the conflict. A peace accord was signed in Rome, Italy, in October 1992, followed two years later by the country's first democratic elections. A large United Nations peacekeeping mission oversaw the transition to peace.

Vast Natural Wealth Fails to Benefit Poor

Although the postwar economy has grown at impressive rates and the country has vast natural resources wealth, it remains one of the poorest nations in the world. The United Nations Development Program's 2013 Human Development Index ranked Mozambique 185 out of 187 countries on measures of life expectancy, educational attainment, and income. According to the African Development Bank (ADB), "despite more than a decade of sustained high economic growth, Mozambique's economy did not undergo any significant structural change, limiting its capacity to sustainably reduce poverty and foster human development, still one of the lowest in the world." Economic growth has been boosted in recent years by inward foreign direct investment in so-called mega projects, which are concentrated in the natural resources sector. However, these projects do little regarding domestic employment, government revenue, and the diversification of the economy, according to the ADB. Moreover, Mozambique's business environment is plagued by corruption, weak infrastructure, and a poorly trained labor force.

In 2012, Mozambican waters were home to the largest natural gas discovery in over a decade. According to the U.S. Energy Information Administration, the country's offshore reserves total 4.5 trillion cubic feet. A liquefied natural gas terminal is expected to open in 2018, and will be the second-largest export terminal in the world.

Despite the positive economic growth and democratic pluralism in the postwar era, significant concerns remained and tensions between the main opposition Renamo and the ruling Frelimo simmered. Chief among the political concerns of civil society groups and Renamo was the apparent decrease in political pluralism and authoritarian tendencies of Frelimo in recent years. In particular, the main opposition party has called for electoral reforms, arguing that the system is flawed and has been manipulated to give Frelimo an advantage over its opponents.

Frelimo has also been criticized for its economic policies. Indeed, despite strong economic growth, the majority of the country still lives in poverty. According to the 2013 Human Development Index, more than 59 percent of the country's population lives on less than $1.25 a day (in purchasing power parity terms). Moreover, critics argue that the country's natural resources have been mismanaged and that the mega projects associated with the extractive industries should take into account environmental and social considerations. Renamo has also called for a more equitable share of the profits from the country's natural resources, although the party has failed to clarify how this would work in practice.

April 2013 Violence

The longstanding political and economic tensions dissolved into violence on April 4, 2013, after a Renamo political meeting was disrupted by the police and fifteen of its members were arrested. Renamo retaliated by attacking a police station, killing five officers. Although Frelimo publicly condemned the police disturbance of Renamo's activities, the incident followed months of similar reported incidences in which the police harassed peaceful political gatherings. Dhlakama took responsibility for ordering the attack on the police station and called on the government to release the fifteen group members arrested and for government security forces to pull back from their position along the perimeter of the party's bush camp.

While some of Renamo's grievances were substantiated (e.g., concerns over democratic pluralism), the tensions followed a period of political decline for the main opposition party. Renamo posted strong showings in the country's first three democratic elections, but subsequently lost ground, in large part reflecting poor leadership as Frelimo moved to solidify its grip on power. In addition, the emergence of the Movimento Democrático de Moçambique as a significant political force in the country has diminished Renamo's support base. The latter's political decline was reflected in its occasional violent reactions to Frelimo provocations. Dhlakama's aim was to force the ruling party into high-level negotiations.

POLITICAL TENSIONS PEAK

On October 21, 2013, government forces attacked Renamo's bush camp stronghold in Satunjira in the central Sofala province. A defense ministry spokesman stated in a news conference that there were no fatalities in the attack and that government forces took control of the camp. Dhlakama escaped the attack and took refuge in a nearby mountain range. Fernando Mazanga, a spokesperson for the group, said at a separate press conference, "Dhlakama is alive and in good health despite that attack . . . the attack definitely puts to an end the Rome peace agreement and from now on we cannot assure what will happen."

Subsequent efforts to engage the two sides in dialogue were largely unsuccessful. The United Nations Secretary General, Ban Ki-moon, and the African Union called on both sides to enter a dialogue. Ban said in a statement that both sides should "fully engage in an inclusive dialogue to resolve differences within the established democratic order and to ensure that the country continues to achieve social inclusion and sustainable development for all." In early November, President Chissano invited Dhlakama to a face-to-face meeting in the capital, Maputa. The latter declined, and the group's spokesperson stated that the offer was "a political propaganda campaign without minimal respect for ethics." Renamo boycotted the local elections on November 20, allowing political seats held by Frelimo to be uncontested, further solidifying the latter's political dominance.

In the months that followed, both sides agreed to engage in negotiations in Maputo. Key among Renamo's grievances was electoral reform, and in particular greater participation on the part of Renamo in the country's highly politicized CNE, which will oversee the October 2014 presidential election. On February 21, 2014, the two sides formally agreed to increase the size of the Commission to seventeen members, up from thirteen previously. Renamo gained two of the new seats, bringing its total representation up to four. Lawmakers voted unanimously to pass the changes.

Despite the progress made in addressing the political tensions and resulting violence, concerns remain about the politicization of the country's electoral body. A July 2013 report from the European Commission Election Follow-Up Mission noted that "the CNE faces a credibility challenge as its action has been seen as lacking transparency, fairness and impartiality and as showing links with ruling party interests." The changes passed in February 2014 are unlikely to lead to significant improvement in these areas.

—Hilary Ewing

Following is a press release from the African Union and a statement from the United Nations, both on October 23, 2013, related to the collapse of the peace accord in Mozambique and subsequent escalation of violence.

African Union Condemns Violence in Mozambique

October 23, 2013

The Chairperson of the Commission of the African Union (AU), Dr. Nkosazana Dlamini-Zuma, is following closely the recent developments in Mozambique. She is particularly concerned by the announcement made by the Resistência Nacional Moçambicana (Renamo) to withdraw from the 1992 Peace Accord signed with the Government of Mozambique. She underlines the AU's total rejection of any attempt to undermine stability in Mozambique and the remarkable economic gains made to date.

The Chairperson of the Commission stresses the need for all concerned stakeholders to act in a spirit of restraint and dialogue, to allow Mozambique to continue on its remarkable path of development and growth, and to continue to consolidate its democratic institutions, including the successful and peaceful holding of the local elections planned for November 2013. In this respect, she welcomes the commitment of the Mozambican Government to talks in order to address the current challenges, and calls on the Renamo leadership to respond positively and unconditionally to this offer.

SOURCE: African Union. "The African Union Condemns Any Attempt to Undermine Peace, Stability and Development in Mozambique." October 23, 2013. http://www.peaceau.org/uploads/auc-com-mozam bique-23-10-2013.pdf.

UN Secretary General Expresses Concern on Situation in Mozambique

October 23, 2013

The Secretary-General is concerned by the recent escalation of violence in Mozambique between government forces and members of the Mozambican National Resistance (RENAMO).

The Secretary-General calls on all parties to refrain from any act that can threaten the peace and stability that has prevailed during the past 21 years, since the 1992 Rome General Peace Accords.

He urges them to fully engage in an inclusive dialogue to resolve differences within the established democratic order and to ensure that the country continues to achieve social inclusion and sustainable development for all.

SOURCE: United Nations. "Statement attributable to the Spokesperson for the Secretary-General on Mozambique." October 23, 2013. http://www.un.org/sg/statements/index.asp?nid=7226.

November

Department of Justice Gives Consent for Largest Airline Merger

NOVEMBER 13, 2013

Just months after entering bankruptcy protection in 2011, American Airlines began work on a merger agreement with US Airways. The merger resulted in the creation of the world's largest airline. Unlike previous similar mergers, which have taken years to complete, the American Airlines/US Airways deal was hammered out and agreed to in short order and received final approval from the Justice Department on December 9, 2013.

MERGER TAKES SHAPE

Throughout their history, American Airlines and US Airways have been fierce competitors, most recently as the third and fourth largest airlines, respectively. They have typically attempted to undercut each other through discount and frequent flier bonus programs. American Airlines services more than 250 destinations worldwide, while US Airways serves 193 destinations in twenty-four countries. In the last decade, both airlines hit dire straits financially largely due to decreasing demand after September 11, 2001, and the price differential of low-cost carriers. To avoid bankruptcy protection, US Airways announced plans in 2000 to be acquired by United Airlines, but the federal government instantly objected to the merger, and the offer was withdrawn when it became clear that the government would not clear the deal. In August 2002, US Airways entered Chapter 11 bankruptcy protection, and with the help of a government-backed loan, US Airways emerged from bankruptcy in 2003, only to file again in 2004. To exit bankruptcy the second time, US Airways merged in 2005 with America West Airlines and retained the US Airways name. American Airlines faced a similar problem, falling victim to the global financial crisis that began in 2007. The company entered bankruptcy protection in November 2011.

Drawing on the financial situation at American Airlines, in early 2012, US Airways unofficially approached some creditors at AMR, the American Airlines parent company, to discuss the benefits of merging the two airlines. According to the *Wall Street Journal*, a total of $1.5 billion in cost savings and revenue could be anticipated with a successful merger. American refused to talk about a possible merger with its rival until March 2012 when AMR CEO Tom Horton said they would be open to negotiations. In April, the three major unions at American Airlines—the Allied Pilots Association, Association of Professional Flight Attendants, and the Transport Workers Union—forged an agreement to encourage their company to enter merger negotiations. "We are pleased to confirm our support of a possible merger between our airline and US Airways," the unions announced. The union decision was predicated on the notion that more than 6,000 jobs could be saved. If American were to move on as a stand-alone airline, it would need to cut at least 15 percent of its workforce, or 13,000 union jobs, to stay afloat.

On August 31, 2012, US Airways announced that it had signed a nondisclosure agreement with AMR to officially discuss a merger. It was not until six months later, in February 2013, that the two airlines announced the intent to combine their operations. As initially outlined, the newly integrated airline would be run as American Airlines, and its holding company would be known as American Airlines Group Inc. The merger would include both the flagship US Airways and American Airlines planes, as well as the companies' subsidiaries: Envoy, Piedmont Airlines, PSA Airlines, US Airways Shuttle, American Eagle, and US Airways Express. Seventy-two percent of the company would be owned by AMR stakeholders, while 28 percent would be retained by US Airways shareholders.

For the merger to be approved, US Airways and American Airlines would have to get approval from their shareholders and antitrust authorities like the Justice Department. If able to do so, American would be allowed to come out of Chapter 11 as part of the merger agreement. On March 27, 2013, the airlines passed their first major hurdle when Judge Sean Lane gave the merger approval to commence. US Airways won shareholder approval on July 12, with American following shortly thereafter.

JUSTICE DEPARTMENT LAWSUIT AND RESOLUTION

On August 13, 2013, the Department of Justice, in cooperation with seven attorneys general from six states and Washington, D.C., filed an antitrust lawsuit against the merger. The lawsuit argued that the $11 billion merger would "substantially lessen competition" in the airline industry, which would lead to higher prices for passengers. The Justice Department expressed its concern that in regional markets across the country, a joint airline would control too much of the takeoff and landing spots. It also said that there was no proven financial necessity for the merger and that it would likely allow other airlines to raise their prices because they would no longer be competing against discount programs offered by US Airways, which were expected to be terminated under the merger.

In the debate over the merger, a major point of contention was Ronald Reagan National Airport (DCA) in Washington, D.C. The airport not only serves as a hub for business and recreational travelers coming to and from the nation's capital, but is also one of the most frequently used D.C. airports for members of Congress when traveling to their home districts. If the merger were approved, the new airline would control more than 60 percent of all outbound nonstop routes from DCA.

The lawsuit came as a surprise, because previous mergers, such as those between Delta and Northwest in 2008, and United and Continental in 2010, were easily approved without challenge. However, airline analysts said the new position of the Justice Department was largely fed by growing airline profits as fares and fees have increased. In the earlier cases, the Justice Department saw the mergers as a necessity for survival. In a response, the parent companies of American Airlines and US Airways expressed a joint opinion "that the DOJ is wrong in its assessment of our merger. Integrating the complementary networks of American and US Airways to benefit passengers is the motivation for bringing these airlines together. Blocking this procompetitive merger will deny customers access to a broader airline network that gives them more choices."

On November 12, the Justice Department reached an agreement with AMR and US Airways Group Inc. to allow the merger to proceed. To win approval, the two airlines would give up gates and landing slots at key airports to low-cost carriers to ensure continuing competition and a variety of price options. "This agreement has the potential to shift the landscape of the airline industry. By guaranteeing a bigger foothold for low-cost carriers at key U.S. airports, this settlement ensures airline passengers will see more competition on nonstop and connecting routes throughout the country," said Attorney General Eric Holder. "This is vital to millions of consumers who will benefit from both more competitive prices and enhanced travel options," he added.

The airports most heavily impacted under the agreement with the Justice Department are DCA and New York LaGuardia (LGA). At DCA, American Airlines and US Airways were required to sell 104 air carrier slots, while 34 slots would be divested at LGA. This would give the newly merged airline limited capacity to operate out of those two airports, reducing the number of DCA departures by forty-four and the number of LGA departures by twelve. JetBlue would be given the opportunity to purchase any of the slots it currently leases from American Airlines at DCA, and Southwest would be given the chance to purchase its leased slots at LGA before the slots would be sold to other airlines. In addition to DCA and LGA, American Airlines and US Airways were required to give up two gates and ground facilities at Boston Logan, Chicago O'Hare, Dallas Love Field, Los Angeles International, and Miami International airports. These gates would be distributed under terms developed by the Justice Department, with preference given to airlines that do not currently have a large stake at any of the five airports.

MERGER APPROVED

On December 9, the two airlines were given the final go-ahead by the Justice Department to complete their merger activities, although it could take months or even years for all the operations to become seamless. "American has a tremendous legacy and knows what it feels like to be the best," said CEO Doug Parker. "The new American is about getting that feeling back," he added. The merger created the largest airline in the world, with more than 100,000 employees, 6,700 daily flights to more than fifty countries. The airline now has a total of nine hubs—Dallas, Texas; Charlotte, North Carolina; Chicago, Illinois (O'Hare); Philadelphia, Pennsylvania; Phoenix, Arizona; Miami, Florida; Washington, D.C. (DCA); Los Angeles, California; and New York City (JFK).

January 7, 2014, was the first date when passengers would begin to recognize the effects of the merger. This date marked the point at which each airline would begin to recognize and award the frequent flier miles of the other. During the following two months, the airlines planned to begin incorporating their flight codes. Starting March 31, those passengers holding US Airways frequent flyer miles would now only be able to use them for travel within the newly merged company, or on American's alliance, the Oneworld global alliance. This marked a change for US Airways passengers who previously had the privilege to use their miles on any carrier in the Star Alliance. For the next couple of years, passengers will still likely see both American Airlines and U.S. Airways ticket counters and gates at airports.

The executives at US Airways took over most of the top spots in the newly merged company. This included CEO Parker, who led the merger process, and former US Airways president, Scott Kirby, who maintained the same role in the new company. Executives at the new company announced their intent to retain both American and US Airways employees. With the merger complete, four airlines—American, United, Delta, and Southwest—now control 85 percent of the flight market in the United States.

—Heather Kerrigan

Following is the text of a press release from the Department of Justice on November 12, 2013, announcing an agreement with US Airways and American Airlines to allow their merger to proceed.

Department of Justice Announces Merger Agreement

November 12, 2013

The Department of Justice today announced that it is requiring US Airways Group Inc. and American Airlines' parent corporation, AMR Corp. to divest slots and gates at key constrained airports across the country to low cost carrier airlines (LCCs) in order to enhance system-wide competition in the airline industry resulting in more choices and more competitive airfares for consumers.

The department said the proposed settlement will increase the presence of the LCCs at Boston Logan International, Chicago O'Hare International, Dallas Love Field, Los Angeles International, Miami International, New York LaGuardia International and Ronald Reagan Washington National. Providing the LCCs with the incentive and ability to invest in new capacity and permitting them to compete more extensively nationwide will enhance meaningful competition in the industry and benefit airline travelers.

"This agreement has the potential to shift the landscape of the airline industry. By guaranteeing a bigger foothold for low-cost carriers at key U.S. airports, this settlement ensures airline passengers will see more competition on nonstop and connecting routes throughout the country," said Attorney General Eric Holder. "The department's ultimate goal has remained steadfast throughout this process—to ensure vigorous competition in airline travel. This is vital to millions of consumers who will benefit from both more competitive prices and enhanced travel options."

Six state attorneys general—Arizona, Florida, Pennsylvania, Michigan, Tennessee and Virginia—and the District of Columbia joined in the department's proposed settlement, which was filed in the U.S. District Court for the District of Columbia. If approved by the court, the settlement will resolve the department's competitive concerns and the lawsuit.

"The extensive slot and gate divestitures at these key airports are groundbreaking and they will dramatically enhance the ability of LCCs to compete system-wide," said Assistant Attorney General Bill Baer of the Department of Justice's Antitrust Division. "This settlement will disrupt the cozy relationships among the incumbent legacy carriers, increase access to key congested airports and provide consumers with more choices and more competitive airfares on flights all across the country."

On Aug. 13, 2013, the department, six state attorneys general and the District of Columbia filed an antitrust lawsuit against US Airways and American alleging that US Airway's $11 billion acquisition of American would have substantially lessened competition for commercial air travel in local markets throughout the United States. The department alleged that the transaction would result in passengers paying higher airfares and receiving less service. In addition, the department alleged that the transaction would entrench the merged airline as the dominant carrier at Reagan National, where it would control 69 percent of take-off and landing slots, thus effectively foreclosing entry or expansion by competing airlines.

The settlement requires US Airways and American to divest slots, gates and ground facilities at key airports around the country. Specifically, the settlement requires the companies to divest or transfer to low cost carrier purchasers approved by the department:

All 104 air carrier slots (i.e. slots not reserved for use only by smaller, commuter planes) at Reagan National and rights and interest in other facilities at the airport necessary to support the use of the slots;

Thirty-four slots at LaGuardia and rights and interest in other facilities at the airport necessary to support the use of the slots; and

Rights and interests to two airport gates and associated ground facilities at each of Boston Logan, Chicago O'Hare, Dallas Love Field, Los Angeles International and Miami International.

The Reagan National and LaGuardia slots will be sold under procedures approved by the department. Under the terms of the settlement, JetBlue at Reagan National and Southwest at LaGuardia will be given the opportunity to acquire the slots they currently lease from American. The remaining 88 slots at Reagan National and 24 slots at LaGuardia plus any JetBlue or Southwest decline to acquire will be grouped into bundles, taking into account specific slot times to ensure commercially viable and competitive patterns of service for the recipients of the divested slots. The parties will divest these slot bundles and all rights and interests in any gates and other ground facilities (e.g., ticket counters, baggage handling facilities, office space and loading bridges) as necessary to support the use of the purchased slots.

The gates at the five airports will be transferred on commercially reasonable terms to the new acquirers. The acquirers of the slot and gate divestitures also require approval of the department. Preference will be given to airlines at each airport that do not currently operate a large share of slots or gates.

The proposed settlement allows the department to appoint a monitoring trustee to oversee the divestitures or transfers of the slots and gates. The settlement also prohibits the merged company from reacquiring an ownership interest in the divested slots or gates during the term of the settlement. The companies must also provide advance notice of any future slot acquisition at Reagan National regardless of whether or not it is a reportable transaction under the premerger notification law and further provides for waiting periods and opportunities for the department to obtain additional information in order to review the transaction.

AMR is a Delaware corporation with its principal place of business in Fort Worth, Texas. AMR is the parent company of American Airlines. Last year American flew more than 80 million passengers to more than 250 destinations worldwide and took in more than $24 billion in revenue. In November 2011, American filed for bankruptcy reorganization.

US Airways is a Delaware corporation with its principal place of business in Tempe, Ariz. Last year US Airways flew more than 50 million passengers to more than 200 destinations worldwide and took in more than $13 billion in revenue.

SOURCE: U.S. Department of Justice. Office of Public Affairs. "Justice Department Requires US Airways and American Airlines to Divest Facilities at Seven Key Airports to Enhance System-wide Competition and Settle Merger Challenge." November 12, 2013. http://www.justice.gov/opa/pr/2013/November/13-at-1202.html.

Same-Sex Marriage Approved in Hawaii and Illinois

NOVEMBER 13 AND 20, 2013

In 2013, supporters of same-sex marriage celebrated another handful of victories as the governors in Delaware, Hawaii, Illinois, Minnesota, and Rhode Island signed legislation permitting the practice within their borders, while court orders in New Jersey and New Mexico made legalization possible. Many of these victories came on the heels of two momentous Supreme Court same-sex marriage rulings released in June. Even though the tide seemed to be turning in favor of same-sex marriage legislation, and with seventeen states and the District of Columbia allowing the practice by the end of 2013, opponents still promised to mount campaigns and fight gubernatorial decisions at the ballot box or in the courts.

THE HISTORY OF SAME-SEX MARRIAGE IN THE STATES

Across the country, states remain fiercely divided on their support for, or opposition to, same-sex marriage. Over the past decade, some states have chosen to strengthen language in their constitutions to uphold the definition of marriage as between one man and one woman, while in other states voters have approved amendments that opened the doors for same-sex civil unions and marriage. The differing views have largely been based on the political leanings of the governor and legislature.

The debate over same-sex marriage in the states dates back to 1993, when the Hawaii Supreme Court determined that it was unconstitutional to afford different rights—in this case, marriage—to certain groups of people. As such, the court ruled that it was in direct violation of its own equal protection clause, unless the state could prove a compelling reason for denying same-sex couples the right to marry. This decision sparked a nation-wide call to action on both sides of the debate. During the next two decades, thirty-two states moved to define marriage as between one man and one woman, thus erasing any constitutional ambiguity. Hawaii voters decided in 1998 to limit the issuance of marriage licenses to only heterosexual couples.

Seven years after the Hawaii ruling, the Vermont Supreme Court ruled that same-sex couples must be given the same benefits as married heterosexual couples. In April 2000, Vermont became the first state to approve legislation allowing for same-sex civil unions. Three years later, Vermont's southern neighbor, Massachusetts, faced a similar court ruling, and, in 2004, under court order it became the first state to allow for same-sex marriage that was on-par with heterosexual marriage. Connecticut, New Jersey, and New Hampshire followed in 2005, 2006, and 2007, respectively, setting up civil unions for same-sex couples. In 2008, Connecticut became the second state to allow same-sex marriage, followed by Iowa in 2009. Also in 2009, the Vermont legislature passed a same-sex marriage bill later vetoed by the governor but which the legislature was able to override. Vermont was the first state to pass legislation allowing for same-sex marriage rather than being required to do so by judicial mandate. The Maine legislature successfully passed a same-sex marriage law in 2009; however, voters overturned the law. The District of Columbia and New Hampshire passed same-sex marriage laws in 2009, and New York followed in 2011.

The year 2012 marked a turning point for same-sex marriage supporters when the first three states—Maine, Maryland, and Washington—legalized the practice by popular vote. Given the changing tide of public opinion on same-sex marriage—in 2013, a *Washington Post*-ABC News poll showed that 58 percent of Americans supported same-sex marriage, while 36 percent said it should be illegal—this was an unsurprising outcome. Also in 2012, Minnesota voters became the first in the nation to vote against an amendment that would define marriage as between one man and one woman (the state went on to pass its own same-sex marriage law in 2013). The one possible loss for same-sex marriage supporters in 2012 was in New Jersey where the legislature passed a bill allowing the practice, but it was vetoed by the governor. The case moved to the state Supreme Court, which ruled in October 2013 to overturn the governor's veto, allowing same-sex marriages to begin taking place immediately.

The case that brought the debate of same-sex marriage front and center in public consciousness started in 2008 in California, when the Supreme Court ruled it unconstitutional to prevent same-sex couples from marrying. Traditional marriage supporters mounted a campaign against the ruling, known as Proposition 8, and were able to garner enough support to put a referendum on the ballot, asking voters whether they wanted to define marriage as between one man and one woman in the state's constitution. The expensive and fiercely debated referendum was passed in 2008, thus overturning the state Supreme Court's decision. The case was appealed to the state Supreme Court in 2009, and Proposition 8 was upheld, keeping same-sex marriage illegal. Unsatisfied with the outcome, Proposition 8 opponents appealed to a federal judge, who in 2010 said the same-sex marriage ban was a direct violation of the U.S. Constitution's Equal Protection Clause. The case made it all the way to the U.S. Supreme Court, which on June 26, 2013, ruled 5–4 that the group supporting Proposition 8 had no standing to challenge the case in federal court. This technical ruling left in place the decision of the federal appeals court, thus vacating Proposition 8. This ruling was released on the same day that the high court decided on another same-sex marriage case, this one regarding the Defense of Marriage Act (DOMA), a federal statute that defines marriage as between one man and one woman for the purpose of federal benefits. In its 5–4 ruling, the Court determined that DOMA violates the rights of equal liberty offered by the Fifth Amendment.

SAME-SEX MARRIAGE IN 2013

With two decisive cases before the Supreme Court, 2013 was another year of increasing activity in the states surrounding the issue of same-sex marriage. In May, the governors of Delaware, Minnesota, and Rhode Island signed a trio of laws allowing for same-sex marriage. In October and November, Hawaii's legislature debated same-sex marriage in a special session. According to the Gallup organization, Hawaii had the largest population, by percentage, of citizens identifying themselves as LGBT in a state currently considering same-sex marriage legislation. The state house voted on November 8 to give final approval to the bill, and the state senate quickly followed on November 12. Governor Neil Abercrombie signed the measure into law on November 13, and it went into effect on December 2. After signing the law, the governor said, "What happened in this Legislature is people set aside even perhaps their own particular views of what might or might not be the greater good, but listened to what their role was in terms of upholding the Constitution, and in moving forward S.B. 1 in such a manner, and with the motivation of acting as a member of a legislature acting for the greater good."

While Hawaii's bill moved toward approval, Illinois worked on same-sex marriage legislation of its own, having approved civil unions in 2011. Although led by a liberal governor, and with Democratic control in the state house and senate, debate on the bill was delayed for months because sponsors were concerned that they would not have enough support for passage. On November 5, the bill came for a vote on the house floor, and passed 61–54. The state senate passed the bill an hour later 32–29. Governor Pat Quinn signed the bill on November 20, which would make same-sex marriages legal beginning on June 1, 2014. "This new law is an epic victory for equal rights in America," Governor Quinn said after signing the bill. "Illinois is moving forward. We are a model for our country. If the Land of Lincoln can achieve marriage equality, so can every other state in the nation."

New Mexico, the only state without a law on the books banning or permitting same-sex marriage, took up the issue in 2013, led by a ruling at the state's Supreme Court that said the state constitution required that marriage licenses be issued to same-sex couples; otherwise, the state would be in violation of the equal protection clause. The ruling immediately went into effect, but Republicans promised to fight the decision, believing that the voters should have the opportunity to weigh in on the debate. "The issue will not be settled until the people speak," said Bill Sharer, a New Mexico Republican state senator.

By the end of the year, seventeen states and the District of Columbia allowed same-sex marriage within their borders, several states recognized civil unions or another form of domestic partnership, and more than 30 opposed same-sex marriage either through statute or the state constitution.

ANTICIPATED FUTURE ACTION

A number of other states began looking at opening up marriage licenses to same-sex couples toward the end of 2013, possibly signaling action in the coming years. On December 20, 2013, a Utah court ruled that the state's ban on same-sex marriage is unconstitutional. The ruling was challenged, and the U.S. Supreme Court put a stay on it. The state is in the process of appealing the December 20 decision, and until a final ruling is made, same-sex couples will not be able to obtain marriage licenses. In North Carolina, where voters passed a constitutional amendment in 2012 banning same-sex marriage, supporters have taken to the courts to open up marriage to all citizens. At one point, the Buncombe County Register of Deeds began accepting same-sex marriage licenses on the grounds that the Supreme Court's DOMA ruling allowed him to do so. He was eventually forbidden from doing so by the state's attorney general.

In Oregon, same-sex marriage supporters are hoping to put a referendum on the 2014 ballot to overturn the state's constitutional ban on the practice. If the referendum goes before voters, it is expected to pass because public opinion polls conducted in the state have shown a majority of the population backing same-sex marriage.

Supporters in other states are looking toward the 2016 general election for potential referendums, knowing that voters are more likely to be coming to the polls. Many of the states that could have referenda on their ballots are in the Midwest, which has traditionally been more socially conservative than Eastern and Western states where same-sex marriage passage has been easier. But those like Evan Wolfson, the founder of Freedom to Marry, believe things may be changing. "We've won in Minnesota and Iowa. With Illinois, we have 37% of American people living in a freedom-to-marry state, including states in the heartland with more to come," Wolfson said.

—Heather Kerrigan

Following is the text of a statement by the Governor of Hawaii on November 13, 2013, upon signing a law to permit same-sex marriage; and a press release from the office of the Governor of Illinois on November 20, 2013, announcing the signing of same-sex marriage legislation.

Hawaii Governor Signs Law Permitting Same-Sex Marriage

November 13, 2013

Gov. Neil Abercrombie:

Aloha everyone, thank you, mahalo nui. Before I begin my remarks . . . I commented to some today and to my wife that it never, ever, occurred to me that I would one day have both the opportunity and responsibility to do something that is as profound as the change that is to come in a few moments as Patsy Mink was able to accomplish with Title IX that literally changed the universe for women for all time.

Another universe is about to change for all time, and I could not have sustained my commitment—and had the support necessary emotional and otherwise to do that—without my wife, Dr. Nancie Caraway. And, together, we have been instructed and informed in a way that helped us sustain our perspective and our perception of what we needed to do by the work of Tony Kushner. We have a particular relationship; we spend a lot of time arguing about Picasso's role in the history of art and so on, and great playwrights, and Tony Kushner has been a singular influence in our life. . . .

Dr. Nancie Caraway:

Aloha, I think we need to get a little sassy; it's very somber. I wanted to use the words of my favorite angel in America, my intellectual and artistic soul mate, the great American playwright—the greatest, I think—Tony Kushner. And this is what I want to say to all of you, through the words of this erudite, soulful artist, Tony Kushner:

"The world only spins forward. We will be citizens. The time has come. Bye now. You are fabulous creatures, each and every one. And I bless you: More life. The Great Work Begins."

Gov. Neil Abercrombie:

We begin virtually every discourse with one another with the word Aloha. And we all cling to that. We all think to ourselves that we know what it is all about, what it should be, what we want it to be . . . and I thought today with this profound change that I mentioned about to take place, that perhaps I ought to re-examine it because I was certainly going to get up like every-body else and say "Aloha," and then I started thinking what am I going to say after that?

I thought maybe I ought to think about that word, about Aloha, about what it means. And I remembered that we actually have Aloha and the Aloha Spirit in our laws. It's in our Constitution. Aloha spirit is the coordination of mind and heart within each person. It brings each person to the self. Each person must think and emote good feelings to others. In the contemplation and the presence of the life force, Aloha means kindness to be expressed with tenderness, unity to be expressed with harmony, agreeableness to be expressed with pleasant-ness, humility to be expressed with modesty, and patience to be expressed with perseverance.

I thought of that especially because, when I was asked what my remarks might be, do I have any remarks from when the Senate agreed to the House version of S.B. 1 and it had passed the legislature, I spoke about courage, I spoke about determination, and I then wanted to thank the Legislature for its patient perseverance.

"Where did I get that from?" I thought to myself. And then I realized I channeled the very words that we have as are the foundation of our very state, our obligations to each other as citizens in the State of Hawaii, to express ourselves through Aloha by patience and perseverance. I think that signifies exactly what this is about.

And so then, having discovered that in myself, I picked up my Constitution of the United States. I have a little history of it; it includes the Declaration of Independence, the chronology of it. It even has the Articles of Confederation, the predecessor to the Constitution. So I decided to re-read and to say today exactly what the Legislature has just done:

> "Congress shall make no law respecting an establishment of religion, or prohibit-ing the free exercise thereof; or abridging the freedom of speech, or of the press; or the right of the people peaceably to assemble, and to petition the government for a redress of grievances."

I submit to you that S.B. 1 is the epitome of the First Amendment in action.

It's easy to criticize the legislators, and it's easy to criticize individual legislators. It's easy to critique or criticize the actions and words that are spoken, but I will tell you in time to come when the history of S.B. 1 is recorded and commented upon, as it will be, there will be a lot of master's degrees and Ph.D.s put together around this process over the past 20 years. What the Legislature had in mind all the way through including those who ended up in opposition to the bill as it finally emerged, was to see to it that we were able to coor-dinate civic responsibility and to show respect for and pay attention to the religious beliefs of others that might have put them in opposition.

We're human beings. We cannot guarantee that the hard work the AG and his staff did in working with Clayton (Hee) and Karl (Rhoads) will make certain this respect mani-fested itself in the language of the bill. We cannot be certain every word and every nuance have been met. That is what amendments are all about. I just read the First Amendment to the Constitution. We couldn't even pass the Constitution originally without putting ten amendments in.

So, it doesn't strike me as strange that we may not have a perfect vehicle here today. But we understand that this is in fact the result of a legislative process which had as its fundamental premise, fidelity to support for upholding the Constitution of the United States and the State of Hawaii. And that was done by legislators, legislators who acted on a premise to represent the greater interest of the public, not necessarily to express their own particular views. And I had re-called and was grateful to have my good friend Professor Henningsen of the University of Hawaii remind me of what I knew was a quote and I couldn't remember where it exactly came from; from Edmund Burke's quote in his acceptance speech when he was elected by the voters of the city of Bristol to the Parliament of Great Brittan in 1774.

And I quote:

"Your representative owes you, not his industry only, but his judgment; and he betrays, instead of serving you, if he sacrifices it to your opinion . . . Parliament is not a congress of ambassadors from different and hostile interests; which interests each must maintain, as an agent and advocate, against other agents and advocates; but parliament is a deliberative assembly of one nation, with one interest, that of the whole; where, not local purposes, not local prejudices, ought to guide, but the general good, resulting from the general reason of the whole. You choose a member indeed; but when you have chosen him, he is not member of Bristol, but he is a member of parliament."

And what happened in this Legislature is people set aside even perhaps their own particular views of what might or might not be the greater good, but listened to what their role was in terms of upholding the Constitution, and in moving forward S.B. 1 in such a manner, and with the motivation of acting as a member of a legislature acting for the greater good.

We all have special interests. Everybody in this room has special interests. This bill is a special interest. It's not a question of whether it's a special interest, it's whether it's a special interest that manifests the public interest and not a private interest, and that is what this bill represents, a melding of the special interest involved, that is to say the equity associated with marriage, and the common good, and the public interest as a whole, which is the upholding of the constitution that binds us.

There have been commentaries in our history with regard to the question of religion and democracy. This is not new to us here in the 21st Century. Thomas Jefferson wrote in the Virginia Act for Religious Freedom, in 1786:

"Subject opinion to coercion: whom will you make your inquisitors? Fallible men; men governed by bad passions, by private as well as public reasons. And why subject it to coercion? To produce uniformity. But is uniformity of opinion desireable [sic]? No more than of face and stature."

Madison in 1833 said:

"I must admit moreover that it may not be easy, in every possible case, to trace the line of separation between the rights of religion and the civil authority with such distinctness as to avoid collisions and doubts on unessential points. The tendency to a usurpation on one side or the other or to a corrupting coalition or alliance between them will be best guarded against by entire abstinence of the government from interference in any way whatever, beyond the necessity of preserving public order and protecting each sect against trespasses on its legal rights by others."

That's what has been the process here in achieving S.B. 1. The history is there. But, now that I have gone over the history to myself in thinking about this and establishing a solid, I think, legal and legislative foundation. You come down to the question that moves me the most, and that is to say the human dimension. The dimension of depth. Our relationship to one another.

One of the first things that I was able to absorb when Nancie and I visited Queen Liliuokalani's home, Washington Place, that is now my honor and privilege to take responsibility for such time as I am allowed to be governor. . . . There was a picture there as we explored the home of the Queen, and for reasons that are entirely obscure to us, someone had affixed to this picture of the Queen in all her regal splendor, the following words:

"If we could but see our likenesses, could we not learn to be tolerant of our differences?"

That's the Queen speaking; that's the legacy of Aloha; that's the guiding principle that I try to follow. I feel very deeply about the responsibility of being the Kiaʻaina, the Governor. It's more than just words; it's more than just Aloha. It's a profound, deep and abiding responsibility.

"If we could but see our likenesses, could we not learn to be tolerant of our differences?"

That's the Queen's admonition to us. I think that S.B. 1 satisfies the Queen's desire that we look to see our likenesses with one another and not to see our differences.

And finally, I was moved deeply by some words given to me by our dear friend, of both my wife and I, someone with whom we've shared our highs and lows, our friendship, who has had to be hidden for all of her life, in her heart; feeling that she was marginalized and shut away. She said to us:

"Today is a moment that my community has fought for, for many, many decades. I have spent my entire life waiting for equality. I have spent my entire life waiting for equality to be visible in the world I live in, to be a part of the whole; this courageous, colorful, inspirational, endlessly talented, brilliant like a star community."

Finally, today, now, all those who have been invisible will be visible to themselves and the whole world.

(Immediately prior to signing S.B. 1)

I know there have been other occasions when, because of the significance of the situation, multiple pens have been used with multiple strokes in order to sign. But today I hope, with all of your indulgence and with your Aloha, you'll allow me to take this koa pen and sign fully and completely, and that you will all approve, that I intend to give this pen that signs this bill, this day, to Judge Levinson.

(Upon signing S.B. 1)

Done.

SOURCE: Office of the Governor of Hawaii. "Governor's Remarks from the Signing of Marriage Equality Legislation." November 13, 2013. http://governor.hawaii.gov/blog/governors-remarks-from-the-signing-of-marriage-equity-legislation.

Illinois Governor Signs Marriage Equality Legislation

November 20, 2013

In front of a crowd of thousands at the University of Illinois at Chicago's UIC Forum, Governor Pat Quinn today signed historic legislation making Illinois the 16th state in the nation to embrace full marriage equality. The legislation permits all couples in the Land of Lincoln to receive the rights and protections of marriage.

As part of his agenda to ensure Illinois embraces all people, Governor Quinn made marriage equality a top legislative priority this year, featuring it in his 2013 State of the State address.

"This new law is an epic victory for equal rights in America," Governor Quinn said. "Illinois is moving forward. We are a model for our country. If the Land of Lincoln can achieve marriage equality, so can every other state in the nation."

Governor Quinn pushed for marriage equality throughout the 2013 legislative session. In 2011, the Governor signed into law historic civil union legislation. Since then, more than 6,000 couples from across Illinois have joined in a civil union.

Senate Bill 10, sponsored by State Senator Heather Steans (D-Chicago) and State Representative Greg Harris (D-Chicago), requires that all Illinois laws pertaining to civil marriage must apply equally to all couples. The law will guarantee equal access to status, benefits, protections, rights and responsibilities for all couples entering into marriage and their families. The law also allows the voluntary conversion of a civil union to a marriage and protects the religious freedom of churches, mosques, synagogues, temples and other religious organizations.

"I couldn't be prouder of Illinois today as we become the 16th state to write equality into our marriage laws," Senator Steans said. "This is a day to celebrate the hard work of so many Illinois families whose commitment to human rights and basic fairness made this moment possible."

"This is a very proud day for the state of Illinois and a happy day for thousands of Illinois families who will now be treated equally in the eyes of the law," Representative Harris said. "I want to thank Governor Quinn, Speaker Madigan and my colleagues for making this day possible."

The law takes effect June 1, 2014.

SOURCE: Office of Governor Pat Quinn. Illinois Government News Network. "Governor Pat Quinn Signs Marriage Equality Into Law; New Law Makes Illinois the 16th State in Nation to Embrace Equal Rights for All Couples." November 20, 2013. http://www3.illinois.gov/PressReleases/ShowPressRelease.cfm?SubjectID=3&RecNum=11727.

OTHER HISTORIC DOCUMENTS OF INTEREST

Saudi Arabia Declines UN Security Council Seat; Jordan Fills Vacancy

NOVEMBER 14 AND DECEMBER 6, 2013

In a first-of-its kind decision, in October 2013, the Kingdom of Saudi Arabia announced that it would not be accepting the United Nations Security Council seat to which it had been elected. The move came as a surprise to the international community because the Middle Eastern nation had long lobbied for inclusion in the body. In December, Jordan was chosen to fill the Security Council vacancy. Saudi Arabia, meanwhile, continued to work closely with the United Nations General Assembly on the country's highest priority issues such as the ongoing civil war and humanitarian crisis in Syria.

Saudi Arabia Elected to UN Security Council; Rejects Seat

On October 17, 2013, two years of lobbying by Saudi diplomats came to fruition with the country's successful election to the United Nations Security Council. Within twenty-four hours, however, Saudi Arabia shocked the international community by refusing to accept the seat. No other UN member had ever declined a Security Council seat, prompting several theories for the kingdom's motivation.

Some observers noted that Saudi Arabia had traditionally preferred backstage diplomacy and would not welcome the scrutiny applied to its votes within the council. This observation countered a growing perception that Saudi Arabia was pursuing a more activist foreign policy in response to multiple crises in the region. Others interpreted the rejection of the seat as an expression of frustration with the rules governing the council, particularly the outsized influence held by the permanent veto-wielding members: the United States, United Kingdom, China, Russia, and France.

The most prevalent theory, however, held that Saudi Arabia derived more power from its rejection of the seat than its acceptance of it, affording the country an opportunity to trumpet long-simmering frustrations regarding attempted United States rapprochement with Iran, its traditional rival in the region. Saudi Arabia, an austere Sunni monarchy committed to orthodox Wahhabi theology, views Shiite Iran as a source of regional instability, abetting bloodshed in Syria among other places. The Saudi government voiced dissatisfaction with the U.S. and Russian stances on Syria, criticizing the United States as ineffectual in deterring abuses by Syria's government under Bashar al-Assad, and accusing Russia of actively supporting Assad's government. King Abdullah bin Abdulaziz Al Saud of Saudi Arabia was said to be especially provoked by the U.S. decision not to take military action after confirmation of Syrian chemical attacks on civilians in 2013. The United States had instead accepted a Russian proposal to dispose of Syrian chemical weapon stockpiles by 2014. In March 2014, the United States reported that just a third of the stockpile had been destroyed. In the same month, the UN also confirmed that the chemical weapons used to attack civilians had been sourced from the Syrian army.

For its part, Saudi Arabia's refusal letter bolstered all three theories. It highlighted the slow pace of reform within the council, which continues to reflect the balance of power immediately after World War II. Saudi Arabia also identified itself as a protector and representative of all Arab and Islamic peoples, arguing that the crises facing the region were not being addressed by the UN Security Council. Its language was unusually firm for a diplomatic missive, reflecting exasperation with its traditional allies within the council. Saudi Arabia announced that it would not accept a seat without significant reforms to address "double standards" that prevented the council from "preserving international peace and security." While acknowledging the honor of being appointed to the preeminent body within the United Nations, the kingdom argued that the structure of the council rendered it incapable of fulfilling its intended purpose. The failure of the council, and indirectly the United States, to resolve the Israeli-Palestinian crisis provided another notable grievance. The letter was well received by other Gulf monarchies. Saudi Arabia waited until November 12 to formally decline the position, allowing nearly a month to elapse after the initial appointment.

IMPLICATIONS AND INTERNATIONAL RESPONSE

American policymakers responded that Saudi Arabia's refusal of the seat would limit its ability to solve the problems highlighted in its letter and reduce its influence over policy toward Iran. However, while Saudi Arabia's decision was seen as a temporary embarrassment for the UN Security Council and the United States, it was not expected to have long-term strategic implications.

The kingdom's retreat left the Group of Asia-Pacific States, which was due to name a member to the council, in search of an alternative candidate. Jordan, another traditional Arab monarchy, was chosen as the replacement in a special election in December 2013, with the apparent approval of Saudi Arabia. Jordan typically coordinates its foreign policy with that of its larger neighbor and is expected to advance similar positions within the council. The country also viewed the appointment as recognition of its role as a moderate voice within the region. Jordan aimed to use its term to highlight its importance as a host for Syrian refugees, potentially winning additional concessions. Jordan also withdrew from the race to sit on the UN Human Rights Committee, allowing Saudi Arabia to stand in its stead. Some analysts posited that the two countries had previously agreed to swap candidacies, although this was not confirmed by either party.

While Saudi Arabia may have preferred a position on the Human Rights Committee due in part to its comparatively lower profile, its candidacy for the aforementioned committee attracted attention from multiple human rights groups, which asserted that repression within the kingdom increased in 2013. Activists who would have conceded the kingdom's regional influence as justification for membership on the Security Council questioned its commitment to human rights after joining the committee. In November 2013, the international organization Human Rights Watch called for the kingdom to adhere to the values of the committee by tolerating internal dissent. The group charged that independent activists had been imprisoned and mistreated in Saudi Arabia and noted that seven requests for visits by the committee's human rights investigators remained outstanding at the time of the country's election. In October 2013, Human Rights Watch had recommended that the kingdom review social policies including the death penalty, particularly as prescribed for children; the male guardianship system; and treatment of migrant workers. Saudi Arabia has long attempted to include local participation in the private sector by discouraging cheaper and more productive foreign employees. As of December 2013, 70,000 Ethiopians had left the country on flights collectively valued at $25 million.

Saudi Arabia was not alone in attracting criticism in its candidacy for the Human Rights Committee. During the electoral cycle Syria and Iran withdrew themselves from consideration in response to protests by watch groups. Conditions in Syria were considered particularly acute as the country continued to struggle amidst a civil war.

Saudi Arabia is expected to counter Russian and Chinese positions on Syria within the Human Rights Committee; both countries also won three-year terms on the committee in November 2013. In addition to the Syrian conflict, the committee was expected to evaluate abuses in the Central African Republic and in Sri Lanka during the latter's own civil war.

Saudi Arabia's Continued Work in the United Nations

Despite rejecting a Security Council seat, Saudi Arabia has remained active within the United Nations. In early 2014, it appeared to have reverted to its traditional position in favor of discreet diplomacy coupled with generous funding to support its vital interests. In January of that year Saudi Arabia announced through state-owned media that it had donated $100 million to the United Nations International Center for Counterterrorism, founded in 2011. The kingdom continues to prioritize action against Shiite-inspired terrorism, particularly as endorsed by its political and religious rival, Iran. It will continue to view negotiations regarding Iran's nuclear program with skepticism, despite decreasing wariness among European partners. Loosened sanctions against Iran have implications for Saudi accounting as well, because a new oil source on international markets could reduce vital revenues for public finances. Europe, in contrast, could benefit from access to Iranian oil, decreasing its dependence on Russia and thus affording it greater leverage on issues like Russian intervention in Crimea. Europe is also evaluating the feasibility of transiting liquid natural gas through the Black Sea via mainland Ukraine and Turkey. Turkey is considered a rising Sunni hegemon in the region.

Syria, however, remains the most pressing public concern for Saudi Arabia. In February 2014, the kingdom called for an emergency meeting in the General Assembly to discuss alleged war crimes committed by the Syrian government. It listed state abuses including starvation and the use of destructive, wide-ranging barrel bombs in the deliberate mass slaughter of civilians. Saudi Arabia called on the body to implement a 2013 Security Council resolution in favor of prompt humanitarian aid, particularly along battle lines. Apart from its activities at the UN, Saudi Arabia is believed to be funding various opposition groups within Syria.

Saudi diplomats will continue to adopt positions largely in line with U.S. foreign policy, notwithstanding recent bilateral tensions. Saudi Arabia will also likely take a position against Russian intervention in Crimea, given its self-appointed role as guardian of all Muslims, implicitly including Crimean Tatars. Sanctions against Russia in response to its Crimean intervention could strengthen Russian ties to Syria and Iran, however, because it could reduce Russian engagement in European and U.S. markets. While Saudi positions on these crises are unlikely to merit historical notice, its unprecedented refusal of a Security Council seat will likely interest diplomatic scholars for years to come.

—Anastazia S Clouting

Following is the text of a letter, released on November 14, 2013, by the United Nations, announcing Saudi Arabia's decision not to accept its position on the Security Council; and a press release from the United Nations on December 6, 2013, announcing the decision to give Jordan the vacant Security Council seat.

DOCUMENT

Saudi Arabia Declines Security Council Seat

November 14, 2013

I wish to inform you that the Government of the Kingdom of Saudi Arabia has decided to advise you that Saudi Arabia will, regrettably, not be in a position to assume the seat on the Security Council to which it was elected on 17 October 2013, for the period 2014–2015. The reasons for this decision have been articulated in the statement issued by the Ministry of Foreign Affairs of Saudi Arabia dated 18 October 2013, a copy of which is enclosed (see annex).

In doing so, Saudi Arabia wishes to reaffirm its commitment to the United Nations and its various organizations and its appreciation of the valuable leadership that you are providing in world affairs. I assure you of my determination to work closely with you for the advancement of the cause of peace and development in the world.

(*Signed*) Abdallah Y. Al-Mouallimi
Ambassador Extraordinary and Plenipotentiary
Permanent Representative of Saudi Arabia to the United Nations

Annex to the letter dated 12 November 2013 from the Permanent Representative of Saudi Arabia to the United Nations addressed to the Secretary-General
Statement of the Ministry of Foreign Affairs on Saudi Arabia's apology for not accepting Security Council membership

The Ministry of Foreign Affairs has issued a statement after the election of the Kingdom of Saudi Arabia as a non-permanent member of the Security Council for two years. Following is the text of the statement:

First of all, the Kingdom of Saudi Arabia is pleased to extend its sincere thanks and deep gratitude to all countries that have given it their confidence by electing it as a non-permanent member of the Security Council for the next two years.

The Kingdom of Saudi Arabia, a founding member of the United Nations, is proud of its full and permanent commitment to the purposes and principles of the Charter of the United Nations, believing that the commitment of all Member States, made honestly, truthfully and accurately, as agreed upon and stipulated in the Charter, is the real guarantee for world security and peace.

If the Member States of the United Nations consider winning membership in the Security Council, which is, according to the Charter of the Organization, the sole agency responsible for preserving world peace and security, as a high honour and a great responsibility for participating directly and effectively in the service of international issues, the Kingdom of Saudi Arabia believes that the manner, mechanisms of action and double standards existing in the Security Council prevent it from performing its duties and assuming its responsibilities towards preserving international peace and security as required, leading to the continued disruption of peace and security, the expansion of the injustices against peoples, the violation of rights and the spread of conflicts and wars around the world.

In this regard, it is unfortunate that all international efforts that have been exerted in recent years, and in which Saudi Arabia participated very effectively, did not result in reaching the reforms required to be made to enable the Security Council to regain its desired role in the service of the issues of peace and security in the world.

The current continuation of the Palestinian cause without a just and lasting solution for 65 years, which resulted in several wars and threatened international peace and security, is irrefutable evidence and proof of the Security Council's inability to carry out its duties and assume its responsibilities.

The failure of the Security Council to make the Middle East a zone free of all weapons of mass destruction, whether because of its inability to subject the nuclear programmes of all countries in the region, without exception, to international control and inspection or to prevent any country in the region from possessing nuclear weapons, is additional irrefutable evidence and proof of its inability to carry out its duties and honour its responsibilities.

Allowing the ruling regime in Syria to kill and burn its people with chemical weapons while the world stands idly by, without applying deterrent sanctions against the Damascus regime, is also irrefutable evidence and proof of the inability of the Security Council to carry out its duties and responsibilities.

Accordingly, the Kingdom of Saudi Arabia, based on the basis of its historical responsibilities towards its people, Arab and Islamic nations as well as towards the peoples aspiring to peace and stability all over the world, announces its apology for not accepting membership in the Security Council until the Council is reformed and enabled, effectively and practically, to carry out its duties and responsibilities in maintaining international peace and security.

SOURCE: United Nations. "Letter dated 12 November 2013 from the Permanent Representative of Saudi Arabia to the United Nations addressed to the Secretary-General." November 14, 2013. http://www.un.org/Docs/journal/asp/ws.asp?m=a/68/599.

Jordan Elected to Fill Vacant Security Council Post

December 6, 2013

The United Nations General Assembly has elected Jordan as a non-permanent member of the Security Council to fill a seat that Saudi Arabia had, in an earlier election, won but declined to accept.

Jordan, endorsed by the African and Asian regional group, was elected to serve on the Council for two-years beginning on 1 January 2014. The country will be seated alongside Chad, Chile, Lithuania and Nigeria, which the Assembly elected on 17 October.

Saudi Arabia was also elected in the October vote, but shortly thereafter began to signal it would not accept the position. In a 12 November statement annexed to a letter from the Ambassador of Saudi Arabia to UN Secretary-General Ban Ki-moon, the Saudi Foreign Ministry formally confirmed that stance.

In that statement, the Ministry apologized for its non-acceptance, explaining that the country could not serve on the Council until the body is "reformed and enabled, effectively and practically, to carry out its duties and responsibilities in maintaining international peace and security." The Kingdom nevertheless reaffirmed its commitment to the UN and the goals of the Organization.

"The Kingdom of Saudi Arabia believes that the manner, mechanisms of action and double standards existing in the [Council] prevent it from performing its duties and assuming its responsibilities towards preserving international peace and security as required, leading to the continued disruption of peace and security, the expansion of the injustices against peoples, the violation of rights and the spread of conflicts and wars around the world," the statement continues.

The Foreign Ministry cited the situation of the Palestinian cause, lacking a just and lasting solution for 65 years, as "irrefutable evidence and proof of the Security Council's inability to carry out its duties and assume its responsibilities.["] It also laments the Council's "failure . . . to make the Middle East a zone free of all weapons of mass destruction."

Finally, the ministry said that "allowing the ruling regime in Syria to kill and burn its people with chemical weapons while the world stands idly by, without applying deterrent sanctions against the Damascus regime, is also irrefutable evidence and proof of the inability of the Security Council to carry out its duties and responsibilities."

In light of those concerns, Saudi Arabia, "on the basis of its historical responsibilities towards its people, Arab and Islamic nations as well as towards the peoples aspiring to peace and stability all over the world, announces its apology for not accepting membership in the Security Council," the statement concludes.

The five permanent Council members, which each wield the power of veto, are China, France, Russia, the United Kingdom and the United States. Non-permanent members Argentina, Australia, Luxembourg, the Republic of Korea and Rwanda will remain on the Council until the end of 2014.

Under the UN Charter, the 15-member Council has primary responsibility for the maintenance of international peace and security, and all Member States are obligated to comply with its decisions.

In addition, the Council takes the lead in determining the existence of a threat to the peace or act of aggression. It calls on the parties to a dispute to settle it by peaceful means and recommends methods of adjustment or terms of settlement.

In some cases, it can resort to imposing sanctions or even authorize the use of force to maintain or restore international peace and security.

SOURCE: United Nations. News Centre. "Jordan elected to serve on UN Security Council." December 6, 2013. http://www.un.org/apps/news/story.asp?NewsID=46678#.UzWKKNzDRkh.

OTHER HISTORIC DOCUMENTS OF INTEREST

FROM THIS VOLUME

FROM PREVIOUS *HISTORIC DOCUMENTS*

China Announces Relaxation of Some Social Policies

NOVEMBER 15 AND DECEMBER 6, 2013

On November 15, 2013, Chinese Premier Xi Jinping announced the decisions from a meeting of top Chinese leaders to restructure the economy and relax some of the country's social policies, most notably the one-child rule. The moves came as a surprise to many in the West, given that the policies have been long-standing strongholds of Chinese socialism. Together, the policy changes are intended to strengthen the Chinese position in the global economy and silence unrest. In announcing the results of the annual meeting, Xi encouraged Chinese citizens and leaders to "have the courage and conviction to renew" themselves. While the social policy changes made by the Central Committee were hailed around the world, no dates for implementation were attached to the proposal, and the Chinese government still has leeway to dilute or overturn the proposed changes.

The announcements made at the annual meeting of the leaders of the Communist Party were in line with the persona Xi had created during his first eight months in office. Marking a change from earlier leaders, Xi has strived to pursue a decidedly liberal social and economic agenda, such as those put forth by the Central Committee, while still maintaining solid one-party rule. International observers have questioned whether this means that Xi has truly consolidated his power at the top of the party, or whether his tenure will be short lived because traditional, hard-line Communist leaders will fail to support him.

HISTORY OF THE ONE-CHILD POLICY

In the 1960s under Chairman Mao, Chinese families were encouraged to have as many children as they desired, following his belief that population growth was interconnected with global power. The population skyrocketed to nearly one billion people by 1976, prompting Chinese officials to encourage families to instead limit themselves to two children. In 1979, the central government cracked down even further, officially enforcing what became known as a "one-child policy." Some exemptions existed for ethnic minorities (such as Tibetans), rural farming families with a disabled or female first born, parents who are both only children, Chinese citizens who previously lived overseas, and any children born outside of China who do not receive citizenship (the latter of which gave rise to birth tourism). Any family allowed to have a second child was forced to wait a set number of years.

To enforce the policy, the government relied on work units, or the places of employment of Chinese citizens, although enforcement varied widely between provinces. At times, employers would track fertility and advise married female employees about when it was their turn to have a child. Any person found in violation of the one-child policy was subject to stiff monetary penalties and could be denied work bonuses. The fine was to be paid by both the mother and father and was calculated based on annual income. No penalties were applied in the case of multiple births.

The one-child policy has drawn sharp criticism from human rights organizations and a number of Western nations, including the United States and United Kingdom, who point to the high rate of child abandonment, infanticide, and sex-selective abortions that all favor males over females. All these practices are illegal under Chinese law, but a number of high-profile studies have proven their use. The one-child policy is also a violation of international human rights conventions.

The Chinese government has long touted the benefits of the one-child policy, including free women's health care that allows the family to spend less on rearing children and thus invest more money into the Chinese economy, and emphasized the importance of financial planning and saving because one child may not be able to care for the parents. The policy is also intended to reduce unemployment, reduce the demand on natural resources, and create a stable workforce. The policy did create a number of financial barriers for the first children born under it because, by the time they had their own children, they were also caring for two parents and four grandparents—a phenomenon known as 4–2–1. In 2011, the Chinese government stated that its policy was beneficial to world population growth, because it had prevented 400 million births, a figure strongly debated by researchers like Cai Yong, an assistant professor at the University of North Carolina at Chapel Hill, who said the data was an attempt at "rewriting China's fertility reduction history."

RELAXATION OF THE ONE-CHILD POLICY

From November 9 to November 12, 2013, Chinese leaders gathered for the third Plenary Session of the 18th CPC Central Committee in Beijing, China. The session was intended to implement economic and social reforms that China would follow for at least the next decade. Perhaps the most notable change announced at the conclusion of the session was the relaxation of the one-child policy. While the Central Committee, the governing body of the Communist Party, did not outlaw the policy altogether, it did revise its implementation. The changes would allow a couple to have two children if either the mother or father is an only child.

The changes were thought to be a reaction to the economic impact of a rapidly aging population—on its current trajectory, the ratio of taxpayers to pensioners will drop to approximately two to one by 2030; by 2050, one quarter of the population will be over age 65. This poses a large burden for both elderly care and the nation's workforce, which must keep pace with the country's economic growth. In 2012, for the first time in nearly fifty years, the number of Chinese laborers decreased (by more than three million). Another consideration raised by demographers is the estimation that by the end of the current decade, twenty-four million men will be unable to find wives due to the severe gender imbalance.

Both Chinese citizens and those around the globe hailed the decision to relax the one-child policy. "This shift is historical. It's fundamental. To change the mentality of the society of policy makers has taken people more than a decade," said Wang Feng, a demographer at Fudan University in Shanghai. However, there is some question regarding what impact it might have. The high cost of urban living coupled with education may prevent many families from having a second child, even if they desire to do so. "There could be a slight rise, but this policy will not cause dramatic growth in the birth rate," said Li Jianmin, a professor at Nankai University. "A majority of only-child parents are living in the cities, where the cost of raising a child is very high, and many young parents cannot afford to have a second child," Li continued.

OTHER SOCIAL AND ECONOMIC CHANGES

The final document that included all recommendations made by the Central Committee during its meeting, called The Decision on Major Issues Concerning Comprehensively Deepening Reforms, was released on November 15 after four days of secretive debate. In the document, sixty policy objectives were addressed, and all the goals outlined were intended to be reached by 2020. "The environment both at home and globally is going through wide-ranging yet profound changes," said Xi, adding, "Our nation's development is facing a series of prominent challenges, creating numerous problems and questions for the road ahead." In addition to relaxing the one-child policy, the Central Committee also agreed to loosen restrictions to give the private sector more influence in the economy and give additional property rights to rural farmers. Moving forward, the Chinese government also intends to allow an increase in overseas investment.

Another significant social change announced by the Central Committee was the end of re-education through labor camps, known internationally as gulags, where prisoners face harsh conditions and relentless factory labor. The practice has been in place for five decades and today houses tens of thousands of prisoners. In its early years, the camps were used to silence political opponents, but today they house Chinese undesirables like prostitutes and drug users. The labor camps have long been criticized by human rights organizations, who decry the lackadaisical policy of allowing police to convict and sentence citizens to the camps without a trial. While international observers noted that Xi was well aware of how unpopular the labor camps are both at home and abroad, the decision came as a surprise because, in his first year as president, Xi has heavily cracked down on political dissent.

The Chinese government initially announced in early 2013 that it would get rid of the camps, only to retract its decision until the Central Committee annual meeting. As with the relaxation of the one-child policy, human rights advocates cautiously applauded the decision. "It doesn't mean that China is going to be kinder to dissent and to its critics," said Human Rights Watch senior researcher Nicholas Bequelin, "but it's an important step to do away with a system that not only profoundly violated human rights, but was also standing in the way of any further legal reform." A report by Amnesty International noted that the closure of the labor camps coincided with an apparent increase in use of drug rehabilitation clinics and what it called "brainwashing centers." The report noted, "There is a very real risk that the Chinese authorities will abolish one system of arbitrary detention only to expand the use of other types." Even so, Ambassador to China Gary Locke said that the United States would "look forward to progress on China's recent decisions to end the re-education through labor system and to strengthen the rule of law." It is thought that Xi may have pressed for the end of these camps as a personal mission, perhaps without the support of other leaders, because his father, a former vice premier, served seven years in a labor camp.

In related decisions, the Central Committee agreed to reduce the number of offenses that can result in the death penalty—China carries out capital punishment sentences more than all other nations in the world combined—and "improve the transparency and public credibility of the judiciary." At the same time, the government announced that it would continue to tighten its control of the Internet, calling the available information "a real and pressing problem facing us."

—Heather Kerrigan

Following is the edited text of a press conference held by the U.S. Department of State on November 15, 2013, discussing U.S. response to the Chinese social policy reforms; and a December 6, 2013, statement from the U.S. Ambassador to China encouraging implementation of the reforms.

DOCUMENT

State Department Responds to Chinese Social Policy Changes

November 15, 2013

[All portions of the press conference not related to the one-child policy or labor camps have been omitted.]

Question: Sorry. On China, what's your reaction to some of the reform announcements that have been coming out of China, especially the announcement today about ending reeducation through labor camps?

Ms. Psaki: I know there have been a range of announcements that have come out over the past couple of days. Obviously, we're looking closely at those. I don't have anything particular for you to convey about each of those announcements at this point.

Question: But obviously, if it's true, it's encouraging for your discussions on human rights with China?

Ms. Psaki: Of course human rights and—is of great concern, and one we raise every time we speak with the Chinese, but I don't want to get too ahead of our team looking at the various proposals and announcements that have come out over the past couple of days about a range of issues.

Question: Can you take that question?

Ms. Psaki: Sure, I'm happy to. I'm happy to.

Question: But I'm—surely it's a good thing.

Ms. Psaki: Of course. Of course. But I don't—we haven't looked at all of the details yet, so I don't want to give too much commentary in analyzing it.

Question: Is that the same for the end to the one-child policy as well, which was announced?

Ms. Psaki: Again, that's one that I know that they have announced in the past. Obviously, we'll be looking at that, but I don't have anything specific on it at this point.

Question: Just a quick follow-up. These reforms announcements are generally opaque and take weeks to sort of digest, but it seems that there's quite a few very quick policies coming out that the U.S. would find encouraging at face value, correct?

Ms. Psaki: Well, again, we—for specifics on them, I would certainly refer you to the Chinese. We'll take a look at them. We're in close touch. And if there's more we have to say in reaction, I'm sure we'll do that.

SOURCE: U.S. Department of State. IIP Digital. "State Department Daily Press Briefing." November 15, 2013. http://translations.state.gov/st/english/texttrans/2013/11/20131115286963.html#ixzz2yp0wqX00.

Ambassador Locke on Chinese Social Policy Reforms

December 6, 2013

Today we celebrate International Human Rights Day and commemorate the 65th anniversary of the Universal Declaration of Human Rights, a document President Obama called "revolutionary" because it "recognized the inherent dignity and inalienable rights of all people as the 'foundation of freedom, justice, and peace in the world.'" This is a time to reflect on progress made and work yet to be done.

As China prepares to implement new reforms, we encourage attention to human rights and look forward to progress on China's recent decisions to end the re-education through labor system and to strengthen the rule of law. All persons, including the accused, must be treated with dignity and fairness. The attorneys who defend sensitive clients should be protected, not punished. Gao Zhisheng and other rights lawyers who are in jail or have had their law licenses revoked should be set free and permitted to return to their important work.

We continue to see official acts of harassment and retribution against family members of rights defenders and activists. We call on China to restore Liu Xia's freedom and free her husband Liu Xiaobo—the only Nobel Peace Prize laureate in the world who remains imprisoned.

As Vice President Biden said recently in Beijing, innovation thrives where people can speak freely. Yet, several Chinese citizens, including Xu Zhiyong, Wang Gongquan, and Yang Maodong, recently were jailed for their activism in support of transparency and clean government. Equally troubling is a vague and broad legal interpretation that justifies charges of criminal defamation for spreading "online rumors," a development that greatly threatens freedom of expression online. China's creativity will be fully unleashed only when its people are free from censorship.

As Ambassador, I have witnessed China's rich diversity first-hand. I have also seen cases where heavy-handed policies deny basic freedoms to ethnic and religious minorities, including ethnic Uighurs, Tibetans and Mongolians, undermining the trust that binds diverse societies. The United States calls on the Chinese government to protect the fundamental freedoms of all its citizens without discrimination. We also urge China's leaders to engage in constructive dialogue with the Dalai Lama or his representatives, as a means to reduce tensions.

As we celebrate the 65th anniversary of the Universal Declaration of Human Rights today, we are reminded that all countries, including the United States and China, have a responsibility to protect the human rights and fundamental freedoms enshrined in this important document. I am hopeful that China's leaders will soon bring substance to the notion that certain inalienable rights pertain to all citizens. With this recognition, I can imagine an unlimited future for China and its great people.

SOURCE: U.S. Embassy in Beijing, China. "Ambassador Locke 2013 Human Rights Day Statement." December 6, 2013. http://beijing.usembassy-china.org.cn/ambassador-locke-2013-human-rights-day-statement.html.

OTHER HISTORIC DOCUMENTS OF INTEREST

FROM PREVIOUS *HISTORIC DOCUMENTS*

- UN on World Population Reaching Six Billion People, *1999*, p. 584

Justice Department Reaches Settlement With J.P. Morgan Chase

NOVEMBER 19, 2013

In late 2012, the U.S. Department of Justice announced legal action against one of the nation's largest banks, J.P. Morgan Chase Bank (J.P. Morgan), which stood accused of misconduct related to the sale of mortgage-backed securities that contributed to the 2008 financial crisis. Just over a year later, both parties announced a record-breaking settlement totaling $13 billion. The settlement is one of many paid out by the bank related to its actions prior to and during the financial crisis. Of the total 2013 settlement, $4 billion was designated to consumer relief to be distributed by the end of 2017. The remainder was split between fines and investor compensation. While the bank acknowledged misconduct, it maintained that it had not violated any laws. The settlement does not prevent further legal action against J.P. Morgan by the government or individuals as it relates to conduct covered in the agreement, and indeed the Department of Justice is pursuing criminal investigations. The firm has set aside a fund for its legal expenses totaling $23 billion.

LEGAL ACTION AGAINST J.P. MORGAN CHASE

On October 2, 2012, the Department of Justice released a statement indicating that the first legal action to be undertaken by the Residential Mortgage-Backed Securities (RMBS) Working Group since its inception in early 2012 would be against J.P. Morgan Securities LLC (formerly known as Bear Stearns & Co. Inc.), J.P. Morgan Chase Bank N.A., and EMC Mortgage LLC "for making fraudulent misrepresentations and omissions to promote the sale of residential mortgage-backed securities (RMBS) to investors." The lawsuit accused the defendants of deceiving investors with regard to the state and riskiness of the investments during the period prior to the collapse of Bear Stearns in early 2008. J.P. Morgan bought the beleaguered Bear Stearns investment bank in mid-2008, and purchased the assets and some liabilities of Washington Mutual (WaMu), a savings and loan association, in September of the same year. The alleged misconduct resulted in investor losses valued at more than $22 billion.

The lawsuit was the first legal action from the RMBS Working Group, a state-federal taskforce created by President Barack Obama to investigate those responsible for misconduct contributing to the financial crisis through the pooling and sale of residential mortgage-backed securities. The RMBS Working Group is comprised of both federal and state law enforcement officials, totaling more than two hundred attorneys, investigators, and others from numerous agencies. The investigations into J.P. Morgan's activities by RMBS were a multi-year and multi-stakeholder effort.

RECORD-BREAKING SETTLEMENT

On November 19, 2013, it was announced that J.P. Morgan Chase would pay a record $13 billion in a settlement with the U.S. government. The settlement includes a $2 billion penalty fee to be paid to the federal government, $4 billion in consumer relief, and the remainder in compensatory payments for investors. The agreement resolved the federal and state civil claims related to the "packaging, marketing, sale and issuance of residential mortgage-backed securities (RMBS) by JPMorgan, Bear Stearns and Washington Mutual prior to Jan. 1, 2009." In a statement, J.P. Morgan admitted to serious misrepresentations of information related to its RMBS, but denied breaking any laws.

U.S. Attorney General Eric Holder placed significant blame on J.P. Morgan for helping cause the mortgage meltdown. "J.P. Morgan was not the only financial institution during this period to knowingly bundle toxic loans and sell them to unsuspecting investors, but that is no excuse for the firm's behavior," the Attorney General said in a statement, adding that his department would continue to investigate and prosecute those responsible for events precipitating the financial crisis.

J.P. Morgan's Chairman and Chief Executive Officer, Jamie Dimon, said in a statement, "We are pleased to have concluded this extensive agreement with the President's RMBS Working Group and to have resolved the civil claims of the Department of Justice and others. Today's settlement covers a very significant portion of legacy mortgage-backed securities-related issues for JPMorgan Chase, as well as Bear Stearns and Washington Mutual." Indeed, the bank indicated that around 80 percent of the bad loans covered by the settlement originated from Washington Mutual and Bear Stearns.

The statement of facts published with the settlement indicated that J.P. Morgan acknowledged that its representatives regularly provided investors with incorrect information regarding RMBS, namely that the RMBS met underwriting guidelines. Moreover, the bank admitted that in a number of instances its employees knew that the mortgages underpinning the RMBS did not meet underwriting guidelines and were not appropriate for securitization. Nevertheless, such loans were securitized and subsequently sold, while the investors were left in the dark about crucial financial information. The Department of Justice holds that these actions at J.P. Morgan and other banks contributed to the financial crisis. The U.S. Attorney for the Eastern District of California Benjamin Wagner stated that the actions of companies like J.P. Morgan turned the housing crisis into the larger global financial meltdown. And despite the end of the global recession, the impact of the sale of toxic mortgages is still ongoing. "Credit unions, banks and other investor victims across the country, including many in the Eastern District of California, continue to struggle with losses they suffered as a result," Wagner said.

BROAD SETTLEMENT DISTRIBUTION

The resolution—the largest ever between the federal government and a private entity—included payments to both federal and state entities. The $2 billion civil penalty paid to the Department of Justice falls under the Financial Institutions Reform, Recovery, and Enforcement Act (FIRREA). Together the National Credit Union Administration, the Federal Deposit Insurance Corporation (FDIC), and the Federal Housing Finance Agency will be awarded nearly $5 billion ($1.4 billion, $515.4 million, and $4 billion, respectively).

A number of states will also receive compensation, including: California ($298.9 million); Delaware ($19.7 million); Illinois ($100 million); Massachusetts ($34.4 million); and New York ($613 million).

J.P. Morgan has also agreed to pay $4 billion in consumer relief for individuals negatively impacted by the actions of the bank (including Bear Stearns and Washington Mutual). According to the Department of Justice, this relief will take many forms, including principal forgiveness, loan modification, targeted originations, and efforts to reduce blight. Under the terms of the settlement, J.P. Morgan is required to have an independent auditor verify its compliance in this area. The bank committed to reaching this target by the end of 2017. If it misses this deadline, J.P. Morgan will be required to pay the shortfall to NeighborWorks America, a nonprofit organization dedicated to affordable housing and community development. The U.S. Department of Housing and Urban Development Secretary, Shaun Donovan, issued a statement in which he said, "This agreement ensures that accountability includes assistance to American consumers and communities hardest hit by the housing crisis by providing $4 billion in relief that could benefit more than 100,000 borrowers."

During a conference call with analysts after the settlement was announced, the bank's chief financial officer, Marianne Lake, said that $2 billion of the settlement (i.e., the fine paid to the Justice Department) would not be tax deductible, but that $7 billion in payments would be deductible. She also indicated that the bank had set aside a fund totaling $23 billion to cover the firm's ongoing legal battles. The $13 billion total settlement will be paid for from the fund.

Ongoing Investigations and Other Settlements

Investigations into J.P. Morgan's actions are ongoing. The settlement does not protect the bank or its representatives from criminal prosecution, nor does it prevent individual employees from facing civil charges. The settlement also states that J.P. Morgan will fully cooperate with any subsequent investigations related to the conduct covered by the settlement.

The $13 billion settlement is just one of many legal woes for J.P. Morgan. Just days before the record-breaking settlement was announced, the bank agreed to pay $4.5 billion to institutional investors who lost money on mortgage-backed securities. The twenty-one institutional investors, including BlackRock and MetLife, alleged that the firm misrepresented the true value of the securities, which later lost value. Investments sold between 2005 and 2008 by both J.P. Morgan and Bear Stearns are covered by the deal. However, investments sold by Washington Mutual are not covered. The settlement funds will go to trustees who have oversight for more than 300 residential mortgage-backed securities trusts. According to the bank's financial statements, its legal fees amounted to more than $9 billion in the third quarter of 2013 alone.

—Hilary Ewing

Following is a press release from the Department of Justice on November 19, 2013, announcing the settlement reached with J.P. Morgan Chase for misleading investors.

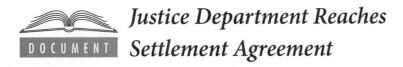

Justice Department Reaches Settlement Agreement

November 19, 2013

The Justice Department, along with federal and state partners, today announced a $13 billion settlement with JPMorgan—the largest settlement with a single entity in American history—to resolve federal and state civil claims arising out of the packaging, marketing, sale and issuance of residential mortgage-backed securities (RMBS) by JPMorgan, Bear Stearns and Washington Mutual prior to Jan. 1, 2009. As part of the settlement, JPMorgan acknowledged it made serious misrepresentations to the public—including the investing public—about numerous RMBS transactions. The resolution also requires JPMorgan to provide much needed relief to underwater homeowners and potential homebuyers, including those in distressed areas of the country. The settlement does not absolve JPMorgan or its employees from facing any possible criminal charges.

This settlement is part of the ongoing efforts of President Obama's Financial Fraud Enforcement Task Force's RMBS Working Group.

"Without a doubt, the conduct uncovered in this investigation helped sow the seeds of the mortgage meltdown," said Attorney General Eric Holder. "JPMorgan was not the only financial institution during this period to knowingly bundle toxic loans and sell them to unsuspecting investors, but that is no excuse for the firm's behavior. The size and scope of this resolution should send a clear signal that the Justice Department's financial fraud investigations are far from over. No firm, no matter how profitable, is above the law, and the passage of time is no shield from accountability. I want to personally thank the RMBS Working Group for its tireless work not only in this case, but also in the investigations that remain ongoing."

The settlement includes a statement of facts, in which JPMorgan acknowledges that it regularly represented to RMBS investors that the mortgage loans in various securities complied with underwriting guidelines. Contrary to those representations, as the statement of facts explains, on a number of different occasions, JPMorgan employees knew that the loans in question did not comply with those guidelines and were not otherwise appropriate for securitization, but they allowed the loans to be securitized—and those securities to be sold—without disclosing this information to investors. This conduct, along with similar conduct by other banks that bundled toxic loans into securities and misled investors who purchased those securities, contributed to the financial crisis.

"Through this $13 billion resolution, we are demanding accountability and requiring remediation from those who helped create a financial storm that devastated millions of Americans," said Associate Attorney General Tony West. "The conduct JPMorgan has acknowledged—packaging risky home loans into securities, then selling them without disclosing their low quality to investors—contributed to the wreckage of the financial crisis. By requiring JPMorgan both to pay the largest FIRREA penalty in history and provide needed consumer relief to areas hardest hit by the financial crisis, we rectify some of that harm today."

Of the record-breaking $13 billion resolution, $9 billion will be paid to settle federal and state civil claims by various entities related to RMBS. Of that $9 billion, JPMorgan will pay $2 billion as a civil penalty to settle the Justice Department claims under the Financial Institutions Reform, Recovery, and Enforcement Act (FIRREA), $1.4 billion to settle federal and state securities claims by the National Credit Union Administration (NCUA), $515.4 million to settle federal and state securities claims by the Federal Deposit Insurance Corporation (FDIC), $4 billion to settle federal and state claims by the Federal Housing Finance Agency (FHFA), $298.9 million to settle claims by the State of California, $19.7 million to settle claims by the State of Delaware, $100 million to settle claims by the State of Illinois, $34.4 million to settle claims by the Commonwealth of Massachusetts, and $613 million to settle claims by the State of New York.

JPMorgan will pay out the remaining $4 billion in the form of relief to aid consumers harmed by the unlawful conduct of JPMorgan, Bear Stearns and Washington Mutual. That relief will take various forms, including principal forgiveness, loan modification, targeted originations and efforts to reduce blight. An independent monitor will be appointed to determine whether JPMorgan is satisfying its obligations. If JPMorgan fails to live up to its agreement by Dec. 31, 2017, it must pay liquidated damages in the amount of the shortfall to NeighborWorks America, a non-profit organization and leader in providing affordable housing and facilitating community development.

The U.S. Attorney's Offices for the Eastern District of California and Eastern District of Pennsylvania and the Justice Department's Civil Division, along with the U.S. Attorney's Office for the Northern District of Texas, conducted investigations into JPMorgan's, Washington Mutual's and Bear Stearns' practices related to the sale and issuance of RMBS between 2005 and 2008.

"Today's global settlement underscores the power of FIRREA and other civil enforcement tools for combatting financial fraud," said Assistant Attorney General for the Civil Division Stuart F. Delery, co-chair of the RMBS Working Group. "The Civil Division, working with the U.S. Attorney's Offices and our state and agency partners, will continue to use every available resource to aggressively pursue those responsible for the financial crisis."

"Abuses in the mortgage-backed securities industry helped turn a crisis in the housing market into an international financial crisis," said U.S. Attorney for the Eastern District of California Benjamin Wagner. "The impacts were staggering. JPMorgan sold securities knowing that many of the loans backing those certificates were toxic. Credit unions, banks and other investor victims across the country, including many in the Eastern District of California, continue to struggle with losses they suffered as a result. In the Eastern District of California, we have worked hard to prosecute fraud in the mortgage industry. We are equally committed to holding accountable those in the securities industry who profited through the sale of defective mortgages."

"Today's settlement represents another significant step towards holding accountable those banks which exploited the residential mortgage-backed securities market and harmed numerous individuals and entities in the process," said U.S. Attorney for the Eastern District of Pennsylvania Zane David Memeger. "These banks packaged and sold toxic mortgage-backed securities, which violated the law and contributed to the financial crisis. It is particularly important that JPMorgan, after assuming the significant assets of Washington Mutual Bank, is now also held responsible for the unscrupulous and deceptive conduct of Washington Mutual, one of the biggest players in the mortgage-backed securities market."

This settlement resolves only civil claims arising out of the RMBS packaged, marketed, sold and issued by JPMorgan, Bear Stearns and Washington Mutual. The agreement does not release individuals from civil charges, nor does it release JPMorgan or any individuals from potential criminal prosecution. In addition, as part of the settlement, JPMorgan has pledged to fully cooperate in investigations related to the conduct covered by the agreement.

To keep JPMorgan from seeking reimbursement from the federal government for any money it pays pursuant to this resolution, the Justice Department required language in the settlement agreement which prohibits JPMorgan from demanding indemnification from the FDIC, both in its capacity as a corporate entity and as the receiver for Washington Mutual.

"The settlement announced today will provide a significant recovery for six FDIC receiverships. It also fully protects the FDIC from indemnification claims out of this settlement," said FDIC Chairman Martin J. Gruenberg. "The FDIC will continue to pursue litigation where necessary in order to recover as much as possible for FDIC receiverships, money that is ultimately returned to the Deposit Insurance Fund, uninsured depositors and creditors of failed banks."

"NCUA's Board extends our thanks and appreciation to our attorneys and to the Department of Justice, who have worked closely together for more than three years to bring this matter to a successful resolution," said NCUA Board Chairman Debbie Matz. "The faulty mortgage-backed securities created and packaged by JPMorgan and other institutions created a crisis in the credit union industry, and we're pleased a measure of accountability has been reached."

"JPMorgan and the banks it bought securitized billions of dollars of defective mortgages," said Acting FHFA Inspector General Michael P. Stephens. "Investors, including Fannie Mae and Freddie Mac, suffered enormous losses by purchasing RMBS from JPMorgan, Washington Mutual and Bear Stearns not knowing about those defects. Today's settlement is a significant, but by no means final step by FHFA-OIG and its law enforcement partners to hold accountable those who committed acts of fraud and deceit. We are proud to have worked with the Department of Justice, the U.S. attorneys in Sacramento and Philadelphia and the New York and California state attorneys general; they have been great partners and we look forward to our continued work together."

The attorneys general of New York, California, Delaware, Illinois and Massachusetts also conducted related investigations that were critical to bringing about this settlement.

"Since my first day in office, I have insisted that there must be accountability for the misconduct that led to the crash of the housing market and the collapse of the American economy," said New York Attorney General Eric Schneiderman, Co-Chair of the RMBS Working Group. "This historic deal, which will bring long overdue relief to homeowners around the country and across New York, is exactly what our working group was created to do. We refused to allow systemic frauds that harmed so many New York homeowners and investors to simply be forgotten, and as a result we've won a major victory today in the fight to hold those who caused the financial crisis accountable."

"JP Morgan Chase profited by giving California's pension funds incomplete information about mortgage investments," California Attorney General Kamala D. Harris said. "This settlement returns the money to California's pension funds that JP Morgan wrongfully took from them."

"Our financial system only works when everyone plays by the rules," said Delaware Attorney General Beau Biden. "Today, as a result of our coordinated investigations, we are holding accountable one of the financial institutions that, by breaking those rules, helped cause the economic crisis that brought our nation to its knees. Even as the

American people recover from this crisis, we will continue to seek accountability on their behalf."

"We are still cleaning up the mess that Wall Street made with its reckless investment schemes and fraudulent conduct," said Illinois Attorney General Lisa Madigan. "Today's settlement with JPMorgan will assist Illinois in recovering its losses from the dangerous and deceptive securities that put our economy on the path to destruction."

"This is a historic settlement that will help us to hold accountable those investment banks that played a role in creating and exacerbating the housing crisis," said Massachusetts Attorney General Martha Coakley. "We appreciate the work of the Department of Justice and the other enforcement agencies in bringing about this resolution and look forward to continuing to work together in other securitization cases."

The RMBS Working Group is a federal and state law enforcement effort focused on investigating fraud and abuse in the RMBS market that helped lead to the 2008 financial crisis. The RMBS Working Group brings together more than 200 attorneys, investigators, analysts and staff from dozens of state and federal agencies including the Department of Justice, 10 U.S. attorney's offices, the FBI, the Securities and Exchange Commission (SEC), the Department of Housing and Urban Development (HUD), HUD's Office of Inspector General, the FHFA-OIG, the Office of the Special Inspector General for the Troubled Asset Relief Program, the Federal Reserve Board's Office of Inspector General, the Recovery Accountability and Transparency Board, the Financial Crimes Enforcement Network, and more than 10 state attorneys general offices around the country.

The RMBS Working Group is led by five co-chairs: Assistant Attorney General for the Civil Division Stuart Delery, Acting Assistant Attorney General for the Criminal Division Mythili Raman, Co-Director of the SEC's Division of Enforcement George Canellos, U.S. Attorney for the District of Colorado John Walsh and New York Attorney General Eric Schneiderman.

SOURCE: U.S. Department of Justice. "Justice Department, Federal and State Partnerships Secure Record $13 Billion Global Settlement with JPMorgan for Misleading Investors About Securities Containing Toxic Mortgages." November 19, 2013. http://www.justice.gov/opa/pr/2013/November/13-ag-1237.html.

OTHER HISTORIC DOCUMENTS OF INTEREST

FROM PREVIOUS *HISTORIC DOCUMENTS*

Federal Leaders on Changes to the Filibuster Rule

NOVEMBER 21, 2013

In a response to the partisan gridlock that has had a stranglehold on Congress over the past few years, on November 21, the Senate approved landmark legislation that would limit its use of the filibuster, a tool commonly used by the party in opposition to a specific bill to prevent the bill from being voted on. The change to Senate rules specifically disallowed the filibuster to be used to block presidential executive and judicial nominees, unless the nomination was for the U.S. Supreme Court. This meant that instead of requiring a supermajority of sixty votes to approve a nomination, only a simple majority of fifty-one would now be needed. The filibuster rule still remained intact for debate on any legislation.

THE FILIBUSTER RULE

The original Senate rules required a procedure called moving the "previous question." If a member invoked this procedure, which essentially called for the end of debate, his or her motion would be voted on, and, if passed, the Senate would move to a vote on the bill in question. In 1837, this procedure was dropped but not replaced, leading to lengthy filibusters. In 1890, with the absence of a rule, Sen. Nelson Aldrich, R-R.I., attempted to end a filibuster by forcing an immediate vote through the appeal from the chair procedure. If the appeal was overruled, by Senate rules, a vote would be called on ending the filibuster. After a decision by the Supreme Court, starting in 1892, the Senate was given the power to begin making procedural rules as long as they were approved by simple majority vote. In 1917, the Senate changed the filibuster rule to install a method for requiring the end of debate known as cloture. Before that time, the minority party could block anything without any recourse for the majority party. Prior to 2013, the last time the filibuster rule was changed was in 1975 when the Senate voted to reduce the number of votes needed to break a filibuster from two-thirds to sixty.

The "nuclear option," the idea of making procedural rule changes by simple majority, is often linked to then-Vice President Richard Nixon who wrote in 1957 that the Constitution granted the Senate's presiding officer the ability to overturn a standing Senate rule as long as it was upheld by a majority vote. Use of the nuclear option was first attempted, unsuccessfully, in 1963, and again in1967 and 1969.

Increasing use of the filibuster started in the early to mid-1990s, when Democrats held the presidency. In 1995, *The New York Times* called the filibuster "the tool of the sore loser." Republicans in the Senate were able to filibuster the nomination of Judge Richard Paez to the United States Court of Appeals for the Ninth Circuit for four years (Paez was ultimately confirmed in 2000 by a simple majority). As the Paez filibuster wore on, Republicans used their slim majority to block a total of sixty judicial nominees of then-President Bill Clinton.

DEMOCRATS THREATEN CHANGES

While the filibuster has been invoked many times in history, it has been used most recently by Republicans in the Senate during the presidency of Barack Obama to block his nominations to federal courts and cabinet posts. While federal agencies are still allowed to conduct day-to-day business, they are somewhat limited in the strength of their actions when they do not have a director in place. For example, the federal appeals court—the highest appeals court in the nation—is often called on to rule on key White House policies, but without three of its eleven justices, decisions were sometimes left up in the air. Similarly, the Consumer Financial Protection Bureau (CFPB), an agency dedicated to educating consumers and enforcing certain financial regulations, was unable to issue binding regulations until a director was installed.

Both Republicans and Democrats have threatened over time to use the nuclear option of removing the filibuster from Senate nominee debate. In 2005, during his time as senator, Obama stood up in support of the filibuster, saying that what the American people "don't expect is for one party, be it Republican or Democrat, to change the rules in the middle of the game so they can make all the decisions while the other party is told to sit down and keep quiet." At the time, there was a Republican president, George W. Bush, and Republicans had control of the Senate. Democrats had blocked a number of the president's nominees and Republicans began considering whether to invoke the nuclear option. However, the Gang of 14, a group of fourteen senators from both sides of the aisle, vowed that they would block such action. The seven Republicans in the group agreed not to vote for the nuclear option, while the seven Democrats said they would stop blocking President Bush's nominees.

Invocation of the nuclear option did not seriously come up again until 2013 when Republicans began blocking President Obama's nominees at the start of his second term. This included the drawn-out process of confirming former Senator Chuck Hagel to the position of Secretary of Defense, and blockage of nominees to head the National Labor Relations Board and the CFPB. The final push came in November when Republicans blocked the appointment of three judges to the Federal Appeals Court for the District of Columbia Circuit, the second highest court in the nation. Republicans wanted to narrow the number of seats from eleven to eight, but Democrats considered that a nonstarter, so Republicans said until the issue was hammered out, they would not approve any more of the president's nominees. Majority Leader Harry Reid, D-Nev., called for a November 21, 2013, vote on the nuclear option, saying that there had "been unbelievable, unprecedented obstruction" in the Senate. "The Senate is a living thing, and to survive it must change as it has over the history of this great country. To the average American, adapting the rules to make the Senate work again is just common sense," Reid said.

Republicans, arguing that they had already approved 99 percent of the president's judicial nominees, came out swinging against the decision. "I say to my friends on the other side of the aisle, you'll regret this. And you may regret it a lot sooner than you think," said Senate Minority Leader Mitch McConnell. "The solution to this problem is at the ballot box," McConnell said. "We look forward to having a great election in 2014." The Republican argument against the rule change was that Democrats were simply using it as a tool to give the executive, in this instance President Obama, almost virtual authority to install any of his nominees and enforce his liberal policies across government.

Democrats Pass Bill With Slim Majority

Throughout the debate, Republicans accused Democrats of violating the intent of the Founding Fathers in setting up the filibuster rule, and warned that the party, which at the time controlled the White House and Senate, would see the ramifications of its actions if a Republican president was put in office in 2016 or if Republicans regained control of the Senate in 2014.

The November 21 vote was split down party lines 52–48, with three Democrats voting against the bill and no Republicans voting in favor. In past rule change votes a two-thirds majority was required for passage, so the use of the simple majority to pass in this case was considered historic. President Obama applauded the victory. "A deliberate and determined effort to obstruct everything, no matter what the merits, just to refight the results of an election is not normal, and for the sake of future generations we can't let it become normal," the president said. "The consequences of action or inaction are very real. The American people deserve better than politicians who run for election telling them how terrible Government is and then devoting their time in elected office to trying to make Government not work as often as possible," he added. Obama concluded, "The gears of Government have to work, and the step that a majority of Senators took today, I think, will help make those gears work just a little bit better."

Republicans decried the outcome. "We have weakened this body permanently, undermined it for the sake of an incompetent administration," said Sen. Pat Roberts, R-Kan. "This is a mistake—a big one for the long run. Maybe not for the short run. Short-term gains, but I think it changes the Senate tremendously in a bad way," said Sen. Richard Shelby, R-Ala. And Sen. John McCain, R-Ariz., said Democrats would eventually "pay a very, very heavy price" for passage of the rules.

The changes apply to more than 1,000 positions in the executive branch that require the approval of the Senate, from cabinet seats and judicial posts to other seats on federal boards and positions at federal agencies. Senators will still be able to use marathon speeches to rail against nominees, but once the speech is over, a vote will only need a simple majority to pass. At the time of the filibuster rule vote, there were seventeen federal judiciary nominees and fifty-nine federal agency nominees awaiting Senate approval. Unsurprisingly, the first nominee the Senate took up under the new rules was that of one of the federal appeals court nominees. How the change might play out beyond 2013 remains to be seen—the Senate has long considered itself the more bipartisan of the two houses of Congress, and the filibuster has given broad powers to the minority party. This shift ensures almost virtual nomination control for any party that holds both the White House and Senate, but the looming 2014 midterm Congressional elections, in which political analysts have said Republicans stand to take back control of the Senate, could make the rule change a bane to Democrats.

—Heather Kerrigan

Following is a floor statement by Sen. Harry Reid, D-Nev., on November 21, 2013, in support of the nuclear option; a floor statement by Sen. Chuck Grassley, R-Iowa, on November 21, 2013, in opposition to the new Senate filibuster rule; and a statement by President Barack Obama on November 21, 2013, applauding passage of the Senate filibuster rule.

Sen. Reid in Support of the Nuclear Option

November 21, 2013

Mr. REID. Mr. President, the American people believe Congress is broken. The American people believe the Senate is broken. And I believe the American people are right.

During this Congress—the 113th Congress—the United States Senate has wasted an unprecedented amount of time on procedural hurdles and partisan obstruction. As a result, the work of this country goes undone.

Congress should be passing legislation that strengthens our economy and protects American families. Instead we are burning wasted hours and wasted days between filibusters.

Even one of the Senate's most basic duties—confirmation of presidential nominees—has become completely unworkable. For the first time in history, Republicans have routinely used the filibuster to prevent President Obama from appointing his executive team or confirming judges. It is a troubling trend that Republicans are willing to block executive branch nominees even when they have no objection to the qualifications of the nominee. Instead, they block qualified executive branch nominees to circumvent the legislative process. They block qualified executive branch nominees to force wholesale changes to laws. They block qualified executive branch nominees to restructure entire executive branch departments. And they block qualified judicial nominees because they don't want President Obama to appoint any judges to certain courts.

The need for change is so very obvious. It is clearly visible. It is manifest we have to do something to change things.

In the history of our country—some 230-plus years—there have been 168 filibusters of executive and judicial nominations. Half of them have occurred during the Obama Administration—so 230-plus years, 50 percent; 4½ years, 50 percent. Is there anything fair about that?

These nominees deserve at least an up-or-down vote—yes or no—but Republican filibusters deny them a fair vote and deny the President his team.

Gridlock has consequences, and they are terrible. It is not only bad for President Obama and bad for this body, the Senate, it is bad for our country, it is bad for our national security, and it is bad for our economic security.

That is why it is time to get the Senate working again—not for the good of the current Democratic majority or some future Republican majority, but for the good of the country. It is time to change. It is time to change the Senate before this institution becomes obsolete.

At the beginning of this Congress, the Republican leader pledged that, "This Congress should be more bipartisan than the last Congress."

We are told in the Scriptures—and let's take, for example, the Old Testament, the Book of Numbers, that promises, pledges, a vow—one must not break his word.

In January, Republicans promised to work with the majority to process nominations in a timely manner by unanimous consent, except in extraordinary circumstances. Exactly three weeks later, Republicans mounted a first-in-history filibuster of a highly qualified nominee for Secretary of Defense.

Despite being a former Republican Senator and a decorated war hero, having saved his brother's life in Vietnam, Defense Secretary Chuck Hagel's nomination was pending in the Senate for a record 34 days—more than three times the previous average. Remember, our country was at war.

Republicans have blocked executive branch nominees such as Secretary Hagel not because they object to the qualifications of the nominee but simply because they seek to undermine the very government in which they were elected to serve.

Take the nomination of Richard Cordray to lead the Consumer Financial Protection Bureau. There was no doubt about his ability to do the job. But the Consumer Financial Protection Bureau, the brainchild of Elizabeth Warren, went for more than two years without a leader because Republicans refused to accept the law of the land, because they wanted to roll back a law that protects consumers from the greed of Wall Street.

I say to my Republican colleagues: You don't have to like the laws of the land, but you do have to respect those laws and acknowledge them and abide by them.

Similar obstruction continued unabated for seven more months, until Democrats threatened to change Senate rules to allow up-or-down votes on executive nominations. In July, after obstructing dozens of executive nominees for months—and some for years—Republicans once again promised that they would end the unprecedented obstruction.

One look at the Senate's Executive Calendar shows nothing has changed since July. Republicans have continued their record obstruction as if no agreement had ever been reached. Again, Republicans have continued their record of obstruction as if no agreement had been reached.

There are currently 75 executive branch nominees ready to be confirmed by the Senate. They have been waiting an average of 140 days for confirmation.

One executive nominee to the agency that safeguards the water my children and my grandchildren drink and the air they breathe has waited more than 900 days for confirmation.

We agreed in July that the Senate should be confirming nominees to ensure the proper functioning of government.

Consistent and unprecedented obstruction by the Republican Caucus has turned "advise and consent" into "deny and obstruct."

In addition to filibustering a nominee for Secretary of Defense for the first time in history, Senate Republicans also blocked a sitting Member of Congress from an administration position for the first time since 1843.

As a senior Member of the House Financial Services Committee, Congressman Mel Watt's understanding of the mistakes that led to the housing crisis made him uniquely qualified to serve as Administrator of the Federal Housing Finance Agency.

Senate Republicans simply do not like the consumer protections Congressman Watt was nominated to develop and implement, so they denied a fellow Member of Congress and a graduate of Yale School of Law even the courtesy of an up-or-down vote.

In the last three weeks alone, Republicans have blocked up-or-down votes on three highly qualified nominees to the DC Circuit Court of Appeals. This does not take into consideration they twice turned down one of the most qualified people in my 30 years in the Senate who I have ever seen come before this body: Caitlin Halligan. So we have three more to add to that list.

The DC Circuit is considered by many to be the second highest court in the land, and some think maybe the most important. It deals with these complex cases that come from Federal agencies and other things within their jurisdiction.

Republicans have blocked four of President Obama's five nominees to the DC Circuit, whereas Democrats approved four of President Bush's six nominees to this important court.

Today the DC Circuit Court—at least the second most important court in the land—has more than 25 percent in vacancies. There is not a single legitimate objection to the qualifications of any of these nominees to the DC Circuit that President Obama has put forward. Republicans have refused to give them an up-or-down vote—a simple "yes" or "no" vote. Republicans simply do not want President Obama to make any appointments at all to this vital court—none, zero.

Further, only 23 district court nominations have been filibustered in the entire history of our country—23. And you know what. Twenty of them have been in the last 4½ years. Two hundred thirty-plus years: 3; the last 4½ years: 20. That is not fair. With one out of every 10 federal judgeships vacant, millions of Americans who rely on courts that are overworked and understaffed are being denied the justice they rightly deserve.

More than half the nation's population lives in a part of the country that's been declared a "judicial emergency." No one has worked harder than the President pro tempore to move judges. The President pro tempore is the chairman also of the Judiciary Committee. No one knows the problem more than the President pro tempore.

The American people are fed up with this kind of obstruction and gridlock. The American people—Democrats, Republicans, Independents—are fed up with this gridlock, this obstruction. The American people want Washington to work for American families once again.

I am on their side, which is why I propose an important change to the rules of the U.S. Senate. The present Republican leader himself said—and this is a direct quote—"The Senate has repeatedly changed its rules as circumstances dictate."

He is right. In fact, the Senate has changed its rules 18 times, by sustaining or overturning the ruling of the Presiding Officer in the last 36 years—during the tenures of both Republican and Democratic majorities.

The change we propose today would ensure executive and judicial nominees get an up-or-down vote on confirmation—yes or no. This rule change will make cloture for all nominations other than for the Supreme Court a majority threshold vote—yes or no.

The Senate is a living thing, and to survive it must change, as it has over the history of this great country. To the average American, adapting the rules to make the Senate work again is just common sense.

This is not about Democrats versus Republicans. This is about making Washington work—regardless of who is in the White House or who controls the Senate.

To remain relevant and effective as an institution, the Senate must evolve to meet the challenges of a modern era.

I have no doubt my Republican colleagues will argue the fault is ours, it is the Democrats' fault. I can say from experience that no one's hands are entirely clean on this issue. But today the important distinction is not between Democrats and Republicans. It is between those who are willing to help break the gridlock in Washington and those who defend the status quo.

Is the Senate working now? Can anyone say the Senate is working now? I do not think so.

Today Democrats and Independents are saying enough is enough. This change to the rules regarding Presidential nominees will apply equally to both parties. When Republicans are in power, these changes will apply to them as well. That is simple fairness, and it is something that both sides should be willing to live with to make Washington work again. That is simple fairness.

Source: Sen. Harry Reid. "Rules Reform." *Congressional Record* 2013, pt. 159, S8414-S8415. November 21, 2013. http://www.gpo.gov/fdsys/pkg/CREC-2013-11-21/pdf/CREC-2013-11-21-pt1-PgS8413-5.pdf.

Sen. Grassley Against the Procedural Rules Change

November 21, 2013

Mr. GRASSLEY. Mr. President, we didn't have a chance to debate the change in rules, and we should have, so I am going to speak now on some things I think should have been said before we voted—not that it would have changed the outcome but because we ought to have known what we were doing before we vote rather than afterward. So I will spend a few minutes discussing what the majority leader did on the so-called nuclear option.

Unfortunately, this wasn't a new threat. Over the last several years, every time the minority has chosen to exercise his rights under the Senate rules, the majority has threatened to change the rules. In fact, this is the third time in just the last year or so that the majority leader has said that if he didn't get his way on nominations, he would change the rules. Ironically, that is about as many judicial nominees as our side has stopped through a filibuster—three or so.

Prior to the recent attempt by the President to simultaneously add three judges who are not needed to the DC Circuit, Republicans had stopped a grand total of 2 of President Obama's judicial nominees—not 10, as the Democrats had by President Bush's fifth year in office; not 34, as one of my colleagues tried to suggest earlier this week; no, only 2 had been stopped. If we include the nominees for the DC Circuit, we have stopped a grand total of 5—again, not 10, as the Democrats did in 2005; not 34, as one of my colleagues tried to argue earlier this week but 5. During that same time we have confirmed 209 lower court Article III judges. That is a record of 209 judges approved to 5 who were not approved. So this threat isn't based on any crisis. There is no crisis.

I would note that today's *Wall Street Journal* editorial entitled "DC Circuit Breakers: The White House wants to pack a court whose judges are underworked" lays out the caseload pretty clearly.

I ask unanimous consent to have printed in the RECORD the editorial to which I just referred.

[The text of a Wall Street Journal *editorial has been omitted.]*

Mr. GRASSLEY. This is about a naked power grab and nothing more than a power grab. This is about the other side not getting everything they want, when they want it.

The other side claims they were pushed to this point because our side objected to the President's plan to fill the DC Circuit with judges the court does not need, but the other side tends to forget history. History is something we ought to learn from, so let's review how we got here.

After the President simultaneously nominated three nominees who are not needed for the DC Circuit—a blatant political power grab in its own right—what did the Republicans do? Well, we did something quite simple: We said we want to go by the rules the Democrats set in 2006. We said we would hold those Democrats to the same standard they established in 2006 when they blocked a nominee of President Bush's by the name of Peter Keisler.

Let's be clear about why the Democrats are outraged. Democrats are outraged because Republicans actually had the temerity to hold the other political party to a standard they established, and because we did, because we insisted we all play by the same rules, they came right back and said: Then we will change the rules. In effect, the other side has said: We don't want to be held to the standard we established in 2006. And not only that, but if you don't give us what we want, we are willing to forever change the Senate. And that is what happened today.

We hear a lot of ultimatums around here, but this ultimatum was not run-of-the-mill. It was very different. It was different because this threat was designed to hold the Senate hostage. It was different because it is designed to hold hostage all of the Senate's history and traditions and precedents. It was different because its effectiveness depends on the good will of Senators who don't want to see the Senate as we know it destroyed or function other than as the constitutional writers intended.

I would note that today's majority didn't always feel that way—the very way we have seen expressed today. Not too many years ago my colleagues on the other side described their fight to preserve the filibuster with great pride. For instance, in 2006 one of my colleagues on the other side said:

> The nuclear option was the most important issue I have worked on in my public life. Its rejection was my proudest moment as a minority leader. I emerged from the episode with a renewed appreciation for the majesty of Senate rules. As majority leader, I intend to run the Senate with respect for the rules and for the minority rights the rules protect.

In 2005 another of my Democratic colleagues had this to say, referring to when Republicans were in the majority:

> Today, Republicans are threatening to take away one of the few remaining checks on the power of the executive branch by their use of what has become known as the nuclear option. This assault on our traditions of checks and balances and on the protection of minority rights in the Senate and in our democracy should be abandoned. Eliminating the filibuster by nuclear option would destroy the Constitution's design of the Senate as an effective check on the executive.

So here we have two quotes from Democrats in the 2005–2006 timeframe very strongly supporting the precedent of the Senate in using the filibuster to protect minority rights. But that was when they were in the minority. Now they are in the majority, and the tradition of the Senate doesn't mean much.

Here is another quote from the late Senator Byrd in 2005:

> And I detest this mention of a nuclear option, the constitutional option. There is nothing constitutional about it. Nothing.

But, of course, that was way back then—just 6, 7 years ago when today's majority was in the minority and there was a Republican in the White House. Today the shoe is on the other foot. Today the other side is willing to forever change the Senate because Republicans have the audacity to hold them—the majority party of today—to their own standard. Why? Why would the other side do this? There clearly isn't a crisis on the DC Circuit. The judges themselves say that if we confirm any more judges, there won't be enough work to go around. And it is not as if all of these nominees are mainstream consensus picks despite what the other side would have us believe, that they are somewhat mainstream. . . .

The point is this: Voting to change the Senate rules is voting to remove one of the last meaningful checks on the President—any President—voting to put these views on this important court.

So I ask again, why would the other side do this? It is nothing short of a complete and total power grab. It is the type of thing we have seen again and again out of this administration and their Senate allies, and you can sum it up this way: Do whatever it takes.

You can't get ObamaCare passed with Republican support? Do whatever it takes: Pass it at 7 a.m. on Christmas Eve with just Democratic votes.

You can't get all of your side to support ObamaCare? Do whatever it takes: Resort to things like the "Cornhusker kickback."

You lose your 60th vote on ObamaCare due to a special election? Do whatever it takes: Ram it through anyway using reconciliation.

The American people don't want to be taxed for not buying health care? Do whatever it takes: Tell the American people it isn't a tax and then argue in the court that it is a tax.

The American people want to keep their health care? Do whatever it takes: Promise them "if you like your health care, you can keep it" and then issue regulations making it impossible.

Your labor allies want out from under ObamaCare? Do whatever it takes: Consider issuing them—labor—a waiver from the reinsurance tax.

You can't find consensus nominees for the National Labor Relations Board? Do whatever it takes: Recess-appoint them when the Senate is still in session.

You can't convince Congress to adopt your gun control agenda? Do whatever it takes: Issue some Executive orders.

You can't convince moderate Democrats to support cap-and-trade fee increases? Well, do whatever it takes: Do the same thing through EPA regulation.

Frustrated that conservative groups' political speech is protected under the First Amendment? Do whatever it takes: Use the IRS to harass and intimidate those same conservative groups.

Frustrated when the court stands up for religious freedom and issues a check on the ObamaCare contraception mandate? Do whatever it takes: Stack the DC Circuit Court in your favor.

Frustrated when the court curbs your power on recess appointments? Do whatever it takes: Stack the DC Circuit with your favorite appointees—people who will rule in your favor.

Worried EPA's regulations on cap-and-trade fee increases might get challenged in the court? Do whatever it takes: Stack the DC Circuit in your favor.

Frustrated because Senate Republicans have the nerve to hold you to the same standard you established during the last administration? Do whatever it takes: Change the rules of the Senate. That is what we have witnessed today, nothing but an absolute power grab.

The majority in the Senate and their allies in the administration are willing to do whatever it takes to achieve their partisan agenda. They know there will be additional challenges to ObamaCare. They know that if they can stack the deck on the DC Circuit they can remove one of the last remaining checks on Presidential power.

But make no mistake, my friends on the other side will have to answer this question: Why did you choose this moment to break the rules to change the rules? Why now? Why, when we are witnessing the collapse of this massive effort to centrally plan one-sixth of this wonderful Nation's economy—why, when millions of Americans are losing their health care—why did you choose this moment to hand the keys to the kingdom over to the President, a President with less check on his authority?

Because the fact of the matter is this: any vote to break the rules to change the rules is a vote to ensure ObamaCare remains intact.

I will conclude by saying this. Changing the rules of the Senate in this way was a mistake. But if the last several years have taught us anything, it is that the majority won't stop making these demands. We can't always give in to these constant threats. Sooner or later you have to stand up and say: Enough is enough.

But if there is one thing which will always be true, it is this: Majorities are fickle. Majorities are fleeting. Here today, gone tomorrow. That is a lesson that, sadly, most of my colleagues on the other side of the aisle haven't learned for the simple reason that they have never served a single day in the minority.

So the majority has chosen to take us down this path. The silver lining is that there will come a day when roles are reversed. When that happens, our side will likely nominate and confirm lower court and Supreme Court nominees with 51 votes, regardless of whether the Democrats actually buy into this fanciful notion that they can demolish the filibuster on lower court nominees and still preserve it for Supreme Court nominees.

I yield the floor.

SOURCE: Sen. Chuck Grassley. "Nuclear Option." *Congressional Record* 2013, pt. 159, S8419–S8421. November 21, 2013. http://www.gpo.gov/fdsys/pkg/CREC-2013-11-21/pdf/CREC-2013–11–21-pt1-PgS8418-2.pdf.

President Obama on the Passage of the Nuclear Option

November 21, 2013

Good afternoon, everybody. It's no secret that the American people have probably never been more frustrated with Washington. And one of the reasons why that is, is that over the past 5 years, we've seen an unprecedented pattern of obstruction in Congress that's prevented too much of the American people's business from getting done.

All too often, we've seen a single Senator or a handful of Senators choose to abuse arcane procedural tactics to unilaterally block bipartisan compromises or to prevent well-qualified, patriotic Americans from filling critical positions of public service in our system of Government.

Now, at a time when millions of American have desperately searched for work, repeated abuse of these tactics have blocked legislation that might create jobs. They've defeated actions that would help women fighting for equal pay. They've prevented more progress than we would have liked for striving young immigrants trying to earn their citizenship. Or it's blocked efforts to end tax breaks for companies that are shipping jobs overseas. They've even been used to block commonsense and widely supported steps to protect more Americans from gun violence, even as families of victims sat in the Senate Chamber and watched. And they've prevented far too many talented Americans from serving their country at a time when their country needs their talents the most.

It's harmed our economy, and it's been harmful to our democracy. And it's brought us to the point where a simple majority vote no longer seems to be sufficient for anything, even routine business, through what is supposed to be the world's greatest deliberative body.

Now, I realize that neither party has been blameless for these tactics. They've developed over years, and it seems as if they've continually escalated. But today's pattern of obstruction, it just isn't normal. It's not what our Founders envisioned. A deliberate and determined effort to obstruct everything, no matter what the merits, just to refight the results of an election, is not normal. And for the sake of future generations, we can't let it become normal.

So I support the step a majority of Senators today took to change the way that Washington is doing business, more specifically, the way the Senate does business. What a majority of Senators determined by Senate rule is that they would restore the longstanding tradition of considering judicial and public service nominations on a more routine basis.

And here's why this is important: One of a President's constitutional responsibilities is to nominate Americans to positions within the executive and judicial branches. Over the six decades before I took office, only 20 Presidential nominees to executive positions had to overcome filibusters. In just under 5 years since I took office, nearly 30 nominees have been treated this way. Now, these are all public servants who protect our national security, look out for working families, keep our air and water clean.

This year alone, for the first time in history, Senate Republicans filibustered a President's nominee for the Secretary of Defense who used to be a former Republican Senator. They tried everything they could to hold up our EPA Administrator. They blocked our nominee for our top housing regulator at a time when we need more help for more families to afford a home and prevent what has caused mortgage meltdowns from happening again.

And in each of these cases, it's not been because they opposed the person, that there was some assessment that they were unqualified, that there was some scandal that had been unearthed. It was simply because they opposed the policies that the American people voted for in the last election.

And this obstruction gets even worse when it comes to the judiciary. The Constitution charges the President with filling vacancies to the Federal bench. Every President has exercised this power since George Washington first named Justices to the Supreme Court in 1789. But my judicial nominees have waited nearly two and a half times longer to receive yes-or-no votes on the Senate floor than those of President Bush. And the ones who eventually do get a vote generally are confirmed with little, if any, dissent.

So this isn't obstruction on substance, on qualifications. It's just to gum up the works. And this gridlock in Congress causes gridlock in much of our criminal and civil justice systems. You've seen judges across the country, including a Bush-appointed Chief Justice to the Supreme Court, say these are vital vacancies that need to be filled and this gridlock has not served the cause of justice; in fact, it's undermined it.

Over the past 3 weeks, Senate Republicans again denied a yes-or-no vote on three highly qualified Americans to fill three vacancies on the Nation's second highest court, even though they have the support of a majority of Senators. Four of President Bush's six nominees to this court were confirmed. Four out of five of my nominees to this court have been obstructed.

So the vote today, I think, is an indication that a majority of Senators believe, as I believe, that enough is enough. The American people's business is far too important to keep falling prey, day after day, to Washington politics.

I'm a former Senator. So is my Vice President. We both value any Senate's duty to advise and consent. It's important, and we take that very seriously. But a few now refuse to treat that duty of advise and consent with the respect that it deserves. It's no longer used in a responsible way to govern. It's rather used as a reckless and relentless tool to grind all business to a halt. And that's not what our Founders intended, and it's certainly not what our country needs right now.

And I just want to remind everybody, what's at stake here is not my ability to fulfill my constitutional duty. What's at stake is the ability of any President to fulfill his or her constitutional duty. Public service is not a game, it is a privilege. And the consequences of action or inaction are very real. The American people deserve better than politicians who run for election telling them how terrible Government is and then devoting their time in elected office to trying to make Government not work as often as possible.

Now, I want to be clear, the Senate has actually done some good bipartisan work this year. Bipartisan majorities have passed commonsense legislation to fix our broken immigration system and upgrade our courts—our ports. It's passed a farm bill that helps rural communities and vulnerable Americans. It's passed legislation that would protect Americans from being fired based on their sexual orientation. So we know that there are folks there, Republican and Democrat, who want to get things done. And frankly, privately they've expressed to me their recognition that the system in the Senate had broken down and what used to be a sporadic exercise of the filibuster had gotten completely out of hand.

I believe—I'm confident—that that spirit will have a little more space now. I want us to make sure that we can do more work together to grow the economy and to create jobs. And if there are differences in the Senate, then debates should be had. People should vote their conscience. They should vote on behalf of their constituents. But they should vote. That's what they're there to do. And ultimately, if you've got a majority of folks who believe in something, then it should be able to pass.

Americans work hard. They do their jobs, and they expect the same from everybody who got sent here. And as long as I have the privilege of being in this office, I'll keep working as hard as I know how to make sure that the economy is growing, and we're creating good jobs, and we're widening prosperity and opportunity for everybody. And I know that that's what the majority of folks in the Senate believe as well. But the gears of Government have to work, and the step that a majority of Senators took today, I think, will help make those gears work just a little bit better. . . .

Source: Executive Office of the President. "Remarks on Procedural Rule Changes in the Senate." November 21, 2013. *Compilation of Presidential Documents* 2013, no. 00795 (November 21, 2013). http://www.gpo.gov/fdsys/pkg/DCPD-201300795/pdf/DCPD-201300795.pdf.

OTHER HISTORIC DOCUMENTS OF INTEREST

FROM THIS VOLUME

■ President Obama Delivers Second Inaugural Address, p. 3

International Leaders Reach Agreement on Iranian Nuclear Program

NOVEMBER 24, 2013

In November 2013, representatives from the United States, United Kingdom, Russia, China, France, and Germany, a group known as the P5+1 in the United States (and known as the EP3+3 in Europe), reached a landmark agreement with Iranian representatives on a short-term plan for resolving the international dispute over Iran's nuclear program. Western countries and the UN had for many years sought to limit Iran's nuclear activities, primarily through economic sanctions, amid suspicions that the country has been attempting to build nuclear weapons in violation of the Nuclear Non-Proliferation Treaty (NPT). Iran claims that its nuclear program is intended to generate electricity for its citizens, but the country has a history of attempting to conceal these activities and their possible military applications from the international community.

Many speculated that the June election of Iranian President Hassan Rouhani, a moderate reformer, would result in greater cooperation and an easing of tensions between Iran and the West, particularly given his calls for more negotiations and "mutual confidence-building" around the nuclear issue. Rouhani's predecessor, former President Mahmoud Ahmadinejad, had been unwilling to negotiate with Western countries and had significantly restricted the International Atomic Energy Agency's (IAEA) ability to inspect and collect information on the country's nuclear activities.

A series of talks between Iran and the P5+1 ultimately led to the November agreement, which was met with mixed reactions from world leaders. Meanwhile, U.S.-Iranian relations appeared to thaw, although many Members of Congress cautioned the Obama administration against being too lenient with Iran.

A HISTORIC PHONE CALL

One of the first signs of eased tensions between the United States and Iran occurred on September 27 when President Barack Obama and President Rouhani spoke on the phone. The fifteen-minute conversation marked the first time leaders from the two countries had directly communicated since the 1979 Iranian Revolution. It followed Rouhani's participation in the UN General Assembly meeting in New York, where he had stated that Iran posed "absolutely no threat to the world" and would never develop nuclear weapons. While characterizing U.S. sanctions as "intrinsically inhumane," Rouhani also said the atmosphere between the United States and Iran was "quite different from the past" and that "our goal is resolving problems." He further called for a nuclear deal with the international community in the next three to six months.

Obama said that during their phone call, he and Rouhani primarily discussed Iran's nuclear program. "I reiterated to President Rouhani what I said in New York: While there will surely be important obstacles to moving forward, and success is by no means guaranteed, I believe we can reach a comprehensive agreement," said Obama. He added that their conversation "underscores the deep mistrust between our countries, but also indicates the prospect of moving on that difficult history."

The day before, U.S. Secretary of State John Kerry met with Iranian Foreign Minister Javad Zarif, the first time in a generation that the two countries had publicly met one-on-one. Kerry described the meeting as "constructive" and said Zarif's presentation "was very different in tone and very different in the vision that he held out with respect to possibilities of the future" than past statements by Iranian officials. Iran observers speculated that these conversations could signal the opening of an ongoing communications channel between the United States and Iran.

THE JOINT PLAN OF ACTION

Less than a month later, on November 20, the P5+1 and Iran met in Geneva, Switzerland, for the latest round of multiparty talks on Iran's nuclear program. The group sought a mutually agreed on, long-term, comprehensive solution to the dispute over Iran's nuclear program. Their goal was to obtain Iran's assurance that it would not seek or develop nuclear weapons, while also establishing a program with certain built-in transparency measures that would enable Iran to develop nuclear energy for peaceful purposes. If Iran agreed to and complied with the requirements of such a program, the UN Security Council and Western countries would agree to lift sanctions related to Iran's nuclear activities.

The same group had met five times since February, but made little progress. Meanwhile, as the Associated Press (AP) later reported, U.S. and Iranian officials had engaged in a series of at least five secret high-level talks since March. The meetings were reportedly authorized by President Obama and involved Deputy Secretary of State William Burns and Vice President Joe Biden's senior foreign policy adviser, Jake Sullivan. The meetings took place in Oman and were mediated by Sultan Qaboos bin Said Al Said. According to the AP, the last four of those meetings, which were held after Rouhani took office, "produced much of the agreement later formally hammered out in negotiations in Geneva."

After four days of negotiations, the Geneva group reached an agreement, signing the Joint Action Plan at the UN's Palace of Nations on November 24. The plan was meant to establish a short-term agreement, lasting approximately six months, to be in place while negotiators worked out a longer-term agreement. Through the plan, Iran agreed to reduce some of its nuclear activities in return for approximately $7 billion worth of sanctions relief from the UN, United States, and EU. One of the plan's key elements was a requirement that Iran either dilute its stockpile of uranium, which had been enriched to 20 percent, down to a maximum of 5 percent or convert that uranium into oxide so that it couldn't be used militarily. Uranium that has been enriched to 20 percent is considered medium-grade purity and can easily be further enriched to become weapons-grade material. Uranium enriched between 3.5 and 5 percent is sufficient to run nuclear power stations. Iran also promised that it would not enrich any additional uranium over the 5-percent level during the six-month agreement period. In addition, Iran agreed that it would not advance its work at its Natanz, Fordo, or Arak facilities; build any new uranium enrichment facilities; install new centrifuges at existing facilities; begin using facilities that already existed but were not yet operational; reprocess nuclear material; or build any facilities that could reprocess such material. Iran also agreed to participate in enhanced monitoring of its nuclear activities, such as providing detailed information about operations at its nuclear facilities to the IAEA and greater access to those facilities, including daily access to the Natanz and Fordo sites, to IAEA inspectors.

Prior to the deal, Iran had enough equipment and low-level enriched uranium to be able to produce fuel for a nuclear weapon within one to two months, according to the Institute for Science and International Security (ISIS). Due to the Geneva deal's stipulations on equipment and uranium enrichment, ISIS estimated that the plan would add several weeks to a month to that timeframe, thus providing other countries with more time to react should Iran decide to pursue a weapon.

In return for compliance with these measures, the P5+1 would halt efforts to further reduce Iran's crude oil sales; allow Iran to repatriate approximately $4.2 billion of oil sales revenue that is currently held in foreign banks; suspend U.S. and EU sanctions on insurance and transportation services related to crude oil sales, petrochemical exports, and Iran's auto industry; not implement any new nuclear-related sanctions; and establish a financial channel to facilitate humanitarian trade for Iran's domestic needs. Despite the suspension of some sanctions around Iran's oil exports, the deal did not allow for any additional Iranian oil to enter the market or permit Western energy investors to invest in Iran. The Western embargo of Iranian oil and a ban preventing Iranians from using the international banking system would also remain in place until a final agreement was reached.

The plan envisioned a final agreement, to be negotiated and agreed on no more than one year after the interim plan was adopted, that would reflect the rights and obligations of all parties to the NPT and IAEA Safeguards Agreements and lift all nuclear-related sanctions on an agreed-upon schedule. The final plan would "involve a mutually defined enrichment programme with mutually agreed parameters consistent with practical needs, with agreed limits on scope and level of enrichment activities, capacity, where it is carried out, and stocks of enriched uranium, for a period to be agreed upon." Among other elements, it would also allow for international civil cooperation with Iran on matters such as acquiring modern light water power and research reactors and would fully implement a number of transparency measures and enhanced nuclear monitoring.

A Joint Commission of the P5+1 and Iran will monitor implementation of the short-term measures and address any issues that arise. The IAEA will be responsible for verifying compliance with nuclear-related measures.

WORLD LEADERS AND U.S. CONGRESS REACT

After announcing the agreement in the United States, President Obama described the deal as the most "significant and tangible" progress made in the diplomatic efforts ever to be under way during his time in office, and said it would "help prevent Iran from building a nuclear weapon." He did acknowledge concerns that were voiced by some leaders in Israel, Saudi Arabia, and other United States allies in the Persian Gulf that the deal would not be successful, and he warned that the United States "will turn off the relief and ratchet up the pressure" if Iran does not honor the commitments it made as part of the agreement.

President Rouhani and Foreign Minister Zarif heralded the deal as a recognition of Iran's right to enrich uranium. "No matter what interpretations are given, Iran's right to enrichment has been recognized," said Rouhani. For their part, U.S. officials denied conceding this point, arguing that the NPT does not provide Iran a "right to enrich." The deal also enjoyed the backing of Supreme Leader Ayatollah Ali Khamenei, and Zarif pledged to act quickly to implement the agreement. "In the coming weeks—by the end of the Christian year—we will begin the programme for the first phase," Zarif said. "At the same time, we are prepared to begin negotiations for a final resolution as of tomorrow," Zarif continued.

Reaction among other world leaders was mixed. UK Foreign Secretary William Hague, for example, said the agreement was "good news for the whole world," but Israeli Prime Minister Benjamin Netanyahu claimed it was a "historic mistake" and that Israel would not be bound by the deal. "Today the world became a much more dangerous place because the most dangerous regime in the world made a significant step in obtaining the most dangerous weapons in the world," Netanyahu said. Others, such as Russian President Vladimir Putin, emphasized that the six-month deal was only a first step in a longer process. "What is done is a breakthrough but it is merely the first step on a long and difficult road," said Putin. He continued, "In conjunction with our partners we are ready to continue the patient search for a mutually-acceptable, broader and comprehensive solution that upholds Iran's inalienable right to develop a peaceful nuclear programme."

The U.S. Congress was also divided on the agreement. House Foreign Affairs Committee Chairman Ed Royce, R-Calif., said he had "serious concerns that this agreement does not meet the standards necessary to protect the United States and our allies. Instead of rolling back Iran's program, Tehran would be able to keep the key elements of its nuclear weapons-making capability." President Obama can use his executive powers to temporarily suspend some U.S. sanctions on Iran, meaning he does not need Congress's approval. However, the Senate was already considering increased sanctions on Iran when the deal was announced, and some argued that Congress should proceed with such legislation in case Iran failed to abide by the agreement. "I do not believe we should further reduce our sanctions, nor abstain from preparations to impose new sanctions on Iran should the talks fail," said Sen. Robert Menendez, D-N.J. "I expect the forthcoming sanctions legislation to be considered by the Senate will provide for a six month window to reach a final agreement . . . but will at the same time be immediately available should the talks falter or Iran fail to implement or breach the interim agreement," Menendez continued.

Iran and the P5+1 are set to meet in early 2014 to begin discussing a long-term agreement.

—Linda Fecteau

Following is the text of the Joint Plan of Action developed by the P5+1 in Geneva, Switzerland, released on November 24, 2013; and the edited text of a press conference with Secretary of State John Kerry on November 24, 2013, on the progress made at the P5+1 meetings.

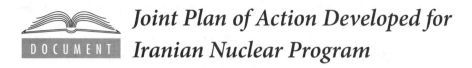

Joint Plan of Action Developed for Iranian Nuclear Program

November 24, 2013

Preamble

The goal for these negotiations is to reach a mutually-agreed long-term comprehensive solution that would ensure Iran's nuclear programme will be exclusively peaceful. Iran reaffirms that under no circumstances will Iran ever seek or develop any nuclear weapons. This comprehensive solution would build on these initial measures and result in a final step for a period to be agreed upon and the resolution of concerns. This comprehensive solution would enable Iran to fully enjoy its right to nuclear energy for peaceful purposes under the relevant articles of the NPT in conformity with its obligations therein. This comprehensive solution would involve a mutually defined enrichment programme with practical limits and transparency measures to ensure the peaceful nature of the programme. This comprehensive solution would constitute an integrated whole where nothing is agreed until everything is agreed. This comprehensive solution would involve a reciprocal, step-by-step process, and would produce the comprehensive lifting of all UN Security Council sanctions, as well as multilateral and national sanctions related to Iran's nuclear programme.

There would be additional steps in between the initial measures and the final step, including, among other things, addressing the UN Security Council resolutions, with a view toward bringing to a satisfactory conclusion the UN Security Council's consideration of this matter. The E3+3 and Iran will be responsible for conclusion and implementation of mutual near-term measures and the comprehensive solution in good faith. A Joint Commission of E3/EU+3 and Iran will be established to monitor the implementation of the near-term measures and address issues that may arise, with the IAEA responsible for verification of nuclear-related measures. The Joint Commission will work with the IAEA to facilitate resolution of past and present issues of concern.

Elements of a first step

The first step would be time-bound, with a duration of 6 months, and renewable by mutual consent, during which all parties will work to maintain a constructive atmosphere for negotiations in good faith.

Iran would undertake the following voluntary measures:

- From the existing uranium enriched to 20%, retain half as working stock of 20% oxide for fabrication of fuel for the TRR. Dilute the remaining 20% UF6 to no more than 5%. No reconversion line.
- Iran announces that it will not enrich uranium over 5% for the duration of the 6 months.

- Iran announces that it will not make any further advances of its activities at the Natanz Fuel Enrichment Plant[1], Fordow[2], or the Arak reactor[3], designated by the IAEA as IR-40.
- Beginning when the line for conversion of UF6 enriched up to 5% to UO2 is ready, Iran has decided to convert to oxide UF6 newly enriched up to 5% during the 6 month period, as provided in the operational schedule of the conversion plant declared to the IAEA.
- No new locations for the enrichment.
- Iran will continue its safeguarded R&D practices, including its current enrichment R&D practices, which are not designed for accumulation of the enriched uranium.
- No reprocessing or construction of a facility capable of reprocessing.
- Enhanced monitoring:
  - Provision of specified information to the IAEA, including information on Iran's plans for nuclear facilities, a description of each building on each nuclear site, a description of the scale of operations for each location engaged in specified nuclear activities, information on uranium mines and mills, and information on source material. This information would be provided within three months of the adoption of these measures.
  - Submission of an updated DIQ for the reactor at Arak, designated by the IAEA as the IR-40, to the IAEA.
  - Steps to agree with the IAEA on conclusion of the Safeguards Approach for the reactor at Arak, designated by the IAEA as the IR-40.
  - Daily IAEA inspector access when inspectors are not present for the purpose of Design Information Verification, Interim Inventory Verification, Physical Inventory Verification, and unannounced inspections, for the purpose of access to offline surveillance records, at Fordow and Natanz.
  - IAEA inspector managed access to:
    - centrifuge assembly workshops[4];
    - centrifuge rotor production workshops and storage facilities; and,
    - uranium mines and mills.

---

1. Namely, during the 6 months, Iran will not feed UF6 into the centrifuges installed but not enriching uranium. Not install additional centrifuges. Iran announces that during the first 6 months, it will replace existing centrifuges with centrifuges of the same type.

2. At Fordow, no further enrichment over 5% at 4 cascades now enriching uranium, and not increase enrichment capacity. Not feed UF6 into the other 12 cascades, which would remain in a non-operative state. No interconnections between cascades. Iran announces that during the first 6 months, it will replace existing centrifuges with centrifuges of the same type.

3. Iran announces on concerns related to the construction of the reactor at Arak that for 6 months it will not commission the reactor or transfer fuel or heavy water to the reactor site and will not test additional fuel or produce more fuel for the reactor or install remaining components.

4. Consistent with its plans, Iran's centrifuge production during the 6 months will be dedicated to replace damaged machines.

In return, the E3/EU+3 would undertake the following voluntary measures:

- Pause efforts to further reduce Iran's crude oil sales, enabling Iran's current customers to purchase their current average amounts of crude oil. Enable the repatriation of an agreed amount of revenue held abroad. For such oil sales, suspend the EU and U.S. sanctions on associated insurance and transportation services.
- Suspend U.S. and EU sanctions on:
  - Iran's petrochemical exports, as well as sanctions on associated services.[5]
  - Gold and precious metals, as well as sanctions on associated services.
- Suspend U.S. sanctions on Iran's auto industry, as well as sanctions on associated services.
- License the supply and installation in Iran of spare parts for safety of flight for Iranian civil aviation and associated services. License safety related inspections and repairs in Iran as well as associated services.[6]
- No new nuclear-related UN Security Council sanctions.
- No new EU nuclear-related sanctions.
- The U.S. Administration, acting consistent with the respective roles of the President and the Congress, will refrain from imposing new nuclear-related sanctions.
- Establish a financial channel to facilitate humanitarian trade for Iran's domestic needs using Iranian oil revenues held abroad. Humanitarian trade would be defined as transactions involving food and agricultural products, medicine, medical devices, and medical expenses incurred abroad. This channel would involve specified foreign banks and non-designated Iranian banks to be defined when establishing the channel.
  - This channel could also enable:
    - transactions required to pay Iran's UN obligations; and,
    - direct tuition payments to universities and colleges for Iranian students studying abroad, up to an agreed amount for the six month period.
- Increase the EU authorisation thresholds for transactions for non-sanctioned trade to an agreed amount.

Elements of the final step of a comprehensive solution*

The final step of a comprehensive solution, which the parties aim to conclude negotiating and commence implementing no more than one year after the adoption of this document, would:

- Have a specified long-term duration to be agreed upon.
- Reflect the rights and obligations of parties to the NPT and IAEA Safeguards Agreements.
- Comprehensively lift UN Security Council, multilateral and national nuclear-related sanctions, including steps on access in areas of trade, technology, finance, and energy, on a schedule to be agreed upon.

---

5. "Sanctions on associated services" means any service, such as insurance, transportation, or financial, subject to the underlying U.S. or EU sanctions applicable, insofar as each service is related to the underlying sanction and required to facilitate the desired transactions. These services could involve any non-designated Iranian entities.

6. Sanctions relief could involve any non-designated Iranian airlines as well as Iran Air.

- Involve a mutually defined enrichment programme with mutually agreed parameters consistent with practical needs, with agreed limits on scope and level of enrichment activities, capacity, where it is carried out, and stocks of enriched uranium, for a period to be agreed upon.
- Fully resolve concerns related to the reactor at Arak, designated by the IAEA as the IR-40. No reprocessing or construction of a facility capable of reprocessing.
- Fully implement the agreed transparency measures and enhanced monitoring. Ratify and implement the Additional Protocol, consistent with the respective roles of the President and the Majlis (Iranian parliament).
- Include international civil nuclear cooperation, including among others, on acquiring modern light water power and research reactors and associated equipment, and the supply of modern nuclear fuel as well as agreed R&D practices.

Following successful implementation of the final step of the comprehensive solution for its full duration, the Iranian nuclear programme will be treated in the same manner as that of any non-nuclear weapon state party to the NPT.

*With respect to the final step and any steps in between, the standard principle that "nothing is agreed until everything is agreed" applies.

SOURCE: European Union External Action Service. "Joint Plan of Action." November 24, 2013. http://eeas.europa.eu/statements/docs/2013/131124_03_en.pdf.

DOCUMENT   *Secretary Kerry on the P5+1 Talks*

November 24, 2013

SECRETARY KERRY: Well, good very early morning to all of you. It's been a long day and a long night, and I'm delighted to be here to share some thoughts with you about the recent negotiations. I particularly want to thank the Swiss Government. I want to thank the United Nations. . . . I particularly want to thank my colleagues from the United Kingdom, Germany, France, Russia, China, and especially Lady Cathy Ashton, who is not only a good friend but a persistent and dogged negotiator and somebody who's been staying at this for a long period of time. And we're very grateful for her stewardship of these negotiations. . . .

At the United Nations General Assembly in September, President Obama asked me and our team to work with our partners in order to pursue a negotiated settlement or solution with respect to the international community's concerns about Iran's nuclear program. Last month, the P5+1 entered into a more accelerated negotiation after a number of years of meetings in various parts of the world and efforts to engage Iran in serious negotiations. The purpose of this is very simple: to require Iran to prove the peaceful nature of its nuclear program and to ensure that it cannot acquire a nuclear weapon. And the reason for this is very clear. The United Nations Security Council found that they were not in compliance with the NPT or other IAEA and other standards. And obviously, activities such as a secret, multi-centrifuge mountain hideaway, which was being used for enrichment, raised many people's questions, which is why ultimately sanctions were put in place.

Today, we are taking a serious step toward answering all of those important questions that have been raised through the United Nations Security Council, through the IAEA, and by individual countries. And we are taking those steps with an agreement that impedes the progress in a very dramatic way of Iran's principal enrichment facilities and parts of its program, and ensures they cannot advance in a way that will threaten our friends in the region, threaten other countries, threaten the world. The fact is that if this step—first step—leads to what is our ultimate goal, which is a comprehensive agreement that will make the world safer. This first step, I want to emphasize, actually rolls back the program from where it is today, enlarges the breakout time, which would not have occurred unless this agreement existed. It will make our partners in the region safer. It will make our ally Israel safer. This has been a difficult and a prolonged process. It's been difficult for us, and it's been difficult for our allies, and it's obviously been difficult for the Government of Iran. The next phase, let me be clear, will be even more difficult, and we need to be honest about it. But it will also be even more consequential.

And while we obviously have profound differences with Iran yet to be resolved, the fact is that this agreement could not have been reached without the decision of the Iranian Government to come to the table and negotiate. And I want to say tonight that Foreign Minister Zarif worked hard, deliberated hard, and we are obviously, we believe, better that the decision was made to come here than not to, and to work hard to reach an agreement. And we thank the Foreign Minister for those efforts.

Together now, we need to set about the critical task of proving to the world what Iran has said many times—that its program is in fact peaceful. Now, with this first step, we have created the time and the space in order to be able to pursue a comprehensive agreement that would finish the work that President Obama began on the very first day in office, and that is to ensure that Iran does not obtain a nuclear weapon. President Obama worked intensively and his Administration worked intensively before I even came in; when I was in the Congress and voted for sanctions, the President worked in order to put in place a significant sanctions regime, an unprecedented regime. And he worked with countries around the world in order to ensure broad participation and support for these sanctions. That has been essential to the success of these sanctions. And we believe that it is the sanctions that have brought us to this negotiation and ultimately to the more significant negotiation to follow for a comprehensive agreement.

Make no mistakes, and I ask you, don't interpret that the sanctions were an end unto themselves. They weren't. The goal of the sanctions was always to have a negotiation. And that is precisely what is now taking place, and that negotiation's goal is to secure a strong and verifiable agreement that guarantees the peacefulness of Iran's nuclear program. For more than 40 years, the international community has been united in its willingness to negotiate in good faith. And we have been particularly crystal clear that we will do whatever is necessary in order to prevent Iran from having a nuclear weapon. We have also said that we prefer a peaceful solution, a peaceful path for Iran to respond to the international community's concerns. And as a result of those efforts, we took the first step today to move down that path.

The measures that we have committed to will remain in place for six months, and they will address the most urgent concerns about Iran's nuclear program. Since there have been many premature and even misleading reports, I want to clearly outline what this first step entails. First, it locks the most critical components of a nuclear program into place and impedes progress in those critical components in a way that actually rolls back the stockpile of enriched uranium and widens the length of time possible for breakout. That makes people safer. With daily access—we will gain daily access to key facilities. And that will enable us to determine more quickly and with greater certainty than ever before that Iran is complying. Here's how we do that: Iran has agreed to suspend all enrichment of uranium above 5 percent. Iran has agreed to dilute or convert its entire stockpile of 20 percent enriched uranium.

So let me make clear what that means. That means that whereas Iran today has about 200 kilograms of 20 percent enriched uranium, they could readily be enriched towards a nuclear weapon. In six months, Iran will have zero—zero. Iran will not increase its stockpile of 3.5 percent lower-enriched uranium over the next six months, and it will not construct additional enrichment facilities. Iran will not manufacture centrifuges beyond those that are broken and must be replaced. Very importantly, Iran will not commission or fuel the Arak reactor—Arak, A-r-a-k, reactor—an unfinished facility, that if it became operational would provide Iran with an alternative plutonium path to a nuclear weapon.

And to ensure that these commitments are met, Iran has agreed to submit its program to unprecedented monitoring. For the international community, this first step will provide the most far-reaching insight and view of Iran's nuclear program that the international community has ever had. This first step—let me be clear. This first step does not say that Iran has a right to enrichment. No matter what interpretive comments are made, it is not in this document. There is no right to enrich within the four corners of the NPT. And this document does not do that. Rather, the scope and role of Iran's enrichment, as is set forth in the language within this document, says that Iran's peaceful nuclear program is subject to a negotiation and to mutual agreement. And it can only be by mutual agreement that enrichment might or might not be able to be decided on in the course of negotiations.

So what is on the other side of the ledger here? Again, there have been a number of premature reports and reactions, so I want to be clear about what this step provides, this first step, and what it doesn't provide. In return for the significant steps that Iran will take that I just listed—and there are more, incidentally, than I just listed; those are the principal—the international community will provide Iran with relief that is limited and, perhaps most importantly, reversible. The main elements of this relief would hold Iran's oil sales steady and permit it to repatriate $4.2 billion from those sales. And that would otherwise be destined for an overseas account restricted by our sanctions. In addition, we will suspend certain sanctions on imports of gold and precious metals, Iran's auto sector, and Iran's petrochemical exports, potentially—potentially—providing Iran with about $1.5 billion in additional export revenues.

For the benefit of the Iranian people, we will also facilitate humanitarian transactions that are already allowed by U.S. law. No U.S. law will be changed. Nothing will have to be different. In fact, the sanctions laws specifically exempt humanitarian assistance. So this channel will not provide Iran any new source of funds, but we will help them in order to try to provide the people of Iran with additional assistance. It simply improves access to goods that were never intended to be denied to the Iranian people.

Now, I want to emphasize the core sanctions architecture that President Obama, together with allies and friends around the world, have put together, that core architecture remains firmly in place through these six months, including with respect to oil and financial services. To put this number in perspective, during this six-month phase, the oil sanctions that will remain in place will continue to cause over 25 billion in lost revenues to Iran, or over $4 billion a month. That is compared to what Iran earned before this took effect—the sanctions. And while Iran will get access to the 4.2 billion that I talked about of the restricted oil revenues, 14 to 16 billion of its sales during this period will be locked up and out of reach.

Together with our partners, we are committed to maintaining our commitment to vigorously enforcing the vast majority of the sanctions that are currently in place. Again, let me repeat: This is only the first step. But it is a first step that guarantees while you take the second step and move towards a comprehensive agreement, Iran's fundamentals of its program are not able to progress—Fordow, Natanz, Arak, and other centrifuge and other things that matter. So that is a critical first step.

And I will say to all of you that as we conclude this first round of negotiation, with the beginning of the possibility of a much broader accomplishment down the road, it is our responsibility to be as firmly committed to diplomacy and as relentless in our resolve over the years as we have been to bring the concerted pressure that brought us to this moment. For the Iranian Government, it's their responsibility to recognize that this first phase is a very simple test. Many times, Iran, I think you heard the Foreign Minister here tonight reiterate, that they have a peaceful program and that's their only intention. Folks, it is not hard to prove peaceful intent if that's what you want to do. We are anxious to try to make certain that this deal ultimately will do exactly that—prove it.

And I will just say finally, I know that there are those who will assert that this deal is imperfect. Well, they too bear a responsibility, and that is to tell people what the better alternative is. Some might say we should simply continue to increase pressure—just turn up the screws, continue to put sanctions on, and somehow that's going to push Iran towards capitulation or collapse. Not by any interpretation that we have from all the experts and all of the input that we have, and from all of the countries—the P5+1—that took place in this today, none of them believe that would be the outcome.

Instead, we believe that while we are engaged in that effort, Iran's program would actually march forward. It would gain. And while it gains, it would become more dangerous in the region and countries like Israel and the Emirates, other people in the region who are threatened, would in fact be more threatened.

So we believe that you would wind up with an Iran with bigger stockpiles, with more advanced centrifuges and more progress at pursuing a plutonium track. And President Obama believes that doesn't benefit anybody.

In 1973–19—excuse me, in 2003, when the Iranians made an offer to the former Administration with respect to their nuclear program, there were 164 centrifuges. That offer was not taken. Subsequently, sanctions came in, and today there are 19,000 centrifuges and growing. So people have a responsibility to make a judgment about this choice. And I am comfortable, as is President Obama, that we have made the right choice for how you proceed to get a complete agreement.

Moreover, making sanctions the sum total of our policy will not strengthen the international coalition that we have built in order to bring Iran to the negotiating table. Instead, it would actually weaken that coalition, and many people believe that to merely continue at a time where Iran says, "We're prepared to negotiate," would in fact break up the current sanctions regime. Others argue for military action as a first resort. Well, President Obama and I do not share a belief that war is a permanent solution, and it should never be the first option. Instead, that particular option involves enormous risks in many different ways, and as President Obama has often said, while that option remains available to us—and the President will not take it off the table—he believes that that can only be entertained after we have made every effort to resolve the dispute through diplomacy, barring some immediate emergency that requires a different response.

So I close by saying to all of you that the singular objective that brought us to Geneva remains our singular objective as we leave Geneva, and that is to ensure that Iran does not acquire a nuclear weapon. In that singular object, we are resolute. Foreign Minister Zarif emphasized that they don't intent to do this, and the Supreme Leader has indicated there is a fatwa, which forbids them to do this. We want to see the process put in place by which all of that is proven, not through words but with actions. And we are prepared to work in good faith, with mutual respect, to work in a way as we did in the last days—cordially, with an atmosphere that was respectful, even as it was tough, as we move towards the process of making certain that this threat will be eliminated. In that singular object, we are absolutely resolute, and in that mission, we are absolutely committed, and in that endeavor, we will do everything in our power to be able to succeed.

[The question and answer section has been omitted.]

SOURCE: U.S. Department of State. "Press Availability After P5+1 Talks." November 24, 2013. http://www .state.gov/secretary/remarks/2013/11/218023.htm.

OTHER HISTORIC DOCUMENTS OF INTEREST

FROM THIS VOLUME

FROM OTHER *HISTORIC DOCUMENTS*

Preparation for the 2014 Olympic Games; Terrorist Attacks Raise Concerns

NOVEMBER 28 AND DECEMBER 30, 2013

Russia spent nearly seven years preparing itself to host its first ever Olympic Winter Games in the seaside resort town of Sochi. The games were the most expensive in Olympic history and in their run-up were overshadowed by a number of issues including President Vladimir Putin's crackdown on homosexual propaganda. However, perhaps the largest issue of all was security concerns, especially those raised following two terrorist bombings in late December 2013.

PREPARATION FOR THE GAMES

Sochi, Russia, won the right to hold the 2014 Winter Olympics in 2007, after beating out Pyeongchang, South Korea, and Salzburg, Austria, in two rounds of voting. The weather was a point of concern for electors, who noted that Sochi's subtropical climate would make it the warmest Winter Olympic host city in history. The Russian Federation had never before hosted the Olympic Games, although the Soviet Union did play host to the Summer Olympics in 1980. The nation promised to spend $12 billion to transform Sochi, a former Black Sea resort town, into a destination that could host tens of thousands of athletes and spectators. Nearly all the sporting venues and accommodations would have to be built from the ground up, but Putin guaranteed that everything would be completed on time. After winning the bid, Dmitry Chernychenko, who was charged with securing the Olympics for Russia, called the choice "a historic decision for all countries" that means "Russia will become even more open, more democratic."

Nearly seven years later, and with only weeks to go, Russia was still hard at work prepping everything necessary to host the games. And the price tag had soared from $12 billion to more than $51 billion, making the Sochi games the most expensive in Olympic history (the next closest was Beijing at an estimated $44 billion for the 2008 Summer Olympics; for comparison, $8 billion was spent on the 2010 Vancouver Winter Olympics). Only $10 billion of the total was funded directly by the Russian government, with the rest coming from private investors and commercial partnerships. The venues were split into two separate clusters—the Sochi Olympic Park and Krasnaya Polyana. The former would host the main Olympic Village, the international broadcasting center, the Olympic ceremony stadium, and the venues for ice hockey, speed skating, figure skating, and curling. Krasnaya Polyana, the Mountain Cluster, would host the skiing, luge, and bobsled events, as well as a secondary Olympic Village for athletes competing in those sports. Building also included more than 200 miles of roads and thirty miles of railway, an upgrade to existing transportation infrastructure, and changes to the existing power grid and telecommunications capability. After the Olympics, the plan was to use the main venues to host Formula One racing. The intent of the Russian government was also to maintain the resort atmosphere and make Sochi an international tourist destination.

The branding development for the games began in 2009 when the official logo was unveiled. It deviated from other earlier Olympics, which have incorporated graphics or pictures. Instead, Russia chose a simple word/number only combination, with Sochi and 2014 reflecting each other, the symbolism being that the games were being held in a place where the sea meets the Caucasus Mountains. The official mascots were chosen by the public and consisted of a polar bear, hare, and snow leopard. The official slogan of the games was "Hot. Cool. Yours." According to the Russian Olympic committee, the slogan was intended to represent the passion of the athletes, the climate in Sochi, and overall inclusiveness, respectively. The iconic torch relay began in October 2013 and would be the longest in history, traveling a total of 40,000 miles through all of Russia's eighty-three regions.

LATE DECEMBER TERRORIST ATTACKS SPARK FEARS

Six weeks ahead of the start of the Olympic Games, twin bombings took place in the city of Volgograd, a major transit hub 400 miles northeast of Sochi. The first bomber, thought to be a woman, set off an explosive device near a train station, killing seventeen and wounding more than thirty. Less than twenty-four hours later, a second explosion killed at least fourteen people and wounded upwards of twenty on a bus. Initially, one claimed responsibility for the bombings, which were deemed terrorist attacks, but they came just months after Chechen rebel leader Doku Umarov called for attacks against Russian citizens with an aim of preventing the Olympics from happening. In a July video, Umarov called the games "Satanic dancing on the bones of our ancestors." Chechen Muslim rebels have long believed that the Sochi region along the Black Sea was stolen by Russia from the Muslim people. Russia has struggled to maintain control over the area since 1999, when Russia voided the region's claim of independence. Over the past few years, Umarov has claimed responsibility for a number of bombings, including the 2010 attacks on Moscow's subway system and the 2011 bombing at the Moscow airport. Umarov himself has come and gone from the public eye over the years, and security analysts are unsure of how much power he might be able to exert regarding a terrorist attack. "In the field of terrorists," said Dmitry Tenin, director of the Carnegie Moscow Center, "we have a lot of franchises." In early January, a week after an unsubstantiated claim that Umarov was dead, an Islamic militant group, Vilayat Dagestan, which operates out of the North Caucuses, claimed responsibility for the twin attacks, noting that it was encouraged, but not ordered, by Umarov's call to action.

The Russian Foreign Ministry as well as countries and international bodies around the world instantly condemned the attacks. "The strike cynically planned on the eve of the New Year celebrations is another attempt by terrorists to open the internal 'front,' to set off panic and chaos, to arouse intersectarian strife and conflicts in Russian society. We will not step back and we will continue tough and consistent fighting against a treacherous enemy, who does not know borders and can be stopped by joint effort alone," the Russian Foreign Ministry said in a statement. International Olympic Committee (IOC) President Thomas Bach called the bombings "a despicable attack on innocent people," adding that the body had "confidence in the Russian authorities to deliver safe and secure Games in Sochi."

The attacks raised concern around the world for the safety of athletes and spectators at the upcoming Olympic Games. "Although fear of terrorist attack has been a staple of Olympics security for the past four decades, the back-to-back blasts yesterday and today, coupled with another attack in the same city in October, are likely intended to be the opening salvos in a sustained terrorist campaign," Bruce Hoffman, the director of the Center for Security Studies, told FoxNews.com. "This would be unprecedented in Olympic history and likely reflects the perpetrators' intention to disrupt the games even before the opening ceremony," he added.

For his part, Putin fervently worked to maintain a sense of security in Russia and had already deployed tens of thousands of troops, police, and security guards to Sochi. A so-called security zone was set up around the venues that would be used during the games, and strict security screenings and policies were put in place. However, security analysts said that it was possible that Chechen rebels, or anyone else who might be involved in a potential terrorist attack, could already be inside the security zone and able to escape detection. While he said a terrorist attack at the games was likely, James Phillips, a senior research fellow at the Heritage Foundation, said that it would be "difficult to move weapons or explosives around inside the zone," thus making a major attack less viable. Following the bombings in Volgograd, Alexander Zhukov, the president of the Russian Olympic Committee, said that tight security was already in place to protect those coming to the games, so "no additional security measures will be taken in Sochi in light of the terrorist attack." Russia had support of the United States, which, according to National Security Council spokesperson Caitlin Hayden, "would welcome the opportunity for closer cooperation for the safety of the athletes, spectators, and other participants." The Russian government did not request additional assistance from the Americans.

PUTIN'S ANTI-GAY POLICIES

Security was not the only pressure facing Russia ahead of the games. In June, Putin sparked international condemnation when he outlawed so-called gay propaganda directed at children. This followed on the heels of comments the president made in April expressing concern that Russia and Europe as a whole face demographic and population challenges created by non-childbearing homosexual relationships. At the time, he called it his duty to protect Russians from such nontraditional relationships. In public opinion polls, Russian citizens have long displayed intolerance for same-sex relationships, and a crackdown has been occurring across the country in recent years. A May 2013 poll conducted by Russia's Levada Center found that 38 percent of those surveyed believed that homosexuals needed treatment for their lifestyle and 13 percent thought those engaged in such activity should face fines or jail time. In 2012, Moscow moved to ban any gay-pride parades in the city limits for the next 100 years, and a number of territories have moved to ban what they consider homosexual propaganda materials.

Putin's propaganda law sought to prevent children from seeing a "distorted conception of the equivalence between traditional and non-traditional sexual relationships" and also prohibit "obtrusive spreading of information about non-traditional sexual relationships that may arouse interest in such relationships." The June law would impose a fine of upwards of 4,000 rubles ($122) on individuals convicted of the crime. Public officials could pay ten times that much, while individuals who use the Internet or other forms of mass media to distribute such propaganda could be fined up to 100,000 rubles.

Putin's homosexual propaganda law was followed in July by a law banning same-sex couples from adopting children. According to the Kremlin, the law would protect children from "non-traditional sexual behavior" and help them avoid "distresses of soul and stresses, which according to psychologists' research, are often experienced by children raised by same-sex parents." Putin has continued to deny that the Russian Federation discriminates against homosexuals, saying, "I want everyone to understand that in Russia there are no infringements on sexual minorities' rights," adding, "they're people, just like everyone else, and they enjoy full rights and freedoms." Such comments have raised the ire of human rights organizations, and even the European Union, which considers Russia's laws in direct violation of the European Convention on Human Rights, to which Russia is party.

Ahead of the Olympics, it was announced that demonstrations in or near the Sochi venues would not be tolerated. Russian investigative journalists also said that Russian authorities were planning to monitor Internet and phone traffic and would limit access to athletes, spectators, and journalists to the areas surrounding Sochi. These moves were thought to be a method of keeping journalists focused on the games instead of Russia's internal politics.

—Heather Kerrigan

Following is the text of a statement delivered by Russian President Vladimir Putin on November 28, 2013, during a meeting on the preparation for the 2014 Winter Olympics in Sochi; a December 30, 2013, statement from the Russian Ministry of Foreign Affairs regarding the terrorist attacks in Volgograd; and a December 30, 2013, statement from IOC President Thomas Bach regarding security for the Games.

Russian President Addresses Winter Olympic Meeting

November 28, 2013

PRESIDENT OF RUSSIA VLADIMIR PUTIN: Good afternoon,

We agreed to literally compare notes as we work during the final weeks of preparations for the Olympic Games.

Much has been done—almost everything—but when I say 'almost,' this means that some things still have to be refined. The main facilities are ready, and test events have been held virtually everywhere. But we still need to talk more carefully and in more detail about, for example, the main stadium [Fisht Central Olympic Stadium] where the opening and closing ceremonies will take place. This is because the equipment needs to be installed and all the necessary preparatory work has to be done.

We need to act particularly carefully with regards to the so-called ticket programme, one we have already talked about. We must give people from different Russian regions the opportunity to attend this sporting festival, while proceeding from the assumption that pricing will be flexible, and enable people with different income levels to attend the Olympics.

Naturally, preparations for the Paralympic Games are a separate issue. We must do everything possible for our Paralympians; they are not merely courageous and talented people, they are also star athletes. In Russia they achieve simply outstanding results. And ensuring all necessary conditions for them—in addition to everything else, in addition to paying due attention to people with disabilities (and of course this is not a very relevant term for Paralympians)—represents a more pragmatic, essential interest than points, goals, seconds or medals. For us, it is more fundamental than that. We certainly have high expectations for them, and therefore must provide them with appropriate facilities for training and participating in competitions.

Yesterday we visited some facilities, and tomorrow we will continue to examine where our preparations stand in others, namely the coastal cluster in the Imeretin Valley.

Now, let's talk in detail about all the issues I raised, and discuss problems if there are any.

I did not mention questions related to public transport and the way the city itself will function. I hope that the regional and municipal authorities will also talk about the relevant issues in this case. . . .

VLADIMIR PUTIN: I think it is obvious not only for us, but for all observers, that an enormous amount of work—and high-quality work, as we saw today—has been carried out. The truth of this statement will be tested as we use the Olympic facilities and infrastructure. I hope that it will stand. Anyway, today it looks that way: the amount of work is clear and the quality is very good. Of course we all know this, and I do too, so why did I come here now?

A little over two months remain in the run-up to the Olympics. Still, as I already said, and you confirmed, there are some things that must be completed and polished. With such large-scale events the final stage is always the most difficult. A great deal during the Olympic Games will depend on how you pass this stage, on how we pass it together.

But before the Olympics we have New Year's holidays and then Christmas. I want to tell you and I think this will be clear: for you the New Year begins the day the Paralympic Games end, on March 17. Your New Year will begin on March 18—yours and that of everyone who works at Olympic venues. It is necessary that all those engaged in work to implement this large-scale—and I would even say grandiose—project understand this. I want you to work accordingly during the final stages of preparations for the Olympic Games.

Source: President of Russia. Speeches and Transcripts. "Meeting on preparations for the 2014 Olympics." November 28, 2013. http://eng.kremlin.ru/transcripts/6342.

Russian Foreign Ministry Responds to Terrorist Attacks

December 30, 2013

Dozens of civilians, including women and children, have become victims of bandit terrorist attacks in Volgograd over the last two days. Currently, investigation activities are continuing, the necessary medical aid is being provided and the lists of victims are being updated.

The strike cynically planned on the eve of the New Year celebrations is another attempt by terrorists to open the internal "front," to set off panic and chaos, to arouse intersectarian strife and conflicts in Russian society.

We will not step back and we will continue tough and consistent fighting against a treacherous enemy, who does not know borders and can be stopped by joint effort alone. Criminal sorties in Volgograd, like terrorist attacks in the United States, Syria, Iraq, Libya, Afghanistan, Nigeria and other countries, are organised according to a single template, they have the same inspirators. Against the backdrop of ongoing, sincerely provocative appeals from crime bosses like Doku Umarov, to combine forces under the flag of jihad, to involve new militants in the terrorist war, the malignancy of position of some politicians and political technicians, who still attempt to divide terrorists into "right" and "wrong," depending on their geopolitical objectives being resolved, is evident.

This type of play has returned like a boomerang many times and led to the most tragic consequences. Terrorism is always a crime and punishment for it should be inevitable. Now, more than ever, we need joint condemnation of terrorism and true international solidarity in counteracting it and the ideology of violence and extremism, which feeds it. We express our deep gratitude to all the world leaders, who made their statements from positions of decisive condemnation immediately after the statement of the UN Security Council on the 29 December. We highly value the words of solidarity, which we have heard from many capital cities, in the statements of the UN Secretary-General Ban Ki-moon and representatives of other international organisations.

We view this as a confirmation of the determination of the world community to build up the fight against terrorists in every corner of the planet, irrespective of the slogans they use to justify their ruthless crimes.

SOURCE: Ministry of Foreign Affairs of the Russian Federation. "Statement by the Russian Ministry of Foreign Affairs in connection with the terrorist attacks in Volgograd." December 30, 2013. http://www .mid.ru/bdomp/brp_4.nsf/e78a48070f128a7b43256999005bcbb3/14d33fec2e9d190b44257c5c005926c8! OpenDocument.

IOC President Thomas Bach on Security for the Games

December 30, 2013

This is a despicable attack on innocent people and the entire Olympic Movement joins me in utterly condemning this cowardly act. Our thoughts are with the loved ones of the victims.

I have personally written to the President of the Russian Federation, Vladimir Putin, to express our condolences to the Russian people and our confidence in the Russian authorities to deliver safe and secure Games in Sochi. I am certain that everything will be done to ensure the security of the athletes and all the participants of the Olympic Games.

Sadly terrorism is a global disease but it must never be allowed to triumph. The Olympic Games are about bringing people from all backgrounds and beliefs together to overcome our differences in a peaceful way. The many declarations of support and solidarity from the international community make me confident that this message of tolerance will also be delivered by the Olympic Winter Games in Sochi.

SOURCE: Official Website of the Olympic Movement. "Statement from the IOC President on terrorist attacks in Russia." December 30, 2013. http://www.olympic.org/news/statement-from-the-ioc-president-on-terrorist-attacks-in-russia/218843.

OTHER HISTORIC DOCUMENTS OF INTEREST

FROM PREVIOUS *HISTORIC DOCUMENTS*

- Putin on His Reelection as President of Russia, *2012*, p. 127
- Moscow Subway Attacked by Suicide Bombers, *2010*, p. 109
- Concern over the 2008 Beijing Summer Games, *2008*, p. 296

EU Responds to Protests in Ukraine; Blocked Trade Agreement

NOVEMBER 29 AND 30, 2013

The decision by Ukraine's President Viktor Yanukovych to cancel the planned signing of a free trade agreement with the European Union (EU) sent shockwaves through his country and beyond. The signing was supposed to be the centerpiece of a summit of EU leaders in the Lithuanian capital, Vilnius, on November 28 and 29. But after Ukraine's easterly neighbor, Russia, warned that signing the pact would lead Moscow to erect new trade barriers against Ukrainian products, Yanukovych got cold feet. While the EU was humiliated by his last-minute move, its disappointment paled in comparison to the outrage sparked back home among pro-Western Ukrainians who viewed the deal as a stepping stone to Ukraine joining the EU. Near daily protests were organized, the largest at Independence Square in the Ukrainian capital Kiev. By the end of the year, an anti-Yanukovych, pro-EU movement dubbed Euromaidan—meaning Eurosquare—was gaining in momentum and Yanukovych's political future looked to be in peril.

BATTLE OF THE INTEGRATIONS

The underlying spark for the crisis was a battle of the integrations that has been playing out between the EU and Russia in recent years as both seek to entice the East European nations formerly part of the Soviet Union into their spheres. In 2008, the EU adopted a new strategy called the Eastern Partnership that targeted six countries: Armenia, Azerbaijan, Belarus, Georgia, Moldova, and Ukraine. Each of them had been under Russian domination for most of the twentieth century until emerging as independent nations after the Soviet Union was peacefully dissolved in 1991. Three other former Soviet republics— Estonia, Latvia, and Lithuania—had acted more swiftly to reorientate themselves westward, joining the EU and NATO in 2004. Not coincidentally, these three Baltic countries were also ardent champions of the EU's Eastern Partnership policy, which foresaw the conclusion of deep and comprehensive free trade agreements with the targeted countries. As for the long-term relationship, the Eastern Partnership neither promised nor precluded full EU membership.

Russia viewed this policy with suspicion given that the targeted countries had strong historical, cultural, and economic ties with Russia. Moscow was especially worried about Ukraine due to its large size and population (45 million people) and because many Ukrainians, especially in eastern Ukraine and the Crimean peninsula, were Russian-speaking and felt a strong affinity with Russia. Meanwhile, just as the EU was negotiating free trade agreements with several of these nations, Russia was constructing its own free trade zone, a project called the Eurasian Economic Union. Russia saw the former Soviet republics as prime candidates to sign onto its customs union project. Belarus, one of the Eastern Partnership countries, had already decided to join the customs union, as had

Kazakhstan. Russia was keen for Ukraine to join and was concerned that this "prize" would slip through its fingers if Ukraine were to go ahead with the EU trade pact.

The trade talks between the EU and Ukraine took about five years, with both sides agreeing on the accord's technical details by early 2012. Under its terms, trade barriers would be removed, saving Ukrainian exporters €487 million ($668 million) a year and EU exporters €391 million. In return for opening up its market of 500 million consumers to Ukraine, the EU required it to reform its political and judicial system to reduce corruption and make the judiciary a genuinely independent arm of government. As the date for signing the pact drew closer, the EU told the Ukrainian government that it needed to release from prison a powerful opposition leader, former Prime Minister Yulia Tymoshenko. She had been imprisoned in 2011 on what the EU claimed were politically motivated charges of corruption. While Yanukovych wanted to move ahead with the EU trade deal, he did not want to release Tymoshenko, his arch political rival whom he defeated in the 2010 presidential election. Tymoshenko's support base was located in western Ukraine, whereas Yanukovych's base was in the pro-Russian eastern part of the country.

As pressure from the EU intensified in the summer of 2013, Yanukovych experienced equally strong countervailing pressures from the east. Russian President Vladimir Putin made it clear to countries in his region that if they concluded free trade agreements with the EU, they could then not be part of the Russian-backed customs union. In case Ukraine doubted the seriousness of Russia's intentions, Moscow started tightening border controls on Ukrainian imports and threatening to impose new tariffs if Ukraine signed the EU deal. Russia took similar actions with the three other countries planning to conclude deep and comprehensive free trade agreements with the EU: Armenia, Georgia, and Moldova. For instance, Russia banned Moldovan wine imports, ostensibly on health and safety grounds. Viewing all these developments with alarm, the United States became more vocal in expressing solidarity with the EU and in urging Ukraine and other Eastern Partnership countries to orientate themselves toward the EU. Meanwhile, Ukraine's fragile economy was teetering on the brink of collapse. Yanukovych asked the International Monetary Fund (IMF) to provide a rescue package worth billions of dollars to help his country avoid defaulting on its mounting debts. But the IMF refused to do this because Ukraine would not adopt the economic reforms demanded by the Fund.

Vilnius Summit

The EU summit at Vilnius was supposed to showcase the success stories of the Eastern Partnership. Apart from the Ukraine deal, Georgia and Moldova were scheduled to initial trade agreements. Initialing is the stage in treaty-making that marks the successful conclusion of the negotiations, after which agreed texts are consolidated, translated into all necessary official languages, and prepared for signing. The EU-Ukraine agreement had already been initialed in March 2012. On November 21, Yanukovych announced that he would not release opposition leader Tymoshenko as the EU demanded, and therefore Ukraine would not sign the trade agreement in Vilnius. Although not entirely unexpected, the announcement caused great upset among EU leaders who quickly pointed a finger of blame at Russia, alleging Moscow had coerced Kiev into reneging on the EU trade deal. Russia in turn accused the EU of trying to blackmail Ukraine into signing it. And Yanukovych slammed the EU for demanding Tymoshenko's release, saying it had no right to make such a demand.

Despite this sour atmosphere, the summit went ahead and Yanukovych attended. The EU took comfort in Georgia's and Moldova's decision to defy Russia's warnings and initial their trade agreements. The EU was disappointed with Armenia, however, because it had concluded talks on an EU trade agreement in early 2013, but then in September, its President Serzh Sargsyan announced suddenly that Armenia would join the Russian-backed customs union instead. The announcement came just after Sargsyan met with Russian President Putin in Moscow.

Back in Ukraine, pro-Westerners took to the streets to protest Yanukovych's ditching of the EU deal. When they clashed with Ukrainian police, EU leaders made it clear where their sympathies lay. In a joint statement adopted at the Vilnius summit, the EU leaders "strongly condemn[ed] the excessive use of force last night by the police in Kyiv." They added that the support voiced by the protesters for the EU "had been welcomed yesterday by the participants" at the summit. Images from the protests showed Ukrainian flags being waved alongside EU flags.

The protests continued after the summit and evolved into a political movement called Euromaidan, in reference to the pro-European sympathies of the crowds that gathered at Kiev's Independence Square. In the ensuing weeks, the Ukrainian authorities' strategy wavered between confronting the protesters and allowing them to demonstrate. The protesters were a mix of moderate pro-Westerners and more radical anti-Russian, Ukrainian nationalists. Russian media coverage of the Euromaidan highlighted the more radical elements, while the Western media focused on the moderate elements.

Meanwhile, Ukraine's economic situation continued to deteriorate. The EU and the United States took the position that they would be willing to help Ukraine out of its dire financial straits only if an IMF program was in place. In December, Russia stepped into the fray, announcing a bailout package worth $15 billion for Ukraine. The Russian aid comprised a loan to prevent Ukraine defaulting on its debts and a lowering of Russian gas prices, which was extremely valuable to Ukraine because it relied heavily on Russian energy. The Russian aid package was viewed as a decisive step in bringing Ukraine into the Russian camp. However, by the end of the year, the volatility of the situation on the ground left lingering doubts about which direction Ukraine was headed.

CRIMEA ANNEXED BY RUSSIA

A tipping point in the Euromaidan was reached on February 18, 2014, when Ukrainian riot police opened fire on protesters in Kiev, killing around one hundred people over the next three days. The protesters responded to the police attacks by erecting barricades and hurling back Molotov cocktails. On February 21, President Yanukovych announced a compromise deal with his political opponents under which a new government of national unity was to be formed. But just a few hours later, the president unexpectedly fled the city for his political heartland in eastern Ukraine. The Ukrainian parliament voted to remove him from office, appointed a new more pro-Western-oriented interim government, and scheduled presidential elections for May 25.

Russia responded to the seismic shift in the political power balance by deploying military forces to Crimea, a peninsula in Ukraine that was once part of Russia and whose population is mostly Russian-speaking. Russia gained control of the entire peninsula quickly because it already had a military base in the Crimean port of Sevastopol, having signed a lease with Ukraine until 2042. A referendum paving the way for Russia to annex

Crimea took place on March 16, with voters opting overwhelmingly for annexation. While Russia recognized the vote, the Ukrainian government, EU, and United States denounced the referendum as illegal. Many view the crisis as the most serious that Europe has faced since the end of World War II. Some predict the emergence of a new Cold War as Russia competes with the EU for influence over Eastern Europe, with Ukraine a key battleground.

—Brian Beary

Following is the joint declaration released by the Council of the European Union on November 29, 2013, following their Vilnius Summit; and a November 30, 2013, statement by the European Union's High Representative and Commissioner condemning excessive use of force in Ukraine.

DOCUMENT *Vilnius Joint Declaration*

November 29, 2013

The Heads of State or Government and the representatives of the Republic of Armenia, the Republic of Azerbaijan, the Republic of Belarus, Georgia, the Republic of Moldova and Ukraine, the representatives of the European Union and the Heads of State or Government and representatives of its Member States have met in Vilnius on 28–29 November 2013. The President of the European Parliament and representatives of the Committee of the Regions, the European Economic and Social Committee, the European Investment Bank (EIB) and the European Bank for Reconstruction and Development (EBRD) the Conference of Regional and Local Authorities of the Eastern Partnership (CORLEAP) and the Euronest Parliamentary Assembly were also present at the Summit.

The Prague Summit in May 2009 launched a strategic and ambitious Eastern Partnership, as a specific dimension of the European Neighbourhood Policy, to further support the sustainable reform processes of all Eastern European countries, States participating in the Eastern Partnership, with a view to accelerating the political association and economic integration of interested partners with the European Union (EU). The agenda agreed in Prague and Warsaw contains the guiding principles of the Eastern Partnership. The participants of the Vilnius Summit re-confirm their commitment to implement them fully.

The participants of the Vilnius Summit reviewed the considerable progress made in the Partnership since the September 2011 Warsaw Summit bringing Eastern European partners closer to the EU and agreed on an ambitious agenda for the way ahead. In this context, they stressed the crucial necessity of implementing agreed commitments, in particular on political, economic and social reforms.

The Summit participants reaffirm the importance they attach to the Eastern Partnership founded on mutual interests and commitments as well as on shared ownership, responsibility, differentiation and mutual accountability. The Partnership is based on commitments to the principles of international law and to fundamental values, including democracy, the rule of law and the respect for human rights and fundamental freedoms, as well as to market economy, sustainable development and good governance. All countries participating in the Eastern Partnership are committed to these values and principles of international law through the relevant international instruments and any EU Member State is also committed to them through the Treaty of the European Union.

While recognising and welcoming the progress that has been made, they also recall that much remains to be done to tackle the persisting challenges posed to democracy, the respect for fundamental freedoms and the rule of law. In this regard, Summit participants underline that progress on respect for those common values will be essential notably through strengthening the efficiency and independence of the judiciary; effectively tackling corruption; and implementing public administration reform.

The Summit participants welcome the steps taken since the Warsaw Summit to strengthen the Eastern Partnership with the objective of building a common area of shared democracy, prosperity, stability and increased interactions and exchanges. Emphasizing the importance of developing strong ties between the EU and the Eastern European countries, the Summit participants agree that achieving closer cooperation is essential to ensure stability and prosperity on the European continent. The resolution of conflicts, building trust and good neighbourly relations are essential to economic and social development and cooperation in the region.

The participants of the Vilnius Summit warmly welcome the significant step forward achieved in establishing ambitious, new Association Agreements, including Deep and Comprehensive Free Trade Areas (DCFTAs) between the EU and some partner countries. Today, following the recent finalisation of the respective negotiations, the EU-Republic of Moldova and EU-Georgia Association Agreements including DCFTAs have been initialled. The participants of the Vilnius Summit take note of the decision by the Ukrainian Government to suspend temporarily the process of preparations for signature of the Association Agreement and Deep and Comprehensive Free Trade Area between the EU and Ukraine. They also take note of the unprecedented public support for Ukraine's political association and economic integration with the EU. The EU and Ukraine reiterate their commitment to the signing of this Agreement on the basis of determined action and tangible progress in the three areas emphasised at the 2013 EU-Ukraine Summit. To this end, important progress has already been achieved. These Association Agreements, including DCFTAs, are designed to support far reaching political and socio-economic reforms and facilitate comprehensive approximation towards the EU, its rules and standards. The participants of the Vilnius Summit welcome the progress made in the negotiations on an Association Agreement between the EU and the Republic of Azerbaijan and, building on existing bilateral contractual relations, call for progress to continue. The EU stands ready to launch negotiations on a DCFTA, as part of an Association Agreement, following Azerbaijan's accession to the World Trade Organisation (WTO). The EU and Armenia have today reconfirmed their commitment to further develop and strengthen their cooperation in all areas of mutual interest within the Eastern Partnership framework, stressing the importance of reviewing and updating the existing basis of their relations. In the framework of the European Neighbourhood Policy and the Eastern Partnership, the Summit participants reaffirm the sovereign right of each partner freely to choose the level of ambition and the goals to which it aspires in its relations with the European Union.

Enhancing mobility in a secure and well-managed environment remains a core objective of the Eastern Partnership. The participants of the Vilnius Summit warmly welcome the progress made by some partners towards Visa Liberalisation through the implementation of the Visa Liberalisation Action Plans. In this context they also welcome the conclusion and implementation of Visa Facilitation and Readmission Agreements.

The participants of the Vilnius Summit reaffirm their acknowledgement of the European aspirations and the European choice of some partners and their commitment to build deep and sustainable democracy. In this context, they take note of the commitment of those partners to pursue these objectives. The participants reaffirm the particular role for the Partnership to support those who seek an ever closer relationship with the EU. The Association Agreements, including DCFTAs, are a substantial step in this direction. Respect for the common values and implementation of Association Agreements will contribute to the future progressive developments in our relationship.

The participants of the Vilnius Summit set the following goals to be attained by the Partnership by 2015:

- Further deepening relations and cooperation between the EU and partners;
- Making further steps in strengthening democracy, guaranteeing respect of human rights and rule of law including through the pursuit of reform of the judiciary and strengthening law enforcement;
- Securing where applicable signature by Autumn 2014 and provisional application of the Association Agreements/DCFTAs thereby launching the implementation phase and ensure that the Agreements' ratification processes are well advanced;
- Establishing where applicable Association Agendas as soon as possible in 2014 as the means of preparing for and implementing the Association Agreements/ DCFTAs and to serve as the key monitoring tool;
- Continuing to provide EU assistance to support partners' reform agendas including taking into account the provisional application and implementation of the Association Agreements including Deep and Comprehensive Free Trade Areas;
- Accession by the Eastern European partners concerned to the regional Convention on pan-Euro-Mediterranean preferential rules of origin and making progress towards their accession to the Common Transit Convention as further steps in the process of economic integration;
- Advancing through gradual steps towards visa free regimes, in due course on a case by case basis, provided that conditions for well-managed and secure mobility are in place;
- Strengthening the business dimension of the Eastern Partnership including through improving the business environment in partner countries to the benefit of local, regional and European SMEs and businesses;
- Gradually developing a Common Knowledge and Innovation Space to pull together several existing strands of cooperation in research and innovation;
- Further strengthening the multilateral dimension of the Eastern Partnership;
- Seeking further regulatory approximation in all transport areas and implementing transport infrastructure projects, along the Eastern Partnership transport network through existing EU programmes and instruments, seeking closer involvement of European and International Financial Institutions and prioritizing projects that improve connections with the TEN-T core network;
- Promoting and strengthening strategic multilateral projects, through creating a conducive, transparent, regulatory, and financial environment for the implementation of projects of Common Interest and Projects of Energy Community Interests for the countries concerned;

- Further strengthening of public institutional capacity with support from the EU;
- Promoting and strengthening visible and effective multilateral Flagship Initiatives including where appropriate combining policy dialogue and support for infrastructure;
- Further strengthening people to people contacts—including through the opening of the new "Erasmus +," "Creative Europe" and the Marie Skłodowska-Curie strand within Horizon 2020 to the participants from the Eastern Partnership countries;
- Implementing a Visibility Strategy for the Eastern Partnership.

Summit participants stress that effective future implementation of Association Agreements and, where relevant, DCFTAs, accompanied by reforms will bring about the comprehensive approximation with EU legislation and standards leading to the gradual economic integration of partners in the EU internal market and therefore to the creation of an economic area. They undertake to review at the next Summit the possible further steps that could be taken to advance economic integration with a view to creating an economic area in light of implementation of the relevant parts of this Declaration and the Association Agreements/DCFTAs. To this end, the European Commission is invited, to conduct a feasibility study in due time. Summit participants agree that such an ambitious long-term vision for economic integration between partners and the EU is desirable—contributing also to the longer-term goal of a wider common area of economic prosperity based on WTO rules and sovereign choices throughout Europe and beyond.

The growing relationship between the EU and its Eastern European partners in particular in the field of economic integration can make a significant contribution to strengthening Europe's international competitiveness and to creating sustainable, inclusive, smart growth and jobs thereby enhancing stability.

Greater differentiation and mutual accountability will allow individual partners better to meet their aspirations and needs. The pace of reforms will continue to determine the intensity of cooperation and those partners most engaged in reforms will benefit most from their relationship with the EU, in line with the incentive based approach ("more-for-more") of the renewed European Neighbourhood Policy. Reinforced and sustainable reform efforts serve a common interest to help the Eastern European countries progress towards deep and sustainable democracies where good governance and the rule of law prevail with economies developing on market-based principles to underpin equitable and sustainable development. Summit participants underline that this ambitious agenda requires the engagement of the broader society and they therefore welcome the increased involvement of parliaments, civil society, local and regional authorities, business community and other relevant stakeholders in the Eastern Partnership agenda.

Summit participants agree the above general political guidelines for the Partnership in 2014–15. This declaration, together with the new Association Agendas and other existing and future documents guiding bilateral relations and Work Programmes of the multilateral Platforms, will constitute a clear plan of action for the Eastern Partnership in 2014–15.

[The remainder of the joint declaration has been omitted.]

SOURCE: Council of the European Union. "Joint Declaration of the Eastern Partnership Summit, Vilnius, 28–29 November 2013." November 29, 2013. http://www.consilium.europa.eu/uedocs/cms_Data/docs/pressdata/EN/foraff/139765.pdf.

DOCUMENT

European Commission Condemns Violence Against Protesters in Ukraine

November 30, 2013

The European Union strongly condemns the excessive use of force last night by the police in Kyiv to disperse peaceful protesters, who over the last days in a strong and unprecedented manner have expressed their support for Ukraine's political association and economic integration with the EU. This support had been welcomed yesterday by the participants of the Vilnius Eastern Partnership Summit. The unjustified use of force goes against the principles to which all participants of the Vilnius Summit, including the President of Ukraine, yesterday reaffirmed their adherence.

We call on Ukraine, also in its capacity as Chairmanship in Office of the OSCE, hosting its Ministerial Conference on 5–6 December in Kyiv, to fully abide by its international commitments to respect the freedom of expression and assembly.

We call upon the President and the Ukrainian authorities to carry out investigations into the events last night and to hold responsible those who acted against the basic principles of freedom of assembly and of expression.

SOURCE: European Union. Press Release Database. "Statement by High Representative Catherine Ashton and Commissioner Stefan Füle on last night's events in Ukraine." November 30, 2013. http://europa.eu/rapid/press-release_MEMO-13-1077_en.htm.

OTHER HISTORIC DOCUMENTS OF INTEREST

FROM PREVIOUS *HISTORIC DOCUMENTS*

December

White House Report Details Benefits of Unemployment Insurance

DECEMBER 5, 2013

In 2013, the U.S. unemployment rate continued to decline, but the public and private sectors were still not creating jobs the way they had before the 2007–2009 recession. With millions of Americans relying on federal unemployment insurance to help make ends meet until a job became available, the impending expiration of benefits for some 1.3 million Americans could have dealt a significant blow not only to the individuals affected but also to the economy. Recognizing the potential impact, in December the White House Council of Economic Advisers released a report touting the benefits of extending unemployment insurance.

Economy Continues Upswing

The economy continued improving in 2013, although slowly, well short of where it was in 2007 before the start of the recession. By the end of 2013, eleven million Americans remained unemployed, even as tens of thousands of jobs were created each month. In the wake of the recession, the economy shed 8.7 million jobs, and by the end of 2013, had added back more than seven million. Job creation was largely led by the blue-collar sectors of manufacturing and construction, but by the close of 2013, higher quality jobs were being added back as well. Economists such as Rajeev Dhawan, the director of Georgia State University's Economic Forecasting Center, said that the momentum from 2013 would likely carry into 2014 and, as long as the government avoided a shutdown, it could be a banner year. "The economy is poised for takeoff," Dhawan said.

When December jobs data was released on January 10, 2014, the addition of 74,000 jobs was weaker than expected and marked the smallest increase since January 2011. Jobs were mainly in the retail and manufacturing sectors; health care and construction both lost jobs. Economists had initially estimated that nearly 200,000 jobs would be added in December, especially in light of temporary holiday hiring. Although disappointing, the jobs numbers still left 2013 with overall positive growth in many sectors. On average, 182,000 jobs were added per month. However, according to the Economic Policy Institute's Heidi Shierholz, that is too few jobs to get the economy back to prerecession levels. In her report released in January 2014, Shierholz estimated that the economy needs to add a total of 7.9 million jobs to get back to where it was in 2007. "At 200,000 jobs per month, pre-recession labor market conditions would not be regained for another five years," she wrote in her report.

The unemployment rate in 2013 continued to decline, reaching 6.7 percent by December. While seemingly positive, this is a contentious piece of data—some argue that it does not accurately reflect the number of jobs being created or overall economic improvement because it does not include working-age adults who have stopped looking for a job or have taken part-time work instead of full-time. The workforce participation rate hovered near 63 percent by the end of the year. While the December 2013 unemployment rate was the lowest since October 2008, the workforce participation rate among working-age adults of 62.8 percent was the lowest since February 1978, meaning that people were continuing to leave the job market, likely frustrated by the inability to find work. "Disappointingly, not all of this decrease in the unemployment rate came about because of people moving into employment. A large part of the decrease was driven by people dropping out of the labor market completely. . . . If the labor force participation had not fallen at all over the past year, we would have had 2 million more people in the labor force today," said Lisa Lynch, a former economist for the Department of Labor. She surmised that the decrease is due in part both to young workers delaying employment by staying in school and by the retirement of older workers. However, Lynch added, "Hundreds of thousands of prime-aged workers have dropped out of the labor market in spite of job growth and a falling unemployment rate. Many of these workers have become discouraged . . . have currently stopped looking because they believe no jobs are available or there are none for which they are qualified." If these two million workers had remained in the labor force, according to Shierholz, the unemployment rate would be above 10 percent.

FEDERAL UNEMPLOYMENT BENEFITS SET TO EXPIRE

Nearly four million Americans are considered long-term unemployed, meaning that they have been out of work for six months or more, and of those, 1.3 million received federal unemployment benefits as of the end of 2013. Federal unemployment benefits begin once state unemployment benefits run out. Someone receiving federal benefits can expect to receive benefits from anywhere between fourteen and forty-seven weeks. The number of weeks is dependent on the state in which the person lives. Benefits average $300 per person per week. From the Emergency Unemployment Compensation (EUC) program's inception in 2008 through 2013, approximately 24 million Americans have received federal unemployment insurance under this program. According to the White House, in 2012, the benefits helped 2.5 million Americans out of poverty.

When EUC was developed, the unemployment rate was 5.6 percent, and the number of Americans relying on the program was minimal. In light of the recession, which raised unemployment rates above 10 percent, Congress has consistently extended benefits during its annual budget negotiations. As the federal government extended benefits, states were cutting back, especially as revenue improved and the jobless rate fell.

Congress renewed unemployment insurance on January 2, 2013, for the eleventh time, but as the December 28, 2013, expiration deadline approached, there was little consensus as to how to move forward. House Speaker John Boehner, R-Ohio, indicated a willingness to review proposals put forth by the Democrats, but more conservative members of his party refused to negotiate unless the total cost of an extension, estimated by the Congressional Budget Office at $26 billion, was offset. Democrats and a number of economists agree that·while there is a spending component involved in the program, the overall economic benefit outweighs any cost.

During the ongoing Congressional debate, economists offered other supporting information to illustrate what might happen if the benefits were not renewed. One surprising change was a drop in the unemployment rate, up to as much as 0.5 percentage points. Without benefits coming in, the unemployed might become more willing to take a job they would have otherwise turned down, but more likely the unemployment decrease will be driven by workers dropping out of the labor force because they are no longer bound by the requirement to provide proof of active job seeking. This happened in North Carolina when the state made itself ineligible to receive federal unemployment benefits, and its unemployment rate fell only because people were being pushed out of the workforce. In the estimate of many economists, if more than a million Americans are left without benefits or a job, poverty will likely increase, and the number of those being lifted out of poverty will decline. The gradual decline in this statistic was already being seen as the EUC was slowly phased down. In 2010, the program lifted 3.2 million Americans out of poverty, but this number fell to 1.7 million just two years later.

As Democrats touted the economic benefits of an extension, vocal Republicans looked at the negatives. Sen. Rand Paul, R-Ky., a favorite of the tea party, said in a Fox News interview that he would support unemployment benefits, so long as they were paid for. He added, if you extend benefits beyond twenty-six weeks, "you do a disservice to these workers." He continued, "When you allow people to be on unemployment insurance for 99 weeks, you're causing them to become part of this perpetual unemployed group in our economy." Other Republicans joined Paul in asserting that extending unemployment benefits removes the incentive for recipients to find work. Economists, however, have found in numerous studies that this only applies to a small number of those who receive the benefit.

WHITE HOUSE REPORT ON UNEMPLOYMENT BENEFITS

As the unemployment benefit debate has been revived in each recent budget cycle, President Barack Obama has been a strong supporter of extension, touting the economic benefits of helping America's most vulnerable. On December 5, the White House Council of Economic Advisers released a joint report with the Department of Labor on the impact of benefit extension. According to the report, if Congress failed to vote to extend benefits, 240,000 jobs would be lost in 2014, gross domestic product (GDP) could fall between 0.2 and 0.4 percentage points, and more Americans would leave the job force frustrated by their inability to find employment. Overall spending would decline, because Americans who lost their benefits would have less on-hand cash to infuse into the economy. The White House also contended that the current 2013 unemployment rate was higher than the rate at any time since 2008 when benefits were extended, while the long-term unemployment rate of 2.6 percent in October was twice as high.

Noting that families are "still struggling to regain the foothold they had prior to the crisis," the report's authors found that "allowing EUC to expire would be harmful to millions of workers and their families, counterproductive to the economic recovery, and unprecedented in the context of previous extensions to earlier unemployment insurance programs." According to the report, the economy was still fragile enough that it would not be able to withstand the loss of such a program. President Obama encouraged Congress to recognize the potential economic impact, and the impact to families, and pass an extension before the holiday recess. "Christmas-time is no time for Congress to tell more than 1 million of these Americans that they have lost this unemployment insurance," Obama said.

PRESIDENT PUSHES EXTENSION OF BENEFITS

Democrats had hoped that unemployment benefits would be extended in the budget passed in December, but Congress was not able to reach a consensus, and the issue was left out of the bill. With the budget passed, and with knowledge that members would not be facing another battle, at least in the short term to keep the government funded, Congress recessed until the New Year, meaning no unemployment legislation would be passed by the December 28 deadline. Democrats used the intervening recess weeks to try to shame Republicans. "I don't know if our colleagues who have opposed passing the unemployment-insurance legislation know or care about the impact on families," said House Minority Leader Nancy Pelosi, D-Calif.

On December 27, President Obama called on members of Congress to address what he called an "urgent economic priority" as soon as they returned to Washington. He encouraged support of a bipartisan bill drafted by Senators Jack Reed, D-R.I., and Dean Heller, R-Nev., which would extend unemployment insurance for three months and give Congress more time to negotiate a longer-term solution. "As the President has repeatedly made clear, it defies economic sense, precedent and our values to allow 1.3 million Americans fighting to find jobs to see their unemployment insurance abruptly cut off—especially in the middle of the holiday season," said Director of the National Economic Council Gene Sperling. When they returned from recess, Congress failed to act to pass an extension, and the unemployment benefits for 1.3 million Americans were left in limbo until a new deal could be reached.

—Heather Kerrigan

Following is the Executive Summary and Introduction of a report released by the White House Council of Economic Advisers and the Department of Labor on December 5, 2013, regarding the economic benefits of extending unemployment insurance.

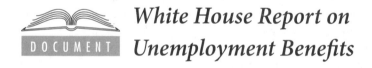

White House Report on Unemployment Benefits

December 5, 2013

[All footnotes and text boxes have been omitted.]

Executive Summary

The United States economy continues to recover from the worst economic crisis since the Great Depression, and while substantial progress has been made, more work remains to boost economic growth and speed job creation. Despite ten consecutive quarters of GDP growth and 7.8 million private sector jobs added since early 2010, the unemployment rate is unacceptably high at 7.3 percent, and far too many families are still struggling to regain the foothold they had prior to the crisis.

The Emergency Unemployment Compensation (EUC) program authorized by Congress in 2008 has provided crucial support to the economy and to millions of Americans who lost jobs through no fault of their own. Under current law, EUC will end on December 28, 2013. This report argues that allowing EUC to expire would be harmful to millions of workers and their families, counterproductive to the economic recovery, and unprecedented in the context of previous extensions to earlier unemployment insurance programs.

Since their inception in 2008, extended unemployment insurance (UI) benefits have provided critical support to millions of workers and their families:

- Nearly 24 million workers have received extended UI benefits
- Recipients are a diverse group: roughly half have completed at least some college, including 4.8 million with bachelor's degrees or higher
- Including workers' families, nearly 69 million people have been supported by extended UI benefits, including almost 17 million children
- In 2012 alone, UI benefits lifted an estimated 2.5 million people out of poverty

Millions of workers stand to lose access to UI benefits if no action is taken:

- Approximately 1.3 million workers currently receiving extended UI benefits are set to lose them at the end of the year
- 3.6 million additional people will lose access to UI benefits beyond 26 weeks by the end of 2014

Allowing UI to expire would be damaging to the macro-economy and the labor force:

- Failing to extend UI benefits would put a dent in job-seekers' incomes, reducing demand and costing 240,000 jobs in 2014.
- Estimates from the Congressional Budget Office and JP Morgan suggest that without an extension of EUC GDP will be .2 to .4 percentage points lower.
- In 2011, CBO found that aid to the unemployed is among the policies with "the largest effects on output and employment per dollar of budgetary cost"
- In over a dozen studies, economists have found that any disincentive to find new work that could result from extended UI benefits is, at most, small
- Expiration of extended UI benefits may also lead some long-term unemployed to stop looking for work and leave the labor force, reducing the number who could eventually find jobs as the economy heals

Allowing EUC to expire would be unprecedented in the context of previous extensions to earlier unemployment insurance programs:

- The unemployment rate (7.3% in October) is currently higher than it was at the expiration of any previous extended UI benefits program
- The long-term unemployment rate (2.6% in October) is at least twice as high as it was at the expiration of every previous extended UI benefits program
- In this cycle, EUC was first signed into law in June 2008 by President Bush when the unemployment rate was 5.6 percent and the average duration of unemployment was 17.1 weeks. Today, as of October 2013, the unemployment rate is 7.3 percent and the average duration of unemployment is 36.1 weeks.
- Consistent with previous programs, the EUC program has been gradually phasing down—the median number of weeks one can receive benefits across states is down from a peak of 53 weeks in 2010 to 28 weeks currently and phasing down to 14 weeks under the proposed extension

I. Introduction

Ten consecutive quarters of economic growth have raised the output of the American economy to an all-time high, more than five percent above its peak before the Great Recession. The labor market has grown steadily as America's resilient businesses have added jobs for 44 consecutive months. Due to the depth of the recession that began in 2007, however, more work must be done to aid workers who continue to struggle to find jobs and to ensure that the economy continues to grow. As of October 2013, 11.3 million workers are unemployed, including 4.1 million who have been out of work for more than 26 weeks.

The Emergency Unemployment Compensation (EUC) program authorized by Congress in 2008 has provided crucial support to the economy and to millions of Americans who lost jobs through no fault of their own. Under current law EUC will end on December 28, 2013 at which point more than 1.3 million workers will lose benefits immediately. By the end of 2014 another 3.6 million workers will lose access to EUC benefits when they exhaust their regular unemployment insurance (UI) benefits before finding employment. As this report details, extending EUC would support these workers and the approximately 9 million others in their families. It would also provide an important boost to economic growth and job creation. Since 1948 Congress has never allowed extended unemployment benefits to expire with unemployment rates as high as they are now and the long-term unemployment rate is currently twice as high as in any previous month in which benefits expired.

Nearly 69 million workers and family members have benefitted from the EUC and EB programs since 2008. Direct beneficiaries of Emergency Unemployment Compensation (EUC) represent a broad cross-section of the population: younger and older workers are roughly equally represented; about 40 percent have household incomes, prior to job loss, between $30,000 and $75,000; and while 13 percent did not finish high-school, 20 percent have a four-year college degree, and the remaining two-thirds of the recipients have education through high school or some college. For many of these Americans and their families, EUC is all that stands between them and poverty: the Census Bureau estimates that unemployment benefits lifted 2.5 million people from poverty in 2012 alone and has kept over 11 million out of poverty since 2008.

There is broad agreement amongst economists that the extended unemployment benefits provided to families during times of high unemployment do *not* noticeably reduce incentives for workers to find jobs. For example, a recent study of EUC in the Great Recession finds that extensions raised the unemployment rate at the end of 2010 by only 0.2 percentage points, about 2 percent of the 9.3 percent unemployment rate in that month. Moreover, recent research has shown that whatever disincentive effects may exist, they are even smaller when jobs are scarce as strategic considerations are dominated by the urgent need to find a job. This logic suggests that unemployment benefits should increase when jobs are scarce and contract when the labor market is strong, which is exactly how EUC is currently designed. As state unemployment rates fall, the program essentially is phased down as states are phased out of eligibility for additional weeks of support.

An often overlooked benefit of extended unemployment compensation programs is that these programs keep the long-term unemployed from exiting the labor market since benefits are contingent on continued job-search. Transitions out of the labor force generally occur at a higher rate for those unemployed 27 weeks or more than for those unemployed for shorter periods. After the EUC legislation was enacted in 2008, however, the rate of transition out of the labor force among those who were unemployed for 27 to 52 weeks and those unemployed over a year actually fell to the lowest level on record. Though the job-finding rate is low for the long-term unemployed (currently about 10 percent per month for those unemployed 27 weeks or more), keeping them in the labor market increases the number who eventually do find jobs.

According to the Congressional Budget Office, EUC is among policies with "the largest effects on output and employment per dollar of budgetary cost." The benefits unemployed Americans receive are often spent immediately on necessary goods like food, clothing, and shelter, supporting local businesses in their communities. Without an extension, the Council of Economic Advisers estimates that the economy will generate 240,000 fewer jobs by the end of 2014.

The Administration has supported reforms to the unemployment insurance system, and the last EUC extension created opportunities for states to improve the program and test new strategies to help get the long-term unemployed back to work. The administration supports a variety of reforms to the UI system that help workers find jobs quicker. It also expanded "work-sharing" programs across the country, which will help prevent layoffs by encouraging struggling employers to reduce hours for workers rather than laying them off. Additionally, for the first time, the reforms allowed the long-term unemployed who were receiving federal benefits to start their own businesses while providing support to states to expand entrepreneurship programs.

The progress made since the depths of the recession in 2010 is a testament to the resilience of the American economy and the American people. Yet more must be done. Extending EUC will enable beneficiaries to search for jobs that utilize their skills, continue to support their families, and support job creation and economic growth in their communities.

[The remainder of the report has been omitted.]

Source: The White House. "The Economic Benefits of Extending Unemployment Insurance." December 5, 2013. http://www.whitehouse.gov/sites/default/files/docs/uireport-2013-12-4.pdf.

OTHER HISTORIC DOCUMENTS OF INTEREST

FROM THIS VOLUME

- Census Bureau Reports on Poverty in the United States, p. 437

FROM PREVIOUS *HISTORIC DOCUMENTS*

- House and Senate Debate Temporary Payroll Tax Extension, *2011*, p. 686

Organisation for the Prohibition of Chemical Weapons Awarded 2013 Nobel Peace Prize

DECEMBER 10, 2013

Almost every year since 1901, the Norwegian Nobel Committee has awarded the Nobel Peace Prize to a person, group of people, or organization selected from a list of more than 200 nominees. On October 11, 2013, the committee announced that the annual prize would be awarded to the Organisation for the Prohibition of Chemical Weapons (OPCW) for its work to eliminate the use and existence of these deadly arms. OPCW received its award in a ceremony in Oslo, Norway, on December 10, 2013. The timing of the award was significant—just months earlier, the United States and United Nations had declared that they had proof that chemical weapons had been used against civilians in Syria. The OPCW was at the time of the award working in the nation to eliminate the weapons stocks, but Syrian civilians complained that the Nobel Committee was placing too much focus on chemical weapons when a majority of those killed were targeted with conventional bombs and weapons.

SUPPOSED NOMINEES

A select group of nominators is invited by the committee to submit a potential candidate for the prize. It is the practice of the Nobel Committee not to release the names of those who were nominated for the prize until fifty years after the prize is awarded. However, the committee does release the number of nominations received, which in 2013 totaled 259—the highest number ever—and included fifty organizations. "This year's nominations come from all over the world . . . well-known names, well-known presidents and prime ministers and also lesser well-known names working in humanitarian projects, human rights activists," said committee secretary Geir Lundestad in March 2013.

Although the Nobel Committee does not reveal the nominees, often the nominators will reveal their picks. Those thought to be the top contenders among names that were released included a variety of traditional and controversial figures. In the latter category was Bradley Manning, the U.S. soldier convicted of leaking classified documents to the WikiLeaks website and sentenced to thirty-five years in prison. Manning was nominated by peace activist Mairead Maguire for what she called an "incredible disclosure of secret documents" that "helped end the Iraq War, and may have helped prevent further conflicts elsewhere." Similarly, Edward Snowden, the NSA worker who uncovered the federal government's wiretapping activities, was nominated by Stefan Svallfors, a Swedish sociology professor. Snowden has been living in Russia since he was charged with espionage by the United States in June 2013.

Among the more mainstream nominees thought to be in contention for the prize was Claudia Paz y Paz, Guatemala's attorney general who has fought against organized crime and political corruption. A trio of Russians—Lyudmila Alexeyeva, Svetlana Gannushkina, and Lilya Shibanova—were nominated for their human rights work. Alexeyeva, the nation's oldest human rights activist at age eighty-six, had recently been a vocal opponent of President Vladimir Putin's decision to ban same-sex marriage.

The two perceived front-runners were Denis Mukwege and Malala Yousafzai. The former is a Congolese doctor who, with his colleagues, has treated more than 30,000 rape victims who were targeted during the civil war in the Democratic Republic of Congo. In 2012, Mukwege survived an assassination attempt. Yousafzai is a Pakistani education activist who, in 2012 at age fourteen, was shot in the head on her way home from school by Taliban militants. Yousafzai now lives in the United Kingdom, and she told a radio station that she still needs "to work a lot." Yousafzai said, "In my opinion, I have not done that much to win the Nobel Peace Prize."

Award Winner Announcement

Despite speculation that the award would go to a human rights or social welfare activist, on October 11, 2013, the Nobel Committee announced that it would be awarding the 2013 Peace Prize to the OPCW for "its extensive efforts to eliminate chemical weapons." According to the press release announcing the award, since 1997 when the Chemical Weapons Convention—an international prohibition of producing and storing chemical weapons—went into effect, "the OPCW has, through inspections, destruction and by other means, sought the implementation of the convention." The committee added, "By means of the present award to the OPCW, the Committee is seeking to contribute to the elimination of chemical weapons."

In its announcement, the committee noted the tragic history of the use of chemical weapons during World War I and World War II and also drew on the ongoing civil war in Syria as a major example of why the work of the OPCW is necessary and important. The announcement also criticized the United States and Russia for failing to meet the convention deadline to destroy their chemical weapons by April 2012. By late 2013, 189 countries were signatories of the convention. Angola, Egypt, Israel, Myanmar, North Korea, and South Sudan are currently not party to the convention.

The OPCW is based in The Hague in the Netherlands and is backed by the United Nations. The group is largely unknown outside its membership and international partners, but its goal is to enforce the 1997 Chemical Weapons Convention. To do this, the body undertakes inspections and declaration evaluations of its 189 members to determine which nations have destroyed their chemical weapons. To date, it has completed approximately 5,000 inspections in nearly ninety countries. Most recently, the body was called to Syria in October 2013 to ensure the safe disposal of chemical weapons controlled by Syrian leader Bashar al-Assad under an agreement forged by the United States and Russia. Upon successful removal of the weapons, Syria will become the OPCW's 190th member.

After learning that his organization would receive the award, OPCW Director General Ahmet Üzümcü said, "We were aware that our work silently but surely was contributing to peace in the world," adding that "the last few weeks have brought this to the fore. The entire international community has been made aware of our work." Üzümcü went on to say that he hoped his organization would be successful in helping "achieve peace in Syria" and end the Syrian peoples' suffering.

As with all Nobel Peace Prize awards, the choice of OPCW had its supporters and opponents. The Syrian government did not release an official response, but Syrian citizens expressed outrage given the current focus on chemical weapons even though they have only impacted a fraction of the more than 100,000 killed during the Syrian civil war. Ryan Crocker, a former U.S. ambassador to Afghanistan, Iraq, and Syria, added that the work by the OPCW, while noble, would not end the civil war. "Getting rid of chemical weapons anywhere is a good thing," Crocker said. "But to make this worthy of the Nobel Peace Prize, I just don't get it," he added. Supporters included UN disarmament official Angela Kane who said that if Alfred Nobel, the prize's namesake, were still alive he "would be gratified indeed that his committee has once again recognized disarmament for its great benefit to humanity." Mikhail Gorbachev, the former leader of the Soviet Union and a former recipient of the Nobel Peace Prize, called OPCW "a deserved winner of the Nobel Peace Prize."

Nobel Peace Prize Ceremony

On December 10, 2013, OPCW accepted its award and a $1.2 million prize. The award was presented by Thorbjørn Jagland, the chairman of the Norwegian Nobel Committee, who said that the prize was going "most deservedly to an organization and its personnel, who have been quietly working to remove an entire category of weapons." Jagland said that because of the work of the OPCW, a future free of chemical weapons is well within reach. In his speech, which detailed the history of the use of chemical weapons by countries around the world, Jagland also urged those countries that have not yet become party to the convention to do so without delay, especially given the convention's success. "The members represent 98 per cent of the world's population and territory as well as 98 per cent of the world's total chemical industry. 80 per cent of the chemical weapons have been removed. 90 per cent of the production capacity has been destroyed," Jagland said. Jagland noted that the OPCW has not always been successful in its mission, specifically because it did not meet the April 2012 target of destroying all chemical weapons and chemical weapon production capability. But, Jagland said, "we should never underestimate the policy of small steps. The follow-up on the Chemical Weapons Convention by the OPCW has shown how small steps can produce large results." Jagland also spoke at length about the ongoing civil war in Syria and the work of the OPCW in that country, even addressing the controversy of "whether it really makes any difference whether one is killed by chemical weapons or by conventional means." He continued, "On the road to a more peaceful world, it is nevertheless important to combat the most monstrous weapons first, the weapons of mass destruction."

Üzümcü accepted the award on behalf of his organization, speaking briefly about the horrors caused by chemical weapons. "You cannot see them. You cannot smell them. And they offer no warning for the unsuspecting," Üzümcü said, adding, "We only need to look at the fate of the survivors of such attacks—people destined to spend the rest of their lives suffering unbearable physical and psychological pain—to understand why such weapons must be banned."

—Heather Kerrigan

Following is the text of the Nobel Peace Prize award ceremony speech delivered on December 10, 2013, by Thorbjørn Jagland, the chairman of the Norwegian Nobel Committee.

Nobel Peace Prize Award
Ceremony Speech

December 10, 2013

Your Majesties, Your Royal Highness, representatives of the Laureate, Excellencies, ladies and gentlemen,

The entry into force of the Chemical Weapons Convention in 1997 prohibiting the development, production, storage and use of chemical weapons states that the parties to the Convention are "Determined for the sake of all mankind, to exclude completely the possibility of the use of chemical weapons."

Is that not beautiful?

Still more beautiful: it can be achieved. We are in fact close to the target.

This is to a large degree due to the work of the Organisation for the Prohibition of Chemical Weapons (OPCW), which was created to ensure the implementation of the Convention.

The Nobel Peace Prize for 2013 therefore goes most deservedly to an organisation and its personnel, who have been quietly working to remove an entire category of weapons.

Our congratulations!

And with this year's prize, we prompt those states that have not acceded to the convention to do so.

The use of chemicals in warfare is nearly as old as mankind. For thousands of years, spears and arrows have had poison applied to them to enhance their effect. Homer's Iliad and Odyssey tell us that such poisoned arrows were used by the parties to the Trojan War. Chinese Sun Tzu mentions the use of fire with various weapons. In Hinduism, the Law of Manu favours a ban on poison and fire arrows, recommending the poisoning of food and water instead.

Up through the centuries, there are masses of examples of the use of various chemical weapons.

In due course there followed demands for bans on such weapons. The Hague Convention from the Peace Congress of 1899, and the Convention from the Congress of 1907, recommended the prohibition of "poison and poison weapons" in the waging of war.

But it was so little use.

World War One marked the first massive use of chemical weapons in war. By the end of the war, a total of 124,000 tonnes of gas had been produced. 85,000 are reckoned to have lost their lives owing to chemical weapons, while almost 1.2 million were injured.

In the wake of World War I, international efforts to ban the use of chemical weapons and prevent such suffering from being inflicted again, on soldiers and civilians, intensified. The result of this renewed global commitment was the 1925 Geneva Protocol for the Prohibition of the Use of Asphyxiating, Poisonous or Other Gases, and Bacteriological Methods of Warfare. But it did not have much effect, because it did not forbid the production and storage of such weapons. As long as possession of such weapons was permitted, there was a strong temptation to use them. Hitler used chemical means to take the lives of millions of people during World War Two, but surprised many by not making direct use of chemical weapons when waging the war itself. In Berlin they were probably afraid of what the Allied response might be if the Germans were the first to use such weapons. Their own forces might also suffer from their use on the battlefield.

Since World War Two, chemical weapons have been used frequently. The former regime in Iraq made extensive use of chemical weapons both in the war on Iran in the 1980s and on its own Kurdish population. Terrorists have also used such weapons.

The Geneva Protocol of 1925 had in other words not had the required effect.

A more comprehensive agreement was clearly needed. The new Chemical Weapons Convention was drawn up in 1992–93. It prohibits the use, production and storage of such weapons. The Convention entered into force in 1997. The OPCW was established to see that the Convention was implemented.

The OPCW's objective, then, is not arms control, as so often in such connections; the objective is disarmament in the form of elimination of chemical weapons. In effect a huge step in human history. Because never before has a weapon, previously integrated in the armed forces and doctrines of states, been banned and its removal sought from the earth's surface.

The Convention, which entered into force in 1997, has rendered chemical weapons taboo under internatonal [sic] law.

The Convention imposes many and detailed obligations. All countries that ratify the agreement undertake to submit a full survey of whatever they may possess of chemical weapons and equipment for the production of such weapons. They furthermore undertake to destroy whatever they possess of such weapons and production facilities, and to admit international inspectors to ensure that such destruction has taken place. The destruction must be carried out in cooperation with the OPCW. The OPCW has the right to inspect any production facility in a signatory state at 76 hours' notice.

190 countries are currently members of the OPCW. The members represent 98 per cent of the world's population and territory as well as 98 per cent of the world's total chemical industry. 80 per cent of the chemical weapons have been removed. 90 per cent of the production capacity has been destroyed.

We are accordingly quite close to achieving the highly ambitious target of totally eliminating chemical weapons. This is the result not only of cooperation between many countries, but also of cooperation undertaken between the business and industry, research institutions and organisations of those countries. Without such cooperation, the implementation of many of the provisions in the Convention would not have been possible.

This year's prize is therefore being awarded to a form of international cooperation of which we need more in other areas.

But it has not all been successes. The OPCW was unable to observe the deadline, which was April 2012, for the destruction of declared chemical weapons. Some 20 per cent, chiefly American and Russian weapons, have not yet been destroyed. It is of course not acceptable that two leading powers, themselves so eager to see others destroying their stores as quickly as possible, have not yet themselves managed to do the same. Please, speed up the process!

Now that Syria has joined the OPCW, only 6 states remain non-members. Two, Israel and Myanmar, have signed, but not ratified, the Convention. Please ratify it!

Angola, North Korea, Egypt and South Sudan have neither signed nor ratified. Please do so!

It marks a big step forward that Syria has joined the OPCW, and that plans are now being drawn up for the destruction of all its chemical weapons. It is of course a huge challenge for the OPCW to manage to destroy all these weapons under the conditions of war and chaos prevailing in the country, and in much less time than is normally available.

The anonymous inspectors from the OPCW do an extremely important and difficult job. That makes the presence of many of you here today so significant. Today's prize is also your prize.

The target of removing chemical weapons from the surface of the earth is highly ambitious, but it is not necessarily the case that it will be achieved once and for all. Development does not stop. We suspect the emergence of new forms of warfare, new types of chemical weapons, types which the world has not seen up to now and which are potentially dreadful in their consequences. Discussion of possible new substances that are not currently defined in the Convention will confront the OPCW with new challenges.

We should never underestimate the policy of small steps. The follow-up on the Chemical Weapons Convention by the OPCW has shown how small steps can produce large results.

The dominant direction of the Norwegian Nobel Committee's work over the years has partly been the struggle for disarmament, but still more the struggle for international cooperation, whether through the League of Nations or the United Nations. The OPCW has its feet firmly planted in both traditions, which also figure so prominently in Alfred Nobel's will.

The current situation in the Middle East and the Persian Gulf lends an important perspective to the Chemical Weapons Convention and the existence of the OPCW, namely that such a multilateral framework once again became a platform from which to attempt to resolve a current crisis without the use of weapons. We were on the verge of a new military confrontation in the Middle East which could have unimaginable consequences. That has so far been avoided.

The improved climate this creates may pave the way for negotiations for a solution to the whole conflict in Syria. We know from experience that one good step may be followed by others.

I hope everyone is with me in a plea to the parties: lay down your arms, stop the bloodbath, come to the negotiating table.

That the leadership of the Russian Federation saw that the Chemical Weapons Convention and the OPCW could be used to shift the conflict over chemical weapons onto a new track, and that President Obama responded favourably, may also have contributed to creating a new climate around Iran's nuclear program. President Rouhani went to the UN General Assembly with a more favourable message than we have heard before. A telephone conversation between the Presidents of Iran and the United States took place for the first time for over 30 years. An important, though as yet only preliminary, agreement has been concluded to limit Iran's nuclear program.

We know that a political solution in Syria and a peaceful solution to Iran's nuclear weapons program are difficult. But developments are more promising than for a long time.

Peace is a difficult issue, as we see even in the debate on the Nobel Peace Prize. Many feel that the prize should always go to bold individuals with firm principles. We need such role models to create hope in a complicated and for many a threatening world. The prize has often gone to such outstanding individuals. Many of them have moved the world in the right direction.

But peace is not brought about by individuals and idealists alone. We also need practical politicians, capable of moving the world away from confrontation within often narrow limits. We also need institutions, not least the global ones within the United Nations.

It is the interplay between all of these that can create peace. The Nobel Peace Prize has accordingly honoured all these directions.

This must remain the Nobel Committee's platform.

Alfred Nobel's will is a visionary document. And concrete at the same time. He wrote that the prize should go to whoever had done most for fraternity between nations, the reduction of standing armies, and the holding of peace congresses.

The agreement of 2010 between Presidents Obama and Medvedev concerning strategic nuclear arms was important because the alternative was a new nuclear arms race. So it fitted in with a modern understanding of Alfred Nobel's demand for the reduction of standing armies.

The Chemical Weapons Convention and the work of the OPCW meet all of Alfred Nobel's requirements. They concern disarmament, are a form of modern peace congress, and strengthen fraternity between nations.

What is more: while negotiations concerning nuclear arms have been based on the exclusive right claimed by the nuclear powers to have nuclear arms, the Chemical Weapons Convention contains no such right. It is a real disarmament agreement. All countries must eliminate their chemical weapons. All nations are treated equally.

This must be the perspective also where nuclear arms are concerned, as was resolved by the UN Security Council meeting called by President Obama in 2009.

Nuclear weapons, too, must vanish from the face of the earth!

Many people ask, not least in Syria itself, whether it really makes any difference whether one is killed by chemical weapons or by conventional means. For those who are hit, the answer is no, though no one should underestimate the suffering that chemical weapons impose on their victims.

On the road to a more peaceful world, it is nevertheless important to combat the most monstrous weapons first, the weapons of mass destruction. We have banned the biological weapons. The Norwegian Nobel Committee has awarded many prizes to the struggle against nuclear weapons.

Today the focus is on chemical weapons, and on the progress we have made. The honour for that goes to the 1997 Convention and to the OPCW. We praise today's laureate and extend our best wishes for success in the important tasks remaining.

Thank you for your attention.

SOURCE: The Nobel Foundation. "Award Ceremony Speech." December 10, 2013. © The Nobel Foundation 2013. http://www.nobelprize.org/nobel_prizes/peace/laureates/2013/presentation-speech.html.

OTHER HISTORIC DOCUMENTS OF INTEREST

FROM THIS VOLUME

FROM PREVIOUS *HISTORIC DOCUMENTS*

U.S. and South African Presidents Eulogize Nelson Mandela

DECEMBER 10 AND 15, 2013

On December 5, 2013, Nelson Rolihlahla Mandela, the former president of South Africa who was affectionately known as Madiba, died at the age of 95. Mandela was known worldwide for not only his struggle for equality during the apartheid era, but also for his work in the global community. On December 10, 2013, U.S. President Barack Obama delivered a eulogy that drew connections to historical figures and called for action to continue the work of building equality for all. The eulogy delivered on December 15, 2013, by South African President Jacob Zuma paid homage to Mandela's great impact around the world. Mandela's death came as the African National Congress (ANC), the party of Mandela's political career, faced accusations of elitism and controversy.

MANDELA'S SOUTH AFRICA

Mandela was born on July 18, 1918, into the Madiba clan in the village of Mvezo, Transkei, located in the Eastern Cape of South Africa. After his father died, Mandela became a ward of the Acting King of his tribe. He attended grade school in Qunu, and it was there that Mandela was given the name Nelson, in accordance with the school's tradition of giving each of the children more traditional "Christian" names. He completed secondary school at a boarding school and then pursued a college education. After some delay due to his activism and lack of funding for his education, Mandela graduated from the University of South Africa in 1943.

He joined the ANC in 1944. During this time of apartheid, South Africa was controlled by the all-white National Party. In the early days of his activism, Mandela advocated only for nonviolent protest against the ruling party. Under apartheid, the black majority was subject to harsh rule by the controlling white minority, which included outlawing shared use of any areas and strictly limiting contact between racial groups.

As tensions surrounding apartheid escalated, Mandela's position regarding nonviolence changed as a direct result of the Sharpeville massacre that left sixty-nine black South Africans dead. On March 21, 1960, scores of people gathered outside municipal buildings in Sharpeville, South Africa, to protest the newly enacted Pass Laws that restricted the movement of black South Africans in white areas. The Pass Laws required all non-white South Africans to carry documentation of their racial classification at all times. The laws also banned intermarriage or sexual relations outside one's classification. Interracial families were split; in some cases a parent could be classified white, while their children were considered non-white. In addition, the majority of all lands in South Africa were seized and held for white use only. Non-whites were denied participation in government through a series of strategic legislative acts.

During the Pass Laws protest, police open fired on the demonstrators. No police officer involved in the massacre was ever convicted. As a result of the increasing violence after the shooting, the ruling party outlawed the ANC and declared a state of emergency. The ANC created a new military branch within the party called Spear of the Nation, and Mandela was appointed as leader of this branch.

Mandela left South Africa to receive training in military tactics and to stir up international support for the armed struggle against apartheid. After returning to South Africa, Mandela was arrested in 1962 and convicted of sabotage and attempting to violently overthrow the government. In 1964, he was sentenced to life in prison. He spent the majority of his sentence in a small cell on Robben Island and was later transferred to Pollsmoor Prison in Cape Town. While in prison, he studied and received a law degree by correspondence. He was freed from prison in 1990 and began the hard work of reconciliation. For his efforts, Mandela was awarded the Nobel Peace Prize in 1993 along with then-President F. W. de Klerk, a white president who helped begin to dismantle the construct of apartheid.

In 1994, Mandela was elected as the first black president of South Africa in the country's first election open to all races. He served only one term as president, though he remained in the public eye until officially announcing his retirement from public life in 2004. Mandela continued to privately campaign for equality. He announced in 2005 that his son died of an HIV/AIDS-related illness. In a public statement after the death of his son, Mandela stated that South Africans should "give publicity to HIV/AIDS and not hide it, because the only way to make it appear like a normal illness, like TB, like cancer, is always to come out and to say somebody has died because of HIV." Critics have said, however, that this statement was too long delayed and expressed regret that Mandela had not spoken out years earlier. The Nelson Mandela Foundation, established in 1999, contends that the fight against AIDS had long been a priority of both Mandela and the Foundation.

MANDELA'S GLOBAL IMPACT

After Mandela's passing, British Prime Minister David Cameron issued a statement saying, "A great light has gone out in the world. Nelson Mandela was a towering figure in our time; a legend in life and now in death—a true global hero." That light was mourned by millions. Memorial services were held around the globe—from India to the United States—and flags were lowered to half-staff in a period of mourning. Those invited to eulogize the late South African president remarked on his life story and encouraged the world to continue his work.

Mandela has long been portrayed as the great unifier of South Africa, working to reconcile racial and gender inequalities. During his imprisonment, the struggle in South Africa captured the attention of the world, prompting "Free Mandela" concerts and protests. In his address on December 10, 2013, President Obama recognized Mandela's achievements and called on the world to take up the work of spreading equality. Obama recalled the memories of American heroes such as Abraham Lincoln and Dr. Martin Luther King Jr. and likened Mandela's actions to their courage and struggles. President Obama urged leaders to speak out for those "still persecuted for what they look like and how they worship and who they love." This statement came as many nations continued to be embattled by disagreements regarding same-sex partnerships.

In his remarks, President Obama took aim at repressive regimes, such as that in Cuba, asking them to "uphold freedom and human rights." Obama added, "There are too many people who happily embrace Madiba's legacy of racial reconciliation, but passionately resist even modest reforms that would challenge chronic poverty and growing inequality."

ANC in Crisis

President Zuma's tribute to Mandela delivered at the State Funeral on December 15, 2013, recalled the early days of the ANC and called on the people of South Africa to build on the principles of the ANC that Mandela helped shape. "These are unity, selflessness, sacrifice, collective leadership, humility, honesty, discipline, hard work and mutual respect," President Zuma stated. "These ideals define your organisation the ANC," he continued. At the time of Mandela's death, criticism of the ANC majority had threatened to lessen the ANC's strong mandate in South African politics. The statements by President Zuma clearly seek to align the ANC's future with the legacy of Mandela, though opponents would question the party's moral compass.

Alleged malfeasance on the part of current ANC leaders and controversy surrounding President Zuma's purported extravagant lifestyle plagued the ANC in the months leading up to this address. Increasingly, the ANC has been branded by critics such as those in the labor movement as too cozy with big business and out of touch with the electorate. In the months leading up to Mandela's death, President Zuma has been at the center of multiple inquiries regarding government funds allocated for improvements to his private home. Zuma's administration contends that the upgrades were made for the president's security. According to an October 2012 report by *The New York Times*, the newly improved compound includes "dozens of smooth, contractor-built dwellings, a helicopter landing pad, a tennis court and a soccer field." The same report also mentions that a "sports stadium and some underground bunkers are in the works." There are a number of newly paved and improved roads leading to the compound, which the Department of Public Works has stated were related to security concerns and that funding was allocated appropriately between public and private sources. Though an official dollar amount has not been released, estimates have been as high as $27 million. President Zuma continues to deny knowledge of the extensive costs.

This scandal came on the heels of a bevy of particularly violent mining strikes. One such strike in 2012 left more than thirty dead, while miners demanded sharp increases in pay for the dangerous work they perform. Mining unions have attempted to broker deals, but the union most closely associated with the ANC has fallen increasingly out of favor. Critics of the ANC claim that the party has left behind their ideals of equality and has become the oppressive ruling party that they themselves struggled against. The ANC continues to face criticism from outside the party and remains divided internally regarding President Zuma's leadership. Questions still remain regarding potential rivals to challenge his plans for a second term.

—Sarah Gall

Following is the text of U.S. President Barack Obama's eulogy for Nelson Mandela, delivered on December 10, 2013; and the text of the eulogy given by South African President Jacob Zuma on December 15, 2013.

President Obama Speaks on Nelson Mandela's Legacy

December 10, 2013

Thank you. To Graça Machel and the Mandela family; to President Zuma and members of the Government; to heads of states and government, past and present; distinguished guests: It is a singular honor to be with you today, to celebrate a life like no other. To the people of South Africa—people of every race and walk of life—the world thanks you for sharing Nelson Mandela with us. His struggle was your struggle. His triumph was your triumph. Your dignity and your hope found expression in his life. And your freedom, your democracy, is his cherished legacy.

It is hard to eulogize any man, to capture in words not just the facts and the dates that make a life, but the essential truth of a person: their private joys and sorrows; the quiet moments and unique qualities that illuminate someone's soul. How much harder to do so for a giant of history, who moved a nation toward justice and, in the process, moved billions around the world.

Born during World War I, far from the corridors of power, a boy raised herding cattle and tutored by the elders of his Thembu tribe, Madiba would emerge as the last great liberator of the 20th century. Like Gandhi, he would lead a resistance movement, a movement that at its start had little prospect for success. Like Dr. King, he would give potent voice to the claims of the oppressed and the moral necessity of racial justice. He would endure a brutal imprisonment that began in the time of Kennedy and Khrushchev and reached the final days of the cold war. Emerging from prison, without the force of arms, he would—like Abraham Lincoln—hold his country together when it threatened to break apart. And like America's Founding Fathers, he would erect a constitutional order to preserve freedom for future generations: a commitment to democracy and rule of law ratified not only by his election, but by his willingness to step down from power after only one term.

Given the sweep of his life, the scope of his accomplishments, the adoration that he so rightly earned, it's tempting, I think, to remember Nelson Mandela as an icon, smiling and serene, detached from the tawdry affairs of lesser men. But Madiba himself strongly resisted such a lifeless portrait. Instead, Madiba insisted on sharing with us his doubts and his fears, his miscalculations along with his victories. "I am not a saint," he said, "unless you think of a saint as a sinner who keeps on trying."

It was precisely because he could admit to imperfection—because he could be so full of good humor, even mischief, despite the heavy burdens that he carried—that we loved him so. He was not a bust made of marble, he was a man of flesh and blood: a son and a husband, a father and a friend. And that's why we learned so much from him, and that's why we can learn from him still. For nothing he achieved was inevitable. In the arc of his life, we see a man who earned his place in history through struggle and shrewdness and persistence and faith. He tells us what is possible not just in the pages of history books, but in our own lives as well.

Mandela showed us the power of action, of taking risks on behalf of our ideals. Perhaps Mandela was right that he inherited, "a proud rebelliousness, a stubborn sense of fairness" from his father. And we know he shared with millions of Black and colored South Africans the anger born of, "a thousand slights, a thousand indignities, a thousand unremembered moments . . . a desire to fight the system that imprisoned my people," he said.

But like other early giants of the ANC—the Sisulus and Tambos—Madiba disciplined his anger and channeled his desire to fight into organization and platforms and strategies for action so men and women could stand up for their God-given dignity. Moreover, he accepted the consequences of his actions, knowing that standing up to powerful interests and injustice carries a price. . . .

Mandela has taught us the power of action, but he also taught us the power of ideas, the importance of reason and arguments, the need to study not only those who you agree with, but also those who you don't agree with. He understood that ideas cannot be contained by prison walls or extinguished by a sniper's bullet. He turned his trial into an indictment of apartheid because of his eloquence and his passion, but also because of his training as an advocate. He used decades of prison to sharpen his arguments, but also to spread his thirst for knowledge to others in the movement. And he learned the language and the customs of his oppressor so that one day, he might better convey to them how their own freedom depend upon his.

Mandela demonstrated that action and ideas are not enough. No matter how right, they must be chiseled into law and institutions. . . .

But as he showed in painstaking negotiations to transfer power and draft new laws, he was not afraid to compromise for the sake of a larger goal. And because he was not only a leader of a movement, but a skillful politician, the Constitution that emerged was worthy of this multiracial democracy, true to his vision of laws that protect minority as well as majority rights and the precious freedoms of every South African.

And finally, Mandela understood the ties that bind the human spirit. There is a word in South Africa, *ubuntu,* a word that captures Mandela's greatest gift: his recognition that we are all bound together in ways that are invisible to the eye; that there is a oneness to humanity; that we achieve ourselves by sharing ourselves with others and caring for those around us.

We can never know how much of this sense was innate in him or how much was shaped in a dark and solitary cell. But we remember the gestures, large and small—introducing his jailers as honored guests at his Inauguration, taking a pitch in a Springbok uniform, turning his family's heartbreak into a call to confront HIV/AIDS—that revealed the depths of his empathy and his understanding. He not only embodied *ubuntu,* he taught millions to find that truth within themselves.

It took a man like Madiba to free not just the prisoner, but the jailer as well; to show that you must trust others so that they may trust you; to teach that reconciliation is not a matter of ignoring a cruel past, but a means of confronting it with inclusion and generosity and truth. He changed laws, but he also changed hearts.

For the people of South Africa, for those he inspired around the globe, Madiba's passing is rightly a time of mourning and a time to celebrate a heroic life. But I believe it should also prompt in each of us a time for self-reflection. With honesty, regardless of our station or our circumstance, we must ask, how well have I applied his lessons in my own life? It's a question I ask myself, as a man and as a President.

We know that, like South Africa, the United States had to overcome centuries of racial subjugation. As was true here, it took sacrifice—the sacrifices of countless people, known and unknown—to see the dawn of a new day. Michelle and I are beneficiaries of that struggle. But in America and in South Africa and in countries all around the globe, we cannot allow our progress to cloud the fact that our work is not yet done.

The struggles that follow the victory of formal equality or universal franchise may not be as filled with drama and moral clarity as those that came before, but they are no less important. For around the world today, we still see children suffering from hunger and disease. We still see run-down schools. We still see young people without prospects for the future. Around the world today, men and women are still imprisoned for their political beliefs and are still persecuted for what they look like and how they worship and who they love. That is happening today.

And so we too must act on behalf of justice. We too must act on behalf of peace. There are too many people who happily embrace Madiba's legacy of racial reconciliation, but passionately resist even modest reforms that would challenge chronic poverty and grow-ing inequality. There are too many leaders who claim solidarity with Madiba's struggle for freedom, but do not tolerate dissent from their own people. And there are too many of us on the sidelines, comfortable in complacency or cynicism when our voices must be heard.

The questions we face today—how to promote equality and justice, how to uphold freedom and human rights, how to end conflict and sectarian war—these things do not have easy answers. But there were no easy answers in front of that child born in World War I. Nelson Mandela reminds us that it always seems impossible until it is done. South Africa shows that is true. South Africa shows we can change, that we can choose a world defined not by our differences, but by our common hopes. We can choose a world defined not by conflict, but by peace and justice and opportunity.

We will never see the likes of Nelson Mandela again. But let me say to the young people of Africa and the young people around the world: You too can make his life's work your own. Over 30 years ago, while still a student, I learned of Nelson Mandela and the struggles taking place in this beautiful land, and it stirred something in me. It woke me up to my responsibilities to others and to myself, and it set me on an improbable journey that finds me here today. And while I will always fall short of Madiba's example, he makes me want to be a better man. He speaks to what's best inside us.

After this great liberator is laid to rest, and when we have returned to our cities and villages and rejoined our daily routines, let us search for his strength. Let us search for his largeness of spirit somewhere inside of ourselves. And when the night grows dark, when injustice weighs heavy on our hearts, when our best laid plans seem beyond our reach, let us think of Madiba and the words that brought him comfort within the four walls of his cell:

It matters not how strait the gate,

How charged with punishments the scroll,

I am the master of my fate:

I am the captain of my soul.

What a magnificent soul it was. We will miss him deeply. May God bless the memory of Nelson Mandela. May God bless the people of South Africa.

SOURCE: Executive Office of the President. "Remarks at the Memorial Service for Former President Nelson R. Mandela of South Africa in Johannesburg, South Africa." December 10, 2013. *Compilation of Presidential Documents* 2013, no. 00843 (December 10, 2013). http://www.gpo.gov/fdsys/pkg/DCPD-201300843/pdf/DCPD-201300843.pdf.

South African President Eulogizes Nelson Mandela

December 15, 2013

[Opening acknowledgments of Mandela's family, distinguished guests, and heads of state have been omitted.]

Today marks the end of an extra-ordinary journey that began 95 years ago.

It is the end of 95 glorious years of a freedom fighter, a dedicated and humble servant of the people of South Africa, a fountain of wisdom, a pillar of strength and a beacon of hope to all those fighting for a just and equitable world order.

We are truly honoured to be part of the final journey of this great son of our country and the founding President of a free and democratic South Africa, Isithwalandwe Nelson Rolihlahla Mandela.

Tata,

It has been a long painful week for us, your people, since you took your last breath on the 5th of December 2013.

When you became critically ill last year, we were gripped with fear and anxiety. We did not want to confront the reality of your mortality.

Over the past 9 days of mourning, people have expressed their grief in various ways. What truly stands out, is the spectacular display of admiration by the thousands who descended upon the Union Buildings in Pretoria to spend just one moment with you, as you lay in state.

As we observed the long, patient queues lining the streets to the Union Buildings, some silent, some singing, many crying, we asked ourselves: what is it about this man that elicits this outpouring of sincere emotion.

The answer is that when people see goodness in a person, they respond by reflecting goodness back at that person, and on their fellow men and women.

We wish today, to express two simple words. Thank you.

Thank you for being everything we wanted and needed in a leader during a difficult period in our lives.

Siyabulela, enkosi.

Tata,

Whilst your long walk to freedom has ended in the physical sense, our own journey continues.

We have to continue building the type of society you worked tirelessly to construct. We have to take your legacy forward.

In doing so, we will continue drawing lessons from your very rich and extraordinary life.

We will always remember you as a man of integrity who embodied the values and principles that your organisation, the ANC promotes.

These are unity, selflessness, sacrifice, collective leadership, humility, honesty, discipline, hard work and mutual respect.

We will promote these values and practise them, in order to build the type of society you wanted.

That society is outlined in the ideals you espoused, the ideals you lived for and which you were prepared to die for.

These ideals define your organisation the ANC. You summarised them in your timeless statement in court in 1964. You said:

> During my lifetime I have dedicated myself to this struggle of the African people. I have fought against white domination, and I have fought against black domination. I have cherished the ideal of a democratic and free society in which all persons live together in harmony and with equal opportunities. It is an ideal which I hope to live for and to achieve. But if needs be, it is an ideal for which I am prepared to die.

When democracy was ushered in on the 27th of April 1994, you set out to build this ideal society.

You actively promoted the achievement of a united, democratic, non-racial, non-sexist and prosperous South Africa.

You taught us to embrace one another as compatriots, regardless of race, ethnicity, religion or creed.

You did this because you hated racism.

In your first court statement in October 1962, where you objected to being a black man in a white man's court, being tried by a white court which was enforcing laws you had had no hand in making, you had also spoken out strongly against racism. You said:

> I hate race discrimination most intensely and in all its manifestations. I have fought it all during my life; I fight it now, and will do so until the end of my days.

We pledge today to continue promoting non-racialism and tolerance in our country and to build a South Africa that truly belongs to all.

We also cherish the lessons you taught us, of the importance of reconciliation, forgiveness and compassion.

You forgave those who had taken away most of your adult life and who had dehumanised the majority of your compatriots.

We learned from you, that to build a new South Africa from the ashes of apartheid colonialism, we needed to rise above anger and the human desire for retribution.

In this way, you offered hope in the place of hopelessness.

Tata,

You did not only believe in gender equality, you practised it.

Gender equality gained prominence and seriousness under your presidency, leading to an increase in the numbers of women in public office, especially in parliament and cabinet.

We dare not reverse your achievements in this regard.

Yemyem,

As your journey ends today, ours must continue in earnest.

One thing we can assure you of today Tata, as you take your final steps, is that South Africa will continue to rise.

Your abiding revolutionary spirit will prevail on us to not rest, until the poor and the working class have truly benefited from the material fruits of freedom and democracy which you fought for.

Therefore, today we undertake to take forward your promotion of an improved quality of life for all.

We commit to work more intensively to deal a decisive blow against the persistent poverty, unemployment and inequality.

We pledge to take your vision forward for good schools and hospitals, quality housing and utilities, decent jobs and working conditions as well as efficient and accountable public services.

Learning from your goodself, we will continue to use education as a weapon to improve the quality of life and bring about change and to invest in the development of children and the youth.

You loved children dearly.

Therefore, in your memory, South African children must grow up in a country that is not only politically free, but which is also free and safe from violence; free and safe from crime, free and safe from poverty, ignorance and disease, free and safe from indignity.

That is the type of country we are building.

In doing all this and more, we will be able to complete this country's transformation into the global force for social and economic leadership that you believed we were capable of being.

Indeed, South Africa will continue to rise because we dare not fail you.

The children of the accomplished strategic thinker and consummate man of action that you were, must succeed and will succeed to build the South Africa of your dreams.

Tata,

As your triumphant journey comes to an end, we sincerely thank you for dedicating your life to building a free and democratic South Africa, in which all shall live in equality and dignity.

We sincerely thank your family for sharing you with us and the world.

We acknowledge the suffering of your own children, who had an absent father, and a father who was called a dangerous man and a terrorist, by the apartheid regime and its surrogates.

They are no doubt, truly proud today, to have been brought to this planet by a man so great and yet so humble.

[Words of thanks directed to Mandela's late, first wife and his second wife have been omitted.]

We thank your dear wife, Mama Graca Machel, who has been at your side providing love, strength, and companionship.

The past year has not been easy for her due to your ill health. She ensured your care and comfort, until the final moments.

Given Mama Graca's own passion for children's rights and well-being, the two of you made a formidable pair, for the benefit of children.

We acknowledge your impressive grand-children who have matured way beyond their ages, because of the type of family they have been born into.

Many have looked after you over the years, providing support and love and doing many things that would have made you proud.

In many of them, we see you.

We thank abaThembu, amaDlomo onke, for being the pillar you needed in undertaking tasks of building this great country.

We extend our deep-felt condolences to your organisation, the ANC as well as COSATU, the SA Communist Party and the SA National Civics Organisation for whom your departure is a monumental loss.

We thank the ANC in particular for providing the space for you to lead us to freedom and to influence humanity.

Our thoughts are with the Eastern Cape Province and the community of Qunu and surroundings who have lost their famous son.

We extend our condolences to the entire South African nation, whose pain we share deeply, as a Government whose foundation you laid in 1994.

[Recognition of other South African leaders who worked with Mandela has been omitted.]

We owe it to them and to countless South Africans and foreign nationals who died in pursuit of our freedom, to take your vision of a better life for all forward.

[Words of thanks to Mandela's medical staff have been omitted.]

You were an internationalist, which is why Africa and the world descended on this country to bid your farewell.

We will continue to contribute to building a better Africa and a more just and equitable world order.

We thank Africa and the world again for the solidarity and support since your passing.

Madiba,

Yemyem,

We will miss your smile, your laughter, your love and your leadership.

We will cherish every moment we spent with you.

You were indeed an extra-ordinary human being.

You will remain our guiding light, illuminating the path as we continue the long journey to build the South Africa of your dreams.

We shall not say goodbye, for you are not gone.

You will live forever in our hearts and minds.

Hamba kahle Madiba, Yemyem, Zondwa, Ngqolomsila, Velambhentsele!

Siyabulela.

I thank you.

SOURCE: South Africa Government Online. Speeches & Statements. "Eulogy by President Jacob Zuma at the State Funeral of the late former President of the Republic and former Commander in Chief of the Armed Forces, His Excellency Nelson Rolihlahla Mandela, Qunu, Eastern Cape." December 15, 2013. © GCIS2014: ALL RIGHTS RESERVED. http://www.gov.za/speeches/view.php?sid=42723.

OTHER HISTORIC DOCUMENTS OF INTEREST

FROM PREVIOUS *HISTORIC DOCUMENTS*

Federal Review of NSA Surveillance Program Issued

DECEMBER 12, 2013

In August 2013, President Barack Obama created a formal panel to review and consider changes to a National Security Agency (NSA) program that monitored millions of phone calls, text messages, e-mail, and other communications, including those of U.S. citizens, without warrants. The panel was established following the publication of a series of documents, leaked by government contractor Edward Snowden, that detailed top-secret surveillance programs conducted by the United States. The revelations caused a public outcry, raising concerns of privacy violations, and prompted the government to reexamine its intelligence operations for opportunities to better protect civil liberties while maintaining national security. The panel presented its recommendations in December 2013, the same month in which two district courts issued starkly different rulings on the phone monitoring program's constitutionality.

REVIEW GROUP RECOMMENDATIONS

On August 12, President Obama issued a presidential memorandum that called for the Director of National Intelligence to establish the Review Group on Intelligence and Communications Technologies. The Review Group was meant to assess "whether, in light of advancements in communications technologies, the United States employs its technical collection capabilities in a manner that optimally protects our national security and advances our foreign policy while appropriately accounting for other policy considerations, such as the risk of unauthorized disclosure and our need to maintain the public trust." By the end of the month, the five-member group had been formed and included Richard Clarke, chief counterterrorism advisor on the National Security Council for former Presidents Bill Clinton and George W. Bush; Michael Morell, former deputy director of the CIA; Geoffrey Stone, a University of Chicago law professor and author of several books about government surveillance; Cass Sunstein, former "regulatory czar" for President Obama at the Office of Information and Regulatory Affairs; and Peter Swire, former chief counselor for privacy at the Office of Management and Budget for President Clinton and special assistant to President Obama for economic policy.

The Review Group was directed to provide a final report and recommendations to the president within sixty days of beginning its work. Members solicited public comments on the country's intelligence programs and met with civil libertarian organizations, technology companies, and academics to help inform their deliberations.

On December 18, the Review Group publicly released its report, titled "Liberty and Security in a Changing World: Report and Recommendations of the President's Review Group on Intelligence and Communications Technologies." The report included a total of 46 nonbinding recommendations for the country's surveillance of U.S. citizens, non-U.S.

citizens, and foreign nations, as well as several organizational changes. Perhaps the most notable items in the Review Group's report recommended changes to how the NSA stores and accesses "bulk telephony meta-data," which includes the phone numbers that originate and receive calls of interest, as well as the date and time of those calls. In particular, the Review Group recommended that the government transition from storing that meta-data itself to a system in which the information is held by a private company. The government could query that information whenever necessary for national security purposes but would need to identify a specific suspicion motivating a search before conducting such a query. Currently, the government collects bulk data from phone companies every day and retains that data for five years in case of a need to search it in the future. The Review Group also recommended requiring the government to get an order from the Foreign Intelligence Surveillance Court (FISC) for each search, which is not currently mandated. The Review Group expressed some skepticism about the value and effectiveness of the current meta-data collection program, noting that it "has generated relevant information in only a small number of cases" and claimed that "current storage by the government of bulk meta-data creates potential risks to public trust, personal privacy, and civil liberty." At the same time, the Review Group said that "a robust foreign intelligence collection capability is essential if we are to protect ourselves against such threats" and that "the National Security Agency, with its impressive capabilities and talented officers, is indispensable to keeping our country and our allies safe and secure."

In addition, the Review Group proposed new restrictions on the FISC's ability to compel third parties, such as phone service providers, to disclose private information to the government, and similar limitations on the FBI's use of National Security Letters to compel businesses to share private records. The group also called for legislation that would require the government to make information about surveillance programs available to Congress and the public to the greatest extent possible, as well as legislation authorizing communications providers to publicly disclose general information about the related orders they receive from the government.

With regard to surveillance of non-U.S. citizens, the Review Group recommended that any such program be required to meet six criteria. It must be authorized by duly enacted laws or executive orders, directed exclusively at protecting the national security interests of the United States or its allies, and not targeted at individuals based solely on their religious or political beliefs, among other things. The Review Group also recommended that President Obama create a new process requiring "highest-level approval" of all sensitive intelligence-gathering in foreign nations, including intelligence on foreign leaders, to help avoid unjustified or unnecessary surveillance. That process should consider whether the requested surveillance is motivated by especially pressing national security concerns, and whether it would involve leaders of nations "with whom we share fundamental values and interests" or "whose leaders we should accord a high degree of respect and deference." It should also consider whether there are other ways to obtain the needed information and the consequences of such surveillance activities becoming public.

Also among the Review Group's recommendations was a series of proposed organizational changes, including that the NSA director be a Senate-confirmed position, that civilians should be eligible to serve as NSA director, and that the positions of NSA director and the leader of U.S. Cyber Command should no longer be held by the same person. Additionally, the Review Group called on Congress to create a Public Interest Advocate position on the FISC, with responsibility for representing privacy and civil liberties interests before the court. To help reduce "internal threats" such as leaks by individuals such as

Edward Snowden, the Review Group said the government should stop using for-profit corporations to conduct personnel investigations, establish greater differentiation between security clearance levels, and establish an ongoing monitoring program for employees with high-level clearance.

"We are not in any way recommending the disarming of the intelligence community," said Review Group member Michael Morrell after the report's release. Fellow group member Richard Clarke added, "Although we found no evidence of abuse by NSA or the FBI, the potential for abuse in the future is there . . . we tend to believe there should be further judicial oversight than there has been."

POLICYMAKERS, THIRD-PARTY GROUPS REACT

The recommendations drew mixed reactions from Members of Congress, the intelligence community, and organizations focused on issues of technology and civil liberties. Supporters of the NSA's meta-data collection program argued that transferring ownership of the phone records from the NSA to a private company would complicate and slow the surveillance process, decreasing the agency's ability to detect terrorist plots. "Though I am still studying the details, I have serious concerns with some of the report's 46 recommendations," said Rep. Mike Rogers, R-Mich. "Any intelligence collection reforms must be careful to preserve important national security capabilities," Rogers continued. Joel Brenner, a former NSA inspector general, claimed the group's recommendations "would put us back before 9/11 again."

Several organizations applauded the report, including the Brennan Center for Justice. "The review committee has reaffirmed that national security neither requires nor permits the government to help itself to Americans' personal information at will," said Elizabeth Goitein, co-director of the center's Liberty and National Security Program. She added, "The recommendations would extend significant privacy protections to Americans." American Civil Liberties Union (ACLU) Executive Director Anthony Romero said that ending the meta-data collection program was "the most necessary recommendation of the review group" and went to "the very heart of NSA dragnet surveillance."

In a statement, the White House said President Obama would spend the coming weeks working with his national security team to evaluate the Review Group's report and determine which recommendations he would pursue. Adopting a majority of the recommendations would constitute the first major restrictions on the powers acquired by the NSA following September 11. The president is expected to announce his proposed reforms in January 2014.

CONFLICTING JUDICIAL RULINGS

Two days before the Review Group publicly released its report, U.S. District Judge Richard Leon ruled that the NSA's meta-data collection was "almost certainly" unconstitutional. Leon's ruling occurred in the case of *Klayman v. Obama*, a lawsuit filed by conservative legal activist and Freedom Watch founder Larry Klayman, who claimed that the NSA program violated the Fourth Amendment's privacy protections against unreasonable searches.

In his decision, Leon challenged the government's claims that the program was limited in scope. "I cannot imagine a more 'indiscriminate' and 'arbitrary invasion' than this systematic and high tech collection and retention of personal data on virtually every single citizen for purposes of querying and analyzing it without prior judicial approval," he wrote. "Surely, such a program infringes on 'that degree of privacy' that the founders enshrined in the Fourth Amendment." Leon granted Klayman's request for an injunction blocking the collection of his and a co-plaintiff's phone data and ordered the government to destroy any records that may already have been gathered on them. However, he stayed action on his ruling pending a government appeal.

A similar case was decided on December 27 by U.S. District Judge William Pauley, III. Yet Pauley came to a different conclusion, ruling that the meta-data collection program was in fact legal. His decision was given in *ACLU v. Clapper*, a case brought against Director of National Intelligence James Clapper by the ACLU. "The collection of breathtaking amounts of information unprotected by the Fourth Amendment does not transform that sweep into a Fourth Amendment search," Pauley wrote. He described the program as the United States' "counter-punch" to al Qaeda and concurred with arguments made by some government officials that the program might have caught the September 11 hijackers had it been in place before the attacks. He said the program cast "a wide net that could find and isolate gossamer contacts among suspected terrorists in an ocean of seemingly disconnected data," and that it "only works because it collects everything."

The government claims the U.S. Supreme Court case of *Smith v. Maryland* provides the legal justification for the NSA's meta-data collection. In that case, the Court ruled that Americans have no expectation of privacy in the phone meta-data that companies retain as business records; therefore, a warrant is not needed to collect that information. Subsequent rulings by the FISC have further affirmed the government's argument. Judge Pauley held that the precedent set by *Smith* still applies, while Judge Leon argued that the *Smith* ruling had been rendered moot by vast advances in technology and the government's surveillance capabilities.

It is expected that both cases will be appealed. *Klayman v. Obama* will next be reviewed by the U.S. Court of Appeals for the District of Columbia Circuit, while the ACLU plans to appeal its case to the U.S. Court of Appeals for the 2nd Circuit.

—Linda Fecteau

Following is the edited text of the President's Review Group's December 12, 2013, report on the National Security Agency (NSA) secret surveillance program.

DOCUMENT   *Review Board Issues NSA Report*

December 12, 2013

[The first seven pages have been excerpted from the full, 316-page report released by the President's Review Group on Intelligence and Communications Technologies. They comprise the report's preface and executive summary of the group's recommendations.]

Preface

On August 27, 2013, the President announced the creation of the Review Group on Intelligence and Communications Technologies. The immediate backdrop for our work was a series of disclosures of classified information involving foreign intelligence collection by the National Security Agency. The disclosures revealed intercepted collections that occurred inside and outside of the United States and that included the communications of United States persons and legal permanent residents, as well as non-United States persons located outside the United States. Although these disclosures and the responses and concerns of many people in the United States and abroad have informed this Report, we have focused more broadly on the creation of sturdy foundations for the future, safeguarding (as our title suggests) liberty and security in a rapidly changing world.

Those rapid changes include unprecedented advances in information and communications technologies; increased globalization of trade, investment, and information flows; and fluid national security threats against which the American public rightly expects its government to provide protection. With this larger context in mind, we have been mindful of significant recent changes in the environment in which intelligence collection takes place.

For example, traditional distinctions between "foreign" and "domestic" are far less clear today than in the past, now that the same communications devices, software, and networks are used globally by friends and foes alike. These changes, as well as changes in the nature of the threats we face, have implications for the right of privacy, our strategic relationships with other nations, and the levels of innovation and information-sharing that underpin key elements of the global economy.

In addressing these issues, the United States must pursue multiple and often competing goals at home and abroad. In facing these challenges, the United States must take into account the full range of interests and values that it is pursuing, and it must communicate these goals to the American public and to key international audiences. These goals include:

Protecting The Nation Against Threats to Our National Security. The ability of the United States to combat threats from state rivals, terrorists, and weapons proliferators depends on the acquisition of foreign intelligence information from a broad range of sources and through a variety of methods. In an era increasingly dominated by technological advances in communications technologies, the United States must continue to collect signals intelligence globally in order to assure the safety of our citizens at home and abroad and to help protect the safety of our friends, our allies, and the many nations with whom we have cooperative relationships.

Promoting Other National Security and Foreign Policy Interests. Intelligence is designed not only to protect against threats but also to safeguard a wide range of national security and foreign policy interests, including counterintelligence, counteracting the international elements of organized crime, and preventing drug trafficking, human trafficking, and mass atrocities.

Protecting the Right to Privacy. The right to privacy is essential to a free and self-governing society. The rise of modern technologies makes it all the more important that democratic nations respect people's fundamental right to privacy, which is a defining part of individual security and personal liberty.

Protecting Democracy, Civil Liberties, and the Rule of Law. Free debate within the United States is essential to the long-term vitality of American democracy and helps bolster democracy globally. Excessive surveillance and unjustified secrecy can threaten civil liberties, public trust, and the core processes of democratic self-government. All parts of the government, including those that protect our national security, must be subject to the rule of law.

Promoting Prosperity, Security and Openness in a Networked World. The United States must adopt and sustain policies that support technological innovation and collaboration both at home and abroad. Such policies are central to economic growth, which is promoted in turn by economic freedom and spurring entrepreneurship. For this reason, the United States must continue to establish and strengthen international norms of Internet freedom and security.

Protecting Strategic Alliances. The collection of intelligence must be undertaken in a way that preserves and strengthens our strategic relationships. We must be respectful of those relationships and of the leaders and citizens of other nations, especially those with whom we share interests, values, or both. The collection of intelligence should be undertaken in a way that recognizes the importance of cooperative relationships with other nations and that respects the legitimate privacy interests and the dignity of those outside our borders.

The challenge of managing these often competing goals is daunting. But it is a challenge that the nation must meet if it is to live up to its promises to its citizens and to posterity.

Executive Summary

Overview

The national security threats facing the United States and our allies are numerous and significant, and they will remain so well into the future. These threats include international terrorism, the proliferation of weapons of mass destruction, and cyber espionage and warfare. A robust foreign intelligence collection capability is essential if we are to protect ourselves against such threats. Because our adversaries operate through the use of complex communications technologies, the National Security Agency, with its impressive capabilities and talented officers, is indispensable to keeping our country and our allies safe and secure.

At the same time, the United States is deeply committed to the protection of privacy and civil liberties—fundamental values that can be and at times have been eroded by excessive intelligence collection. After careful consideration, we recommend a number of changes to our intelligence collection activities that will protect these values without undermining what we need to do to keep our nation safe.

Principles

We suggest careful consideration of the following principles:

1. The United States Government must protect, at once, two different forms of security: national security and personal privacy.

In the American tradition, the word "security" has had multiple meanings. In contemporary parlance, it often refers to national security or homeland security. One of the government's most fundamental responsibilities is to protect this form of security, broadly understood. At the same time, the idea of security refers to a quite different and equally fundamental value, captured in the Fourth Amendment to the United States Constitution: "The right of the people to be *secure* in their persons, houses, papers, and effects, against unreasonable searches and seizures, shall not be violated . . ." (emphasis added). Both forms of security must be protected.

2. The central task is one of risk management; multiple risks are involved, and all of them must be considered.

When public officials acquire foreign intelligence information, they seek to reduce risks, above all risks to national security. The challenge, of course, is that multiple risks are involved. Government must consider all of those risks, not a subset, when it is creating sensible safeguards. In addition to reducing risks to national security, public officials must consider four other risks:

- Risks to privacy;
- Risks to freedom and civil liberties, on the Internet and elsewhere;
- Risks to our relationships with other nations; and
- Risks to trade and commerce, including international commerce.

3. The idea of "balancing" has an important element of truth, but it is also inadequate and misleading.

It is tempting to suggest that the underlying goal is to achieve the right "balance" between the two forms of security. The suggestion has an important element of truth. But some safeguards are not subject to balancing at all. In a free society, public officials should never engage in surveillance in order to punish their political enemies; to restrict freedom of speech or religion; to suppress legitimate criticism and dissent; to help their preferred companies or industries; to provide domestic companies with an unfair competitive advantage; or to benefit or burden members of groups defined in terms of religion, ethnicity, race, and gender.

4. The government should base its decisions on a careful analysis of consequences, including both benefits and costs (to the extent feasible).

In many areas of public policy, officials are increasingly insistent on the need for careful analysis of the consequences of their decisions, and on the importance of relying not on intuitions and anecdotes, but on evidence and data. Before they are undertaken, surveillance decisions should depend (to the extent feasible) on a careful assessment of the anticipated consequences, including the full range of relevant risks. Such decisions should also be subject to continuing scrutiny, including retrospective analysis, to ensure that any errors are corrected.

Surveillance of US Persons

With respect to surveillance of US Persons, we recommend a series of significant reforms. Under section 215 of the Foreign Intelligence Surveillance Act (FISA), the government now stores bulk telephony meta-data, understood as information that includes the telephone numbers that both originate and receive calls, time of call, and date of call. (Meta-data does not include the content of calls.) We recommend that Congress should end such storage and transition to a system in which such meta-data is held privately for the government to query when necessary for national security purposes.

In our view, the current storage by the government of bulk meta-data creates potential risks to public trust, personal privacy, and civil liberty. We recognize that the government might need access to such meta-data, which should be held instead either by private providers or by a private third party. This approach would allow the government access to the relevant information when such access is justified, and thus protect national security without unnecessarily threatening privacy and liberty. Consistent with this recommendation, we endorse a broad principle for the future: as a general rule and without senior policy review, the government should not be permitted to collect and store mass, undigested, non-public personal information about US persons for the purpose of enabling future queries and data-mining for foreign intelligence purposes.

We also recommend specific reforms that will provide Americans with greater safeguards against intrusions into their personal domain. We endorse new steps to protect American citizens engaged in communications with non-US persons. We recommend important restrictions on the ability of the Foreign Intelligence Surveillance Court (FISC) to compel third parties (such as telephone service providers) to disclose private information to the government. We endorse similar restrictions on the issuance of National Security Letters (by which the Federal Bureau of Investigation now compels individuals and organizations to turn over certain otherwise private records), recommending prior judicial review except in emergencies, where time is of the essence.

We recommend concrete steps to promote transparency and accountability, and thus to promote public trust, which is essential in this domain. Legislation should be enacted requiring information about surveillance programs to be made available to the Congress and to the American people to the greatest extent possible (subject only to the need to protect classified information). We also recommend that legislation should be enacted authorizing telephone, Internet, and other providers to disclose publicly general information about orders they receive directing them to provide information to the government. Such information might disclose the number of orders that providers have received, the broad categories of information produced, and the number of users whose information has been produced. In the same vein, we recommend that the government should publicly disclose, on a regular basis, general data about the orders it has issued in programs whose existence is unclassified.

Surveillance of Non-US Persons

Significant steps should be taken to protect the privacy of non-US persons. In particular, any programs that allow surveillance of such persons even outside the United States should satisfy six separate constraints. They:

1. must be authorized by duly enacted laws or properly authorized executive orders;

2. must be directed exclusively at protecting national security interests of the United States or our allies;

3. must not be directed at illicit or illegitimate ends, such as the theft of trade secrets or obtaining commercial gain for domestic industries;

4. must not target any non-United States person based solely on that person's political views or religious convictions;

5. must not disseminate information about non-United States persons if the information is not relevant to protecting the national security of the United States or our allies; and

6. must be subject to careful oversight and to the highest degree of transparency consistent with protecting the national security of the United States and our allies.

We recommend that, in the absence of a specific and compelling showing, the US Government should follow the model of the Department of Homeland Security and apply the Privacy Act of 1974 in the same way to both US persons and non-US persons.

Setting Priorities and Avoiding Unjustified or Unnecessary Surveillance

To reduce the risk of unjustified, unnecessary, or excessive surveillance in foreign nations, including collection on foreign leaders, we recommend that the President should create a new process, requiring highest-level approval of all sensitive intelligence requirements and the methods that the Intelligence Community will use to meet them. This process should identify both the uses and the limits of surveillance on foreign leaders and in foreign nations.

We recommend that those involved in the process should consider whether (1) surveillance is motivated by especially important national security concerns or by concerns that are less pressing and (2) surveillance would involve leaders of nations with whom we share fundamental values and interests or leaders of other nations. With close reference to (2), we recommend that with a small number of closely allied governments, meeting specific criteria, the US Government should explore understandings or arrangements regarding intelligence collection guidelines and practices with respect to each others' citizens (including, if and where appropriate, intentions, strictures, or limitations with respect to collections).

Organizational Reform

We recommend a series of organizational changes. With respect to the National Security Agency (NSA), we believe that the Director should be a Senate-confirmed position, with civilians eligible to hold that position; the President should give serious consideration to making the next Director of NSA a civilian. NSA should be clearly designated as a foreign intelligence organization. Other missions (including that of NSA's Information Assurance Directorate) should generally be assigned elsewhere. The head of the military unit, US Cyber Command, and the Director of NSA should not be a single official.

We favor a newly chartered, strengthened, independent Civil Liberties and Privacy Protection Board (CLPP Board) to replace the Privacy and Civil Liberties Oversight Board (PCLOB). The CLPP Board should have broad authority to review government activity relating to foreign intelligence and counterterrorism whenever that activity has implications for civil liberties and privacy. A Special Assistant to the President for Privacy should also be designated, serving in both the Office of Management and Budget and the National Security Staff. This Special Assistant should chair a Chief Privacy Officer Council to help coordinate privacy policy throughout the Executive branch.

With respect to the FISC, we recommend that Congress should create the position of Public Interest Advocate to represent the interests of privacy and civil liberties before the FISC. We also recommend that the government should take steps to increase the transparency of the FISC's decisions and that Congress should change the process by which judges are appointed to the FISC.

Global Communications Technology

Substantial steps should be taken to protect prosperity, security, and openness in a networked world. A free and open Internet is critical to both self-government and economic growth. The United States Government should reaffirm the 2011 International Strategy for Cyberspace. It should stress that Internet governance must not be limited to governments, but should include all appropriate stakeholders, including businesses, civil society, and technology specialists.

The US Government should take additional steps to promote security, by (1) fully supporting and not undermining efforts to create encryption standards; (2) making clear that it will not in any way subvert, undermine, weaken, or make vulnerable generally available commercial encryption; and (3) supporting efforts to encourage the greater use of encryption technology for data in transit, at rest, in the cloud, and in storage. Among other measures relevant to the Internet, the US Government should also support international norms or agreements to increase confidence in the security of online communications.

For big data and data-mining programs directed at communications, the US Government should develop Privacy and Civil Liberties Impact Assessments to ensure that such efforts are statistically reliable, cost-effective, and protective of privacy and civil liberties.

Protecting What We Do Collect

We recommend a series of steps to reduce the risks associated with "insider threats." A governing principle is plain: Classified information should be shared only with those who genuinely need to know. We recommend specific changes to improve the efficacy of the personnel vetting system. The use of "for-profit" corporations to conduct personnel investigations should be reduced or terminated. Security clearance levels should be further differentiated. Departments and agencies should institute a Work-Related Access approach to the dissemination of sensitive, classified information. Employees with high-level security clearances should be subject to a Personnel Continuous Monitoring Program. Ongoing security clearance vetting of individuals should use a risk-management approach and depend on the sensitivity and quantity of the programs and information to which individuals are given access.

The security of information technology networks carrying classified information should be a matter of ongoing concern by Principals, who should conduct an annual assessment with the assistance of a "second opinion" team. Classified networks should increase the use of physical and logical separation of data to restrict access, including through Information Rights Management software. Cyber-security software standards and practices on classified networks should be at least as good as those on the most secure private-sector enterprises.

[The remainder of the report has been omitted.]

SOURCE: The White House. "Liberty and Security in a Changing World." December 12, 2013. http://www.whitehouse.gov/sites/default/files/docs/2013-12-12_rg_final_report.pdf.

OTHER HISTORIC DOCUMENTS OF INTEREST

FROM THIS VOLUME

China Successfully Lands Spacecraft on the Moon

DECEMBER 13, 2013

On December 14, 2013, China became the third country to successfully land a spacecraft on the moon when its *Change 3* probe and Yutu rover touched down on the lunar surface. This achievement marked the second phase of China's lunar program and another step forward in the country's rapid advancement of its broader program of space exploration, which has lagged behind the United States and Russia for decades. The *Change 3* mission continued to lay the groundwork for future lunar missions, which have as their ultimate goal the construction of a moon base, and demonstrated the further evolution of China's technological and scientific capabilities.

MILITARY BEGINNINGS

Since its inception, the Chinese government has viewed the country's space program as a way for the country to demonstrate China's technological, scientific, and military strength, and become a global, respected power. The program had its beginnings in 1956 when the government established the Fifth Academy of the National Defense Industry under the control of the People's Liberation Army and initiated the country's first ballistic missile program in response to perceived threats of a nuclear strike by the United States. Following the former Soviet Union's launch of the orbital satellite *Sputnik* in 1957, Communist Party Chairman Mao Zedong called for China to place a similar satellite in orbit by 1959—a goal the country did not achieve until 1970. Initially, the Soviet Union provided some support for China's fledging space program, including helping train Chinese students, but withdrew this support following the Sino-Soviet split that began in the 1960s as the two countries' Communist Parties diverged politically and ideologically. China continued to develop and test various missiles throughout the 1960s.

In 1968, China took its first steps toward developing a crewed space program, establishing its Space Medical Institute to begin identifying and training astronaut candidates and to research the necessary technologies for manned spaceflight. Yet the country made little progress in its space program following Chairman Mao's death in 1976, and two separate manned spaceflight programs were canceled before the government authorized the Shenzhou program in 1992. The following year, the China National Space Administration (CNSA) was founded within the State Administration for Science, Technology and Industry for National Defense (SASTIND). Since then, CNSA has been responsible for the planning and development of space activities.

CNSA conducted four unmanned test flights as part of the Shenzhou program before sending China's first astronaut into space in 2003 aboard *Shenzhou 5.* In 2008, astronaut Zhai Zhigang completed China's first spacewalk, spending thirteen minutes outside of the *Shenzhou 7* spacecraft. China launched its first space lab, *Tiangong 1,* one year later. The lab is meant to serve a test module for other Shenzhou spacecraft to practice docking and other skills that astronauts will need to master before China builds a permanent space station, which the country plans to do by 2020. In December 2011, China's State Council released a white paper outlining a new five-year plan for expanding the space program, which includes the launch of orbiters that can make soft lunar landings, survey the lunar surface, and collect samples of rock and soil. The plan also called for improving conditions for human spaceflight, which would involve, in part, launching more advanced space laboratories, manned spacecraft, and space freights, as well as advancing key space station technologies such as regenerative life support. Additionally, China would focus on upgrading its satellite technology and developing its own global positioning system by 2020. Officials reiterated that these goals were not meant to have military implications. "China always adheres to the use of outer space for peaceful purposes, and opposes weaponization or any arms race in outer space," the State Council wrote.

LUNAR ASPIRATIONS

SASTIND began planning the country's lunar program in 1998, although it was not approved by the government until 2004. More than three million Chinese citizens voted to name the program "Chang'e" after a Chinese mythical moon goddess. The program would initially consist of three phases: orbiting the moon, landing on its surface, and bringing a spacecraft back to Earth with rock and soil samples. Once these three phases were complete, China would next attempt manned spaceflight to the moon and eventually establish a lunar base.

The program's first phase began with the October 2007 launch of *Chang'e 1*, which entered the moon's orbit on November 7. Nearly three weeks later, China published its first picture of the lunar surface, as transmitted by the spacecraft. In January 2008, the government published its pictures of the moon's polar regions taken by *Chang'e 1*, and in November it published a hologram of the whole moon created from data collected by the probe. On March 1, 2009, *Chang'e 1* hard-landed on the moon's surface in a controlled crash.

This spacecraft was followed by *Chang'e 2*, which launched on October 1, 2010. The mission sought to test new technologies that would be used in phase two spacecraft, *Chang'e 3*, and to photograph the chosen landing site for that upcoming mission. *Chang'e 2* entered lower elliptical lunar orbit on October 26, and transmitted photos of the landing site on October 29. The spacecraft continued to circle the moon for several months before leaving its orbit. In December 2012, *Chang'e 2* entered deep space at a distance of seven million kilometers from Earth and surveyed the Toutatis asteroid, which is classified as a potentially hazardous object given its frequent close approaches to terrestrial planets. *Chang'e 2* has since traveled approximately 60 million kilometers from Earth and continues to fly into deep space.

CHANG'E 3'S LAUNCH AND LANDING

On August 28, 2013, state-run Xinhua News Agency reported that Chinese officials planned to soft-land an unmanned rover on the moon by the end of the year and that the launch rocket and spacecraft had already been assembled and tested. Spacecraft that are soft-landed still function afterward, as opposed to those that are hard-landed. "The *Chang'e 3* mission will be our country's first soft landing on an extraterrestrial body,"

Dr. Ma Xingrui, CNSA administrator, told Xinhua. It would also be the first time since 1976 that a spacecraft had soft-landed on the moon.

Chang'e 3 would consist of a landing vehicle, which would operate for a year as a stationary probe upon arrival on the moon, and a six-wheeled rover, which would operate for about three months. The rover was named Yutu, or "jade rabbit," because according to Chinese folklore the moon goddess Chang'e had a pet rabbit. Yutu was designed to survey the moon's geological structure and surface substance and to look for natural resources such as helium-3. Scientists consider helium-3 to be a possible source of fusion energy that could replace oil and gas. "Everyone knows fossil fuels such as gas and coal will be used up one day, but there are at least 1 million metric tons of helium-3 on the moon," said Ouyang Ziyuan, chief scientist of the Chinese Lunar Exploration Program. According to Ouyang, if China was able to mine the moon for helium-3 and create nuclear power from it, that supply of resources could generate power for more than 10,000 years. The rover's instruments included ground-penetrating radar to help gather measurements of the lunar soil and crust, and both the rover and the lander were equipped with high resolution cameras that were able of capturing images far more clearly than those used during the lunar missions of the 1970s. Another unique feature of the *Chang'e 3* lander was its capability to survey the landscape of its landing site to identify the safest spot to land, and then make quick course adjustments as it descended. Neither U.S. nor Soviet lunar spacecraft had such capabilities. The rover and lander would be managed by the Xichang Satellite Launch Center and would test China's abilities to track objects and communicate across deeper space. This in turn had national security implications; such capabilities can be leveraged for space surveillance.

Chang'e 3 launched on December 2 at 1:30 a.m. Beijing time and landed on the moon at 9:11 p.m. on December 14. Yutu separated from the lander and rolled to the moon's surface the following morning. State television broadcast pictures of the moon's surface as the spacecraft made its descent and released an eye-level view of the landing site later in the evening. The next day, China shared photos that the lander and rover took of each other. Staff at the launch center celebrated their achievement and received praise from scientists and space experts around the world. "China becomes the third space faring nation to accomplish such a monumental achievement and has demonstrated that they are serious about making their mark in pursuing the final frontier," said James Longuski, a Purdue University professor and associate fellow at the American Institute of Aeronautics and Astronautics. Paul Spudis, lunar scientist at the Lunar and Planetary Institute in Houston, Texas, shared similar sentiments. "This is a very big deal indeed," Spudis said. "Landing on the moon is not something easily attained—it requires precision maneuvering, tracking, computation and engineering. It is a delicate task and the Chinese success reflects a mature, evolving and capable program," he continued. Former CNSA Administrator Luan Enjie described the lunar program as a "springboard" for deep space exploration. "We've embarked on deep space exploration for 10 years, and we still have a long way to go," said Luan. "Many of our scientists are studying Mars, and how Chinese will land on it," he said.

However, the landing prompted some concern among U.S. officials that China may overtake the United States in space exploration in the coming decades, particularly in light of budget cuts at NASA, and that China's achievements may have more than scientific implications. Reps. Frank Wolf, R-Va., and Mike Rogers, R-Ala., for example, wrote to Director of Intelligence James Clapper questioning the national security implications of China's space-related accomplishments and stating that they "are among those who have grown concerned that while the People's Republic of China commits significant resources and sense of national purpose to its space program, the United States is at risk of losing its space leadership." Rep. Wolf previously led an effort to pass a law in 2011 that forbade NASA from cooperating with China on any space activities, claiming that the law was necessary to keep the Chinese from stealing NASA technology that it might then use for military purposes. Others dismissed these concerns. Roger Lanius, associate director for Collections and Curatorial Affairs at the Smithsonian Institution's National Air and Space Museum, said China's moon landing was "no small achievement," but also noted that China was doing what the United States and the Soviet Union had done before and what private companies are attempting to do again. "Some people who might be concerned that the Chinese are demonstrating these capabilities, and who are running around with their hair on fire—I'm not sure that's appropriate," said Lanius.

On December 16, Chinese officials announced during a news conference that they plan to launch phase three of their lunar program by 2017. "There are many break-through technologies required, including technology to take off from the moon, packaging samples taken from the surface of the moon, docking in lunar orbit and high-speed re-entry to Earth, all things China hasn't done before," said Wu Zhijian, spokesman for SASTIND. Wu continued, "According to our present understanding, if all goes smoothly, the construction of *Chang'e 5* and its launch will occur around 2017."

—Linda Fecteau

Following is an article released on December 13, 2013, by the National Aeronautics and Space Administration (NASA) on the potential impact of Chang'e 3's *mission on U.S. space exploration.*

NASA Says Chang'e 3 Could Provide Valuable Space Data for United States

December 13, 2013

[Images have been omitted.]

After sending 12 humans to the moon's surface during the Apollo Program, NASA remains committed to lunar science. Building on modern missions such as Clementine and Lunar Prospector and recent missions like LCROSS and GRAIL, NASA science has helped to map the moon, determine the presence of water ice, and understand our satellite's irregular gravity field. NASA's current missions to the moon are helping the agency understand our solar system better, informing future exploration efforts to other planetary bodies, and bringing us closer to the technologies we'll need to explore future destinations like an asteroid and Mars.

Scientists using four NASA spacecraft currently studying our lunar neighbor may get an opportunity to gather new data from the Dec. 14 landing of the *Chang'e 3* lunar rover. U.S. and international researchers view the pending arrival as a new scientific opportunity that could potentially enhance studies and observations of the lunar atmosphere.

The robotic lander will arrive as NASA's *Lunar Atmosphere and Dust Environment Explorer (LADEE), Lunar Reconnaissance Orbiter (LRO),* and two probes called the

Acceleration, Reconnection, Turbulence and Electrodynamics of Moon's Interaction with the Sun (ARTEMIS) continue their science missions.

Although there is no cooperation between the U.S. and China on these missions, U.S. researchers could see potentially interesting science from the landing. The data will be made available to the international science community.

LADEE

LADEE, the *Lunar Atmosphere and Dust Environment Explorer,* is equipped with technology to measure atmospheric species and dust particles, and may be able to detect changes in the atmosphere caused by dust and exhaust introduced above the surface as the Chinese lander touches down on the surface.

The spacecraft's initial objective is to study the pristine lunar atmosphere and orbital dust environment. Using its instruments, scientists hope to address a long-standing question: Was lunar dust, electrically charged by sunlight, responsible for the pre-sunrise glow above the lunar horizon detected during several Apollo. [missions?]

LADEE has been gathering science data since lowering its orbit on Nov. 10 to begin its 100-day prime mission. The science team has already established a baseline of data for the tenuous lunar atmosphere, or exosphere, and dust impacts. Prior to the landing of *Chang'e 3*, the LADEE team will have gathered data for a full lunar cycle, or 29.5 days.

Before and after the landing, *LADEE* will be using its Neutral Mass Spectrometer (NMS) instrument to obtain additional observations. The NMS will monitor the specific masses of the products (e.g., H_2O, N_2, CO and CO_2, H_2) the team expects the propulsion system will generate during landing based on the descriptions of the landing system available. In addition, *LADEE* will continue its baseline observations, which will allow it to see if the landing generates a detectable change in the moon's background dust and gas environment.

LADEE was launched Sept. 6 and is the first spacecraft designed, developed, built, integrated and tested at NASA's Ames Research Center at Moffett Field, Calif. Ames manages the overall mission and serves as a base for mission operations and real-time control of the probe. NASA's Goddard Space Flight Center in Greenbelt, Md., manages the science instruments and technology demonstration payload, the science operations center and overall mission support. NASA's Marshall Space Flight Center in Huntsville, Ala., manages *LADEE* within the Lunar Quest Program Office.

LRO

Launched in June 2009, the *Lunar Reconnaissance Orbiter, LRO,* has been conducting science activities and returning unique results on the lunar exosphere. The spacecraft also has returned a treasure trove of unprecedented images of the lunar surface.

On the day of the anticipated *Chang'e 3* landing, the spacecraft will do up to eight spacecraft maneuvers to scan an area near the landing site with the Lyman-Alpha Mapping Project (LAMP) instrument, an ultraviolet imaging spectrometer. LAMP will be looking for a signature of the exhaust plume from the spacecraft.

Beginning in December, the LRO Camera (LROC) will be able to image the lander and rover at approximately 2 meter per pixel resolution on a monthly basis as the rotation of the moon brings the landing site underneath the LRO orbit plane. Repeated imaging of the landing site by LROC will allow for detailed measurements of changes to the surface caused by the landing and movement of the Chang'e 3 rover.

LROC can image the surface to identify changes caused by *Chang'e 3's* descent engine, similar to what has been observed from previous lunar landers. Lighting conditions will not be ideal for the first attempt, with the sun low on the horizon, but will improve in later months. The resulting atmospheric and surface changes will provide LRO with a new scientific opportunity to observe the transport of gases on the moon and the effects of local disturbances on the lunar regolith.

Not only has *LRO* delivered all the information that is needed for future human and robotic explorers, but it has also revealed that the moon is a more complex and dynamic world than scientists had ever expected. *LRO* will continue to send back lunar data until October 2014, with the possibility of an additional two years.

LRO is managed by NASA's Goddard Space Flight Center, Greenbelt Md.

ARTEMIS

The *ARTEMIS* spacecraft will assist *LADEE* in the interpretation of its measurements from the landing.

The two spacecraft comprising the ARTEMIS mission or Acceleration, Reconnection, Turbulence and Electrodynamics of Moon's Interaction with the Sun have been in lunar orbit since 2010. They are probes from the 5-spacecraft Heliophysics constellation Time History of Events and Macroscale Interactions during Substorms (THEMIS). The ARTEMIS mission allowed NASA to repurpose two in-orbit spacecraft to extend their useful science mission.

The first ARTEMIS spacecraft (*P1*) will pass within 124 iles (200 km) of the lunar surface on December 14. According to current plans, the spacecraft will look for any plume signatures in the plasma or magnetic field associated with *Chang'e 3's* landing. The second spacecraft (*P2*) will observe pristine solar wind plasma and magnetic field conditions. This information is needed to determine how dust is lofted from the lunar surface.

Current ARTEMIS investigations are focusing on measuring the electrostatic charging of the lunar surface, the plasma wake that the moon carves out in the supersonic solar wind, and the interaction of the solar wind.

ARTEMIS is managed by NASA's Goddard Space Flight Center in Greenbelt Md.

SOURCE: National Aeronautics and Space Administration. "China's Lunar Lander May Provide Additional Science for NASA Spacecraft." December 13, 2013. http://www.nasa.gov/content/chinas-lunar-lander-may-provide-additional-science-for-nasa-spacecraft/#.U0s80NzDRkh.

OTHER HISTORIC DOCUMENTS OF INTEREST

FROM THIS VOLUME

FROM PREVIOUS *HISTORIC DOCUMENTS*

Index

Names starting with al- or el- are alphabetized by the subsequent part of the name.